Venice, Austria, and the Turks
in the
Seventeenth Century

Venice, Austria, and the Turks
in the
Seventeenth Century

Kenneth M. Setton

THE AMERICAN PHILOSOPHICAL SOCIETY
Independence Square · Philadelphia
1991

MEMOIRS OF THE
AMERICAN PHILOSOPHICAL SOCIETY
Held at Philadelphia
For Promoting Useful Knowledge
Volume 192

Library of Congress Catalog Card No: 90-55269 ∞
International Standard Book No. 0-87169-192-2
US ISSN: 0065-9738

In memoriam
Margaretae

CONTENTS

PREFACE

This book is in many ways a sequel to the four volumes of my *Papacy and the Levant (1204–1571)*, although the emphasis has shifted northward from the Holy See to Venice and Austria. Far more time and effort have thus been spent in the Venetian than in the Vatican Archives, although the latter have as always been very useful. In most works one's plans may change somewhat as one gets more deeply into a subject. It was originally my intention to pursue certain questions in the Haus-, Hof- und Staatsarchiv in Vienna—*talia publica diligo tabularia*—but the book was becoming much longer than I thought it should be. Therefore I gave up the idea of working in the archives in Vienna, and confined myself to those in Venice and the Vatican. As a result it soon seemed advisable to reduce the coverage of Austria, which I did by a full third, *et tantae molis erat*, and I think, at least I hope, it was not a mistake. As for the Austrians vis-à-vis the Turks, however, we must always bear in mind that the Venetian successes in Greece after the Turkish failure at Vienna in 1683 were largely the consequence of the Turks' being obliged to direct their chief armament against the Austrian imperialist forces, not against those of the so-called Serene Republic. We must also accept the fact that such was the strain of Turco-Venetian relations that, as far as the Serenissima was concerned, the end of the seventeenth century came not with the peace of Karlowitz (in 1699) but rather, as we shall see, with that of Passarowitz in 1718.

Nevertheless, to return to the archival sources, I have tried to put them before the reader to the extent it has proved practicable, whatever the variations in spelling to be found in the texts (hence Costantinopoli and Constantinopoli, Morosini and Moresini, provveditore and proveditor, as well as giovane, giovine, and giovene, principe and prencipe, etc.). I mention these inconsequential differences because it is possible they may annoy or perplex some readers.

As one puts aside the page proofs of a book, and turns to the Preface, one feels the strong desire to acknowledge the various forms of assistance received through the years. It is a pleasure thus to express my gratitude to Mrs. Gladys Krieble Delmas and to Mrs. Boris Nedelev, both friends of many years, for the help and encouragement they have given me. In her generous gifts to the American Philosophical Society, Gladys Delmas has helped subsidize the publication of this book. Mrs. Nedelev, known as Eileen Turner during the years that she managed the publishing firm of Variorum, has made available her apartment in London whenever I had need of the Public Record Office. She has also read proofs, copied documents, and been helpful in numerous other ways.

In recounting further debts, I must begin with my friends Professors Christian Habicht and Hans Eberhard Mayer, both of whom have read the entire typescript, and offered valuable suggestions for improvement. Professor Mayer has also been most helpful in dealing through the years with the successive volumes of *A History of the Crusades.* Also I owe much to several friends in Venice, especially (continuing my indebtedness in alphabetical order) Marino and Renata Berengo, Vittore and Olga Branca, Gaetano and Luisa Cozzi, the Rev. Giorgio Fedalto, Marino and Rosella Zorzi. Professors Berengo and Cozzi both came to my rescue in connection with the eighteenth century, into which I have boldly ventured at the conclusion of this book. Dr. Zorzi, director (and historian) of the Biblioteca Nazionale Marciana, and his staff produced every manuscript I needed, and cheerfully rendered whatever other assistance they could. My thanks go also to Dr. Maria Francesca Tiepolo and the staff of the Archivio di Stato di Venezia, where I first began working some forty years ago. Needless to say, I also owe much to the librarians of the Institute for Advanced Study and Princeton University. And not the least of my indebtedness is to Dr. Herman H. Goldstine, Executive Officer of the American Philosophical Society, and Carole N. Le Faivre and Dr. Susan M. Babbitt, who manage the editorial staff of the Society, all three of whom are (like several others mentioned in this Preface) friends of many years.

Mrs. Enid Bayan and Mrs. Suki Lewin have prepared the typescript, and Mr. Mark Darby of the Library of the Institute has been largely responsible for the Index. When the Royal Society and the American Philosophical Society held a joint meeting in Philadelphia (in April 1986), I was called upon to give a lecture, for which I used selections from this book relating to the Venetians in Greece and the destruction of the Parthenon. Although the lectures read at this meeting were published, they received but slight circulation.

My friends will understand the need to dedicate this book to my late, ever-generous wife Margaret. She shared in every way my love of Italy and the Italian Archives, and her "ready help was ever nigh."

K.M.S.

The Institute for Advanced Study
Princeton, N.J.
1 August 1990

I

Austrians and Turks in the Long War (1592–1606), the Bohemian Succession, and the Outbreak of the Thirty Years' War

❧

t was Saturday, 7 March 1573, a day long to be remembered in Europe and the Levant. That day at Pera, the suburb of Istanbul north of the Golden Horn, the Venetians made peace with Sultan Selim II, abandoning their alliance with Spain and the Holy See and surrendering the island of Cyprus to the Turks. The high point of the Cypriot war had been the Christian victory at Lepanto, which quickly became an inspiration to painters and poets, historians, newsmen, and printers. Lepanto, however, turned out to be of but slight naval importance to Christendom, for the Turks soon rebuilt their armada, occupying the Tunisian outpost of La Goletta after a month-long siege in August 1574 and taking the fortress town of Tunis in September. The Turks thus remained masters of the eastern Mediterranean, and strengthened their hold upon the Maghreb, "the West," i.e., Tripolitania and Tunisia, Algeria and even Morocco. A long peace usually followed a Turco-Venetian war, and after the notable events of 1573–1574 the Republic and the Porte refrained from serious hostility for a full seventy years, until in 1645 the Turks embarked upon the conquest of the Venetian island of Crete in the long "war of Candia."

In many ways, however, these seventy years were not years of peace. The Christians seem to have been more of a disruptive force in the

1

Mediterranean than the Moslems. One or more squadrons of Spanish, Tuscan, Neapolitan, Sicilian, and Hospitaller galleys made annual voyages into the Levant, ranging as far as Rhodes, Cyprus, Tenedos, and even the Dardanelles, looting the Turkish convoys on the route between Alexandria and Istanbul. The Hospitallers of Malta, the so-called Knights of S. John of Jerusalem, were the most aggressive. Usually more enterprising at sea than the Turks, the Christians attacked the Barbary strongholds of La Goletta and Tunis, Tripoli, Bizerte, and Algiers. To the distress of the Venetians, who always feared embroilment with the Turks, Spanish-Italian agents of Philip III encouraged the natives of Maina on the central prong of the Morea as well as those of Syria to revolt against the Porte, providing them with arms and supplies to add effect to their dissidence.

The Venetians had rarely got along well with the Casa d'Austria, and now they were having trouble with the Hapsburgs' cousin in Madrid. Nevertheless, Philip III did intervene in September 1617 to help arrange peace between the Austrian Hapsburgs who, as we shall see, were having difficulties of their own, and the Venetian Signoria. It was agreed that the Uskoks should be expelled from Segna (Senj) and other places belonging to the house of Austria, and in return the Venetians would restore to the Hapsburgs certain places which they had occupied both in Istria and in Friuli.[1] The Uskoks were pirates, a plague to Venetian shipping in the Adriatic and a ceaseless nuisance to the Turks in the borderlands of Dalmatia. In fact the Uskoks had been harassing the Venetians and the Turks for almost a century, a matter which the Austrian Hapsburgs had never found inconvenient. Philip III's mediation helped calm the troubled waters. Encounters at sea between the Venetians and the Spanish-Italian (i.e., Neapolitan) galleys had been frequent. A state of almost warfare had existed through much of the second decade of the seventeenth century, especially whenever the galleys of Philip III entered the "Venetian Gulf," i.e., the Adriatic.[2] From time to time, to be sure, a Turkish armada moved into the Spanish-Italian waters; indeed the Turks sacked Reggio di Calabria (in 1594) and Manfredonia (in August 1620).

---

[1] J. Dumont, *Corps universel diplomatique*, V-2 (Amsterdam and The Hague, 1728), no. CLXX, pp. 304–5, doc. dated 26 September 1617. The French had assisted in the formulation of the treaty (*ibid.*, no. CLXIX, pp. 302–4).

[2] On Venetian-Spanish relations during the second decade of the seventeenth century and on the long-controversial legend of the Spanish conspiracy against Venice (in 1618), which involved a number of shady characters with whom the Spanish government in Naples would in fact have nothing to do, see Giorgio Spini, "La Congiura degli Spagnoli contro Venezia del 1618," *Archivio storico italiano*, CVII (1949), 17–53, and CVIII (1950), 159–74. Pedro Téllez Girón, duke of Osuna, was viceroy of Naples from 1616 to 1620. It was he who rejected the overtures of the disreputable would-be conspirators then resident in Venice, although the Venetians later charged him with conspiring to put an end to the Republic.

The modes of naval warfare were changing, especially from about the year 1600, as square-rigged sailing ships, "battleships," with heavy broadside cannon were replacing the galleys as the most effective armament at sea. As time passed, "three-deckers" were built with heavy guns on three levels, the lower calibers being put on the top deck. Manuals were written to instruct gunners in the employment of their ordnance in battles at sea. The Hospitallers, the "Knights of Malta," following the lead of the Dutch and English, took on the square-rigged vessels more quickly than did the Venetians, and (even more than the Venetians) the Turks seemed to find the change difficult of acceptance. By the later seventeenth century, however, the Venetians were apparently relying as heavily on the square-rigged battleship as on the galleass, which had won the battle of Lepanto. The broadside cannon of the big square-riggers rendered out-of-date the "ramming and boarding" practices of galley warfare.

The last years of the sixteenth century and the first years of the seventeenth were filled with warfare on land, much less so at sea, bringing about changes in central and eastern Europe that were long to endure. As the Turks were moving toward another invasion of Europe, Christendom was a house divided against itself. The Protestant princes and burghers in Germany and the Protestant bourgeoisie in Holland, France, and England, as well as the Venetian nobles and merchants were at constant odds with the Hapsburgs in Austria and Spain, the Holy See, the Spanish-dominated states in Italy, and the Catholic kingdom of Poland. The Protestants of the Northwest had kindred spirits among the Calvinists (and Lutherans) in Hungary and Transylvania. In the years before and after 1600 the Hapsburgs were also at the nadir of their history, and owing to Hapsburg ineffectiveness, the Turks were again a great menace.

As the Protestants in Holland were struggling to survive and to preserve their independence, treaties of one sort or another were negotiated by representatives of the United Provinces with England in 1585,[3] with the French in 1589,[4] and with the Rhenish Palatinate and the electorate of Brandenburg in 1605.[5] During these years the Dutch were taking giant strides forward, economically and militarily, and Spain would never be able to reassert her dominance over the northern Netherlands. Indeed, in these critical years before and after 1600 the economic and

---

[3] Dumont, *Corps universel diplomatique*, V-1 (1728), nos. CC, CCIII-CCIV, pp. 446, 454–57, docs. dated 6 June and 10 August 1585 and 6 February 1586, which pact was nullified by the "perpetual alliance" which James I of England made in 1604 with Philip III of Spain and the Archdukes Albrecht and Isabella of the southern (Belgian) Netherlands (*ibid.*, V-2, no. XVII, pp. 32–36).

[4] Dumont, V-1, no. CCXVI, pp. 479–81, doc. dated 31 May 1589, an agreement somewhat altered by Henry IV's commercial treaty with Philip III and the Archdukes Albrecht and Isabella in 1604 (*ibid.*, V-2, no. XII, p. 42).

[5] Dumont, V-2, no. XVII, pp. 53–54, doc. dated 25 April 1605.

military dominance of Europe was shifting from the Mediterranean world of the Italian and Spanish peninsulas to the Northwest, to the Netherlands, England, and the Germanies. The Venetians were feeling the impact of Dutch and English naval enterprise in the Levantine ports. The strange strengthening of the Germanies extended into Austria, and contributed to the decline of the Ottoman empire.

Searching for economic advantages and military alliances everywhere in non-Catholic Europe and the Mediterranean, the Dutch managed to obtain a rich commercial "capitulation" from Ahmed I, the fourteenth sultan of the house of Osman. It was a notable concession, dated at Istanbul at the beginning of July 1612. Thenceforth the Dutch would be seen in eastern waters, like the French and the English, "trafiquant et négociant par tout," under the protective aegis of the sultan, "seigneur et patron de la forteresse des vertus."[6] There was a long-standing entente between France and the Ottoman Empire, since 1536 in fact;[7] but, for the rest, Protestantism was always an advantage when dealing with the Turks, who rarely put aside their hostility to the Catholic Hapsburgs.[8]

The world of warfare was changing, especially in Holland and the European northland, as we shall have occasion to note again. A wide range of armaments was improved upon, and new ones concocted, during the later sixteenth and throughout the seventeenth centuries—cannon and culverins, falcons and falconets, with varying bores and weights, arquebuses and petronels fired by wheel locks, muskets fired by matchlocks and flintlocks, with a diversity of lengths, weights, and names (calivers, curriers, carbines, blunderbusses, dragons, etc.), pistols (dags), hand grenades, incendiary bombs, petards, and wheeled rigs loaded with explosives to roll downhill against the enemy. By the mid-sixteenth century gunsmiths and foundries were to be found everywhere in Europe, and so were powder-mills, making gunpowder of saltpeter (potassium nitrate), charcoal, and sulphur. The recipes for gunpowder varied from place to place, but the ingredients were always the same.

Crossbows, "arbalests," had become almost useless in the face of firearms on the battlefield. They were, of course, employed as a major weapon into the seventeenth century. Hunters used crossbows for shooting game even into the eighteenth century, but that was sport, not warfare. In the era of the crossbow the mercenary owned his own weap-

---

[6] Dumont, V-2, no. CXXIV, pp. 205–14, doc. dated "l'an d'après la manifestation du Prophète 1021, qui est au commencement de Juillet de l'année de nôtre Seigneur Jésus Christ 1612."

[7] Cf. Kenneth M. Setton, *The Papacy and the Levant (1204–1571)*, 4 vols., Philadelphia: American Philosophical Society, 1976–1984, III, 400–1.

[8] Cf. K.M. Setton, "Lutheranism and the Turkish Peril," *Balkan Studies*, III (Thessaloniki, 1962), 133–68, and Carl Göllner, "Die Türkenfrage im Spannungsfeld der Reformation," *Südost-Forschungen*, XXXIV (1975), 61–78.

onry, and to some extent the practice continued into the age of firearms. Until the organization of the "standing army" (*stehendes Heer*) toward the end of the seventeenth century the gunners were sometimes entrepreneurs who owned their guns or worked for those who did. They were in fact civilians, strictly speaking, not part of the military. They even provided the wagons for the transport of their cannonry, their property being leased for service when troops were recruited at the outbreak of war. And when the war ended, like the mercenaries they were out of work.

Such gunners were thus not unlike the captains of galleys and ships which were often leased from private owners (and in the seventeenth century the Turks sometimes hired English and Dutch ships which they used perforce in naval combat). The gunners, like the captains, might worry more about protecting their own or their employers' property than about the outcome of a field battle or a hostile encounter at sea. With the appearance of the standing army, however, artillery gradually became an abiding branch of governmental service, the cannonry being owned and transported by the state, the artillerymen being enrolled in the military and trained to operate the state-owned guns (*Geschützbedienungsmannschaft*).[9]

Although the years had given a clumsy complexity to Ottoman military organization, the Turks always remained a formidable foe, making a fearful impact upon their enemy to the blare of drums, tambourines, trumpets, and diverse other instruments. When the first attack failed, however, there was little likelihood of effective tactics, and the Turks lacked a mobile field artillery. Indeed the disparate structure of the Ottoman army, with various units tending to go each its own way on the spur of a critical moment, made tactics almost impossible after the initial assault. In the seventeenth century the Turks, like the Spanish, tended to follow past practices. The Spanish were caught in an era of religious

---

[9] On the manufacture of various forms of artillery, light and heavy, the production of munitions, and the tactical employment of cannonry on the battlefield and in siege warfare in the sixteenth and seventeenth century, with much attention given to the *Türkenkriege*, see Anton Dolleczek, *Geschichte der österreichischen Artillerie von den frühesten Zeiten bis zur Gegenwart*, Vienna, 1887, repr. Graz, 1973, pp. 78–288, and cf. Dolleczek's *Monographie der k. und k. österr.-ung. blanken und Handfeuer-Waffen, Kriegsmusik, Fahnen und Standarten seit Errichtung des stehenden Heeres bis zur Gegenwart*, Vienna, 1896, repr. Graz, 1970, which gives some attention to the seventeenth but is chiefly concerned with the eighteenth and nineteenth centuries. More modern and more readable are Charles Ffoulkes, *The Gun-Founders of England*, Cambridge, 1937, and A.R. Hall, *Ballistics in the Seventeenth Century*, Cambridge, 1952, which also deals primarily with England; Frederic C. Lane, *Venetian Ships and Shipbuilders of the Renaissance*, Baltimore, 1934, and cf. Lane, *Venice and History*, Baltimore, 1966, pp. 3–24, 143ff.; also C.M. Cipolla, *Guns and Sails in the Early Phase of European Expansion, 1400–1700*, London, 1965. Well equipped with guns, Cipolla sails from the Atlantic and the Mediterranean to India and China in an interesting little book.

bigotry, the Turks in a renewal of Islamic fanaticism, and neither people could keep abreast of the technological innovations which had been altering European society from at least the mid-sixteenth century.

The Ottoman government had made peace with Venice in 1573 and with the Hapsburgs and Poland in 1577. With peace on the European front the Turks embarked on some twelve years of costly, exhausting warfare with Persia (1578–1590), from which the Porte appeared to emerge victorious, having established a semblance of authority over Kurdistan, Georgia, Azerbaijan, Shirvan, and Dagestan. The young Abbas, later known as "the Great," who had become the sophi or shah of Persia in 1587, had no alternative but to accept the unfavorable peace of 1590, which seemed likely to assure the Porte a widespread political and economic dominance west and south of the Caspian Sea. The Porte, however, had paid a heavy price for the Turks' apparent success.

Despite the alleged peace which had existed between Austria and the Porte since the time of Rudolf II's accession to the imperial throne (in 1576), the Turks had made frequent raids into the emperor's kingdom of Hungary. In 1590 not only did the Persian war come to an end, but the Porte again made peace with Poland. An abundance of soldiery now became available, and the Turks were short of funds. Warfare would employ the troops, for whom plunder might help take the place of wages. In June 1592 the Turks seized the imperial town of Bihać (Wihitsch) on the Una river in southern Croatia to the distress of Clement VIII, who had recently been elected pope. Clement now proposed, as his predecessors had often done, a league against the Turks. From Bihać the Turks might move north to Ljubljana and thence into Friuli, but the Venetian Signoria could not be moved to join an anti-Turkish league, which would of course disrupt the Levantine trade.

According to a contemporary "warhafftige newe Zeitung aus Ungern, Graitz und Wien," the Turks killed five thousand Christians and carried off eight hundred children when they captured Bihać.[10] From July through October 1592 the raids of Hassan Pasha of Bosnia into the areas of Neuhäusel (Nové Zámky) in Bohemia, Karlstadt (Karlovac) in Croatia, and Raab (Györ) in Hungary are said to have netted the Turks 35,000 captives.[11]

From the time of the Turkish capture of the town of Bihać (Wihitsch) in 1592 until the end of the Long War (in 1606) journalists and pamphleteers, preachers and propagandists kept Europe well informed with a deluge of *Zeitungen, Beschreibungen, avvisi, ragguagli, orationes,* and

---

[10] Carl Göllner, ed., *Turcica: Die europäischen Türkendrucke des XVI. Jahrhunderts,* II (Bucharest and Baden-Baden, 1968), no. 1895, p. 470, and cf. *Cal. State Papers . . . , Venice,* IX (1897, repr. 1970), nos. 197, 209, pp. 96, 101.

[11] Göllner, *Turcica,* II, no. 1896, p. 471.

various other publications. They rolled off the presses in Nuremberg, Leipzig, Graz, Prague, Dresden, Freiburg, Vienna, Frankfurt am Main, Paris, London, Rome, Florence, Verona, and elsewhere. Hundreds were published, recalling the anti-Turkish exploits of Scanderbeg, Martin Luther's *Büchlein vom Krieg wider den Türcken*, the Christian victory at "Strigonia" (Gran, Esztergom), "la défaite des Turcs en Allemagne devant la ville de Sissik, le 22 de Iuin dernier, 1593," and so on year after year. Sisak (Sziszek) is in northern Croatia on the river Sava, and it was quite true that Hassan Pasha had been defeated at Sisak, then Hungarian Sziszek.[12]

The rejoicing did not last long, however, for the Turks took the town of Sisak in late August (1593), as other *Zeitungen* sadly relate. Every Christian or Turkish victory or defeat became the subject of a pamphlet or a "newspaper." These remain among the chief sources for the military exploits and tragedies of the time.[13] As with all newspapers, however, one would be ill-advised to believe all the details they recount, but in alignment with other sources they help make clear the extent to which the last decades of the sixteenth century were a period of turmoil and confusion.

Most generalizations concerning Ottoman society, perhaps concerning any society, tend to break down under the weight of factual data. The historical record makes clear, however, that with the advent of the seventeenth century the Turks' expansion into Hungary and the western Balkans, and eastward into Persia, had reached the limits of their capacity for conquest. As castles were built and towns were fortified, especially in the West, and the countryside was plundered from year to year, Turkish campaigning became more difficult and less profitable.

On the whole large armies did not remain in the field during the cold season. Winter quarters were unpopular. Most Turkish expeditions started from Istanbul-Edirne, and the campaigning season was largely finished by the time the army had reached Hapsburg Hungary or Persia. As for the Turkish ventures into Hungary, a look at the map is deceptive. In medieval and early modern times the Danube was a poor passageway.

---

[12] Cf. Ludwig von Pastor, *Gesch. d. Päpste*, 16 vols. in 22, Freiburg im Breisgau, 1926–33, IX (1927), 200 and, *ibid.*, note 9; *Cal. State Papers . . .* , Venice, IX (1897, repr. 1970), nos. 181, 187, 197, pp. 78ff.; and for the contemporary *Zeitungen, Anzeigungen,* "chronicles," propaganda, etc., see Karl Vocelka, *Die politische Propaganda Kaiser Rudolfs II. (1576–1612)*, Vienna: Österreichische Akademie der Wissenschaften, 1981, esp. pp. 219ff. On the historical background, note J.V. Polišenský, "Bohemia, the Turk and the Christian Commonwealth (1462–1620)," *Byzantinoslavica*, XIV (Prague, 1953), 82–108, esp. pp. 96ff.

[13] Göllner, *Turcica*, II, nos. 1897–2463, pp. 471–729, has collected the *Zeitungen*, etc., which appeared from 1593 until the year 1600. They were published in Latin, German, Czech, Italian, Dutch, French, English. On the Turkish occupation of Sisak, cf. *Cal. State Papers . . .* , Venice, IX, no. 228, p. 111. Vocelka's *Politische Propaganda* covers the entire period of Rudolf II's reign.

Trade was confined to narrow limits. Navigation was always difficult. Downstream traffic was impeded by political and ethnic hostilities, fortified outposts, watermills, and banditry. Bandits did not interfere with Ottoman armies, but upstream traffic was hard going. Despite strenuous effort it usually took some twelve weeks to get from Istanbul-Edirne to Buda[pest]. Expeditionary forces usually encountered heavy rains, swollen rivers, flooded plains, broken bridges, and washed-out roads, as they moved in and out of the Danube valley.

As the western frontiers became more heavily fortified and the imperialist forces better equipped to deal with the Turks, the sultan's soldiery garnered less plunder. His troops required more pay and had become less disciplined, especially the janissaries—the central corps of the Ottoman armament—who were beginning two full centuries of rapine, robbery, and revolt. The sipahis, the rank and file of the cavalry, were no better behaved. The unruly troops brought about the downfall and death of many a grand vizir. Even the sultan was not safe in Istanbul. But as Sir John Finch, the English ambassador to the Porte in the later seventeenth century, once observed, "the Turke cannot live without a warr."[14] And so the Turks went to war with Austria and the Hapsburg hereditary states in the summer of 1593, beginning the "Long War,"[15] which was to last until 1606. The war cast a long shadow. Judgments were made, and stands were taken, that would last a century and more.

Meanwhile, as Matteo Zane, the Venetian bailie in Istanbul (1591–1593), wrote the doge and Senate (on 24 July 1593), "Many here think that the Sultan's anxiety for war is caused by the dread of a rising among the troops which have just come home from the Persian war." When the English ambassador in Istanbul, Edward Barton, delivered letters from Queen Elizabeth to the Porte, recommending the preservation of peace between the Holy Roman Empire and the Turks, and requesting fulfillment of "the engagements repeatedly made to her of attacking Spain and assisting her in the [English] war [with Spain] . . . ," he caused the grand vizir Sinan Pasha no end of agitation. Elizabeth had written that "to begin a war was in the hands of princes, its successful conclusion was in the hands of God." Barton noted "that the world did not hold the Imperialists responsible for what had happened in Bosnia, while the Queen always hoped that war would be made upon Spain, and to move in so many directions was not advisable."

Having heard this,

the Pasha flew into a rage, and declared that the forces of the Sultan were so numerous that he was equal to facing the whole world; and this war would not

---

[14] G. F. Abbott, *Under the Turk in Constantinople*, London, 1920, p. 281.
[15] Cf. *Cal. State Papers . . . , Venice*, IX (1897, repr. 1970), nos. 159, 164–65, 176–77, 180, 187, 189, 190–91, 197–98, 211, 213, pp. 70ff.

end in Hungary, but would spread to Vienna, and he himself would not be satisfied till he had levelled the walls of Rome. In order to prove that this war was just,
he declared that the Imperialists had seized on a place in Croatia where they
were exhorted to turn the mosques into taverns and pigsties; the Turks were not
going to war for an increase of territory nor of subjects, for of these they had
enough, but in obedience to their laws; and even if they did not win, it was a
great good fortune to die as martyrs, but victory was certain. He added that if the
Emperor chose to surrender all his possessions in Hungary, it would then be
possible to treat of peace, and to allow him to enjoy the rest in quiet; but if he
were to offer thirty tributes, he would find a deaf ear turned to his proposals. The
Pasha boasted that in fifteen days he had collected and despatched a very powerful army, a feat no one else could have accomplished. As to the King of Spain, the
Pasha announced that war by sea would be declared. That this had not been
done before was due to the operations in Persia.[16]

Clement VIII's response to the Turks' aggression was certainly
prompt. He dispatched missions to the Emperor Rudolf II, Philip II of
Spain, and other princes. At the beginning of the year 1594 Clement sent
Aleksandar Komulović, rector of the Yugoslav church of S. Girolamo in
Rome and abbot of Nona, on a prolonged embassy into central and eastern Europe. Komulović went by way of Venice, Trent, Innsbruck, and
Vienna to Alba Iulia (Weissenburg, Gyulafehérvár), the capital of Transylvania. His purpose was to try to persuade the prince of Transylvania,
the voivodes of Moldavia and Wallachia, the king of Poland, and the tsar
of Muscovy to join a western alliance against the Turks.

Komulović was also to try to enlist the aid of the Zaporozhian Cossacks
against the Turks. The Cossacks could be useful. Theoretically subject to
Poland, they made frequent raids into Turkish territory and into the
Tatar Khanate of the Crimea, which was subject to the Porte. Furthermore, Komulović was to appeal to the Serbs to free themselves of the
Turks. In the spring or summer of 1597, after a long and arduous itiner-
ary, Komulović set out on his return journey, stopping at Prague, where
he suggested to the Emperor Rudolf II the recovery from the Turks of the
border fortress of Klis (Clissa) in southern Croatia, which the adventur-
ous Uskoks had occupied for a brief while about a year before.[17]

---

[16] *Cal. State Papers . . .* , Venice, IX, no. 190, pp. 83–84.

[17] Cf. Pastor, *Geschichte der Päpste*, XI (1927), 202–4, 210; Peter Bartl, " 'Marciare
verso Costantinopoli:' Zur Türkenpolitik Klemens' VIII.," *Saeculum*, XX (1969), 47–49,
repeated with corrections in Bartl's monograph on *Der Westbalkan zwischen spanischer
Monarchie und osmanischem Reich: Zur Türkenkriegsproblematik an der Wende vom
16. zum 17. Jahrhundert*, Wiesbaden, 1974, pp. 47–50. According to the papal nuncio in
Venice, Komulović had sewed up his instructions and letters in a cushion which he inad-
vertently left behind upon his departure from the city. When discovered, they were turned
over to the Signoria. While in Venice, Komulović stayed with the well-known Albanian
Tommaso Pelessa, who is said to have claimed that Komulović was equipped with false
seals and letters (*ibid.*, pp. 47, 119), the significance of which seems to be unclear.

The war started badly for the imperialists. On 2 October 1594, owing to the apparent incompetence of the Austrian commander Ferdinand von Hardegg, the Turks (much assisted by the Crimean Tatars) occupied the heavily fortified town of Raab (Győr) in northern Hungary at the confluence of the river Raab and the Danube. It was a case of "the sleeping Germans against the wakeful Turks" (*die schlaffende Teutschen wider die wachende Türcken*).[18] The latter failed, however, to take Komárno in October,[19] and that ended the year's campaign. Shocking as the loss of Raab (or rather Győr) was to both Austria and the Holy See, the Turks were to lose the fortress town four years later.

Before the Turks could resume their offensive in 1595, an alliance was formed between Rudolf II and Sigismund Báthory, the prince of Transylvania. The voivodes Michael the Brave of Wallachia and Aaron of Moldavia also threw in their lot with the imperialists, and began to take action against the Turks.[20] Their adherence to the imperialist cause was serious, for Wallachia and Moldavia were the breadbaskets of Istanbul. The Turks put in their claim for grain, and shipped it to the Bosporus from Galati, Braila, and Silistra. Most inopportunely for the Ottoman government and its army Sultan Murad III died in mid-January 1595, and it was some months before Turkish troops could take the field. On 1 July, however, an imperial army under the able Count Karl von Mansfeld laid siege to the great fortress city of Gran (Esztergom), the birthplace of S. Stephen (d. 1038), the "apostolic king" of Hungary. On 4 August, von Mansfeld defeated a Turkish relief force of (it is said) 20,000 men. Shortly thereafter von Mansfeld died, an irreparable loss to the Christian cause.

In late August the imperialist army was reinforced by several thousand papal auxiliary troops under the command of Clement VIII's nephew Gian Francesco Aldobrandini. Other Italian troops under their own commanders, among whom was Duke Vincenzo I Gonzaga of Mantua, also joined in the siege, helping to bring about the Turkish surrender of Gran

---

On the early history of the Zaporozhian or Dnieper Cossacks (as opposed to the Don Cossacks), note W.E.D. Allen, *The Ukraine: A History*, Cambridge, 1940, pp. 72–79, 120–23; Gunter Stökl, *Die Entstehung des Kosakentums*, Munich, 1953, pp. 157ff. (Veröffentlichungen des Osteuropa-Institutes, München, III), and C.M. Kortepeter, *Ottoman Imperialism during the Reformation: Europe and the Caucasus*, New York and London, 1972, pp. 16, 32–33, *et alibi*.

[18] Göllner, *Turcica*, II (1968), nos. 1948, 2003, 2075, pp. 494, 519, 554–55. Today, as one enters the city of Győr from Pápa, one first encounters a massive public-housing development, and thereafter finds little or no trace of the Turks except for a so-called Turkish house and the site of an alleged Turkish fountain or bath.

[19] Cf. Göllner, *Turcica*, II, nos. 1967, 2002, 2010, 2012, pp. 504, 519, 522, 523.

[20] As usual the Venetian bailie in Istanbul kept the Signoria well informed, for which note *Cal. State Papers . . .* , *Venice*, IX, nos. 317, 319, pp. 147ff., where "Bogdania" means Moldavia, and see in general Walter Leitsch, "Rudolf II und Südosteuropa, 1593–1606," *East European Quarterly*, VI-3 (1972), 301–20, esp. 307ff.

on 2 September.[21] Thereafter Aldobrandini succeeded in taking nearby Visegrád from the Turks. The Christian recovery of Gran was hailed as a miraculous victory; considering the topography and fortifications of the city, it certainly seemed so. The Turks had held Gran for more than half a century, having taken it on 9 August 1543, when they were alleged to have killed everyone they found within the walls.[22]

Although the imperialists recovered a few towns in Croatia, the Christian campaign of 1595 was over. The imperialists sought refuge in their winter encampments. The papal forces and their allies were recalled to Italy. Clement VIII's subsidies to the Hapsburgs and to the campaign had cost the Holy See some 600,000 scudi during the years 1594–1595.[23] In retrospect contemporaries may not have regarded it as quite worth the effort and the cost, for the Turks soon recovered Gran (in 1605), and held it until late October 1683 when, after the failure of the Turks before Vienna, they were forced to surrender the city to the imperialist commander Charles V of Lorraine and John III Sobieski of Poland.[24]

Although Sigismund Báthory of Transylvania, in union with Michael the Brave of Wallachia, achieved some measure of success against the Turks, their efforts were undone by the great Ottoman campaign of 1596. The imperialist commander, the Archduke Maximilian, also began with some measure of success, seizing and sacking the town of Hatvan in northern Hungary. His undisciplined troops slaughtered the inhabitants in early September (1596).[25] As the Turkish army approached Szeged, at the juncture of the Theiss (Tisza) and Maros (Mureş) rivers, Maximilian retreated westward to Gran (Esztergom). The Turks then proceeded northward up the valley of the Theiss to Erlau (Eger), which they had failed to take in September and October 1552 in a dramatic and indeed famous siege.[26]

This time the Turks did take possession of Erlau (Eger, *Agria*) on 12 October 1596, after a siege of three weeks, the Archduke Maximilian having arrived on the scene too late to relieve the city. As a result of the

---

[21] Göllner, *Turcica*, II, nos. 2076, 2082–84, 2091–92, 2096–98, 2106, 2111, 2114–15, *et alibi*, pp. 555ff. On the career of Karl von Mansfeld, note the *Allgemeine Deutsche Biographie*, XX (1884, repr. 1970), 234–35.

[22] Cf. K.M. Setton, *The Papacy and the Levant, 1204–1571*, III, 472 note, 479, and cf. vol. IV, 697a.

[23] J.W. Zinkeisen (1803–1863), *Geschichte des osmanischen Reiches in Europa*, 7 vols., Gotha, 1857–63, III, 585–602; N. Jorga, *Gesch. d. osmanischen Reiches*, 5 vols., Gotha, 1908–13, III, 295–315; Pastor, *Gesch. d. Päpste*, XI (1927), 198–214, and *Hist. Popes*, XXIII, 265–88; P. Bartl, "Marciare verso Costantinopoli," *Saeculum*, XX (1969), 55; C.M. Kortepeter, *Ottoman Imperialism during the Reformation*, pp. 136–47.

[24] Thomas M. Barker, *Double Eagle and Crescent: Vienna's Second Turkish Siege and its Historical Setting*, Albany, N.Y., 1967, pp. 356–60, and see below, pp. 271, 276, 364.

[25] Göllner, *Turcica*, II, nos. 2221, 2234, 2238, 2240, pp. 621, 627, 628, 629–30, *et alibi*.

[26] Setton, IV, 585.

advent of Sigismund Báthory with reinforcements, however, Maximilian decided to meet the Turks head-on. The hard-fought battle began near the little town of Mezökeresztes, to the southeast of Erlau, on 23 October, lasted for three days with fierce, intermittent encounters, and ended in disaster for the Christian allies on the long-lamented 26th of October. Once more the Crimean Tatars had rendered their Ottoman overlords an inestimable service on the battlefield. Sigismund Báthory's forces suffered heavy losses at Mezökeresztes.[27]

The strength of the Turkish movement westward was a threat not only to Austria and the hereditary lands of the Hapsburgs but also to Italy. Ever since the fall of Constantinople it had been said from time to time (and was now being said again) that, as the successors of Constantine and the Byzantine emperors, the sultans claimed Italy as their rightful possession. The Curia Romana was well aware of the alleged Ottoman ambition. Clement VIII sought throughout his reign to do as Pius V had done before him, to create an effective Holy League against the Turks, but his appeals to Spain were hardly productive and those to Venice quite futile. In fact the Venetians professed to believe that the formation of a Holy League would only lead the Turks to increased effort and a heavier armament while, league or no league, the Christian states would remain disunited and weak. The Venetian outposts of Corfu, Zara, and Cattaro as well as Candia, Cerigo, and Zante were Christian bulwarks against the westward advance of the Turks whether through the southern Balkans or via the Mediterranean.

In November 1595 the historian Paolo Paruta returned to Venice from Rome, where he had served the Signoria for thirty-eight months as ambassador to the Holy See. He lies buried today in the church of the S. Spirito on the Zattere. Paruta apparently made his report to the doge and Senate after February 1596. He provides us, as he did the doge and Senate, with a remarkably complete and discerning summary of the *status quo* of the Holy See during the reign of Clement VIII. Speaking of the formation of leagues among the Christian princes in times past, Paruta noted that alliance with the papacy was of the greatest importance, not for the popes' temporal powers, "although these are also of some importance," but for the papal capacity to gain adherents to an alliance, to give it repute and emphasize its justice and legitimacy. This had been very much the case "in the enterprises undertaken against the infidels," for the crusade had been the pontiff's especial responsibility as the head of Christendom.

---

[27] Göllner, *Turcica*, II, nos. 2221a, 2227, 2242, 2307, pp. 621–22, 624, 630–31, 662, and on the battle of Mezökeresztes, note *Calendar of State Papers . . .* , *Venice*, IX, no. 524, pp. 247–48, a report of Marco Venier, Venetian bailie in Istanbul to the doge and Senate, dated 24 December, 1596.

In the days of yore, "when the zeal for religion was greater," the influence of the papacy had been enough to put great armies into the field "contra Saraceni e altri infedeli." Yes, even in recent times the Republic had itself been obliged to have recourse to the Holy See "nelle guerre contra Turchi." Paul III had taken the lead in putting together the Holy League of 1537, and Pius V in that of 1570. But the popes had not always acted with justice. They had sometimes employed their spiritual weapons to achieve temporal objectives, like Julius II in the war of the League of Cambrai, which had been directed against Venice. Prudent princes, says Paruta, had taken care to maintain the "friendship and grace" of the popes, often condoning "grandissime imperfezioni" to be found in many of those who had attained the pontificate. Paruta was far more aware of the imperfections of the popes than those of his self-seeking fellow countrymen who always turned to the Holy See and the Christian princes, pleading for help against Turkish attacks (which the papacy always provided), but never rendering others aid when they were attacked. Such was the situation as Paruta addressed the Senate. Clement VIII was pouring vast sums into the imperialist efforts against the Turks. The Venetians were doing nothing.

Weaving in and out of occasional references to the Turks, Paruta felt no need to justify to the doge and Senate their decision not to come to the assistance of the Emperor Rudolf II. Clement did not think highly of the emperor, who fell below the level of his lineage, and whose idleness made him unequal to his great responsibility.[28] For the Swedish king of Poland, Sigismund III Vasa (1587–1632), however, Clement had the highest admiration, seeing in him a prince of the utmost virtue, commending especially his zealous advocacy of the Catholic religion, which was in fact to help cut short his possession of the kingdom of Sweden (1592–1599).

Clement was pleased with Sigismund's anti-Turkish promises and plans. When the king failed to do something or tried to do it too late, the pope would blame it on the disagreements of "the barons of the realm," on the weakness of the king in Poland, and on his lack of money. To assist Sigismund in his anti-Turkish designs and to encourage him, Clement had often urged the Venetian Signoria to unite with the Holy See to help provide the necessary funds. Sigismund had promised to take up arms against the Turks "con potenti forze" for a subvention of 400,000 scudi a year. Clement had not been pressing the matter of late, according to Paruta, but he had not given up the idea.

---

[28] Paolo Paruta, "Relazione di Roma," in Eugenio Albèri, ed., *Le Relazioni degli ambasciatori veneti al Senato durante il secolo decimosesto*, X (ser. II, tom. IV, Florence, 1857), 359, 365–66, 424–25: ". . . e [l'imperatore] sia amatore dell'ozio e della quiete troppo più di ciò che a chi sostiene quel grado di dignità e alla qualità di questi tempi saria conveniente" (p. 424). On Paolo Paruta, note Paolo Preto, *Venezia e i Turchi*, Florence, 1975, pp. 302–13.

Clement was also full of praise for Sigismund Báthory, prince of Transylvania: *lo lauda di bontà, di religione, di prudenza civile, e di valor
militare.* As the doge and Senate were well aware, Clement hoped that
one day the Signoria would finally agree, especially when the affairs of
the imperialists were changing for the better, "to unite in a league with
them and with other Christian princes against the Turks." He had often
regaled Paruta with word of the disorders in the Turkish government and
in the armed forces, which were the consequence of the effeminate nature of the last two sultans, "dati in preda all'ozio e alle delizie." Dwelling constantly upon the assumed weakness of the Ottoman state, Clement was inclined in Paruta's opinion to exaggerate certain recent defeats
which the imperialists and the prince of Transylvania had inflicted on the
Turks.[29] However that might be, it was quite clear that Clement VIII was
as dedicated as Pius V had been to the idea of a great Christian offensive
against the Turks.

Little was achieved by the Christian campaign of 1597, to which
Clement VIII again contributed an auxiliary force under his nephew
Gian Francesco Aldobrandini. The allied army was assembled toward the
end of July at Hungarian Altenburg (present-day Mosonmagyaróvár),
some twenty miles northwest of Raab (Györ) in northwestern Hungary.
On 20 August the Christians occupied the town of Pápa (between Raab
and Veszprém), failed to recover Raab from the Turks, managed to keep
an enemy force at bay, and closed another sorry year of warfare against
the hereditary enemy.[30]

The spring of 1598 did bring the imperialists a striking success, however, for Adolf von Schwarzenberg and the Hungarian commander Nik-
las Pálffy suddenly appeared before Raab on 28 March, and stormed the
fortress on the following day. The recovery of Raab was an event of the
greatest importance.[31] The name of Schwarzenberg resounded throughout Christendom, and Adolf was later knighted by the Emperor Rudolf II
at Prague (on 5 June 1599). There were some further conquests in the
imperialists' campaign of 1598, for after recapturing Raab they went on
to take Eisenstadt (Kismarton), Veszprém, and Várpalota. Pest, the
lower part of Buda (Ofen) on the left bank of the Danube, was occupied,
but the imperialists could not make their way into the upper city on the
right bank, which was the fortress. At that time Pest was of little strategic
importance.

In April 1599 Schwarzenberg tried again to gain the fortress of Buda
for the imperialists, but once more the effort was crowned with failure.

---

[29] Paruta, "Relazione di Roma," pp. 431, 433, 435, 436–37.
[30] Cf. Göllner, *Turcica,* II, no. 2322, p. 668. In 1597 the Christians also took the fortress
of Totis (Tét) in Hungary (*ibid.,* II, nos. 2317–18, p. 666).
[31] Cf. Göllner, *Turcica,* II, nos. 2340–41, 2346, 2349, 2351–54, 2358, 2361, 2365,
2368–74, pp. 676ff., *et alibi.*

The Turks had taken possession of Buda at the beginning of September 1541,[32] and they were to hold it until Charles V of Lorraine reconquered it, along with Pest, in 1686. In the meantime Schwarzenberg also failed in 1599 in an attempt to take Stuhlweissenburg (*Alba Regia*, Székesfehérvár), the coronation site of the kings of Hungary. Clement VIII had provided the imperialists with huge subventions to assist them in their struggle against the Turks. He was, therefore, much distressed to learn of their attempts to negotiate peace with the Porte. Indeed, according to Giovanni (Zuan) Dolfin, who had succeeded Paolo Paruta as the Venetian ambassador to the Holy See, Clement had, as of the latter part of 1598, "twice sent his nephew [Gian Francesco Aldobrandini] into Hungary with a large number of infantry and cavalry at a cost of more than 1,500,000 gold [scudi]. He has also helped the Transylvanian with money, and has wanted to give the Poles a great sum of gold to unite them to the others."[33]

Paruta has informed us that at this time the revenues of the Holy See, all told (*le entrate. . . in tutto fra obbligate e libere*), amounted to about 1,600,000 scudi. Of this sum actually only 570,000 scudi were available for expenditure, for the remaining 1,030,000 scudi were spent in advance or otherwise already committed.[34] It is small wonder, therefore, that Clement should have been disturbed by what he learned of the imperialists' efforts to negotiate a peace with the Porte. The intermediary was Gazi Giray, the khan of the Crimean Tatars, one of the notable figures in the history of the years before and after 1600. The imperialists suggested that they would exchange Gran (Esztergom) for Turkish-held Erlau (Eger). Sultan Mehmed III rejected the proposal. The Porte never gave up territory won by the sword.

In the meantime Sigismund Báthory's great hopes of a united Christian offensive against the Turks having come to nothing, the melancholic prince gave up his sovereignty in May 1598, but resumed authority in August of the same year. In March 1599, however, he abdicated again, and was replaced as the ruler of Transylvania by his cousin, Cardinal Andras Báthory. The latter was soon displaced by Michael "the Brave" of Wallachia, who not only took over Transylvania late in the year 1599, but succeeded in overrunning Moldavia in the spring of 1600. Michael had captured the imagination and won the allegiance of the Vlachs (Rumanians) in the three principalities. He was carried along for a while by a strong current of Rumanian nationalism, for there were many who hoped that, when the Turkish yoke had been thrown off, the principalities might be united under one regime as in the old days of the Byzantine

---

[32] Cf. Setton, III, 459.
[33] Giovanni Dolfin, "Relazione di Roma (1598)," in Albèri, *Le Relazioni degli ambasciatori veneti*, X (ser. II, vol. IV, 1857), 453–54.
[34] Paruta, "Relazione di Roma," *ibid.*, p. 406.

empire, which of course the Turks had destroyed. After all, Michael's predecessor in Moldavia, Jacobus Heraclides, had ruled in 1561–1563 under the titles Βασιλεὺς Μολδαβίας and *defensor libertatis patriae*. Although the Rumanian princely families had become attached to Catholicism, the Protestants in the principalities were often in close touch with the Greek patriarchate in Istanbul, and the lure of anti-Turkish Orthodoxy apparently helped Michael along his hazardous course. Minor insurrections against the Porte were breaking out in many areas throughout the Balkans. Michael the Brave was becoming a legend in his own day, and untold numbers of villagers were eager to see him march on to Byzantium and rule there as the *basileus*.[35]

Michael's ascendancy would prove short-lived, but it was distressing to the imperialists, the Poles, and the Turks. Also distressing to the imperialists was the news of the mutiny of the emperor's troops at Pápa in late July 1600. The soldiers were prepared to surrender the town to the Turks. When Adolf von Schwarzenberg tried to bring them back to obedience, he was killed by a musket shot (on 29 July). And his death was not the only serious loss which the imperialists suffered in the gloomy year 1600.

On 20 October of that gloomy year the Turks took the fortress town of Nagykanizsa less than twenty miles from the frontier of the Austrian duchy of Styria. The loss caused consternation at the imperial court and at the Holy See. Clement VIII decided that he must send an armed force into embattled Hungary for the third time, and he did so, once more under his nephew Gian Francesco Aldobrandini, who died of illness on the campaign, and was later buried in the church of S. Maria sopra Minerva in Rome.

The unpredictable Sigismund Báthory was restored to his former dominion by the Transylvanian diet in January 1601, and in the following month with Ottoman aid he embarked upon an apparently successful military expedition from Turkish-held Temesvár (Timişoara).[36] Fighting now against the Hapsburgs to achieve some measure of independence in Transylvania, Sigismund's success would not last long. His change of sides was discouraging to Clement VIII and the Curia Romana, but on 5 April 1601 there suddenly appeared in Rome an embassy from Abbas I, the shah of Persia.

The envoys were Hussein Ali Beg and the English adventurer Sir Anthony Shirley; they had already been to Moscow, Prague, and various

---

[35] Cf. the interesting article by Andrei Pippidi, "Résurrection de Byzance ou unité politique roumaine? L'Option de Michel le Brave," in *Hommes et idées du Sud-Est européen à l'aube de l'âge moderne*, Bucharest, 1980, pp. 53–65. Michael the Brave received much attention in the contemporary *Zeitungen.*

[36] Temesvár (Timişoara) was taken by the Turks in 1552 (Setton, IV, 584). They held the city until it was recovered in 1716 by Eugene of Savoy.

German courts. They brought the pope a letter from the shah, in which the latter announced his intention of going to war against the Turks (which he did a year later). Abbas had granted the Christians freedom of trade and religion in his realm to the great pleasure of Clement, who replied to the shah's embassy by a letter dated 2 May (1601), urging him to take up arms against the Turks and assuring him of the continuance of papal and imperial efforts against the Porte.[37]

Michael of Wallachia had already been ousted from Moldavia by the Poles, and defeated in Transylvania by the imperialists. Both the Poles and the Turks moved into Wallachia; they avoided conflict with each other, and Michael avoided them both. Reestablishing his accord with the imperial court at Prague, Michael joined forces with the emperor's general Giorgio Basta to drive Sigismund Báthory from Transylvania. When Michael sought to play off the Turks against the imperialists, however, his "treachery" was discovered, and he was put to death by Basta in mid-August 1601.

The Austro-Turkish war was indeed the "Long War," a costly business. Failure accompanied success. The Christians occupied Stuhlweissenburg (Székesfehérvár) in October (1601), and lost it back to the Turks in late August of the following year. While the principalities were being reduced to a shambles, the scene was becoming a bit less crowded. Michael of Wallachia was gone. The political career of Sigismund Báthory (d. 1613) ended after another briefly successful campaign early in 1602 against the imperialist general Giorgio Basta. By mid-year, however, Basta had become the dominant figure in Transylvania, where he soon began a vigorous drive against the Lutherans, Unitarians, and other "heretics." The Calvinists were supposed to be spared for a while. They were too numerous to deal with so quickly. In any event the elimination of Sigismund Báthory and Michael of Wallachia seemed for a little while to reduce the confusion on the eastern fronts.

A policy of religious toleration in the kingdom of Hungary and in the principality of Transylvania might possibly have added most of the former state and much of the latter to the Hapsburg dominions. The Christians were anti-Turkish, but the Turks were tolerant of the disparate faiths in Hungary and Transylvania, provided non-Moslems paid the *kharaj* or poll-tax. The Hapsburgs, especially Rudolf II and the Archduke Ferdinand of Styria, were intolerant. Papal-imperial policy was designed to restore Catholicism to its religious dominance both in the kingdom and in the principality. In mid-July 1603 Giorgio Basta stamped out local religious and ethnic opposition to Austrian-Catholic rule (or

---

[37] Pastor, *Gesch. d. Päpste*, XI (1927), 221–22; Peter Bartl, "Marciare verso Costantinopoli," *Saeculum*, XX, 50, and *Der Westbalkan zwischen spanischer Monarchie und osmanischem Reich* (1974), p. 51.

tried to do so) at Kronstadt (Brassó, Braşov) in the foothills of the Transylvanian Alps, the chief center of the Lutheran Saxons in the harassed principality. Such harshness was bound to cause trouble. With regard to liberty of conscience, however, it must be admitted that the Protestants were hardly more tolerant than the Catholics. The Curia Romana and the Hapsburg court feared that granting religious freedom in areas in Hungary and Transylvania (as in Germany), where the Protestants were in a majority, would lead to the Protestants' taking over Catholic bishoprics, monasteries, property, and jurisdiction (in violation of the religious peace of Augsburg), as in fact they had often done.

The Emperor Rudolf II was somewhat deranged, and his archducal brothers incompetent; the reason and restraint of the Austrian-Hapsburg past were gone. Basta sought to uproot Protestantism in Transylvania. Calvinist Magyars, Szeklers, Vlach-Rumanians, and even Lutheran Saxons were subjected to reckless slaughter and unbridled pillage, religious oppression, and the confiscation of property. Years of warfare, added to Basta's ruthless regime, produced the almost inevitable famine and plague in Transylvania. It is thus not strange that despite the successes of Abbas, the shah of Persia, and the sudden death of Sultan Mehmed III (on 22 December 1603),[38] the imperialists made no progress against the Turks. A spirit of nationalism, a desire for religious freedom, and antagonism to the Hapsburgs—hardly new sentiments in Hungary and Transylvania—pervaded the kingdom and the principality. Rudolf II's policy set the course for a century, and eastern Hungary and Transylvania would not be free of the Turks until the treaty of Karlowitz in 1699.

From the military maelstrom in Hungary and Transylvania two nobles emerged in the year 1604, both Calvinists who had been loyal to the Hapsburgs, Stephen Bocskay and his chief supporter Gabriel (Gábor) Bethlen. Bocskay was a relative of Sigismund Báthory, whom he had served, and like him (although Sigismund was always somewhat ambivalent toward the Hapsburgs) Bocskay had become gravely disillusioned by the harsh fatuity of imperial policy in the kingdom and in the principality. Before long Bocskay and Bethlen were at war with the Hapsburgs. After enjoying a minor victory in the field in mid-October (1604), Bocskay's forces were twice defeated by Giorgio Basta the following month. The Turks came immediately to Bocskay's assistance, and most of the Haiduk mountaineers rallied to his cause. In Germany the Lutheran princes had no intention of helping the Emperor Rudolf to obliterate Protestantism in Hungary and Transylvania. In fact one form or another of Protestantism made up the dominant faiths in Hungary and Transyl-

---

[38] *Cal. State Papers . . . , Venice*, X (1900, repr. 1970), nos. 173, 178, pp. 125, 127.

vania, for Catholicism had suffered a marked decline throughout southeastern Europe during the later sixteenth century.[39]

The Turkish sultan Ahmed I recognized Bocskay not only as prince of Transylvania but also as king of Hungary. Bocskay declined the latter title, but was enthroned with all due ceremony as prince of Transylvania in the fortress town of Medgyes (Medias), to the east of Alba Iulia, on 14 September 1605. Many a person present on that occasion must have given thought to the violent death of Lodovico Gritti at Medgyes on a September day some seventy years before (in 1534). The Venetian doge Andrea's son, Gritti had been in his day one of the most powerful figures at the Porte, and was said to have nurtured hopes of winning some such position as Bocskay had now achieved.

As for the Venetians, they remained at peace with the Porte, and continued to appoint their *giovani della lingua,* as they had been doing for long generations. Thus on 31 October 1609 the Senate granted the petition of the young Battista Navon for the Turkish bursary. Battista's father Pasquale and his brother Tommaso had served the Signoria faithfully as dragomans. The Turkish language ran in the Navon family. Being a dragoman was a "carico laborioso e travaglioso;" he must be able to read, write, and speak Turkish easily and accurately. The holder of the bursary lived and was fed in the house of the bailie in Istanbul. There were several such students at the *bailaggio.* Battista's remuneration was to be fifty ducats a year "et quelle regalie che sono solite darsi a gli altri giovani della lingua."[40]

Such students were almost always Venetian citizens by birth (*cittadini originari*). The Signoria's need of reliable and loyal interpreters is obvious. The bailie had no other way to communicate with the sultan or the grand vizir. The Collegio had no other way of reading Turkish texts when they were delivered to Venice. When the student had achieved the required linguistic proficiency, he would be appointed to the secretarial staff in Venice, and might eventually be sent as a translator to the Bosporus. When the Republic was at war with the Porte, however, obviously such bursaries usually had to be suspended.[41]

---

[39] On Hungarian society, politics, and religion at the beginning of the seventeenth century, see in general Kálmán Benda, "Absolutismus und ständischer Widerstand in Ungarn am Anfang des 17. Jahrhunderts," *Südost-Forschungen,* XXXIII (1974), 85–124.

[40] Archivio di Stato di Venezia (ASV), Senato Mar, Reg. 69 (1609–1610), fol. 15ᵛ [37ᵛ], doc. dated 31 October 1609.

[41] Few such appointments could be made during the Turco-Venetian war for possession of the island of Crete (1645–1669), but in 1668 one Giacomo Tarsia, *giovene di lingua,* came to Larissa from Istanbul to serve the Venetian ambassador Alvise da Molin when the latter was trying to negotiate some kind of peace with the Turks at Larissa, where Sultan Mehmed IV had gone hunting (*Diario della Speditione dell'ill. et ecc. signor Alvise da Molin . . . alla Porta,* MS. Marc. It. VII, 1608 [7514], p. 47). When peace was made (in

The Christian revolt against the Hapsburgs in 1604 and the elevation of Stephen Bocskay to princely sovereignty in Transylvania were a boon to the Turks, who looked upon him as their vassal. Bocskay drove the imperialists out of upper Hungary while Gabriel Bethlen, who was himself later to become prince of Transylvania (1613–1629), was gaining control of the principality in Bocskay's name. The Poles were restraining their ambitions in Transylvania and Moldavia because of the threatening attitude of the Crimean Tatars and the increasing effectiveness of the Turkish soldiery. The sultan's forces had been doing well in Hungary, in alliance with Stephen Bocskay, and this despite the prolonged revolt of the Celālīs in Asia Minor and the onset of another war with Persia to which we have already referred. The war had begun in 1602–1603, and would eventually lead to the Turks' losing their conquests in the Caucasus. Meanwhile, however, although the Turks were said to be interested in making peace in the spring of 1605,[42] during the summer they went on to recover Visegrád and Gran (Esztergom), which the Christians had wrested from them ten years before.

The Christian losses brought fear and sadness to the Curia Romana, but Clement VIII was spared the news, for he had died on 5 March, 1605. He was succeeded for twenty-six days by Leo XI de' Medici, and thereafter by Camillo Borghese, who took the name Paul V at his election on 16 May. Paul V's difficulties with Venice are well known.[43] At times it seemed almost as if the Long War would never draw to a close, but in imperialist circles the fear was growing that when it did, it might also be the end of Hapsburg hegemony in Hungary. Subject to mental disorders, the Emperor Rudolf II was adding instability to incompetence. On 25 April 1606 the Archdukes Matthias, Maximilian, Ferdinand, Maximilian Ernst, and later the Archduke Albrecht, "brothers and paternal cousins," affirming Rudolf's inability to rule (*ex quadam animi indis-*

1669) the Senate had to look again to "la necessaria provisione de' giovini di lingua" in Istanbul (ASV, Delib. Costantinopli, Reg. 32, fol. 109^r [200^r], doc. dated 27 December 1670).

About this time Paul Rycaut, who distinguished himself as consul of the Levant Company at Smyrna, recommended the setting-up of "a seminary of young Englishmen of sprightly and ingenious parts" to learn Turkish and certain other oriental languages (Sonia P. Anderson, *An English Consul in Turkey: Paul Rycaut at Smyrna, 1667–1678*, Oxford, 1989, pp. 108–9), but no English school of *giovani di lingua* was ever established.

[42] *Cal. State Papers . . . , Venice*, X (1900, repr. 1970), no. 350, p. 226, doc. dated 14 March 1605.

[43] Ludwig von Pastor, *Geschichte der Päpste*, XII (Freiburg im Breisgau, 1927), 82–93 and ff.; Gaetano Cozzi, *Il Doge Nicolò Contarini: Ricerche sul patriziato veneziano agli inizi del Seicento*, Venice, Rome, 1958, pp. 93ff.; William J. Bouwsma, *Venice and the Defense of Republican Liberty: Renaissance Values in the Age of the Counter Reformation*, Berkeley and Los Angeles, 1968, pp. 339ff. In the Biblioteca Nazionale Marciana, MS. It. VII, 1689 (7757), there is a heavy quarto volume of 370 fols., which contains a miscellany of documents ranging from the years 1602–3 to 1617 relating to the background and consequences of the interdict which Paul V laid upon Venice (on 17 April 1606), with the most important texts coming from the years 1605–7.

positione et infirmitate, quae sua periculosa intervalla habet), en-trusted the fortunes of their house to Matthias, who was to exercise the "power and authority" of the Empire.[44]

Thereafter on 23 June, after lengthy negotiations, Matthias accepted the treaty of Vienna with Stephen Bocskay and the latter's Hungarian adherents, granting a limited freedom of religion in the kingdom of Hun-gary "without prejudice, however, to the Roman Catholic religion," which meant that the Catholic clergy and churches were to remain un-disturbed. A palatine was to be chosen, "according to the ancient cus-tom," at the next meeting of the Hungarian diet, and along with Hungar-ian councilors the palatine was to recognize the Archduke Matthias, in accordance with the *plenipotentia* granted him by the emperor, as the supreme authority in the kingdom of Hungary. In the absence of Matthias the palatine was to represent him "in negotiis regni." His impe-rial and royal Majesty was indeed to possess (through Matthias) Hungary and its annexes, i.e., Slavonia, Croatia, and Dalmatia, but all major and minor offices in the realm were to be conferred upon Hungarians en-tirely without religious discrimination. The rights and properties of various Hungarian families were to be restored.

Stephen Bocskay was recognized as prince of Transylvania, being given *iure haereditario* the castle (*arx*) of Tokaj and the counties of Ugocsa, Beregh, and Szatmár, which were to revert to the Hungarian crown, however, if he died without male heirs. Stephen Bocskay de-clared that he had not accepted the crown offered to him by the Turkish grand vizir [Lala Mehmed Pasha] "in derogation of the king and kingdom of Hungary and of the ancient crown." And in accordance with their past tradition the Transylvanians were to have the right to elect their own princes.[45] Rudolf confirmed the treaty on 6 August (1606), although he

---

[44] J. Dumont, *Corps universel diplomatique*, V-2, no. XLIV, p. 68, "actum Viennae 25 die Aprilis, anno salutis humanae 1606."

[45] Dumont, *Corps universel diplomatique*, V-2, no. XLIV, pp. 68–72: "acta et conclusa sunt haec Viennae Austriae 23 die mensis Iunii, anno 1606;" and see in general Jos. von Hammer-Purgstall, *Gesch. des osmanischen Reiches*, IV (1829, repr. 1963), 265–393, trans. J.-J. Hellert, VII (1837), 323–76, and VIII (1837), 1–108, who deals in large detail with the years 1596–1606 from the Turkish standpoint; J.W. Zinkeisen, *Gesch. d. osman-ischen Reiches*, III (1855), 604–17; N. Jorga, *Gesch. d. osmanischen Reiches*, III (1910), 319–43, with emphasis on the Turks and the Rumanians; Pastor, *Gesch. d. Päpste*, XI (1927), 215–29, and *Hist. Popes*, XXIII, 289–310; C.M. Kortepeter, *Ottoman Imperi-alism during the Reformation* (1972), pp. 148–210; P. Bartl, *Der Westbalkan zwischen spanischer Monarchie und osmanischem Reich* (1974), who is concerned solely with the years just before and after 1600; J.V. Polišenský, *The Thirty Years' War*, trans. from the Czech by Robert Evans, Berkeley and Los Angeles, 1971, pp. 66–74. Although without direct references to the sources, Polišenský's book is very useful. As one of the early editors of the *Documenta bohemica Bellum Tricennale illustrantia* (1971ff.), Polišenský was as well acquainted with the archival sources as with the secondary literature. It is not surprising that, as a Czech, Polišenský should put a perhaps undue emphasis upon Bohe-mia (Zlín as well as Prague) after the crucial years 1618–1620.

protested *secrete* that he had acted under duress. His secret repudiation of the peace was meaningless, for the settlement at Vienna took immediate effect, providing the background for another treaty which finally ended the Austro-Turkish war.

After a few weeks of negotiation at "Zsitvatorok," the mouth of Zsitva creek by the Danube, representatives of the Empire and the Porte reached agreement on 11 November 1606, *in festo S. Martini,* to end the Long War. The Emperor Rudolf confirmed the peace of Zsitvatorok on 9 December. According to the first article of the treaty, the sultan and the emperor were to behave toward each other as father and son (*unus in patrem, alter vero in filium se suscipiant*), and were so to deal with the ambassadors which the one sent to the other. In all texts and on all occasions they were to refer to each other as emperor, not as king, which was the first time the Porte appears to have recognized the emperor as the equal of the padishah. The peace of Zsitvatorok, moreover, was the first treaty made by the Porte outside Istanbul.

The Crimean Tatars were included in the treaty, and as long as the peace lasted they were not to cause loss or damage to any Christian lands. Peace was to obtain between the two *imperatores* everywhere, on land and at sea, "especially in Hungary," and if the king of Spain should wish to be included in the treaty, he was to be allowed to do so. There were to be no more "raids" (*excursiones*); pirates and plunderers were to be imprisoned, and dealt with by local commanders; "and stolen goods returned." Neither of the high contracting parties was to attack or seize fortresses belonging to the other; "moreover, that which has been granted to the most illustrious lord [Stephen] Bocskay is to remain his according to the peace made at Vienna." Prisoners of war were to be exchanged "on the basis of equality." Minor affairs were to be handled locally, "but if other matters of great moment should come up, which cannot be decided by local authorities, then the attention of each emperor may be required."

Fortresses might be rebuilt on their former sites (*in suis antiquis locis*), but the treaty forbade the building of any new *castra et castella.* The emperor was sending an envoy to Istanbul with gifts for the sultan. The grand vizir Murad Pasha was to send an envoy to the Archduke Matthias with gifts, "and when our envoys come to Constantinople for the ratification of the peace, the emperor of the Turks should also send an envoy to our city of Prague [Rudolf's residence] with greater gifts than has been his custom." The imperial envoy would take to the Porte a gift of 200,000 florins, as had been promised, which gift was never to be repeated (*semel pro semper*).

The peace was to last for twenty years, beginning on 1 January (1607). Embassies were to be exchanged after three years with further gifts without obligation, and they were to be called gifts, i.e., not any form of

tribute. The peace was to endure for the said twenty years, binding the heirs of both emperor and sultan to its observance. Imperial envoys were to be free to make whatever requests of the sultan that they might wish. A dozen or so villages, which are specified in the treaty, were to be free of the "Turkish yoke." Hungarian nobles living in villages under Ottoman control were to pay the Turks neither tribute nor tithes, but in all things, "whether as to their property or their persons," were to be free. Those who paid nothing to their legal sovereign were to pay nothing to the Turks.[46] The Treaty of Zsitvatorok is a milestone in the history of Ottoman relations not only with Austria but with the whole of Europe.

The success of the Emperor Rudolf II and Duke Maximilian I of Bavaria in December 1607 in imposing Catholicism upon largely Protestant Donauwörth, a "free city" in Swabia, some twenty miles or more northwest of Augsburg, led to a large increase in the smouldering religious unrest in Germany. The municipal council in Donauwörth had refused to allow freedom of worship to the Catholic minority in the town. Maximilian seized Donauwörth, reasserted Catholicism, and continued to hold the town to the angry resentment of the Protestant princes.[47] At the end of April 1608 the Calvinist Elector Friedrich IV of the Palatinate and his adherents withdrew in a huff from the Regensburger Reichstag, where a vain effort had been made to restore and make adjustments in the old religious peace of Augsburg of 1555. Immediately thereafter, in the week of 12–16 May (1608) at Auhausen bei Nördlingen a number of Protestant princes—the Elector Friedrich, Duke Johann Friedrich of Württemberg, the Margrave Joachim Ernst of Brandenburg-Ansbach, the Margrave Georg Friedrich of Baden-Durlach, together with Philipp Ludwig, count palatine of Neuburg am Rhein, and Christian, the margrave of Kulmbach—formed a union against the Catholic powers. It was an ominous beginning, but there was more to come.[48]

In the spring of 1608 Matthias, the eldest of Rudolf's three surviving

---

[46] Dumont, *Corps universel diplomatique*, V-2, no. XLVIII, pp. 78–80, "datum in castris infra Danubium et Fluvium Situa [Situa Torock] positis, in festo S. Martini, A.D. MDCVI," and cf. von Hammer-Purgstall, *Gesch. d. osmanischen Reiches*, V (1829, repr. 1963), 393–96, trans. J.-J. Hellert, VIII (1837), 108–111, and Setton, *The Papacy and the Levant*, IV (1984), 1097–98, with refs.

[47] Cf. Dumont, V-2, no. LXXXIV, pp. 126–35.

[48] The conflicts at Donauwörth led to a series of events which soon produced the Evangelical Union of the Protestants and, *par réaction*, the Catholic League of the princely adherents to the Church of Rome. The Capuchin father S. Lorenzo da Brindisi, having been assailed with venomous insults by the Lutherans of Donauwörth (in the spring of 1606), launched against them the campaign, which soon brought about the intervention of Rudolf II and Maximilian da Bavaria, resulting in the Catholic dominance in Donauwörth, on which see Arturo da Carmignano, "La Part de S. Laurent de Brindes dans le ban de Donauwörth (1607)," *Revue d'histoire ecclésiastique*, LVIII-2 (1963), 460–86, and cf. Geoffrey Parker *et al.*, *The Thirty Years' War*, London and Boston, 1984, pp. 22–24.

brothers, was prepared to take the field with Protestant help to give the fullest effect to the Hapsburg archdukes' declaration (of 25 April 1606), granting him the exercise of imperial sovereignty. Rudolf was now forced by a series of pacts of June 1608 to yield to Matthias full authority in the kingdom of Hungary, the archduchy of Austria, and the margraviate of Moravia. If Rudolf died without male heirs, Matthias was to succeed him as king of Bohemia. Furthermore, Rudolf was to propose on Matthias's behalf at the next meeting of the Reichstag that funds be provided "pour payer les gens de guerre qu'il fait entretenir sur les frontières du Turc en Hongrie." All the rights, liberties, and privileges of the Bohemian Estates were to be preserved inviolably.[49]

The Protestants in Austria asserted their right to the free exercise of the evangelical faith (on 30 August 1608),[50] and Rudolf conceded the free *exercitium religionis . . . sub utraque specie* to their coreligionists in Bohemia (in 1609).[51] By an edict dated at Prague on 11 July (1609) Rudolf extended freedom of worship to the Silesians and Lusatians.[52]

To halt his brother Matthias's rise in power, the most Catholic Emperor Rudolf was prepared to make almost any concession to the Protestants to lure them away from Matthias. Rudolf was now giving more and more time to alchemy, to which he had devoted his chief attention for years.[53] He was failing in health; his sanity was slipping away. He gave no heed to Pope Paul V's persistent pleas to accept reconciliation with his rebellious brother Matthias, and help secure the latter's election as king of the Romans to make sure that succession to the Empire would thus remain within the house of Hapsburg. Matthias had managed to get himself elected king of Hungary, and was crowned on 19 November (1608), to the ever-increasing exasperation of Rudolf, who had come to hate his brother.

Indeed, to hold his own against Matthias, on 9 July 1609 Rudolf signed the well-known "Letter of Majesty" (*Majestätsbrief*), and thereafter accepted a "Compromise" (*Vergleich*) between Catholics and Protestants, extending the right to build churches and full freedom of worship (as we have just noted) to a wide range of the inhabitants of Bohemia. To the distress of the Curia Romana, Rudolf was soon obliged to address an-

---

[49] Dumont, *Corps universel diplomatique*, V-2, nos. LVIII, LXI, LXII, LXIV, pp. 91–95.

[50] Dumont, V-2, no. LXV, pp. 95–97.

[51] *Ibid.*, V-2, no. LXVII, pp. 98–99, and cf. nos. LXXIII, LXXVII, pp. 111–13, 116–18.

[52] *Ibid.*, V-2, no. LXXVI, pp. 115–16: ". . . ut inter omnes . . . tam sub una quam sub utraque specie communicantes, his et futuris temporibus, pax et amicitia pro amplificando regno isto [Bohemiae] conservetur, utraque pars religionem suam, unde salutem aeternam consequi sese posse sperent, libere et absque nullo impedimento exerceant. . . ."

[53] On Rudolf's interest in alchemy and the other "occult arts," see R.J.W. Evans, *Rudolf II and His World: A Study in Intellectual History*, Oxford, 1973, pp. 196ff.

other "Letter of Majesty" to the Silesians. For a while there seemed almost to be no bounds to the success of the Bohemian Brethren and their Protestant allies.[54] Nationalism was also playing its part, tending to separate Hungarians, Bohemians, Transylvanians, Silesians, and others from the Austrian-Catholic house of Hapsburg.

In March 1609 Duke Johann Wilhelm of Jülich, Cleves, Berg, and Ravensburg finally died. Half-mad and childless, he had been a serious problem. The duchies were claimed by Philipp Ludwig, count palatine of Neuberg am Rhein, and Johann Sigismund, the elector of Brandenburg; they were also claimed by Christian, the elector of Saxony; and all three claimants were Protestants. Neuburg and Brandenburg regarded the duchies as theirs because they were related by marriage to the deceased Johann Wilhelm; Saxony based his demand for the duchies upon an imperial promise. And at Prague on 7 July 1610 Rudolf II, with a review of the recent history of the duchies, signed a letter of investiture granting Christian of Saxony the duchies of Jülich, Cleves, and Berg as fiefs of the Empire.[55] Rudolf's grant did not take effect; Saxony did not get the duchies.

The Jülich-Cleves contention twice brought Europe to the brink of war but, most surprisingly, it was settled on 12 November 1614 by the "provisional" treaty of Xanten, dividing the disputed lands into two parts without prejudice to the claims of either Brandenburg or Neuburg (*sans préjudice de l'union d'iceux*). The provisional treaty was to last for two centuries. Brandenburg was assigned the duchy of Cleves, the county of La Marck, Ravenstein, and the county of Ravensburg, while Neuburg acquired Jülich and Berg.[56]

In the meantime the Empire as well as the house of Hapsburg seemed to be falling apart. On 3 July 1610, however, upon the intervention of the Archduke Ferdinand of Styria, the Elector Ernst of Cologne, and Duke Heinrich of Brunswick, "Articles of Reconciliation" between Rudolf and Matthias were finally accepted at Vienna. The articles were designed to preserve Rudolf's dignity as emperor, king of Bohemia, margrave of Moravia, "et le premier de la maison d'Austriche," as well as to recognize Matthias's royal right to the crown of Hungary. Provision was made for the defense of Hungary, should there be need of "la guerre contre le

---

[54] On the emperor's advisors (and his problems), cf. Evans, *Rudolf II* (1973), pp. 63–74.

[55] Dumont, V-2, no. XCI, pp. 144–47, and on the rival claims to Jülich, Cleves, and Berg, see, *ibid.*, nos. LXXXI–LXXXIV, pp. 121–35. By a treaty of 11 February 1610, Henry IV of France joined the Protestants Friedrich IV of the Palatinate and Johann Sigismund of Brandenburg to keep the disputed duchies and the county of La Marck "aux plus proches héritiers" (*ibid.*, no. LXXXV, pp. 135–37, and cf. nos. LXXXVI–LXXXVII, CCLII, CCCXXX).

[56] For the text of the treaty of Xanten, "fait et conclu à Santen le 12 Novembre 1614," see Dumont, V-2, no. CXLII, pp. 259–61, cf. no. CXLIII, and note Geoffrey Parker *et al.*, *The Thirty Years' War*, London and Boston, 1984, pp. 26–31, 35–37.

Turc.''[57] Like other attempts to heal the breach between the brothers, the Articles of July 1610 soon proved to be futile.

As the religious cauldron continued to boil in central Europe, outsiders added further ingredients of hostility to the coming flare-up between Catholics and Protestants. King Henry IV of France, a onetime Huguenot, gave his support to the formation of the Protestant or Evangelical Union, while the opposing Catholic League turned for sustenance to Spain, Bavaria, and the Holy See. Henry IV had been preparing for war against the Hapsburgs when he was assassinated by the half-mad schoolmaster François Ravaillac in mid-May 1610. His death, together with that of the Elector Friedrich IV of the Palatinate in September and the Bavarians' apparent readiness for conflict, diverted the Evangelical Union from any serious thought of warfare, at least for the time being.

From the Catholic standpoint that was just as well, for there was no reconciling Rudolf with his brother Matthias; in the spring of 1611 Matthias marched upon Prague, removed Rudolf from the throne, and was himself crowned king of Bohemia.[58] Matthias also took over Silesia. Although he had not been elected king of the Romans when Rudolf died (on 20 January 1612), Matthias succeeded his brother as emperor, being chosen by the Electors on 13 June after a brief but worrisome interregnum. In his electoral capitulation of 18 June Matthias acknowledged his responsibilities as advocate and protector of the Holy See and the "Christliche Kirch." He also declared his intention to maintain peace in both religious and secular affairs in accord with the decrees of the Reichstag of Augsburg in 1555.[59]

During the seven years of Matthias's reign (1612–1619) his chief minister was Melchior Klesl (Khlesl), bishop of Vienna and Wiener Neustadt. Klesl's elevation to the cardinalate (on 2 December 1615) remained *in pectore* until 11 April 1616, when Paul V published it in the consistory. The son of a Protestant baker in Vienna, Klesl became a Catholic in his youth; although he seems to have been a sincere churchman in his later years, he was also a politician. To the great ire of both Maximilian I, duke of Bavaria and (from 1623) an imperial elector, and Ferdinand, archduke of Styria and (from 1619) the Holy Roman Emperor, Klesl pursued a policy of religious moderation. To the annoyance of Paul V and the Curia Romana, Klesl had gone along with Matthias's concessions to the Protestants in Hungary and Transylvania in the treaty of Vienna in June 1606.

---

[57] Dumont, *Corps universel diplomatique*, V-2, no. XC, pp. 143–44.
[58] Dumont, *Corps universel diplomatique*, V-2, nos. XCVII, CII–CIII, pp. 160, 166–68. Matthias promised to preserve all the rights, liberties, and privileges granted to the Bohemians in the past.
[59] Dumont, V-2, no. CXXII, pp. 198–203, esp. p. 199a.

In 1608 the Elector Friedrich IV (d. 1610) of the Palatinate helped establish, as we have seen, the Evangelical Union, and in the course of the year 1609 Maximilian of Bavaria helped found the Catholic League, along with the three ecclesiastical electors of Mainz, Trier, and Cologne. At Würzburg in 1610 the Articles of the Catholic League were approved for nine years. Maximilian was recognized as leader (*zum Obersten*), and the bishops of Würzburg, Passau, and Augsburg were added to the league.[60]

Matthias proved to be less energetic as emperor than he had been as his brother's opponent, having clearly decided to enjoy the empire which God had given him. He left almost all decisions to Melchior Klesl. Like his brother Rudolf, Matthias had no heir; the imperial succession was the major problem of Catholicism in central Europe. Paul V made repeated appeals to Klesl to help bring about the election of a king of the Romans, but time passed, and nothing was done. In any event the Turks were quiet. At the beginning of July 1612 Sultan Ahmed I granted the same extensive privileges to Dutch merchants as the French and English already possessed, "aller et venir dans toutes les villes de mon empire et . . . trafiquer librement et sans être inquiettez."[61] Ahmed also accepted a renewal of the treaty of Zsitvatorok for another twenty years; all the old "puncta et articuli" were retained, and some new articles were added. Matthias ratified the treaty at Prague on 1 December, 1615.[62]

If the Turks were quiet, the Protestants were not. For some years they had been alarmed by the Catholic restoration in Europe. In Germany the Catholic recovery was strongest in the south, and the Protestants began to fare very badly in such places as Mainz, Trier, and Cologne, Regensburg, Augsburg, Bamberg, Würzburg, Eichstätt, and Passau. Under Duke Maximilian I, Bavaria was a Catholic stronghold; Protestantism was a lost cause in the Tyrol. Cardinal Melchior Klesl was trying to pursue a policy of compromise with the Protestants to avoid war. The great problem, fraught with peril, was the imperial succession. Klesl wanted to postpone a meeting of the electoral college until he could assure the Protestants of some measure of religious freedom, to the indignation of the Emperor Matthias's brother, the Archduke Maximilian, and his cousin, the Archduke Ferdinand of Styria.

The Hapsburg archdukes had decided upon Ferdinand of Styria as the successor of Matthias, for the latter was sixty years of age (in 1617), in poor health, and childless. Matthias's brother Maximilian was fifty-nine

---

[60] Dumont, *Corps universel diplomatique*, V-2, no. LXXIX, pp. 118–19.

[61] Dumont, V-2, no. CXXIV, pp. 205–14, esp. p. 207.

[62] Dumont, V-2, no. CXLVII, pp. 264–66, and note no. CLXXV. On the religious and, especially, the economic problems which the Bohemians and Moravians faced during the first two decades of the seventeenth century, note Polišenský, *The Thirty Years' War*, pp. 75–86 and ff.

and childless, and his other surviving brother Albrecht was fifty-eight and also childless. The archdukes, fearing for the future of their house, insisted upon the immediate election of Ferdinand as king of the Romans. Ferdinand had two sons. Some twenty years younger than his cousins, Ferdinand was an ardent Catholic, having stamped out Protestantism in Styria, Carinthia, and Carniola. Now at least the picturesque villages in these areas were no longer rent by religious dissent and disturbance, and peace reigned amid the rolling green hills, winding rivers, and pine-clad mountain sides.

Ferdinand's eventual election as emperor seemed assured, for in the spring of 1617, at the apparent behest of Matthias, King Philip III of Spain renewed and confirmed for himself and his heirs his mother Anna's renunciation (on 29 April 1571) of her rights of succession to the kingdoms of Hungary and Bohemia. Anna (d. 1580) was the daughter of the Emperor Maximilian II (d. 1576). She had been the fourth (and last) wife of Philip II of Spain. Philip III yielded all such rights of succession to Ferdinand of Styria and his male heirs, and male heirs only, for Ferdinand's female descendants would have to yield, *casu ita eveniente,* to the male heirs of the Spanish king. Ferdinand accepted the condition, and the final documents were ratified by Matthias in the royal castle at Prague.[63]

In return for his compliance Philip III was promised Alsace, which would also be a source of trouble. In 1617 Ferdinand settled his differences with the Venetians with regard to the piratical Uskoks,[64] turning his full attention to Bohemia, where the Estates despite a Protestant majority elected or rather accepted him as king (on 17 June, 1617).[65] As king of Bohemia Ferdinand had a vote in the imperial electoral college. In fact he had what might be the deciding vote, for while the archiepiscopal electors of Mainz, Trier, and Cologne were obviously Catholics, the electors of Saxony, Brandenburg, and the Palatinate were Protestants. Ferdinand thus seemed almost assured of election as emperor for he could, if necessary, vote for himself. Nevertheless, it must be borne in mind that the elector of Trier might have to yield to the wishes of the

---

[63] Dumont, V-2, nos. CLXV–CLXVIII, pp. 298–302, docs. dated 6 and 15 June, 1617: ". . . dicta Regis Catholici [Philippi III] linea masculina praeferatur foemineae lineae paternae stirpis memorati Archi-Ducis Ferdinandi."

[64] Dumont, V-2, nos. CLXIX–CLXX, pp. 302–5, and on the so-called "Uskok War," note Parket *et al., The Thirty Years' War* (1984), pp. 40–42, 248, note 5. On the Uskoks themselves, cf. Setton, II, 297, and esp. IV, 608, 843–44, *et alibi.* The contest between Ferdinand and Venice was also caused by their rival claims to the fortress of Gradisca d'Isonzo in Gorizia, which Ferdinand looked upon as a hereditary possession, on which note Heinrich Kretschmayr, *Geschichte von Venedig,* 3 vols., 1905–34, repr. Aalen, 1964, III, 281–83, and esp. Cozzi, *Il Doge Nicolò Contarini* (1958), pp. 149ff.

[65] Anton Gindely, *Geschichte des Dreissigjährigen Krieges,* 4 vols., Prague, 1869–1880, I, 165–73. With some hesitation Ferdinand accepted Rudolf's Letter of Majesty.

French government. In 1618 Ferdinand was elected king of Hungary. Although he had acknowledged the Protestants' right to exercise their freedom of conscience (on the basis of the religious peace of Augsburg of 1555 and the Letter of Majesty), the Bohemian Brethren, the Lutherans, and the Calvinists soon discovered they had good reason not to trust him. In July 1618, after the outbreak in Prague (to which we are now coming), Ferdinand arrested Cardinal Melchior Klesl, the would-be peacemaker, and confined him to a castle in the Tyrol. Although later released, Klesl's political career was ended, and there were few articulate advocates of peace in a position to be heard.

Despite the Evangelical majority in Bohemia, in 1617–1618 Johann Lohel, the archbishop of Prague, with Hapsburg support, embarked upon a series of attacks upon the Protestants, all in grave violation of Rudolf's Letter of Majesty. The Protestants began by summoning their co-religionist members of the Bohemian diet to come together again at Prague, where they met on 21 May (1618) to make a formal remonstrance to the royal councilors. On the next day Count Heinrich Matthias von Thurn, Wenzel von Ruppa, Ulrich Kinský, Colonna von Fels, and other radicals held a secret meeting at which they decided to take action against the councilors whom they held responsible for the anti-Protestant policy of the Hapsburgs, which Melchior Klesl had been unable to avert.

It was on the following day, 23 May, that von Thurn and his fellows invaded the "castle village" (in the Lesser Town, the Malá Strana) on the towering height of the Hradčany. They entered the Old Royal Palace (Starý Královský Palác) next to the cathedral church of S. Vitus. From Vladislav Hall they passed on into a small room, the then chancellery, where they engaged in a hostile exchange with four [of the ten] royal councilors present in the chamber, and ended up by throwing two of them, Jaroslav von Martinitz and Wilhelm von Slawata (along with the secretary Philipp Fabricius), out of a castle window into the moat then some eighty feet below. Surprisingly enough, no one of the three was seriously injured. Such was the "defenestration of Prague," *der Prager Fenstersturz.*[66] The Thirty Years' War had begun.

---

[66] E. Charvériat, *Histoire de la Guerre de Trente Ans,* 2 vols., Paris, 1878, I, 89–99; Gindely, *Geschichte des Dreissigjährigen Krieges,* I, 269–99. On the counts von Thurn, see Gindely, I, 88ff.

On the Thirty Years' War, especially as it bore upon Bohemia, see the *Documenta bohemica Bellum Tricennale illustrantia,* eds. Josef Polišenský, Josef Kŏcí, Gabriela Čechová, Josef Janáček, Miroslav Toegel, *et al.,* 7 vols., Prague, 1971–81. A survey of modern works on the Bohemian war (1618–1621) is given, *ibid.,* I, 54ff. Geoffrey Parker *et al., The Thirty Years' War,* London and Boston, 1984, provides a good introduction to the major events, problems, and bibliography of the long, destructive conflicts which tore Germany to pieces. Among the countless general histories (and monographs) on the war in question see, on the events leading up to and following the Defenestration, Polišenský, *The*

The Protestants in Silesia, Moravia, and Austria took their stand with Heinrich Matthias von Thurn. The Dutch might have joined them, but were dissuaded by the neutrality of the French and the English. One could also be sure of Venetian neutrality, although the interests of the Republic seemed always to be at variance with those of the Hapsburgs at both Vienna and Madrid. After the death of the Emperor Matthias (on 20 March 1619) the Bohemian Estates felt obliged to reconsider their future. Although they had accepted Ferdinand of Styria as king of Bohemia (in 1617), they now looked forward to the election of a new king, as the Estates were being convened in a Protestant assembly. The Estates were a sort of parliament, made up of the landowning nobles, the knighthood, and the burghers. One hundred articles were now passed (on 31 July 1619) as binding upon the next king. There had been strong support, especially among the higher nobility, for the elevation of the Elector Johann Georg of Saxony to the Bohemian throne, but he had persistently declined the risk and risen above the temptation. Hence there was little doubt as to whom the throne would be offered, and also little doubt that he would accept the conditions.

The sovereign to be elected must employ no Jesuits in his councils or on his legations. Indeed, the Jesuits and their pupils (*discipuli*) were to be "proscribed forever," and all their properties expropriated for public use. Neither the king nor the queen could introduce any "new order of monks into the kingdom." The king must observe every article and every clause in Rudolf II's "Letter of Majesty." The Evangelicals were to continue to hold all the churches they then possessed "in all the cities, towns, and country districts." The Moravians and Lusatians who had no Letter of Majesty were, nevertheless, to enjoy the same rights of religious and civil freedom, for the "exercise of religion must be free to everyone" (*exercitium religionis unicuique liberum sit*).

In Catholic communities members of the local town council (*senatus*) were required to abjure the decrees of the Councils of Constance and Trent to the effect that heretical faiths should not be allowed safety. Catholics must not be permitted dominance in ecclesiastical affairs. In

---

Thirty Years' War, pp. 98ff., and Georges Pagès, *The Thirty Years' War*, New York, 1970, pp. 45–54 and ff. Herbert Langer's work *Hortus Bellicus—Der Dreissigjährige Krieg*, Leipzig, 1978, trans. C.S.V. Salt, *The Thirty Years' War*, Poole, Dorset, 1980, is richly illustrated. Incidentally, Pagès' book, although rather a small one, is rich in factual data held together and placed in their historical context by an overall chronological narrative.

Having agreed to a renewal of the treaty of Zsitvatorok in 1615 (see above) and having made peace with Persia in late August 1618, the Turks continued at peace with their neighbors, for they had trouble enough within their own government, on which see in general Reinhard Rudolf Heinisch, "Habsburg, die Pforte und der Böhmische Aufstand (1618–1620)," *Südost-Forschungen*, XXXIII (1974), 125–65, and XXXIV (1975), 79–124. Incidentally, the moat below the castle on the Hradčany (or what is left of it) is now about fifty feet deep, time and debris having filled in the moat to a considerable extent.

those places in which the town council consisted solely of Catholics it must be altered to allow for a membership of one half Protestants. On the other hand, where Evangelicals were a majority, they alone were to serve on the council (an obvious abridgment of the civil rights of Catholics!). The elected king of Bohemia must observe these articles. Otherwise no one was to owe him obedience.

The next king of Bohemia could not go to war without the consent of the Estates. Only Evangelicals—Bohemian Brethren, Utraquists, Lutherans—were to serve in the offices and ministries of the Bohemian Chancery. Foreigners must be shown consideration and kindliness. The rights of respectable Catholics were to be protected by the present compact, but this did not include those who were trying to contravene the Letter of Majesty. Matters of great importance must be referred to the Estates. Bohemian subjects (*subditi*) should be trained in the military arts, but not the peasants (*coloni*), to whom arms were not allowed. In case of necessity one area of Bohemia must furnish assistance to another within four weeks.

The Bohemians were to provide an armament of horse and foot to the Silesians, Moravians, and Lusatians, who had joined them as Protestant allies. Those who stood in opposition to the Protestant confederation must be punished, and those who had been proscribed were to remain in banishment (*extorres maneant*). Their properties were to be confiscated and sold.[67] Such were the major articles intended to form the basis of the Bohemian monarchy, from which Ferdinand of Styria was deposed (on 22 August 1619), and to which the Elector Friedrich V of the Palatinate was elected (on 26 August).[68] Friedrich was the scion of the elder branch of the Wittelsbach family (Maximilian I of Bavaria headed the younger branch). Friedrich had married Elizabeth Stuart, the only daughter of James I of England, from whom Bohemia would get no help, for James soon decided to keep out of the fray.

The Bohemian rebels as well as the Hungarians and Transylvanians were bound sooner or later (and from time to time) to turn to the Turks, the enemies of the Hapsburgs, for help in one form or another. In fact the Thirty Years' War might have seemed to give the Turks a splendid opportunity to move further westward into Europe. Actually, however, the Turks had been exhausted by their war with Persia and Abbas the Great (1602–1618) and by the Long War with Austria (1592–1606). Sultan Murad IV (d. 1640) would be remarkably successful in further warfare with the Persians and, as we shall see in some detail, the Turks would eventually wrest almost all the island of Crete from the Venetians in

---

[67] Dumont, V-2, no. CLXXXV, p. 326, doc. dated 31 July 1619, a Latin summary, and, *ibid.*, no. CXCIV, pp. 338–46, the full German text.

[68] On the background, cf. Dumont, V-2, nos. CLXXXIX, CXCIII–CXCIV, pp. 331ff.

another "long war" (1645–1669). Furthermore, until the grand vizirates of Mehmed Köprülü (1656–1661) and his son Ahmed (d. 1676) there was no end of turbulence in Istanbul. Although Turkish irruptions on the Christian eastern front were not infrequent, and there was another Austro-Turkish war in 1663–1664 (as well as Ottoman strife with the Poles and Russians thereafter), there was a surprising measure of peace and quiet on the Christian eastern front (it has been called "stagnation") lasting from the peace of Zsitvatorok (in 1606) until the siege of Vienna (in 1683).[69]

Although the Dutch and the Venetians were rivals for the Levantine trade, fear of the Hapsburgs brought them together. The Dutch had rendered Venice assistance during the second decade of the century, as the Serenissima sought to suppress Uskok piracy in the Adriatic. The Uskoks, whose chief stronghold was Segna (Senj) in Hapsburg Croatia, were subjects of the archduchy of Austria. In 1619, as the Twelve Years' Truce between Spain and Holland was drawing to a worrisome close, the Venetians and the Dutch came together in a defensive alliance. If either of the two high contracting parties was attacked by Hapsburg forces, the one would aid the other to the extent of 50,000 florins a month. If they were both attacked, the treaty would fall into abeyance, and each state would conduct its own defense.

The Veneto-Dutch treaty was to last for fifteen years (1619–1634). Indeed, when Spain and Holland returned to warfare upon the expiration of the Twelve Years' Truce (in 1621), Venice lived up to her obligations, and was alleged to have disbursed more than one million ducats on behalf of her Dutch allies from April 1622 to March 1626. The resumption of peace between France and Spain, however, in the treaty of Monzón (on 5 March, 1626),[70] the war of the Mantuan succession, and the terrible plague of 1630, which laid the Venetians low, all helped to remove the Serenissima from the scenes of conflict. It was just as well, for presently (in 1645) a quarter-century of warfare with the Turks lay before

---

[69] On Austrian, Transylvanian, Bohemian, and Hungarian relations with (and embassies to) the Turks at the beginning of the Thirty Years' War, see Reinhard Rudolf Heinisch, "Habsburg, die Pforte und der Böhmische Aufstand (1618–1620)," *Südost-Forschungen,* XXXIII (1974), 125–65, and XXXIV (1975), 79–124, who covers somewhat more time and territory than his title suggests. Heinisch has also made good use of materials to be found in the Haus-, Hof- und Staatsarchiv in Vienna.

In like fashion and with emphasis on Gabriel Bethlen (Bethlen Gábor), Helfried Valentinitsch has explored the entanglements of the Styrians and Hungarians with the Ottoman Empire during the half-century or more of Austro-Turkish peace which lasted from the treaty of Zsitvatorok to the war of 1663–1664 and the battle of S. Gotthard (Szentgotthárd)—"Die Steiermark, Ungarn und die Osmanen (1606–1662)," *Zeitschrift des Historischen Vereines für Steiermark,* LXV (1974), 93–128.

[70] Dumont, V-2 (1728), no. CCLXXI, pp. 487ff., "fait à Monçon le cinquième Mars 1626," and cf. Heinrich Kretschmayr, *Geschichte von Venedig,* 3 vols., 1905–34, repr. Aalen, 1964, III, 294–95.

the Venetians for possession of the island of Crete. When the fifteen-year alliance with Holland ended in 1634, the Dutch claimed that Venice was some 1,200,000 ducats in arrears in her payments, which the Serenissima denied on the grounds that the Dutch war with Spain was fully as offensive as it was defensive.[71] That was the end of cordial relations between Holland and Venice, and in any event commercial rivalry rarely makes for friendship.

The Bohemians had caught the attention of all Europe and the Levant. Heinrich von Thurn, the leader of the revolt, had already invaded Austria with widespread Protestant support, reaching the very walls of Vienna. He soon had to fall back into Bohemia, however, for his ally Ernst von Mansfeld, the hireling general of Friedrich of the Palatinate (with some financial help from Savoy), was defeated on 10 June 1619 near the modern town of Horní Vltavice to the west of Budweis (České Budějovice). In the late summer (of 1619) Gabriel Bethlen, the Calvinist prince of Transylvania, moved into Hungary, occupied Pressburg (Bratislava) as well as a number of lesser places, and was soon advancing upon Vienna, which for some time he subjected to a futile siege. With the world around him falling apart Ferdinand of Styria, *rex alter Bohemiae*, once he saw that Vienna was safe, made haste to Frankfurt am Main, where on 28 August 1619 he was chosen Holy Roman Emperor by the electoral college.[72]

As a personality Ferdinand was dowdy and unimpressive, but he proved to be almost imperturbable. Deeply religious, he was also energetic and amiable. Friedrich V of the Palatinate was no match for him.

---

[71] Alfred van der Essen, "L'Alliance défensive hollando-vénitienne de 1619 et l'Espagne," in the *Miscellanea historica in honorem Leonis van der Essen*, 2 vols., Brussels and Paris, 1947, II, 819–29, has (despite his title) traced the relations of Venice and Holland in connection with the alliance of 1619 from the latter date until 1643. Cf. Kretschmayr, *Venedig*, III, 290ff., 299–300.

On the economic advance of the United Provinces (in the age of "mercantilism") in the sixteenth century and their paramount importance in the seventeenth and earlier eighteenth centuries, see the articles by Immanuel Wallerstein, Pierre Jeannin, and Charles Carrière in Maurice Aymard, ed., *Dutch capitalism and world capitalism*, Cambridge Univ. Press, 1982, pp. 93–196, and note the interesting little book by Peter Burke, *Venice and Amsterdam: A study of seventeenth-century élites*, London, 1974, who draws contrasts and comparisons between almost Catholic Venice and almost Calvinist Amsterdam, with especial consideration of the urban "élites" in each case, who tended gradually to move from being merchants (entrepreneurs) to becoming rentiers (land-holding aristocrats).

[72] Ferdinand II's electoral capitulation (*Wahlkapitulation*), defining the terms under which he was elected emperor of the Holy Roman Empire, is given in Dumont, V-2, no. CXCV, pp. 349–54, doc. dated 28 August 1619. On the role of Gabriel Bethlen (Bethlen Gábor) at the beginning of the Thirty Years' War, see Maja Depner, *Das Fürstentum Siebenbürgen im Kampf gegen Habsburg: Untersuchungen über die Politik Siebenbürgens während des Dreissigjährigen Krieges*, Stuttgart, 1938, pp. 36ff.

And the Evangelical Union was no match for the revived Catholic League. The Union was sadly lacking in funds, while Paul V now began to pour money into Ferdinand's coffers.

Paul also gave financial support to the League and to Bavaria whose ruler, Duke Maximilian I, agreed by the treaty of Munich in early October (1619) to put his own resources and those of the League, of which he was the head, into the field against Friedrich of the Palatinate.[73] Maximilian was promised possession of whatever territories the forces of the League might wrest from the Palatinate as well as the electorate itself, of which Friedrich was to be deprived. The only support, such as it was, that Friedrich managed to get was to be found in the alliance which he made at Pressburg (Bratislava) with Gabriel Bethlen on 15–20 January 1620. The treaty was made between Friedrich as king of Bohemia, margrave of Moravia, duke of Silesia, and margrave of Upper and Lower Lusatia, and Bethlen as *rex vel princeps Hungariae . . . princeps Transylvaniae*. Their confederacy was to last "eternally," *aeternum foedus, perpetuaque ac inviolabilis pax*.[74] A treaty designed for eternity was not likely to last long, and a treaty with Bethlen was not likely to be of much benefit to anyone but Bethlen.[75] Calvinists both, Friedrich and the Transylvanian could not enlist the aid of the Lutherans, who hated Calvinists, and constantly equated them with Moslems.

Holland, Denmark, Sweden, Venice, and the Evangelical Union all recognized Friedrich of the Palatinate as king of Bohemia, but no significant assistance was forthcoming from any one of them. Bethlen was as untrustworthy as he was able; also he had his own problems in Transylvania. The day after his agreement with Friedrich, Bethlen accepted a truce (on 16 January 1620) with Ferdinand II, which was to last until 29 September. This truce was renewed in February.[76] Friedrich had no capacity for leadership. Handsome and good-natured, he was entirely under the influence of his ambitious wife and his advisor Christian of Anhalt.

As king of Bohemia, however, Friedrich had two electoral votes, which did not endear him to the Lutheran Elector Johann Georg of Saxony. If

---

[73] Dumont, V-2, no. CXCVI, pp. 354–56, doc. dated at Munich on 8 October 1619.

[74] Dumont, V-2, no. CXCVII, pp. 356–58, "actum Posonii [i.e., Hung. Pozsony, Germ. Pressburg] in comitiis publicis decimo quinto Januarii, anno Christi millesimo sexcentesimo vigesimo." Cf. Depner, *Das Fürstentum Siebenbürgen im Kamp gegen Habsburg* (1938), pp. 49–54.

[75] Although caught between the imperialists and the Turks, Gabriel Bethlen, who died on 15 November 1629 at the age of forty-nine, proved to be a successful and effective prince of Transylvania. Fighting for his own advancement and that of his people, Bethlen generally and perhaps necessarily tended toward the Turks. An excellent sketch of his career (and a sympathetic appraisal of his character) may be found in D. Angyal, "Gabriel Bethlen," *Revue historique*, CLVIII (May–June 1928), 19–80, and see also R.R. Heinisch, "Habsburg, die Pforte und der Böhmische Aufstand," *Südost-Forschungen*, XXXIII, esp. pp. 152–65, and XXXIV, 79ff. (cited above).

[76] Dumont, V-2, nos. CXCVIII, CC, pp. 358–59.

Friedrich could hold the Bohemian throne, he would become too power-ful. Not surprisingly, therefore, when Johann Georg was promised Lusa-tia as well as continued possession of church property expropriated con-trary to the religious peace of Augsburg (of 1555), he joined the ranks of the imperialists. Also the election of the Calvinist Friedrich to the Bohe-mian throne had been especially galling to the Lutheran elector of Sax-ony. Thus there was reason for Johann Georg's letting the Protestants down, just as he would find reasons for letting the emperor down in 1631 and the Swedes in 1635. And, of course, the princes, Protestant as well as Catholic, did not take kindly to the republican sentiments expressed by the revolutionaries, especially the Calvinists, at recent assemblies of the Estates in Prague.

Despite French hostility to the Hapsburgs (which would increase with the passing years), the government of the young Louis XIII sided with the imperialists, and sought support for Ferdinand II against Friedrich of the Palatinate by sending ambassadors, *wolansehenliche Gesandten,* into Germany. With no faith in Friedrich, in fear of possible French intervention, and lacking the necessary funds and forces to carry on against the Catholic League, the Evangelical Union gave way. At Ulm on 3 July 1620 Maximilian I, duke of Bavaria and general of the League, and Joachim Ernst, margrave of Brandenburg-Ansbach and lieutenant-gen-eral of the Union, along with their allies, made a treaty which was de-signed to remove the misunderstanding (*Missverstand*) which had arisen between the two religious coalitions. The text of the agreement acknowledges the importance of the French intervention.[77] The Evan-gelical Union had abandoned Friedrich of the Palatinate.

Having marshaled their forces, the enemies of Friedrich soon de-scended upon him. Ambrosio Spínola, the Genoese-Spanish commander in the Netherlands, moved into the Palatinate, and the elector of Saxony into Lusatia. Maximilian of Bavaria and the imperialist army took the expected offensive against Bohemia. Now had come the day of judgment, for which the western world had been waiting. At the White Mountain (Bílá Hora), some four miles west of Prague, the Protestant forces under the Calvinist general Christian of Anhalt were defeated by the army of the imperialists and the Catholic League under Johan Tserclaes, count of Tilly. The battle was fought on 8 November 1620.[78]

---

[77] Dumont, V-2, no. CCV, p. 369, "geschehen Ulm den 3. Julii neuen Calend. anno 1620," and cf., *ibid.,* no. CCXVII, p. 391, doc. dated 12 April 1621; also C.V. Wedgwood, *The Thirty Years' War,* London, 1947, pp. 111–12, and Dieter Albrecht, *Die auswärtige Politik Maximilians von Bayern, 1618–1635,* Göttingen, 1962, pp. 45–47 (Schriftenreihe der Historischen Kommission bei der Bayerischen Akademie der Wissenschaften, VI).

[78] Hans Delbrück, *Geschichte der Kriegskunst im Rahmen der politischen Geschichte,* IV (Berlin, 1920), 223–32. On the composition and the financing of the opposing forces at the White Mountain, cf. Polišenský, *The Thirty Years' War,* pp. 124–32, who believes that the commercial rivalry between England and Holland was the major cause of the Bohemian

Christian of Anhalt had been the right hand of Friedrich IV of the Palatinate (d. 1610), and he had helped build the Evangelical Union. A strong Calvinist, Anhalt had been the mentor of Friedrich V, who now became the "winter king." Both he and Anhalt were placed under the ban of empire (on 22 January 1621)[79] and, what was worse, Friedrich would soon lose the Palatinate to Maximilian of Bavaria. In the meantime, five days after the White Mountain, the Estates of Bohemia made their full obeisance to the Emperor Ferdinand II (on 13 November), acknowledging their error in opposing their true royal and imperial sovereign. They promised to recognize him and no other as king of Bohemia, to remain steadfast in the loyalty they now declared, and to give up all alliances and associations contrary to his interests.[80]

Gabriel Bethlen accepted a treaty with Ferdinand II (on 26 January 1622), by which he renounced the claim he had made to the title and dignity of king of Hungary, and promised to send the emperor the sacrosanct crown of the Magyar realm. He also agreed to withdraw from all the fortresses he then held on the frontier. Everyone might continue to practice the religion he followed at the time of the emperor's accession. The Jesuits could return to all the places from which they had been evicted, but they were not henceforth to acquire or to possess landed property in Bethlen's domain. Ferdinand made Bethlen a prince of the Empire, "et lui laisseroit jouïr sa vie durant en la Hongrie de huict comtez avec la ville de Cassovie" [Kaschau, Košice].[81]

Estates' being unable "to create a great 'anti-Habsburg coalition,' " which seems rather doubtful. Bílá Hora is about four miles west of the Powder Tower in the center of the Old Town (Staré Město) of Prague; it is not east southeast of the city, as stated in the *Columbia Lippincott Gazetteer* (1962), p. 2087. Bílá Hora is at the end of the tram line on Vělohorská ulice, where one now finds the Velká Hospoda na Bílé Hoře, an inn. The battle of the White Mountain is depicted in a large painting on the north wall of the dining room of the inn. The White "Mountain" is not a mountain, not even a hill. It is a flat plain somewhat higher, to be sure, than the ground level of the Old Town.

[79] Dumont, V-2, nos. CCX–CCXI, pp. 371–78, and cf. Wedgwood, *The Thirty Years' War* (1947), pp. 123–35, who dates the imperial ban on 29 January.

[80] Dumont, V-2, no. CCVIII, pp. 370–71, "actum in der königlichen Hauptstadt Prag den 13. Tag Novembris, anno 1620."

[81] Dumont, V-2, no. CCXXVII, pp. 407–8, text of the peace of Nikolsburg, dated 26 January 1622, which was followed (after another outbreak of hostilities between Ferdinand and Bethlen in 1623) by the treaty of Vienna of 8 May 1624 (*ibid.,* no. CCLI, pp. 444–46), and after Bethlen again had recourse to arms, another treaty was made in 1626, on which see below, and cf. Depner, *Das Fürstentum Siebenbürgen* (1938) pp. 90–91, 102, 106ff. Although on the whole the Turks were not a serious problem to the Hapsburgs for a long time after the peace of Zsitvatorok, the Ottoman government did assist Bethlen with a fair number of horse and foot in 1623 (cf. Polišenský, *The Thirty Years' War*, pp. 155–57), but little came of it.

There are surveys of Ottoman history from the treaty of Zsitvatorok (1606) to the accession of Murad IV (1623) in von Hammer-Purgstall, *Gesch. d. osman. Reiches*, IV (1829, repr. 1963), 397–608, trans. Hellert, VIII (1837), 112–376; Zinkeisen, *Gesch. d. osman. Reiches*, III (1855), 673–762; Jorga, *Gesch. des osman. Reiches*, III (1910), 339–57 and ff.

Protestantism had received a serious blow in the battle of the White Mountain. There was understandable rejoicing in Rome, where the ailing Pope Paul V led an exultant procession from the church of S. Maria sopra Minerva to the German church of the Anima near Piazza Navona. As the months and years passed, Bohemia was ravaged and enslaved by the victorious Hapsburgs, who put an end to Protestantism in the land of the Hussites and Brethren, Lutherans and Calvinists. The pitiless execution of all apprehended opponents of the Hapsburgs, the widespread confiscation of property, the corruption of coinage, and the suppression of the old parliamentary and judicial institutions brought about the complete ruination of Bohemia. Paul V died on 28 January 1621, and on 9 February Gregory XV Ludovisi was elected his successor. Like Paul before him, Gregory poured great sums into the imperialist coffers and those of Bavaria and the Catholic League. Ferdinand II was in firm control of Bohemia, and by the close of 1621 the forces of Maximilian I of Bavaria had overrun the Upper Palatinate in the region of the river Main, bordering upon Bohemia. Now the war went on in the Lower or Rhenish Palatinate.

Friedrich V's chief supporters were the fiery, young Christian of Braunschweig-Wolfenbüttel, the Margrave Georg Friedrich of Baden-Durlach, and Ernst von Mansfeld. Christian, administrator of the diocese of Halberstadt, was known as "der Halberstädter." He sacked the northern city of Paderborn, and ravaged the countryside over a wide area, amassing loot enough to finance his military endeavors, while Mansfeld plundered the dioceses of Speyer and Strasbourg to the south. On 22 May (1622), however, the count of Tilly and the Spanish general González de Córdoba overwhelmed the forces of the margrave of Baden at Bad Wimpfen on the Neckar, some seven miles northwest of Heilbronn. Baden dropped out of the struggle. Thereafter, on 20 June (1622) Tilly and Córdoba defeated Christian at Höchst on the right bank of the Main, and on 19 September they occupied Heidelberg, the capital of the Palatinate. Six weeks later (on 2 November) they seized Mannheim, an important inland port on the right bank of the Rhine.

After the capture of Heidelberg, Maximilian I presented the famous Palatine Library to Pope Gregory XV, and in 1622–1623 the Greek scholar Leone Allacci prepared the library for shipment to Rome. Allacci not only gathered together the Bibliotheca Palatina from the Heiliggeist-kirche in Heidelberg, but he also raided the Elector's private library in

---

Papal interests were wide-ranging, and Pastor, *Gesch. d. Päpste,* XII (1927), 498–583, and *Hist. Popes,* XXVI, 255–376, has given us a general account of papal relations with the Hapsburgs during the reign of Paul V (1605–1621), including the last years of the Long War with the Turks, the Protestant revolt in Bohemia, and the outbreak of the Thirty Years' War.

the castle as well as those of the university and the college of the Sapientia. Allacci transported some 3,500 manuscripts and 5,000 printed books from Heidelberg to Rome by way of Munich in 196 chests aboard fifty wagons guarded by Bavarian musketeers. The books and manuscripts reached the Vatican under Allacci's guidance two or three weeks after Gregory XV's death (on 8 July 1623). The papal acquisition of the Palatine Library remains, in historical retrospect, one of the most important results of Tilly's campaign in 1622.[82] If the library had not been removed to Rome (in 1623), it might well have been plundered and scattered when the French ravaged Heidelberg seventy years later.

During this period various imperialists emerged from obscurity, and became more than wealthy. Thus by the year 1623 Albrecht Wenzel Eusebius von Wallenstein (Waldstein) had become a prince of the Holy Roman Empire. Now forty years of age he had served the Hapsburgs with marked distinction on the battlefield. Daring and intelligent, well educated and ambitious, he yearned for eminence, even majesty, knowing that in his day (as today) wealth was the stairway to power. After the battle of the White Mountain he acquired vast estates for paltry sums. Among the rebellious Protestants who were put to death (in 1623) was Václav (Wenceslas) Budovec of Budov, whose large estate at Mnichovo Hradiště was seized, and fell into the hands of Wallenstein. A monument to Václav Budovec now stands at the west end of the mansion or so-called castle of Mnichovo Hradiště.

In 1627 Wallenstein sold or gave the rich estate to his nephew Maximilian von Wallenstein. Mnichovo Hradiště became a fief in Wallenstein's duchy of Friedland (Frýdlant). It is a short drive north of Prague, and although few tourists go to see it, Mnichovo Hradiště is well worth a visit, even if it is not so impressive as Wallenstein's palace in the Malá Strana in Prague. After Wallenstein's fall (in 1634) Mnichovo Hradiště remained in the family for three centuries. Some years ago a body, alleged to be that of Wallenstein, was brought to Mnichovo Hradiště, and buried in the chapel of S. Anne, which lies just south of the mansion. A

---

[82] Cf. Gindely, *Gesch. d. Dreissigjährigen Krieges*, IV (1880), 353–79; Pastor, *Gesch. d. Päpste*, XIII-1 (1928), 180–88, and *Hist. Popes*, XXVII, 237–47; Wedgwood, *The Thirty Years' War*, pp. 149–57. On the Palatine Library, now in the Vatican, note the manuscript catalogues by Henry Stevenson and his archaeologist son Henry Stevenson, Jr. (Rome, 1885ff.), and see above all the splendid work on the *Bibliotheca Palatina: Katalog zur Ausstellung vom 8. Juli bis 2. November 1986, Heiliggeistkirche, Heidelberg*, eds. Elmar Mittler *et al.*, 2 vols., Heidelberg, 1986, II, 458ff. The Bibliotheca Palatina also contained the library of Ulrich Fugger, the Augsburg banker, who had lived in Heidelberg for some twenty years (*ibid.*, II, 368ff.). The ousted Friedrich V of the Palatinate had been much concerned for his library, as shown by a letter which he addressed to the Heidelbergers from his exile in Holland on 9/19 November 1621, warning them to see to its safety (*ibid.*, II, 460).

tombstone in the chapel declares it to be the site of the great soldier's burial.[83]

Now that Johan Tserclaes, the count of Tilly, who served Maximilian I of Bavaria and the Catholic League, had conquered the Lower Palatinate, Ferdinand, proceeding cautiously, finally invested Maximilian with the Palatine electorate. Gregory XV had done his best to take the electoral dignity and vote away from the Calvinist Friedrich V. But the opposition, including England and Spain, Saxony and Brandenburg, was great; Maximilian was, therefore, granted the electorate only for his lifetime, reserving the rights (whatever they might prove to be) of Friedrich's heirs.[84] Johann Georg I, the elector of Saxony, received Lusatia.[85] Thus the seeds were planted for another twenty-five years of destructive warfare.

---

[83] Cf. Mojmír Horyna, Luboš Lancinger, Vojtěch Láska, *Mnichovo Hradiště*, Prague, 1984.

[84] Dumont, V-2, nos. CCXXXVI–CCXXXVII, pp. 418–20, docs. dated at Regensburg on 25–26 February 1623; cf., *ibid.*, nos. CCXCVII–CCC, pp. 538ff.; and see Gindely, *Gesch. d. Dreissigjährigen Krieges,* IV (1880), 438–49, and Pastor, *Gesch. d. Päpste*, XIII-1 (1928), 189–202.

[85] Dumont, V-2, no. CCXLVII, pp. 438–40, doc. dated 13/23 June 1623.

II

Continuance of the War, Gustavus Adolphus, Cardinal Richelieu, and the Hapsburgs, the Increasing Importance of France

❧

When Tilly inflicted a crushing defeat upon Christian, the "mad Halberstädter," on 6 August (1623), and destroyed his forces at Stadtlohn on the Berkel River to the west of Münster, the Austrian-Bavarian triumph was complete. Friedrich of the Palatinate was forced to drop out of the contest for a while, and so did Ernst von Mansfeld, who sought refuge and employment in England. But now the Hapsburg-Valois struggle of the preceding century seemed likely to be renewed, for Armand du Plessis, cardinal de Richelieu (since 1622), was taking over the reins of government in France as Louis XIII's prime minister. Richelieu found the Hapsburgs' territorial encirclement of Bourbon France as dangerous and distressing as had the Valois. Also, like them, Richelieu was becoming interested in Italy.

The Spanish were not popular in England, especially after James I failed to marry his son Charles [I] to the Infanta Maria.[1] Thereupon

---

[1] Cf. Dumont, *Corps universel diplomatique,* V-2, no. CCXLVIII, pp. 440–42, projected marriage contract between Charles, prince of Wales, and Maria, infanta of Spain, dated at Westminster on 20 July 1623.

Henriette-Marie, daughter of Henry IV and sister of Louis XIII, suddenly looked attractive at Westminster.[2] As the wheel of fortune spun around, it seemed for a brief spell as though it might unwind the victories of the Hapsburgs. On 6 August 1623, the day that Tilly did away with the Halberstädter's army at Stadtlohn, Maffeo Barberini was elected pope as Urban VIII. He had been papal legate in France. He disliked and feared the Hapsburgs, who had the Holy See caught in the Milanese-Neapolitan vise. Almost by leaps and bounds, in 1624–1625, the enemies of the Hapsburgs drew together in a series of separate treaties—France, the Protestant Netherlands, England, and Brandenburg, even the rivals Denmark and Sweden, as well as Venice and Savoy.[3]

The French, Venetians, Savoyards, Swiss Protestants, and Urban VIII himself wanted to clear the Hapsburgs out of the Valtellina,[4] and in 1624–1625 they did so, but lost the valley back to the Spanish the following year when the French were obliged to make peace with Philip IV of Spain.[5] The would-be allies were in fact still not ready for concerted action against the Hapsburgs. Richelieu had moved too quickly. He could not solve the Huguenot problem until he could take La Rochelle, which did not happen until 1628, when he found himself in a silly war with the English under George Villiers, the first duke of Buckingham (d. 1628), who tried in vain to help the Huguenots. Richelieu thus had to become reconciled with Spain. He had to postpone, but of course he did not abandon, his anti-Hapsburg plans.

From Vienna the European landscape had, for a brief while, begun to look murky, but on 5 June 1625 the Genoese-Spanish general Ambrosio Spínola had wrested from the Dutch the important fortress of Breda in North Brabant. Every visitor to the Prado in Madrid has admired Velázquez's painting of the surrender of Breda. With the war clouds gathering in the west, Ferdinand II sought to maintain peace on his eastern frontier by renewing the treaty of Zsitvatorok with Sultan Murad IV (on 26 March 1626).[6] After another conflict with Gabriel Bethlen, peace was restored in December (1626). The Transylvanian remained a prince of the Empire, and was to hold for his lifetime the seven counties

---

[2] Dumont, V-2, nos. CCLVII, p. 468, and CCLXV, pp. 476–78, docs. dated 20 November 1624 and 8 May 1625.

[3] Cf. Dumont, V-2, nos. CCLIII–CCLIV, CCLVI, CCLVIII–CCLXII, CCLXVII, CCLXIX, and note no. CCLXXIII, pp. 458ff.

[4] Dumont, V-2, nos. CCLVIII–CCLIX, pp. 469–70, and cf. no. CCLX, pp. 469–70.

[5] Dumont, V-2, no. CCLXXI, pp. 487–97, texts dated at Monzón on 5 March 1626, with documentary addenda extending to 28 January 1628.

[6] Dumont, V-2, no. CCLXIV, pp. 475–76, and cf. no. CCLXXIX.

of the Upper Theiss, which he had been granted "par la bénignité de sa Majesté."[7]

At all times in all places it would seem that the rich and powerful seek to take advantage of their position. Bethlen was no exception. On 3 March 1627 the Venetian Senate voted by a large majority "in gratificatione del Signor Prencipe di Transilvania" to allow him to export certain goods without paying a toll of fifty ducats.[8] To a Venetian citizen fifty ducats was no small sum; to the Signoria it was nothing. Why not please Bethlen? He might some day be useful. On 19 November of the same year, however, the Senate declined the request of Bethlen's agents to forego an export toll of 400 ducats despite the obvious desire of many members "tenir buona intelligenza col Prencipe di Transilvania."[9] The Signoria was well aware of the political risks of establishing unwise precedents. Would Bethlen want to avoid a toll of a thousand ducats next time? Who else would expect similar concessions to be granted to them?

One by one Ferdinand II was trying to find solutions for his numerous problems. He made the Bohemian monarchy hereditary in the Hapsburg family by the well-known decrees of 1627, expelling all non-Catholics from the kingdom and establishing the higher Catholic clergy as the dominant Estate in the realm, which now became a mere appendage to

---

[7] Dumont, V-2, no. CCLXXV, pp. 498–99, and cf., *ibid.*, nos. CCLXXVI–CCLXXVII. In March 1626 Gabriel Bethlen had proposed to the French government an alliance, which he promised he would never break, whatever misfortune might overtake him. The alliance was to be "against our common enemy" (obviously Ferdinand II), and peace would be made only "unamini consensu et consilio." Bethlen claimed, however, that five years of warfare had almost exhausted his treasury. To be of use to Louis XIII and Cardinal Richelieu he would require a monthly subsidy of at least 40,000 imperial dollars as long as a state of war existed (. . . *quadraginta dumtaxat thalerorum imperialium millia menstruatim durante bello in subsidium numerari et dari poscimus*), for his proximity to the Austrian Hapsburgs and the king of Poland exposed him to especial danger. Bethlen concluded his request to the king and cardinal with the assurance that if they were also exposed to danger, they could rely upon him, *quod et nos suis Serenitatibus in casu simili reciproce praestituros promittimus* (Public Record Office [PRO], Chancery Lane, London, State Papers [SP] 97, XI, fol. 249). Richelieu was not yet ready, however, for any direct intervention into the Thirty Years' War.

In early May 1626 Sultan Murad IV had word that a Hapsburg embassy was likely to come from Spain or Naples to ask for a formal statement of friendship from the Porte. Murad informed the beys and kadis of Greece, however, that the self-seeking Spanish sought only "their own fraudulent ends," and that the beys and kadis were not to allow them passage through Greece (*ibid.*, State Papers 97, XII, fols. 21, 23, 25, "written in Constantinople in the middle of the moon of Saban [Sha'ban] anno 1035, that is 8 May 1626" [*sic*]). Although Murad was willing to adhere to the treaty of Zsitvatorok with the Hapsburgs of Vienna, he had apparently no intention of accepting the "friendship" of their cousins in Madrid.

[8] Arch. di Stato di Venezia (ASV), Senato Mar, Reg. 85, fol. 1ʳ [26ʳ].

[9] *Ibid.*, fols. 297ᵛ–299 [323ᵛ–325]. After Gabriel Bethlen's death (in 1629) his brother Stephen aspired to the principality of Transylvania, but had to give way before George Rákóczy (cf. PRO, SP 97, XV, fol. 64).

Austria. The Bohemian diet was stripped of all authority to make laws, the Bohemian nobility was crushed, the peasants reduced to a lowly state of serfdom, and seizures of property carried out on a vast scale.[10] German was declared an official language along with Czech, and the latter language remained subdued until the Czech literary revival of the early nineteenth century.

Seeking to take fish from the troubled waters of northern Germany in 1625–1626, Christian IV of Denmark, the brother-in-law of James I of England, almost drowned in the torrent of his own ambition. His endeavors to secure control of the secularized bishoprics of Bremen, Osnabrück, Verden, Minden, Halberstadt, and Magdeburg as well as to exert his sway over the river Elbe's exit into the North Sea and that of the Oder into the Baltic were all frustrated by failures on the battlefield. Equipped with English money, Ernst von Mansfeld had returned to the continent, but he was now defeated by Wallenstein at the bridge of Dessau (on 25 April 1626). Four months later Christian IV was himself crushed by Tilly near the village of Lutter am Barenberge in Brunswick (on 27 August). Christian's own duchies of Schleswig and Holstein were overrun by Tilly and Wallenstein. Presently Mansfeld died in retreat to Dalmatia. Once more the forces of the imperialists and those of the Catholic League had been victorious everywhere despite the intervention of France and England against the Hapsburgs. The future of Protestantism in the German northland, Luther's own *Heimat*, was obviously imperiled.[11] Europe was drifting into near chaos, however, with the corruption of coinage in Spain, Bohemia, and throughout the Empire, the disruption of trade and commerce, the widespread confiscations of the urban and landed properties of the Protestants (and of other rebellious subjects), the reestablishment of Catholicism wherever the Hapsburg arm could reach, driving out Calvinists and (despite earlier compacts) the Lutherans as well, and the rapacity of the unpaid Spanish troops in Flanders, the Rhineland, and the Milanese.[12]

Nevertheless, the Austrian Hapsburgs were doing well, very well. They had little or nothing to fear from the Turks, their most dreaded enemies, for the treaty of Zsitvatorok (of 11 November 1606) had been renewed on 1 July 1615, on 1 May 1616, on 27 February 1618, and on 26 May 1625. Now it was renewed again for twenty-five years on 13 September

---

[10] Dumont, V-2, no. CCLXXVIII, pp. 500–1, and esp. no. CCLXXXII, pp. 507–15, dated 10 May, 1627, and cf. no. CCCIX.

[11] On the political and military confusion caused by Christian IV of Denmark's entry into the European fray, cf. Geoffrey Parker *et al., The Thirty Years' War* (1984), pp. 72–81, and Polišenský, *The Thirty Years' War*, pp. 169–75.

[12] Cf., Parker, pp. 72–109.

1627.[13] The following year (on 20 July 1628) Hans Ludwig von Kuefstein left Vienna as Ferdinand II's envoy to the Porte. His entourage was loaded with gifts for the Sultan Murad IV and the more important participants in the affairs of the Ottoman court. Kuefstein's purpose was to clear up various discrepancies between the Latin and the Turkish texts of this last treaty of 1627. He was to proceed with care, and must not upset the Turks unduly, for what could not be obtained immediately might sometime in the future be won by force of arms. One has learned a fair amount about conditions in Turkey and life at the sultan's court from Kuefstein's diary and correspondence. He arrived back in Vienna on 8 December (1628), and had a long audience with the emperor the following day.[14]

At Vienna on 25 March 1629, Ferdinand II published the text (dated 6 March) of the long-awaited Edict of Restitution, restoring to Catholics all

---

[13] Gabriel Noradounghian, *Recueil d'actes internationaux de l'empire ottoman*, I-1 (Paris, 1897), nos. 205, 218, 219, 224, 246, pp. 39, 41–42, 43, 46. The treaty of Zsitvatorok, like other international conventions, was renewed as the sultanate passed from one ruler to another; thus there was another ratification of the treaty on 19 March 1642 (*ibid.*, no. 251, p. 48), of which a summary of the text is given *ibid.*, I-2, no. VIII, pp. 120–21. The Latin text of the renewal of Zsitvatorok dated 1 May 1616 may also be found, *ibid.*, I-2, no. VII, pp. 113–20.

[14] Karl Teply, *Die kaiserliche Grossbotschaft an Sultan Murad IV. im Jahre 1628: Des Freiherrn Hans Ludwig von Kuefsteins Fahrt zur Hohen Pforte*, Vienna, no date of publication given. Both the Austro-Turkish peace and that which Ferdinand II had made with Gabriel Bethlen in December 1626 remained uncertain, according to a memorial which Sir Thomas Roe is said to have addressed to Frederick Henry, prince of Orange, on 27 December 1628 (O.S.), i.e., 6 January 1629: ". . . All the ministers of the Grand Signor [Murad IV] know and confess their dishonor and disadvantage by this peace, to which they were constrayned to yield by the Asian war [i.e., with Persia], wherein, having now some ease, they wilbe ready to review their accounts with the Emperor and, having reconciled Gabor [Gabriel], he is able by his arts or by necessitye to engage the Turkes at his pleasure. . . . It is desired by Gabor that the Kyng of Sweveland [Gustavus Adolphus] may appeare in Silesia, to whom he will obey and, making the territories of Austria the seate of the war, he offereth to spoyle all the countrye round about and to burne whatsoever is found without the walled townes as far as Bavaria, when he shalbe secured of his retrayct by the King, and to serve him with his horse in all other occasions" (*Letters Relating to the Mission of Sir Thomas Roe to Gustavus Adolphus, 1629–30*, ed. S.R. Gardiner, Camden Society, 1875, p. 4). Gabriel Bethlen died on 15 November 1629. On Roe's activities in Istanbul, see in general *The Negotiations of Sir Thomas Roe* [1581?–1644], *in his Embassy to the Ottoman Porte, from the year 1621 to 1628 inclusive* . . . , vol. I [no more published], London, 1740.

In 1630–1631 the Turks were still deeply involved in an invasion of Persia, and Sultan Murad IV was engrossed in his efforts "to prohibit the takinge of tobacco, havinge commanded yt upon paine of death . . . , and so greate is his hatred that in person he doth walke up and down (daie and night disguised) in search thereof, and hath commanded present infliction upon the [guilty] parties" (Public Record Office [PRO], Chancery Lane, London, State Papers [SP] 97, XV, fols. 33, 64–65ʳ, 74, on the sultan's pursuit of the tobacco smokers, Wyche to Dorchester). Sir Peter Wyche (he usually spelled his name Wych) was the English ambassador to the Porte from 1627 to 1641, succeeding Sir Thomas Roe; Sir Dudley Carleton, Viscount Dorchester, was Charles I's secretary of state from December 1628 until his death in February 1632.

the ecclesiastical properties and rights usurped by the Protestants since the peace of Passau (of 1552). This involved, of course, the archbishoprics of Bremen and Magdeburg as well as the bishoprics of Minden, Verden, Halberstadt, and nine others. As one might have assumed, however, the current claims of the elector of Saxony had eventually to be recognized. Had it been possible to put the edict entirely into effect, which it was not, more than a hundred important abbatial and monastic properties, hospitals, and other foundations might have been recovered by the Catholics. The more recent Protestant nobility would have been impoverished, losing the social status that accompanies wealth. It was sinful and illegal to buy, sell, or usurp church lands; no matter how one had acquired ecclesiastical properties since Passau, he must give them up. The edict recognized, moreover, only Catholics and adherents of the Confession of Augsburg (of 1530), "ceux de l'ancienne religion Catholique et ceux de la Confession d'Ausbourg non changée," for all other doctrines and sects were excluded and prohibited, "and must not be suffered or endured," which meant the exclusion of the Calvinists.[15]

The rivalry of the Hapsburgs and the Wittelsbachs of Bavaria for governance of disputed dioceses had delayed issuance of the Emperor Ferdinand's edict of restitution. Also Maximilian feared the growing power of Wallenstein. Efforts to bring about some kind of reconciliation between Friedrich V, the erstwhile elector palatine, and Ferdinand II had proved futile,[16] while the emperor's son and namesake Ferdinand [III], now king of Hungary and Bohemia, was invested with the electoral dignity which accompanied the crown of the latter kingdom.[17] The Austrian Hapsburgs were riding high in Germany and eastern Europe. Furthermore, the bond with their Spanish cousins was strengthened when a marriage contract between the younger Ferdinand and the Infanta María, sister of Philip IV of Spain, was prepared in Vienna in August 1627 and ratified at Madrid in September 1628.[18] This was the bride that James I had failed to secure for his son and successor Charles.

The imperial claims of Ferdinand II and the massive forces of Wallenstein were getting out of hand, almost as distressing to Catholics as to Protestants. Late in the year 1628 and early in 1629 the four Catholic

---

[15] Dumont, V-2, no. cccix, pp. 564–69, "donné en nostre ville de Vienne le 6 jour du mois de Mars l'an 1629;" cf. Pastor, *Gesch. d. Päpste*, XIII-1 (1928), 349–65, and *Hist. Popes*, XXVIII, 169–92, and esp. Robert Bireley, *Religion and Politics in the Age of the Counterreformation*, Univ. North Carolina Press, 1981, pp. 74–79, 81–94, 122ff., on the bewildering complications which the Edict involved.

[16] Dumont, V-2, no. cclxxxiv, pp. 519–22, doc. dated at Colmar, "die freye Reichsstadt," on 18 July 1627. On the hopes of the English for the restoration of the Palatinate to Friedrich V, Charles I's brother-in-law, as late as March 1629/1630, cf. Public Record Office [PRO], State Papers [SP] 97, XV, fol. 17.

[17] Dumont, V-2, no. ccxciv, p. 537, doc. dated at Prague on 26 January 1628.

[18] Dumont, V-2, no. cccv, pp. 554–58.

electors—Georg Friedrich von Greiffenklau of Mainz, Philipp Christoph von Sötern of Trier, Ferdinand von Wittelsbach of Cologne, and Cologne's brother Maximilian I of Bavaria—chose deputies to wait upon the Emperor Ferdinand to plead for peace for the "afflicted empire, that dear and precious peace for which all good patriots are longing." His Majesty had reduced all the empire to his devotion. There was no longer an enemy to be feared. The electors hoped that Ferdinand would now lighten the burden of soldiery upon the empire by dismissing and removing the *gens de guerre*, making a firm peace, and effecting the "réintégration de la foi germanique entre les états de l'Empire."

To achieve this important objective "une diette impériale" was declared to be absolutely necessary.[19] The electors should attend the diet in person to air their differences and resolve them. Protestants of the Augsburg Confession should be protected and left to their faith. The electors complained of the emperor's generalissimo Albrecht von Wallenstein, the duke of Friedland, who harassed their troops and those of the Catholic League, depriving them of their quarters. The four Catholic electors wanted the Circles of Franconia and Swabia for their own forces. The empire was, incidentally, divided into ten "circles" (as it had been since the end of the fifteenth century), and they often went their own way, adding to the hopeless confusion of what was called the governance of the empire.

The deputies of Christian IV of Denmark also submitted proposals upon which peace could be reestablished, pleading for restoration of the status quo ante bellum. The imperial demands were harsh, however, for Ferdinand wanted Christian to give up the duchies of Schleswig and Holstein as well as to make other important concessions, to which the Danish deputies could not agree.[20]

The Protestants had been poorly led. Defeated, they were being trod under foot. The imperialist generals Wallenstein and Tilly were, however, disturbed by the warlike preparations of Gustavus Adolphus, the Protestant king of Sweden. Wanting to solve the Danish problem to help clear the atmosphere, Wallenstein advocated peace with Christian IV, who was happy to accept the treaty of Lübeck in May 1629. The imperi-

---

[19] This "imperial diet," as we shall note shortly, was to be an electoral diet or convention (a *Kurfürstentag*), not a meeting of the imperial parliament or Reichstag, on which note Hermann Weber, "Empereur, Électeurs et Diète," *Revue d'histoire diplomatique*, LXXXIX (1975), 281–97. On the Electors (*Kurfürsten*) and Princes (*Reichsfürsten*) of the Empire in the sixteenth and seventeenth centuries, see Fritz Dickmann, *Der Westfälische Frieden*, Münster, 1959, pp. 25ff.

[20] Dumont, V-2, no. CCCVIII, pp. 561–64, the last text being dated at Lübeck on 15 March 1629; note also the *Documenta bohemica*, IV, nos. 728–29, 737–38, 741–46, 770, pp. 286ff. Although the emperor's son Ferdinand [III] was one of the "Catholic electors," and had a vote in an imperial election, he was also king of Bohemia, a "foreign" monarch, and could not share in councils of the empire.

alist-Danish peace provided for an abiding friendship between Ferdinand II and Christian. Their heirs and successors were always to keep the peace, "zu ewigen Zeiten untereinander rechtschaffene ungefärbte Freundschafft zu Wasser und Land [zu] halten." The emperor would not interfere in Danish affairs, nor would the king of Denmark in those of the empire, i.e., Christian gave up all claim to the secularized archbishoprics and bishoprics in Germany. The emperor would seek no war indemnity from Denmark despite the damage Christian had done. The duchies of Schleswig and Holstein were to be restored to Christian (and they would remain Danish until the Prussians moved in, in 1864–1866) save for such feudal rights as the emperor possessed in the said duchies and in whatever other lands, cities, and fortresses the emperor would now return to Christian. The kings of Spain and Poland as well as Maximilian of Bavaria and the other electors were all included in the treaty.[21]

The house of Hapsburg and Catholicism seemed to have emerged triumphant from the first dozen years of the Thirty Years' War. Bohemia was no longer Protestant, and had been virtually removed from the political map of Europe. Denmark had been subdued. A number of secularized bishoprics had been returned to Catholicism. The entire Palatinate was in Catholic hands. Protestants were expelled from the revered Lutheran city of Augsburg, a free city of the empire, in August 1629. Ferdinand's *Restitutionsedikt* was wreaking havoc.

Most of the Catholic princes, especially Maximilian of Bavaria, who feared and hated Wallenstein, were rendered extremely uneasy by the extent of the Hapsburg success. It seems not to have occurred to various Catholic leaders that they might need Wallenstein's prowess on the battlefield, even when on 25 September 1629 the Swedish chancellor Axel Oxenstierna concluded a six years' peace with Sigismund III Vasa of Poland,[22] presumably to free the forces of King Gustavus II Adolphus for a descent into Germany.

The "diette impériale" demanded by the Catholic electors was held at Regensburg during the summer and fall of 1630. Although the Protestant electors Johann Georg I of Saxony and Georg Wilhelm of Brandenburg declined to put in an appearance at the diet (or *Kurfürstentag*), the Emperor Ferdinand did not fare well. The electors present rejected his efforts to secure the designation of his son Ferdinand [III] as king of the Romans (and therefore his successor); refused to support the imperialist-Spanish candidate for the duchies of Mantua and Montferrat; and

---

[21] Dumont, V-2, no. cccxviii, pp. 584–86, doc. dated at Lübeck on 22 May 1629, and see Michael Roberts, *Gustavus Adolphus: A History of Sweden, 1611–1632*, 2 vols., London and New York, 1953–58, II, 380–88.

[22] Dumont, V-2, no. cccxxi, pp. 594–96, "fait au camp d'Altemmarck le quinzième Septembre, stil vieil [i.e., the 25th], mil six cens vingt-neuf;" the treaty was ratified by Sigismund III at Warsaw on 8 October 1629, and cf., *ibid.*, no. cccxxiii, p. 598b.

granted exoneration to Friedrich V of the Palatinate provided he would give up his avowed rights to the crown of Bohemia and surrender his electoral dignity and vote (which he declined to do). It appeared as though Maximilian I of Bavaria and his confederates of the Catholic League had successfully asserted their control over Germany, leaving Ferdinand II those rights attendant upon the imperial dignity and, of course, the kingdoms of Hungary and Bohemia, the archduchy of Austria, and the hereditary lands of the Hapsburgs.[23]

Maximilian of Bavaria feared the rising greatness of Wallenstein who, by his success on the battlefield and with the initial support of two rich wives, had created the duchy of Friedland (Frýdlant, in 1625), purchased that of Sagan (in 1628), and conquered that of Mecklenburg (in 1628).[24] A military entrepreneur, Wallenstein raised his own forces and paid them well, relieving the imperial treasury, but imposing a terrible burden upon the lands in which they were quartered. His own huge estates, however, he managed with some measure of forbearance, reaping in capitalist fashion rich rewards of an economic nature. Wallenstein

---

[23] The "diette impériale" was held during the unsuccessful Spanish siege of Casale Monferrato, an important episode in the war of the Mantuan succession (1627–1631), which the French won with the establishment of Charles of Gonzaga-Nevers on the ducal thrones of Mantua and Montferrat (even with the imperialist seizure and sack of Mantua in 1630). Despite an occasional success, 1630 was a bad year for Ferdinand II (cf. *Documenta bohemica Bellum Tricennale illustrantia*, IV [1974], esp. docs. nos. 1030ff., pp. 393ff.).

Charles of Nevers, along with the interesting Jachia ben Mehmet [Yahya ibn Mehmed] and even Wallenstein, was one of several persons who entertained various far-fetched schemes for a crusade against the Turks and the restoration of the Byzantine throne. Jachia was active from about 1610 to his death in 1649/50 (Dorothy M. Vaughan, *Europe and the Turk*, Liverpool, 1954, pp. 217–36), an important but forgotten figure.

The French domination of Mantua-Montferrat disrupted the Milan-Naples axis of the Hapsburgs, to which fact we shall make reference later. On the Kurfürstentag of Regensburg, see Dieter Albrecht, *Die auswärtige Politik Maximilians von Bayern* (1962), pp. 263ff., who explores the background of events, including the consequences of Maximilian's hostility to Wallenstein; note also Roberts, *Gustavus Adolphus*, II (1958), 437–39, and esp. Robert Bireley, *Religion and Politics in the Age of the Counterreformation* (1981), pp. 113–30.

[24] Before the imperialist-Danish peace (of May 1629) Sir Thomas Roe, the English ambassador in Istanbul, in a report on the alleged plans of the Austrians, had picked up the rumor that Wallenstein was also to be given the kingdom of Denmark, "but upon condition that the royall crowne shall be kept from him, and that he shall only hold it with the title of a duke," as a fief of the Empire (Public Record Office, Chancery Lane, London, State Papers 97, XIV, fol. 41, doc. dated January 1627 [1628?]). A number of the "desseigns of the Austrians," which Roe thus reported, do seem unlikely. Sir Thomas Roe resided in Istanbul, as the ambassador of James I (d. 1625) and Charles I, from late December 1621 to early June 1628; like his predecessors and successors he also served as representative of the Levant Company at the Porte (see Michael J. Brown, *Itinerant Ambassador: The Life of Sir Thomas Roe*, Lexington, Kentucky, 1970, pp. 118–65).

On Wallenstein (Waldstein, Valdštejn), note the observations of Polišenský, *The Thirty Years' War*, pp. 71, 74–75, 116–18, 172ff., 177–84, 193–206, 211–14, and see the detailed work of Golo Mann, *Wallenstein*, Frankfurt am Main, 1971, with extensive references to the sources. Mann's biography of Wallenstein has been translated by Charles Kessler, London and New York, 1976, without refs. to sources.

apparently planned the unification of the German empire under the Hapsburgs (at the obvious expense of the princes), and looked forward to domination over Sweden, Denmark, Brandenburg, and Saxony as well as over Poland and Bavaria, after which his dream is alleged to have been a great movement against the Turks, the Hapsburgs' most formidable enemy. But, as the years passed, Wallenstein built air castles in various places, depending upon where he believed his self-interest lay. It was clear to the German princes, however, that their self-interest did not coincide with his, and so Ferdinand II was finally obliged to dismiss him in mid-August 1630.

Having made peace with the Poles (and the Muscovites), Gustavus Adolphus accepted a commercial treaty with the city of Danzig (Gdańsk) on 28 February 1630,[25] and thereafter moved into Pomerania, where on 20 July (1630) he made a treaty of alliance with Bogislaus, the duke of Stettin (Szczecin), "avec très-grande compassion," declaring that Bogislaus had for three years suffered "les très-griefves et inouies oppressions." In 1628 Wallenstein had laid siege—unsuccessfully—to the important city of Stralsund, strategically placed in Pomerania on an outlet to the Baltic Sea. Gustavus Adolphus's treaty with Bogislaus was for their mutual defense, "non point pour l'offence." It was directed, according to the text, against neither the sacred Majesty of the emperor nor the empire, but was intended solely for the preservation of religious freedom and secular peace. Stralsund figures prominently in the treaty. With certain provisos Gustavus Adolphus was designated as Bogislaus's heir if the latter died "without male descendants."[26] Stripped of its verbiage, the treaty meant that the Swedes had taken over Pomerania, to the distress of Georg Wilhelm of Brandenburg.

In France, meanwhile, Louis XIII's chief minister, Cardinal Armand de Richelieu, having taken care of the French Huguenot problem by the occupation of La Rochelle (in 1628) and by the peace of Alais (in 1629), was prepared to venture abroad to do such damage as he could to the Hapsburgs in Austria as well as in Spain. In March 1630 he made a defensive alliance with Maximilian I of Bavaria and the Catholic League, which seemed appropriate for a cardinal of the Roman church. Richelieu, however, had his eyes firmly fixed upon the stalwart Lutheran Gustavus Adolphus, who in the summer of 1630 published a manifesto setting forth the reasons which obliged him to take up arms and enter Germany.

Actually, according to Gustavus, there was no need to dilate on his

---

[25] Dumont, V-2, no. cccxxiii, pp. 598–99, "actum Tiegenhoff [Nowy Dwór Gdański] die decimo octavo Februarii stili veteris [i.e., the 28th] anni 1630."

[26] Dumont, V-2, no. cccxxvii, pp. 606–8, "au vieil Stetin le dixiesme jour de Juillet, vieil stil, l'an mil six cens trente."

reasons, for they were known to all the peoples and states of Christendom, "sçavoir est le dessein perpétuel des Espagnols et Maison d'Austriche à la monarchie universelle." At any rate, still according to Gustavus, the Hapsburgs of Spain and Austria were aiming at the conquest of the states of western Christendom, and especially the principalities and free cities of Germany. Although Gustavus's reasons for embarking upon his "just war" were thus said to be well known, he set them forth at great length.[27]

In response to an embassy which Richelieu sent to Gustavus Adolphus in June 1630, the latter wrote both Louis XIII and Richelieu from Stralsund (on 17 September), requesting in the usual roundabout fashion of the day funds with which to raise troops for the common good.[28] Maximilian and the Catholic League had apparently abandoned the Hapsburgs. Pope Urban VIII Barberini was no friend of the house of Austria, and now Richelieu was prepared to finance Gustavus's "just war" against Ferdinand II.

By the well-known treaty of Bärwalde of 23 January 1631 between Louis XIII and Gustavus Adolphus, the most serene sovereigns of France and Sweden undertook the defense of their common friends and the security of the Baltic Sea and the Atlantic Ocean. They would restore conditions in Europe to the state in which they had been "before the German war." To this end the king of Sweden undertook to put 30,000 foot and 6,000 horse into the field in Germany "at his own expense." To help meet the said expense the king of France would make an annual contribution of "400,000 imperial dollars" (*quadringenta millia talerorum imperialium*), one half to be paid on 15 May, the other half on 15 November, at Paris or Amsterdam, as the Swedish ministers should think best.

Soldiers and sailors might be conscripted in either French or Swedish territory. Ships and military equipment could be exported from the domains of either power free of charge. If God granted the king of Sweden success in areas of the empire and in other places, "in which the exercise of the Roman Catholic religion shall be found," he was not to disturb the faith. Gustavus was to maintain friendship "or at least neutrality" with the duke of Bavaria and the Catholic League if they dealt with him in like fashion. The Franco-Swedish treaty was to last for five years. Since Gustavus had already encountered many expenses in the current war, he was

---

[27] Dumont, V-2, no. CCCXXVIII, pp. 608–11. On 12 August 1630 Gustavus also formed an alliance with the Protestant landgrave of Hessen-Kassel (*ibid.*, no. CCCXXIX). On the changes and complications which time and the hazards of warfare brought about in Gustavus' policies in Germany, note Michael Roberts, "The Political Objectives of Gustav Adolf in Germany, 1630–2," in *Essays in Swedish History*, London, 1967, pp. 82–110, with an extensive bibliography in the notes.

[28] Dumont, V-2, no. CCCXXXIII, p. 615, doc. dated 17 September 1630.

forthwith to receive 400,000 imperial dollars upon the signing of the present treaty, which sum was not to be counted against the five years' subsidy which lay ahead.[29]

The war had begun in earnest. At the beginning of April 1631 Johann Georg of Saxony, Georg Wilhelm of Brandenburg, and their Protestant

---

[29] J. Dumont, *Corps universel diplomatique,* VI-1 (Amsterdam and The Hague, 1728), no. I, pp. 1–2, "actum in Stativis Bernvaldi in nova Marchia Brandeburgensi [i.e., Bärwalde in Neumark in Brandenburg], decima tertia Januarii 1631 stylo veteri [i.e., 23 January *stylo novo*]." In article 3 of Dumont's text of the treaty 400,000 (*quadringenta millia*) is incorrectly given as 40,000 (*quadraginta millia*) by a slip of the penman or the printer, but the figure appears correctly in art. 11. On the negotiations which led to the treaty of Bärwalde, see Lauritz Weibull, "Gustave-Adolphe et Richelieu," *Revue historique,* CLXXIV (July–August 1934), esp. pp. 218–25; cf. Dieter Albrecht, *Die auswärtige Politik Maximilians von Bayern* (1962), pp. 304–5, and Roberts, *Gustavus Adolphus,* II (1958), 466–69.

The military world was remade in the late sixteenth century and the seventeenth. A large bibliography has grown up on the subject in the last two or three generations, of which no account can be taken here, but mention may be made of Michael Roberts' lectures on "Gustav Adolf and the Art of War" (1955) and "The Military Revolution, 1560–1660" (1956), in *Essays in Swedish History,* London, 1967, pp. 56–81, 195–225, on which note also Maury D. Feld, "Middle-Class Society and the Rise of Military Professionalism: The Dutch Army 1589–1609," in *Armed Forces and Society,* I-4 (1975), 419–42; Geoffrey Parker, "The 'Military Revolution,' 1560–1660—a Myth?" in *The Journal of Modern History,* XLVIII (1976), 195–214; and Parker *et al., The Thirty Years' War* (1984), pp. 190ff., 205–8.

The first and most important innovations in drill, tactics, and siegecraft were made by the Dutch under Maurice of Nassau (d. 1625), and new tactical offensives on the battlefield were devised by Gustavus Adolphus, king of Sweden (d. 1632), who drew his ideas from the contemporary Spanish as well as the Dutch models. In tactics Gustavus exerted a considerable influence upon his military successors, including the later Austrian generals (among them Raimondo Montecuccoli) who were to fight successfully against the Turks. Although by the later seventeenth century, the era of Sébastien de Vauban, the modes of warfare had changed considerably, the Dutch-Swedish impact upon military operations remained strong. See in general Werner Hahlweg, *Die Heeresreform der Oranier und die Antike,* Berlin, 1941, who has described the creation of the "modern army" (between 1589 and about 1630) which, oddly enough, was the consequence of the study of the work on tactics (the *Tactica*) of the Greek Aelian (from the second century A.D.) as well as on that attributed to the Byzantine emperor Leo VI (d. 911). Beginning in the Netherlands with Maurice of Nassau and his cousins, the "Heeresreform" was quickly taken up in Germany, France, England, and Italy, and thereafter in Switzerland and Spain—and especially by the Swedish commanders in Germany during the Thirty Years' War.

Hahlweg has also edited the so-called *Kriegsbuch* of Count John VII of Nassau-Siegen (d. 1623), who sought to link theory and practice in the fine art of warfare (*Die Heeresreform der Oranier: Das Kriegsbuch des Grafen Johann von Nassau-Siegen,* Wiesbaden, 1973, with various other texts). Hahlweg's introduction to this work sketches in ample detail the reform of the military in the Netherlands, especially as instituted by Maurice of Nassau and other members of the house of Orange in the later sixteenth and earlier seventeenth centuries. John of Nassau deals in his *Kriegsbuch* with the necessity of drills and practice in the use of pikes, muskets, heavy artillery, and other types of firearms and explosives, mining (in siegecraft) and countermining (in the defense of a fortress), military watchwords and routine commands, tactical formations in marching as well as the "countermarch" in battle, problems of encampment, the current truisms and maxims of warfare and strategy, peace and politics, etc., with historical examples illustrating the success or failure of one method or another. Count John also established the first German military academy (at Siegen in Westphalia).

allies signed an agreement at Leipzig in defense of "unser geliebtes Vaterlandt Teutscher Nation," which had been severely tried "by God's
righteous wrath for our manifold sins." They lamented the notorious
violations of the *Reichsconstitutionen*, the disregard of princely dignity
and privileges, and the utter derogation of German liberty. The Emperor
Ferdinand II must take note of their warning. They did not say that as
Protestants they would join Gustavus Adolphus, but the implication that
they might was easily read between the lines. Saxony and Brandenburg
were joined by two dozen or more lesser princes of some importance and
by delegates from Strasbourg, Nuremberg, Lübeck, Frankfurt-am-Main,
Mühlhausen, Nordhausen, and "the evangelical cities in Swabia."[30] The
idea was that if Ferdinand would revoke the edict of restitution, and
reach a satisfactory compromise with the Protestants, they would, as
Germans, presumably join him in defense of the "Vaterlandt" against
Gustavus Adolphus, a Lutheran but a foreigner.

On 13 April (1631), however, Gustavus II stormed the city of Frankfurt an der Oder, which was a good beginning. The imperialist army
under Tilly was disintegrating for lack of financial support, but he and his
lieutenant Gottfried zu Pappenheim looked to the capture of the Protestant stronghold of Magdeburg on the Elbe. Pappenheim had had the city
under siege for some time. Gustavus sent Dietrich von Falkenberg to
conduct its defense, while he appealed to his fellow Protestants, the
electors of Saxony and Brandenburg, to join him and save the threatened
city. They did nothing; Gustavus could not tell which side they were on;
and neither could they. The two Protestant electors wanted to defend
Germany and also to remain neutral. Their policy was at odds with itself.

The neutrality of Brandenburg, who had but slender resources, was
broken when Gustavus occupied Spandau, just to the west of Berlin, and
made the elector his reluctant ally. Gustavus, unfortunately for Magdeburg, hung back, uncertain of Johann Georg of Saxony, who might or
might not take the field against him. Saxony was unreliable even when he
was sober. Tilly and Pappenheim redoubled their efforts to take Magdeburg, hoping to acquire booty enough to provide them with desperately
needed supplies and wages for their unruly troops.

At long last on the morning of 20 May (1631), after three full days of
ceaseless cannonading, the imperialist forces under Pappenheim
stormed and captured the city of Magdeburg, which was subjected to
merciless sack and slaughter. Before they could gather much booty,
however, fires broke out in several places. Falkenberg, who was killed in
Pappenheim's final onslaught, may conceivably have planned the fires in
advance. The imperialists saved their troops with difficulty, having

---

[30] Dumont, VI-1, no. IV, pp. 6–9, doc. dated 2 April 1631.

gained little by way of provisions and hard cash. Some twenty thousand Magdeburgers perished in the mass destruction of their city. It horrified a Europe accustomed to butchery and conflagration, and was long remembered as the major disaster of the Thirty Years' War.[31]

After Magdeburg, Georg Wilhelm of Brandenburg was obliged to ratify his agreement with Gustavus Adolphus, virtually surrendering the fortress towns of Spandau (a few miles west of Berlin) and Küstrin (on the Oder) to the embattled Swedes, according to the treaty dated 22 June 1631.[32] Gustavus was making progress. On 30 May a treaty had been signed at Fontainebleau between Louis XIII and Maximilian I of Bavaria, who were "désirans . . . confirmer une bonne amitié et une mutuelle deffense." It was a mutual-defense pact, and was to last for eight years. Louis or rather Richelieu undertook to furnish Maximilian with nine thousand foot and two thousand horse "avec canons et provisions convenables et nécessaires pour la défense de l'Électeur de Bavière et de ses provinces héréditaires et acquises en cas que l'on y entrast hostilement." Maximilian might choose either the aforesaid troops or money "in proportion."

On the other hand Maximilian must make available to the French three thousand foot and one thousand horse "for the defense of the most Christian king and his hereditary and acquired lands." Louis XIII, like his new ally, might also demand money in lieu of troops. The French would supply neither men nor money to anyone who proposed to "trouble or molest the said elector or his lands." The French promised to recognize, defend, and maintain Maximilian and the Bavarian Wittelsbachs in the electoral dignity. The Franco-Bavarian treaty was to be kept secret, but the said treaty was not to be understood in any way to contravene the Bavarian promises and commitments to the Emperor Ferdinand II and the Empire. And in evidence of good faith the most Christian king signed the treaty with his own hand.[33]

The French thus bound themselves to maintain Maximilian in the electoral dignity which Gustavus Adolphus proposed to give back to Friedrich V of the Palatinate. They also agreed to defend Maximilian from attack, but the latter's general Tilly was not only generalissimo of the

---

[31] E. Charvériat, *Hist. de la Guerre de Trente Ans*, II (1878), 81–89; Anton Gindely, *History of the Thirty Years' War*, trans. Andrew Ten Brook, 2 vols., New York, 1884, II, 58–67; Wedgwood, *The Thirty Years' War*, pp. 286–91; Parker *et al.*, *The Thirty Years' War* (1984), p. 125; Roberts, *Gustavus Adolphus*, II (1958), 469–74, 480–83, 490ff., 496ff., who places the fall of Magdeburg on 10 May, old style (*ibid.*, II, 495–96); and see esp. Werner Lahne, *Magdeburgs Zerstörung in der zeitgenössischen Publizistik*, Magdeburg, 1931.

[32] Wedgwood, *The Thirty Years' War*, pp. 291–92; Roberts, *Gustavus Adolphus*, II (1958), 490–93, 509–13.

[33] Dumont, VI-1, no. VIII, p. 14.

imperialists but also of the Catholic League, at the head of which was
Maximilian, who was helping to finance the imperialist defense of Catholicism and the German Empire. Since Tilly had to obtain plunder
somewhere to provide his troops with food and funds, he found himself
in a hopeless plight. As the imperialist general, he was at war with Gustavus; as the Bavarian commander, he was the ally of Gustavus's confederates Louis XIII and Richelieu. The French would make available neither
men nor money, according to the secret treaty of 30 May (1631), to
anyone who sought to "trouble or molest the said elector or his lands."
They were very largely financing Gustavus's campaign. What would they
do if and when the Swedes entered Bavarian territory with hostile
intent?

Rendered desperate by the need to find provisions for his troops, Tilly
finally moved into the domain of the Elector Johann Georg of Saxony, to
whom Maximilian was also bound as an ally by the Protestant resolution
of Leipzig (of 2 April 1631). Tilly's action immediately drove Johann
Georg into the arms of Gustavus Adolphus, with whom he signed a pact
of mutual defense on 1 September at Torgau on the Elbe, a city sacred to
the Lutherans, about thirty miles northeast of Leipzig. Gustavus also
confirmed the pact at his camp in the village of Werben, about thirteen
miles southeast of Wittenberge. Werben had been Gustavus's command
post since Tilly and Pappenheim had destroyed Magdeburg, where the
Swedes had hoped to establish their forces.

Gustavus made a solemn pledge to defend the elector of Saxony, his
lands, and his subjects against all enemies, and especially against the
general "Graff von Tilly," who is mentioned in the text.[34] Johann Georg
agreed to unite his forces with those of Gustavus as soon as his Swedish
Majesty had crossed the Elbe to the south, and to give him "full direction" of the coming campaign "so lange die Gefahr von dem Feinde
wehren wird," i.e., "as long as danger from the enemy shall continue."[35]

Meanwhile Tilly was hard at work in Saxony, seizing Halle an der
Saale, some twenty miles or more northwest of Leipzig, as well as Eisle-
ben to the west of Halle, and Merseburg to the south. Each conquest
strengthened his hand against Leipzig, which he occupied in mid-September (1631). The Swedish and Saxon armies now came together at the
town of [Bad] Düben on the river Mulde, a dozen miles east of Bitterfeld.
Düben is something over twenty miles north of Leipzig. The opposing
forces were getting closer, and the reckless Pappenheim ventured out on
his own from the area of Leipzig to determine the whereabouts of Gustavus Adolphus and Johann Georg of Saxony. Finding them, he sent an

---

[34] Dumont, VI-1, nos. XII–XIII, pp. 18–19, docs. dated 1 September 1631.
[35] Dumont, VI-1, no. XII, p. 18b.

urgent appeal to Tilly to join him, which the latter did with grave misgivings.

The famous battle took place at Breitenfeld, a few miles northwest of Leipzig, on Wednesday, 17 September (1631). As the two armies confronted each other on the field, they exchanged cannon fire for several hours before either side began to make an attack. Less than mid-way through the later violence of the contest Johann Georg fled from the field. The Saxon infantry melted away quickly. The cannoneers took to their heels, leaving the heavy artillery behind. Most of the cavalry followed the elector, stopping along the way to steal what they could from the Swedish baggage train behind the lines.

Abandoned by their Saxon allies, Gustavus Adolphus and the Swedish army had to face the imperialist host by themselves. For some time it looked as though the emperor's banner of the double-headed eagle had indeed been unfurled for victory, which was quite unexpected, for the combined Saxon-Swedish soldiery had outnumbered the imperialist forces. Now Tilly and Pappenheim should have had the advantage, but a new era had dawned in warfare.

Gustavus's small, loosely deployed squads of cavalry interspersed with groups of infantry—with little rows of musketeers put among them at intervals—met the far less maneuverable masses of Tilly's horse and foot, and finally defeated them in prolonged and bloody encounters. The aged Tilly, now in his early seventies, was severely wounded; helped off the battlefield, he escaped capture. A mighty warrior, a matchless strategist, Gustavus had achieved the victory at Breitenfeld by his own daring as well as by his strange capacity for leadership.[36] He became the idol of Protestant Europe, as Breitenfeld came to mean the salvation of Protestantism in Germany. As in the case of Lepanto, contemporaries probably exaggerated the military importance of Breitenfeld but, again as with Lepanto, it long remained an inspiration to those whose forebears had won the victory.

After the crushing defeat at Breitenfeld, Tilly wound his way southwestward some three hundred miles to Nördlingen to regroup what was left of his forces and to recruit such additional soldiery as he could find. Pappenheim moved westward into the Weser valley to await the next turn of events. If Gustavus Adolphus defeated the imperialists, as he had

---

[36] Cf. Hans Delbrück, *Geschichte der Kriegskunst im Rahmen der politischen Geschichte*, IV, 232–40, who puts the strength of the Saxon-Swedish army at about 39,000 men, and that of the imperialists at about 36,000. These figures include some 13,000 Saxon-Swedish and 11,000 imperialist cavalry. Needless to add, perhaps, estimates of the sizes of the two armies vary (cf. Parker *et al., The Thirty Years' War*, p. 126; Roberts, *Gustavus Adolphus*, II [1958], 250–53, 534–38). Roberts dates the battle on 7 September, old style.

hoped (and as he had now done), it had been his intention to march upon Vienna. But he distrusted Johann Georg of Saxony, who might well have made peace with Ferdinand II behind his back. Leaving the Saxon elector to proceed against Ferdinand's domains to the extent he dared to do so, Gustavus made his way down the "priestly catwalk," the Pfaffengasse, into the German center of Catholic wealth and authority.

From the beginning of October to the end of December (1631) Gustavus Adolphus seized, one after the other, a half-dozen important Catholic cities—Erfurt, Würzburg, Hanau, Aschaffenburg, Frankfurt am Main, and Mainz. Frankfurt was the site of imperial elections; the archiepiscopal see of Mainz was itself an electorate. At Höchst on 19 November (1631) at the time of Gustavus's entry into Hessen, between the occupation of Hanau and that of Aschaffenburg, the landgrave Georg of Hessen-Darmstadt surrendered to him the important fortress town of Rüsselsheim. Three days later at Frankfurt am Main, Gustavus promised to restore Rüsselsheim, which is only a few miles east of Mainz, to the landgrave "as soon as the present state of war has been brought to an end."[37]

Within hours of Gustavus's capture of Mainz the archiepiscopal elector of Trier, Philipp Christoph von Sötern, put himself, his subjects, and his cities of Trier, Speyer, "et autres" under the protection of Louis XIII of France. The diverse movements of warfare, which Philipp Christoph said had come upon the Roman Empire, "principalement és environs de nos archevêché et évêché de Trèves et Spire," had led him to seek the king's assurance of safety. His neighbors at Mainz and Würzburg had been ruined. The emperor's troops had withdrawn from the fray. The king of Spain could not guarantee the safety of his own subjects "contre tant de puissantes forces jointes ensemble." Christoph, therefore, sent word to all his subjects that they must recognize the most serene king of France as their "seigneur assistant," and receive his soldiers in all Christoph's garrisons.[38]

In mid-November (1631) Wallenstein, who had been of late the virtual ruler of his native Bohemia, abandoned Prague in an enigmatic move. He could easily have held the city against Johann Georg's general Hans Georg von Arnim, who occupied the Bohemian capital a week or so later. The winter of 1631–1632 was the great period of Gustavus Adolphus's life; there was ample rejoicing among his followers at Mainz and Frankfurt am Main, where he was spending most of his time. It was at Mainz on 29 January (1632) that he signed with his own hand a treaty of neutrality with Maximilian I of Bavaria and the Catholic League, although they had taken the emperor's side, "and deserved only hostility." At the interces-

---

[37] Dumont, VI-1, nos. XVII–XVIII, pp. 21–23, docs. dated 19 and 22 November, 1631.
[38] Dumont, VI-1, no. XX, pp. 24–25.

sion of the king of France, however, Gustavus would accord them a neutral status

provided the duke of Bavaria and the princes and states of the Catholic League of Germany establish a firm and assured neutrality which they will observe religiously and inviolably, and give adequate assurance thereof to the king of Sweden . . . , his realms, lands and subjects, both hereditary and acquired in Germany, as well as to his allies, the electors, princes, counts, nobles, towns, states, communities, and Orders, and especially the elector of Saxony.

The duke of Bavaria and his Catholic associates must abstain from all acts of hostility to his Swedish Majesty and the Protestant princes and states, and they must restore to the Protestants, "de quelque condition qu'ils soient," everything which had been taken from them since the year 1618, "the year in which this war began." That meant the restitution of all castles, fortresses, towns, territories, and provinces in Lower Saxony, which must be returned to their rightful owners "in the same state as they were before the war." The duke and his Catholic confederates must withdraw their forces from all the possessions of the Evangelical princes.

The duke and his Catholic confederates must also reduce their armed forces to ten or twelve thousand men, who were to be dispersed and distributed throughout their towns and territories. Such forces as well as those to be dismissed by the Catholic duke and his confederates were not to be put at the disposal or in the service of the emperor "neither openly nor clandestinely," nor could the house of Austria or other enemies of his Swedish Majesty recruit troops in Bavaria and the other lands of the Catholic League. As for the king of Sweden and his allies, they promised to observe the neutrality of the duke of Bavaria and his confederates of the Catholic League, if the latter acceded to the terms given above and to certain other lesser requirements.[39]

It almost seemed as though Germany lay at the feet of the Swedish king. As a consequence of his success a military alliance was ratified at Vienna on 14 February 1632 between Philip IV of Spain and Ferdinand II, ruler of the Holy Roman Empire, "through the superior strength of which for eight hundred years and more the affairs of Christendom have clearly flourished both by withstanding the fury of barbarous peoples and by promoting amity among the Christian princes." The alliance was directed, as stated in the text of the treaty, against Gustavus Adolphus, *rex Sueciae*. To combat his unrighteous aggressions Ferdinand was to

---

[39] Dumont, VI-1, no. xxiv, pp. 29–30, "en foi de quoi nous avons signé ces présentes de nos mains et scellé de nos armes, donné à Maience le 29 Janvier, stile nouveau, 1632."

provide at least 30,000 foot and 8,000 horse, and Philip was to make ready 21,000 foot and 5,000 horse, "with all things necessary for an effective expedition."

The alliance was to last for six years. Those who joined Ferdinand and Philip against the Swedes were to make appropriate contributions in men or money. Wages for officers and soldiers were to be computed in gold coinage and the equivalents in the imperialist, Spanish, German, Italian, and Belgian currencies of the time. If the war should end before the lapse of six years, the alliance was still to continue for the specified period "pro majori pacis stabilimento." If the war lasted longer than six years, however, the alliance was to be extended "ad aliud tempus."[40]

Appalled by Swedish success and dismayed by Gustavus Adolphus's terms for neutrality, on 1 April (1632) Maximilian of Bavaria joined his general Johan Tserclaes, count of Tilly, at Ingolstadt. As we have seen, Tilly was the commander-in-chief of both the imperialist troops and those of the Catholic League. Maximilian feared for Bavaria. Richelieu might still regard him as neutral and Bavaria as beyond the range of Swedish attack, but hereafter Gustavus could only look upon Maximilian's domain as enemy territory. As the new campaign season was beginning in Germany, almost every prince, Catholic or Protestant, looked for allies. Georg Wilhelm of Brandenburg made a three years' pact with the United Provinces at The Hague (on 2 April 1632).[41]

Philipp Christoph von Sötern, the elector of Trier, bound himself more closely to Louis XIII, who undertook to put a garrison of a thousand foot and a hundred horse into Christoph's castle of Eberstein (Ehrenbreitstein), "qui est le plus considérable de nostre archevêché de Trèves." According to the agreement of 9 April (1632), the French were to hold and guard the castle until the conclusion of peace in Germany, after which they were supposed to return it to Christoph or his successor in the same state as it was when they took possession of it. Since Christoph felt hard-pressed for funds because of the "recent ravages" in his electorate, he wanted to pay only a third of the cost of maintaining the French garrison in the castle of Eberstein until such time as his subjects could meet the considerable expenses involved.

As soon as the French had taken over the castle, they were to drive out of the archdiocese of Trier "not only the troops of his Swedish Majesty but all others who will be found therein." When Eberstein was safely under French protection, Christoph proposed also to put "our castle of Philippsburg into the hands of his Most Christian Majesty under the same conditions and in the same manner," i.e., as in the case of Eberstein,

---

[40] Dumont, VI-1, no. xxv, pp. 30–31, "datum Viennae die 14 Febr. 1632."

[41] Dumont, VI-1, no. xxviii, pp. 33–35, "actum Hagae-Com. secundo die Aprilis, anno 1632."

Philippsburg would receive a French garrison of a thousand foot and a hundred horse. Louis XIII or rather his minister Richelieu must also see to it "that the king of Sweden and his adherents shall evacuate all the bishopric of Speyer and all [other] places of our state." On 30 April (1632) Louis XIII ratified the agreement with Christoph at the royal castle of S. Germain-en-Laye northwest of Paris.[42]

At Mainz on 22 April the Swedish chancellor Axel Oxenstierna had imposed stringent terms of neutrality upon Christoph, which the latter accepted.[43] Since Oxenstierna came close to being Gustavus Adolphus's alter ego, the agreement with his Grace of Trier would presumably stand, but it still awaited the king's confirmation. Although Richelieu was help-ing to subsidize Gustavus's various armed forces in Germany, the king had gone his own way, disregarding the desires and cautions of the French. Annoyed with the Swedes' independence, Richelieu wished, nev-ertheless, to keep them in the field against the Hapsburgs. Gustavus needed the cardinal's funds to advance the Protestants' cause in Ger-many and, as he hoped, to acquire Pomerania for Sweden.

Gustavus Adolphus might be willing to regard Philipp Christoph of Trier as neutral, but certainly not the elector of Bavaria, who had joined the Catholic armies under Tilly. The Elector Maximilian's plight became desperate when, on 15 April (1632), Gustavus once more defeated Tilly near the town of Rain, six miles southeast of Donauwörth. The battle took place by the river Lech, which flows into the Danube about three miles north of Rain. The imperialists were aghast. Was there no stopping the king of Sweden? Was he indomitable? Were Catholic Germany and the house of Austria to be trod under foot? Although Maximilian with-drew the shattered Catholic forces from the fields by the Lech, Tilly had been fatally wounded in the battle, and toward the end of April he died within the stout walls of the imperialist city of Ingolstadt, a Jesuit center.

As the Hapsburgs faced the disaster for which Wallenstein had been waiting, the latter finally yielded to their entreaties to rejoin their ranks and defend the Catholic cause. Uncertainty still cloaks the precise terms

---

[42] Dumont, VI-1, no. xxix, pp. 35–36, "le tout fait et passé dans nostre Chasteau d'Eber-stein le 9 Avril 1632," and cf., *ibid.*, no. xxx. Owing to the intervention of the French, Gustavus Adolphus also accepted a treaty of neutrality with Maximilian of Bavaria's brother Ferdinand von Wittelsbach, the archiepiscopal elector of Cologne. However, "au cas que le Comte de Papenheim [who was then in the Weser valley] ou autres chefs de la Ligue Catholique viennent à loger leurs troupes dans les evêchez ou païs dudit Sieur Électeur, le Roi de Suède et ses alliés pourront aussi venir avec leurs troupes aux mesmes lieux sans que cela empesche que le présent traité demeure en sa vigueur" (*ibid.*, VI-1, no. xxxvii, p. 43, doc. dated 27 October, 1632). On the difficulties faced by Christoph von Sötern as elector of Trier, cf. Fritz Dickmann, *Der Westfälische Frieden* (1959), pp. 26, 286–87, 290, 292–93, *et alibi.*

[43] Dumont, VI-1, no. xxxi, pp. 36–38, "[datum] Moguntiae die 12 mensis Aprilis stylo veteri, . . . anno millesimo sexcentesimo trigesimo secundo."

under which Wallenstein placed his own large army and seemingly limitless resources at the service of the house of Austria and its allies. The
terms were, however, such as to put him in almost absolute control of
Hapsburg policy and troops, at least for as long as the king of Sweden
ravaged the once-prosperous hills and dales of Catholic Germany.

To the extreme annoyance of Gustavus Adolphus, and to his peril, the
Saxon forces under the Protestant general Hans Georg von Arnim now
pulled out of Bohemia, and on 25 May (1632) Wallenstein returned to
Prague after an absence of something more than six months. It looked as
though there might be collusion between von Arnim and Wallenstein.
When the Saxon troops were withdrawn from Bohemia, seeking cover in
war-ridden Silesia, Gustavus dared not continue on toward Vienna, for
he could get caught between Wallenstein's army in Bohemia and the
imperialists in Austria. He was also worried lest Johann Georg might
make peace with Ferdinand II, for the Saxon elector was as timorous as
the Swedes' other doubtful ally, Georg Wilhelm of Brandenburg.

Wallenstein's duchies were storehouses of vast quantities of foodstuffs
and military supplies. Recruits were flocking to his paymasters in large
numbers, even as they had previously responded to Gustavus's victories,
when Swedish success in the field had opened up great opportunities to
pillage Catholic lands. If Gustavus were to suffer a serious defeat—a
contingency for which he seemed to make no provision, because experience had shown him that God was on his side—could he marshal his
scattered forces in Germany or get safely back to Sweden to recover his
losses? Would not Wallenstein advance upon his rear from Bohemia?

From February to November 1632 the king of Sweden moved from the
area of Mainz, Hanau, and Frankfurt am Main eastward to Schweinfurt
and Nuremberg, thence southwestward to Nördlingen. On 7 April he had
been at Donauwörth, after which (as we have seen) he defeated Tilly by
the river Lech, and then went on to Augsburg (on 24 April). Thereafter
toward the end of April he made his way north and east to well-fortified
Ingolstadt, which he did not try to take. Turning southward, he reached
Munich by the middle of May, destroying the crops and plundering the
towns and villages as he traversed the countryside. It was at Munich on
20 May that he ratified the pact of neutrality which Philipp Christoph,
the ecclesiastical elector of Trier, had managed to secure from the
Swedish chancellor Oxenstierna as a result of French intervention.[44]

Gustavus Adolphus stayed in and around Munich for three weeks or
so, and then took the long road north to Nuremberg, which he reached on
20 June. He remained for some time in the general area of Nuremberg,
where famine and disease diminished his forces. In late October Gusta-

---

[44] Dumont, VI-1, no. XXXI, p. 38a, "[datum] Monachii, die 20 Maii anno 1632."

vus ventured farther north to Arnstadt in Thuringia, where Bernhard von Sachsen-Weimar and his troops awaited him, arriving about 2 November. Thereafter he continued north and east through Naumburg and Merseburg to Leipzig and Lützen, back to the region of his great victory at Breitenfeld.

Meanwhile Wallenstein had marched westward from Prague the hundred and fifty or so miles to Bohemian Eger (Cheb) at the foot of a spur of the Fichtelgebirge. Swerving southeastward, he skirted Nuremberg, and went on the ten miles to Schwabach, where he came together with Maximilian of Bavaria (on 11 July 1632). Maximilian soon left him in dudgeon and disagreement, however, and fell back into Bavaria, which the Swedes had plundered in fearful fashion. Their destruction was a grievous sight to Maximilian, who had ruled and loved Bavaria for thirty-five years. His family, the younger branch of the Wittelsbachs, had held sway in Bavaria since 1180 (and, indeed, when the Bavarian line of the family died out in December 1777, the duchy passed to the elder, the Palatine, branch of the family which held the reins of government until 1918). After Maximilian's departure from Schwabach, Wallenstein summoned Pappenheim from the Weser valley (in the area of Göttingen), and then proceeded northward into the heart of old Saxony to Weissenfels, Merseburg, Leipzig, and Lützen.

Gustavus Adolphus and Wallenstein had approached each other slowly and by circuitous routes. They were seeking each other cautiously. Somewhere along their straggly lines of march they would collide. That somewhere proved to be the little town of Lützen. On 16–17 November (1632) in a desperately fought battle, which took place in the fields to the southeast of Lützen, Gustavus again defeated the imperialists, but for the last time, for he was killed in the encounter, as was Wallenstein's right hand, the stormy Pappenheim. Gustavus and Pappenheim were both in their thirty-eighth year. Wallenstein, alive but ailing, retreated from the gory scene the few miles north to Halle. The failure at Lützen had diminished his reputation, and discouraged the imperialists, who were also perplexed. While Pappenheim's death was a serious loss, how would the Swedes manage without their bellicose king? What if any change would there be in Richelieu's policy?[45]

---

[45] On the battle of Lützen, note K. Deuticke, *Die Schlacht bei Lützen (1632)*, Giessen, 1917; Delbrück, *Gesch. d. Kriegskunst*, IV, 240–43; Wedgwood, *The Thirty Years' War* (1938), pp. 324–28; Josef Seidler, *Untersuchungen über die Schlacht bei Lützen, 1632*, Memmingen, 1954, esp. pp. 31–95; Roberts, *Gustavus Adolphus*, II (1958), 253–55, 763–73; Polišenský, *The Thirty Years' War*, pp. 210–11; Parker *et al.*, *The Thirty Years' War* (1984), pp. 130–32. On Gustavus Adolphus's fatal victory at Lützen, note the report of Vincenzo Gussoni, the Venetian ambassador in England, to the doge Francesco Erizzo and the Senate in the *Cal. State Papers . . .*, *Venice*, XXIII, no. 68, pp. 41–42, doc. dated 10 December 1632.

The death of the warrior king of Sweden did not bring peace to Europe. The chancellor Axel Oxenstierna and his countrymen believed that the Swedes must hold on to Pomerania, which made it necessary for the elector Georg Wilhelm of Brandenburg to receive territorial compensation elsewhere in the Northland. This meant continued strife, as did Cardinal de Richelieu's determination to maintain France's position on the Rhine. The Hapsburgs in Spain as well as in Austria also harbored ambitions that could only be fulfilled by warfare. Wide areas of Germany lay in ruins. Bohemia was a wasteland. Homeless peasants and townsmen were beset by famine and plague.

Although the elector Johann Georg of Saxony and his field marshal Hans Georg von Arnim wanted to see peace restored to the Empire, Oxenstierna managed to negotiate a treaty of alliance between the crown of Sweden and the Protestant states of the four Circles of the "electoral Rhine," Franconia, Swabia, and the Upper Rhine (*die Evangelische Stände des Churfürstlichen Rheinischen, Fränckischen, Schwäbischen, und Ober-Rheinischen Creysses*). The treaty was declared in effect at Heilbronn on 23 April 1633; its purpose was to defend and maintain Protestantism in "the Holy Empire of the German Nation," which meant continuance of the war against the Austrian Hapsburgs. Financial provision was made (in unrealistic fashion) for the maintenance of a large army of horse and foot. Control over the League of Heilbronn devolved upon the chancellor Oxenstierna, who would now carry on in place of the late Gustavus Adolphus.[46]

Two days later, on 25 April, Oxenstierna enlisted the support of the free knights of the four Circles.[47] His success at Heilbronn, however, was mitigated by the presence of Richelieu's envoy Manassés de Pas, marquis de Feuquières, who induced the Protestants to put themselves under the aegis of France as well as under that of Sweden. Furthermore, Feuquières arranged that the French military subsidy should be given in the name of the newly formed League rather than in that of Sweden. In any event Johann Georg of Saxony, the advocate of peace, was removed from any prospect of becoming the leader of Protestant Germany. The death of Gustavus Adolphus had enhanced the ambitions of both the Austrian and the Spanish Hapsburgs, who were anxious to clear the

---

[46] Dumont, VI-1, no. XLIII, pp. 51–52, "geschehen zu Heylbrunn den dreyzehenden Monatstag Aprilis im Jahr . . . sechzehen hundert dreissig und drey," old style.

[47] *Ibid.*, VI-1, no. XLIV, pp. 52–54, "geschehen in Heylbronn den fünffzehenden Aprilis . . . ," old style. Oxenstierna also made a treaty with Philipp Ludwig of Pfalz-Zimmern, brother of the late Friedrich V of the Palatinate, and regent for the young Karl Ludwig, Friedrich's son and heir (Wedgwood, *The Thirty Years' War*, p. 339). On the imperial Circles in the first half of the seventeenth century, see Ferdinand Magen, "Die Reichskreise in der Epoche des Dreissigjährigen Krieges: Ein Überblick," *Zeitschrift für historische Forschung*, IX-4 (1982), 409–60, with an extensive bibliography.

French out of the Rhineland and to frustrate their ambition to acquire the southern part of the Spanish Netherlands.

The failing health and the erratic policies of the imperialist general Albrecht von Wallenstein, the duke of Friedland, were then evoking no less suspicion in Vienna, Madrid, and Brussels than they were causing confusion in Paris and in the electorates of Saxony and Bavaria. Wallenstein had become much feared and widely hated. He seemed no longer to be loyal to the emperor. By a secret rescript, dated 24 January 1634, Ferdinand II removed Wallenstein from his command of the imperial forces, which led to the famous (or infamous) conspiracy against the generalissimo. Wallenstein was stabbed to death in his bedchamber at Eger (Cheb) by the English soldier Walter Devereux on the night of 25 February (1634). The plot against him, however, had been at least a month in the making. The chief conspirators were the Italian-born general Ottavio Piccolomini and the Italo-Austrian Matthias Gallas (Galasso), together with Johann von Aldringen. They were aided by a dozen other officers of lesser stamp, including Walter Butler, Fabio and Giulio Diodati, Rodolfo Colloredo, and Baltasar Marradas. The removal of Wallenstein from the scene helped for a while to clarify the issues and hostilities which were to prolong the war for another fourteen years. More than a century and a half after Wallenstein's death, as his memory lived on in Germany, the dramatist Schiller depicted his fall as the sacrifice of a hero to the inevitability of fate. Something of an enigma to his contemporaries, Wallenstein remains no less so to us today.[48]

After the death of Wallenstein the imperialists occupied the two important Danubian cities of Regensburg and Donauwörth, but their success was to be merely the prelude to a far more notable triumph. On 6 September (1634) the Austrian and Spanish armies under the joint command of the young Hapsburg cousins—Ferdinand [III], king of Hungary, and the Cardinal-Infante Ferdinand, brother of Philip IV—defeated the German and Swedish forces under Bernhard of Sachsen-Weimar and the

---

[48] On the death of Wallenstein, see (among numerous other works) A.E.J. Hollaender, "Some English Documents on the End of Wallenstein," *Bulletin of the John Rylands Library*, XL (1958), 358–90, esp. pp. 381ff., on details of the murder, and pp. 387ff., on Wallenstein's character; *Cal. State Papers . . . , Venice*, XXIII, nos. 276, 281, pp. 206, 209, letters of Vincenzo (or Vicenzo) Gussoni, Venetian ambassador in England, to the doge Francesco Erizzo and the Senate; cf. Wedgwood, *The Thirty Years' War*, pp. 46–60, with refs; Thos. M. Barker, *Army, Aristocracy, Monarchy: Essays on War, Society, and Government in Austria, 1618–1780*, New York, 1982, esp. pp. 79–93; Parker *et al.*, *The Thirty Years' War* (1984), pp. 137ff.; Polišenský, *The Thirty Years' War*, pp. 212–14; Golo Mann, *Wallenstein* (1971), pp. 1092–1126. Mann writes after the fashion of a novelist. When Wallenstein was removed from the scene, a large part of his duchy of Friedland was turned over to Matthias Gallas, on whom see the *Allgemeine Deutsche Biographie*, VIII (1878, repr. Berlin, 1968), 320–31. There is, needless perhaps to add, an enormous literature on Wallenstein (cf. Parker *et al.*, *The Thirty Years' War*, pp. 290, 294–95).

marshal Gustavus Horn in the fields to the south of Nördlingen. Count Matthias Gallas had accompanied the two Ferdinands; to no small extent the victory was the consequence of his presence. The battle was a disaster for Protestantism. As Wedgwood has put it, "All that had been lost at Lützen had been won again at Nördlingen." Horn was captured. Bernhard escaped to the town of Göppingen on the river Fils in northern Württemberg.[49]

Axel Oxenstierna lost his dominance in Protestant Germany, for the Swedish hegemony ceased with the battle of Nördlingen. Bernhard of Sachsen-Weimar lost the duchy of Franconia, which Oxenstierna had recently ceded to him; the imperialists quickly overran Württemberg and thereafter almost the whole of central and southern Germany. The marquis de Feuquières, Richelieu's envoy, stepped into Oxenstierna's shoes. France assumed the political guidance and economic support of what was left of the League of Heilbronn. With the apparent elimination of Sweden, the Thirty Years' War became a territorial, dynastic struggle between the Bourbons and the Hapsburgs.

At Paris in early November 1634 a treaty was arranged between Louis XIII of France and the Protestant princes "pour l'établissement d'une bonne et sure paix dans l'Empire et mesme dans la Chrestienté maintenant et à l'avenir. . . ." It was to be a general peace "among the Christian princes, and especially in Germany." His Majesty and the lord Oxenstierna, grand chancellor of the crown of Sweden, together with their confederates, "n'aians autre dessein que le bien commun de l'Empire: déclarent et conviennent par ce présent traité de s'emploier sincèrement et à tout leur pouvoir pour aider à pacifier les présens troubles de l'Allemagne. . . ." His Majesty bound himself to furnish, in the event of strife, "12,000 foot, whether Germans or of another nation." He also promised the prompt payment of 500,000 *livres* for the support of the [Protestant] allies' cavalry and other troops "in order to give them the means of recrossing the Rhine in short order and taking action against the enemy."

The electors of Saxony and Brandenburg as well as the other princes and states of Upper and Lower Saxony had already given expression to their ardent desire for the maintenance of their freedom "and the restitution to the princes and states of the Empire of their immunities, privileges, and franchises according to the constitutions of the Holy Empire." The twelve thousand foot, whom Louis XIII proposed to maintain "beyond the Rhine," were to form a single corps. Their commander was to be one of the allied princes, although his Majesty would appoint the lieutenant general.

---

[49] On the Protestant disaster at Nördlingen (27 August to 6 September 1634), see Delbrück, *Gesch. d. Kriegskunst*, IV, 243–48; Wedgwood, *The Thirty Years' War*, pp. 371–80; Parker *et al., The Thirty Years' War*, pp. 140–41.

The Catholic faith was to be protected in Germany, and the French must be given possession of Benfeld and Sélestat (Schlettstadt). The two towns were (and are) in Alsace, ten miles apart on the river Ill. The French must also have control of the bridge at Strasbourg, which was just to the north of Benfeld and Sélestat, all three places being in the valley of the lower Rhine. They were needed "pour y faire passer et repasser les troupes que Sa Majesté jugera estre requises pour le bien commun. . . ." His Majesty wanted assurance that the electors of Saxony and Brandenburg as well as the other princes and states of Upper and Lower Saxony would make no truce or peace with the Hapsburg enemy.[50] Despite the royal desire expressed in this last clause, Louis XIII and Richelieu were unlikely to get the cooperation of the electors of Saxony and Brandenburg, who wanted peace in the Empire.

Meanwhile at The Hague the lords of the States General of the Netherlands had authorized (on 30 May 1634) the dispatch of an embassy to the French court to take up with his Majesty the important question of Spanish aggression, "le maintien et subsistance de la cause commune contre les progrés de l'ambition du Roy d'Espagne." The French were of course prepared for the continuance of war against the Hapsburgs. On 30 January 1635 Louis XIII signed at Paris a treaty of alliance with the United Provinces of the Netherlands against the Emperor Ferdinand II and his cousin Philip IV of Spain and their adherents, Louis's purpose being "to support and assist our allies in order to help maintain them against the enterprises of their enemies." When the red-and-gold seal of the States General was attached to the text of the treaty, the king's officers added thereto the royal seal, "le cachet de nos armes," on 8 February (1635).

Louis XIII committed himself to send an army of 25,000 foot and 5,000 horse into the Netherlands, along with cannon and all the other necessary accoutrements of war. The Netherlanders also agreed to put 25,000 foot and 5,000 horse into the field "avec le canon et attirail nécessaire à un tel corps." The Spanish would be driven from the towns of the Dutch Lowlands. There was to be a division of territory between the French and Dutch allies, the area of Luxembourg, the counties of Namur and Hainaut, Artois and Flanders being assigned to the French.[51]

Three weeks later, on 28 February (1635), an armistice (*Waffenstill-*

---

[50] Dumont, VI-1, no. LX, pp. 79–80, "fait à Paris le premier jour de Novembre 1634," and cf., *ibid.*, nos. LVI–LIX. Despite the free employment of his name in the treaty, Oxenstierna was quite dissatisfied with it.

[51] Dumont, VI-1, no. LXI, pp. 80–85. Certain secret articles added to the treaty were ratified at The Hague on 11 April and thereafter at Compiègne on 23 April (1635). Cf., *ibid.*, no. LXIV, p. 88, an agreement between Louis XIII and Queen Christina of Sweden, whereby Axel Oxenstierna, "le chancelier de Suède promet et s'oblige au nom de la Reine et Roiaume de Suède de conserver le libre exercice de la religion catholique dans les églises soumises à son pouvoir, occupées dans l'Empire depuis l'an 1618 . . . ," a provision which of course Cardinal Richelieu required.

stand) was negotiated between the Emperor Ferdinand II and the elector Johann Georg of Saxony. The agreement was signed at Laun (Louny) on the river Ohre in northwestern Bohemia.[52] This was followed by the long, elaborate treaty of Prague on 30 May (1635) between Ferdinand II and Johann Georg, whereby the imperialists recognized only the Lutherans, adherents to the Augsburg Confession (of 1530), as legally possessing the right to the free exercise of their faith, i.e., a *Religionsfriede* now existed between the Lutherans and Catholics in Germany. The ecclesiastical lands and properties, to which the emperor had no direct claim, and which had been taken over before the religious peace of Passau (negotiated between the Hapsburgs and Maurice of Saxony in 1552), were to remain in perpetuity in possession of their current owners. Other such ecclesiastical lands and properties were to remain for forty years (from 12 November 1627 *stylo novo*) in the hands of their current owners, and thereafter, if no further legal adjustments were made, they were henceforth to be held in such fashion as they had been in 1627.

Johann Georg of Saxony received the whole of Lusatia (Germ. Lausitz, Pol. Łużyca) as his permanent possession, and his second son, Duke August, was given the archbishopric of Magdeburg for his lifetime (*seine Lebtage*). Many political and religious details of the contemporary scene were dealt with in the treaty of Prague. A general amnesty (*Amnisti*) was declared, and those who wished could subscribe to the terms of Prague, and be accepted as Christian allies, but the rebels of Bohemia were to be excluded, as were the exiled Wittelsbach claimants to the Palatinate. The emperor wished to maintain friendly relations and freedom of trade (*freie Commercia*) with the rest of Europe, and he hoped for a wide extension of peace.[53] The religious animosity had lessened a good deal, but there was not to be peace and freedom of trade. The French would see to that.

After battering the pro-imperialist dukes Charles IV of Lorraine and old Charles Emmanuel of Savoy (who had died in late July 1630), the French finally made a treaty with the latter's successor Vittorio Amadeo on 11 July 1635 against the Spanish, who had been "for these last years encroaching upon the general freedom of Italy." The purpose of the Franco-Savoyard pact was the conquest of the plague-wracked Spanish duchy of Milan, "en exécution de laquelle [ligue] ils s'obligent de faire guerre ouverte contre le Roi d'Espagne." Louis XIII would furnish 12,000 foot and 1,500 horse as well as the 6,000 foot and 500 horse he

---

[52] Dumont, VI-1, no. LXII, pp. 85–86, "datum Laun den 28. Feb. an. 1635."

[53] Dumont, VI-1, nos. LXV–LXVIII, pp. 88–105, the imperial grant of Lusatia being made to Johann Georg, *ibid.*, no. LXVIII. Cf. also no. LXX, pp. 108–9. On the recent literature relating to the treaty of Prague, note Parker *et al.*, *The Thirty Years' War* (1984), p. 295; see also Fritz Dickmann, *Der Westfälische Frieden* (1959), pp. 70ff., and Robert Bireley, *Religion and Politics in the Age of the Counterreformation* (1981), pp. 209–30.

was then maintaining in the "Valtellina," the valley of the upper Adda. The French duke of Mantua, Charles of Gonzaga-Nevers, would also enter the league, providing 3,000 foot and 300 horse, and so would Duke Odoardo of Parma, who would add 4,000 foot and 500 horse to their forces.[54] The French were planning carefully the warfare which lay ahead.

On 27 October (1635) Louis XIII formed a pact with Bernhard of Sachsen-Weimar, who was by now commander-in-chief of the forces of the anti-imperialist confederation of German princes and states. Bernhard was to raise and maintain an army of 18,000 men, for which the French would provide an annual subsidy of 4,000,000 *livres tournois,* to begin on the 15th of the following month. Payments would be made on a quarterly basis. Bernhard was not to reach any sort of "accommodation" with the emperor and the latter's allies, his primary commitment being to his Most Christian Majesty of France. The text of this treaty, as given by Dumont, pays little or no attention to the fact that Bernhard was promised Alsace for his services to the French crown.[55]

At long last, on 20 March 1636, a treaty of alliance was made between Louis XIII and the little Queen Christina of Sweden. It was signed in Wismar (on Wismar Bay) on the southwestern shore of the Baltic in Mecklenburg. Having established "la paix et le repos dans nos états" for some years, Louis and Richelieu were ready to look to their principal concern—the support of their allies against the enemy, *les Impériaux et Espagnols.* They had always had, they said (or at least Louis said), a particular affection for the states of Germany and for the crown of Sweden. They wanted now to reduce the Spanish to such terms as would assure peace in Christendom. The main purpose of the Wismar alliance was not only to maintain the defense of the two kingdoms, but also (it was said) "to preserve the immunities [*les franchises*] and freedom [*libertés*] of Germany."

The French would carry the war into the hereditary provinces of the house of Austria "beyond the Rhine," while the Swedes would do so "in other hereditary provinces of the said house, namely the kingdom of Bohemia and Silesia." The conditions and affairs of states would be reestablished as they had been when the war first broke out in 1618. Both the French and the Swedes would allow the "free exercise of religion" in the territories which they occupied. Every year Louis XIII

---

[54] Dumont, VI-1, no. LXXI, pp. 109–10, "fait, signé et scellé à Rivolles [Rivoli] en présence de Madame la Duchesse de Savoie [regent of the duchy], ce 11 jour du mois de Juillet 1635." Louis XIII (and Richelieu) were gradually preparing the French for war with Spain (cf., *ibid.,* no. LXIX, pp. 105–8).

[55] Dumont, VI-1, no. LXXVII, pp. 118–19, "fait à S. Germain en Laye le vingt-septiesme Octobre mil six cens trente-cinq. . . ."

would pay the queen of Sweden, according to the Wismar text, 1,000,000 *livres tournois* in two installments as well as an additional 500,000 livres "pour le passé." Neither side would make a separate peace or truce with "the emperor and his adherents." The treaty was to last for ten years. It was ratified by Louis XIII in the town of S. Germain en Laye, thirteen miles northwest of Paris, on 15 April (1636).[56]

Inclined in these troublous times to run with the hare and hunt with the hounds, Axel Oxenstierna avoided any formal Swedish ratification of the treaty of Wismar. The years 1635–1636 were very difficult for the French. An invasion of the valley of the Somme by an army of Spaniards and imperialists, coming down from the southern Netherlands, ended on 14–15 August 1636 with their seizure of the fortress town of Corbie, ten miles east of Amiens on the road to Paris. In the French capital the populace was terrified; without Louis XIII's consistent support Richelieu might have fallen from power. The French did not recover Corbie until 9 November. The cardinal had endless problems, for at this time France had neither the military nor the financial capacity to embark upon full-scale open warfare with the Hapsburgs and their German allies.

With an ineffective soldiery, an unreliable nobility, and a disorganized fiscal administration, Louis XIII and Richelieu were soon trying to maintain armies of varying strengths in the Netherlands, Lorraine, Savoy, the Valtellina, and the Rhineland. The chief allies of the Most Christian King and the Catholic Cardinal were the Protestants Oxenstierna and Bernhard of Sachsen-Weimar. The king and cardinal were, to be sure, *au fond* enemies of all the Hapsburgs, but they feared Philip IV more than Ferdinand II, for Madrid and the Spanish Netherlands were closer to the French borders than was Vienna.

As the French were floundering, Ferdinand II finally succeeded in securing the election of his son Ferdinand [III] as king of the Romans on 22 December 1636, toward the end of the electoral assembly at Regensburg.[57] The usual restrictions were placed upon the imperial authority, but the Hapsburgs had succeeded in keeping the *imperium* in their family. As the French were doing badly, however, their Swedish allies seemed suddenly to be experiencing a military renascence. Oxenstierna had left Richelieu to worry about the Rhineland, and had returned to Stockholm to take over and tighten the reins of government. He saw to it that the forces of his country were now supplied with men and munitions, which began a new era of Swedish aggression.

Withdrawing his army from Pomerania, the Swedish field marshal Jo-

---

[56] Dumont, VI-1, no. LXXX, p. 123, and cf. Fritz Dickmann, *Der Westfälische Frieden* (1959), pp. 91ff., 152, 182–83.

[57] Dumont, VI-1, no. LXXXVII, pp. 129–37, and cf., *ibid.*, no. LXXXVIII, pp. 137–46, docs. dated 22–24 December 1636.

han Banér won a remarkable victory over the imperialists and Saxons under Melchior von Hatzfeldt on 4 October (1636) at Wittstock, on the river Dosse in Brandenburg. Wittstock did much to restore both the confidence and the reputation of the Swedes.[58] Georg Wilhelm, the elector of Brandenburg, was left in a helpless quandary, and his fellow Protestant imperialist Johann Georg, the elector of Saxony, was now in some danger himself. The Emperor Ferdinand II died at Vienna on 15 February 1637, but the accession of his son and namesake Ferdinand III had but little impact upon the European scene. The Dutch were doing well, for on 10 October 1637 Frederick Henry, prince of Orange (and son of William the Silent), finally recovered Breda from the Spanish, who had held the fortress town for some twelve years.

The year 1637 started out well for Banér, who took Erfurt and Torgau, and menaced Leipzig, but the year was ending badly when Banér had to retreat into Stettin (Szczecin) in Pomerania. The imperialists occupied a good deal of the disputed province, and everything that Banér had won at Wittstock seemed in danger of being lost. The sorry plight in which Sweden now found herself thus led Oxenstierna by the treaty of Hamburg on 5 March 1638 to "l'échange des ratifications du Traité conclu à Wismar le 20 Mars 1636 entre les ambassadeurs du Roi de France et de la Reine de Suède, aiant esté remis jusqu' à présent pour plusieurs raisons." During the next three years, namely from 15 May 1638 "to the same day of the year 1641," the Swedes would receive (at Amsterdam) an annual grant of one million livres tournois from the French, i.e., payments of 500,000 livres were to be made twice a year. No peace was to be made with the Hapsburgs by either France or Sweden "except by mutual consent." The administration of French affairs was to be managed at Cologne, those of Sweden at Hamburg or Lübeck.[59]

Although the French might be hard put to maintain these payments, it was clear that the war was going to be renewed with vigor. Attention was now diverted from Banér to Bernhard of Sachsen-Weimar, who commanded the French forces (largely German mercenaries) in the field. On 3 March 1638 Bernhard defeated the imperialists at Rheinfelden, and thereafter occupied the town (on 24 March). A month later he took

---

[58] On the battle of Wittstock, note Hans Delbrück, *Gesch. d. Kriegskunst,* IV (1920), 248–51; Wedgwood, *The Thirty Years' War* (repr. 1947), pp. 414–15. On the career of Hatzfeldt, see the *Allgemeine Deutsche Biographie,* XI (1880, repr. Berlin, 1969), 35–36.

[59] Dumont, VI-1, no. xcvii, pp. 161–62, "fait à Hambourg le 5 Mars 1638." In Dumont's text the treaty of Wismar is misdated 1626 by a typographical error. The dates 15 Mai and 15 Mars are also confused in Dumont's text. On Charles I's futile efforts (carried on at Hamburg immediately after the Swedish ratification of the treaty of Wismar) to regain the Rhenish Palatinate for his nephew Karl Ludwig, see E.A. Beller, "The Mission of Sir Thomas Roe to the Conference at Hamburg, 1638–40," *English Historical Review,* XLI (1926), 61–77, and cf. M.J. Brown, *Itinerant Ambassador: The Life of Sir Thomas Roe* (1970), pp. 215–20.

Freiburg (in southwestern Württemberg), defeated the imperialists at Wittenweiher (on 9 August), and after a terrible siege took possession of Breisach on the right bank of the Rhine (on 17 December). Just across the river from the French Neuf-Brisach (*Neubreisach*), where Vauban would later build a well-known fortress, Breisach was the entryway into Württemberg.

Possession of Breisach strengthened Bernhard's hold upon Alsace, to which he claimed full right of possession, for this had been assured (as he saw it) by his contract with the French in the treaty of S. Germain (of 27 October 1635). He refused to give up Breisach and certain other places. He had been ill, however, for some time, and in mid-July 1639 Richelieu was relieved of a perhaps insoluble problem by Bernhard's death at the age of thirty-five. Bernhard bequeathed Alsace to his eldest brother Wilhelm,[60] and if he could not accept it (and he could not), Alsace was to go to Louis XIII, who was (he declared) anxious to maintain "la liberté germanique."

Bernhard of Sachsen-Weimar's army was in effect left to his chief officer Johann Ludwig von Erlach, who had no alternative to accepting a French contract of employment. Karl Ludwig, who claimed the Palatine Electorate as the son of Friedrich V, aspired to the command of Bernhard's army but, foolishly making his way through France, was captured at Moulins and thereafter imprisoned at Vincennes. The army had to be paid. Where could Karl Ludwig find the money? How could he have resisted Richelieu? Erlach had had a long experience of warfare; he was forty-four years of age when Bernhard died. On 9 October 1639 Erlach and his fellow officers made a "treaty" with Louis XIII, who agreed to accept Bernhard's army "en un corps ainsi que [Monsieur le Duc de Weimar] a témoigné le désirer par son testament . . . ," i.e., the Weimarian forces were to remain intact under their then commanders, who were to keep all Bernhard's artillery.

If the army suffered from any "mauvaise rencontre ou accident inévitable," the French king promised Erlach and his fellow officers the complete rehabilitation of both cavalry and infantry, to which apparently generous financial commitments were now made, "suivant et conformément aux capitulations que l'on avoit avec feu M. le Duc de Weymar." The agreements were signed (on 9 October) at Breisach, of which town Erlach was appointed governor, having recognized French suzerainty over Alsace as well as Breisach and Freiburg.[61] In the view of

---

[60] Bernhard of Sachsen-Weimar had three brothers—Wilhelm, Albrecht, and Ernst, all dukes of Sachsen-Weimar (of the Wettin family). In September 1641 they divided their heritage into three parts (Dumont, VI-1, no. cxxxvi, pp. 222–28, docs. dated at Gotha on 22 September 1641 and at Vienna on 19 August 1642).

[61] Dumont, VI-1, no. cxii, pp. 185–87, texts dated 9 and 22 October 1639. On Erlach's career, see the account in the *Allgemeine Deutsche Biographie,* VI (1877, repr. Berlin 1968), 216–20.

some historians Bernhard was becoming something of a German nationalist at the time of his death—his troops were of course almost all German—and the treaty of 9 October has been called "the betrayal at
Breisach."

While the German nationalists (let us refer to them as such) may have
felt betrayed at Breisach, a far worse "betrayal" awaited Philip IV of
Spain and his prime minister Gaspar de Guzmán, the count-duke of Olivares. In 1640 both the Catalans and the Portuguese revolted against
Spain. The facts are well known. On 16 December (1640) Louis XIII
entered into an "everlasting treaty of alliance and brotherhood with the
. . . principality of Catalonia, the county of Cerdagne [*Cerdaña*], . . .
and the county of Roussillon, which are in the power of the Catalans.
. . . ." The French would provide the rebels with army officers to command their troops, "horse and foot as well as their artillery." His Majesty
would also provide the Catalans with six thousand foot and two thousand
horse, "that is, three thousand infantry and a thousand cavalry for the
present and the remainder in the coming month of March. . . ." The
Catalans would also receive arms and munitions, and in return for loyalty
to France would be fully protected from oppression by the king of Spain.
At an assembly in Barcelona on 23 January 1641 the representatives of
Catalonia, Cerdagne, and Roussillon made obeisance to Louis XIII under
certain articles and conditions which he accepted at Péronne on 19
September.[62] As far as Spain was concerned this was more than bad
enough, but of course it was not all.

Portugal had also risen in revolt, and Duke John of Braganza was pro-
claimed king as John IV, receiving the support of the three estates of the
realm, "that is to say, the Church, the Nobility, and the People of the
kingdom of Portugal." The proclamation was first made in Lisbon on 1
December 1640, and was justified and ratified by a written declaration
on 28 January (1641).[63] As was to be expected, John IV soon received
recognition from France, and was promised assistance against Spain (on
1 June 1641).[64] The treaty with France was followed immediately by a
detailed commercial pact with the Dutch, establishing peace, friendship,
and mutual assistance between Portugal and the United Provinces, both
on land and at sea, ranging from the East Indies and Brazil to the European continent.[65] The United Provinces had already made an alliance
and commercial pact with Sweden, which guaranteed them (they hoped)
libertas navigationis et commerciorum on both the Baltic and the

---

[62] Dumont, VI-1, nos. CXXI–CXXII, pp. 196–200; cf., *ibid.,* no. CXXIII; and see John H.
Elliott, *The Revolt of the Catalans,* Cambridge, 1963, and *The Count-Duke of Olivares,*
New Haven and London, 1986, esp. pp. 576ff.

[63] Dumont, VI-1, no. CXXIV, pp. 202–7, and note Elliott, *The Count-Duke of Olivares*
(1986), esp. pp. 597ff.

[64] Dumont, VI-1, no. CXXX, p. 214.

[65] *Ibid.,* VI-1, no. CXXXII, pp. 215–18, doc. dated at The Hague on 12 June 1641.

North Seas.[66] Louis XIII and Richelieu also turned to Sweden to help maintain the "privileges and liberties" of the Holy Roman Empire as well as "to acquire a good general peace for Christendom,"[67] which meant that the French were now well prepared to press forward more vigorously with the war against the Hapsburgs.

The devastation and depopulation in the German states had been appalling. Most of the princes longed for peace. After Bernhard of Sachsen-Weimar's death Johan Banér had brought Swedish victory into northern Germany. The French were a threat to the south. At the year-long Reichstag of Regensburg (1640–1641) the Emperor Ferdinand III made an apparently sincere and sensible attempt to achieve a *pax Germanica* on the basis of a modified Peace of Prague. Finally he even gave way on the Edict of Restitution despite papal objections. Those who had held ecclesiastical property since 1627 were to retain it. Ferdinand's efforts were frustrated, however, when on 1 December 1640 Georg Wilhelm, the elector of Brandenburg, died (at the age of forty-three).[68] His reign had been a confusion. A Calvinist, he had ruled a Lutheran people; his chief minister, Adam von Schwarzenberg, was a Catholic, and always played a pro-imperialist game.

Easily frightened and usually irresolute, Georg Wilhelm was succeeded by his bold and calculating son Friedrich Wilhelm, who would become known as the Great Elector. Friedrich Wilhelm was to create the grandeur of the house of Hohenzollern. Profiting from his father's hardships and disappointments, Friedrich Wilhelm had apparently come to the conclusion that, to be successful, a statesman must learn to rise above principle. Georg Wilhelm had been the emperor's ally as a consequence of his subscribing to the Peace of Prague. His soldiery had lost heavily in the field, and the Swedes had laid waste his lands, driving him into Königsberg in Prussia (in 1638). His son and successor Friedrich Wilhelm needed peace and time and money to pay the debts incurred by his father and to restore the battered electorate of Brandenburg (which was now in pieces) to some semblance of its former state.

As early as February 1641 the Hapsburg commander Ottavio Piccolomini saw the first signs of Friedrich Wilhelm's possible defection from the imperialist cause, which would make it hard to strike an effective

---

[66] *Ibid.*, VI-1, no. cxix, pp. 192–95, doc. dated at Stockholm on 11 September 1640 (n.s.).

[67] *Ibid.*, VI-1, nos. cxxv–cxxvi, pp. 207–9, docs. dated (with some confusion) in 1641.

[68] According to a letter addressed to Alvise Contarini, the Venetian bailie in Istanbul, dated at The Hague on 7 January 1641, "La morte dell'Elettore di Brandenburg pervenuta qui ultimamente raffredda le trattationi incaminate di matrimonio tra il figliuolo del morto Duca e la primogenita del Conte d'Oranges, sperando Brandenburg di poter ottenere la Regina di Suezia e mettersi in capo per questa via una corona" (Biblioteca Nazionale Marciana [Venice], MS. It. VII, 1208 [8853], fol. 138ʳ).

blow at the enemy, i.e., the Swedes.[69] It was a difficult period for the imperialists. The French had invaded Württemberg, and plundered the area. There was also fear of a Turkish invasion of Hungary.[70] The Swedish field marshal Johan Banér died at Halberstadt on 10/20 May 1641 after an illness of seven weeks.[71] He had been by and large militarily successful, but even his fellow Swedes had found Banér unruly and unreliable. Nevertheless, at the time he seemed to be Sweden's only important soldier.

Friedrich Wilhelm had of course already made overtures to the Swedes, who apparently became more receptive after Banér's death. In fact on 24 July the Swedes agreed to abstain from hostilities with Brandenburg. When the anti-imperialist Duke Georg of Brunswick [Braunschweig]-Lüneburg died (in 1641), however, his heirs made peace with Ferdinand III. Thus if the latter had lost the active support of Brandenburg, the Swedes had lost that of Brunswick-Lüneburg. Europe was more than tired of war. Negotiations for peace were carried on by the representatives of Vienna, Paris, and Stockholm, but no one wanted to give up any territory or any advantage that he thought he had gained. No one wanted to accept losses he had sustained,[72] and yet, it would appear, everyone wanted peace.[73] Life had been hard; it would continue to be so. Restlessness, riot, and revolt were spreading throughout Europe, not only in Portugal and Catalonia, but also in England and France, Naples and the Netherlands. The rebellious spirit seemed to be contagious although differing political and economic difficulties inspired unruliness in different places, increased by nationalistic hostilities which, however submerged, had long been smouldering in Europe. Religious antagonism also remained a potent force.

The erratic Johan Banér's command of the crumbling Swedish forces was taken over by the gout-ridden but rigorous Lennart Torstensson,

---

[69] *Documenta bohemica Bellum Tricennale illustrantia,* VI (Prague, 1979), no. 1150, pp. 391–92, dispatch dated at Monheim (near Donauwörth) on 15 February 1641. On the Regensburger Reichstag of 1640–1641, note Fritz Dickmann, *Der Westfälische Frieden* (1959), pp. 100–3, 179–80, 374ff.

[70] *Documenta bohemica,* VI, no. 1136, p. 389, dispatch of the imperialist officer Walter Leslie to Ott. Piccolomini. Current events had made Ferdinand III "melancholisch." As to the fear of a Turkish invasion, cf. the *avviso* from Istanbul, which the imperialist field marshal Rodolfo Colloredo sent Piccolomini from Prague on 22 May 1641 (*ibid.,* no. 1192, pp. 401–2).

[71] *Ibid.,* VI, no. 1193, p. 402, a dispatch dated 12 May 1641 (or 22 May, "new style").

[72] Cf. Wedgwood, *The Thirty Years' War* (1947), pp. 436–46; Parker *et al., The Thirty Years' War* (1984), pp. 167–69.

[73] On the general desire for peace and the diplomatic wrangling at this time, note R.B. Mowat, "The Mission of Sir Thomas Roe to Vienna, 1641–2," *English Historical Review,* XXV (1910), 264–75. Roe had gone to Vienna, as he had previously been sent to Hamburg, to try to secure the return of the Rhenish Palatinate to Karl Ludwig, the son of Friedrich V and Charles I's sister Elizabeth Stuart, the "queen of Bohemia."

who (in his twenty-eighth year) had had charge of Gustavus Adolphus's artillery at Breitenfeld in 1631 and at Lech in the following year. Torstensson brought money, munitions, and reinforcements to the Swedish army in northern Germany. A strong, brutal disciplinarian he rebuilt the army, recruiting peasants, feeding them, and providing them with opportunities for plunder. Beginning in the spring of 1642 Torstensson embarked upon a series of spectacular victories. He crushed a Saxon army at Schweidnitz in Lower Silesia, occupied the town, and pushed on into Moravia, where in June he seized and sacked the city of Olmütz (Olomouc) in northcentral Moravia (Czechoslovakia).

At the beginning of November (1642) Torstensson overwhelmed the imperialist forces under the Archduke Leopold Wilhelm in the second battle of Breitenfeld, killing and capturing some thousands of the archduke's troops. Torstensson then seized Leipzig, about five miles south of the battlefield of Breitenfeld, mulcting the inhabitants of 400,000 imperial dollars. The period 1642–1643 was disastrous for the Hapsburgs, more so for the Spanish than for the Austrian branch of the family. The area of Leipzig, however, was very badly hit. The city itself had been put under siege some five times during the preceding decade (1631–1642), and was now to be occupied by the Swedes from 1642 to 1650.

Although Cardinal de Richelieu died (on 4 December 1642), and Louis XIII soon followed him (on 14 May 1643), the cardinal's young protégé Louis II de Bourbon, duke of Enghien (later known as the Great Condé), destroyed the Spanish army (the *tercios*) under Francisco de Melo, governor of the Netherlands, at Rocroi on 18–19 May 1643.[74] The decisive Franco-Spanish encounter at Rocroi (in the Ardennes in northern France) was the first battle in which d'Enghien exhibited that extraordinary capacity for warfare which was to remain with him for more than thirty years, until his last campaigns in 1674–1675. Thereafter illness and fatigue forced him into a retirement relieved by devotion to religion and dedication to literature. Rocroi was thus the beginning of the Great Condé's career. It was also the end of the military superiority of Spain in Europe.

The second battle of Breitenfeld was also a serious blow to Austria, for the Spanish had rendered the Hapsburg emperors much assistance through the years, providing an impediment to French and Dutch expansion in Europe and elsewhere. The able Cardinal-Infante Ferdinand, who had been a threat to France as well as to Holland, had died on 9 November 1641, and the Spanish prime minister Olivares fell from power in January 1643. If the Hapsburgs had their troubles, so did the French.

---

[74] Cf. in general Karsten Ruppert, *Die kaiserliche Politik auf dem Westfälischen Friedenskongress (1643–1648)*, Münster, 1979, pp. 15, 42ff.

Four days after Louis XIII's death his widow Anne of Austria, the sister of Philip IV and sister-in-law of Ferdinand III, was declared the regent of France by the Parlement de Paris (on 18 May 1643). She was a Spaniard; her friend and minister, Cardinal Jules Mazarin, was an Italian; as foreigners they had to proceed carefully with the foreign policy of France. After Rocroi, when the French seemed to be on the pinnacle of victory, it would be hard to make any concession to Austria to achieve peace.

In any event Anne of Austria yielded the conduct of French foreign policy to Mazarin, who was hostile to the Hapsburgs. By and large, however, most of Europe wanted peace, and the Austrians and the Germans, the French and the Swedes were seeking to end the long destructive war in various roundabout ways. While Anne of Austria and Mazarin continued Richelieu's foreign policy, France seemed to be winning, but in the twenty-five years from 1618 to 1643, the French expenditure on warfare had risen by six hundred percent, allegedly from 8,017,934 to 48,550,314 livres tournois.[75]

France had more than financial problems. Despite the successes of d'Enghien and Turenne, she soon lost the notable general Jean Baptiste Guébriant, who had won a number of victories on the field, defeating the imperialists in the battles of Wolfenbüttel (in 1641) and Kempen (in 1642). Having recently received the baton of marshal of France, Guébriant laid siege on 7 November 1643 to Rottweil on the Neckar in southern Württemberg. Ten days later he was killed by a falconet shot.[76] Soon afterwards the imperialist-Bavarian army under Franz von Mercy and Johann von Werth inflicted a crushing defeat upon the French forces in the area of Rottweil and Tuttlingen, driving Turenne back toward the Rhine and preventing his further advance into Württemberg.

The Thirty Years' War sometimes seems to be largely a series of frightful battles causing an appalling loss of life and the widespread destruction of churches, town halls, houses, landed property, and works of art. Devastation had become a way of life. Famine and plague were fatally extensive.[77] However distressed they might be, the Germans had almost become used to disaster. As the French sought to move eastward from

---

[75] Richard Bonney, *The King's Debts: Finance and Politics in France*, Oxford, 1981, pp. 193ff., esp. pp. 306–7, and cf. Parker *et al.*, *The Thirty Years' War*, p. 150.

[76] On the career of Guébriant, see the notice in Johann Heinrich Zedler, *Grosses Vollständiges Universal-Lexikon*, XI (Halle and Leipzig, 1735, repr. Graz, 1961), 1216–17.

[77] Cf. Jürgen Kuczynski, *Geschichte des Alltags des deutschen Volkes, 1600–1650*, Cologne, 1981, esp. pp. 83ff., for an interesting account of the plagues, pillages, famines, and other hardships assailing the German people during the Thirty Years' War. Some readers, however, will find Kuczynski's Marxian emphases rather tiresome. Much briefer than Kuczynski's book (and much better) is the highly factual work of Günther Franz on *Der Dreissigjährige Krieg und das deutsche Volk: Untersuchungen zur Bevölkerungs- und Agrargeschichte*, Stuttgart, 1979, which contains a good deal of numerical data drawn from a wide range of sources.

the Rhine, the imperialist-Bavarian commander Franz von Mercy tried to stop their advance with the troops of Maximilian I. On 27 July (1644) Mercy took the town of Freiburg im Breisgau, which lies some ten miles east of the Rhine and (as the crow flies) 150 or so miles west of the battle grounds of Rottweil and Tuttlingen. Turenne awaited the arrival of d'Enghien in the area of Neuf-Brisach and Breisach, and when d'Enghien arrived with the necessary reinforcements, they got their troops across the Rhine.

The so-called battle of Freiburg was a series of three separate encounters between the French under d'Enghien and Turenne and the imperialist-Bavarian army under Mercy. The engagements took place on 3–5 and 9–10 August 1644; both sides suffered severe losses of manpower. After prolonged maneuvering, however, the French forced Mercy to retire to Rothenburg ob der Tauber. Despite Mercy's retreat, Freiburg was not assailed by the French, although Maximilian is said to have ordered his general not to seek an immediate resumption of hostilities with the French. D'Enghien pressed on to the fortress town of Philippsburg, which he occupied together with the cities of Mannheim on the right bank of the Rhine and Speyer on the left bank. Turenne seized the famous city of Worms, also on the Rhine, a dozen miles north of Mannheim, as well as Oppenheim on the left bank (a dozen miles south of Mainz) and Landau, about ten miles west of the Rhine in the southern Palatinate. Now the French were lording it over the Rhineland from Koblenz in the north to Basel in the south, but Mercy was still keeping them out of the Black Forest.[78]

In the unceasing warfare of these years Franz von Mercy did recover Mannheim, and inflicted a stunning defeat upon Turenne in the battle of Mergentheim in Franconia (on 15 May 1645). Mercy and Johann von Werth soon learned again, however, that the baroque goddess Fortuna was ever fickle, for when on 3 August they met d'Enghien and Turenne on the field of Allerheim near Nördlingen in Swabia, the French won the battle. Mercy was killed by a musket shot. Both sides suffered heavy losses, but the French had certainly carried the day.

---

[78] On Franz von Mercy, see the *Allgemeine Deutsche Biographie*, XXI (1885, repr. 1970), 414–18, and especially the detailed monograph of Hans-Helmut Schaufler, *Die Schlacht bei Freiburg im Breisgau, 1644*, Freiburg, 1979, who provides the reader with contemporary (and modern) maps, portraits of the leading generals, notes on seventeenth-century weaponry, and plans of the battle, together with the numbers of troops involved. Johann (Jan) von Werth is alleged to have said of the battle ". . . seit zweiundzwanzig Jahren mit dem Bluthandwerk vertraut, habe [ich] niemalen so blutigens Treffen beigewohnt" (*ibid.*, p. 7): In twenty-two years of sanguinary warfare von Werth had never experienced such a flow of blood on the battlefield. Cf. Parker *et al.*, *The Thirty Years' War*, p. 271, note 9, and see in general Karsten Ruppert, *Die kaiserliche Politik auf dem Westfälischen Friedenskongress* (1979), pp. 65ff.

In the meantime, during the winter of 1642–1643, the Swedes had gained firm possession of northern and central Moravia, from which the Austrian general Matthias Gallas could not dislodge Lennart Torstensson, who had swept down from Saxony to strengthen the Swedish hold upon the threatened fortress town of Olomouc (Olmütz). War was everywhere in Europe, including England, where armed conflict between the Royalists and the Roundheads was now beginning. In 1643–1644 Torstensson and the Swedish general Hans Christoph, count of Königsmarck, acting upon orders from Stockholm, extended the area of conflict by invading Denmark. The self-seeking antics of Christian IV had become an intolerable nuisance to the Swedish government. Not the least of the Danes' offenses had been their interference with Swedish vessels in the Baltic and the Kattegat. The Swedes conquered Schleswig and Holstein, and moved into Jutland, bringing Christian to heel after the imperialists had made a vain attempt to help him. Christian was humbled in the peace of Brömsebro (of 13/23 August 1645), which assured the safety of Swedish warships and merchantmen.[79]

The unexpected Swedish invasion of Denmark had evoked the indignation of the Protestant Dutch and the suspicions of the Catholic French. It was a *fait accompli*, however, and although the peace of Brömsebro largely removed Denmark from the diplomatic as well as the military scene, the war of course went on to the increasing dissatisfaction of most of the harassed and tax-ridden inhabitants of Europe. When the bulk of the Swedish forces under Torstensson had withdrawn from Moravia (in early September 1643), the imperialists moved back into the area. The poor Moravians could again bear witness to widespread devastation. Actually the Swedes held on to Olomouc and certain other fortress towns until the summer of 1650, by which time peace had been made, and the Swedes finally left Silesia and Wallenstein's castle of Friedland (Frýdlant), now a museum, in northern Bohemia.

Always disabled by gout, Torstensson often had to move from place to place in a litter, but his spirit was as strong as his body was decrepit. Leaving the Danish problem to the Swedish general and admiral Karl Gustav Wrangel after Christian IV's maneuvering off the Pomeranian coast to ward off a Swedish attack upon Copenhagen, Torstensson entered Germany again, defeating the imperialists at Jüterbog in Brandenburg (on 23 November 1644), and thereafter winning another spectacu-

---

[79] Dumont, *Corps universel diplomatique*, VI-1 (Amsterdam and The Hague, 1728), no. CLXXXVII, pp. 314–21, "actum Brömsebroo in finibus 13. Augusti anno 1645," by which treaty the Swedes were assured ". . . quod . . . debeant imposterum habere ac frui jure, libertate, et potestate navigandi tam propriis quam conductis navibus onerariis vel vectariis . . . armatis et militaribus aut inermibus . . ." (*ibid.*, p. 315).

lar victory over the imperialists at Jankau (Jankov) in southern Bohemia (on 6 March 1645),[80] opening up the roads to Prague and Vienna, but he never reached the walls of either place. By December (1645) Torstensson's troops were all worn-out, and so was he. Giving up command of the Swedish forces to Wrangel, Torstensson returned to Stockholm, where in 1647 Queen Christina recognized his achievements by making him a count and giving him a command in Sweden. Always beset by illness, Torstensson died in Stockholm at the age of forty-eight (on 7 April 1651), by which time the long and dreadful war had ended.

---

[80] On the background and importance of the battle of Jankau, see Ruppert, *Die kaiserliche Politik auf dem Westfälischen Friedenskongress* (1979), pp. 72–85.

III

The Last Stages of the Thirty Years' War and the Treaties of Westphalia

❧

he Thirty Years' War exerted a powerful influence upon the German mentality. As the pastors, poets, and writers of the "peace dramas" of the mid-seventeenth century watched with horror the death and degradation to which their people were exposed, they turned to the Almighty for assurance of social as well as spiritual salvation. Theological definitions of dogma, whether of Tridentine or even of Lutheran origin, did not suffice. One needed a more easily intelligible and believable approach to spiritual and social salvation, which could only be transmitted to the masses in the German language. The everlasting intrusion of French, Swedes, Danes, Dutch, Hungarians, and Transylvanians into German affairs as well as the influence of imperialist-Italian commanders and the constant fear of the Turks enhanced in the German mind the fact and the importance of being German (*Deutschtum*). The war stimulated a nationalist awareness of the self, promoted pietism and patriotism, and led to the careful cultivation and purification of the German language.

The pastoral and literary leaders, largely recruited from bourgeois families, found in the German language their own identity and that of their people. It was a matter of *Teutschland über alles*, which blossomed into pietistic patriotism. Neither Swedish Protestants nor French Catholics could share the heavenly gift of the German language. Luther's translation of the Bible (and his other works) had helped combine the

German language with a simple religious fundamentalism. Dialectical differences within the fatherland as well as the seepage of foreign words and phrases into German helped lead to the formation of language societies which extolled the virtues of the language they sought to preserve and to purify.

Adhering to the Christian tradition of centuries, the German poets and dramatists emphasized in their works that the horrors of the war must be seen as God's punishment for the sins of their people. It was a familiar theme, but their prolonged expiation was producing a nation nobler than all others. God was thus purifying the soul of his beloved nation. The French, not the Turks, would seem to have become the Germans' most insidious enemies. As the French language and culture came to dominate the European scene (including the German courts), displacing Italian, various pastors, scholars, poets, and dramatists of the Protestant northland practiced their piety and cultivated their language with increased intensity. They presumably increased the social division between the German nobles, who mimicked the French, and the bourgeois, who preserved their lackluster solidity.

Indeed, a century after the Thirty Years' War the addiction of Frederick the Great of Prussia to the French and their literature is notorious. The seventeenth-century German dramatists, writers of the "peace plays," Justus Georg Schottel and Enoch Gläser were the sons of Lutheran pastors and (unlike Frederick the Great) devoted to the German language and the Christian faith. Their contemporaries Johann Rist and Johann Heinrich Hadewig were imbued with the same linguistic and religious patriotism. As they saw their world falling apart, they tried hard to reassemble the pieces. It is difficult to say how widespread their influence was, but it was enduring.[1]

After the Swedes had defeated the imperialist forces at Jüterbog (in November 1644) and at Jankau (in March '45), the French had overcome the imperialist commanders Mercy and Werth at Allerheim (in August '45). The Emperor Ferdinand III had reached the end of his resources as well as the end of his hopes. His opponents had included not only the French, the Swedes, the Dutch, and certain disgruntled German princes, but also the Protestant prince of Transylvania, George I Rákóczy, who

---

[1] Cf. the interesting article of Leon Stein, "Religion and Patriotism in German Peace Dramas during the Thirty Years' War," *Central European History*, IV (1971), 131–48. There is a useful sketch of the career of Justus Georg Schottel (Schottelius) in the *Allgemeine Deutsche Biographie*, XXXII (1891, repr. 1971), 407–12, but the *ADB* contains no notices of Gläser, Hadewig (Hadewieg), and Rist, on whom brief entries may be found in Zedler's *Grosses Vollständiges Universal-Lexikon*, X (1735, repr. 1961), 1547; XII, 103; and XXXI (1742, repr. 1961), 1744–46, the last one (Rist) receiving the most attention. Of broader scope than the article by Leon Stein and with quite different emphases is the study of R.J.W. Evans, "Learned Societies in Germany in the Seventeenth Century," *European Studies Review*, VII (1977), 129–51, with an extensive bibliography.

like Gabriel Bethlen before him wanted to protect his coreligionists and to extend his territorial possessions. In the spring and summer of 1643 Rákóczy had entered into detailed negotiations with both the French and the Swedes to form an alliance against Ferdinand, although before the agreements could be put into effect, the Transylvanian was to secure the permission and the approval of Sultan Ibrahim I. The French and Swedes promised to give Rákóczy 200,000 *écus* "in German money" and thereafter to pay him 150,000 each year thereafter "as long as the war shall last."[2]

Under the circumstances the sultan's permission could be taken for granted, although the Turks had recently confirmed their treaty with Austria-Hungary (on 19 May 1642).[3] The French government confirmed the agreement with Rákóczy on 22 April 1645,[4] but when the Porte decided to undertake the conquest of the island of Crete from Venice (to which we shall devote a good deal of attention later on), Rákóczy was obliged to give up warfare with the Austrians. The exhausted Ferdinand dealt generously with him, glad to remove the belligerent nuisance from his eastern front. In the Austro-Transylvanian treaty of Linz of 16 December 1645 Rákóczy promised to give up his alliances with the French and the Swedes, to withdraw his forces back into his homeland, and to restore to Ferdinand the places he had occupied. In return Ferdinand granted him the hereditary right to three fortress towns, including Tokay (Tokaj), as well as seven counties "for the remaining days of his life, just as his late Imperial Majesty had granted them to the late Gabriel Bethlen in the year 1622."[5]

---

[2] Dumont, *Corps universel diplomatique*, VI-1 (1728), no. CLIX, pp. 273–76: "Avant toutes choses, il faut que le Prince de Transilvanie obtienne de l'Empereur des Turcs la permission de déclarer et faire la guerre en Hongrie à Ferdinand Troisième, Empereur des Romains: . . . Les Couronnes de France et de Suède et tous leurs Alliez prendront en leur protection et deffense le Prince de Transilvanie, sa Femme, et ses Enfans et ses Héritiers avec toutes leurs Terres et tous leurs biens en quelque lieu qu'ils soient situez, même en Hongrie. . . ." Freedom of religion was also to be guaranteed to both Protestants and Catholics.

[3] Gabriel Noradounghian, *Recueil d'actes internationaux de l'Empire Ottoman*, 4 vols., Paris, 1897–1903, I, no. 8, pp. 120–21.

[4] Dumont, VI-1, no. CLXXXIV, pp. 310–11; Fritz Dickmann, *Der Westfälische Frieden* (1959), pp. 122–23.

[5] Dumont, VI-1, no. CXCIII, pp. 329–32, "datum in Arce nostra Lyntzene Austriae superioris die 16. mensis Decembris A.D. 1645," and cf., *ibid.*, nos. CXCV, CCV, pp. 333–35, 348–50. On Rákóczy, Torstensson, Wrangel, von Königsmarck, and other leading figures of this period, cf. the brief monograph of Peter Broucek, *Der Schwedenfeldzug nach Niederösterreich, 1645/46*, Vienna, 1967, pp. 6ff. (Militärhistorische Schriftenreihe, Heft 7), and see Ruppert, *Die kaiserliche Politik auf dem Westfälischen Friedenskongress* (1979), pp. 16–17, 74–75, and esp. pp. 120–21.

Both Venice and the Curia Romana were kept more or less well informed on recent events in central Europe, as we perceive from the Arch. Segr. Vaticano, Cod. Urb. lat. 1109 [1644–1645], fols. 14–15ʳ, *Di Venetia li 6 di Gennaro 1645* [i.e., 1646], including the fact "che sua Maestà Cesarea si era contentata a concedere quasi tutto quello che pretende il

Peace with George Rákóczy was a relief to the Emperor Ferdinand, but Friedrich Wilhelm of Brandenburg had already come to terms with the Swedes, and now on 6 September 1645 Johann Georg I of Saxony sought and received a six months' truce with Lennart Torstensson, the Swedish field marshal. The terms of the armistice "unter diesen 6. monatlichen Stillstand" were signed at Kötzschenbroda, a part of the modern town of Radebeul in Saxony, a few miles northwest of Johann Georg's capital of Dresden.[6] In other words Saxony, like Brandenburg, had now quit the field. The Saxon-Swedish truce, which was in effect a peace, removed the sole remaining bulwark in the way of Torstensson's entry into the hereditary lands of the Hapsburgs.

Meanwhile negotiations for peace had been going on for some time. Agents and delegates of a number of the German princes and states had gathered at Frankfurt as early as January 1643 to deal with the multiplicity of problems they faced. At the same time envoys of the other European states and sovereigns were coming together at Münster and Osnabrück in Westphalia. The representatives of the Catholic powers, including France and Spain, assembled at Münster, while the Swedish envoys and their Protestant associates made Osnabrück their headquarters. The imperialists were to deal with France at Münster and with Sweden at Osnabrück. Protocol, the perennial bone of contention of who took precedence over whom, was an obstacle to trying to settle any question for months and months. The Saxon truce with Torstensson, however, finally moved Ferdinand III seriously and promptly to seek some sort of compromise with his enemies, above all of course with France and Sweden. He therefore sent Count Maximilian von Trauttmannsdorff, his close friend and trusted advisor, to Münster, where (unlike some of his predecessors) Trauttmannsdorff made a most unpretentious entry on 29 November 1645, just twelve weeks after the Saxon-Swedish "truce."[7]

While Trauttmannsdorff was carrying on at Münster and Osnabrück,

---

Ragozzi, ch'è la maggior parte dell'Ungaria superiore con la città di Cassovia [Košice in Slovakia] metropoli, rivocando da tutta quella parte li Padri Giesuiti, et ciò nonostante nel serrare delle lettere capitò nuova alla marciata del Getz [the imperialist general Johann von Goetz] che detto Ragozzi si moveva per inoltrarsi nel regno." The writer of this *avviso* was also well informed concerning the movements of Torstensson, von Königsmarck, and others at this time. Cf., *ibid.*, fols. 35ᵛ–36.

[6] Dumont, VI-1, no. CXC, pp. 325–26, "so geschehen zu Ketzschebernreda den 27. Augusti anno 1645," O.S., i.e., 6 September, and cf., *ibid.*, no. CXCVII, pp. 340–42.

[7] The instructions which Trauttmannsdorff received from Ferdinand III were dated at Linz on 16 October 1645; they may be found in the *Acta Pacis Westphalicae*, ser. I, vol. I (1962): *Instruktionen: Frankreich, Schweden, Kaiser*, pp. 440–52, "geben auf meinem Schlos zu Linz den 16. October 1645." Trauttmannsdorff's instructions make clear Ferdinand's fear of French intrusion into the affairs of the Empire [art. 14]: "Es ist auch wol zu vermuten dass Frankhreich im Reich sessionem et votum praetendiren und behaubten wirdt wollen, welliche praetension dann genzlichen zu rejiciren und sich derselben mit allen khreften zu widersezen sein wirdt. . . ."

seeking the best terms he could for the Emperor Ferdinand, the Swedish general Karl Gustav Wrangel invaded Bavaria (in 1646–1647), devastating the duchy and frightening the Elector Maximilian out of his wits. On 14 March (1647), however, Wrangel's onslaught was halted by a general truce initiated at Ulm, establishing peace among France, Sweden, Hessen-Kassel, and Bavaria. Bavaria, threatened with overall destruction, was actually the chief subject of the truce, an important prelude to the subsequent peace of Westphalia. The truce was "à commencer d'aujourd'hui jusqu'à la prochaine Paix universelle, qui doit être concluë en Allemagne et dans la Chrétienté," i.e., the truce would last until the delegates at Münster and Osnabrück arrived at the "universal peace" for which they had been dickering for some four years.

Special provision was made for Bavaria:

> . . . d'autant que la plûpart desdites provinces [de la Haute et Basse Bavière, etc. . . . avec le Haut et Bas Palatinat de deçà le Rhin] sont épuisées par les ravages de la guerre et réduites à une extrême misère, on laissera pour cet effet à l'Armée de Bavière tous les états et cantons situez entre les rivières de Mindel et de Lech, comme aussi les lieux qui y sont compris et ceux qui sont voisins du Danube . . . afin de lui donner les moyens de subsister.

As for the rival claims of Karl Ludwig, son of the late Elector Friedrich V of the Palatinate, and Maximilian of Bavaria, "on en laissera la décision entière aux conférences du Congrès de Münster et Osnabrug."

As the truce went into effect, it was agreed that the Bavarian troops should not pass into the service of the emperor, the king of Spain, or any of the Hapsburg confederates. Other provisions were made concerning garrisons, munitions, and food supplies, along with various details which in this context need not detain us. Ferdinand von Wittelsbach, the elector of Cologne (1612–1650) and the brother of Maximilian, was included in the truce, which required him (to the fullest extent he could) to force the withdrawal of the imperialists and their adherents from all places in his possession or under his jurisdiction. Those whom the Wittelsbachs could not expel, the Franco-Swedish forces would.

Maximilian must return to the prince of Württemberg all the towns, castles, and fortresses then being occupied by Bavarian garrisons, although he was permitted to take therefrom all his armaments. Freedom of trade was to be allowed in the Wittelsbachs' territories, but no contraband of any kind was to be given or sold to the Austrian or Spanish forces. The truce of Ulm was ratified by Maximilian of Bavaria on 19 March (1647), by Karl Gustav Wrangel on 25 March, and by the Elector Ferdinand of Cologne on 2 May—it was a stepping-stone to the treaties of Westphalia.[8]

---

[8] Dumont, VI-1, nos. CCXV–CCXVI, pp. 375–86, "signatum Ulm 4/14 Martii anno 1647;" Dickmann, *Der Westfälische Frieden* (1959), pp. 397–98, 424–25, 429–30.

If the modern historian finds it difficult to keep track of the intrigues and chicanery of these years, so did contemporaries. When the young King Louis XIV's government proposed to the Spaniards the exchange of French-held Catalonia for the southern Netherlands (Belgium), the Spaniards played the game with them until it was profitable to disclose it all to the States General of the United Provinces. As Spain had weakened, and France had grown in power, the Dutch were coming to fear the nearby French more than their distant enemies in Spain. The Dutch dreaded the thought of having the French as their immediate neighbors, and so lost little time in making a provisional peace with Spain. Philip IV now recognized and asserted the freedom and sovereignty of the United Provinces in a truce dated 15 December 1646.

The proposed peace between Spain and Holland was to be "bonne, ferme, fidelle, et inviolable, et qu'en suitte cesseront tous actes d'hostilité . . . entre lesdits Seigneurs Roi [Philip IV] et États Généraux tant par mer . . . que par terre." The proposed peace was to be on the basis of their current holdings, *uti possidetis,* taking stock of their territories overseas as well as those in Europe. The Spanish-Dutch agreement would also take account of trade and commerce, excise taxes and tolls, salt being always a matter of importance. Restitution was to be made *réciproquement* of all goods and properties improperly confiscated, including the properties of churches and colleges.

Philip IV would undertake to secure for the United Provinces "la continuation et observation de la neutralité, amitié, et bonne voisinance de la part de Sa Majesté Impériale et de l'Empire," which would remove something of a load from the shoulders of the Dutch. Spanish subjects would henceforth be assured of safety in Holland, and the Dutch in Spain. A judicial chamber composed of one-half Spanish and one-half Dutch would be established to pass judgment on commercial and other disagreements and disputes between the two contracting parties. Various provisions were made for the house of Orange-Nassau. The text of the truce of 15 December 1646 is long and detailed. It was accompanied by more than a little debate, but was ratified by the Spanish envoys Count Guzmán de Peñaranda and the scholarly Antonio Brun. It was also signed by seven representatives of the United Provinces.[9] Nevertheless, it was still not a final treaty of peace.

When the Spanish refused to give up the southern (Catholic) Netherlands in return for a Catalonia they were confident they could regain, the French decided to concentrate their military efforts upon the conquest

---

[9] Dumont, *Corps universel diplomatique,* VI-1, no. ccix, pp. 360–65, with the addition of certain amendments. Philip IV also made special treaties with William II, prince of Orange, son of Frederick Henry (d. 14 March 1647), on 8 January and 30 August 1647, and on 27 December of the same year (*ibid.,* nos. ccx, ccxxviii, pp. 365–66, 427–28).

of the long-disputed county of Flanders. The remains of the late Bern-
hard of Sachsen-Weimar's army, which had been in the employ of the
French since 1635, now revolted against the unpopular leadership of
Turenne. Largely German and Protestant (like Bernhard himself), the
"Bernhardines" had no intention of winning Flanders for the French.
They revolted in the area of Strasbourg on the Lower Rhine (in Alsace) in
the summer of 1647, and went off to join the Swedish forces under Karl
Gustav Wrangel, who received them despite his government's alliance
with France.

Turenne could not invade Flanders, not only because of the desertion
of the Bernhardines, but also because Maximilian of Bavaria now abandoned the peace or truce of Ulm which he had accepted a few months
before (on 14 March 1647). Johann von Werth, disgusted by Maximilian's obeisance to the Swedes and French, turned his back on the court
of Munich, and added himself to the Emperor Ferdinand's staff. When
Wrangel moved again into Bohemia, however, the distraught Maximilian
returned to his alliance with the emperor on 7 September 1647, once
again becoming an imperialist *socius belli et pacis.*[10]

Bit by bit, however, peace was being made. On 11 September 1647
Philip IV's envoys at Münster accepted a commercial treaty with the
Hanseatic League of northern Germany. The misfortune of the times and
the calamities of war, according to the Latin summary of the text, had
caused great loss to the Spanish as well as to the Hanseatic peoples.
Henceforth the old privileges and immunities which the Hanse had acquired over the years "in the kingdoms and provinces of Spain" were to
be observed by both sides in good faith, as had been intended in the first
Hispano-Hanseatic pact of the year 1607. Although the Hanse had suffered a good deal of late from competition with the Dutch and English
merchantmen, the League still existed (the last council of its ministers
would meet in 1669). In any event, having made peace with Holland,
Peñaranda and Antonio Brun had hoped to gain the good will of the
German Hanse as well as, perhaps, some economic advantage.[11] It would
take a good deal to revive the old Hanseatic commerce. In fact Germany
had on the whole sustained severe economic losses during the war, with
a general decline in agricultural production and a diminution of trade.
Peasants fled from the fields as armies approached, and the transport of
such grains and manufactured goods as remained available was much
curtailed by warfare.

---

[10] Dumont, VI-1, no. CCXXIV, pp. 399–400, "geschehen . . . zu Pilsen den 7. September
anno 1647," the treaty (*Traktat*) being confirmed by Ferdinand III on 7 September at
Pilsen in western Bohemia and by Maximilian at Munich toward the end of the month.
[11] Dumont, VI-1, nos. CCXXVI–CCXXVII, pp. 402–27, with Philip IV's personal ratification
of the treaty dated at Madrid on 26 January 1648, and reaffirmed at Münster on 3 May and
6 June 1648, and cf., *ibid.*, no. CCXXXIV, pp. 445–46.

At long last, however, on 30 January 1648 Philip IV of Spain and the States General of the United Provinces, "touchés de compassion Chrétienne et désirans mettre fin aux calamités publiques," made the long-expected and definitive treaty for which, as we have seen, detailed outlines had been drafted in the preliminary peace of 15 December 1646. The final peace was signed at Münster, bringing to an end "the long course of bloody wars, which have afflicted for so many years the peoples, subjects, kingdoms, and lands owing obedience to the lord King of the Spains and [the] States General of the United Provinces of the Netherlands." Philip recognized of course the fact already emphasized (in 1646) that the United Provinces were "libres et souverains Estats"—"and from the day of the conclusion and ratification of this peace, the King will order the discontinuance on the Rhine and the Meuse of the [Spanish] collection of all the tolls which before the war were under the territorial jurisdiction of the United Provinces, above all the toll of Zeeland, so that this toll will not be collected by his Majesty in the town of Antwerp nor elsewhere. . . ."

In fact heavy charges were now laid on the states of Zeeland but, more importantly still, the United Provinces acquired the right to close the river Scheldt (Schelde), Antwerp's easy access to the North Sea. Furthermore, from 1648 to 1863, except for the Napoleonic era, the Netherlanders levied tolls on non-Dutch freight brought up the Scheldt. After Westphalia, Antwerp declined rapidly, and Amsterdam in northern Holland became one of the commercial and banking centers of Europe.

When it came to the public exercise of religious practice, the subjects of the Spanish kingdoms and the United Provinces must behave themselves with all modesty "sans donner aucun scandale de parole ou de fait." Merchants, masters of ships, pilots, and seamen as well as their merchandise and other possessions were to be free from seizure under any command or pretext, whether on the grounds of war or otherwise. Just seizures of property for debts or the violation of contractual obligations were, however, another matter, and were to be dealt with by "right and reason." Certain vested interests of the house of Orange-Nassau were considered and protected.

The definitive treaty of 30 January (1648) is a meticulous expansion in seventy-nine articles of the preliminary peace of 15 December 1646. The bipartite tribunal (*chambre mypartie*) set up in 1646 was to settle the disputes and doubts which might and did still exist from 1567 to the beginning of the twelve years' truce between Spain and Holland (in 1609) as well as from the latter period to the year 1648,[12] and with that assurance we may omit any further detail.

---

[12] Dumont, VI-1, no. ccxxxi, pp. 429–35, with various legal addenda, *ibid.*, pp. 435–41. In article xlix of the preliminary peace of 15 December 1646 between Spain and the United Provinces, Philip IV had undertaken "effectively to secure the continuation and

Long years of enmity between Spain and the United Provinces had now, officially at least, drawn to a close. Monarchical Catholic Spain had made a political, economic, and religious peace with republican Protestant Holland. The representatives of the Catholic princes, ecclesiastics, and cities had been fighting among themselves at Münster, some ready to accept religious toleration, others doggedly against it. At Osnabrück the Protestants, despite the differences between Lutherans and Calvinists and their territorial disputes, found general agreement easier to achieve than the Catholics, some of whom left Münster in irate dissatisfaction about the time of the Dutch-Spanish treaty. When the religious problem was solved (to the extent it could be), the solution would be to the marked advantage of the Protestants, as we shall note presently. In any event the treaties of Münster and Osnabrück were not the consequence of such accommodations as were reached in 1648. They embodied the final agreements of the participants after the past four years of diplomatic as well as military contention.[13]

While the Dutch and Spanish were making peace, the Swedes and French were invading southern Germany. Wrangel and Turenne almost crushed the remaining forces of Ferdinand III and Maximilian of Bavaria on 17 May (1648) near Zusmarshausen in Swabia, some sixty or seventy miles north of the far western border of Austria. Once more Bavaria was ravaged, and Ferdinand and Maximilian were almost disarmed. Presently another Swedish army under Hans Christoph von Königsmarck descended upon Bohemia, laying violent siege to now devoutly Catholic Prague. The inhabitants resisted the Protestant assaults with extraordinary courage and an intense religious zeal.

Although on 26 July (1648) von Königsmarck's forces fought their way into the (western) Lesser Town (the Malá Strana, "Small Side") as well as into the Hradčany, where Prague Castle stands on the hill, they could not take the larger, eastern part of the city, the Old Town (Staré Mešto) and the New Town (Nové Mešto), for the inhabitants fiercely defended the Charles Bridge. The bridge crosses the Vltava river from east to west, connecting the two parts of the city. It is still one of the great monuments of Prague, and is now closed to motor vehicles of all kinds. It was the right bank of the Vltava, the larger (eastern) area, which von Königsmarck failed to get into his clutches.

A half century before this final siege of 1648, the Lesser Town (Malá Strana) on the left bank of the Vltava had been a thriving commercial

---

observation of neutrality, friendship, and good neighborliness on the part of his imperial Majesty and the Empire" (*ibid.*, VI-1, no. CCIX, p. 363a), to which Ferdinand III was to respond affirmatively on 6 July 1648 (*ibid.*, no. CCCXXXV, p. 446, which refers, however, to "art. LIII" of the preliminary peace).

[13] See in general the detailed study of Fritz Dickmann, *Der Westfälische Frieden*, Münster, 1959, to which several references have already been made.

and intellectual center with extensive colonies of Italian, Dutch, German, and English merchants and intellectuals.[14] Now, however, it showed the sad effects of political, economic, and social erosion, which must await the gradual reconstruction of the later seventeenth and eighteenth centuries to help remake Prague into the impressive city of modern times.[15]

In any event the Old Town of Prague was now spared further depredation by the final agreements signed in Westphalia on 24 October 1648, almost bringing peace to Europe. It had taken a long time. Eight years before this, in fact, on 8 October 1640 Johann Adolf von Schwarzenberg had written his kinsman Georg Ludwig from Regensburg that all the states involved in the war wanted peace, but that negotiations with the Swedes had been bogged down by nothing more than the unseemly wording of what had appeared (to Schwarzenberg at least) a possible agreement.[16] Despite some four years of negotiations, peace was indeed long in coming. At Lens, then in the southern Netherlands, now in northern France, Louis d'Enghien de Condé defeated the imperialists (on 20 August 1648) in the last important battle of the war. Meanwhile at Münster, as at Osnabrück, demands and concessions were still dependent upon victory or defeat in the field.

Diplomatic protocol, however, delayed the proceedings at Münster and Osnabrück quite as much perhaps as the vagaries of warfare. France would not yield precedence to Sweden, nor the latter to France. Thus it was better that their negotiations with the imperialists should not be held in the same place. If, for example, the ambassadors of the two kingdoms found themselves together, neither could allow the other to enter a room before him, sit above him at an assembly or a dinner, sign a document before he had attached his own signature thereto, and so the contest could go on indefinitely, as the envoys and ecclesiastics at the Council of Trent had sometimes made painfully clear. Such diplomatic clashes, whether involving ambassadors or mere agents, were inevitable. They were also time-consuming, for one of the two contestants would leave the scene, and nothing would get done.[17] Hence France and Sweden each had to make a separate treaty with the Empire. The French and Swedish ambassadors were, however, prepared to acknowledge the

---

[14] J.V. Polišenský, *The Thirty Years' War*, trans. Robert Evans, Berkeley and Los Angeles, 1971, pp. 12–13, 16–17, and cf., *ibid.*, pp. 43ff.

[15] Cf. the brief article of A. Klima, "Industrial Development in Bohemia, 1648–1781," *Past and Present*, XI (April 1957), 87–97. Despite the widespread "feudalization" (or we should say manorialization) of Bohemia, with the large increase of serfdom after 1648, the textile industries grew in almost remarkable fashion during this period.

[16] *Documenta bohemica Bellum Tricennale illustrantica*, VI (1979), no. 1088, p. 375.

[17] On the always vexed question of protocol as well as the divisions and disagreements at Münster and Osnabrück, note Alvise Contarini, *Relatione . . . per la pace universale al convento di Münster* (1650), Biblioteca Nazionale Marciana (Venice), MS. It. VII, 1107 (9016), esp. fols. 13ff.

higher status which an age-old tradition had accorded to the emperor and therefore to his ambassador.

Thus a treaty of peace was accepted at Münster in Westphalia on 24 October 1648 by the representatives of the Emperor Ferdinand III and his adherents, King Louis XIV and his *foederati et adhaerentes,* and the electors, princes, and states of the Holy Roman Empire. Of Louis XIV's *foederati* Queen Christina of Sweden was foremost, and was included in the peace. A similar treaty was concluded and signed on the same day at Osnabrück in Westphalia by the plenipotentiaries of the emperor, the queen of Sweden, and the deputies of the electors, princes, and states of the Empire. The emperor included, on his part, the king of Spain, the Hanseatic League, the duke of Savoy, and certain other sovereigns and princes. Among her "allies and adherents" the queen of Sweden put Louis XIV foremost, *principalement le Roi Très-Chrestien,* as well as (for the most part) the princes and sovereigns whom Ferdinand had ranked among his "alliez et adhérens," all of whom were thus included in the imperialist-Swedish peace.[18] In Münster, however, the papal nuncio Fabio Chigi, who was to be elected pope as Alexander VII (in April 1655), protested against the damage being done to the Catholic Church and the faith by various articles in the treaties, and (on 26 November 1648) Pope Innocent X added his own solemn protestation against the evil peace.[19]

The peace of Westphalia altered the political and social structure of Europe. It gave the Protestants the right to retain all the church lands they had taken and still held as of 1 January, 1624,[20] as opposed to their

---

[18] The Westphalian treaties reestablishing peace between Ferdinand III and Louis XIV, "et consentientibus Sac. Rom. Imperii Electoribus, Principibus, ac Statibus ad Divini Numinis gloriam et Christianae Reipublicae salutem in mutuas pacis et amicitiae leges consenserunt . . ." may of course be found in Dumont, VI-1, no. CCXXXVIII, pp. 450–59: "Acta sunt haec Monasterii Westphalorum die 24. Octob. anno 1648." The French text of the treaty between Ferdinand III and Christina of Sweden, which included Louis XIV, is given, *ibid.,* no. CCXLIV, pp. 469–90: "Aussi-tost que le Traité de Paix aura esté souscrit et signé par les Plénipotentiaires et Ambassadeurs, tout acte d'hostilité cessera . . ." (art. XVI): "Ce qui a esté ainsi arresté et conclu à Osnabruch le 14. ou 24. Octobre l'an 1648." Besides the Latin and French texts of these treaties, copies were prepared in German and other languages.

[19] *Ibid.,* VI-1, nos. CCXL–CCXLI, pp. 462–64, and note Hermann Bücher, *Der Nuntius Fabio Chigi (Papst Alexander VII) in Münster, 1644–1649,* Münster, 1958. Chigi had previously been the apostolic delegate in Malta from 1634 to 1639; his official correspondence during these years has been published by Vincent Borg (Città di Vaticano, 1967, Studi e Testi, 249).

[20] As declared in the imperialist-Swedish treaty (Dumont, VI-1, no. CCXLIV, art. V, 2, p. 473), "Que le terme duquel on doit commencer la restitution dans les choses ecclésiastiques, et en ce qui a esté changé à leur égard dans les politiques, soit le premier jour de Janvier 1624, et partant que le rétablissement de tous les Électeurs, Princes, et Estats de l'une et l'autre religion, compris la noblesse libre de l'Empire comme aussi les communautez et villages immédiats, se fasse pleinement et sans restriction de ce jour-là . . . , et toutes exécutions faites en ces sortes d'affaires demeurent nuls et supprimez et le tout réduit en l'estat qu'il estoit aux jour et an susdits."

more limited possessions recognized by the treaty of Passau (1552) and the religious peace of Augsburg (1555). The principle *cuius regio, eius religio,* which had been restricted to Catholics of the imperial states and to the Lutheran adherents of the Confession of Augsburg (1530), was now largely abandoned. Although religious freedom was granted to the inhabitants of Silesia, Ferdinand III refused toleration in the hereditary lands of the Casa d'Austria. Catholicism remained the sole authorized faith in the *Erblande* of the Hapsburgs. For the rest, in Germany as in most of Europe, Calvinism became an acceptable faith. The "ecclesiastical reservation" was retained, however, and so if a Catholic archbishop, bishop, or prelate, should change his religion, he must give up his ecclesiastical office and all its attendant revenues which was, according to the imperialist-Swedish treaty, to be damaging to neither his honor nor his reputation.[21]

Owing to the concessions made to the Protestants (under Swedish pressure at Osnabrück) by the Emperor Ferdinand III, the Elector Maximilian I of Bavaria, and Johann Philipp von Schönborn, who had been recently appointed the (ecclesiastical) elector of Mainz, Westphalia seemed to be a victory for the Protestants and a defeat for the German Catholics and their Church. The princes, cities, and towns had already seized upon a wide range of ecclesiastical property, and now the Catholics also lost two archbishoprics, a dozen bishoprics, and a half-dozen abbeys. As the emperor's chief representative, Count Maximilian von Trauttmannsdorff, was well aware, the emperor needed peace for several important reasons, one of them being the Swedish threat to Prague, another the recent French victory over the imperialists' Spanish allies at Lens, and a third the ever-present possibility of renewed Turkish aggression.[22] Nevertheless, despite the opportunity presented by the Hapsburgs' constant involvement in the Thirty Years' War, the Turks had directed their bellicose attention toward Venice, as we shall see, for Crete appeared to be an obtainable prize.

During the course of the long war religious issues had gradually given way (to some extent) to the political and economic needs and ambitions of the combatants. The individual treaties of Westphalia are too long and detailed to attempt full summaries in a survey as brief as this, but France at long length received imperial recognition of her perpetual and irrevocable possession of the bishoprics and cities of Metz, Toul, and Verdun,

---

[21] Dumont, VI-1, no. CCXLIV, art. v, 3, p. 474, and cf. Contarini, *Relatione,* MS. Marc. It. VII, 1107 (9016), fol. 19.

[22] Pastor, *Gesch. d. Päpste,* XIV-1 (1929), 73–108, esp. pp. 82ff., 91ff., and the [carelessly proofread] *Hist. Popes,* XXX, 94–142, esp. pp. 106ff., 118ff. On Innocent X's protest against the Catholic concessions to the Protestants in the peace of Westphalia, note Pastor, XIV-1, 96–101.

which she had been holding since the time of Charles V (from 1552). The emperor and the Empire also "ceded and transferred" to the most Christian king of France the city and citadel of Pinerolo in Piedmont (where the Man in the Iron Mask is said to have been kept a prisoner in the later seventeenth century) as well as the "town of Breisach, the landgraviate of Upper and Lower Alsace, . . . and governance of the provinces of ten imperial cities in Alsace," all ten of which are of course identified in the text. Since these cities remained within the Empire, France thus acquired the right to be represented in the Reichstag.[23]

On 15 November (1648), however, Philip IV of Spain issued a long and detailed protest in the name of the "Burgundian Circle" against the imperialist-French treaty which the emperor had accepted without the agreement of Spain. The king of Spain and the emperor had always had the same enemies. The house of Hapsburg in Madrid had always assisted their cousins in Vienna, and now the Spanish government and Spanish arms had been shamefully deserted.[24]

The French might have gained more from their victories in the field, but the revolts known as "la Fronde" (1648–1653) were now beginning against the ever increasing power of the Crown. Mazarin's government was opposed by the Parlement de Paris, which refused to accept an order for an increase in taxation. The unruly French nobility were soon up in arms; the people were tired of war and the financial burdens being laid upon them. The Fronde would eventually prove a stepladder to the almost absolutist authority of the Crown, but in the meantime Mazarin's position was seriously threatened. He needed peace even more than France did, and the French representatives at Münster had been directed to reach an accord with the emperor and his allies as soon as they could. Yes, Mazarin knew he needed peace, but not with Spain. The Franco-

---

[23] As stated in the imperialist-French treaty (Dumont, VI-1, no. CCXXXVIII, p. 455), it was agreed "quod supremum dominium, jura superioritatis, aliaque omnia in episcopatus Metensem, Tullensem, et Virodunensem, urbesque cognomines eorumque episcopatuum districtus . . . , eo modo quo hactenus ad Romanum spectabant Imperium, in posterum ad Coronam Galliae spectare eique incorporari debeant in perpetuum et irrevocabiliter. . . .

"Secundo, Imperator et Imperium cedunt transferuntque in Regem Christianissimum . . . jus directi dominii, superioritatis, et quodcumque aliud sibi et Sacro Romano Imperio hactenus in Pinarolum competebat et competere poterat.

"Tertio, Imperator pro se totaque serenissima Domo Austriaca itemque Imperium cedunt omnibus juribus . . . ac jurisdictionibus, quae hactenus sibi, Imperio, et Familiae Austriacae competebant in oppidum Brisacum, Landgraviatum superioris et inferioris Alsatiae, . . . praefecturamque provinciarum decem civitatum imperialium in Alsatia sitarum, . . . omnesque pagos et alia quaecumque jura, quae a dicta praefectura dependent, eaque omnia et singula in Regem Christianissum Regnumque Galliarum transferunt. . . ." On the imperial cession of Breisach, Upper and Lower Alsace, the ten imperial cities in Alsace, and other territory, note, *ibid.,* no. CCXLVI, pp. 490–91. Carlo II Gonzaga had some reason to protest against this treaty (*ibid.,* no. CCL, pp. 493–94). Note also Contarini, *Relatione,* MS. Marc. It. VII, 1107 (9016), fol. 14ᵛ, and cf. fols. 17ʳ, 18ᵛ.

[24] Dumont, VI-1, no. CCXLII, pp. 464–67, doc. dated at Münster on 15 November 1648.

Spanish war continued for more than a decade—until the peace of the Pyrenees in 1659[25]—until within two years of Mazarin's death (in 1661).

The queen and kingdom of Sweden were henceforth to hold as fiefs of the Empire the duchy of Pomerania and the principality of Rügen, in addition to which the Swedes were given, *en fief perpétuel et immédiat de l'Empire,* the town and port of Wismar plus the archbishopric of Bremen and the bishopric of Verden to be held as secular duchies. With possession of the duchies of Bremen, Verden, and Pomerania, the principality of Rügen, and the lordship of Wismar, the sovereigns of Sweden were to be duly summoned to assemblies of the imperial Reichstag. Gliding over various complications, we may finally note that the electorates, principalities, and other states of the Empire must furnish the crown of Sweden with 5,000,000 imperial dollars (*risdales, Reichstaler*) for the demobilization of the numerous mercenary forces which the Swedes still had in the field.[26] As soon as the plenipotentiaries and the ambassadors had affixed their signatures to the imperialist-Swedish treaty, every act of hostility was to cease, and one was to start putting into effect the numerous provisions set forth in the treaty.

Maximilian I of Bavaria retained the (eastern) Upper Palatinate and the electoral dignity, while he agreed to the annulment of a debt of 13,000,000 imperial dollars and gave up all claim to Upper Austria. Maximilian would turn over to the emperor all documents relating to this

---

[25] Dumont, *Corps universel diplomatique,* VI-2 (1728), no. CVIII, pp. 264–83, texts dated from 7 November 1659 to 1 June 1660, and note, *ibid.,* no. CIX.

[26] Taking a few extracts from the imperialist-Swedish treaty (Dumont, VI-1, no. CCXLIV, arts. X, 1–4, and XVI, pp. 481ff.), we may note that "Sa Majesté et le Royaume de Suède tiendra et possedera dès ce jourd'huy à perpétuité en fief héréditaire ce duché de Poméranie et la principalité de Rügen. . . . L'Empereur, du consentement de tout l'Empire, céde aussi à la Reyne Sérénissime . . . la ville et le port de Wismar. . . . L'Empereur . . . céde aussi, en vertu de la présente transaction, à la Sérénissime Reine . . . l'archevesché de Bremen et l'evesché de Verden. . . .

"L'Empereur . . . reçoit pour estat immédiat de l'Empire la Reyne Sérénissime et ses successeurs au Royaume de Suède en sorte que la susdite Reyne et lesdits Roys seront désormais appellez aux Diètes Impériales avec les autres estats de l'Empire sous le titre de Ducs de Brémen, de Verden, et de Poméranie, comme aussi sous celuy de Princes de Rügen et de Seigneurs de Wismar . . . [art. X, 1–4]. Aussi-tost que le Traité de Paix aura esté souscrit et signé par les plénipotentiares et ambassadeurs, tout acte d'hostilité cessera, et les choses qui ont esté accordées cy-dessus seront de part et d'autre en même temps mises à exécution. . . . Finalement pour ce qui regarde le licentiement de la soldatesque Suèdoise, tous les Électeurs, Princes, et autres Estats . . . seront tenus de contribuer la somme de cinq millions de risdales en espèces de bon aloy ayant cours dans l'Empire . . . [art. XVI]."

Cf. Contarini, *Relatione,* MS. Marc. It. VII, 1107 (9016), fol. 18ʳ: "In Febraro del '47 restò parimente aggiustata la sodisfatione della corona di Suezzia, che in sostanza fu la ritentione della miglior e maggior parte della Pomerania, compresi li forti, l'isole, e le città migliori sopra il Baltico, li vescovati di Bremen e Ferden, l'uso libero del porto di Wismar, datasi per questo ai duchi di Mechlemburgh, che ne furono patroni, una conveniente ricompensa in conformità del pratticatosi coll'Ellettore di Brandemberg per la cessione della Pomerania" (and cf., *ibid.,* fols. 14ʳ, 22ʳ).

debt, "pour estre cassez et annullez." An eighth electorate was now created for Karl Ludwig, the son of Friedrich V, "the winter king."[27] Karl Ludwig was thus confined to the Lower or Rhenish Palatinate, extending from the left bank of the Rhine to the Saarland and the French border, with his capital in the devastated city of Heidelberg.[28]

In order to provide proper compensation to Friedrich Wilhelm, the elector of Brandenburg, "who to advance the cause of universal peace has given up the rights he had to Hither Pomerania, Rügen, and the provinces and places connected therewith," Brandenburg now received the bishoprics of Halberstadt, Minden, and Cammin (Kamien) "en fief perpétuel et immédiat de l'Empire." Needless to add, Friedrich Wilhelm possessed "en ce nom scéance et voix aux Dietes Impériales." Friedrich Wilhelm was also granted "the expectancy of the archbishopric of Magdeburg upon its becoming vacant either by the death of the then administrator, Duke August of Saxony, or by the latter's accession to the electorate [of Saxony]."[29] As for old Johann Georg, the elector of Saxony, he did no better than retain Lusatia, which he had acquired in the treaty of Prague (of 1635), but that was a considerable gain.

These were trying years for the Emperor Ferdinand III, who saw no way of helping to make peace between his Hapsburg cousin in Spain and the government of Louis XIV. The Turks were quiet, however, even friendly, for on 1 July 1649 the Porte renewed the treaty of Zsitvatorok, which had been the cornerstone of the generally peaceful relations between the Ottoman and the Catholic empires for more than forty years.[30] The government of the boy sultan Mehmed IV was torn by interior dis-

---

[27] Dumont, VI-1, no. ccxliv, art. iv, p. 470. In order for Karl Ludwig "to discharge in some fashion what he owed his brothers by way of appanage," the emperor undertook to pay the brothers 400,000 imperial dollars over a period of four years, beginning with the year 1649 (*ibid.*, pp. 470–471).

Despite the destruction in their territories (particularly that of Bavaria) on the whole Maximilian and the Emperor Ferdinand fared well in the Westphalian agreements (cf. Contarini, *Relatione*, MS. Marc. It. VII, 1107 [9016], fol. 21ʳ): "Il Palatinato Superiore, che prima era della Casa Palatina, rimane al Duca di Baviera contiguo a suoi stati, per il qual ogetto Baviera rilascia poi a Cesare l'Austria Superiore, impegnatali già per tredici millioni, che la Casa Imperiale doveva poi a quella di Baviera, sì che in questa pace si può dire con verità che l'Imperatore benchè angustiato da pericoli, nemici, et necessità abbi fatto per lui una pace vantaggiosissima. Ha conseguito la corona di Boemia ereditaria nella sua dissendenza, che fu l'origine della presente guerra, mentre li Boemi la prettendevano ellettiva. Ha presservato li suoi stati patrimoniali dalla libertà di conscienza, concedendola liberamente in tutti gl'altri d'Alemagna. Ha ricuperato l'Austria Superiore impegnata per tredici millioni alla Casa di Baviera senza esborsare un quatrino. In somma ha fatto per lui una pace avantaggiosa altretanto quanto dannosa all'auttorità e forze imperiali per la cognitione che si è datta ai stati dell'Impero delle proprie loro forze e del modo ancora di maneggiarle per non rimaner assogettiti."

[28] Cf. Dumont, VI-1, no. ccxlviii, p. 492, doc. dated 1649.

[29] Dumont, VI-1, no. ccxliv, arts. xi–xii, pp. 482–83. August of Saxony died in 1680.

[30] Dumont, VI-1, no. cclxiv, pp. 521–22, "actum Constantinopoli 1. Julii anno Christi 1649."

sension, and was having a hard time carrying on the war it had started with Venice four years before in an effort to wrest the island of Crete from the Signoria.

The Dutch and the Swiss were content, for the independence of the United Provinces—together with that of the cantons of Uri, Schwyz, Unterwalden, and the rest—was now internationally recognized. There was a widespread fear in Europe, however, with large numbers of mercenaries who had little or no prospect of employment, that maybe the war was not really over. In fact the Swedish troops stationed at Vechta in Oldenburg (in northwestern Germany), some thirty miles or more northeast of Osnabrück, did not leave the scene until the spring of 1654. Mutinies were frequent. Many erstwhile mercenaries turned to brigandage for a living. Bohemia, Germany, and the other areas caught up in the Thirty Years' War had not only been subjected to widespread destruction, but had also suffered year after year from typhus fever (*mal di petecchie*), the scourge of armies in the sixteenth and seventeenth centuries, and sometimes the bane of the populations upon which they intruded. Famine became widespread in areas disrupted by the war. The bubonic plague which, as we shall note, struck at the mercenary army that Venice sent into Greece two generations after the peace of Westphalia, also took its toll during these thirty years of dismal conflict. So did dysentery and influenza, but the Germans were generally spared the cholera and malaria which, later on, afflicted the Venetians in Greece. At least the Germans were spared something, for by 1648 no little of their homeland was a shambles.

It was a disastrous and turbulent era, even more confusing to contemporaries than to modern historians. Alvise Contarini, the Venetian emissary at the negotiations in Westphalia, was one of the most astute observers of the current of events in his time.[31] In 1650 Contarini

---

[31] The original texts of Contarini's dispatches to the doge and Senate during his years in Westphalia are to be found in the Venetian Archives (ASV), Senato, Dispacci Münster [where Contarini maintained his residence until 1649], Filze 1–11. The first dispatch is dated 31 July 1643, the last 19 June 1650. There are copies of these dispatches in seven volumes in the Bibl. Nazionale Marciana (Venice), MSS. It. VII, 1098–1104 (8148–8154)—*Registro di lettere scritte al Serenissimo Senato di Venetia dal Signor Cavalier Alvise Contarini, ambasciator straordinario al Convento per la Pace universal di Christianità in Mü[n]ster* (the first of these letters being dated at Venice on 31 July 1643; the last, no. 424, being dated 28 December 1649, apparently at Brussels).

There are also two volumes of *Lettere del Senato al Cavalier Alvise Contareni, ambasciator a Münster per la Pace di Christianità* [more than three hundred letters from 8 August 1643 to 4 June 1650]—MSS. Marc. It. VII, 1105–1106 (8155–8156), the first volume covering the period from 1643 to 1646. Another collection in the Marciana (MS. It. VII, 1926 [9055]) contains a large group of letters written by princes, ministers, and other important personages to Contarini, who was at Münster and Paris from 1644 to 1649. The letters are all originals, signed by the senders, with attached seals still adhering to the

presented to the Signoria a retrospective summary of the objectives of the leading powers as well as of some of the major problems created by the Thirty Years' War. He seemed still to be consoled by the recollection that in 1643 it had finally become clear there was going to be a European congress. The mediators and plenipotentiaries of the emperor and the other crowned heads had come together at Münster and Osnabrück; proceedings began on 10 April (1643) when the mass of the Holy Spirit was sung "to implore the divine assistance in the managing of such important business." Thereupon Contarini plunged into the difficulties caused by the Spaniards' initial abstention from the proceedings. The papal nuncio Fabio Chigi also remained aloof, which did not bother the Protestants.

Contarini has shown in brilliant fashion how changing events in the last half dozen years of the war had determined the varying attitudes and stands of the ministers and plenipotentiaries at Münster and Osnabrück. Peace had been made in August 1645 between the crowns of Sweden and Denmark, a peace advantageous for Sweden, shameful for Denmark, *per Francia mediatrice gloriosa*. The Emperor Ferdinand III's policy "varied according to the capacity shown by Swedish arms." Among the numerous problems, with which the negotiators in Westphalia were wrestling, were two to which modern historians have given little attention. The first was the question whether passports should be granted to deputies of George I Rákóczy, the prince of Transylvania, who had been at war with the emperor in 1644–1645. The second related to Portugal and "the freedom of Prince Edward of Braganza, brother of the king of Portugal, now a prisoner in the Castello of Milan," which need not concern us here, and was no worry to Contarini.

Rákóczy's request to be represented in Westphalia was another matter. Rákóczy was not included in the preliminaries of the congress (because his deputies had received no passports), and also, says Contarini,

---

texts. Contarini's prominence and importance are attested to by the bulk of this correspondence and by the great respect shown by those who wrote to him.

A full coverage of the archival and other sources relating to Contarini's Westphalian mission is to be found in the excellent study by Stefano Andretta, "La Diplomazia veneziana e la Pace di Vestfalia (1643–1648)," *Annuario dell' Istituto storico italiano per l'età moderna e contemporanea*, XXVII–XXVIII (1975–1976), Rome, 1978, pp. 3–128. Andretta explores the diplomatic intricacies and clarifies the important issues debated at Münster and Osnabrück, setting his account against the background of the entire Thirty Years' War. Note also A.M. Bettanini, "Alvise Contarini ambasciatore veneto (1597–1651)," *Rivista di studi politici internazionali*, IX (1942), 371–416, who gives us a survey of Contarini's early career, a sketch of his years at Münster, and a list of the relevant archival sources; A. Zanon Dal Bo, *Alvise Contarini mediatore per la Repubblica di Venezia nel Congresso di Vestfalia (1643–1648)*, Lugano, 1971, which I have not seen; and G. Benzoni's sketch of Contarini's career in the *Dizionario biografico degli Italiani*, XXVIII (1983), 82–91, with an extensive bibliography. Contarini arrived in Münster on 20 November 1643.

"because I knew that by such means the Turks would certainly have been able to penetrate to the very heart of these negotiations: I strove and succeeded in preventing [his deputies] from coming, and although this matter went on for some months, it finally ended quietly, for soon afterwards Rákóczy made peace with the emperor."[32]

In most accounts of Westphalia the Turks receive little attention.[33] At one point in the proceedings, however, the negotiators did give thought to the Turks. Trauttmannsdorff, "along with the states of the Empire," declared that Ferdinand

as emperor and archduke of Austria should not be allowed to assist the Spaniards without the consent of the Empire, but [according to Trauttmannsdorff] as king of Hungary he could not fail to meet the obligations of the blood relationship and the mutual interests of the two houses [of Hapsburg] in Germany and Spain.

To this, of course, the French took immediate exception, asserting that under the guise of king of Hungary the emperor would give his full support to the Spanish against France. Seeking a resolution of this problem the negotiators, according to Contarini,

took the opportunity to propose a war against the Turk, especially upon the basis of some secret article, under which the French would bind themselves to come to the emperor's aid in such a [noble] cause[!], but in the end the proposal came to nothing, owing to the fear which the Court of Vienna had and still has of the Turk. The negotiators declared that war against the Turk would be a guarantee without any other legal pronouncement that the emperor could not render assistance to the Spaniards, but the French and the states of the Empire took a contrary stand, insisting that the emperor must not be left powerfully armed for any reason, because although his arms were assumed to be for use against the Turk, they might well be employed either against France or merely to renew the [Hapsburg] oppressions within the Empire. There was a greater hatred of Austria than of the Turk; all the efforts expended on the proposal [against the Turk] came to nothing. May it please God that the same views, as well as the widespread fear, not still prevail today [i.e., in 1650] as objections to war against the Turk.

Current circumstances, however, in Contarini's Venetian opinion, were such that the imperialists would never again have as good an oppor-

---

[32] Contarini, *Relatione . . . per la pace universale al convento di Münster* (1650), MS. Marc. It. VII, 1107 (9016), fols. 5ᵛ, 7ʳ 12ʳ. On Rákóczy's peace with Ferdinand III (on 16 December 1645), see above, p. 81, Joseph Fiedler, *Die Relationen der Botschafter Venedigs über Deutschland und Österreich im siebzehnten Jahrhundert*, I (Vienna, 1866), 293–366, has published the text of Contarini's *Relatione* from a later copy (in a Viennese manuscript).

[33] Andretta, "La Diplomazia veneziana," esp. pp. 72–93, does deal at some length with the Turkish problem.

tunity as then existed "to take advantage of the common enemy."[34] At any rate, considering the fact that the Turks had embarked upon war with Venice five years before for possession of the island of Crete, the Signoria could wish for nothing more than a European ally against the Porte.

Contarini informs us in some detail of Trauttmannsdorff's arrival in Münster in December 1645, his departure in July 1647, and his return to the congress thereafter. When he came back, he made every effort to bring the Emperor Ferdinand III and Maximilian of Bavaria together again, "distraendo questo [Maximilian] dall'amicitia de' Francesi." He could not do so, however, because Maximilian distrusted the emperor. Contarini seems to heave a sigh of relief when he reaches the point that "seguì finalmente col favore del Signor Dio la sottoscritione della pace d'Impero con le Corone di Francia e Suezzia a 24 d'Ottobre 1648."

On the day that the treaties of Westphalia were signed, Contarini says, couriers were sent to Vienna, Paris, and Stockholm with instructions to bring back ratifications from the imperial and royal courts within two months. Other couriers were dispatched to the generals of the armies in the field "to suspend hostilities." At Münster (and Osnabrück) on 25 October the signing of the treaties of peace was celebrated with a volley of cannon fire to mark "the jubilation of all Germany after thirty years of the most painful and hideous warfare."[35]

After the signing of the treaties there followed two years of convalescence (*convalescenza*), as Contarini calls it, during which the troops had to be disbanded and the soldiers paid. The plenipotentiaries lacked the authority and the information necessary to effect this final resolution of the remaining problems of the long war,

in which context there were assigned to the Swedish militias seven of the ten "circles" of the Empire until the emperor could pay them the five million dollars [*tollari*] agreed upon for their discharge. The circle of Austria was reserved as quarters for the emperor's militias, that of Bavaria for the Bavarian [militias], and that of Burgundy remains free, the state having been excluded from the treaty for the aforesaid reasons [Contarini had already dealt with Burgundy].

The Swedes in the seven circles were so paid off that when I left Münster they got, the lot of them, as enforced contributions 108,000 dollars a day—I say a day—an almost incredible sum which does, however, give evidence of the strength of that great society [*corpo*] of Germany, even though it has been

---

[34] Contarini, *Relatione*, MS. Marc. It. VII, 1107 (9016), fol. 19ʳ.

[35] Contarini, *Relatione*, fols. 14ᵛ, 15ff., 16ʳ, 20, 22ᵛ. On 12 November 1648 the Venetian doge Francesco Molin wrote Contarini (his letter reached Münster on 26 November), "A 7 del corrente gionse il vostro dispaccio de 24 passato [24 October] con l'aviso della Pace d'Imperio conclusa et sottoscritta" (*Lettere del Senato al Cav. Alvise Contareni, ambasciator a Münster*, MS. Marc. It. VII, 1106 [8156], fol. 238ᵛ).

beaten down by so many evils for so many years. Therefore it is no surprise if the Congress of Nuremberg, assembled to carry out [the terms of the peace], has labored for two entire years in order to do so. As for the settlement with the militias, there were many objections raised over the 5,000,000 dollars finally agreed to, for Germany would have saved so much more if instead of quarters [being provided for the troops], prompt recompense had been decided upon from the beginning, because payment has been made ten times over.[36]

Contarini pauses for a moment over two of the many advantages which the peace of Westphalia brought to the participants. The first related to all the states bordering upon the Empire which in earlier times had suffered from Hapsburg ambitions or prejudices. Now conditions had changed, to the benefit of Italy especially, but most of all Venice, which had long had trouble with the Hapsburgs. As a result of the peace, however, the Hapsburgs had been subjected to the laws of the Empire no less than to the presence of France and Sweden, both of which had in fact made their way into the Empire. In one of his dispatches (dated 30 March 1646), two years before the Westphalian settlement, Contarini expressed the belief that France, Sweden, and the Netherlands then formed "a trinity of self-interest," but in the increasing fear of nearby France, the Netherlands soon withdrew from the trinity. As for the other advantage in question, Contarini declared that it accrued only to Venice. It was the gratitude now felt by the princes and cities of Germany as a consequence of the effectiveness of Venetian diplomacy in dealing with all the parties involved but, alas, with small profit to the Republic as regards the war with the Turk despite their commiseration and praise, for no large support had yet been forthcoming.[37] Nevertheless, both the Austrian Trauttmannsdorff and the papal legate Fabio Chigi had been advocating assistance for Venice against the Porte:

The nuncio [Fabio Chigi] on the contrary has protested against this peace, and the protests have lately been given validity by a papal bull which annuls whatsoever agreement was made by the Catholics as to the alienation of church properties, absolving them from whatsoever promise they made or oath they took in this context. . . . And this is to leave the door open to the Catholics themselves to regain whatever they gave up when the fortune of arms may become favorable, as happened after the so-called "Religious Peace" of 1555, against which some of the more zealous prelates of Germany had protested, owing to the alienation of church properties which took place at that time. As a result of that protest, however, many such properties were recovered when Catholic arms did

---

[36] Contarini, *Relatione*, fol. 35ʳ.
[37] Contarini was of course always acutely aware of Venice's Turkish problem; it is almost the main theme of his *Relatione*. Three volumes of letters, largely from 1639 on, addressed to him (MSS. Marc. It. VII, 1207–9 [8852–4]), include letters sent to him when he was the Republic's bailie at the Porte.

prevail, a fact which at present is compelling the Protestants to exercise particular caution to retain among themselves the possessions acquired from the Catholics.[38]

At this point Contarini felt that he had at least "touched upon" the most important parts of the Westphalian texts, covering the gains of France and Sweden, Bavaria and the Rhenish Palatinate, "come li più beneficati—il resto ho tralasciato per evitare le maggiori longhezze." In any event there was, he believed, no prince, no state, no city, no lordling with sovereignty who had not wanted to be named in so grand a treaty of peace, some to increase their territory, others to give stronger confirmation to their prerogatives.[39] Thereafter Contarini goes on to deal with the final resolution of the major problems and with the various personalities which were dominant in the prolonged negotiations at Münster and Osnabrück.[40]

Ending the war meant the demobilization of tens of thousands of troops, who must be paid upon the termination of their service. They must also be removed from the numerous garrisons in which they had been stationed and from the extensive territories which they had been holding. It was a problem to send them home; many of them had no home but the regiment in which they had lived. For almost three years, however, from late in the year 1648 to the midsummer of 1651, efforts were made at an international congress held in Nuremberg to find practicable means of putting into effect the treaties of Westphalia.[41] The most pressing problem was to find and allot the funds for the disbandment of the troops, but eventually the negotiators did find their way out of what had often seemed to be an impasse. Most of Europe could rejoice in peace.

The commercial enterprise and military reforms of the Dutch had made a deep impression upon Europe. With easy access to the Mediterranean as well as to the Atlantic their international trade had grown by leaps and bounds. By the beginning of the seventeenth century the Germans and Austrians had probably been falling behind economically, and so apparently had the Venetians, although the latter could still live comfortably on their Mediterranean transport. The French were now advancing most of all. The tactical efficiency of Condé and Turenne in the field and, as time went on, the skillful management of French economic resources by Colbert also made a large impact upon Europe. Gov-

---

[38] Contarini, *Relatione*, fol. 23ᵛ.
[39] Contarini, *Relatione*, fol. 23.
[40] Contarini, *Relatione*, fols. 24ff.
[41] Cf. Dumont, VI-1, no. CCLXXVII, pp. 549–61, texts dated at Nuremberg from 21 September 1649 to 5 October 1650, and note, *ibid.*, no. CCLXXIX.

ernments tended henceforth to give increased attention to technological improvements in industry as well as in warfare. The Austrians and the Germans had learned a good deal about tactics and armaments during the Thirty Years' War.

The Turks and Spanish, however, although they were dominant in the territorial waters of the eastern and western Mediterranean, were falling behind the French, English, Dutch, Germans, and Austrians in the various aspects of mathematics, science, and technology with which we associate the names of Bartolommeo Crescenzio (fl. 1607), Giovanni Branca (d. 1645), Marin Mersenne (d. 1648), Athanasius Kircher (d. 1680), and Otto von Guericke (d. 1686). Geared mechanisms were becoming useful in industry and warfare. Having noted elsewhere the ways in which the Spanish and the Turks were lagging behind their European contemporaries, I fear that I can do no better than repeat what I have already said in this context:

> There is a remote resemblance between the Spanish and Ottoman empires as to the time and causes of their decline. Each was attached to past practices, to "tradition," to an intellectual stagnation which meant failure to keep up with the technological innovations of the later sixteenth century and the seventeenth. Each was unable, therefore, to share to any appreciable extent in the advances being made in mining and metallurgy, medicine and pharmacology, the production of hardware, textiles, glass, clocks, and especially firearms and shipbuilding. The Spanish and Turks were both impeded by inefficient governments and by the failure to produce a middle class strong enough to face the increasing economic competition of the seventeenth century.
>
> The Spanish Church and the Inquisition were obstacles to social change and scientific progress in Spain, while the growth of Moslem fanaticism among the Turks had an even more deleterious effect upon the understanding and use of any scientific improvement or instrument. Weakened central governments, hard-pressed for money, met increasing difficulties in maintaining the infrastructure of roads, canals, and dikes, bridges, warehouses, and docks—all essential to commercial, military, and naval efficiency.[42]

Destruction had varied from one area to another; some towns and villages were almost spared, others became uninhabited or nearly so. Conditions were, for example, much worse in Württemberg than in Lower Saxony. Although an abundance of local records still exist to attest to the depopulation of this village or that, agreement as to the overall loss of life has been difficult to achieve. Doubtless prolonged hunger and disease did more to decimate the population than the carnage of the battlefield plus the mercenaries' pillaging of the countryside. Undefended areas would lose their people when the latter took refuge

---

[42] *The Papacy and the Levant*, IV, 1098.

within the walls of nearby or not so nearby cities. Generalizations concerning the results of the Thirty Years' War are not easy to formulate, for a large bibliography (and almost as much controversy) has grown up in the last century or so.[43] In any event the conclusion of the conflict was hardly the end of warfare in mid-seventeenth century Europe.

In June 1654 Queen Christina of Sweden gave up her father's throne, being succeeded by her ambitious cousin Charles X, whose accession brought further strife to northern Europe. During the brief period of his reign Charles embarked upon some four years of warfare with Poland, which led to the Danes' and Russians' entering the contest against Sweden. Charles actually occupied Warsaw and Cracow, the two chief cities of Poland (in 1655) but when, after a prolonged siege, he failed to take the monastery on the height of Jasna Gora at Częstochowa, the Poles responded to the inspiration of the Black Virgin of Częstochowa, still the chief object of pilgrimage in Poland, and Charles had eventually to withdraw from the country. He invaded Denmark in 1657, made an ally and then an enemy of Friedrich Wilhelm of Brandenburg,[44] and nearly exhausted the resources of Sweden. But, upon the bellicose Charles's death in mid-February 1660, peace returned to the Northland for a while in the Swedish treaty of Oliva of 3 May 1660 with King John Casimir of Poland and his *foederati* (the Emperor Leopold I and Friedrich Wilhelm of Brandenburg), by which treaty Poland ceded Livonia to the Swedes.[45] The new king of Sweden, Charles XI, reached an agreement also with Frederick III of Denmark in June 1660; the treaty was made "in our castle at Copenhagen," and subsequently ratified in Stockholm.[46] The belligerents were tired. Peace seemed to be in the atmosphere. A year later, in July 1661, Charles XI subscribed to a *perpetua quies et pax* with the grand duke of Muscovy.[47] But there was still little or no peace for the remainder of the century. When France emerged as the dominant

---

[43] Cf. Parker *et al.*, *The Thirty Years' War*, pp. 190–226; Theodore K. Rabb, "The Effects of the Thirty Years' War on the German Economy," *Journal of Modern History*, XXXIV (1962), 40–51; J. V. Polišenský, "The Thirty Years' War," *Past and Present*, VI (Nov. 1954), 31–43; Polišenský, "The Thirty Years' War and the Crises and Revolutions of Seventeenth-Century Europe," *ibid.*, XXXIX (April 1968), 34–43; Henry Kamen, "The Economic and Social Consequences of the Thirty Years' War," *ibid.*, XXXIX, 44–61, a very good article. On the various "crises" and numerous problems with which the historian of the seventeenth century has been wrestling for years, note Rabb's interesting essays in *The Struggle for Stability in Early Modern Europe*, New York, 1975.

[44] Dumont, *Corps universel diplomatique*, VI-2 (1728), nos. XLIII, XLIX, LV–LVII, LXXV, pp. 127ff.

[45] Dumont, VI-2, no. CXV, pp. 303–15, "datum Olivae, die tertia mensis Maii, anno 1660." Oliva (*Oliwa*) is in northern Poland, a few miles northwest of Danzig (*Gdańsk*).

[46] Dumont, VI-2, no. CXX, pp. 319–24, "actum in castris ad Hafniam [Copenhagen] 27. Maii [the text gives *Junii* by mistake] anno 1660," with addenda, *ibid.*, pp. 324–26. The 27th May (O.S.) becomes 6 June by the Gregorian Calendar. Note also, *ibid.*, nos. CXXXVIII–CXL, pp. 358–63.

[47] Dumont, VI-2, no. CXLI, pp. 363–64, text dated 21 June/1 July 1661.

power in Europe, Louis XIV plunged the continent into three more wars (1667–8, 1672–8, and 1688–97), always seeking to add territory to his royal domain.

In the opinion of many historians, both past and present, the peace of Westphalia remained the foundation of a balance of power in Europe until the end of the Holy Roman Empire (in 1806), by which time, of course, the wars of religion in Germany, France and elsewhere in Europe were little more than a painful memory. The Holy Roman Empire was over and done with by 1806, but the Hapsburgs were firmly entrenched in the *kaiserliche Erblande,* and became emperors of the so-called Austro-Hungarian empire. In the meantime, however, after 1648, Austria would not become involved in war with France for some time, although the Turkish advance upon the eastern front brought about a renewal of warfare with the Ottoman Empire in 1663–1664.

The experience of the Thirty Years' War had gradually moved the Christians ahead of the Turks in military tactics and armaments. Despite the shortcomings and differences among the states in western and central Europe, and despite enduring religious disaffection, the Christians had developed and were maintaining more efficient governmental administrations than the Turks. Although corruption of various sorts was almost rampant in the military as well as in the civil service of various Christian states, it was far less destructive than the widespread deterioration in Ottoman society. The Christian military organization, especially in Sweden, France, Brandenburg-Prussia, Bavaria, and Austria was more effective than the Turks' military medley—the infantry corps of janissaries, the mounted sipahis, diverse other bodies of foot and horse, the akinjis, and the accompanying rabble. The Christian armies took on the beginnings of a modern cast during the seventeenth century with manageable units in the regiment, battalion, squadron, and company.

Gustavus Adolphus (d. 1632), as we have noted, had been a military organizer and innovator of genius, fighting successful wars against Denmark, Russia, Poland, and the Holy Roman Empire. Raimondo Montecuccoli (d. 1680), an Italian general in the Hapsburg service, the peer and the opponent of Condé and Turenne, also made notable advances in the military arts of his day. A soldier with immense experience of the battlefield, Montecuccoli defeated the grand vizir Ahmed Köprülü in the important battle of S. Gotthard (Szentgotthárd) on 1 August, 1664, although the Emperor Leopold I, who had succeeded his father Ferdinand III a half-dozen years before, derived but slight advantage from the Austro-Turkish treaty of Vasvár of 10 August which did, however, provide for twenty years' peace between the Holy Roman and the Ottoman Empires.[48] Montecuccoli left behind him the well-known *Memorie della*

---

[48] Dumont, VI-3, nos. xi–xii, pp. 23–25, "actum in castris Turcicis apud Vasvarum decima mensis Augusti anno MDCLXIV:" ". . . pax in viginti annos prorogata. . . ."

guerra, which helped determine the modes of warfare into the nineteenth century. A captain of infantry early in his career, Montecuccoli
rose to the top as a commander of cavalry, and in due time turned his
attention to matchlock musketry as well as to field artillery. Among the
military arts to which Montecuccoli gave time and thought was that of
fortification, which led him to convert the important north-Hungarian
town of Raab (Györ) into an almost impregnable fortress, at least as far
as seventeenth-century siegecraft was concerned. When the treaty of
Vasvár had reached its termination—actually the Ottoman government
violated its terms by a year, renewing its aggression in 1683—the fortifications on the eastern front delayed the advance of the Turks, and
helped save the city of Vienna from a conquest that might have been
disastrous for Europe.[49]

---

[49] Cf. John A. Mears, "The Influence of the Turkish Wars in Hungary on the Military
Theories of Count Raimondo Montecuccoli," in C. K. Pullapilly and E. J. Van Kley, eds.,
Asia and the West: Essays in Honor of Donald F. Lach, Notre Dame, Indiana, 1986, pp.
129–45, and see esp. Thomas M. Barker, *The Military Intellectual and Battle: Raimondo
Montecuccoli and the Thirty Years' War,* Albany, N.Y., 1975, pp. 1–71.

IV

Venice, Malta, and the Turks, the Beginning of the Long War of Candia

∿

Despite the interference of the dominant French every now and then, Spain and the Holy See ruled Italy for the most part from the treaty of Cateau-Cambrésis (1559) to that of the Pyrenees (1659), and for some years thereafter, but that did not mean there was any more peace in the peninsula than on the Mediterranean. We have dwelt at some length on the extent to which the Thirty Years' War spread unrest throughout Europe. The Protestant Grisons, France, Venice, and Savoy entered a prolonged contest with Spain, Austria, and the Holy See (1620–1639) for control of the picturesque Valtellina (the valley of the upper Adda), which led from the Milanese into Germany and Austria. Free access to the Valtellina was essential for both the Austrian Hapsburgs in the hereditary lands and for the Spanish Hapsburgs in the Milanese. Therefore they kept the pass open. The availability of the passage through the Valtellina was also important to Venice,[1] and the

---

[1] Giov. Battista Nani, *Historia della republica veneta*, Venice, 1663, pp. 203–15, 217ff., 225, 233ff., etc., 555ff., and note Jean Dumont, *Corps universel diplomatique,* V-2 (1728), nos. CCXIX, CCXXVI, CCXXIX, CCXXXIV–CCXXXV, CCLXXI, pp. 395ff., and (as given above) nos. CCLVIII–CCLIX. For a miscellany of contemporary texts relating to the Valle di Valtellina, see the Bibl. Nazionale Marciana (Venice), MS. It. VII, 1181 (8879), docs. dated from March 1617 to November 1635, and note Victor Cérésole, *Relevé des manuscrits des Archives de Venise se rapportant à la Suisse . . .* , Venice, 1890, pp. 100, 103ff., 121ff.

Republic (like the French) could not tolerate the thought of the hostile Hapsburgs' controlling the valley which marked the northwestern boundary of the Veneto, leading to the Rhine and the Netherlands as well as to the Inn and Austria. The Valtellina remained an unsolved problem for a generation.

During these years the war of the Mantuan succession (1627–1631) again pitted Spain and the Empire against France, Venice, and this time the Holy See.[2] The war also involved old Charles Emmanuel of Savoy, who advanced his own claims to Mantua and Montferrat,[3] as well as the Emperor Ferdinand II, who tried to assert his right of adjudication since Mantua was an imperial fief. In fact the Hapsburg forces occupied Mantua on 18 July 1630, and ten days later Wallenstein sent his congratulations from Memmingen to the imperialist commander Johann von Aldringen.[4] The French claimant Charles of Gonzaga-Nevers, however, finally succeeded to the war-torn duchies as one result of the treaties of Cherasco of 6 April and 19 June 1631.[5] The fatuous policy of Philip IV of Spain and his erratic minister Olivares in the affair of Mantua had inevitably involved Ferdinand II in open hostility with Pope Urban VIII, who was strongly pro-French. The Mantuan question had also reduced the tension between England and France by bringing them together against their common enemy Spain.

As was widely known at the time, the year 1630 was a disaster for northern Italy. Venice was engulfed in the plague. It was thought that 46,490 persons died in Venice alone from July 1630 to 21 November 1631.[6] Where the old parish records survive, as in the church of S. Giovanni in Bragora in Venice, one will find almost endless lists of those who died, especially young sailors, lesser tradesmen, workers, and other lowly folk. As Sir Peter Wyche, the English ambassador in Istanbul, wrote Viscount Dorchester, Charles I's secretary of state, on 24 December (1630): "The great sickness of plague which is at Venice doth alter much the intercourse of letters, and makes all verie uncertaine. God be praysed for the decrease thereof in Englande, and preserve theire Majesties."[7] Just as the church of the Redentore was built on the Giudecca in Venice in thanksgiving for the cessation of the plague of 1575–1576, so now (in 1631) the church of the Salute was begun on the

---

[2] Dumont, V-2, nos. cccxii, cccxiv, pp. 572–73, 580, docs. dated 11 March and 8 April 1629, and note no. cccxxxiv, pp. 615–19, doc. dated 13 October 1630.

[3] Dumont, V-2, no. cccxvii, pp. 583–84, doc. dated 10 May 1629.

[4] *Documenta bohemica Bellum Tricennale illustrantia*, IV (1974), no. 1039, p. 396, and note nos. 1020, 1044, and 1082. On "the taking of Mantua by the Imperialls," cf. Public Record Office [PRO], Chancery Lane, London, State Papers [SP], XV, fol. 45.

[5] Dumont, VI-1, nos. v, ix, pp. 9–13, 14–18. Montferrat remained subject to Mantua (from December 1566) until June 1708, when it was taken over by the Savoyards.

[6] S. Romanin, *Storia documentata di Venezia*, 3rd. ed., VII (Venice, 1974), 216–17.

[7] PRO, SP 97, XV, fol. 65ʳ.

Grand Canal near the Dogana to commemorate the passing of the plague which one feared (it would seem) from Istanbul to England.

Another war broke out in Italy in 1641 when Urban VIII seized the town of Castro from Odoardo Farnese, the duke of Parma, but the latter's brother-in-law, the grand duke of Tuscany, and the Venetians came to his assistance.[8] In 1644 Urban restored Castro to the Farnesi, and died soon after;[9] five years later Castro came once more into papal hands, and again provoked by the Farnesi, Urban's successor Innocent X reoccupied Castro, and demolished the place entirely.[10]

The Venetians had thus become involved in the "guerra Valtellinese," the war of the Mantuan succession, and the war of Castro. All three were serious, grueling affairs, and soon after the conclusion of the war of Castro (in 1644) the long-drawn-out war with the Turks began for possession of the island of Crete. Europe was still caught up in the prolonged agony of the Thirty Years' War. The French were adding whatever they could to the warfare and disunion of Christendom. The prolonged war was a serious blow to the Venetians, cutting them off, as it did to a large extent, from the German markets.

The Turks chose the opportune time to strike, for the Venetians had borne a heavy burden of expenditure in the recent Italian wars. The Signoria had held the important island of Crete for 434 years, since shortly after the Fourth Crusade (1204), but during the first two centu-

---

[8] For the terms of the league of the Republic of Venice, the grand duke of Tuscany, and the duke of Modena against Urban VIII, dated 31 August 1642 and 26 May 1643, see Dumont, *Corps universel diplomatique*, VI-1 (1728), no. CLX, pp. 276–79, and note, *ibid.*, nos. CLI, CLXI, and CLXXIV, docs. dated 26 July 1642, 22 June 1643, and 31 March 1644, and cf. *Acta Pacis Westphalicae, Die Kaiserlichen Korrespondenzen*, ser. II A, I (1643–1644), Münster, 1969, no. 236, p. 371, doc. dated 25 April 1644.

[9] Giov. Battista Nani, *Historia della republica veneta* (1663), pp. 653–89, 702–14, 739–44, which volume ends with the Farnesi's recovery of Parma and the peace with Urban VIII. According to Joseph Grisar, "Päpstliche Finanzen, Nepotismus und Kirchenrecht unter Urban VIII," *Miscellanea Historiae Pontificiae*, VII (Rome, 1943), 207–8, "Toward the end of his reign Urban VIII undertook the very expensive and useless war of Castro, the military costs of which alone amounted to six million scudi in the two years of warfare (1642–1643), so that at the pope's death the debt [of the Holy See] had reached 30 million scudi." Grisar has dealt at some length with papal revenues during Urban's reign, his constant expenditures, and the problems which ensued as a result of his disbursements of funds.

[10] The failure of Odoardo's unruly young son and successor Ranuccio II, duke of Parma (1646–1694), to repay his creditors for their loans in the *monti Farnesi*, which were supposed to be guaranteed by the revenues of Castro and Ronciglione, together with the apparent participation of Farnese supporters in the murder of Cristoforo Giarda, the bishop of Castro, in March 1649, moved the peaceful Innocent X to warfare. Papal troops not only destroyed the fortifications of Castro, an episcopal see, but also the churches and the little Palazzo Farnese. Castro was replaced by Acquapendente as the diocesan center (Pastor, *Gesch. d. Päpste*, XIV-1 [Freiburg im Breisgau, 1929], 270–71, and *Hist. Popes*, XXX, 369–71).

ries of this period the Cretans had almost never taken peaceably to Venetian dominance. Revolts had been frequent, and resentment never ceased.[11]

When the Turks landed west of Canea in late June 1645, and the natives hardly raised a finger to oppose them, the Venetians could not fail often to quote the biblical text (Titus 1:10–13) to the effect that among the Cretans "there are many unruly men, vain talkers and deceivers. . . . One of themselves [Epimenides?], a prophet of their own, said, 'Cretans are always liars, evil beasts, idle gluttons.' This testimony is true." The Cretans' animus against Venice is not strange, for the Greeks had manifested their discontent under foreign rule in the Latin empire of Constantinople (1204–1261) and in the Latin kingdom of Thessalonica (1204–1224), which were also products of the Fourth Crusade. Oddly enough, however, there seem to have been no serious upheavals among the Greeks in the Latin principality of Achaea (1204–1432), the lordship and duchy of Athens (1204–1456), and the Venetian duchy of Naxos (1205–1566). But by the mid-seventeenth century the Venetians had other troubles to add to the Cretan unrest.

The descendants of the original Venetian colonists, nobles and commoners alike, had become largely Hellenized in the past two centuries or so, often abandoning Catholicism for Orthodoxy and joining the Greeks. The profits of the Levantine trade had dwindled. The Dutch and English had become serious competitors. Although the Holy See would always support a Christian state against the Turks, the Venetians had no ally, at least no friend, in Europe. Always fearful of Turkish attack, they had left their confederates in the lurch more than once in the long series of wars with the Porte.

The Cretans looked upon the Venetian administration of their island as harsh and corrupt, and on the whole they were justified in regarding it as such. Negligence and lack of funds had left the Cretan garrisons shorthanded from the early years of the seventeenth century. Although colossal sums had been spent upon the island fortresses, century after century, the Italian wars had been a costly distraction. The fortifications had not been properly maintained.[12] Having taken Cyprus, it was inevita-

---

[11] Cf. K. M. Setton, *The Papacy and the Levant, 1204–1571*, 4 vols., Philadelphia, 1976–84, I, 16–17, 177ff., 249–57.

[12] Although Emmanuele Mormori, a Veneto-Cretan noble, begins his history of the war of Candia with the observation that "risciedeva il regno di Candia sotto la benignità del Veneto dominio in una lunga e tranquilissima pace," such was hardly the case (Mormori, *Guerra di Candia. . .: Testimonio* de visu *dall'anno 1644 sino il 1655, 30 settembre*, Bibl. Nazionale Marciana [Venice], MS. It. VII, 1563 [7596], fol. 1ʳ, and esp. MS. It. VII, 101 [8382] fol. 1ʳ). Emmanuele, son of Giovanni, was superintendent of artillery in the time of the war of Candia. He begins his work with the further notice of the "notable modern

ble that the Turks should seek to acquire Crete. The Venetians had feared such a move for at least a hundred years, and during the war of Cyprus the Turks had landed troops on Crete.

Relations between Venice and the Porte had been strained for some years, although the commercial ties had remained unbroken. In the early summer of 1638, however, sixteen north-African corsairs under Ali Picenino pillaged towns along the coast of Calabria, venturing almost as far north as Loreto. Being informed of their depredations, the Venetian provveditore Antonio Marino Cappello set out after them, but since he was delayed by a storm, the corsairs escaped into the Turkish port of Valona. Upon Cappello's approach the cannon of the fortress of Valona opened fire. The provveditore withdrew, setting up a blockade, which lasted from 1 July to 7 August (1638), to prevent the corsairs' escape. At length, learning that a Turkish naval force was on its way to break the blockade, Cappello entered the harbor of Valona under heavy fire, captured all sixteen vessels of the Barbary corsairs, sinking fifteen of them and sending one as a prize to Venice. Although Moslem corsairs were not exempt from pursuit and punishment by the Venetians—according to the terms of peace between the Republic and the Porte—obviously no town or territory belonging to one of the two powers could be invaded by the other.

Pope Urban VIII sent his hearty congratulations to the doge Francesco Erizzo, for his Holiness thought he saw a renewal of Christian maritime strength in Cappello's enterprise. Costantino de' Rossi, who was soon appointed bishop of Veglia, declared that Cappello had "set free the seas of Christendom." The Venetian Signoria was more cautious, and the diplomatic dexterity of Alvise Contarini, the bailie in Istanbul, helped to deflect Turkish anger for a while. According to the terms of the Turco-

---

fortifications" with which the Venetians had girded Candia, Retimo, and other places, supplying them all with Italian garrisons and stradiote cavalry. Actually the fortifications were in wretched condition, and the manpower available for defense quite inadequate, as he soon acknowledges (cf. MS. Marc. It. VII, 1563 [7596], fol. 6^r).

Mormori's original manuscript, with numerous addenda, alterations, and corrigenda scribbled between the lines and in the margins, is preserved in the Marciana, MS. It. VII, 101 (8382), fols. 1–111, together with a copy of bks. II–III (*ibid.*, fols. 41–126). Since MS. Marc. It. VII, 1563, has undergone some further revision, and is more legible (despite some obvious errors of transcription), I have generally followed the latter. Mormori, who was apparently of Greek origin, frequently praises the Greeks, and mentions members of his own family in the struggle against the Turks (MS. Marc. It. VII, 1563 [7596], fols. 31^v–33^r, 37^r, 40^r). On the manuscript, note the *Inventari dei manoscritti delle biblioteche d'Italia*, LXXXI (Florence, 1956), pp. 39–40, and Jacopo Morelli, *Biblioteca manoscritta di Tommaso Giuseppe Farsetti . . .* , 2 pts., Venice, 1771–80, II, no. CXCVI, pp. 139–40. There is a general survey of the sources and the secondary literature relating to the Cretan war in Heinrich Kretschmayr, *Geschichte von Venedig*, III (Stuttgart, 1934, repr. Aalen, 1964), 623ff. On the economic and military resources of Crete (*il regno di Candia*) as well as its strategic and psychological importance to Venice, note *Venezia e la difesa del Levante da Lepanto a Candia, 1570–1670*, Venice, 1986, pp. 97–107.

Venetian capitulations, the port authorities in Valona should not have given refuge to the corsairs, but Sultan Murad IV was furious at what he regarded as the armed effrontery of the Venetians.

Murad's first reaction was to order the slaughter of all Venetians in his domains. He soon grew calmer, however, and had the bailie Alvise Contarini put in confinement, the Venetian port of Spalato (Split) blockaded, and all trade with the Republic stopped. The Turks had been carrying on war with Persia for some sixteen years. Murad was on the road to Baghdad, which he took on 25 December (1638), after which he made peace with Persia on 7 May (1639), and returned to Istanbul. Having reached an amicable accord with Venice, the ferocious Murad died after a brief illness on 9 February 1640, threatening his physicians with death and seeking to kill his benighted brother Ibrahim.[13] Thus, despite Cappello's forcible entry into Valona, the Turks' inevitable return to warfare with the Venetians was postponed for a few more years. The English ambassador in Istanbul, Sir Peter Wyche, seems to provide us with the explanation of the amicable accord between Venice and the Porte. On 6 September (1638) he wrote Charles I's secretary of state:

I have bin eauen now advertised in greate secresie that the Venice bailo [Alvise Contarini] for the accomodation of this business hath made proffers of 100 m.

---

[13] [Gio.] Battista Nani (1616–1679), *Historia della republica veneta*, 3rd ed., 2 vols., Venice, 1676–86, I, 697–701; Jos. von Hammer-Purgstall, *Geschichte des osmanischen Reiches*, 10 vols., Pest, 1827–35, repr. Graz, 1963, V, 246–52, 264–67, 285–86; Heinrich Kretschmayr, *Geschichte von Venedig*, 3 vols., Gotha and Stuttgart, 1905–34, repr. Aalen, 1964, III, 312ff., 620ff., with a good survey of the sources; Samuele Romanin, *Storia documentata di Venezia*, 3rd ed., 10 vols., Venice, 1972–75, VII, 243–45; Tommaso Bertelè, *Il Palazzo degli ambasciatori di Venezia a Costantinopoli e le sue antiche memorie*, Bologna, 1932, pp. 164–65, 176–81; Ekkehard Eickhoff and Rudolf Eickhoff, *Venedig, Wien und die Osmanen: Umbruch in Südosteuropa 1645–1700*, Munich, 1970, p. 20. On the Venetians' invasion of Valona and the career of Antonio Marino Cappello, note also the article by G. Benzoni, in the *Dizionario biografico degli Italiani*, XVIII (1975), 756–58, and cf. Mormori, *Guerra di Candia*, Bibl. Nazionale Marciana, MS. It. VII, 1563 (7596), fol. 1ᵛ. There are many English dispatches from Istanbul giving reports of Murad IV's expedition into Persia in 1638–1639 in PRO, SP 97, XVI, as for example (on fols. 204–5) that of Sir Sackville Crow dated 2 February 1638, i.e., 1639.

Alvise Contarini was elected to the bailaggio in Istanbul in 1635, but he did not arrive on the Bosporus until 31 December 1636. He remained at the Porte until 1 April 1641, when he began the return journey to Venice. He has left a most informative account of conditions at the Porte during the reigns of Murad IV and of the latter's brother Ibrahim, the text of which may be found in Nicolò Barozzi and Guglielmo Berchet, eds., *Le Relazioni degli stati europei lette al Senato dagli ambasciatori veneziani nel secolo decimosettimo*, ser. V, *Turchia*, 2 pts., Venice, 1866–72, I, 329–434. Before his departure for Istanbul Contarini had already served the Republic for fourteen continuous years as an envoy in Holland, England, France, and Rome (*ibid.*, pp. 325, 326–27, 330). He later represented the Republic at Münster, as we have seen, during the negotiations which led to the treaties of Westphalia. See the excellent survey of his career by G. Benzoni, in the *Dizionario biografico degli Italiani*, XXVIII (1983), 82–91, and on his leaving Istanbul in 1641, note MS. Marc. It. VII, 1208 (8853), fol. 81.

[thousand] dollers to the Grand Signor, of tenn thousand dollers to the Captine Bassa, and of tenn thousand dollers to the Caymacam, and heerof the Caymacam doth dispatch advise unto the campe [of the sultan] in all poste haste, and surelie the purse of St. Marke will purchase the accomodation of this business, and whereas the Caymacham would not formerlie suffer to departe two Venetian ships, which were in porte, since those liberall offers hee hath given order for their departure.[14]

As the Moslem corsairs of Tripoli, Tunis, and Algiers sailed through the Mediterranean, seizing Christian merchantmen, the Knights of the Hospital of S. John of Jerusalem were even more venturesome as privateers in attacking Moslem shipping, including the galleys and galleons carrying pilgrims on their way to Mecca. For more than a century the Knights of S. John had held the island of Malta (as a grant from the Emperor Charles V). Although not so enterprising as the Maltese, the Knights of the Tuscan Order of S. Stefano also preyed upon Moslem merchants and pilgrims. The Knights of both Orders could hit and run, as they did, but the Venetian merchants and islands in the eastern Mediterranean were always exposed to Turkish reprisals. For generations, ever since the old days when the Knights of S. John were established on the island of Rhodes, they had never got along well with the Venetians.

The Hospitallers attacked Venetian shipping on the grounds that the merchants of the Republic carried Turkish subjects aboard their vessels, and were forever trading on friendly terms with the infidels, as indeed they were, for it was the Levantine trade that kept Venice afloat. In earlier years compensation for Venetian losses had occasionally been extracted from the Hospitallers by seizing their property in Venetian territories, but the Holy See tended to side with the Maltese Knights, and the Signoria had a hard time. Finally, hardly more than three weeks after the Venetians had delivered a strenuous protest to the Order of S. John (on 3 September 1644),[15] the Knights struck a blow at the Turks, the impact of which fell with a deadly weight upon Venice.

It was on 28 September (1644) that the six Maltese galleys which had been plundering the Moslem vessels in the Archipelago for a decade came upon a small Turkish fleet consisting of a galleon, two other vessels, and seven caïques. The fleet was loaded with riches of one sort or

---

[14] PRO, SP 97, XVI, fols. 168ff., the quotation from fol. 172ᵛ. Sir Sackville Crow, however, was not so sure that the Venetians were out of the woods, "for the gallies beinge suncke (as the Venetians pretend) noe other satisfaction wilbe harkened unto" (*ibid.,* fol. 188, letter dated at Istanbul on 17 November 1638). Wyche had already written the secretary of state of the Venetians' violent intrusion into Valona on 21 July (1638), in which letter he also described at some length the Turks' execution of the "Protestant" Patriarch of Constantinople, Cyril Lucaris (*ibid.,* fol. 166).

[15] ASV (Arch. di Stato di Venezia), Senato I (Secreta), Filza 27 (Deliberation del Senato Corti 1644, no. 189): no. 188 covers the period from March to August, 1644.

another. The galleon was carrying the aged eunuch Sünbüllü, the master of the seraglio (*kislar ağasi*), who, having got into trouble amid the tensions of the harem, was on his way to Mecca with his movable treasure, "frutti delle venalità de' suoi impieghi." After Mecca, Sünbüllü intended to retire to Egypt, the usual refuge for masters of the seraglio. One Mehmed Effendi of Brusa was also on board; he had recently been appointed judge (*kadi*) in Cairo. And, as usual in such convoys, there were many pilgrims aboard. According to Nani, the galleon which was carrying Sünbüllü had six hundred men and sixty cannon on board. The eunuch Sünbüllü was killed in the Hospitallers' violent attack, which lasted eight hours, and so was the Turkish commander Ibrahim Chelebi. The Knights captured the treasures of the eunuch, thirty women, 350 slaves, the judge of Cairo, and a small boy, whose mother was a favorite of the dissolute sultan Ibrahim. In later years the judge of Cairo, who was freed by ransom, rose in rank to become a mufti. The boy was brought up as a Christian, entered the Dominican Order, and was known as Padre Ottomano, for the sultan was assumed to be his father.

Sailing westward with their captives and the booty, the Hospitallers anchored at the naval roadstead of Kalismene on the southern shore of Crete, which was then unguarded. At Kalismene the Hospitallers took on water and supplies, setting ashore horses and some fifty Greeks, who seem to have been hired mariners. Thereafter, skirting the Cretan shoreline in the area of Sfacchia (*Khóra Sfakíon*), they tried to drop anchor at Castel Selino, but the Venetian commandant made them leave. They pushed on to the Venetian island of Cerigo, where they were again forbidden anchorage. Seeking refuge in the cove of S. Niccolò and certain inlets on the island of Cephalonia, they soon ran into stormy weather, and had to abandon the battered Turkish galleon, which was no longer seaworthy. Returning to Malta with their portable spoils, they regarded their attack upon the Turks' Mecca-bound fleet as a profitable undertaking.[16]

---

[16] Battista Nani, *Historia della republica veneta*, II (1686), 17–20. Of the booty taken Nani says, "La preda trapassò due millioni; ma tutto fu posto a ruba, ogn'uno di gioie, e danari, pigliando ciò che trovare potè, e che gli presentò la fortuna." Cf. Mormori, *Guerra di Candia*, MS. Marc. It. VII, 1563 (7596), fol. 2; *Historia della guerra di Candia*, MS. Marc. It. VII, 371 (7526), unnumbered fols. 1ff., which adds little to the history of the Candiote war; von Hammer-Purgstall, *Gesch. d. osman. Reiches*, V (1829, repr. 1963), 359–63, trans. Hellert, X (1837), 76–81; Romanin, VII (1974), 246; Allen B. Hines, ed., *Cal. State Papers . . .*, Venice, XXVII (1926, repr. 1970), nos. 190, 200, pp. 170, 176.

The boy who was captured by the Hospitallers was allegedly the son of Sultan Ibrahim I and the elder brother of Mehmed IV. A decade or so later he was converted by the Dominicans, who had changed his name from Osman to Domenico, after which he became Fra Domenico Ottomano, on which cf. C. D. Rouillard, *The Turk in French History, Thought, and Literature*, Paris, 1938, p. 97; von Hammer-Purgstall, *Gesch. d. osman. Reiches*, V, 362–63, trans. Hellert, X, 79–80; Vaughan, *Europe and the Turk* (1954), p. 256. Fra Domenico cut a considerable figure in Naples, Turin, Rome, Paris, Venice, and elsewhere

When word of the tragic event reached Venice, the Signoria was badly shaken. The Turks would presumably seek to take vengeance on the Hospitallers but, once aroused, would they spare Venice? In Istanbul the news caused an almost indescribable outburst of anger. Sultan Ibrahim was enraged. The culprits were the Hospitallers, of course, but they had landed on Venetian soil at Crete. The Signoria had warned the Hospitallers against such landings, and had forbidden them. Nevertheless, the Knights had taken on water and landed slaves and employees of the Turks at Kalismene, and the Venetians had not intervened. All the ambassadors at the Porte were summoned before Sultan Ibrahim's so-called tutor or preceptor (*khoja*)[17] and the chief judicial officer of the army (*kadiasker*), as the bailie Giovanni Soranzo reported to the Signoria in a dispatch of 20 December 1644, to which Romanin has called attention.

The kadiasker [of Greece] was the first to address the envoys, informing them that the sultan had ordered that they be brought together "in order to learn what we knew of the seizure of the master of the seraglio [*kislaragà*]." The French ambassador [M. Jean Delahaye] was the first to speak; he knew nothing but what he had just learned at the Porte. Soranzo said the same thing; so did the agent of Flanders. The kadiasker replied that the sultan believed one of them certainly must know a good deal and, very likely, be loath to reveal it. The envoys' reply was that such was not the fact; nothing would prevent their informing the Porte of everything they knew. The khoja with his usual arrogance then asserted that this was no time to seek refuge in denials, which would only provoke the disdain of the sultan, who was already beside himself with anger, "upon which he made a certain gesture with his hand, which they commonly use here when they wish to order cutting off someone's head."

The French dragoman was not up to giving an answer, being obviously frightened. Soranzo had the Venetian dragoman, Giovanni Antonio Grillo, respond to the khoja's remarks. He stated that because of the sultan's sense of justice one would expect nothing but the most upright deeds, adding that the ambassadors were at the Porte, as their Turkish lordships were well aware, under the guarantees of treaties and the

---

until his death at the age of thirty-four on 26 October 1676 (H. Missack Effendi, "Le Père Ottoman," *Revue d'histoire diplomatique*, XVII [1903], esp. pp. 360–78); and note Daniele M. Callus, *Il Padre Domenico Ottomano, fu vero principe?* . . . , Rome, 1918, a learned monograph (of 186 pp.), in which see esp. pp. 131–52.

[17] On the troublesome khoja, see Cengiz Orhonlu, "Husayn *Djindji* [Sorcerer] *Khodja*," in the *Encyclopaedia of Islam*, III (1971), 623, and on the sultan, note M. Tayyib Gökbilgin, "Ibrāhīm," *ibid.*, III, 983. The khoja was appointed kadi or judge of Galata in January 1645. After the death of Sultan Ibrahim the khoja's huge fortune was distributed among the janissaries, sipahis, and certain officers of the Porte as the imperial benefice at the accession of his little son Mehmed IV. On the fall of the khoja and the confiscation of his funds, note von Hammer-Purgstall, *Gesch. d. osman. Reiches*, V, 405, 458–61, trans. Hellert, X, 128–29, 188–92.

pledge given by his Majesty. The khoja replied angrily that in cases such as this the sultan would pardon no one, not even his own mother. Everyone knew that the Maltese were guilty of the outrage, "and that they were aided and abetted by all [of us], and that therefore everyone must give an account [of what he knows]."[18] The sultan was determined to learn what had happened to the Turkish galleon. Up to now it had been stated that the master of the seraglio was dead, but that a certain Ussun Mehmed Agha, a Moorish eunuch of whom the sultan's favorite [*casicchi, ḫāṣṣekī*] was very fond, was being held as a slave, and so were the kadi of Mecca and three or four servitors of the seraglio. The sultan required the details of all that had happened. It was necessary to obey him.

The French ambassador calmly observed there was no communication between France and Malta, emphasizing with a gesture the long distance between the two places. Soranzo added that the Hospitallers were entirely independent; they went their own way, and certainly never received aid or support from Venice. The Dutch agent [Henry Cops] thought himself on safe ground in declaring that the Knights of Malta were of a religion opposed to that of his countrymen, whereupon the kadiasker of Greece pinned him down with the statement that, such being the case, the Dutch should surely join the Gran Signore in proceeding against Malta. Soranzo regarded the Dutch agent's response as more prompt than prudent. If the Gran Signore wanted, the Dutchman said, to make war on the enemies of Holland, the Dutch would join the Turks. When the kadiasker asked who these enemies were, he was told, "The Spanish." "Ah, to be sure," the kadiasker replied, "your people should unite with us, for the Spanish are the defenders of the Maltese." Fearing the turn of the conversation, which the Turks had begun apparently for the sole purpose of acquiring information, Soranzo had recourse to the old refrain "that the greatness of the Gran Signore has no need of others' assistance."

In the meantime the khoja had brusquely demanded that a scribe be summoned, and when the latter appeared, the khoja insisted that the envoys should each make a separate statement, so that a summary of

---

[18] ASV, Senato III (Secreta), Filza 126 (Costantinopoli, 1644, Dispacci Giovanni Soranzo, Cavalier, Bailo), fol. 311: "Il Coza con la sua veemente et altiera maniera disse che non era tempo di star nelle negative, chè si provocarà lo sdegno del Re, pur troppo alterato facendo con la mano certo atto, che hanno qui familiare quando vogliono intimare il taglio della testa. Il dragomano di Francia si perde un poco di core, et io feci che il Grillo rifferisse, et alli sudetti concetti disse che dalla giustitia di sua Maestà non si poteva spettare senon attioni molto rette, et che sue Signorie illustrissime bene sapevano che li ambassatori erano qui sotto l'ombra delle capitulationi e con la fede data da sua Maestà. Rispose alteramente [il Coza] che in questi casi il Re non la perdonerebbe nè anco alla propria madre, chè si sapeva certo che Maltesi havevano fatto la preda, et che questi erano protetti et aiutati da tutti, che però bisognava che ogn'uno ne rendesse conto. . . ."

their pronouncements might be prepared for the sultan. The French ambassador began to speak as he had before, declaring that he knew nothing of the Hospitallers' attack upon the Turkish vessels. Soranzo interrupted him, however, pointing out that the Turks' taking their testimony, as though they were being subjected to an interrogation of persons accused, was quite unacceptable. Soranzo stated that for his part he would not go along with any such procedure. The French ambassador stopped talking. Soranzo then had the Venetian dragoman, Grillo, make clear that since the European envoys did not understand Turkish, and could not read the Arabic script, they should not be committed by the notes which the Turkish scribe was prepared to take. As for Soranzo, he would say no more. The khoja then replied with some exasperation that Soranzo intended to disregard the command of the sultan, who had wanted especially to learn the details from the Venetian ambassador, the recipient of numerous reports which had arrived in Istanbul. After all, the Maltese galleys had borne the Turkish galleon to Crete, where they had disembarked horses and men. The sultan wanted the facts, for he was resolved to turn his arms against those who would be found guilty.

Soranzo insisted that he wanted to please his Majesty, but that taking down in writing the verbal assertions of the envoys was neither a common practice nor a proper one. He had already stated in all sincerity that he knew nothing of the Hospitallers' going to Crete. People might make odd and malicious statements, but justice looks for truth. Oftentimes what appear to be irrational actions are shown upon closer scrutiny to be justified by reason. Desiring to deal with the Porte in all sincerity, Soranzo said that he did not want to commit himself to anything, but he was certain the Maltese galleys would never have approached the Cretan shore at any place where the Venetians might have used cannon against them. As always neither the local Venetian governor nor any other representative of the Republic would ever act contrary to the Turco-Venetian peace, the "capitulations." As the dragoman Grillo began to interpret Soranzo's statement, and the scribe began to push his pen, Soranzo drew Grillo back, indicating a desire to leave the scene. He told the French ambassador that he could not assent to this procedure, to which the latter replied, "What can one do?"

Soranzo now had Grillo say that if their Turkish lordships wished him to give them a reply in writing, he would do so. Taking his cue from Soranzo, the French ambassador said through his dragoman that he would do the same thing. The kadiasker of Greece (Rumelia), an able person, spoke in a low voice to the khoja, and then stated that the envoys' written responses would be admissible, but that they must try to give the sultan a satisfactory answer. Meanwhile they should send two or three persons to certain appropriate places to gather information so that within fifteen or twenty days one might know every relevant detail. The khoja told Soranzo that he must send someone to Crete immediately, loudly claiming to be the person who had appeased the sultan, together with other bombast which there was no need to repeat because, as Soranzo says, the Signoria had heard it many times in the past. At this point the meeting broke up and, according to Soranzo, there was no one who had not thoroughly approved of the resolute manner in which he had opposed the khoja's attempt to wring ill-considered statements from them. Furthermore, the French were saying with their inborn freedom of speech that if it were not for the bailie, the cause would have been lost.[19]

As work was being hastened in the Arsenal at Istanbul, and preparations made for a campaign when the spring came, the Venetians were well aware that the Turks might be planning an attack upon the island of Crete. Although the Porte was beset with webs of intrigue and disorganization, there was little evidence so far of much decline in military strength. From late December (1644) the bailie Soranzo had good reason to fear that Crete might be the Turks' objective despite the fact that the pashas said they intended to direct their fire against Malta. In fact Soranzo learned from both the French and the English ambassadors [M. Delahaye and Sir Sackville Crow] that the khoja was claiming, rather inaccurately,[20] that the Byzantine emperor had pawned the island of Crete to the Venetians, who had never restored it to imperial authority. Since the sultan had taken over the erstwhile empire, Crete (like Cyprus) belonged to him.[21]

The Hospitallers had furnished the Porte with a reason to attempt the conquest of Crete. In an audience of 3 January 1645 the young vizir Yusuf Pasha informed Giovanni Soranzo that the Porte was now well informed as to what had happened. Various persons aboard the Turkish galleon seized by the Hospitallers had found their way back to the Bosporus, including the pilot, the helmsman, a cabin boy, and a few others, who told a story which belied Soranzo's efforts to absolve his government of any responsibility in the affair. All the Turkish eyewitnesses were alleged to have stated that the Hospitallers had taken the galleon to Crete, where they had remained for twenty days, disembarking men and horses. They also unloaded and sold on the island the rich haul the galleon was carrying. Thereafter, taking water and supplies on board

---

[19] ASV, Senato III (Secreta), Filza 126 (Costantinopoli 1644), fols. 296–320ᵛ, esp. fols. 306ff., doc. dated 20 December 1644, on which note Romanin, VII (1974), 246–49, and see the reports (especially of the French ambassador Jean Delahaye) given in H. Missak Effendi, "Le Père Ottoman," *Revue d' histoire diplomatique*, XVII (1903), 350–60. After serving Venice faithfully for forty years, the dragoman Giovanni Antonio Grillo was put to death by the Turks in 1649, when the war of Candia had been going on for some years. Cf. von Hammer-Purgstall, *Gesch. d. osman. Reiches*, V (repr. 1963), 490–91.

[20] Cf. Setton, I, 16–18.

[21] Cf. Mormori, *Guerra di Candia*, MS. Marc. It. VII, 1563 (7596), fols. 2ᵛ–3ʳ.

their six galleys, they set sail for Malta, towing away the galleon from which a number of Turkish crewmen had apparently escaped, although the Hospitallers were said still to hold twenty prisoners.

The bailie Soranzo expressed disbelief in the vizir's account, pointing out how unlikely, how impossible, it all was in view of the Signoria's most stringent orders. The provveditore generale of Candia and other officials of the Republic would never have tolerated such an outrageous performance. Yusuf Pasha noted, however, that the Hospitallers' actions on Crete could not have escaped the attention of the provincial government on the island for twenty days. Speaking to Soranzo as a friend, not as a vizir, Yusuf remarked that he must find a stronger reply to the charges than his assertions so far. Yusuf might "speak as a friend," but he was far from being a friend of the Republic. Actually he was a Dalmatian renegade, a convert to Islam named Josef Masković. He hated the Venetians. The depositions of those who had witnessed the events were (he said) quite convincing in their charges against the Venetians at Crete. The Gran Signore would tolerate neither the loss nor the disparagement he had suffered.[22] If the Venetians could not provide more persuasive evidence of their guiltlessness, the Turks would break off relations with them.

Soranzo knew that the Turks' claim the Hospitallers had spent twenty days on the island of Crete was a gross distortion of what had happened. According to dispatches of 16 October (1644) and 10 February (1645) of Andrea Corner, the Venetian provveditore on Crete, the Hospitallers' six galleys and the captured Turkish galleon had been sighted off shore on 8 October. They had landed at night on a deserted and unguarded stretch of beach, put the Greeks taken from the galleon ashore, and promptly resumed their voyage to Malta. The corporal, who was absent from his post in the area where the Hospitallers anchored their galleys, was executed. The Greeks were confined in a lazzaretto as a sanitary precaution.

Corner knew that the galleon was commanded by one Ibrahim Chelebi; it was, he believed, loaded with wood to be delivered to Alexandria. The Hospitallers had captured the galleon 130 miles or so to the south of Rhodes. It was a mercantile vessel with Turks, mariners, merchants, and passengers aboard, about 350 persons. It was also carrying a certain number of cannon. Ibrahim Chelebi was killed in the Hospitallers' assault, together with 150 Turks. The general of the Knights was killed as

---

[22] Arch. Segr. Vaticano, Cod. Urb. lat. 1109, fol. 14, *di Venetia li 6 di Gennaro 1645:* "Di Costantinopoli avvisano che il Gran Turco fusse molto irritato contro li cavalieri di Malta per lo scritto galeone preso, molto ricco, sopra il quale vi era il capo delli neri eunuchi del Gran Turco che andava alla Mecha, minacciando di volere andare a visitare detti cavalieri con poderosa armata. . . ." Cf., *ibid.,* fols. 52ᵛ–53, 59ᵛ–60, 68.

well, and many of his fellow freebooters. The captive Turks were thrown overboard. Such was Corner's report to the doge Francesco Erizzo on 16 October (1644), long before the Turks were charging the Venetians with any sort of complicity in the Hospitallers' evildoing.[23]

---

[23] ASV, Senato, Provveditori da terra e da mar, Filza 795 [no. 65], Dispacci Andrea Corner, dispatch dated "Candia, 16 Ottobre 1644 s[til] n[ovo]:" "Serenissimo Principe: Hoggi mi capita aviso che alli 8 del corrente fossero state vedute al di fuori di questo Regno nelle acque di esso, in luogo rimotto dal comercio, sei galee Maltesi di ritorno da Levante con un ben grosso vascello, e vi havessero sbarcato in terra quaranta otto persone del medesimo, e poi proseguito il camino verso Malta.

"Subito ho fatto volar ordini efficacissimi perchè non fossero lasciati pratticar con alcuno e molto meno entrar in Città quando per avventura vi si fossero avanzati, come poco dopo è seguito con scorta però d'alcuni privileggiati e con le necessarie cautele di sanità.

"Dal costituto, che ne ho fatto levar, ho inteso questi esser stati in qualità de' marinari sopra il medesimo vascello stipendiati, andativi al servitio di loro volontà di natione Greci et Armeni, tutti Christiani e sudditi del Gran Signore, desiderosi e risoluti di portarsi, chi a Rodi e chi altrove, alle proprie case.

"Ne ho anche cavato che il sopradetto vascello sia stato d'un Hibrain Celebi Turco, carico di legne dal Mar Negro per Alessandria, preso fuori di Rodi miglia cento trenta verso ostro.

"Questo era legno di mercantia et haveva dentro tra Turchi marinari, mercanti, e passagieri al numero di trecento cinquanta con parecchi pezzi di cannone.

"Nel conflitto e tre abbordi seguiti è stato amazzato il medesimo Hibrain con cento cinquanta Turchi, e così anco il general Maltese con molti de' suoi, compartiti gli altri Turchi sopra le galee, dalle quali il giorno stesso del combattimento è stato gettato a fondo anco un berton di Costantinopoli che navigava pure per Alessandria.

"Tanto risulta dal sopraccennato costituto che occluso nelle presenti trasmetto alla Serenità vostra ad ogni buon fine.

"In questo mentre, regolandomi nel presente caso con quel partito che concede la necessità, ho stimato bene di far andar esse genti al lazaretto sotto buona custodia con pensiero di licentiarli tutti tosto che haveran purgato il sospetto con la dovuta contumatia. [Signed] Andrea Corner, proveditor general."

On 27 October Corner wrote the doge, *ibid.*, "Dopo chiuso e consegnato il mio humilissimo dispaccio per la Serenità vostra al patron Ughetto, che in Candia si trovava alla vella per cotesta volta, mi capitò a notitia che nel Porto di Caluslimniones nei mari d'ostro altri cinque Greci fossero fuggiti dal vascello preso dalle galee Maltesi e condotto a quella parte, come scrissi riverentemente all'Eccellenze vostre, che da esso pure in distanza di quattro miglia in circa dal medesimo porto fossero stati gettati in mare otto cavalli, venuti prodigiosamente vivi in terra dopo esser stati fieramente battuti dall'empito delle onde e gravemente offesi, nuotando tra sirti e scoglie, e ricuperati in fine dalle genti del paese, sian da esse stati asportati senza sapersi dove.

"Subito con gli opportuni riguardi del publico servitio, fatti ricoverar nel lazaretto di Candia li sopradetti Greci con gli altri quaranta otto primi, ho ispedito fuori il capitan Giacomo da Napoli di Romania con ordini proprii di dover farsi le maggiori diligenze per ritrovar i cavalli sopradetti e per condurli qualche miglio dalla Città a solo fine di potersi riconoscere la qualità e conditione loro.

"In tanto che si sono andate facendo le sopraccennate diligenze, non son restato di voler anco risaper da essi Greci che cavalli siano questi di ragion de chi e dove caricati. Ho cavato che nel detto vascello ve ne fossero in tutto venti tre, levati a Costantinopoli di ragion di Chislar Agà, eunuco deputato alla cura del Serraglio delle Sultane del Gran Signore, che il medesimo Chislar si portava col detto vascello alla Meca, e che nel conflitto con i Maltesi sia stato amazzato, che fossero usciti dalle reggie stalle, che sette nel medesimo conflitto ne sian rimasi stroppiati pur da cannonate, restatine sedici nel vascello et otto di essi tratti in mare come di sopra, non saputosi che farne per mancanza di provisione da sostentarli. . . .

"Così che seben questi cavalli con la presa fatta da Maltesi del vascello siano usciti dalla patronia de' Turchi, e poi anco da quella degli stessi Maltesi con l'esser stati gettati da loro in acqua e lasciati come perduti e derelitti e da me fatti ricuperare, io però senza haver voluto disponerne o riconoscer in essi alcuna ragione, a niente altro mirando che a quanto possa avantaggiar sempre i publici interessi, ho con l'uso di mia solita ingenuità e puntualità creduto miglior partito il farli riponer nel monasterio greco d'Angaranto, ch'è dei principali del Regno fuori della Città, perchè vi sian governati e tenuti sino ad altra commissione. . . .

"Con l'occasione che nel porto di Candia si trovano due vascelli per Costantinopoli, ho voluto valermi dell'incontro loro per l'incaminamento d'esse mie lettere e perchè li sopradetti Greci, che ancora dimorano in lazaretto, mi han fatto ricercar la loro liberatione et assenso per la partenza, ho pur dato ordine che con la sopradetta opportunità si facci goder loro l'imbarco verso le proprie case, e che in tanto siano pur ben trattati, perchè partano ottimamente impressi con buone relationi, e tutto risulti a vantaggio della Serenità vostra con avvertenza che la loro liberatione dalla contumacia segua nel punto del partir d'essi vascelli affinchè in tanto non si disuniscano, ma possano valersi del commodo di quei e d'altri che partissero per l'Archipelago. . . .

"Mi son condotto già con le galee di questa guardia al Castel Bicorna nel territorio di Canea per i progressi della visita generale. Ho havuto occasione d'ammirar con l'ochio proprio la vigilanza dell'illustrissimo signor Zorzi Moresini, capitano di essa guardia, e la sua applicatissima diligenza alla navigatione et a tutti i numeri della sua carica con mia somma sodisfattione. Portatomi poi a drittura a questa parte prima che la stagione maggiormente si avanzi, non ostante la difficoltà delle strade precipitose, horride, e quasi impratticabili, che però ho procurato di superar in ogni maniera, facendole a piedi in buona parte, vi vado formando la solita inquisitione, rivedendo e riconoscendo tutte queste occorrenze, facendo la mostra e rassegna generale delle cernide, dando gli ordini necessarii, ascoltando tutti, contribuendo a cadauno i proprii suffraggi, et edificando tra queste genti fiere et indocili, non visitate dall'eccellentissimo signor general Molino in qua, la conoscenza del dovere, l'obedienza dovuta alla giustitia, et il rispetto che conviene ai publici rappresentanti, et anco riducendo all'unione e pace diverse proli che ho trovato divise e piene di odii intestini e di vecchi rancori, persuadendomi che da questi atti tutti di mia indeffessa applicatione sia per risultar non ordinario vantaggio al publico servitio, come di quanto io vado operando in questo luogo, vostra Serenità haverà poi distintamente notitia da altre mie lettere. Sfacchia, in visita, 27 Ottobre 1644 s[til] n[ovo]. [Signed] Andrea Corner, proveditor general." Cf. Romanin, VII (1974), 250–51.

Corner had a bad reputation in Crete, being accused of arrogance and tyranny, connivance with the Hospitallers, underhanded financial dealings, and getting a corner on the oil market on the island (cf. Amy A. Bernardy, *Venezia e il Turco nella seconda metà del secolo XVII*, Florence, 1902, pp. 7–8); note also *Narrazione de' strani accidenti successi in Candia causati per Signor Andrea Corner, che fu generale di quell'isola*, Bibl. Correr (Venice), MS. Cicogna 2290, pp. 22–25 [pagination is irregular in the MS]:

"Che quel signore superiore a tutti abbia esercitato un severissimo dominio imperioso e crudele in tutte le cose e con tirannia a quei popoli grandissima. Ha ricevuto le robbe de Maltesi, gioie in quantità, cavalli molti, et altro con immenso suo utile, che da essi Maltesi furono tolte al Turco con prigionia di quelle sultane che andavano alla Mecca, e di esse donne goduto l'affetto amoroso con grande applauso. Ha fatto pagare a molti Candiotti, con esecuzioni rigorosissime fuori dell'ordinario, quantità grandissima di danari senza poter questi tali esser ascoltati, con pretesto di aver credito da loro di certe cose vecchie e prescritte da casali.

"Ha anche mandato, come si dice a Venezia, per suo conto più di 200 m. ducati. Ha richiesto con autorità anzi incettato per suo conto tutti gli ogli di quel Regno e mandati a Venezia con avantaggio et avanzo grandissimo. Ha anche bandito senza occasione evidente alquanti gentiluomini principalissimi di quel Regno e di grande autorità in quell'isola con confiscazione de' beni, che ha causato la loro disperazione a tanto più che conforme alla pia e solita clemenza della Repubblica di Venezia per materia così importante, come si vede, era solito in tali occasioni l'essere a questi banditi dal bailo Veneto concesso salvo condotto, ma interpostesi lettere al bailo di questo signore hanno causato che gli è stato negato questo suffraggio di salvo condotto. Onde vedendosi così maltrattati e disperati sono ricorsi alla Porta del Gran Signore Turco, et hanno causato questo incendio di guerra così grande e anco data al Turco ogni informazione dello stato di quel Regno di Candia, anzi loro stessi si sono posti nell'armata Turchesca per indrizzo e cognizione di venire a man salva all'impresa et acquisto del Regno, come si vede.

"Che la Repubblica paga 12 m. fanti all'anno in Candia, e che non ve ne siano nè anco due milla.

"Anzi ora si scuopre la mala custodia et governo di esso Regno, qual in questa neccessità si trova sprovisto di tutte le cose neccessarie, come viene anco scritto da quelli nostri buoni cittadini, che se non li sarà mandata gente et monizioni, non potranno resistere, ma che gloriosamente perderanno le loro vite per la sua cara Patria, che il Signor Dio benedetto e la gloriosa Vergine Maria la guardi da così gran tribulazione, e tutti quelli popoli che innocenti soggiacciono a tanta miseria. . . ."

In another contemporary account, also in the Bibl. Correr, MS. Cicogna 2290, entitled *Relazione dell'invasione fatta da Turchi del Regno di Candia*, p. 10 [pagination is irregular], we are informed "che veramente il pensiero del Turco fosse solo contro Malta, ma che poi il combattimento con le doglianze degli Affricani lo disponesse contro a Veneziani, e finalmente in tutto lo facesse risolvere il ricorso che fecero a lui delle prime famiglie di Candia che disgustate dal governo asprissimo di Andrea Cornaro, non sapendo dove trovar giustizia, per esser in Venezia la famiglia Cornara troppo potente, implorarono il braccio del Gran Signore, rappresentandogli la facilità dell'impresa et il desiderio che haveva quel Regno di soggettarsi a lui. . . ."

Corner's other important dispatch relating to the Maltese seizure of the Turkish convoy in late September 1644 may also be found in the Provv. da terra e da mar, Filza 795 [no. 65], dated "Canea, in visita, 10 Febraro 1644 s[til] n[ovo]," *more veneto*, i.e. 1645: "Serenissimo principe: Sollecitate con l'assistenza e diligenza maggiore le funtioni et occorrenze della visita anco nel Castel Bicorna me ne son lodato Dio sbrigato con l'intero adempimento d'ogni numero del bisogno, e dopo un travaglioso pelegrinaggio per tutti i castelli, fortezze, e luoghi principali di questo territorio con viaggi lunghi, strade precipitose, stagione horrida, e con incommodi patimenti e dispendii grandissimi in tante residenze, son finalmente giunto in questa città, come di dover fare ho humilmente scritto a vostra Serenità nelle ultime mie.

"A Bicorna i concorsi de popoli, i suffraggi impetrati, i sollievi conseguiti sono stati al solito moltiplici a tutte le hore così che ove supeditava l'oppressione, vi ho introdutta l'equità, ove serpeva un'universale miseria, resta in molti risorto il commodo, e chi indebitamente era spogliato delle sostanze, l'ho restituito nel proprio possesso.

"Vi ho pur maturato e colto i frutti dell'inquisitione col castigo di molti rei, con l'estirpatione de malviventi, e con nettar anco quella parte di paese da chi perturbava le vite e le fortune altrui, operando in somma che il sollievo de' boni e la pena di tristi vagliano respettivamente d'essempio e di terrore a tutti.

"Li privilleggiati di quel territorio, essercitati e rassegnati da me con la dovuta diligenza, erano già dui mille cento sessanta nove, et hora sono dui mille cento nonanta [*sic*] cinque.

"Riveduti anco gli angarici, che pur erano mille seicento quattordeci, e sono al presente mille sette cento quaranta nove.

"Qui poi son stato incontrato e ricevuto da questi illustrissimi signori con le forme più decorose e da tutti questi popoli con applausi ben degni al nome che rappresento di vostra Serenità, non essendo certo stato ommesso alcun numero di rispetto e riverenza per honorar il mio ingresso e solennizar le speranze che ogn'uno tiene de proprii sollievi.

"Trovo l'illustrissimo signor rettor Michiel in possesso d'un sommo affetto e stima indifferentemente di tutti, quali benedicono il suo governo e n'essaltano il merito.

"L'illustrissimo signor proveditor Navagier pure con le pari d'una pronta dispositione complisce a tutte le occorenze di sua carica e con quelle di virtù attrahe i cuori d'ogn'uno alle dovute lodi e commendationi.

"Anco monsignor reverendissimo vescovo Bencio [Milano Benzio] riporta l'amore e l'applauso universale come prelato molto degno, di rara bontà e di costumi e talenti singolari.

"Mi son subito applicato alle incombenze della visita che preveggo moltiplici e grandissime anco in questa città e nell'istesso tempo a tutti gli altri affari ben importanti della carica.

"Nella camera faccio rivedere i maneggi di denari, i fondi delle casse, la regola della scrittura, et ogni altro particolare, osservando i disordini che vi fossero per rimediarvi con proprie provisioni.

In view of the extensive preparations going on in the Arsenal at Istanbul, it was clear the Turks intended to mount a major campaign at sea. As galleys came to the Bosporus from the Barbary coast, and troops were being recruited, it was hard to believe that their destination would not be either Crete or Malta. The Venetians had learned through the years, however, that in dealing with the Turks there was only one thing of which they could be certain, namely that they could be certain of nothing. The naval armament the Turks were getting ready was on too grand a scale for mere raids of depredation on the Italian coast. There was no point in their attacking Spain; the French were as always their friends. The building of galleys and the levying of mariners must mean that they were not embarking upon a campaign against the Austrians, the Poles, or the Russians. Yes, they were looking toward Crete or Malta.

The Hospitallers may have been prepared for an attack upon Malta. The colonial government on Crete, however, was in disarray despite the attempts of Andrea Corner, recently appointed the provveditore generale, to rebuild the fortifications with the generous support of the Vene-

---

"All'essatione de publici crediti ho posto pure tutto il pensiero, e se ne riporterà certo il possibile proffitto.

"Per l'affare de' datii invigilo non meno acciò tutto passi in aggiustata maniera senza fraude e senza intacchi.

"Delle munitioni faccio vedere lo stato, le ricevute, le dispense, la scrittura, et ogni altra chiarezza.

"Dell'Arsenale osservo parimenti molti disordini, e vi disponerò e stabilirò ogni miglior regola.

"Ho fatto rivedere il maneggio di cinque patroni di esso Arsenale che sono stati successivamente nella carica dal 1622 in qua, e risultano tra tutti debitori per la summa di lire cento quaranta cinque mille, delle quali restano formati debitori in Camera. La fatica è stata grandissima, principiata sin quando capitai alla carica, ma tanto più mi consolo quanto che con l'essecutioni già incaminate spero che nella maggior parte resterà vostra Serenità reintegrata di così rilevante capitale che per tanti anni è stato sepolto nel torbido e nel silentio, e ch'era prossimo a cader anco nell'oblivione.

"Ho trovato pure nei libri di questa Camera che molti e quasi tutti li provenditori stati alla Sfacchia è così li provenditori alla sanità e castellani di questi castelli hanno tralasciato di salvar li loro maneggi, e restano debitori al presente per la summa di lire cinquanta due mille, per quali parimenti procurarò non solo con tutto lo spirito la dovuta sodisfattione, ma disponerò regole per maggior cautione in avvenire del publico interesse nei medesimi maneggi.

"Rivederò con l'occhio proprio tutte le altre cose, e così le militie, li bombardieri, e le cernide. Regolarò i roli, accrescerò i numeri, darò buone regole, e di tutto avisarò con altre la Serenità vostra che in tanto può esser ben certa di non doversi da me lasciar ommesso alcun numero del bisogno, del mio debito, e del publico servitio. [Signed] Andrea Corner, provveditor general."

Note also the dispatch, *ibid.*, also dated "Canea, in visita, 10 Febraro 1644, stil novo" (1645), beginning "All'eccellentissimo signor bailo in Costantinopoli ho di volta in volta portato puntuale e distinta notitia dei successi che per giornata sono accaduti in questo Regno toccanti Maltesi e Ponentini, et gli ho sempre espresso il merito che dovrebbe havere la Serenità vostra delle operationi fatte da me in castigo dei medesimi et in vantaggio de sudditi del Gran Signore, mentre certo non possono, non dirò esseguirsi, ma ne meno desiderarsi maggiori attestati o più vive dimostrationi di una sincera et ottima volontà. . . ."

tian Senate. The fortifications of the early modern era were costly to maintain. They became rundown with the wear and tear of time, suffered from neglect, and were rendered out-of-date by the improved tactics of siege warfare. The Senate sent 2,500 infantry to Crete, engineers, provisions of wheat and rice, and (on 10 February 1645) 100,000 ducats to help Corner meet his ever-increasing expenses. They decided also to arm two galleasses and thirty light galleys, and authorized Corner to raise a thousand infantry in the Brazzo di Maina and elsewhere in the Archipelago.[24] While the Senate hoped that the self-seeking khoja might be converted to a more friendly attitude by bakshish and by the fact of the Republic's innocence of the Maltese malfeasance, as they wrote the bailie Soranzo in Istanbul on 1 March (1645), they were nonetheless adding another ten galleys to their defenses at Candia. They were also arming six large warships in the Arsenal at Venice, and hastening the recruitment of troops. The recently elected pope, Innocent X, had promised the Signoria a large levy of troops from the papal states. Furthermore, Ferdinand II, the grand duke of Tuscany, could also be depended upon for a sizable force. In the meantime Soranzo was to continue his negotiations with the pashas and others in Istanbul.[25]

The chief cities on the island of Crete were (and are) on the northern coast—Candia (mod. *Herákleion, Iráklion*) at the center of the coastline; Canea (Chaniá, *Khaniá*), about 75 miles west of Candia; Retimo (*Réthymnon*), about midway between Candia and Canea; and Sitía (*Seteía*), then as now the smallest of the four cities, at the eastern end of the island on the little Gulf of Seteía. Candia was the metropolis, the other three cities being suffragan sees. There were another three lesser ports along the northern shore, Grabusa (Vouxa) and Suda (Souda) in the west

---

[24] Romanin, VII (1974), 252–53, doc. dated 25 January 1645 (Ven. style 1644), from the Arch. di Stato di Venezia, Rettori, p. 151. The two galleasses and thirty galleys were apparently more or less ready by 24 June (1645), as we may infer from Senato, Deliberazioni Costantinopli (Secreta), Reg. 28, fol. 172ᵛ: "Sia incaricato il magistrato dell'Arsenale de sollecitare l'allestimento delle due galeazze et trenta galere sottili ordinate già tempo tenerse pronte acciò in ogni caso possano senza dilatione essere adoperate et portino subito in scrittura il stato di esse. . . ." On the Turkish armada, which allegedly now consisted of 170 galleys, 80 ships (*navi*), and 300 *caramusalini* loaded with foodstuffs and munitions, cf. Arch. Segr. Vaticano, Cod. Urb. lat. 1109, fol. 84, *di Roma 25 Marzo 1645.*

[25] ASV, Senato, Deliberazioni Costantinopli (Secreta), Reg. 28 [1644–1646], fols. 128ᵛ–129ʳ: "Nè sarà difficile col vehicolo del denaro l'introddurre le nostre ragioni, che sono tanto vere e chiare, nella consideratione et approvatione del Cozà sicome d'ogni altro. . . . In tanto però andiamo provedendo noi sempre meglio alle nostre diffese, rissoluti di alestersi d'altre dieci galere in Candia oltre le scritte, l'armarsi qui [a Venezia] di sei grossi vasselli da guerra, et l'aumento delle nostre soldatesche, havuta havendo promissione di una buona levata de sudditi dal Pontefice, et altro amassamento su quello del Gran Duca ancora," and cf. Arch. Segr. Vaticano, Cod. Urb. lat. 1109, fols. 52ᵛ–53ʳ, 59ᵛ–60ʳ, 84, 158ᵛ–159ʳ, 181ᵛ–182ʳ, 187–188ʳ.

and Spinalonga in the east, all protected to a large extent by a rocky, fortifiable entryway. The island was defensible, but the resources of the Republic were not what they used to be, nor were the stamina and aggressiveness of a declining nobility what they had once been.

The government of Crete was a reflection of that of Venice. The duke of Candia, who usually served for two years, was the administrative and ceremonial head of the colonial regime.[26] He was chosen in Venice. The provveditore generale served as military overseer of the island, his duties varying with the terms of his commission. In Crete as in Venice there were ducal councilors, a Grand Council (*consilium maius*), official advocates (*avogadori*), a grand chancellor, various magistrates, and a special police force (called on the island, as in Venice, the *signori di notte*). The government was inefficient. The Venetian and Greek feudatories did not meet their obligations in producing an experienced military manpower in either lancers or infantry. The peasant militia (the *cernide*) was on the whole of little use. Venice still lived on the Levantine trade, which had declined in volume as well as in profits. Impoverished nobles could not meet the costs of public office at home, and still less abroad, where salaries often fell far short of expenses. Noble families were dying out. The plagues of 1575–1577 and 1630–1631 had taken their toll of the patriciate as well as of the citizenry.[27]

As the Turks spread word from Istanbul that their armament was being prepared against Malta, the Senate was disturbed by the movements of troops and artillery along the borders of Dalmatia. Conditions were even more worrisome in western Crete, as the doge Francesco Erizzo was warned in a letter from Canea dated on 16 March 1645.[28] Giovanni Soranzo's attempt to reach an amicable accord with the Porte was impeded by the dragoman Grillo's illness, which worried the Signoria. Neverthe-

---

[26] Cf. Setton, I, 177–78.

[27] Cf. Paolo Preto, *Peste e società a Venezia nel 1576*, Vicenza, 1978, esp. pp. 111ff., and Jas. C. Davis, *The Decline of the Venetian Nobility as a Ruling Class*, Baltimore, 1962, pp. 34ff., 75ff. Note also Pastor's remarks on the decline of the Roman nobility (*Gesch. d. Päpste*, XIV-1 [1929], 272–73, and *Hist. Popes*, XXX, 372–73), and on the earlier plague, see Bibl. Nazionale Marciana, MS. It. VII, 194 (8493), Provvedimenti per la peste a Venezia, ann. 1575–1577. We shall find more *aggregazioni alla nobiltà* when we reach the year 1684.

[28] *Raccolta diplomatica della guerra di Candia*, Bibl. Nazionale Marciana, MS. It. VII, 211 (7468), fol. 30ʳ, the writer of which letter, an official at Canea, was most apprehensive "che per lo sprovedimento in cui si trova questa piazza delle cose più necessarie per una lunga et valida ressistenza contro potentissima invasione, è stato di recente qui riconosciuto dall'eccellentissimo signor generale l'esser di tutte le cose, et mi ha assicurato di haver presentata distinta notitia alla Serenità vostra, ma ad ogni modo non sarà disdicevole al mio debito l'abbondare in raguagli in urgenza di tanto rilievo." The available ship's biscuit and wheat would last two months. The four armed galleys assigned to Canea and Retimo were not sufficient for the "mantenimento di questi popoli." Alarm was spreading throughout the Archipelago. Armaments were inadequate in Canea, and apparently little could be expected of the local militia.

less, Soranzo kept his government well informed, at least to the extent he could, of what was going on in Istanbul. In return the Senate sent him the news from Vienna of the Turkish recruitment of 4,000 Tatars and 2,500 Vlachs in Transylvania. The pasha of Buda had, however, assured the Emperor Ferdinand III of "la buona corrispondenza con l'imperio." On 21 March (1645) the doge wrote the sultan Ibrahim that he was sure his Majesty would not allow the Turkish ministers to violate the capitulation of peace which he had himself guaranteed with "la sua reale promessa." A copy of the letter was sent to Soranzo, who was instructed to present it to the sultan or not, depending on the view then prevailing at the Porte of the "affair" of the master of the seraglio (*kislar ağasi, chislaragà*), whom the Hospitallers had killed aboard the Turkish vessel they had captured.[29]

On 18 March (1645) the doge and Senate had written Andrea Corner, the provveditore generale of Candia, concerning the many letters which the bailie Soranzo had written Corner, who had sent summaries of the letters (or the texts themselves) to the doge and Senate. Soranzo had also received letters from Corner which should strengthen his hand at the Porte. The Venetians had allegedly stopped a number of western and Maltese vessels, punished their crewmen (when they were guilty of anti-Turkish activities), and freed many subjects of the Gran Signore, especially mariners taken from the very galleon on which the master of the seraglio, the kislaragà Sünbüllü, had been killed. The Venetians had taken them in, treated them well, and sent them home, receiving from them the reliable information that the Maltese galleys and other vessels had not approached the Cretan shores. Some horses, to be sure, having been badly treated by the Hospitallers, had been thrown overboard and had come ashore at Crete quite by accident. The facts were established by the deposition of three mariners who had been aboard the kislaragà's vessel. After arriving in Malta the three mariners in question had somehow got away, and turned up in Venice on their way back home. On the basis of these facts, which the doge and Senate were relaying to Soranzo, the latter was bound to make an impression on the Turks.[30]

---

[29] Senato, Deliberazioni Costantinopoli (Secreta), Reg 28, fols. 130–139[r]. On Venetian fears of the Turks' next move, cf. *Cal. State Papers . . . , Venice*, XXVII (1926, repr. 1970), nos. 209–13, pp. 181–83. The Hospitallers were marshaling their forces for the defense of Malta (Arch. Segr. Vaticano, Cod. Urb. lat. 1109, fol. 68, *di Roma XI Marzo 1645*).

[30] Senato, Deliberazioni Costantinopoli (Secreta), Reg. 28, fols. 135[v]–136[r]: "Havemo inteso l'arrivo costà [in Candia] di molte lettere scrittevi dal Bailo con tutte le informationi che del contenuto de esse havete mandato a noi. Egli pure ha recevuto le vostre col fondamento delle quali maggiormente si incalorirà a sostenere il vero che tanti vasselli ponentini e Maltesi siano stati fermati, castigate le genti, posti in libertà molti suddeti del Gran Signore, particolarmente li marinari del vassello del Chislaragà, ricoverati et mandati alle case loro con buoni trattamenti colla certezza che le galere et vasselli Maltesi non

Yusuf Pasha's contention that the Hospitallers had spent twenty days on the island of Crete (in October 1644) was certainly untrue. Also, however, the doge's letter of 18 March (1645) seems to belie the widely reported fact that the Hospitallers had indeed landed, however briefly, at Kalismene on the south shore of Crete. In any event we can only read the lines of the doge's letter. Corner, who was much better informed than we are, could read between the lines. After all, Corner had himself reported to the Signoria, as we have seen, that the Hospitallers had been sighted off shore on 8 October, and had disembarked a number of Greeks on the island under cover of darkness.

The Turks declared war on Malta, and Soranzo was instructed to try to win over the avaricious khoja with bakshish. He was also to keep reminding the grand vizir of the importance of Turco-Venetian commerce, emphasizing always the Signoria's desire to maintain peace with the Porte. Although minor incidents here and there kept the Venetians on the alert, they certainly did not expect the coming attack. In a letter to Soranzo of 22 June (1645) the doge and Senate expressed their appreciation of the friendliness and helpfulness of the grand vizir, "il primo visir, che sempre più capace si dimostrava della stima et affetto nostro. . . ."[31] The grand vizir was Sultanzade Mehmed Pasha, and he was a friend of Venice. At least he was opposed to an expedition against the island of Crete. Also he had become jealous and fearful of Yusuf Pasha, the second vizir, whose star was rising. Yusuf had joined the khoja in advocating the attempted conquest of Crete. It usually took a month or more for letters from Istanbul to reach Venice, and of course much could happen between the dispatch of a letter and its delivery to the addressee.

When the doge and Senate wrote the bailie Soranzo in praise of the grand vizir, Soranzo had been a prisoner of the Porte for three weeks. Two days after their letter of 22 June (which was presumably never sent to Soranzo), the latter was able to inform them by way of a courier from Vienna that guards had been placed at his house, the *casa bailaggia* (in the "vineyards of Pera"), and he could not go out, nor could anyone enter. Soranzo had become friendly with the imperial ambassador at the Porte, Count Hermann Czernin, who had presumably sent Soranzo's letter to Venice in the diplomatic pouch to Vienna. The bailie's imprisonment was contrary to international law, the *jus gentium*, and to the Venetians' friendship with the Porte. Istanbul was full of rumors. The Turks' confinement of Soranzo to his house was naturally distressing to

---

sianosi accostati al regno [di Candia]. Che li cavalli gettati siano venuti in terra per accidente, mal trattati particolari, che si accordano pure con la depositione di tre marinari dello stesso vassello del Chislaragà giunti a Malta et capitati qui de passaggio: Onde credemo che il Bailo col fondamento delle nostre lettere con quello della verità haverà fatto buona impressione et sostenuto il nostro servicio. +137, 2, 18."

[31] For details see Senato, Deliberazioni Costantinopoli (Secreta), Reg. 28, fols. 143–63 (with the quoted phrase on fol. 162^r), 166^{v}ff.

the doge and Senate, who sent word of it to the Curia Romana and to the courts of the other Christian princes. The princes must see that it was time to put aside their rancors and hostilities, to establish a peace which would make much easier Christian opposition to such displays of Turkish belligerence. When the Turks saw the Christians at peace, they stopped causing "trouble and travail."[32] Although Soranzo was now a prisoner of the Porte, month after month he found ways of sending dispatches to the doge and Senate, and to others in Venice as well as to receive the dispatches which they sent to him.[33]

---

[32] Senato, Deliberazioni Costantinopoli (Secreta), Reg. 28, fol. 171, dispatch dated 24 June 1645, addressed to Girolamo Morosini, the Venetian provveditore generale da mar, who had replaced the captain-general Francesco da Molin as overall commander, for the latter (who became the doge in January 1646) was ill: "Con lettere di primo corrente spedite per via de Viena con espresso corriero tenemo aviso dal Bailo che siano state poste guardie alla sua casa acciò non esca nè alcuno entri da lui con effetto della maggior violenza tenendolo come prigione. Non haveva potuto esso Bailo saper la causa di effetto tanto barbaro e contrario alla ragion delle genti, all'amicitia della Republica.

"Molte cose si discorrevano in Constantinopoli che l'armata fosse in Candia, a Tine, et altrove, ma tutto senza fondamento [this reference seems to be to the Venetian, not the Turkish fleet]. La rissolutione è stata intesa da noi con molestia, et ci ha dato cause de darne parte a Roma et alli corti delli altri principi Christiani con le debite considerationi de quanto convenga per bene della Christianità lasciar li rancori, stabilire la quiete per maggior commodo da opporsi a tentativi de infideli, et perchè Turchi, quando vederanno li Christiani in pace, s'asteneranno dal promover torbidi e travagli. . . ." The Senate was sending the provveditore 750 footsoldiers, canvas awnings, and a thousand muskets in addition to the five hundred which had already been shipped to Corfu. Cf. *ibid.*, fols. 177ff. On Soranzo's imprisonment, note also Arch. Segr. Vaticano, Cod. Urb. lat. 1109, fol. 231. Count Hermann Czernin was the imperial ambassador to Istanbul from June 1644 to August 1645.

According to Mormori, *Guerra di Candia*, MS. Marc. It. VII, 1563 (7596), fol. 7[r], "Capitò li ii giugno con fregata venuta di Arcipelago una lettera del bailo Soranzo dirretta al Cornaro [Corner], a cui fu subito espedita, nella quale avvisava il suo arresto e la certezza della vicina invasione del regno [di Candia], il medemo in sostanza s'ebbe di bocca di uno da Rettimo, che portò essa lettera . . . ," and now the Turkish grand admiral or kapudan pasha, having tarred his keels at Navarino, was on his way to the island of Crete.

The bailie Giovanni Soranzo had a long, hard road of captivity ahead, on which note Tommaso Bertelè, *Il Palazzo degli ambasciatori di Venezia a Costantinopoli* (1932), pp. 184ff., 239–40, and cf. *Cal. State Papers . . . , Venice*, XXVII (1926, repr. 1970), nos. 234–35, pp. 193–94. Czernin was succeeded as the emperor's resident ambassador at the Porte by Alexander von Wollrath Greifenklau, who got into serious trouble with the Turks, but died before the final resolution of his case (von Hammer-Purgstall, *Gesch. d. osman., Reiches*, V, 392–93, trans. Hellert, X, 114–15).

[33] By 6 February 1647 (Ven. style 1646), the doge and Senate had received some 260 dispatches from Soranzo (Senato, Deliberazioni Costantinopoli [Secreta], Reg. 28, fol. 258[r]). Ivan Dujčev has published a long series of dispatches addressed to the Holy See, as we have noted, detailing Turkish activities and the current of events in Istanbul as seen from Ragusa, in the *Avvisi di Ragusa: Documenti sull'impero turco nel sec. XVII e sulla guerra di Candia*, Rome, 1935 (Orientalia Christiana analecta, 101). These dispatches relate to the Turks' military preparations for the "war of Candia" (doc. xx, pp. 13–15), the sailing of the sultan's fleet of 70 galleys, 20 large ships, 300 karamussals carrying soldiers, sappers, and other military personnel from Istanbul on 30 April 1645 (doc. xxv, pp. 19–20), the arrest of the bailie Soranzo (doc. xxvii, pp. 21–22), etc., etc., and much other such material in some two hundred documents coming down to the year 1663. The events of 1645–1646 are covered in considerable detail.

The sultan's armada sailed from the Dardanelles on 30 April (1645) under the command of Yusuf, the sultan's son-in-law and kapudan pasha. It was said to be a most impressive armament, consisting of some 416 vessels, among them two galleasses, a great galleon called the *Sultana,* ten ships from Alexandria, two from Tunis, ten vessels rented from the Dutch and English, and three hundred smaller craft, including the usual Levantine caïques and karamussals. Little reliance can be placed on such reputed numbers. The karamussal (Turk. *karāmusāl*) had a mainmast, a mizzenmast, an extended bowsprit, and a high poop. It was a common sight in eastern waters,[34] and is often mentioned in the western sources. There were said to be more than fifty thousand men aboard the armada, with seven thousand janissaries, a large contingent of sipahis, sappers, and other troops. After a friendly stop at the Venetian island of Tenos, where the Turks received water and supplies, they went on in stormy weather to Monemvasia, Maina, and Cerigo, rounding the Morea to the harbor of Navarino, as though they were indeed on the road to Malta. After three weeks at Navarino, however, the Turks raised anchor on 21 June, sailing toward Cape Spada (Spátha), the headland of western Crete, where they were sighted two days later, on Friday, the twenty-third.[35] The war of Candia had begun.

On 26 June (1645) the provveditore generale Andrea Corner prepared a detailed dispatch for the Venetian Signoria, reporting the Turkish disembarkation of troops on the shores of the bay of Gognà, some fifteen miles west of Canea. Their landing was at first contested by the local peasantry which fled, however, as the first cannon were fired from the Turkish galleys. Another small force of paid, peasant militia and some five hundred infantry also retreated from the scene, leaving the Turks free to burn and ravage the countryside.[36] Corner put the size of the enemy armada at 78 galleys, three heavy, square-rigged merchant ships

---

[34] On the karamussal (Ital. *caramusalino*), see the *Nouveau glossaire nautique d'Augustin Jal,* rev. ed., Paris and The Hague, 1948, pp. 219–20, and on the caïques, p. 181. On the composition of the Ottoman armada, note Senato, Deliberazioni Costantinopoli (Secreta), Reg. 28, fol. 174, and cf. *Cal. State Papers. . . , Venice,* XXVII (1926, repr. 1970), nos. 310, 314, 335, pp. 225, 227, 239.

[35] Mormori, *Guerra di Candia,* MS. Marc. It. VII, 1563 (7596), fol. 7ᵛ: "Li scoprì finalmente la matina di 13 Giugno in giorno di Venerdì l'armata in grandissimo numero di velle, e s'avvanzava alla volta di Canea da Capo Spada guidata d'alcuni Malvasioti, che avevano lungo tempo esercitato traffico in queste città, et avevano cognizione delli siti e spiaggie. . . ." Friday, 13 June (O.S.), is also given as the date when the Turkish armada hove into sight, in MS. Marc. It. VII, 101 (8382), fol. 10, Mormori's original text, but 13 June fell on a Wednesday in 1645. The twenty-third (N. S.) did of course fall on Friday.

[36] Mormori, *Guerra di Candia,* MS. cit., fol. 8ʳ: ". . . L'inimico . . . , fattosi padrone della campagna, cominciò ad abbruggiare le biade di già segate, le case, e le ville che gli riparavano avanti avanzandosi sempre verso la città [di Canea] perchè la cavalleria doppo aver scaramuciato bon pezzo sotto la condotta de Ser Francesco Vizamano Caropulo, essendo stato esso ferito d'archibuggiata in un braccio nè potendo più resistere, solo si ritirò entro le mura." Cf. the revised and mangled text of MS. Marc. It. VII, 101 (8382), fols. 10ᵛ–11ʳ.

(*bertoni*), and 117 saïques or ketches (Turk. sing. *shāīka*) besides other vessels which also had been seen heading for the bay of Gognà. Despite the precautions which Corner had taken and such forces as he could muster, the Turks quickly occupied the small fortified island of S. Todero.[37]

The fortress had been defended by the Istrian officer Blasio Zulian who, having command of hardly more than thirty soldiers with some worn-out cannon, could see only too clearly that the Turks would take the islet. After having sunk a few Turkish galleys, Zulian had mines planted in the little fortress, set them afire, and blew himself, his men, and the fortress to pieces. The Turks took over the remaining pieces of S. Todero as their first victory of the war,[38] and advanced upon nearby Canea both by land and by sea as early as 27 June, encamping on the hillsides facing the city and taking over the harbor. Unloading their artillery, munitions, and supplies, the Turks began the siege, which lasted fifty-six days. On 22 August (1645) Canea surrendered, and three days later the cathedral church of S. Niccolò and two other churches were converted into mosques.[39] In November Yusuf Pasha left a garrison of at least eight thousand soldiers in Canea with munitions and supplies, and returned to Istanbul,[40] where an unexpected tragedy was awaiting him.

The war had begun which would last a quarter of a century, and prove almost as great a drain on the Turks as on the Venetians. We cannot here

---

[37] ASV, Senato, Provveditori da terra e da mar, Filza 796 (no. 66), Dispacci di Andrea Corner, dispatch no. 126, dated "di Canea, li 26 Giugno 1645."

[38] Andrea Valiero, *Historia della guerra di Candia*, Venice, 1679, p. 21; B. Cecchetti, "Un 'Pietro Micca' dell'Istria," *Archivio Veneto*, XXX-1 (ann. XV, 1885), 170–72, who quotes from a letter of Andrea Corner to the doge Francesco Erizzo dated 27 June, 1645 (Cancell. Secr. Candia, Lettere, fol. 66): "Il Capitan Giuliani però, che vi si trovava con le sue genti rinforzate di ordine mio [but apparently not very well 'reinforced'], veduto superato il porto con l'ingresso de Turchi, dato fuoco alla municione ha più tosto voluto morire generosamente con li suoi et con parte dei medesimi Turchi quali vi erano entrati che mai rendersi. . . ."

[39] Von Hammer-Purgstall, *Gesch. d. osman. Reiches*, V (1829, repr. 1963), 366, 377–83, trans. Hellert, X (1837), 84, 95–102; Romanin, VII (1974), 254–57; Kretschmayr, *Gesch. von Venedig*, III (1934, repr. 1964), 315, 319–20; R. C. Anderson, *Naval Wars in the Levant, 1559–1853*, Princeton, 1952, pp. 121ff.; Mormori, *Guerra di Candia*, MS. Marc. It. VII, 1563 (7596), fols. 15ʳ–20ʳ; and on the Venetian surrender of Canea, note the *Raccolta diplomatica della guerra di Candia*, MS. Marc. It. VII, 211 (7468), fols. 64–73ʳ.

The Turkish siege of Canea, "sostenuto con coraggio e gran valore de diffensori il fiero assedio per lo spacio de mesi due," the Venetian efforts to defend the city, the precautions taken to protect the Dalmatian coast and Corfu, the then current naval and diplomatic news, etc., can also be followed to some extent in Senato, Deliberazioni Costantinopoli (Secreta), Reg. 28, fols. 183ᵛ–197, dispatches dated from 10 July to 2 October 1645, although details are sparse for the month of August; note also Senato, Provveditori da terra e da mar, Filza 932 (Prov. generale Girolamo Morosini, 1645–1646), dispatches dated 5 and 13 August, 1645.

[40] Senato, Deliberazioni Costantinopoli (Secreta), Reg. 28, fol. 201ᵛ, a dispatch to the bailie Soranzo, dated 25 November 1645. Von Hammer-Purgstall, *Gesch. d. osman. Reiches*, V, 383–84, trans. Hellert, X, 103–4, provides Canea with a much larger garrison.

pursue the war of Candia in full detail, but a glance at some of the major events of the long-drawn-out contest will make clear that, after a feeble beginning, the Venetians' performance was extraordinary. In the confusion of July and August (1645) Pope Innocent X dispatched five galleys to assist the harassed Venetians; Ferdinand II, the grand duke of Tuscany, also sent five galleys, as did the Spanish authorities in Naples. And after some delay the Maltese sent their six well-known galleys. When these twenty-one galleys were added to the Venetians' twenty-five, the Christian allies had a fleet of fair size, which was augmented by four galleasses and eighteen other vessels. Since the Turkish armada was in some disarray both at S. Todero and in the harbor of Canea by the beginning of September, it was conceivable that an all-out attack upon the Turks might have rewon Canea, destroyed a good part of their armada, and put a stop to any further operations of the enemy on the island of Crete. The Christian forces, however, were under the cautious command of the papal captain-general Niccolò Ludovisi, a papal nephew and prince of Piombino, and in fear of defeat he may have lost an opportunity for victory. Owing to Ludovisi's indecision or prudence, whichever it may have been, as well as to stormy weather, the allied fleet made no attempt to recover Canea until 1 October. Then the fleet, allegedly consisting of some sixty galleys, four galleasses, and twenty-eight ships, once more achieved nothing but failure and frustration owing to the Turks' defense of the harbor and the allies' divided command.[41] Thereaf-

---

[41] Von Hammer-Purgstall, *Gesch. d. osman. Reiches*, V, 383–85, trans. Hellert, X, 102–5, on the activities of the Turks; Romanin, *Storia documentata di Venezia*, VII (1974), 256–59; Anderson, *Naval Wars in the Levant*, p. 124; Arch. Segr. Vaticano, Cod. Urb. lat. 1109, fols. 217–218ᵛ; Mormori, *Guerra di Candia*, MS. Marc. It. VII, 1563 (7596), fols. 21ʳff.; and cf. *Cal. State Papers . . . , Venice*, XXVII (1926, repr. 1970), no. 288, pp. 215–16. Niccolò Ludovisi, who had married a niece of Innocent X, was the friend and patron of Gian Lorenzo Bernini, and was responsible for Bernini's receiving the commission to do the famous fountain of the four rivers in the Piazza Navona in Rome (cf. Pastor, *Gesch. d. Päpste*, XIV-1 [1929], 292–98, and *Hist. Popes*, XXX, 402–8).

A detailed report of Girolamo Morosini, provveditore da mar, to the doge Francesco Erizzo, dated at Suda on 10 September 1645, depicts his relations with Prince Ludovisi and "questi altri commandanti di squadre ausiliane," i.e., the generals of Malta, Tuscany, and Naples, and adds the (to Morosini) encouraging news that "dalla Canea si hanno avisi continuati delle debollezze de'Turchi" (ASV, Senato, Provv. da terra e da mar, Filza 932, pages unnumbered). Morosini had learned that "delle 23 galere del regno [di Candia] 15 erano già comparse ben all'ordine di tutto punto, che le altre si alestivano parimenti. . . ."

Morosini also writes, however, "Delli affari del regno ha tenuto con me l'eccellentissimo Cornaro lungo preciso discorso, rappresentandomi specialmente la debolezza di militie, in che sono constituiti tutti li pressidii a segno, che in Candia non vi restino più di 400 fanti da servitio oltre li amalati et feriti usciti dalla Canea et in debolissimo numero le altre guarniggioni! . . ." (*ibid.*, undated dispatch). A discouraging assessment of the Venetians' situation on the island of Crete, dated at Suda on 8 December 1645, among other such gloomy reports, may be found in this "file" (*filza*), with seven signatures attesting to its accuracy.

ter naval operations were suspended for the current year, and preparations were hastened for the clashes which lay ahead.[42]

After some five weeks of ineffectual cooperation the allied commanders bade their Venetian friends good-bye, headed for Messina,
which they reached on 23 October (1645), and thereafter returned their
vessels to their own dockyards. The Venetians seemed no longer to have
a safe haven in the Mediterranean. The Signoria sent troops to the Dalmatian coast and Corfu. Local defenses were strengthened at the Lido
and at Malamocco, and additions made to the fortifications of Candia.
The failure to recover Canea was due as much to disagreement among
the allied leaders as to the impediment of stormy weather. A captain-
general was required of the highest rank, whose authority could not be
questioned or challenged by ambitious competitors. In the Senate the
name of the doge Francesco Erizzo, then eighty years of age, was proposed; the motion was made and carried to ask him to accept command
of the fleet. To the admiration of the Senate, and indeed of all Venice, the
old man accepted the charge.

Giovanni Pesaro, however, advanced grave objections to the doge's
appointment. Inevitable ducal ceremonies would take time and money,
which could be better employed against the Turks. Perhaps the sultan
Ibrahim would also be inspired to assume command of the Turkish armada, which would certainly move the Turks to increased effort. And
what confusion at home and abroad might be caused by the doge's death
at sea? Nevertheless, the appointment was confirmed, and two councilors, Giovanni Cappello and Niccolò Dolfin, were chosen to accompany
the aged doge, *sed homo proponit, disponit Deus*, and Francesco Erizzo
died on 3 January 1646. He was buried in the church of S. Martino (near
the Arsenal in Venice), where his funeral monument may still be seen on
the wall to the right as one enters the church. Two days after Erizzo's
death Giovanni Cappello was elected captain-general of the sea to face
the Turks in the year that lay ahead.[43]

Meanwhile in Istanbul the Turks' successful occupation of Canea was
celebrated for three days and nights. As the weeks passed, however,
some persons of note were removed from office, others received kaftans

---

[42] On the naval armament available in the Arsenale di Venezia in October and November
1645, see *Venezia e la difesa del Levante da Lepanto a Candia, 1570–1670*, Venice,
1986, pp. 56–57.

[43] Cf. Romanin, VII (1974), 259; Kretschmayr, *Gesch. von Venedig*, III (repr. 1964),
321; Senato, Deliberazioni Costantinopoli (Secreta), Reg. 28, fol. 204ᵛ, *al Bailo in Constantinopoli*, dispatch dated 6 January 1646 (Ven. style 1645): "Il dolore di questa gran
perdita [i.e., the doge Erizzo's death] habbiamo procurato mitigare con l'elettione seguita
hieri del dilettissimo nostro Gio. Capello fo di Ser Andrea in capitano general del mare, la
prudenza e la virtù ben conosciuta del quale dovemo sperare secondata dal favor del
Signor Dio a vantaggio della nostra giustissima causa."

of honor and new appointments. The grand vizir Sultanzade Mehmed Pasha, who had become inimical to Yusuf Pasha, was demoted, but his life was spared, and he was later given a military command in the continuing war with Venice for possession of the island of Crete. Yusuf Pasha, the conqueror of Canea, declined the grand vizirate, which was given to the imperial treasurer (*defterdar*) Salih Pasha, a Bosnian by birth, who had risen rapidly in the service of the Porte. Musa Pasha, agha of the janissaries, succeeded Salih as the defterdar. The customary rules of advancement were disregarded throughout the reign of Sultan Ibrahim. Some strange doings at the Porte could be attributed to the intrigues of the harem, but it does seem clear that the able Yusuf brought disaster upon himself with little assistance from his enemies.

Sultan Ibrahim summoned Yusuf Pasha one day, and quite unexpectedly ordered him to go back to Crete with thirty vessels to complete the conquest of the island. Yusuf stated that the needed vessels were in the dockyards. Also it was winter, no time for such an expedition. Ibrahim reviled Yusuf for allowing the Christian garrison to withdraw from Canea with all their possessions. As a good Moslem, he should have destroyed the infidels. Yusuf replied that he had done what he could. It might well be that the sultan could send someone else to Crete who would do better. Becoming quite excited, Ibrahim replied that Yusuf could choose between death and departure for Crete. More of a warrior than a wheedler, Yusuf remonstrated, as von Hammer tells us, "Ah, my Padishah, but you know nothing of maritime ventures. We have no oarsmen. Without oarsmen we cannot run the galleys."

"Accursed fool," yelled Ibrahim, "are you trying to teach me seafaring?" And thereupon he straightway ordered Yusuf's execution. Salih Pasha, the new grand vizir, and Musa Pasha, the new defterdar, both pleaded with the irate sultan to spare Yusuf's life. The latter, who had married a daughter of Ibrahim, addressed a petition to the sultan from prison, asking to be sent to a post somewhere in the empire as a merciful gesture to the "sultana" and the sultan's own grandsons. It was no use. Yusuf Pasha was strangled on 21 January 1646. Such was the mindless, murderous regime of the sultan Ibrahim.[44]

The Venetian Signoria was looking everywhere for money. Three nobles who had made generous contributions to the war fund were created Procuratori di S. Marco. Three large vessels had been prepared at Malamocco to send 400,000 ducats eastward to help support the Venetian fleet. Troops and supplies were also on their way into Levantine waters.

---

[44] Von Hammer-Purgstall, *Gesch. d. osman. Reiches,* V, 383–90, trans. Hellert, X, 102–11. On 10 March 1646 the Venetian Senate addressed conciliatory letters to Sultan Ibrahim and Salih Pasha (Senato, Deliberazioni Costantinopoli [Secreta], Reg. 28, fols. 225^v–227^v), congratulating the latter upon his elevation to the grand vizirate. Poor Salih did not last long (von Hammer, V, 410–11).

The passageways into Friuli had to be guarded. The sultan was said to be coming into the Morea with 200,000 combatants. The Turks were rounding up soldiers in Syria and Asia Minor; they were supposed to be in Istanbul by November (1645). One hoped, however, that the building of warships at the Turkish arsenals was proceeding "slowly enough," because of the scarcity of materials, to frustrate the ambitious plans allegedly being entertained at the Porte. There were problems everywhere, and the Signoria was looking in all directions to find solutions. Owing to illness, Francesco da Molin had been relieved of his command as captain-general of the sea, but now he was elected doge on 20 January 1646.[45]

The Signoria had not been taken entirely unawares by the renewal of war with the Porte. As early as 1639 a levy of 400,000 ducats had been imposed upon the Terraferma; it was to be paid in four six-month installments. Hardly a village was spared, and even a little town like Este (Ateste) in the Veneto, about seventeen miles southwest of Padua, was to pay surprisingly large amounts throughout the entire duration of the Turkish war. Este, the original home of the Estensi of Ferrara-Modena, had been under Venetian domination since 1405, and was to remain so until the end of the Republic.[46]

While the Venetian government was imposing heavy financial levies upon the Terraferma, it was trying vigorously—but without avail—to enlist the military support of the Poles, Muscovites, Persians, Swedes, Danes, and others against the Turks, as well as to engage the naval strength of the Dutch and English to help hold on to the island of Crete. The Turks were well aware of conditions in Europe, and had reason to believe they were choosing the right time to attack Crete. The extent of their naval and military preparations was alarming, as Jean Paul de Lascaris Castellar, the grand master of the Hospitallers, warned the Venetians in Suda Bay in a letter dated at Malta on 10 January 1646. The letter reached Suda in early March.[47]

As the Thirty Years' War went on, the French had secured control over the Rhine. Their Swedish allies were victorious in the northlands. George I Rákóczy (1631–1648) was supreme in Transylvania and, en-

---

[45] Arch. Segr. Vaticano, Cod. Urb. lat. 1110, fols. 16–17[r], *di Roma li 6 Gennaro 1646*, and cf., *ibid.*, fols. 20, 35 [also on the election of the new doge, Francesco da Molin], 43[v]–44[r], 48[r], 51, 56[v]–57[r], 97, and note Cod. Urb. lat. 1111, fol. 157[v], to the effect that "in quel Maggior Conseglio era stato eletto Procuratore di San Marco l'eccellentissimo Signore Gio. Luigi Pisano, che haveva pagato 22 m. scudi . . . ," report from Venice dated 18 May, 1647, relating to still another purchase of a Procuratorship of S. Marco.

[46] Linda Fellini, "Le Contribuzioni di Este a Venezia durante la guerra di Candia," *Nuovo Archivio Veneto*, XXXV (1918), 188–205.

[47] ASV, Senato, Provv. da terra e da mar, Filza 932, pages unnumbered. Lascaris expressed apprehension over "tutti quei grand'apparati che si fanno a Constantinopoli con tanta diligenza et ardore."

couraged by the Swedes and French, had advanced into Hungary.[48] Bohemia, Moravia, and Silesia lay in ruins. Saxony had given way to the Swedes. Bavaria had joined the French. The Empire was wearing away, and Ferdinand III wanted to make peace. The Hapsburgs were the great enemies of the Turks, but Ferdinand was in no position to aid the Venetians, who had never been popular in Vienna. As for France, Cardinal Jules Mazarin was unfriendly to both Venice and the Holy See, for he aspired to some measure of dominance in Italy, and as the only two independent states in the peninsula they were opposed to the French ambition. Poland was a disorganized monarchical republic, and would not be ready to venture out against the Turks for another forty years. No help could possibly be expected from Russia.

Portugal had revolted from Spain (in 1640), put John of Braganza on the throne, and years of warfare lay ahead. Catalonia had also revolted from Spain in 1640. Although the Spanish Hapsburgs, like their Austrian cousins, had long been hostile to the Turks, Philip IV could not help the Venetians. He could not help himself. The only assistance which Spain might have rendered Venice would have been by sea (conceivably to send troops to Crete), but less than a half dozen years before (on 21 October 1639) the Dutch admiral Marten Tromp had almost completely destroyed the Spanish fleet off the coast of England. Spain was never thereafter a significant power at sea. Commercial rivals of the English, at war with Spain, fearful of the increasing greatness of France, the Dutch would not assist the Venetians, who had also been competitors for the eastern trade. And, like the English, the Dutch sometimes rented ships to the Turks. As for England, Charles I was engaged in his fateful struggle with Parliament. Indeed, the bailie Giovanni Soranzo wrote the doge and Senate (on 18 October 1645) that the English "would like the Turks to capture Candia so that they may have free trade there in muscat."[49]

---

[48] Cf. Maja Depner, *Das Fürstentum Siebenbürgen im Kampf gegen Habsburg* (1938), pp. 138ff., and Franz Salamon, *Ungarn im Zeitalter der Türkenherrschaft*, trans. Gustav Jurány, Leipzig, 1887, pp. 340–53.

[49] *Cal. State Papers . . . , Venice*, XXVII (1926, repr. 1970), no. 288, pp. 215–16. Long since disillusioned with the Swedes, Protestant Saxony as well as Catholic Bavaria had returned to the imperial allegiance; despite the then current negotiations at Münster and Osnabrück, central Europe was still in turmoil (cf. Arch. Segr. Vaticano, Cod. Urb. lat. 1109, fols. 35ᵛ–36ʳ, *di Venetia 28 detto [Gennaro] 1645*).

With regard to Giovanni Soranzo's observation that the English "would like the Turks to capture Candia so that they may have free trade there in muscat," an earlier Venetian bailie in Istanbul, Piero Foscarini, had written the doge Francesco Erizzo and the Senate a decade before (on 27 June 1635) "that the English devote their attention to depriving our people of the little trade that remains to them in the mart of Constantinople, as they imitate Venetian cloth and make borders after the Venetian manner. . . . It shows that they are trying to imitate everything and to despoil our merchants of all the trade they have left" (*Cal. State Papers . . . , Venice*, XXIII, no. 500, p. 408). On the extent of the English trade in Istanbul, Aleppo, and Smyrna, see the letter of Anzolo Correr, the Vene-

From whom could Venice hope to receive substantial aid? Only from the pope and the Maltese. After the peace of Westphalia the Venetians could renew their appeals for help to the larger states in Europe but, as may be assumed from what has just been said, little help would be forthcoming for some time.[50] The chief allies of the Signoria would still remain the Holy See and the Maltese.

From well before the early seventeenth century the Republic had been losing its hold even upon families of Venetian origin throughout the island of Crete. As in Cyprus during the later fifteenth and the sixteenth centuries, Catholicism had been dwindling and giving way to Greek Orthodoxy,[51] owing to the constantly diminishing number of Latin priests and the prolonged absences of bishops who much preferred residence in the Veneto or elsewhere in Italy to that on the gloomy island of

---

tian ambassador in England, to the doge and Senate (*ibid.*, no. 553, pp. 461–62, doc. dated 5 October 1635).

As the trade of the Levant Company grew in volume, the English became increasingly interested in the history of the Turks, as shown by the popularity of the works of Richard Knolles (d. 1610), *The generall historie of the Turkes, from the first beginning of that nation to the rising of the Othoman familie. . . . Together with the lives and conquests of the Othoman kings and emperours . . . until this present yeare 1603 . . .* , London: A[dam] Islip, 1603, with various subsequent editions, as well as with revisions and continuations (for the years 1623 to 1699) by Sir Paul Rycaut (d. 1700), who wrote *The Present State of the Ottoman Empire. Containing the maxims of the Turkish politie . . .* , London: J. Starkey and H. Brome, 1668, with subsequent editions in English, French, Italian, German, Dutch, and other languages. The first edition of Rycaut's work was published in 1666–67, but almost all copies were destroyed in the "fire of London." On Rycaut (pronounced Rye-court) see the excellent study by Sonia P. Anderson, *An English Consul in Turkey: Paul Rycaut at Smyrna, 1667–1678*, Clarendon Press, London, 1989. A convenient abridgment of the works of both Knolles and Rycaut was published by John Savage, 2 vols., London, 1701.

Although Samuel Johnson, Henry Hallam, Robert Southey, and Lord Byron admired Knolles' *Historie of the Turkes*, the work is of little or no historical value. While Dudley North (d. 1691), treasurer of the Levant Company, was highly critical of the work of Rycaut who, like North, spent years in the Levant, the *Present State of the Ottoman Empire* is still useful.

Certain aspects of the Turco-Venetian war for possession of the island of Crete (1645–1669) as well as a survey of conditions in virtually all Europe may be studied in the sources covered in the *Calendar of State Papers and Manuscripts, relating to English Affairs, existing in the Archives and Collections of Venice, and in other Libraries of Northern Italy*, vols. XXVII–XXXVI, repr. Nendeln/Liechtenstein, 1970.

[50] There were apparently offers of assistance from Odoardo Farnese, the duke of Parma, as well as from Luigi d'Este and others, but the Italian princelings required funds to support their recruits. Note the *avviso* in the Arch. Segr. Vaticano, Cod. Urb. lat. 1109 [1644–1645], fols. 77ᵛ–78, *di Roma 18 Marzo 1645:* "Le lettere di Venetia danno avviso che il Serenissimo di Parma si era offerto d'andare al servitio di quella repubblica con 3,000 fanti, che il Signor Principe Don Luigi d'Este faceva levata di 2,000 combattenti, e mille il marchese Malatesta, che detta republica haveva fatto cavare dall'Arsenale due galeazze quali con altri vascelli sarebbono andate in Candia. . . ." The Turkish peril and the threats coming from Istanbul had spread alarm throughout the Italian states and the island of Malta (cf., *ibid.*, fols. 35ᵛ–36, 52ᵛ–53, 59ᵛ–60, 68, 217–218ᵛ, *et alibi*).

[51] Cf. Setton, *The Papacy and the Levant*, IV, 756–58.

Crete. So-called Latins had long been attending services conducted by priests of the Greek rite. No few young women of families with Venetian names had been entering Greek nunneries as they turned to fathers from the Byzantine past to receive the sacraments.

In a report which Leonardo Mocenigo, archbishop of Candia (1633–1644), made to Pope Urban VIII (in 1637), he noted that every year Christians were furtively giving way to the tyranny of the Turks. His description of the state of the church in Candia, i.e., in Crete, was gloomy. In his archiepiscopal church there were fifteen canonical prebends which brought their holders slender incomes (*fructus tenues*). In Candia there were three nunneries (*monialium coenobia*), of which the most important was the Dominican convent of S. Caterina, where there were twenty-seven veiled nuns, four novices, four converts, and two secular sisters who served the others. They had an ample church, which was well equipped. The nuns were all from families of Venetian origin, following "the Roman rite under the rule of S. Dominic," although their language was demotic Greek, and they could neither read nor refer to religious books in Latin or Italian (*earum licet graeca sit vernacula lingua, et nullis possint vel latinis vel italicis spiritualibus libris . . . excitari. . .*). Mocenigo was doing his best, his very best, to improve the sad situation, "but the lack of clergy renders everything extremely difficult."[52]

Gian Francesco Gozzadini, who became bishop of Retimo (Réthymnon) in August 1641,[53] was presumably well informed on conditions in the Greek islands. He had been born at Naxos, which the Turks had taken over in 1566.[54] Two years after his accession to the cathedra of Retimo, Gozzadini prepared a report for a congregation of cardinals (in 1643) relating to the problems he faced as bishop of the see on the northern shore of Crete. The diocese of Retimo, he wrote, contained some two thousand families or "hearths" (*focularia*), and embraced a circuit of twenty-five miles. The Latin and Greek rites were confusedly mixed up in Retimo, as elsewhere, but the "Latin souls do not exceed the number of two hundred."

There were six canons with prebends in the cathedral church, but their total revenues did not exceed eighty Venetian ducats a year, except for the treasurer, who received forty ducats, and the archdeacon,

---

[52] Marco Petta, "La Chiesa latina di Creta negli ultimi anni del dominio veneto," *Bolletino della Badia greca di Grottaferrata*, n.s., XXII (1968), 20ff., 22, 23, 28–29, with nine well-chosen documents from the Archivio della S. Congregazione di Propaganda Fide. I have depended much more on the documents than on Petta's text. On Leonardo (or Luigi) Mocenigo, cf. C. Eubel and P. Gauchat, *Hierarchia catholica medii et recentioris aevi*, IV (1935), 168.

[53] Eubel-Gauchat, *Hierarchia*, IV, 295.

[54] Cf. Setton, IV, 850, 898–99.

whose annual income was thirty ducats. In the coastal city of Retimo these sums did not go very far. In fact the receipts of the entire diocese did not exceed the sum of one thousand Venetian ducats, a certain portion of which went to Venice and to Rome as a papal tithe.

In Retimo there were two Franciscan convents and a third belonging to the Augustinians "with, however, but a small number of friars in each one of them." The failure of the descendants of Venetian families to preserve their ancestral language was the trouble. The Latin priesthood had not thrived in Crete. "For the conservation of the Latin rite . . . no priest is to be found anywhere in the diocese [of Retimo]; therefore many Latins, abandoning their rite, hasten off to the Greek; and in the city the women are especially lured away for various reasons by the Greek monks [καλόγηροι] of the Order of S. Basil, residents as well as missionaries."[55]

In 1659, ten years before the Turkish occupation of Candia, Giovanni Querini, archbishop of the primatial see (1644–1669),[56] prepared another report as a sequel to that of his predecessor Leonardo Mocenigo. As Latins and Greeks used each others' churches, there was now peace between them, although of course the Greek had by and large replaced the Latin rite. It was not surprising that when Querini made a formal visit to his archdiocese (on 16 October 1659), his formal entry was marked by a turnout of cavalry and footsoldiers as well as "con li cleri latino et greco in habiti sacerdotali." He had obviously not established his permanent residence at Candia.

In the cathedral church there was an altar of the Ten Martyrs, who were held in great veneration by both Greeks and Latins, for it was widely believed that heresy had never entered the "kingdom" of Crete because of the intercession of the Martyrs. Also, while Candia was in grave danger of falling into the hands of the Turks, there were those who believed they had seen the Martyrs combating the enemy "in their white habit, upon the walls with a great slaughter of the enemy."

There were of course signs of Latin ecclesiastical decline everywhere. There should have been fourteen canons in the cathedral church, but now there were no more than five. Once there had been a hundred friars in the seven monasteries at Candia; in 1659, however, there were only thirty, "parte di loro inutili come d'Agostiniani e parte de molto scandalosi come de' Dominicani!" Many years before, "in times of peace," there had been four thousand adherents to the Latin rite. Now there were only about five hundred. In the happy days of yore there had been more than twenty thousand "souls of the Greek rite," but as Querini wrote (in 1659) their total had been reduced to about ten thousand.

---

[55] Petta, *art. cit.*, pp. 5, 33–34, 35.
[56] Eubel-Gauchat, *Hierarchia*, IV, 168.

To be sure, in the Venetian fortress at Spinalonga, fifty miles to the east of Candia, there was a Latin garrison where, according to Querini, the local church was being maintained by the soldiery "with much devotion."[57] Although one may well wonder how much, if anything, devotion had to do with it all, the fact remains that when the Turks finally took possession of Candia, Spinalonga remained (along with the coastal fortresses of Grabusa and Suda) in Venetian hands.

---

[57] Petta, *art. cit.*, pp. 5, 45, 47, 48–49, 50–51.

V

The Turco-Venetian War (1646–1653) and the Turmoil in Istanbul

⌒

The resources of the Turks seemed limitless (they were not), and the Venetians never ceased looking everywhere for money. Interest on loans was running at seven percent, which seemed high for the times. New taxes and imposts were levied. Young men of the patriciate were admitted to the Maggior Consiglio in disregard of the traditional requirement of age. Offices might be purchased at a price. It was also proposed that Venetian citizens or subjects who would make available a thousand soldiers for active duty for a year at the cost of 60,000 ducats would be received into the nobility. Their names would be inscribed in the Libro d'Oro, the register of the nobility, and so would the names of their legitimate descendants to the extent of five families. Outsiders would also be taken into the nobility, under the same terms, at the cost of 70,000 ducats to hire twelve hundred infantry for an entire year. The Avogadori di Comun, the wardens of the state, kept track of the Golden Book and of young nobles' entry into the Maggior Consiglio at the (usual) age of twenty-five.

Angelo Michiel, an avogadore di comune, objected strenuously to the degrading device of ennobling commoners merely to gain money which he said would do little to relieve the plight of the Republic. The ducal councilor Giacomo Marcello defended the proposal. Fatuous pride must not be allowed to endanger the state. Mercenaries must be hired, and the fleet reinforced. It would be more helpful than harmful if one increased

137

the manpower of the nobility, for the holding of an important post should not be the patrimony of birth, but rather one of the rewards of virtue and valor. The motion was approved in the Senate.

Nevertheless, on 4 March 1646 in the Maggior Consiglio, the supreme conciliar authority, the motion received only 368 affirmative votes (*de parte*) as opposed to 528 negative votes (*de non*), with 140 uncommitted votes (*non sinceri*), and so the motion did not pass.[1] Later on, however, it did, and non-noble families were soon enrolled in the patriciate (some ninety from 1646 to 1669), paying a minimum of 60,000 to 70,000 ducats to have their names inscribed in the Golden Book. There was no general decree of ennoblement; the concession was requested, and was granted to appropriate individuals. With the letters N. H. prefixed to their names (*nobilis homo, nobil huomo*), those newly added to the noblesse now found important offices of state and naval commands open to them. The wonder is not that there were those who aspired to noble rank, but that so many persons should have amassed private fortunes of such size. Full payment was supposed to be made within one month but, if necessary, one might pay one-half to start with, and the balance within two months. Candidates for the nobility had to present to the Avogaria di Comun proofs that their fathers and grandfathers had never practiced the "mechanical arts," and that they were "all born of legitimate marriage." The first families thus ennobled (from 22 July to 28 August 1646) were the Labbia, Widman, Gozzi, Ottoboni, Rubin, and Zaguri.[2] Within the next year or two the scions of such families were being given commands at sea.[3]

Very soon after these ennoblements Marforio met Pasquino on the

---

[1] Arch. di Stato di Venezia, Deliberazioni del Maggior Consiglio [Marcus], Reg. 39, fols. 161–162 [179–180].

[2] Bibl. Nazionale Marciana, MS. It. VII, 948 (8958), 232 pp. in MS., giving the ennoblement of some ninety families from 1646 to 1669. Cf. Battista Nani, *Historia della repubblica veneta*, II (1686), 72–74; Romanin, VII (1974), 260–63; H. Kretschmayr, *Gesch. von Venedig*, III (1934, repr. 1964), 375–76. The Marciana has numerous MSS. listing the "aggregazioni di famiglie alla nobiltà veneta," especially for the Cretan and Moreote wars, but also for the Veneto-Genoese war of Chioggia (in 1381)—MSS. Marc. It. VII, 626 (8047), 682 (7891), 683 (7892), 724 (7903), 942 (9014), 945 (7962), 946 (7697), 947 (7429), 948 (8958), 949 (7908), 1539 (7641), and 2470 (10,292). On the "aggregations," note also Jean Georgelin, *Venise au siècle des lumières*, Paris and The Hague, 1978, pp. 623ff., and on the divisions among the social classes in Venice (*nobili, cittadini*, and *popolani*), *ibid.*, pp. 619ff., 684ff.
The number of such MSS. is testimony to the interest and excitement the ennoblements caused. In 1381 thirty citizens had had their names inscribed in the so-called Golden Book as nobles, in payment of their services in defense of Venice against the Genoese, the Carraresi, and the Hungarians (Setton, *The Papacy and the Levant*, I [1976], 322–23).

[3] Arch. Segr. Vaticano, Cod. Urb. lat. 1111, fol. 395ᵛ, *di Roma 28 Decembre 1647:* "Le lettere di Venetia in particolari delli 21 'stante danno avviso che quella Republica haveva eletto 20 nuovi governatori di galere sottili, tra quali il Signor Martino Vidman, Andrea Tasta, Marc'Antonio Ottobono, e Gabriele Gozzi. . . ."

road to Venice; the latter was on his way to get himself made a nobleman. Marforio asked various questions, and Pasquino answered him with some entertaining puns on the family names of all the first new nobles.[4] A source of entertainment to the satirists, the ennoblements created an enduring resentment among some of the older patriciate, who remained unreconciled to the new members of the *nobiltà* until well into the nineteenth century. Although there was need of increased manpower at the level of the patriciate to provide for this office or that command, during a good part of the year 1646 the Senate hoped that French mediation might make peace with the Turks possible, especially "per la mutatione del visir," but nothing came of the French intervention.[5]

With the advent of spring the Venetians attempted a blockade of the Dardanelles to prevent the Turkish armada from putting to sea and to cause the Turks as much annoyance as possible by cutting off the delivery of foodstuffs to the capital. Girolamo Morosini, the provveditore generale da mar, gave the task to his relative Tommaso Morosini, who set out from Suda Bay (*Órmos Soúdhas*) in western Crete on 20 March (1646) with twenty-three ships, exacting heavy tolls from the Turkish islands as he sailed toward Istanbul. Morosini tried to establish a footing on the Turkish island of Tenedos, but did not succeed, losing his lieutenant Lorenzo Venier and some two hundred men when their ship caught fire and exploded. Sultan Ibrahim was incensed by the Venetian blockade impeding the departure of his armada to pursue the conquest of Crete. The new kapudan pasha, Musa, and Mehmed Sultanzade, the former grand vizir, were in command of the sultan's naval armament. Moved by Ibrahim's threat, they tried to leave the Dardanelles with some seventy-five galleys and five galleasses (on 26 May), but Tommaso Morosini launched an attack upon them with only part of the Venetian fleet, and after seven hours of continuous fighting drove them back into the cover of the Sea of Marmara.[6]

Nine days later, on 4 June, the Turkish armada, now with sixty galleys and four galleasses, emerged from the Dardanelles on a calm sea. As the

---

[4] MS. Marc. It. VII, 948 (8958), fol. 232ᵛ.

[5] Senato, Deliberazioni Costantinopoli (Secreta), Reg. 28, fols. 206ᵛff., 223ff., 239ᵛff., 243ʳ, 245ʳ, 254. *et alibi.*

[6] Senato, Deliberazioni Costantinopoli (Secreta), Reg. 28, fol. 242ᵛ, doc. dated 21 June 1646: "In lettere del Capitan de Galeoni Moresini scritte al Capitan Generale [Cappello] habbiamo che sia seguito combattimento per lo spacio d'hore sette continue tra parte de nostri vasselli e l'armata nemica, la quale in fine convenne darsi con danno alla retirata. . . ." A few Turkish galleys did escape Morosini, and went on to Chios (Anderson, *Naval Wars in the Levant*, p. 126). Cf. Mormori, *Guerra di Candia*, MS. Marc. It. VII, 1563 (7596), fols. 29ᵛff., also Arch. Segr. Vaticano, Cod. Urb. lat. 1110, fols. 174–175ʳ, and cf. fols. 181ᵛ–182ᵛ, 188ᵛ–189ʳ, 208ᵛ, 268–69. Further documentation may be found in the Senato, Provveditori da terra e da mar, Filza 932: *Proveditor generale Girolamo Morosini,* from 20 August 1645 to 16 March 1646.

oarsmen rowed vigorously, and the Turkish galleys helped tow the galleasses, Tommaso Morosini could neither prevent their exit nor pursue them, for his square-rigged sailing ships were almost immobilized by the lack of wind. Morosini followed them as best he could to protect the Venetian island of Tenos. The Turkish armada made its way to Chios, where it was reinforced by vessels from the Barbary coast, and sailed on to Canea with heavily armed troops and abundant provisions. The Venetian captain-general of the sea, Giovanni Cappello, although within range of the Turks, as they approached Crete, apparently did not dare to attack them. He was an old man, then seventy-three years of age, timid and fearful of suffering defeat. Musa Pasha's fellow commander, Mehmed Sultanzade Pasha, died of a fever two months after his arrival at Crete.[7]

Old Giovanni Cappello's performance had been far from commendable. Attending to personal affairs of small importance apparently, he did not sail from Venice until 25 March (1646); his voyage to Suda, where he arrived on 21 June, took even longer than his departure. He lamented the strong winds that held him back and the epidemic aboard his fleet, the usual typhus fever. He was said, however, to have wasted a good deal of time inspecting fortifications and taking stock of the garrisons as he made his way to Crete. Cappello complained that now the wind failed the fleet entirely. The ships could not keep up with the galleys, and then violent storms kept him confined in ports along the way. Insecure within himself, Cappello could not reach a decision to take action against the Turks, but he was not alone at fault, for the other commanders of the fleet were at frequent odds with Andrea Corner, the provveditore generale of Candia. The orders which the Signoria sent Cappello were sometimes vague,[8] sometimes inconsistent with previous

---

[7] Von Hammer-Purgstall, *Gesch. d. osman. Reiches,* V (1829, repr. 1963), 400ff., trans. Hellert, X, 123ff.; Romanin, VII (1974), 263ff.; Mormori, *Guerra di Candia,* MS. Marc. It. VII, 1563 (7596), fol. 31ʳ.

[8] As for the vagueness of various instructions which Cappello did receive from the Signoria, the doge and Senate observed to the bailie Soranzo in a dispatch of 24 May 1646 (Senato, Deliberazioni Costantinopoli [Secreta], Reg. 28, fol. 239ʳ): "E perchè per la distanza de luoghi e per la varietà delli accidenti, non è conveniente o possibile prescrivere certa regola, con la quale si possano senza alteratione maneggiare negocii di così alte conseguenze, rimettemo alla virtù vostra dell' incontrare quelle aperture che se vi andassero scoprendo, lassandovi in libertà nel farlo e nel tempo e modo dell' esseguirlo. . . ." If changing circumstances made it necessary for Soranzo to use his own judgment in seeking to deal with the Turks rather than to adhere to a "certa regola," it was even more incumbent upon Cappello to do so as he maneuvered with the Turks at sea.

We are kept abreast of the news by an interesting *avviso* in the Arch. Segr. Vaticano. Cod. Urb. lat. 1110, fols. 112–113ʳ, *di Roma li 7 Aprile 1646:* "Le lettere particolari di Venetia delli 31 passato danno avviso che si era inteso il passaggio che haveva fatto il generalissimo Cappello per li mari d'Istria, navigando con una buona squadra di galere verso Corfu. Che conoscendosi il pericolo che poteva un giorno apportare a quella città il taglio che per le fortificationi si faceva al Lido mentre nelle burasche haverebbe il mare potuto rompere gl'argini et estendersi per quelle lagune con gran danno dell'istessa città era stato sospeso l'ordine di lavorarle più. Che il Prencipe D. Luigi d'Este era ritornato da

instructions. The crews of the ships and galleys were laid waste with the plague and incensed by the arrears in their wages.

After the failure of an attack upon the Turks ensconced in Canea Bay in mid-August (1646), Cappello was no more successful in trying to stop a Turkish convoy carrying munitions from Nauplia to Canea (in September). Thereafter he undertook to break the Turkish blockade of Retimo (*Réthymnon*), but received no help from Corner, who wanted him to keep the Turks out of Suda Bay. As a consequence, therefore, the Turks took the town of Retimo on 20 October and the castello on 13 November (1646). Cappello was soon removed from his command, being replaced by Giovanni Battista Grimani, to whom he surrendered the fleet on 18 February 1647. Going on to Corfu, Cappello had to wait until late May for a ship to take him to Venice, where he was imprisoned for mismanagement of the fleet, but he was soon absolved of the charge on the grounds that the plague had done more damage than he had.[9]

The Venetians had received but slight assistance against the Turks, i.e., only the six Maltese galleys plus five provided by Pope Innocent X.

Modena e si diceva sarebbe andato in Friuli per essercitare la carica di generale della cavalleria.

"Che ivi era comparsa una fregata dal Zante con lettere dell'armata veneta in confirmatione del soccorso entrato nella Canea, dove erano state sbarcate 4 m. stara di grano, et che una saicca Turchesca restata indietro fosse stata presa da vascelli veneti. Che della galeazza Cornara, la quale per burasca di mare si era separata dall'altre senza sapersi dove fosse andata, si era poi inteso si fosse salvata al Cerigo. Che per il grand'adunamento dell'armi che si fa nella Bossina si scopriva li disegni del Turcho essere d'invadere per la parte di terra la Dalmatia et attaccare Zara, la cui città veniva però proveduta d'ogni cosa necessaria. Et tanto più si accresceva il sospetto, vedendosi havere il Bassà di Buda levato molti pezzi di cannoni da diversi luoghi. Et che anco nel Friuli si temeva di qualche invasione de Tartari per essersi saputo che un chiaus era stato mandato al Prencipe Ragozzi a chiedere il passo in nome di essi Tartari per la Transilvania, Ungheria, Croatia, et di là nel Friuli.

"Soggiongono le medesime lettere che in Venetia fossero gionte lettere di Constantinopoli, per le quali si era intesa l'allegrezza che havevano li Turchi havuta del soccorso entrato nella Canea. Che prima il Turcho pareva desse orecchie a qualche trattato all'accomodamento, ma che dopo la nuova del socorso della Canea si era assai insuperbito. Che se bene esso Turcho si portava spesso nell'Arsenale per sollecitare la fabrica delle galere, nondimeno per quest'anno non haveria messo insieme più di 140 galere, delle quali dovendone mandare un numero nel Mar Nero, sarebbe riuscita più debole di quella da venire nel Mar Bianco, e però si credeva che haverebbe atteso solo al mantenimento della Canea con risolutione di non venire a battaglia e di procurare per terra la diversione dell'armi de Signori veneti," and note, *ibid.*, fols. 125^r, 127–128^r, 136, 143^v–144^r, 157^v–158, 165^v–166, 174–175^r, 277–278^r.

[9] On the loss of Retimo, cf. Senato, Deliberazioni Costantinopoli (Secreta), Reg. 28, fols. 256^v–257^r, doc. dated 8 January 1647 (Ven. style 1646); von Hammer-Purgstall, *Gesch. d. osman. Reiches*, V, 402–3, trans. Hellert, X, 126–27; Kretschmayr, *Gesch. von Venedig*, III, 322; Anderson, *Naval Wars in the Levant*, pp. 126–30; Mormori, *Guerra di Candia*, MS. Marc. It. VII, 1563 (7596), fols. 33^r–34^v, 37^{r}ff.; and note the letter of the Turkish commander at Retimo to the Greeks of the city of Candia, offering them freedom (if they assist in the surrender of Candia) and slavery (if they do not), *Raccolta diplomatica della guerra di Candia*, MS. Marc. It. VII, 211 (7468), fol. 102. On Giovanni Cappello's career, see G. Benzoni, in the *Dizionario biografico degli Italiani*, XVIII (1975), 783–86. Cappello died at eighty on 21 December 1653.

For some time Cardinal Jules Mazarin, the prime minister in France, had been promoting intrigue and causing unrest in the Spanish kingdom of Naples. In May 1646 a French fleet had occupied the ports of Talamone and S. Stefano, and tried to take Orbetello on the Tyrrhenian shore of the Tuscan Archipelago; thereafter another fleet seized Piombino, where the French remained for some four years (1646–1650).[10] As Mazarin sought a foothold in Italy, the grand duke of Tuscany, Ferdinand II, became alarmed. He had sent five galleys against the Turks the year before, and so had the Spanish authorities in Naples. In 1646, however, neither Ferdinand nor the Spanish sent any galleys at all.[11]

Current reports regularly brought bad news. According to an *avviso* of 21 July (1646), a special courier sent from Venice to Alvise Contarini, then the Republic's ambassador in Rome,[12] had arrived posthaste with word that the Turks had captured the fortress of Novigrad fifteen miles northeast of Zara (Zadar). Having left a sizable garrison at Novigrad on the Dalmatian coast, the Turks had set out for Spalato (Split) "per impadronirsi di quella città come metropoli della Dalmatia." Contarini had immediately sought an audience with the pope. Novigrad had fallen on 4 July. Its capture was all the more distressing, because it had been regarded as "almost impregnable." On 30 June the Turks had encamped under the walls of the fortress; on 2 July they had put one heavy and two lighter cannon in place; and after one day of bombardment the Venetian commanders were ready to discuss the terms of surrender.

The inhabitants of the village of Novigrad, who had obviously taken refuge within the walls, were prepared to defend the fortress. But the commanders had allowed a Turk to come into the fortress, and had sent out a Venetian captain, to negotiate with the pasha, who promised the besieged generous terms. The pasha sent the commanders a caftan of cloth of gold as a pledge of his good faith. By about 11:00 A.M. of the sixth day of the siege Turks were being admitted, most unexpectedly, within the walls to the distress and confusion of the garrison, which had wanted to resist. No sooner, indeed, did the Turks get into the fortress than the pasha ordered the seizure and execution of allegedly some eight

---

[10] On the French occupation of Talamone, S. Stefano, Piombino, and the failure at Orbetello, note Pastor, *Gesch. d. Päpste*, XIV-1 (1929), 48–49, and *Hist. Popes*, XXX, 60–61. Since Innocent X had given way to Mazarin, and pardoned the Barberini family for peculation, Niccolò Ludovisi was allowed to retain Piombino under French suzerainty.

[11] Cf. Senato, Deliberazioni Costantinopoli (Secreta), Reg. 28, fol. 237ʳ, a dispatch dated 24 May 1646 from the doge and Senate to the bailie Soranzo in Istanbul: "Le galee del Papa e di Malta già si sono mosse per unirsi et incaminarsi verso Levante. Quelle di Spagna e Fiorenza [i.e., of Ferdinand II] sospese ancora per la sopravenienza in Italia dell'armi Francesi . . . ," and cf., *ibid.*, fols. 241ᵛ–242ʳ, 247ᵛ.

[12] On this Alvise Contarini, Venetian ambassador to the Holy See from 1645 to the spring of 1648 (and obviously not the Republic's emissary in Westphalia), see G. Benzoni, in the *Dizionario biografico degli Italiani*, XXVIII (1983), 91–97.

hundred persons—soldiers and peasants—whose heads were cut off one by one "with barbarous savagery." A few persons managed to escape. The Turks had promised to allow everyone to go free.

The lives of the commanders were spared, according to the report, and so were those of the bombardiers and the surgeons. Thus the Turks had acquired another *point de départ* for an attack upon the Italian coast or some other enterprise on the Adriatic. They now possessed all the Dalmatian countryside up to Zara, having already taken the important islands of Veglia (Krk) and Cherso (Cres) as well as that of Pag and other places roundabout. Their recent success had netted them eight large cannon, fourteen small cannon, arms and munitions of all sorts, and of course an increased capacity to impede Venetian vessels taking aid to the Republic's Levantine ports.[13]

---

[13] Cod. Urb. lat. 1110, fol. 227^r, *di Roma li 21 Luglio 1646:* "Gionse quà sabbato sera un corriere straordinario di Venetia spedito a questo signor ambasciatore di quella Republica, quale la mattina seguente fu all'audienza di Nostro Signore, dandoli parte come il Turco per via di assalti si era impadronito di Novegradi, fortezza posta su la marina 7 miglia lontana da Zara, e che dopo haver' lasciato un sofficiente presidio per difesa di quella piazza si era incaminato alla volta di Spalato per impadronirsi di quella città come metropoli della Dalmatia."

A dispatch from Venice, dated 14 July (*ibid.,* fols. 228^{v}ff.), correctly locates "la fortezza di Novegradi lontana 15 e non 7 miglia da Zara," and notes that "resa quasi inespugnabile dalla qualità del sito tanto più grave riesce il dispiacere della sua miserabile caduta alli 4 del corrente in mano de Turchi, quali il sabbato ultimo del passato [30 June] vi si accamporono sotto con l'essercito, et il lunedì seguente [2 July] vi piantorono tre cannoni, il maggiore da 50 et gli altri due da 14, e dopo haverla cannonata per un giorno intiero senza far freccia di sorte alcuna, il Conte Soardo Bresciano, commandante delle armi, che si haveva in gran concetto di valoroso soldato et il podestà o proveditore Loredano cominciorono contro il volere delli habitanti, che si volevano defendere coragiosamente, a trattare del modo di rendersi, essendo stato a questo effetto introdotto dentro un Turco e mandato fuori un capitano a negotiare con il Bassà, che prometteva larghi partiti. Questi rimandasse dentro una vesta d'oro in pegno della sua fede, onde alle 14 hore [11:00 A.M.] del sesto giorno dell'assedio furono quasi improvisamente introdotti li Turchi per la porta del soccorso con molta confusione del presidio, che voleva fare resistenza.

"Entrati li Turchi, il Bassà fece condur' fuori della fortezza in una villa vicina tutto il presidio di 800 [written over '400'] persone tra soldati stipendiati et alcuni paesani, a quali fece ad uno ad uno con barbara ferità tagliare la testa, salvandosi alcuni pochi con la fuga con altri delli borghi sopra di certe barchette, restandone molti annegati per la fretta di salvarsi dalle mani di quei barbari, che sul principio havevano fatto larghe promesse di lasciare ogniuno in libertà. Furono poi salvate le persone del Conte Soardo e Loredano, delli bombardieri e chirurgi, altri dicono di 3 capitani che sono restati prigionieri de Turchi.

"La perdita di questo luogo riesce per diverse circostanze di grandissima consideratione, restando aperto a Turchi più vicino all'Italia un'altro buon porto nel Golfo [the Adriatic], dove per la commodità de legnami vicini possono tenere un'arsenale. Restano similmente padroni di tutta la campagna sino a Zara, sottoposte alle loro invasioni l'isole di Veglia, Pago, Cherzo, et altre convicine oltre l'havervi acquistato 8 pezzi di cannoni, 14 petriere, gran quantità d'arme d'ogni sorte e monitione, e potere con maggior facilità infestare il transito de nostri legni per il soccorso di Levante . . ." (fols. 228^v–229^v, and cf. fols. 237–38, 261^v–262, 324^v–325^r, 353^v–354^r). The Turks were also exerting themselves to take the fortress town of Suda on the island of Crete (fols. 298, 301, 306–307^r, 339^r). References to the seriousness of the loss of Novigrad continue to appear in dispatches of

According to a dispatch from Venice of 12 January 1647, as reported in Rome a week later, the Signoria had imposed new taxes to raise the funds necessary to send more troops to Candia, "seeing that every day things were going from bad to worse, lessening their hopes of being able any longer to defend themselves against the Turkish forces." Soldiers were dying on the island for lack of adequate food and clothing. The Signoria had, therefore, had four large vessels put in order, loaded with ship's biscuit, 200,000 scudi, and 4,000 soldiers to send to Crete.[14]

Another dispatch from Rome dated 19 January (1647), citing an *av-viso* from Venice (also of a week before), contained information from Dalmatia to the effect that [after the Turkish success at Novigrad] the Gran Turco had sent a chavush to the pashas of Clissa (Klis) and Buda with a dire warning. If within four months they had not besieged and taken the Venetian stronghold at Zara, he would remove them from their posts, and cut off their heads. The Turks were said to have 30,000 troops ready for action, with which they apparently planned to attack Spalato. To meet such a challenge the Signoria was apparently able to do no better than send off two thousand soldiers with munitions and provisions to the threatened area.[15] Zara and Spalato were strong fortresses, but they were clearly in danger.

The Curia Romana followed the exploits of the Turks with no less apprehension than did the Venetian Signoria. The Curia, however, had trouble in the West as well as in the East. As the ambassador Alvise Contarini wrote the doge and Senate, while Innocent was concerned that "Christendom is oppressed by the Turks and the heretics," the Scots and English had united to subdue the "Catholic kingdom" of Ireland.[16] Contarini was hoping for more assistance from the Holy See than the Republic had received in 1646, but Innocent could be depended upon to do what his slender resources would allow. In any event, as the year came to an end, the pope granted the Venetians permission to recruit "another thousand soldiers in the papal states for service in the war against the Turk."[17] From Spain no help could be expected when the Neapolitans

---

the time (ee.g., Cod. Urb. lat. 1111, fol. 44, citing a report from Venice dated 2 February 1647, and fol. 118ᵛ, another report from Venice dated 13 April), and on the surrender of Novigrad, note Girolamo Brusoni, *Historia dell'ultima guerra tra Veneziani e Turchi, nella quale si contengono i successi delle passate guerre nei regni di Candia e Dalmazia dall'anno 1644 fino al 1671* . . . , 2 vols., Venice, 1673, I, bk. v, pp. 100–4. Brusoni's work is a detailed year-by-year account of the Turco-Venetian war, with the inclusion of some of the pamphlet literature of the time.

[14] Cod. Urb. lat. 1111, fol. 20, from an *avviso di Roma li 19 Gennaio 1647*, and cf., *ibid.*, fols. 75, 130.

[15] Cod. Urb. lat. 1111, fols. 20ᵛ–21ʳ, *di Roma li 19 Gennaio 1647*, and on the Turkish threat to Spalato, note, *ibid.*, fols. 52ᵛ, 67ᵛ.

[16] *Cal. State Papers* . . . , *Venice*, XXVII, nos. 430, 487, pp. 282, 305, docs. dated 6 October, 1646, and 9 March, 1647.

[17] Arch. Segr. Vaticano, Cod. Urb. lat. 1110, fol. 389ᵛ, *di Roma li 15 Decembre 1646*.

rose in revolt in 1646–1648,[18] and Mazarin preferred to use French naval forces to harry the Spanish rather than to aid Venice against the Turks.

By the beginning of the year 1647, as hopes were rising at Münster and Osnabrück that the Thirty Years' War might indeed be coming to an end, the Venetian Senate was looking toward a change of fortune, a possible union of the Christian princes, which would moderate the Turks' ambition.[19] But rather than continued warfare with the Turks and the conceivable defeat of the Porte, the Venetians wanted (as the Senate reminded Giovanni Soranzo) the reestablishment of peace and a resumption of the Turkish trade.[20] In the meantime the war dragged on in Piedmont and the Milanese, in Flanders and Germany, but there was a slackening of momentum. The Venetian Signoria sent out the usual appeals to the princes. One must defend Candia, the Dalmatian coast, the Adriatic islands, and the cities and towns in Friuli. While in the northlands the Austrians must try to put a stop to the Turkish *Drang nach Westen,* the Venetians had to keep watch on almost fifteen hundred miles of borderland with the Ottoman empire. If Candia should fall, the barrier would be breached. Always eager to extend their sway, always covetous of territory, the Turks would attack the Italian peninsula. The safety of Europe, the well-being of Christendom were at stake. Such at least was the Venetian claim.

The year 1647 began with a dramatic encounter between the Turks and the Venetians. Toward the end of December Gianbattista Grimani, now the captain-general, had moved into the Cyclades with some twenty galleys, three galleasses, and fifteen ships. On 3 January the Venetian fleet met up with two ships from Barbary on the way to Algiers from the

---

[18] J.V. Polišenský, *The Thirty Years' War* (1971), pp. 241–42, has placed the Neapolitan revolt in the background of the war of 1618–1648.

[19] Word was current, however, that the sultan had ordered that almost all his troops be ready for service by the spring of 1647, and that the arsenals produce more "galleys and other ships"—"il tutto per mandare contro Christiani" (Cod. Urb. lat. 1110, fol. 388, *di Venetia 1 Decembre 1646*).

[20] Senato, Deliberazioni Costantinopoli (Secreta), Reg. 28, fol. 255, a dispatch of 8 January 1647 (Ven. style 1646) from the doge and Senate to the bailie Soranzo in Istanbul: "La fortuna pure, che sempre varia et gira il suo corso, potrebbe con l'assistenza del Signor Dio portare una volta qualche respiro alle nostre armi con alcun buon successo che potria rendere le loro pretensioni più moderate. Tanto più che la pace universale si trova vicinissima alla conclusione con speranze anco d'aiuti considerabili, come vedrete dell' aggionte copie de capitoli in lettere delli ambasciatori nostri de Münster e Francia, per la quale gran stima potrebbe far la Porta dell' unione de Principi, et più vigorose sarebbero le nostre forze, le quali ogni giorno si vanno accrescendo per renderle sempre più valide e sussistenti.

"Tuttavia, se bene considerabili siano le promesse e con tant' altre considerationi ben note alla vostra prudenza, potrete però dire esser noi portati da un' special desiderio di voler la pace col Re [i.e., Sultan Ibrahim] et restabilire la quiete con la più cordiale et amorevole corrispondenza tra sudditi dell' una et l'altra parte. . . ."

island of Chios. The Venetian galleasses attacked the two Moslem ships, the crews of which sought refuge on the island of Kea (Zea), but were captured three weeks later. On 8 January the Turkish commander-in-chief Musa Pasha set forth from Canea on his way back to Istanbul with fifty-one galleys, two ships, and fifteen smaller vessels, but running into a storm he lost six galleys, the two ships, and five of the small boats. By the twenty-fifth he had reached the island of Makronisi, just off the southeastern shore of Attica, when he learned that Grimani's fleet had seized the two Barbary ships. With the advent of another storm on 27 January Tommaso Morosini, commander of the sailing ships in the Venetian fleet (*capitano delle navi*), was blown toward Negroponte (Euboea), where he was sighted by the Turks, who bore down upon him quickly, all forty-five galleys.

Morosini's ship was a large square-rigger, the *Nave Nuova*. Since he could not outrun the Turkish galleys, he fired his broadside cannon at them when they got within gunshot range. For a while the Turks seemed to draw back, but presently they moved in for another attack. A number of them boarded Morosini's vessel, even climbing the mainmast to cut down the lion banner of S. Mark and replace it with the crescent. A Turkish arquebusier, bracing himself at a porthole in the captain's cabin (*alla finestra della camera del capitano*), shot through the doorway. The bolt struck Morosini in the head; he died immediately, but his men continued to fight, not yielding to panic. Presently the captain-general Grimani, whom the first roar of the cannon had summoned to the scene, drove the Turks into retreat. Morosini's broadside cannon had taken a heavy toll of the Turks. Even Musa, the kapudan pasha, had fallen. Taking over the *Nave Nuova*, by this time a wreck, Grimani made prisoners of the Turks on board. The banner of S. Mark was again raised to the masthead, and Grimani sailed back to Candia to refit the fleet. The Senate decreed a public funeral for Tommaso Morosini, and all the shops in the city were decked out in black.[21]

When Sultan Ibrahim had learned of the extent to which Morosini's single ship had caused damage to his fleet, he gave vent to the anger that seemed to obsess him at every setback. To punish the failure of Musa Pasha, who had lost his life off the coast of Negroponte, Ibrahim deprived the pasha's heirs of their inheritance. Impelled by the sultan's impa-

---

[21]Battista Nani, *Historia della republica veneta*, II (1686), 102–4; Romanin, VII (1974), 266–67; Anderson, *Naval Wars in the Levant*, pp. 130–31; Mormori, *Guerra di Candia*, MS. Marc. It. VII, 1563 (7596), fol. 44; *Raccolta diplomatica della guerra di Candia*, MS. Marc. It. VII, 211 (7468), fols. 99ᵛ–100ʳ: "La Merciaria et tutte le botteghe della città si adornano di nero . . . ," and cf., *ibid.*, fols. 98ᵛ–99ʳ, a *mandato* of the captain-general Grimani, dated "di galeazza all'Argentiera a VIII Febraro 1646" (Ven. style, i.e., 1647). On the death of Tommaso Morosini, cf. Girolamo Brusoni, *Historia dell'ultima guerra tra Veneziani e Turchi* (1673), I, bk. VI, pp. 155–56.

tience, the Turks directed their forces upon Suda, which had recently received reinforcements from Venice. French adventurers had joined the Venetians in opposition to the Turks. The plague had been ravaging both the Christian and the Moslem troops, lessening their effectiveness. Although by April it had largely ceased at Candia, it was still serious at Canea. The captain-general Grimani had been refurbishing his fleet at Candia, and was now ready for renewed action.[22] Neither side was making much progress at Crete, however, when about the middle of June (1647) under the very walls of Candia a large company of horse and foot in Venetian employ, "già avendo la vittoria in pugno," suddenly and inexplicably turned and fled before a smaller body of Turks, who looked as though they were defeated.[23] A month or so later Hussein Pasha, Sultanzade Mehmed's successor as "serdar" or general of the Ottoman troops in Crete, took the first step toward laying Candia under the siege that was to last for more than twenty years.

The defeat of the Venetian mercenaries in mid-June enabled the Turks to extend their sway throughout the eastern half of the island. They overran the plain of Mesara to the south of Candia, and occupied the seaport of Hierapetra (Ierápetra) on the southeast coast as well as the village of Mirabella (Merabello) on the northeast coast. The nearby town of Sitía (Seteía), on the little gulf of the same name, held out. The Venetian captain-general Gianbattista Grimani and his fellow officers Alvise Leonardo Mocenigo, the provveditore generale, and Bernardo Morosini, who had replaced his deceased brother Tommaso as *capitano delle navi,* were always on the lookout for Turkish vessels from the northern Sporades to the southern Cyclades. While the Turkish armada was assembling at Mytilene, Grimani attacked the port of Chesme (Çesme), capturing some vessels, and moved from place to place until in mid-July (1647) his fleet was strengthened by the addition of five papal and a half-dozen Maltese galleys. He also received further reinforcements from Venice. As the months passed, however, the Christian casualties mounted throughout the island of Crete, and Emmanuele Mormori puts them as high as eighteen thousand, "il ch'è verisimile," for by and large

---

[22] A dispatch from Rome of 4 May 1647, summarizing an *avviso* from Venice dated 27 April, makes known the fact that 4,000 Venetian infantry and abundant supplies had reached Candia, where the captain-general Grimani had just refitted his fleet, which (according to the dispatch) consisted of 28 light galleys, four galeasses, and 12 ships. About 11 April he had sailed northward "per sorprendere qualche fortezza o porto, et ivi trattenersi per impedire all'armata Turcescha, che ancora si trovava in Negroponte per condurre le genti alla Canea, dove tuttavia vi continuava la gran peste, la quale all'incontro era affatto cessata in Candia" (Cod. Urb. lat. 1111, fols. 134ᵛ–135ʳ, *di Roma li 4 Maggio 1647,* and in general cf., *ibid.,* fols. 163, 166, 174ᵛ–175ʳ, 182ʳ, 183ᵛ–185ʳ, 193ʳ, 197ᵛ–198, 208ᵛ, 218, 239, 256ᵛ, 270, 278ᵛ–279ʳ, 303, 311ᵛ, *et alibi,* 388).

[23] Nani, *Historia della republica veneta,* II (1686), 105–7, and note Romanin, VII (1947), 267.

some forty percent of all the islanders had perished in two years or so of warfare.[24]

The Venetians accomplished little by their naval maneuvering in 1647, although Kretschmayr notes that Alvise Leonardo pursued the Turkish armada, now under the command of another kapudan pasha named Musa, from March to June from one port in the Aegean to another, and then from June to September blockaded the Turks first in the channel of Chios and thereafter in Monemvasia. When Musa Pasha went from Crete to the Morea to raise more troops, he was caught in another Venetian blockade, which led the Turks to take over all Christian vessels in Ottoman ports. It was not a good year for the Venetians, at least not at sea. Their efforts seemed all in vain, for Grimani and Mocenigo could not prevent the Turks from conveying troops and supplies to the sultan's army in Crete, which was getting ready to put the capital city of Candia under siege.

In the meantime the Venetians did much better against the Turks on the Dalmatian coast, where Leonardo Foscolo took from the Turks the villages of Obrovac, Nadin, Zemonico, and Vrana in western Croatia in the area of Zara (Zadar). At Vrana the Venetians acquired the "han" or caravanserai which the kapudan pasha Yusuf had built about three years before. It is one of the few Turkish buildings which still exist in present-day Yugoslavia. Foscolo also recovered the village of Novigrad, and seized Scardona (Skradin) some six miles north of Sebenico (Šibenik). He failed to take the town of Sinj, just east of Spalato (Split), but was able to make secure (at least for a while) Venetian possession of the great fortress at Knin. The fortress was soon lost, but the Venetians were to recover it in 1699.[25] Meanwhile the Venetians were enjoying some

---

[24] Mormori, *Guerra di Candia*, MS. Marc. It. VII, 1563 (7596), fols. 40ᵛ–41ʳ, is eloquent on the plight of the Cretans, "non si potendo massime ritirare dalla prattica de' feriti per non consentire l'uso de Turchi, sicchè non meno in città che nelle ville ove si dilatò fece grandissima stragge, ma più nelle donne, particolarmente gravide, delle quali niuna campò, e ne' putti, siccome s'inoltrò in tutte le rimanenti parti del regno, e massime nella città di Candia, dove si dice che li morti di tutte le condizioni ascendevano a 18 m., il ch'è verisimile, perchè universalmente parlando non sono rimaste le due delle cinque porzioni delle anime che abitavano detta isola, sebben anco in alcuni luoghi non è restata meno la quinta . . ." (and cf. the almost illegible text of the original in MS. Marc. It. VII, 101 [8382], fol. 48ᵛ). Pestilence was adding to the Cretan mortality.

[25] Nani, *Historia della republica veneta*, II (1686), 93, 112, 114ff., 144–46; cf. von Hammer-Purgstall, *Gesch. d. osman. Reiches*, V, 408–10, trans. Hellert, X, 132–35, who says, "Ein Anschlag der Venezianer auf Scardona misslang" (V, 409); Kretschmayr, *Gesch. von Venedig*, III, 323–24; Anderson, *Naval Wars in the Levant*, pp. 131–33; and note Cod. Urb. lat. 1111, fol. 142, *di Roma li 11 Maggio 1647*: "Di Venetia delli 4 'stante scrivono che quella Republica havesse di nuovo ordinato le levate di genti delle quali continuamente se ne mandavano in Candia e Dalmatia, di dove in Venetia era venuta la confirmatione della scritta presa al Turcho delle città di Vrana e di Nadin con li luoghi di Carino et Durazzo, havendovi fatti schiavi molti Turchi con acquisto di ricchi bottini e da 500 cavalli, et li Veneti al numero di circa 10 m. si erano incaminati alla volta di Sebenico

success, for on the morning of 28 September (1647) the *Te Deum* was being sung in all the churches on the lagoon in thanks to the Almighty because the Turks had been obliged to abandon a month-long siege of the important Adriatic port of Sebenico and the adjacent Fort S. Giovanni. The Turks had lost some 6,000 men "between death and flight" as well as a large number of wounded. The Venetians had lost only eight hundred men in the siege. The local inhabitants of Sebenico and the Fort had celebrated the Republic's success with "molte feste" and were now looking forward to the replacement of cannon on their walls and burying the bodies of the Turks "che in buon numero si trovavano per la campagna. . . ."[26]

Early in 1648 the Venetian fleet embarked upon a sea of troubles. Although Gianbattista Grimani recovered Mirabella on the east end of Crete, and headed for the Dardanelles to block the exit of the Turkish armada, he ran into a violent storm in mid-March, losing sixteen or so of twenty galleys off the island of Psará. Grimani and most of the crew of his flagship ended their lives in the storm,[27] but the provveditore Giorgio Morosini and his brother Bernardo, the *capitano delle navi*, decided to bring back what was left of the fleet to the island of Standia and the city

---

per scacciare da quei contorni, come havevano fatto li Turchi con la presa di Cardona e di 2 altri luoghi, e che poi marciassero con 3 cannoni all'acquisto della fortezza di Clissa per tentare anco per l'impresa di quella piazza, e che in Venetia erano gionte lettere di Levante con avviso che il generale Grimani pervenuto con l'armata veneta a Negroponte si fosse impadronito de forni et magazzini posti fuori di quella città con saccheggiarli et brugiarli, havendo con tale occasione proveduto essa armata di gran quantità di biscotti, et che detto Grimani havesse anco preso nel porto di Milo 6 vascelli Turchi che carichi di viveri andavano per servitio de la Canea.

"Soggiongono le medesime lettere che in Venetia si fosse attaccato fuocho nell'Arsenale, dove per li buoni ordini di quella Republica non haveva fatto altro danno che abbrugiare il magazzino dei remi, facendosi gran diligenza per venire in cognitione del autore, et che nel serrare delle lettere fosse arrivato un caico di Dalmatia con avviso che il generale Foscolo faceva fabricare un fortino per tenere di là delle montagne li Turchi, havendo in oltre fatto un ricco bottino di più di 20 m. capi d'animali tra grossi e piccoli," and note, *ibid.*, fols. 149ᵛ–150ᵛ, 192ᵛ, 232ᵛ, 273ᵛ, 313, 326ᵛ–327, 357ᵛ.

Foscolo took the important fortress of Clissa on 31 March 1648 (*Raccolta diplomatica della guerra di Candia*, MS. Marc. It. VII, 211 [7468], fols. 124ᵛ–133, esp. fols. 131ff.). Quite understandably, Foscolo became one of the heroes of his time (*Lettere e oration in commendation dell' eccellentissimo Ser Lunardo Foscolo, procurator di San Marco, general di Dalmazia et capitan general da mar*, MS. Marc. It. VII, 340 [7779], 71 fols., with letters and commendations ranging from 1646 to 1653). Girolamo Brusoni gives a good deal of attention to Foscolo in his history of the Turco-Venetian war (2 vols., Venice, 1673).

[26] Cod. Urb. lat. 1111, fol. 313, *di Roma li 5 Ottobere 1647*, and cf., *ibid.*, fol. 319.

[27] Mormori, *Guerra di Candia*, MS. Marc. It. VII, 1563 (7596), fols. 53ᵛ–54ᵛ. Grimani was succeeded as captain-general of the Venetian forces by the provveditore generale Alvise Leonardo Mocenigo (*ibid.*, fol. 55ᵛ). On Grimani's death, note the dispatch of 8 April, 1648, which dates the disaster on 18 March (MS. Marc. It. VII, 211 [7468], fols. 134–136ʳ).

of Candia. They soon received the reinforcement of a squadron under Giacomo da Riva, however, and while Giorgio Morosini continued on to Candia with a half-dozen galleys and as many ships, Bernardo Morosini, Riva, and Antonio Bernardo, *capitano delle galeazze,* proceeded to the Dardanelles to prevent the Turkish armada from entering the Aegean. After refitting his galleys and adding others at Candia, Giorgio Morosini also set out for the Dardanelles, where he arrived on 11 June, having captured a Turkish galley off the island of Kea some two weeks before. The Venetian naval force now consisted of seventeen galleys, three or five galleasses, and some forty-five sailing vessels.

The Turkish armada did not emerge into the Aegean for almost a year. In the meantime the then kapudan pasha Ibrahim was put to death for alleged corruption and treachery as well as for his failure to effect the release of the sultan's armada from the Sea of Marmara and the strait below Gallipoli. The next kapudan pasha, Voinok Ahmed, saw no point in risking his inferior galleys in an encounter with the Venetians. He moved his troops, munitions, and supplies by land to the mainland promontory opposite the island of Chios, where he assembled galleys enough to carry the men and matériel to Canea.[28] The Venetians divided their forces to try to intercept the transport of the Turkish soldiery and provisions, which they failed to do, as well as to continue the blockade of the exit from the Dardanelles, which they succeeded in doing all the long winter of 1648–1649.[29]

The summer of 1648 brought serious losses to the city and government of Istanbul. The Christians' plundering of a rich convoy might have been a matter of great concern except for the fact that a terrible earthquake struck the city in mid-July. It severely damaged the famous mosque of Sultan Ahmed I [built between 1609 and 1616] on a Friday at the very hour some four thousand Turks had gathered to say their prayers. Four campanili were ruined at Hagia Sophia and certain other

---

[28] Cf. Mormori, *Guerra di Candia,* MS. Marc. It. VII, 1563 (7596), fol. 56^r: "Quando alli 18 Giugno [1648] arrivò alla Canea una galera d'un Bei con avviso che attrovandosi con le conserve al numero di 22 a Scio fossero stati caviati dall'armata Veneziana, che con 3 galeazze, 17 galere, e 4 bertoni li seguivano, ma essendo risorto un temporale l'avevano perduti di vista, e perchè li ferri ch'esso gettò per sorgere non fecero presa diede le velle al vento e si ridusse in detto porto, dove di momento sarebbero giunte le altre 21 galere con alquanti minatori e spahi di Anatolia, e con 200 m. reali per dare una paga all'esercito, avvisò anco che il Re avesse fatto levar la vita al nuovo Capitan Passà imputato d'aver ricevuto danari da Veneziani per non sortire a Mustafa Passà, perchè corrotto s'avesse l'anno antecedente rinchiuso a Napoli e per diverse altre cagioni a 6 altri è creato Capitan Passà Voinic Agmet Passà con ordine di sortire, ma perchè per l'impedimento dell'armata Cristiana ciò riusciva impossibile, aveva condotto li dinari per terra sopra le galere predette acciochè li portassero in regno . . ." (the text being slightly altered on the basis of Mormori's original in MS. Marc. It. VII, 101 [8382], fol. 69^r).

[29] The Turks made little or no progress in the siege of Candia during the year 1648 (von Hammer-Purgstall, *Gesch. d. osman. Reiches,* V, 416–18, trans. Hellert, X, 141–44; Kretschmayr, *Gesch. von Venedig,* III, 324–25).

temples. A huge number of houses were destroyed, and more than thirty thousand persons were said to have perished. The chief aqueduct of the city had been demolished, causing a shortage of water, which was selling at a whole *reale* for a single liquid measure, with suffering to many and death to those who could not afford the price, all of which had produced dire predictions as to the future.[30]

Earthquakes did not produce confusion enough, however, and heads continued to fall in Istanbul. One never knew where he stood with Sultan Ibrahim. Annoyed at being impeded by wagons in the city streets, Ibrahim had ordered the grand vizir Salih Pasha to see that no more wagons of any sort should come within the walls. Having then met up with a wagon on 18 September 1647, Ibrahim summoned Salih into his presence, and straightway ordered his execution. Ahmed Pasha, then the highest civil official (a kaïmakam), managed to displace a rival for the grand vizirate, and thereafter attempted to destroy the family and the supporters of the late Salih.[31] Absurd appointments were made at the Porte, where astrologers helped to determine foreign policy. The Ottoman court was ruled by the favorites, the "sultanas" and khassekis, of the harem, to whom the prompt delivery of snow for sherbet counted for more than a military command. Sultan Ibrahim lost touch with all reality beyond the harem; his idiotic cruelty seemed to be mounting into madness. The Ottoman government was falling apart. Distress was inevitable and widespread. Here and there the fearful and the discontented rose in revolt.

While the sultan drowned himself in debauchery and extravagant display, the grand vizir Ahmed Pasha mismanaged the affairs of state with self-seeking savagery. The sultan's idea of taxation was tantamount to

---

[30] Mormori, *Guerra di Candia*, MS. Marc. It. VII, 1563 (7596), fol. 58ᵛ: "Tornava la caravana dal Cairo per la parte di Rodi e di Scio a Costantinopoli, quale fu incontrata dall'armata Cristiana, dalla quale a più potere procurò di fuggirsene, ma non gli sortì, perchè sopraggiunta dalle galere sottil restò in un momento disfatta e presa con danno notabile de' mercanti di Costantinopoli, e con non poco utile de' Cristiani. Ma questo fu un niente in riguardo del danno e del presaggio sinistro che un gran terremoto fece in Costantinopoli, perchè avendo atterrato con la sua violenza la famosa Moschea di Sultan Amurat [*sic*] in giorno di Venerdì nell'ora appunto che oravano appresso da 4 m. Turchi, et avendo ruinato 4 campinili di quelli di Santa Soffia ed altri tempii e numero grandissimo di case, uccise oltre 30 m. e più anime e perchè la stessa violenza aveva dirocato l'aquedotto maggior della città riuscì cotanto penuria di acqua che fu venduta un reale l'utrio [? litro ?] con patimento di molti e morte di alcuni che non avevano il commodo di comprarla a prezzo sì caro, onde li giudiziosi fecero diversi pronostici di future rillevantissime turbolenze nella città e d'imminenti ruine e disaggi" (with an incomplete text in MS. Marc. It. VII, 101 [8382], fol. 72).

[31] Von Hammer-Purgstall, *Gesch. d. osman. Reiches*, V, 410–11, 419ff., 442, trans. Hellert X, 135–36, 144ff., 169. Several Ottoman officials bore the title kaïmakam (*ka'im-ma-kam*), the highest being the kaïmakam pasha, who remained in the capital to exercise the authority of the grand vizir when the latter was absent on a military campaign. The kaïmakam was not permitted to intrude upon the military. Cf. the notice by E. Kuran in *The Encyclopaedia of Islam*, new ed., IV (Leiden, 1978), 461.

confiscation. The grand vizir sold offices of state like merchandise. At length a cabal of Ahmed's enemies, largely composed of the aghas or chief officers of the janissaries, whom he had failed to destroy, took a firm stand against him. They enlisted the support of the mufti and the ulema, and declared Ahmed deposed from the grand vizirate. The rebels did more than effect his deposition, however, and soon had him put to death. Turning their attention to the sultan, they complained of his tyrannical thievery and the hopeless corruption of the court, where the dissolute women of the harem held sway. The peoples of the Ottoman empire had been ruined. The infidel Christians had taken forty castles in Bosnia, and now they were blockading the Dardanelles with eighty vessels while the padishah gave himself over to lust and pleasure, extravagance and corruption. The learned ulema had gathered, and issued a fetva authorizing the sultan's deposition and the accession of his seven-year-old son Mehmed [IV].[32]

The mufti Abdurrahim, the new grand vizir Sofi Mehmed, the ulema, the [two] kadiaskers or chief justices, and the aghas had a throne set up before the Gate of Rapture, the entrance to the harem. The little Mehmed [IV] emerged from the inner chambers of the Seraglio and, as the reigning sultan, he received the obeisance of the vizirs and the ulema. The mufti Abdurrahim was the moving spirit behind it all. After a period of distress and doubt, however, even Sultan Ibrahim's mother, Koesem, the Sultana Valide, accepted the accession of her grandson and the deposition of her worthless son. An irate and indignant Ibrahim was given formal notice of his deposition. When he protested that he was the padishah, he was told: "No, you are not the padishah, for you have held justice and faith for naught. You have ruined the world. You have wasted your life in frivolity and lust. You have squandered the imperial treasury on nothingness. Corruption and cruelty have everywhere ruled in your stead!"

Ibrahim was imprisoned that day (8 August 1648), and when ten days later it was feared that the sipahis might rise up on his behalf, the mufti Abdurrahim, the grand vizir Sofi Mehmed, the kadiaskers, and the other involved officials at the Porte decided that the aberrant Ibrahim must be put to death. The mufti had reached the solemn conclusion that it was right and proper to do away with a padishah who bestowed the responsibilities of law and the sword not upon those who earned them but upon those who bought them. When the mufti, the grand vizir, the kadiaskers, and the other disaffected officials entered the Seraglio, the slaves and servitors fled, for no one of them wanted to be on hand when the sultan

---

[32] Von Hammer-Purgstall, *Gesch. d. osman. Reiches*, V, 442, 448, trans. Hellert, X, 169, 176–77.

was done to death. Even Kara Ali, the chief executioner of the Porte, tried to hide, and then threw himself in tears at the feet of the grand vizir who, striking him with a cudgel, set him to the task.

The grand vizir and the mufti, followed by "black Ali" and the latter's assistant, the porter Ali Hammal, went to the two-room apartment where Ibrahim was imprisoned. They found him clad in a rose-tinted and red garb, reading the Koran. He appealed to them, and reviled them. They had lived on his bounty, and now they had betrayed him. He recalled that Yusuf Pasha had once advised him to put Abdurrahim to death "as a mischief-maker without faith—but I did not kill you, and now you want to kill me. See here the holy writ, the Koran, the word of Allah, which condemns the cruel and the unjust." When the executioners laid their hands upon Ibrahim, he burst into curses and invectives, reviling the Turkish people for their faithlessness toward their ruler. Putting the cord around his neck, the two Alis strangled him into enduring silence (on 18 August 1648). He was buried in the tomb of Sultan Mustafa I (1617–1618, 1622–1623) by the entrance to Hagia Sophia.[33] The young

---

[33] On the deposition and death of Sultan Ibrahim, note Knolles and Rycaut, *Turkish History*, ed. Savage, II (1701), 108–9; see especially von Hammer-Purgstall, *Gesch. d. osman. Reiches*, V, 429–54, trans. Hellert, X, 156–84; and cf. Mormori, *Guerra di Candia*, MS. Marc. It. VII, 1563 (7596), fols. 59ᵛ–63ʳ, who describes the renewal of Turkish assaults upon Candia after the death of Ibrahim (*ibid.*, fols. 64ᵛff.). Although the works of Knolles and Rycaut have long been linked together, only Rycaut's work still retains value (S. P. Anderson, *An English Consul in Turkey: Paul Rycaut at Smyrna* [1989], pp. 229ff., 239–41).

On the near revolt of the sipahis after the deposition and death of Ibrahim, note Mormori, MS. Marc. It. VII, 1563 (7596), fols. 73ᵛ–75ʳ: "Caminavano le cose di Constantinopoli con non saldo piede, perchè doppo la deposizione e morte del Sultan Ibraim venivano machinate di continuo novità et Amurat Agà, che n'era stato potissima causa, doppo fatto per Agà de' Giannizeri aspirava alla suprema carica di primo vizir, quello che avendo addossata a Meemet Bassà la colpa d'aver licenziati li prenominati 14 bertoni, che si rittrovavano alle Smirne con lo esborso di 90 m. reali, ond'era seguita la fazion così dannosa e disonorata per loro a Fochies, fu deposto li 20 Maggio, e creato esso successore della dignità di vizir Atem, e data la carica di Gianizeraga a Mustafa Agà charachiaus uno delli [4] congiurati alla deposizione e morte del Re. . . .

"Ardevano i tumulti in questo tempo in Costantinopoli perchè non potendo sopportar li spai l'ingiuria fatta senza loro participazione al Re erano rissolti alla vendetta, alla quale più ardentemente aspiravano doppo il combattimento tra essi [et] giannizeri, come si scrisse seguito in Costantinopoli, e però uniti sotto il comando di Gengis Delbi si condussero in numero di 50 m., e s'attendarono vicino a Costantinopoli a Scutari, da dove mandarono a chieder al Re la testa di 45 [che] n'erano stati delle dette rivoluzioni cagionate, minacciando in altra maniera di poner il tutto a ferro et a fuoco. Conoscendo Amurat Bassà che questa tempesta minacciava particolarmente il suo capo volse far mossa contra di loro, ma non potendo farlo senza espressa commissione in scrittura dal Re [Mehmed IV] lo ricercò di quello con prettesto che malmenassero i suoi sudditi, e che ricercassero sua madre.

"Rispose il Re ch'esso non vedeva alcun suddito a dolersi contra di loro, e che quanto all'istanza che facevano, esso era pronto a compiacerli non solo nella testa della madre ma in quella di ogni altro che gli avessero ricercato, perchè i suoi schiavi non si uccidessero tra di loro, di che sentì sommo dispiacere nel cuore. Chiamò subito da Babilonia 5 m.

Mehmed IV, who became known as "the Hunter," now began a reign of almost forty years, toward the end of which the Turks were to suffer the major misadventure of their history.

The fall of Sultan Ibrahim and the accession of his little son Mehmed IV helped give rise to near chaos in Istanbul and in Anatolia. The janissaries suppressed an uprising of the sipahis and the attendants of the Seraglio.[34] The grand vizir Sofi Mehmed had a hard time maintaining himself in authority, and in the spring of 1649 the news came from Crete that the Turks had had to raise the siege of Candia for want of men and munitions. Sofi Mehmed and the then kapudan pasha Voinok Ahmed were at odds, but on 6 May the Turkish armada emerged from the long channel south of Gallipoli, sailing toward the port of New Phocaea (Yeni-foça on the Gulf of Candarli). In the meantime the dwindling fleet of the Venetian commander Giacomo da Riva had been reinforced by a half-dozen or so ships from Candia. Steering clear of the shore batteries on

---

Giannizeri e due altri dalle parti di Natolia, ma questi conoscendo il loro svantaggio si unirono con li Spai a Scutari.

"Fece però strozzar il deputato visir, il suo chiagià, et il suo imbroghar [o] mastro di stalla, che vogliamo dire, e depose dalla carica il mufti, restituendo il già deposto nel suo seggio per mitigare l'animo de' spai, che sommamente s'erano contra di essi sdegnati per aver consultata, data, e eseguita la sentenza contro esso Re, ma per questo li spai non si sono acquietati, e li rimanenti Turchi si sono sdegnati contro di lui per aver privato di vita un defterdar per non averli dato luoco nella loro meschita mentre quella nazione conserva stile di dar luoco a' magistri nella chiesa o nei bagni" (and cf. MS. Marc. It. VII, 101 [8382], fols. 93, 94ᵛ–95ʳ, on the basis of which I have emended the above text). On the deposition and execution of the sultan Ibrahim, note also (among numerous contemporary sources) Dujčev, *Avvisi di Ragusa* (1935), nos. cix–cxff., pp. 122ff.

[34] Cf. von Hammer-Purgstall, *Gesch. d. osman. Reiches*, V, 466–83, trans. Hellert, X, 197–217. Almost all Europeans (and especially the Venetians) were interested in the Seraglio, of which there is a well-known *Descrizione del Serraglio di Costantinopoli* attributed to Ottaviano Bon in MS. Marc. VII, 923 (7800), fols. 1–33 (unnumbered), but this same manuscript, fols. 38ʳff., also assigns the *Description of the Seraglio* to the bailie Giovanni Soranzo (*Il Serraglio del Gran Signore descritto dall'eccellentissimo Signore Senator Soranzo, bailo Veneto in Constantinopoli nell'anno 1646*). MS. Marc. VII, 1083 (8531), names Ottaviano Bon as the author, and Pietro and Giulio Zorzanello, *Inventari dei manoscritti delle biblioteche d'Italia*, LXXXV (Florence, 1963), pp. 143–44, give Bon as the author of the *Description of the Seraglio* in MSS. Marc. VII, 976 (7966), and VII, 977 (7631). Of these two latter MSS., 7966 with 103 pp. of text gives some addenda to the *Breve Descrizzione del Serraglio del Turco in Constantinopoli*, and MS. 7631, *Descitione del Serraglio de' Turchi*, has an interesting addendum describing the ceremonial involving ambassadors to the Holy See in Rome, but I find no indication of authorship in either of these two MSS. All these descriptions of the Seraglio have essentially the same *incipits* and *explicits*, all copies of the same work.

Nicolò Barozzi and Guglielmo Berchet, *Le Relazioni degli stati europei lette al Senato dagli ambasciatori veneziani nel secolo decimosettimo*, series V (Turchia), I (Venice, 1866), 59–115, have published the *Description of the Seraglio*, which they ascribe to Ottaviano Bon, adding, *ibid.*, I, 116–24, the *Massime essenziali dell'Impero Ottomano notate dal bailo Ottaviano Bon*. Bon had been the bailie in Istanbul from 1604 to the beginning of 1608. Maybe Bon was the author of the work on the Seraglio, but I keep thinking of Giovanni Soranzo in this connection.

the European side of the Dardanelles, Riva was ill-prepared to try to block the exit of the kapudan pasha. Riva's force would seem to have consisted of no more than 19 sailing ships, which could not be effectively maneuvered on the calm, windless sea, which had assisted Voinok Ahmed's departure from the straits with (it is said) some 65 galleys, six galleasses, and a number of sailing ships. Different figures are given, as usual, for the size of the Turkish armada.

Taking refuge in the harbor of Old Phocaea and along the neighboring shoreline, for the janissaries objected to combat at sea, the kapudan pasha Voinok Ahmed had to meet an attack by Giacomo da Riva on 12 May (1649). The janissaries cut the cables binding their galleys to the anchors, and sought to flee. The Venetians are said to have captured a galleass, one ship, and a galley but, more importantly, they succeeded in setting fire to three galleasses, two galleys, and some nine ships. The Venetian losses were much less heavy, but Riva apparently decided not to press his luck unduly, and withdrew south to the Gulf of Smyrna (Izmir Körfezi). The kapudan pasha regrouped his forces, sailing for the island of Rhodes in early June. There his losses were more than made good by the addition of some eighteen ships from Egypt along with ten galleys and as many galleons from the Barbary coast. After stopping at Tenos and Melos, he set sail for Canea with ample reinforcements to renew the siege of Candia. Although he had encountered the Venetians at Melos, they did not attack him, nor did they impede his disembarkment at Canea.[35]

---

[35] Von Hammer-Purgstall, *Gesch. d. osman. Reiches*, V, 484–85, trans. Hellert, X, 218–19; Kretschmayr, *Gesch. von Venedig*, III (1934, repr. 1964), 326–27; Anderson, *Naval Wars in the Levant*, pp. 136–39; and note Mormori, *Guerra di Candia*, MS. Marc. It. VII, 1563 (7596), fols. 72–73ʳ:

"Pativano in Candia grandissima carestia di biscotto e di panne li cittadini, perchè alli soldati non è mai mancato assegnamento sufficiente, ma giunsero 8 vascelli, e fu condotto un caramusal con formenti preso a' Turchi da' Maltesi, che si consolarono. Arrivarono medemamente alla Canea alcuni vascelli barbari carichi di formento et altre vittuarie dall' Egitto, e fornirono abbondantemente la città e tutto l'esercito. . . . Gionsero intanto 18 vascelli in Candia con vettovaglie e soldati et altre munizioni da guerra e provviddero a sufficienza la città. Gionsero in oltre alli 21 Marzo [1649] alcune galere alla Suda.

"S'erano riddotte le galere di Costantinopoli in numero di 73 e 10 grosse con 12 vascelli alle bocche del stretto [the Dardanelles] per sortire dalli castelli, dove tutto l'inverno [1648–1649] erano stati li bertoni e galere dell'armata Cristiana ad attenderle ed impedire, et osservando ogni opportunità conobbero li 14 Aprile [1649] che per l'absenza delle galere e galeazze Venete, e perchè non dimoravano più di 18 bertoni alle bocche, e quelli s'attrovavano in bonazza, potevano senza ostacolo con la correntia del mare sortire comandate però all'uscita da Voinic Agmet Bassà, che (come si disse) era stato eletto capitano bassà in luogo dello strozzato previo capitano bassà, come persona d'auttorità per la dignità di visir, [in] congionzione col Re [Mehmed IV], e come soggetto di gran bravura et esperienza. Uscirono senza alcun ostacolo, e s'avviorono verso Meteline. . . ."

Although the Turks met with some slight interference from the Christians, "velleggiando più presto l'armata Turca, come più leggiera, non fu raggionta da Cristiani, che però stimando fossero per fare il viaggio a Scio, si riddussero al porto di Foches, e s'avrebbero

da 23 galere de bei, parte delle quali mandorono alle Foches Vecchie per remurchiare e convogliare 4 saiche cariche di munizioni da guerra, dove in capo di due [o tre] giorni arrivorono anche li predetti 18 bertoni, e dato fondi alla bocca stettero fermi fino che col benefficio del vento potessero muoversi. Stimorono li Turchi che per mancamento di aria non avessero progredito, nè facendo gran conto de' Cristiani per il loro picciol numero non prestò men al castellan del luoco orecchie il Bassà, che lo ammoniva a dover per sua sicurezza far poner alcuni cannoni alle bocche di detto porto, e schierasse l'armata in modo che restando nel mezzo un canale dasse adito alli pezzi del castello di giocare quando l'occasione lo richhiedesse. Anzi l'ingiuriò, e fece solo avvanzare le galleazze a detti vascelli alle bocche.

"Sorse intanto il vento, e levandosi 7 bertoni guidati da Giacomo da Riva si scostorono alquanto per prenderlo a loro vantaggio, e quando meno li Turchi lo credevano entrorono li sei nel porto. L'uno si fermò alle bocche, et avvanzando cheti per mezzo de' nemici, fra quali uno s'inoltrò notabilmente, diedero fondo e serrate le velle oltre la chebba del trinchetto per poter girare apersero li portelli dell'artiglieria, scaricando addosso li nemici tempesta di cannonate con [loro] danno e terrore indicibile. S'avanzò il capitano Bassà con la reale seguitato dalla patrona, ma ricevendo [tanto] danno dalle cannonate che avendo perso l'arbore e l'antene 133 Turchi e 17 schiavi fu ganzato da un vascello, e correva rischio di perdersi, essendo massime fuggito in terra lo stesso capitan bassà, se Chischeti Pascagli a forza di rimurchio non l'avesse staccata e liberata. Non successe già così alla patrona perchè affatto rimessa fu abbruggiata con perdita di molte cassette de reali, che in essa erano state caricate. Veduto ciò dalle genti delle altre galere, sortirono tutte in terra, abbandonando li legni perchè le cannonate non fecero esente alcuna galera, uccidendo grandissimo numero sicchè per comun consenso de' Turchi, quando in compagnia de' vascelli vi fossero trovate 10 galere averebbero al sicuro rimurchiata fuori del porto tutta l'armata Turchesca, e a suo talento di quella disposto acquistorono nulladimeno una delle galeazze nuove, che furono in Costantinopoli fabbricate, presero un vascello, acquistorono una galera sottile per essersi li schiavi sollevati, abbruggiorono 6 altri vascelli et una galeazza e liberorono da circa mille schiavi che dall'altre maone e galere sottili fuggirono a quelli con la sola perdita di un bertone che per aver toccato in terra fu spogliato di quanto fu possibile da Cristiani ed arso. Si stima che li Turchi tra morti e fuggiti abbiano perso 4 m. uomini, gran summa di denaro caricato sopra detta maona e patrona detta Gedechio e tutta la riputazione per esser stati in così gran numero strapazzati e malmenati da 6 soli bertoni Cristiani nello spazio di tre ore di giorno ed alcune della notte subseguente. Giunse pertanto una fregata portando avviso ai Cristiani che li barbari in numero di 25 bertoni d'Algier, compreso un' inglese preso sopra Sapienza, e di 5 da Tunesi e di 16 [o 6] galere da Tunesi e Biserta e li Alessandrini in quantità di 29 vascelli, 9 Francesi, 4 Inglesi et un Fiammengo, e il resto de' Turchi venivano, per il che subito si levarono dando respiro a nemici e tempo di racconciar l'armata. Racconciò al meno [meglio] che potè il capitan bassà la sua armata, lasciando per mancamento di ciurma per inabilità due galere sottili et una maona a Fochies, e portati a Scio lasciò ivi due altre galere sottili, e mandò alle Smirne ad ammassar a forza de' soldi quanto maggior numero de leventi che potè per surrogarli in luoco de' morti e fuggiti, non potendo senza detto aiuto proseguir il viaggio o però anco che tre [o tredici] vascelli Inglesi et un Fiamengo che si rittrovavano in detto luoco di Smirne, e che prima con l'esborso fatto di 90 m. reali in mano del primo visir erano stati licenziati si contentassero di ricevere alcune genti e ridurse seco di conserva in Candia, e sebbene ricusorono quanto potero, piegorono finalmente il collo alla forza, facendo accordo di condurli in prima a terra del regno, et occorrendo combattere per viaggio co' Cristiani, ricevuto di mercede 8 m. reali per uno, compresi li soldi datili per la campagna, e promesse d'esenzione e privileggi sicchè con 87 galere, 8 maone, e 73 bertoni si mosse da Scio, tirando verso Napoli di Romania per levar il berlierbei Mustafa Bassà, che con alcune genti si trovava ivi per passare in campo sotto Candia in luoco del morto Ghassan Bassà, avendo espedite le altre con fregate e con le squadre di Napoli in due viaggi in numero di 1,500 incirca" (and cf. MS. Marc. It. VII, 101 [8382], fols. 90^v–92^v, also fols. 117^v–120^r, on the basis of which I have made some obvious corrections in the text).

On Riva's victory at Phocaea, "in Asia nel porto de Focchies a dì 12 Maggio 1649," see also the *Raccolta diplomatica della guerra di Candia*, MS. Marc. It VII, 211 (7468), fols. 142–144: "Si viddero la mattina seguente le genti dell'abbattuta armata [Turca] fuggite alla montagna disperse e vagarono abbandonate le restanti galere, morti di 2,000 Turchi,

The Venetians' burning of the Turkish vessels at Old Phocaea kindled a flame of intrigue at the Porte, in which Mehmed IV's grandmother, the Sultana Valide, and Kara Murad, the agha of the janissaries, brought about the fall of the grand vizir Sofi Mehmed, who was banished from Istanbul, and thereafter put to death.[36] Kara Murad succeeded him as grand vizir but, like all the grand vizirs during these years, he did not last long. With trouble brewing in Anatolia, where a revolt soon broke out, on 1 July 1649 Kara Murad accepted a renewal of the twenty-year peace of Zsitvatorok (of 11 November 1606), according to which the rulers of the Holy Roman and Ottoman Empires were to recognize each other as "emperor." Although in 1606 the Emperor Rudolf had agreed to give the sultan 200,000 florins in cash, the annual tribute to the Porte was forever annulled.[37] According to the treaty of 1649 the Emperor Ferdinand III agreed to make the sultan a once-for-all gift of 40,000 florins to be delivered to the Porte within ten months of the Turkish ratification of the peace (*transmittetur infra spatium 10. mensium . . . sponte promissum illud munus valoris 40. m. fl. pro hac vice et imposterum non amplius . . . Imperatori Turcarum . . .*).[38] It is perhaps superfluous to add that, on the whole, the peace would not be kept.

---

gli altri malcontenti ritornati alle loro case, et l'armata tutta fracassata e disfatta" (fol. 144ᵛ), and note the *Relatione della vittoria ottenuta dalle armi della Serenissima Republica di Venetia sotto il commando dell'illustr. et eccellentiss. Sig. Giacomo da Riva, capitan delle navi, contro l'armata turchesca in Asia nel porto di Fochie 1649 adì 12 Maggio*, Venice, appresso Gio. Pietro Pinelli, *stampator ducale*, 1649.

Giacomo da Riva made his own report (*relazione*) to the doge and Senate on 10 November 1653. See ASV, Collegio, V (Secreta), Relazioni, Busta 80. He began the report with the statement that "il regno di Candia mirabile per il suo sito et insigne per la grandezza et per tanti opportuni commodi, come tale celebrato nelle memorie dell'antichità, reso in questi calamitosi tempi theatro infelice de i più memorabili accidenti, o combatuto dal Cielo con le pestilenze o angustiato dalla fortuna con la fame, e per il corso d'anni nove oggi mai invaso in gran parte, et impugnato dall'armi prepotenti del Turco sarà il sogetto della mia sincera et breve relatione [and contrary to the practice of many of his fellows, da Riva did make his report brief] commandatami con parte espressa dell'eccellentissimo Senato. . . ."

[36] On the fall of Sofi Mehmed, see von Hammer-Purgstall, *Gesch. d. osman. Reiches*, V, 485–88, trans. Hellert, X, 219–22.

[37] On the treaty of Zsitvatorok, cf. Setton IV, 1097; despite the high hopes of 1606, the treaty had not established a full peace between the Hapsburgs and the Porte (*ibid.*, p. 1098).

[38] An important event in the history of imperial-Turkish relations, the treaty of 1 July 1649, was negotiated and signed by the imperial internuncio Johann Rudolf Schmidt von Schwartzenhorn. It was to run for twenty-two and one half years: "Cumque excellentissimus dominus supremus vezirius Murath Bassa ex sua absoluta plenipotentia solito sigillo et subscriptione munitum instrumentum horum tractatuum juxta consuetudinem in lingua Turcica mihi Caesareo Internuntio tradiderit, ego vicissim pro more veteri Latino idiomate instrumentum juxta articulos sequentes [nine articles define the terms of peace] sigillo et subscriptione mea consueta roboratum ad ratificationem tamen Augustissimi Imperatoris Domini mei clementissimi praedicto excellentissimo Domino Vezirio exhibui . . ." (J. Dumont, *Corps universel diplomatique*, VI-1 [1728], no. cclxiv, pp. 521–22, and cf. von Hammer-Purgstall, V, 492–93).

Shortly after his arrival in Crete the kapudan pasha Voinok Ahmed was killed by a cannon ball at the time of a Turkish attack upon Suda. He had had his disagreements with Hussein Pasha, the serdar or general of the land forces on Crete. The Turkish troops were mutinous, refusing to return to the trenches at Candia until the gunsmiths and sappers, who had often been requested, were sent to help in the siege. Hussein's enemies had encouraged the mutiny until they feared their own lives and interests were in jeopardy. When the commanders of the Turkish armada made available to Hussein the needed sappers, sailors, and corsairs to take a firm stand before Candia, the siege was resumed for two months. More than seventy mines were exploded. The Turks lost more than a thousand men, and the besieged lost their valiant commander, Count Giovanbattista Colloredo.[39] Orders now came from Istanbul, however, recalling 1,500 janissaries in whose place another 3,000 janissaries and 1,000 sipahis had (it was said) been enrolled for service in Crete. But when would they actually come to the island? It was only too clear to Hussein, whose enterprise and daring had evoked the jealousy of his competitors both on the island and in the capital, that once more dwindling manpower would bring a halt to the siege of Candia.

Hussein Pasha had declined to serve with the kapudan pasha who had been appointed as Voinok Ahmed's successor, and so the dignity of grand admiral was given to Haideragazade Mehmed Pasha. The grand vizir Kara Murad Pasha was pleased with the thought of Haider's going to Crete, for he suspected that the latter had his eye on the grand vizirate. Little would be done for a while, because the Turkish troops now went into winter quarters. Meanwhile Istanbul was a welter of intrigue which von Hammer-Purgstall has tried to depict, as the little sultan's grandmother Koesem, the Greek Sultana Valide, was engaged in an unending struggle for supreme authority with the younger Sultana Valide, Tarkhan, the sultan's Russian mother. Grand vizirs did not last long; Kara Murad soon lost the paramount post, and was sent off as governor of Buda[pest]. He was to be replaced by Melek Ahmed Pasha in late August 1650.

The Turks kept the Venetian garrison at Candia in close confinement although in July 1650 the provveditore Alvise Mocenigo recovered the small island of S. Todero off shore from Canea.[40] The divan in Istanbul

---

[39] On Colloredo's career, see the article by G. Benzoni, in the *Dizionario biografico degli Italiani*, XXVII (1982), 80–82.

[40] The "reacquisition" of S. Todero is described in the newsletter *Riacquisto di S. Teodoro dalle mani de' Turchi seguito sotto il commando dell'illustrissimo et eccellentissimo Signor Alvise Mocenigo II, proveditor dell'armata della Serenissima Republica di Venetia*, Venice, appresso Gio. Pietro Pinelli, stampator ducale, 1650.

The numerous signed dispatches of Alvise Mocenigo are to be found in the ASV, Senato, Provv. da terra e da mar, Filza 1091, extending (in so far as they are dated) from 16

ordered the construction of three strongholds in the area of Candia, one hard by the lazzaretto, another near the little fort of Castro, and the third at the place where the Turkish troops usually disembarked for assaults upon the city. The kapudan pasha Haideragazade had left Istanbul with the sultan's armada in May (1650), but he could not get out of the Dardanelles owing to the Venetians' vigilant blockade of the exit with (it was reported) 32 galleons, seven galleys, and two galleasses. Haider had trouble with the janissaries, who detested naval warfare and travel by sea. As the blockade went on, they found solace in ravaging both the European and the Anatolian shores of the Dardanelles.

To help insure a better performance of the Turks at sea the government of the Porte ordered the arsenals on the Black Sea to build 29 galleons. The ships' carpenters were to use seasoned timber, for freshly cut wood tended to crack as it got older. There was an increase in taxation. In the late fall of 1650 Hozamzade Ali Pasha of Rhodes was appointed kapudan pasha. Toward the end of the year he took on board eight galleys and some ships of his own a thousand sipahis, four regiments of janissaries, and other troops, sailing in the dead of winter from the Dardanelles with no opposition from the Venetians, who had given up the blockade on the assumption that the Turks would not take to the sea at that time of year. Hozam Ali stopped at Chios, and went on to Crete, where he arrived in a week with all his troops, provisions, and munitions. For such extraordinary service to the Porte he was offered elevation to the vizirate, but since the three horsetails that went with the honor would have cost him 400,000 piasters, he declined the costly distinction.[41] In any event the siege of Candia went on, and Hozam Ali had strengthened the Turkish forces.

The grand vizirate of Melek Ahmed Pasha lasted only a year (1650–1651). His was the second of ten appointments to the Ottoman presidency within the scarcely more than a half-dozen years to come until the appointment of the rugged Mehmed Köprülü in 1656. Melek Ahmed tried with straitlaced sincerity to solve the state's imperial deficit. He began with the *bedeli timar,* a special levy on fiefs, which is said to have taken from the timariots about half their income, causing rebellion in

---

September 1650 to 18 February 1651, S[tilo] N[ovo]. The continuation of his dispatches from 9 March to 15 October 1651 are bound, *ibid.,* in Filza 936. Into both these "files" miscellanies of other texts have been stuffed, most of them in a sad state of decay. Many of the dispatches are given partly (or even wholly) in a numerical cipher; they are written in a rather rapid secretarial hand which reveals little or no trace of calligraphic training. These files also contain texts other than Mocenigo's detailed reports to the doge. The paper documents of the seventeenth century have succumbed to time and moisture to a far greater extent than the parchment texts of earlier eras, but Mocenigo's dispatches are on the whole in good condition.

[41] Von Hammer-Purgstall, *Gesch. d. osman. Reiches,* V, 498–501, 514–17, trans. Hellert, X, 233–37, 250–53.

Anatolia and in Crete. Although he was opposed to the sale of governmental offices, Melek Ahmed sought to relieve pressure on the treasury by allowing self-seekers to purchase their posts, setting up an accounting office to keep track of the income, which hardly amounted to one-tenth of what had been expected. Next he caused consternation in the divan or council of state when he suggested that all the vizirs should give up for two years the revenues they received from the imperial domains. It might be a way of paying the troops, for the treasury had already collected and disbursed the next two years' taxes.

The vizirs were distressed, however, at the thought of their incomes' being diminished. After all, if the grand vizir sold an office at a good price, he was likely to keep forty percent of the return. He could afford to do without the revenues accruing from the imperial domains. But the lesser vizirs lived on such income. Indeed, yes, explained Yusuf Pasha, the second vizir: His assignment from the imperial domains amounted to no more than a million aspers which, when added to the gift at Baïrām (a festival after Ramadan), did not suffice to pay his expenses. It looked as though the vizirs' costs of living would be going up as their incomes went down. The third vizir, old Kenaan Pasha, a true Moslem, remained quiet when his turn came, but the grand vizir pressed him to speak up with full freedom. Well, said Kenaan, the janissaries' wages amounted to 800,000 piasters a year, but of that sum the aghas appropriated 300,000 piasters for themselves. The aghas ought to help provide payment for the soldiery. If one seized the relatively small sums which hardly sufficed to maintain the vizirs and their families, would the proceeds help the treasury very much?

Kenaan's speech shocked the aghas, and Beshiktash remonstrated in a soft voice, "But I have no income beyond my four hundred aspers a day." That was all he had to say. It was clear that the grand vizir was not finding the solution to the huge Ottoman deficit. The burden which the vizirs and the aghas shifted from their own shoulders was thus to fall the more heavily upon the poor, the ulema, the sheiks, the widows, and the orphans by taking away all or part of their state pensions. The treasurer or defterdar Emir Pasha recommended the complete cancellation, for the current year, of the 17,000,000 aspers which was the overall cost of the pensions.

When the old Sultana Valide, the wise Greek widow of Ahmed I (d. 1617), was informed of these deliberations, she summoned the guardians of the state. "So you are taking the bread away from thirty thousand pensioners. On whom do you want them to put the curse?" Sarikiatib, the young jackanapes of a scribe, had the impudence to reply,

Ah, dear lady, since the world began, no one has ever heard tell that fortresses were taken by the prayers of mullahs and dervishes. If one asks who won this battle, who took that fortress, the answer is Ibrahim Pasha the Drunkard or

Someone Pasha the Bore. The prayers of the poor and the dervishes are of no more use to us than their curse is harmful. With no hesitation I will take their curse upon myself!

And so Melek Ahmed seemed to have found the solution to the deficit. Thirty thousand pensions were allegedly suspended for a year. The pensioners had no vote, no voice in the government.[42]

No, Melek Ahmed Pasha had not solved his fiscal problem, but he had added to the social unrest both in the capital and in the provinces. His next move was to corrupt the coinage, issuing at Belgrade a debased asper with only about a third of the silver of the former asper. It now required 150—no longer 50—aspers to vie with the Hungarian ducat. The *bedeli timar,* the levy on fiefs, was producing rebellion in Anatolia, which extended into Syria and reached the Persian borders. A revolt broke out in Smyrna (Izmir) when the local governor, in obedience to orders from Istanbul, closed the warehouses to cut off the exportation of wheat. Rivalries, fears, and suspicions in the capital almost caused a serious break between the grand vizir Melek Ahmed and the aghas. Owing to a corrupt coinage and an unstable government inflation was on the rise, and yet dress and cookery were both attaining ludicrous levels of luxury. As usual in Islam there was religious controversy, the fundamentalists storming against the liberals who condoned the smoking of tobacco and the consumption of coffee. Yielding to pressure from the fundamentalists, the grand vizir forbade the dances and chants of the dervishes and then, yielding to other advice, he forbade anyone to interfere with their dances.

Melek Ahmed did, however, rather dexterously get rid of the mufti Behayi, who annoyed him. Claiming that he had more important matters to attend to, Melek Ahmed turned over to Behayi the resolution of certain demands the English consul in Smyrna was making of the Porte. Irked by the consul's claims and exasperated by the attitude of the English ambassador, whom he summoned into his presence, Behayi heaped insults upon the latter, and had him locked up in the stable. Insulting everyone who remonstrated against his high-handed conduct, Behayi evoked the ire of the aghas who succeeded, to Melek Ahmed's satisfaction, in bringing about his dismissal and replacement by Aziz Effendi. Getting rid of the bothersome Behayi doubtless gave Melek Ahmed some satisfaction, but he had troubles everywhere (in the provinces as well as in the capital), and was proving unable effectively to deal with them.

---

[42] Von Hammer-Purgstall, *Gesch. d. osman. Reiches,* V, 518–21, trans. Hellert, X, 255–58, who gives the total of the annual Ottoman pension (*siebzehn Millionen Aspern*) as "soixante-dix millions d'aspres," and takes the usual liberties with von Hammer's text. On the old Sultana Valide, note Mormori, *Guerra di Candia,* MS. Marc. It. VII, 1563 (7596), fol. 66.

Having debased the asper, Melek Ahmed proceeded to coin piasters with a reduced silver content in the Ottoman mints at Belgrade, in Albania, and in Bosnia. When he tried to force acceptance of this coinage, at the rate of 118 aspers to the piaster, upon the mercantile corporations, he stirred up what became apparently the first irrepressible revolt of the corporations in Turkish history. The difficulties of merchants and artisans were insurmountable when they had to exchange the sounder western coinage for the cheap Ottoman mintage. In a great and boisterous march upon the Seraglio the chiefs of the corporations, supported by the masses of merchants and artisans, loudly demanded the removal of the grand vizir. They claimed to have paid some forty taxes in the course of the current year. The boy sultan and the old Sultana Valide had to give way. Melek Ahmed fell from office on 21 August 1651, and for a brief period Si'ush Pasha replaced him. In the meantime the Porte had paid a heavy price for the apparently well-meaning but certainly ineffectual rule of Melek Ahmed.[43]

The war had been dragging on in Dalmatia as well as in the Aegean. The years 1649–1650 had been a prolonged hardship, as Leonardo Foscolo wrote the doge from Zara on 28 June 1650. Famine and pestilence had beset the Venetian naval station at Zara, even invading Foscolo's own household.[44] During these two years, owing to the war of Castro, Innocent X's galleys had not joined the Venetian fleet. Unsettled conditions in Italian waters and in the peninsula had meant that the papal galleys were needed to protect pilgrims going to Rome for the jubilee year.[45] The Maltese had come, but little or nothing had been accomplished in these two years.

Venetian and Turkish galleys, galleasses, and sailing ships cruised back and forth in the northern Aegean and among the Cyclades without a serious encounter. Profiting by the experience of the past few years the Turks had been adding larger sailing ships with broadside cannon to their galleys and "mahones" (*mawunahs*) or galleasses. The Venetians still thought that their concentration upon the fleet rather than upon an army was the way to save Crete from the clutches of the Turks. Their annual blockade of the Dardanelles, however, had not prevented the Turks from reinforcing their armament on the island by the transport of men, munitions, and provisions to Canea year after year. The Venetians

---

[43] Von Hammer-Purgstall, V, 521–39, trans. Hellert, X, 258–76, with alterations in von Hammer's text.

[44] MS. Marc. It. VII, 340 (7779), fol. 22: "La guerra, la carestia, la peste, che per un anno continuo affligge questa città, et che s'inoltrò già pure nel mio palazzo, si posson chiamare compendii di tutti i mali. . . ."

[45] Pastor, *Gesch. d. Päpste*, XIV-1 (1929), 136–39, 265–66, and *Hist. Popes*, XXX, 180–85, 363.

had certainly been assisted by the rebelliousness induced by Melek Ahmed's grand vizirate. Six weeks before his downfall the Turks had suffered a notable defeat in the first large-scale naval engagement of the Cretan war. The Turkish setback had helped cause Melek Ahmed's undoing.

Yielding to the high cost of leasing (and sometimes insuring) foreign vessels, especially English and Dutch ships, the Venetians gave up the blockade of the Dardanelles early in the year 1651, although they would resume it at a later date. Despite the instability of the Turkish government and the general disquiet in Istanbul, work had gone on in the arsenals, and on 21 June the kapudan pasha Hozambegzade Ali sailed from the Dardanelles without interference. Melek Ahmed and the old Sultana Valide had hoped for some success, for Hozam's armada was said to consist of 53 galleys, 55 ships, and six mahones. The Venetian captain-general Alvise Mocenigo seems to have had on hand and ready for action no more than 24 galleys, 28 ships, and six galleasses. Actually this was a large fleet for the Venetians, whose vessels were well built and seaworthy, as the Turkish vessels often were not. Anchored off the southern shore of Negroponte (Euboea) at the beginning of July, Mocenigo was informed that Hozam Ali's armada had sailed on 29 June from Chios to the island of Patmos.

Anxious to stop the Turkish armada before it could reach Crete, Mocenigo went on to the volcanic island of Santorin, which had been ravaged by a terrible eruption the year before. He reached Santorin late on 5 July (1651), and two days later the sultan's armada under Hozam Ali Pasha was sighted on the eastern horizon. On 8 July the Turks attacked part of the Venetian fleet in determined fashion. Five ships under Girolamo Battaglia had to carry the brunt of the onslaught until relieved by Luca Francesco Barbaro, Riva's successor as *capitano delle navi*. When Alvise Mocenigo approached the scene of action, the Turks withdrew toward the north. By the morning of 10 July the Venetian fleet caught up with them between the islands of Paros and Naxos. The brothers Tommaso and Lazzaro Mocenigo, commanders of the two galleasses on the left wing of the fleet as it approached the Turks, tried to attack some of the pasha's galleys still taking on water at Paros only to find Hozam Ali himself bearing down upon them with his six galleasses and some galleys. Tommaso was killed, Lazzaro wounded, and their men and vessels were in peril until Francesco Morosini, the *capitano delle galleazze*, relieved them. Later on in the century Morosini was to emerge as the major figure in Venice's wars with the Turks. There was another Francesco Morosini, captain of the Gulf, i.e., the Adriatic, who was to be killed (as we shall see) in the first "battle of the Dardanelles" in mid-May 1654.

After Morosini's rescue of the Mocenigos' galleasses the Venetian right wing and *battaglia* broke the Turkish line, the center of which had been dislodged by Hozam Ali Pasha's descent upon the Mocenigo brothers. The Turkish galleys took to flight, leaving those aboard the sailing ships to fend for themselves. With the Turks in almost hopeless disarray the fast-moving Venetian galleys closed in upon them, seizing one mahone and ten or eleven ships. Setting fire to another five Turkish ships, the Venetians took some 965 prisoners.[46] It was a good day's work.

Alvise Mocenigo withdrew with the Venetian fleet and with his captured vessels to Candia. He was soon joined by four papal and four Maltese galleys, but there was no further action of importance for the rest of the year 1651. Hozam Ali Pasha sought refuge at the Turkish naval station of Rhodes, and thereafter sailed with forty galleys to Canea, encountering no obstacles along the way. In mid-September Alvise Mocenigo gave up the captain-general's baton to his successor Leonardo Foscolo, who spent the autumn pillaging the Sporades from Samos to Kos, achieving nothing but the enmity of the Greeks. When Foscolo returned to Candia, Hozam Ali sailed back to Istanbul with 22 galleys, five ships, and his remaining five mahones or galleasses.[47] He was removed from his position as kapudan pasha or grand admiral about a year later, on 3 October 1652, owing to his failure to achieve any success against the Venetians.

In the meantime conditions at the Porte had been deteriorating. Although the new grand vizir Si'ush Pasha checked the revolt of the merchants, assuring them of the abolition of the excessive taxation which had been levied on them, troubles were brewing in the Seraglio, which had become the center of Ottoman government. The merchants nurtured an abiding hatred of the aghas of the janissaries, who had forced them into submission. The aghas remained hostile to the merchants, who had demanded their lives. For years the aghas had got along well with the

---

[46] The Venetians' defeat of the Turkish armada between the islands of Paros and Naxos on 10 July 1651 is described in the *Raccolta diplomatica della guerra di Candia*, MS. Marc. It. VII, 211 (7468), fols. 160ʳ–164ʳ, dispatches dated "in the waters of Paros [*Paris*] on 13 July 1651." Owing to a typographical error, the date appears as 1650 in Setton, IV, 1101a. There is a brief account of the battle of 10 July 1651 (based upon the later literary sources) in Gino Damerini, *Morosini*, Milan, 1929, pp. 66–69, who also notes, pp. 69–73, the dissension within the Venetian high command after the battle.

In a dispatch to the doge and Senate dated 15 July 1651, one of Mocenigo's longest dispatches, he has described the battle of Paros of five days before (ASV, Senato, Provv. da terra e da mar, Filza 936, pages unnumbered). Following Mocenigo's report of 15 July, Filza 936 provides us with a list of the more than fifty Venetian commanders of the galleasses, galleys, and ships which won the battle: "Notta de illustrissimi capi da mar, governatori de galeazze, galee, sopracomiti, et governatori di nave trovatisi al ultimo combatimento con gloriosa victoria contro l'armata nemica, seguito li dieci luglio 1651, S[tilo] N[ovo], nel Canal de Parisi e Nixia sotto la diritione et commando del illustrissimo et eccellentissimo Signor Alvise Mocenigo, Procurator, capitan general da mar."

[47] Anderson, *Naval Wars in the Levant*, pp. 142–45.

"sultanas," as the westerners called them, in the harem, but now two hostile parties had grown up in the Seraglio. One had gathered around Koesem, the old Sultana Valide, who at times had all but ruled the Ottoman empire under her husband Ahmed I, her sons Murad IV and the sex-mad Ibrahim, and now her little grandson Mehmed IV. The other party had rallied around Tarkhan, the young Sultana Valide, the mother of Mehmed IV. Koesem depended upon Begtash, agha of the janissaries; Tarkhan upon the black eunuch Suleiman Agha. Suleiman had gradually wrested power from the old Sultana Valide, and was therefore at serious odds with the aghas. Twelve days after Melek Ahmed had had to step down from the grand vizirate, the enmity between Koesem and Tarkhan reached the point (on 2 September, 1651) from which apparently no return was possible to the superficial sufferance of the past.

Loath to see authority slip from her hands the old Sultana Valide, wise and kindly as she was, undoubtedly did encourage the aghas of the janissaries to intervene on her behalf to remove Suleiman, the chief eunuch in the Seraglio, and to reduce to nothingness the now large importance of her rival, the young Sultana Valide. Von Hammer-Purgstall assures us, however, that there is no evidence to support the charge that the elderly Koesem planned the assassination of her grandson Mehmed IV in order to undo Tarkhan and her partisans in the Seraglio. Koesem might well have preferred to see Mehmed's brother Suleiman on the throne, for the latter's unambitious mother would have been easy to manage. Whether or not there was such a plot against the little Mehmed's life, a slave named Meleki is said to have informed Tarkhan that her enemies were going to feed her son a poisoned sherbet, which gave Tarkhan the idea that she had better do away with the old Sultana Valide.

Working with the old Sultana Valide, the aghas of the janissaries had asked the grand vizir Si'ush Pasha to enroll more troops, and getting together at the janissaries' barracks, they had sent word to the divan that they wanted the black eunuch Suleiman and two of his fellows, the young Sultana Valide's strong partisans, to be banished forthwith to Egypt. Tarkhan's spies had kept her supporters well informed, however, and the eunuch Suleiman realized that the time had come for decisive action. Assuming perhaps that he was more likely to be slain than banished, Suleiman vowed with fourteen other eunuchs to kill the old Sultana Valide, whom they held responsible for the janissaries' address to the divan.

It was night time. The pages of the Seraglio had gone to bed. The eunuchs were sitting up to guard the sultan. Suleiman is said to have armed a hundred and twenty white eunuchs who would do as he charged. Going to the window of the first chamber of the pages, Suleiman cried out to them that while they slept, the janissaries were invading the Seraglio, planning to put them all to death. The janissaries also intended to strangle the little Padishah, and set on the throne the agha Begtash, who was going to marry the old Sultana Valide!

It was a rousing call to arms. The pages responded with alacrity, and were straightway joined by the pages of the other chambers. Those of the first chamber were more than ready to do battle with the janissaries, whose chief agha had closed on them the door which led to advancement, bestowing upon others posts which they regarded as rightfully theirs. After slaying the chief officer of the first chamber, the pages pushed on under the eunuch Suleiman's leadership to the old Sultana Valide's apartments. She was being guarded by her own eunuchs, some of whom were killed while others fled. Suleiman and his followers burst into the Sultana Valide's antechamber. She was expecting the janissaries to invade the Seraglio and solve her problems. Hearing all the commotion, she cried out from behind locked doors, "Have they arrived?" Suleiman answered, "Yes, they have. Now you come out!"

Yes, they had arrived, but she did not come out. She realized who had arrived, and she fled to the farthest corner of her apartment, seeking refuge in a wardrobe. Her assailants broke down the doors, invaded the apartment, and shattered various wardrobes, quickly discovering the old Sultana Valide's hideaway. As they pulled her out, she tried to buy them off, scattering gold and jewels among them. It was no use. One of the attacking mob cut the cords from a curtain. He strangled her with them. A vigorous old woman, it took her some time to die, as blood streaming from her nose and ears stained the garments of those who held her. They had killed the great philanthropist of their time, a builder of khans and mosques, a guardian of widows and orphans, a benefactor of those in hospitals and prisons. The partisans of Tarkhan, the young Sultana Valide, and of her chief counselor, the black eunuch Suleiman, had indeed triumphed over the leading figure at the Porte.

With surprising rapidity the janissaries, who had little confidence in their aghas, were becalmed. New leaders and other officers were assigned them. The three chief malcontents, including the old Sultana Valide's friend Begtash Agha, received appointments as provincial governors to remove them from Istanbul. Begtash was to go to Brusa, the others to Temesvár and Bosnia; the latter went off to their posts, but were overtaken and put to death along the way. Begtash, who doubtless knew what lay ahead, never set out for Brusa, but sought to hide in the city, hoping that the wheel of fortune might turn once more in his favor. It did not do so, for he too was soon caught and strangled by alleged order of the boy sultan Mehmed.

Several others paid the price of their ambition; prominence was a risky business at the Porte. Within two weeks the whole cast of government had changed in Istanbul. As for the old Sultana Valide, twenty-four hours after she had ordered the janissaries to come to the palace to do her bidding, her body was taken to the old Seraglio, with all the court in attendance, and thereafter she was buried near the tomb of her husband Ahmed in the mosque which the latter had built in the capital.[48]

Peace seemed to descend upon the Porte, but a grave unease continued. The grand vizir Si'ush Pasha escaped the trials of September 1651, having exercised a good deal of skill in the management of affairs. Little was done, however, and little was to be done for some time to advance Ottoman interests in the war against Venice. Turkish and Venetian ships and galleys still sailed back and forth in the Aegean, but hardly anything of note occurred during the year 1652 despite another Venetian blockade of the Dardanelles and the kapudan pasha Hozamzade Ali's unsuccessful attempt upon the Venetian island of Tenos.[49] Until mid-August the captain-general Leonardo Foscolo had the assistance of seven Maltese but no papal galleys. Although active through most of the year, he was unable to strike an effective blow at the Turks. In 1653 Foscolo again moved here and there in the Archipelago, being joined at the island of Nisyros in June by the seven Maltese galleys, but once more little was accomplished. The Turks delivered provisions and munitions to their forces on the island of Crete, took the little fortress of Selino on Suda Bay, and repaired the shattered fortifications on the island of S. Todero. By this time the aging Foscolo had rendered the Republic years of bold and devoted service. He had become tired of it all,[50] and who could blame him?

The apparent peace at the Porte did not last long, for the rivalry between the black kislaragà Suleiman and the grand vizir Si'ush Pasha soon developed into extreme hostility. The young Sultana Valide lacked the sound judgment of the late Sultana Koesem. She was also less decisive and, quite understandably, relied unduly upon the self-seeking Sulei-

---

[48] Von Hammer-Purgstall, *Gesch. d. osman. Reiches*, V, 539–52, trans. Hellert, X, 276–91.

[49] Von Hammer-Purgstall, *Gesch. d. osman. Reiches*, V, 564, 590, trans. Hellert, X, 305, 332. Hozamzade Ali was removed from office because of his failure to take Tenos.

[50] Glimpses into Foscolo's naval activities during the spring of 1652 and the fall of 1653 may be found in MS. Marc. It. VII, 340 (7779), fols. 43–50, 55–58, the texts being *avvisi* of March, April, and May 1652 and a signed dispatch of Foscolo to the doge Francesco da Molin dated at Candia on 29 October 1653. Note also Anderson, *Naval Wars in the Levant*, pp. 145–46.

As for Foscolo's increasing fatigue, three years before (on 28 June 1650) he had written the doge, "Cinque anni sono hormai che senza respiro assisto a questa laboriosissima carica, vertendo sempre ne' maggiori disaggi, agitationi, e patimenti fierissimi, per quali se non si fussero estenuate le forze, sarebbe un miraculo della divina omnipotenza, come è gratia sua particolare, che tanto v' habbia potuto ressistere e sussista tutt' hora nelle proprie languidezze aggravate da un peso di sessanta doi anni" (MS. Marc. It. VII, 340 [7779], fol. 22ᵛ). Cf. Nani, *Historia della republica veneta*, II (1686), 241–42, 253–54, 265–67.

man. Although she did not accede to the latter's demand for Si'ush's head, the grand vizir's property was confiscated, and he was sent into exile. To guarantee his own possession of power Suleiman secured appointment to the grand vizirate of an old fool, allegedly ninety years of age, who promptly appointed his brother, another old fool, as provincial governor of Damascus.

The new grand vizir, Gurji Pasha, embarked upon a new series of exiles and confiscations, imprisonments and executions. Before Gurji's elevation to the second post in the empire the Sultana Valide had asked her kiaya, the architect Kasim, who had witnessed the ups and downs of Ottoman government for years, about Gurji's ability. Kasim thought it would be far better to leave Si'ush as grand vizir. Gurji was an imbecile. Kasim's choice for the grand vizirate would have been Mehmed Köprülü. When the Sultana Valide suggested to the kislaragà Suleiman that it might be well to have Mehmed Köprülü work with Gurji in the grand vizirate, Köprülü was soon sent into exile. His sponsor Kasim was imprisoned in the Seven Towers, and thereafter banished to the now sleepy island of Cyprus. Such was the Ottoman government.

Efforts of the Venetians to negotiate what they regarded as a reasonable peace with the Porte were getting nowhere at all, but the grand vizir Gurji Pasha was happy to receive the imperial internuncio von Schwartzenhorn, who brought him Ferdinand III's ratification of the old treaty of Zsitvatorok. One war at a time was enough for the Porte, especially since the shah of Persia had just established diplomatic relations with John Casimir, the king of Poland. But if the Venetians were making no progress in their search for peace, the Turks were making no progress in their prosecution of the war. The kapudan pasha Hozamzade Ali's failure to achieve any worthwhile success against the Venetians led, as we have seen, to his removal from the grand admiralty, to which Dervish Mehmed Pasha was appointed. Considering the distractions and enmities which filled the minds and took the time of the chief officials at the Porte, would Dervish Mehmed do any better? Hozam Ali had been brought back in chains to Istanbul, fined a hundred purses for failure, and then was released and given a lesser naval command.

When the extent of old Gurji Pasha's incompetence had become painfully conspicuous, he was removed from the grand vizirate, which was given to Tarkhunji Ahmed Pasha after long consultations at the divan. Tarkhunji accepted the post with the understanding that he would see to the proper equipment of the sultan's armada (over which the insistent Dervish Mehmed Pasha now presided), continue the war for the conquest of Crete, and levy the required imposts to raise the necessary funds. Like many grand vizirs in the past, Tarkhunji was an Albanian by birth, with a long administrative experience, but his harsh and impracticable efforts to raise the revenues necessary for the Ottoman treasury proved unsuccessful. For a decade expenses, increased by corruption and inefficiency, had grown with every year until now (in 1653) the costs of government allegedly exceeded income by some 120,000,000 aspers, but no one had devised acceptable means of reducing the deficit. Some things were accomplished, however, during Tarkhunji's grand vizirate, among them the banishment of the kislaragà Suleiman, the black eunuch. There seems to be no evidence that the Sultana Valide missed him.

Theological dissension came to the fore again for a while. An earthquake caused widespread ruin in Asia Minor in late February 1653. Something always seemed to be going awry. Tarkhunji Ahmed was using available funds to pay the wages of the restless sipahis, which exasperated the ambitious kapudan pasha Dervish Mehmed. On one occasion this led to a quarrel when Dervish found himself at the Arsenal with Tarkhunji and the defterdar Surnazen. Dervish told the grand vizir, "You simply must give me money!" After all, Tarkhunji had taken the grand vizirate with the realization that he was to prepare the armada for action. The defterdar observed that they could not extract money from the stones, which remark led to a heated quarrel between Dervish and the defterdar.

When Tarkhunji tried to introduce a note of quiet into the violence of their dispute, Dervish turned on him in anger. The grand vizir had been playing fast and loose with him, he said, and henceforth he would not accept a draft to be drawn on the treasury, the payment of which was always being postponed. He must be able to count on three hundred purses of ready cash. It is not hard to see why the Turks should have avoided any large-scale encounter with the Venetians during the years 1652–1653. A serious defeat of the sultan's armada would have made its rebuilding difficult. By weaving in and out of the sealanes, however, the Turks had managed to elude Leonardo Foscolo's sailing ships and galleys and to reinforce their hold upon Crete by transporting men, munitions, and provisions to the island.

The dispute at the Arsenal had unfortunate consequences for Tarkhunji Ahmed Pasha. When informed of the wrangle, Sultan Mehmed IV summoned Tarkhunji and Dervish Mehmed to appear before him. The latter made clear he had received but a paltry sum to maintain the armada. Tarkhunji declared that the drafts to be drawn on the treasury were in every way the equivalent of money. If Dervish could not wait, however, for the dates on which they fell due, he still had no problem. Dervish was rich enough to assume the responsibility of paying the troops from his own pocket. Reimbursement would obviously be made at an appropriate time by the treasury. Tarkhunji's sarcasm was ill-advised; the sultan was offended by it. Indeed, it was doubtless at this time that Mehmed decided quickly to remove Tarkhunji from office. Whenever a grand vizir made a false step, his enemies were sure to come together to undo him.

Tarkhunji's bluntness and the harshness of his administration had given him the full quota of enemies that the grand vizirate was likely to produce. They seem to have convinced Mehmed IV, who was quite willing to listen, that Tarkhunji's fallout with Dervish Mehmed was owing to the fact that Dervish would not join him in a conspiracy to replace Mehmed on the throne by his younger brother, the prince Suleiman. When Mehmed now showered praise and gifts upon the grand vizir, Tarkhunji realized that such gestures were intended to deceive him. His time had come, as he acknowledged to certain friends. To serve the sultan, he had turned the world against him. Death had long been the way the sultans repaid their servitors. And it was not long before Tarkhunji was summoned into the imperial presence, and strangled (on 20 March 1653), Dervish Mehmed being made the grand vizir in his stead.

Dervish Mehmed's accession to power was the prelude to several more executions, some of them apparently not undeserved, and of course to numerous promotions and removals from office. Surnazen, who had acquired Dervish's enmity, was sent off as governor and defterdar to Temesvár, and was soon fined two hundred purses. Some persons, as usual, sought retirement with as ample a pension as they could obtain from the Porte. Despite Dervish's elevation there were long delays in rebuilding the Ottoman armada in the Arsenal at Istanbul. The Turks at court found some encouragement, however, in the fact that Fazli, the enterprising pasha of Bosnia, sent Mehmed IV in March 1654 two hundred Christian heads and some 220 prisoners as evidence of his success against the Venetians in the disputed area of Knin in western Croatia.

The dubious financial operations of the kiaya of the Arsenal as well as the discord which soon arose between Dervish Mehmed and Kara Murad Pasha, the new kapudan pasha, who had himself been the grand vizir three years before, had slowed the pace in the Arsenal. The arrival of a squadron of so-called corsairs from Tunis and Tripoli, however, now quickened work on the Turkish ships and galleys. The Barbary beys were received several times by the sultan, who gave them money and riggings which the reluctant kiaya was obliged to produce.

Murad Pasha and the Turkish commanders decided to adopt the customary order of battle (if they met the Venetians on the open sea) with the Tunisian vessels in the right wing and those from Tripoli in the left. The galley of the kapudan pasha would sail with the *battaglia* or center squadron. After the usual distribution of kaftans to the officers Murad assembled the armada at Beshiktash near the tomb of Khaireddin Bar-

barossa, promptly moved toward the Seven Towers, and despite the objections of the kiaya continued on to Gallipoli. The former kapudan pasha Hozamzade Ali sailed out of the Dardanelles with three galleys, apparently opening up a way through the Venetian ships and galleys under Giuseppe Dolfin, who was trying to blockade the straits. Hozam Ali landed at Tenedos, where the beys of the Archipelago had brought together their forces,[51] and now certain events were about to take place, in which the Venetian populace and the nobility would long take pride.

---

[51] Cf. von Hammer-Purgstall, V, 553–60, 566–85, 598–99, trans. Hellert, X, 292–300, 307–27, 339–40.

VI

Naval Battles at the Dardanelles (1654–1657), the Cretan War, and Papal Aid to Venice

he first of four important naval combats now lay just ahead. Although the final outcome would be another victory for the Turks, the Venetians' performances at sea during the years 1654–1657 remain among the more notable events in the eleven centuries of their history. The first of the famous "battles of the Dardanelles" took place on 16 May 1654. Although the Venetians were loath to admit it, they lost the encounter. We shall deal with the event in some detail, and pass more rapidly over the Venetians' engagements with the Turks in 1655–1657. What seems to be an eyewitness account of the first battle of the Dardanelles is preserved in a bulky manuscript in the Marciana. While the report appears on the whole to be accurate, it was prepared by a Venetian, and is strongly slanted in favor of the forces of the Republic. Having apparently been printed, it was presumably used as propaganda when Venice was seeking aid from the Christian princes.

According to this account, in early May (1654) the kapudan pasha Kara Murad moved south toward the Dardanelles, the "Castelli," with an armada of 79 vessels—33 sailing ships, including four from France and two Barbary *pinchi,* 40 galleys, and six mahones or galleasses. South of the Dardanelles, "at the point of Greece," the beys of the Aegean had assembled 22 galleys, and opposite them "at the point of Troy" the

172

Barbary corsairs had brought together 14 ships, giving Murad a naval force of some 115 vessels. We are informed that as Murad reached the narrows, the beys and the Barbary corsairs were supposed to attack the Venetian fleet under Giuseppe Dolfin, *capitano delle navi,* who had been maintaining a blockade of the strait. As Murad came south, Dolfin's vessels were stationed to the south of the narrows, i.e., the channel between the modern towns of Çanakkale on the east and Kilitbahir on the west. Dolfin had at his command two galleasses, eight light galleys, and 16 sailing ships, some of which were not in good condition. In view of the numbers of the Moslem vessels and the positions they had taken, it was clear that "we were surrounded within and without, but the appearance of so great an armada brought us no fear—because our hearts were given over to service of the faith and of the fatherland, it was not easy to intimidate us."

Considering, however, the situation in which the Venetians now found themselves and the inadequacy of their fleet, our source does acknowledge that not all the captains of the vessels facing the Turks were confident of a favorable outcome. In fact that infamous wretch, captain Zorzi de' Bianchi of the ship *Margarita* had deserted his fellows, and fled to the Turks, informing them of the weakness of the Venetian forces. Murad Pasha had left the waterfront area of Beshiktash on 10 May (1654). He moved toward the Castelli at the mouth of the channel on the fifteenth. Early the next morning he came upon the Venetian fleet within the Dardanelles. Murad, clad as a common sailor, had left his flagship, boarded a small frigate, and then run through the Turkish lines, bow and arrow in hand, giving an example of enterprise and encouraging his forces. Also, if the Venetians aimed at his flagship, they would not find him aboard.

The Turks came on rapidly with a strong northerly wind "con gran fondamento," their ships and galleys so numerous that our informant thought the Venetian fleet would have been lost without the intervention of the Almighty, truly "un patente miracolo." He says it was generally rumored that the grand vizir Dervish Mehmed had come down to see the battle, along with some thirty thousand people who had gathered on both the Anatolian and the European sides of the strait. Turkish boats and brigantines left the shores bringing Murad Pasha's forces still further reinforcements. The Venetian commander Giuseppe Dolfin had sent written orders to the captains of all his ships and galleys to keep their vessels at anchor when the first assaults of the enemy came, "chè dovessero ricever li primi assalti dell'inimico combattendo al ferro." When the northerly wind and the current had carried the bulk of the Turkish armada beyond the Venetian fleet, "as must inevitably happen," then they were to cut the cables, and fight with the wind behind them as their ally, attacking the Turks from the rear.

The captains of a dozen ships, however, failed to obey Dolfin's orders, "whence of 16 ships only four remained [at anchor] to meet the furious attack of so great an armada." Whether the tragic error began with the disobedience of a few captains, and the others followed because they thought Dolfin had changed his tactics, it is impossible to say. At any rate instead of following the dozen ships which were soon seeking an exit from the channel, the Turks believed it more to their advantage to try to capture Dolfin's flagship, "giudicandolo molto glorioso." "Thus very quickly the flagship was surrounded by the entire armada, heavy vessels and light, at the stern, at the prow, on the port and starboard, and everywhere."

Without inquiring into the possibility of 79 vessels surrounding a single ship, we may note that Dolfin invoked the name of the Almighty and of the Blessed Virgin, urging his men to follow his example. Standing conspicuously on deck without armor, he seized a scimitar, and said in a loud voice that true Christians and faithful subjects of the Republic must now make known their loyalty to the state. He was determined to have the enemy pay dearly for his death. He was answered by massive cries of agreement. The seamen and soldiers would rather die than fail in their duty to Christendom and to Venice. Dolfin was much loved by his men, according to our source, because of the good treatment they had received from him. And now the battle started with a fierce attack upon Dolfin's flagship (*capitana*), as the Turks streamed aboard from the flagships of the kapudan pasha and his second-in-command, the two Turkish vessels being loaded with an astonishing range of musketry, "due sultane cariche di tanta moschettaria che facevano stupire."

Dolfin's men fought so vigorously, according to our informant, that the flagship of the kapudan pasha (he was not aboard) was knocked out of the battle, "whence our men went aboard her, and seized all the banners." Two hundred Turks lay dead on deck, "one on top of the other;" the rest of them took such cover as they could. "Continuing the combat in this way we became aware of the fact that our ship had got so close to shore that we thought ourselves lost." Dolfin dropped an anchor,

and the enemy believing us to have gone ashore came upon us with all their mahones, galleys, and ships. Some came aboard by the stern, others by the starboard or port side, still others by the prow, and on all sides we put up a stalwart defense of ourselves with the aid of the blessed Lord God.

Despite the constant intervention from heaven it did look as though Dolfin and those aboard his flagship had reached their end.

But the lord captain Dolfin with his own sword cut down many Turks as they came aboard our vessel. Finally the enemy resolved to retreat to their own ships, nor did they want to try to come aboard us any more, but thereafter they fired at us incessantly with their cannon, the result of which torment was that all the yards of the topsails were broken, all the ropes and rigging which the big masts carry were shattered. And they struck the big masts with such cannonading that one suspected they would fall. Moreover, as a result of the cannon fire the ship was hit at the water line, making holes which admitted water with the danger of sinking. The lord captain, however, running the length of the ship, did everything he could to make possible repairs, promising rewards to this man and that, as it seemed to him they deserved them. Before the fighting was over and done with he had given away more than five hundred reali of his own money.

Having exhausted their martial "art and ingenuity," further resistance to the Turks seemed beyond their strength. They had lost a hundred men between the dead and wounded. Dolfin decided to cut the cable and drift with the wind and current. He therefore summoned the captain of his flagship, telling him to cut the cable.

"But we are too close to land," the captain replied, "we'll go ashore!"

"We're already lost," was Dolfin's answer. "It is true, but what can we do? Cut the cable, because if the Lord God guides us out of here, we may have some hope of saving ourselves. If we go ashore, we'll both make it bravely to the powder. We'll light it, and up into the air we'll go!"

Dolfin was more than determined to do or die. The captain did as he was ordered. Taking an axe in hand, he leapt up onto the prow, and cut the cable. Suddenly—*O miracolo grande!*—a northerly wind began to blow. It was carrying the flagship toward the sea. Making a little sail of cloaks and sheets, they pulled away from the shore, found themselves again in the very midst of the enemy armada,

and making our way, we emerged from the channel, always fighting and firing with a great slaughter of Turks. . . . Thus this [flag]ship escaped from the Turkish labyrinth, towing along with us their flagship, which we had taken and shattered. When, however, those aboard the fourteen vessels from Barbary saw what was happening, they gave themselves to the wind, throwing themselves upon us with terrible cannon shots. With great and prompt force they seized the ship from us without attempting anything else against us, and withdrew to join the rest of their armada below Troy.

As Dolfin's flagship rounded a headland, the dozen vessels and others, which had gone off on their own, had now regrouped, and veering toward the flagship became reunited with it. The Venetian fleet, now in less disorder, kept together all that night, facing the Turks in order to see whether they intended to launch another attack. Since the Turks did not do so, our source assumes they had suffered heavy losses (*grandemente danneficati*). We are told that Dolfin would have been glad to resume the offensive if he had had some way of keeping a sail aloft and if the north wind had allowed it.

The *Pesara* and the *Gabriela*, the two galleasses in Dolfin's fleet, as well as the sailing ship *Margarita* commanded by Antonio Zeno, had met with courage the enemy's first blows. Having cut their cables, however, the galleasses were conveyed out of the channel by force of the current. The eight light galleys, every one of them following the lead of the dozen ships that had failed to obey Dolfin's orders, had also withdrawn from the scene of action. They had all been carried off to safety, except for the galley *Paduana* which, having become separated from the others, fell into the midst of the enemy. She put up a brave defense, but was finally sunk.

The Turks found their chief contestants in Dolfin's flagship and Francesco Morosini's galley. Morosini was captain of the "Gulf," i.e., the Adriatic. His galley had been tied to the stern of Dolfin's flagship when attacked by two Turkish vessels. The galley received a fearful battering from its attackers. Part of Morosini's men were killed by the Turks, and part were drowned, including Morosini himself, who had been hit by a musket shot.[1] About a hundred officers, soldiers, and galley slaves were saved, but some of these also perished as the conflict continued. The galley remained afloat. The Turks could not take it despite their best efforts. When Dolfin saw, however, that it was partly submerged (*mezza a fondo*), and that it could not be salvaged, he had it set afire in several places. When the fire reached the galley's store of munitions, "it flew into the air."

We lost two ships, namely the *Aquila d'Oro* and the *Orsola Bonaventura*, the first being commanded by Andrea [Daniele] Morosini (son of the most excellent lord Andrea), who held the post of admiral [*armirante*]. The captain Raffaele, truly a worthy and valorous subject, was his second in command. They both showed remarkable courage, but were overwhelmed by four other vessels. At first they had got the better of a sultana, but not being able to hold out against so great an attack, in the end they set fire to their own ship along with the sultana rather than surrender, consecrating their lives to God and bequeathing immortal glory to their names.

The *Orsola Bonaventura* was a small vessel in quite poor condition, but it was defended with passion and bravery. Finally, however, this one also went up in smoke with the death of its commander Sebastiano [da] Molin. The rest of the fleet has all been saved without further loss except for some dead and wounded aboard the ships involved in the combat. If everyone had been able to do his duty, . . . we might have gained a complete and glorious victory despite so great a disparity between the forces.

Our "eyewitness" knew for certain—or so he says—that the Turks had suffered heavy losses. One of their galleys had been sunk. A galleass

---

[1] In the account of the first battle of the Dardanelles in MS. Marc. It. VII, 211 (7468), fol. 223^r, we are informed "che il capitan del Golfo Francesco Moresini colpito da moschettata vi rimanesse estinto. . . ."

had run ashore, having collided with the sultana which was burned along with Morosini's *Aquila d'Oro,* and a Barbary vessel also went down. The Turks would have to reckon with still greater losses, since there was no doubt that many thousands had been killed and many of their vessels badly damaged. . . .

The sergeant major Gianbattista Sessa had made himself immortal because, besides his other courageous actions, he had been the first to board the Turkish flagship, from which he had carried off the Ottoman banners to take them to Dolfin. Sessa deserved some appropriate reward, as did those members of his company who had emerged from the fray alive. As for Dolfin himself, according to our source, he would never know any peace of mind until he could again confront the Turk, especially if he could have eight or ten Flemish ships to help him in the encounter, being certain that the Flemings would face no end of peril without abandoning their leader.

Although wounded and badly shaken, Dolfin was alive and in good health. His fleet was soon united with that of the captain-general Leonardo Foscolo in the Cyclades. As a postscript to his account the writer later added that a report had reached Venice to the effect the Turks had lost some six thousand men in the combat, the kapudan pasha had been wounded, and the Turks themselves looked upon the encounter as a defeat, "a fact which is even confirmed by the news which comes of the armada, because it is said that at Chios the kapudan pasha has disarmed ten of his galleys in order to reinforce the others."[2]

After his victory at the Dardanelles the kapudan pasha Murad went south to Mytilene, which he reached on 20 May (1654), and then on to Chios, where he arrived on 26 May. Here he added further vessels to his armada. They had come from Egypt, the Barbary states of Tunis and Tripoli, and the Turkish islands in the Aegean. Although he found it necessary to disarm ten of his galleys to help equip the others, when he resumed his voyage, he had "at his obedience" 54 ships (*vascelli*), 65 galleys, six galeasses, 30 brigantines, and 10,000 infantry besides the 4,000 which he believed were ready for him at Nauplia. Thus reinforced Murad Pasha proceeded to Psará (on 6 June), Skyros (on the eleventh),

---

[2] *Raguaglio del combattimento seguito a Dardanelli tra le navi Venetiane comandate dal nobil homo signor Iseppo Dolfin de Nicolò del 1654 a 27 di Maggio et l'armata dei Turchi,* in the *Raccolta diplomatica della guerra di Candia,* MS. Marc. It. VII, 211 (7468), fols. 183^r–187^r, an account dated 27 May, 1654. After the postscript the statement is made that "la relatione sopra fu come l'altre stampata." Other accounts of the first battle of the Dardanelles may be found, *ibid.,* fols. 237^r–240^r, and Nani, *Historia della republica veneta,* II (1686), 278–81, whose account differs in some details. Nani dates the battle on 16 July (*ibid.,* p. 279). While lamenting the dead and wounded, he states that "nondimeno il danno si compensava con la gloria di sì celebrato cimento, non mai combattutosi con minor forza e con maggior animo . . ." (p. 281).

Castel Rosso on the island of Negroponte (on the twelfth) and, following instructions from Istanbul, he reached the Venetian stronghold of Tenos (on the sixteenth).

Two days of Turkish plundering on the island of Tenos were ineffectively countered by the Venetian fleet under Alvise Mocenigo, who had replaced Foscolo in the high command, with six galeasses, 22 galleys, and 33 sailing ships. On 21 June (1654) a minor engagement took place just west of Melos, near the tiny islands of Andímilos and Anánes. Although Murad Pasha's naval force was obviously much larger than Mocenigo's, he apparently had no desire to risk diminution of the reputation he had gained at the Dardanelles. Outmaneuvering Mocenigo, the kapudan pasha sailed off to New Phocaea (Yenifoça), where he cast anchor on 24 June. Mocenigo moved westward to the Venetian island of Cerigo, where his fleet was strengthened by the arrival (on 5 July) of five papal and six Maltese galleys.

Leaving Phocaea the day after his arrival, Murad Pasha made a three weeks' excursion through the Archipelago, again avoiding the Christian fleet and returning to Phocaea on 20 July. Tarring his keels and putting the armada in order, Murad sailed from Phocaea (on 30 July), and was back at the Dardanelles on 10 August. Now he sailed southward through the Aegean islands again, reaching the Cretan waters off Candia (about 10 September). He had to abandon plans for an attack upon Spinalonga on the northeastern shore of Crete, however, and went on to Rhodes, Patmos, Chios, and Smyrna, then back to Phocaea, and on to Mytilene, where he learned that at S. George of Skyros there was a Christian ship which he might seize. But the janissaries had become restless, "chè per non disgustarli proseguì il suo viaggio, giongendo a' 28 [Settembre] ai Castelli, e di là a Galipoli, poi a Marmorà, nel qual luoco licentiò li Bei. . . ." Thus he was back at the Dardanelles by the end of September (1654), having released the Barbary beys about the same time as the papal and Maltese galleys were homeward bound. Murad had eluded the ailing Mocenigo all the way. He had turned in an impressive performance. As the author of the *Viaggio dell'armata Ottomana del 1654* concludes his account, "Questo è stato il viaggio dell'armata Ottomana di quest'anno, il capitan bassà della quale minacciava non solo impatronirsi di Candia, ma volleva soggiogar l'isole, sottometter l'armata Veneta, e condurla in Costantinopoli . . . !"[3]

---

[3] *Relatione del viaggio dell'armata Ottomana del 1654 col fatto delle armi seguito ai Castelli di Costantinopoli con VIII galere Venetiane, due galeazze, et XV* [sic] *vascelli et incontro della detta armata con la Veneta sopra Millo con tutto il seguito sin al ritorno della medesima in Costantinopoli*, MS. Marc. It. VII, 211 (7468), fols. 217ᵛ–237ᵛ, esp. fols. 225ʳff. The account in this MS. does not record Murad Pasha's arrival at the Dardanelles on 10 August (*A 30 di luglio partito con l'armata da Focchies passò a* . . . [i.e., *ai Dardanelli*, which the copyist, fol. 233ʳ, apparently could not read], *dove gionse al dicesimo de Agosto* . . .).

Leaving his ships at Tenos and Cerigo as a safeguard against Turkish attack, Mocenigo went back to Candia, and there he died. Francesco Morosini, who was now embarked on one of the most notable careers in Venetian history, assumed command of the Republic's forces in the Levant. Stormy seas and wintry winds now lay ahead, however, and naval operations were suspended for the rest of the year.

Morosini began the campaign of 1655 with a destructive attack upon the Turkish fortress on the island of Aegina, a supply depot for the sultan's troops at Crete. Thereafter he sailed with the galleasses and galleys through the northern Sporades to the Gulf of Volos, landing at the fortified town on the northern shore at nighttime on 23 March. Morosini burned the town of Volos, destroyed the fortifications, and seized 27 cannon (*tormenta bellica*) and a large store of ship's biscuit. In the meantime he had sent Lazzaro Mocenigo, *praefectus navium*, to the Dardanelles with the sailing ships. From Volos Morosini went on to the Dardanelles, where six Maltese galleys arrived on 4 June for joint action against the Turks. The sultan's armada, however, showed no signs of seeking to enter the northern Aegean. On 12 June, therefore, Morosini sailed from the Dardanelles southward into the Cyclades to do the Turks such damage as he could and to receive Girolamo Foscarini, who had been named Alvise Mocenigo's successor as captain-general of the sea. Upon his arrival Foscarini died at Andros, which still left Morosini in command.[4]

The Turkish armada had not come down to the Dardanelles. It was not ready for action owing to the continuing chaos in Istanbul. In the fall of 1654 the grand vizir Dervish Mehmed had suffered a paralytic stroke. He was replaced by the arrogant Ipshir Mustafa Pasha, who had been the governor of Aleppo (Haleb) at the time of his appointment. In a triumphant journey from Aleppo to Scutari, Ipshir Mustafa had done away with his enemies and advanced the fortunes of his followers, causing fears and giving rise to nerve-racking rumors in Istanbul. At the outset of his grand vizirate Ipshir had spoken belligerently of settling the troubled affairs of Syria, Egypt, and Anatolia, as well as ridding the capital of the corruption of the court intriguers. Everyone on the Bosporus was afraid. Everyone was corrupt.

Ipshir Mustafa Pasha entered Istanbul with great pomp, and continued to mow down his enemies and his opponents, earning the enmity of the kapudan pasha Murad, who gradually formed a cabal against him, and helped to foment a revolt of the janissaries and sipahis. When the situa-

---

[4] Giovanni Graziani (*Joannes Gratianus Bergomensis*), *Francisci Mauroceni Peloponnesiaci, Venetiarum principis, gesta*, Padua, 1698, pp. 38–44, and cf. Antonio Arrighi, *De vita et rebus gestis Francisci Mauroceni Peloponnesiaci, principis Venetorum . . .* , Padua, 1749, lib. I, pp. 36ff.

tion got entirely out of hand, the young Mehmed IV appointed Murad the grand vizir, ordering the strangulation of the overbearing Ipshir (on 10 May 1655). But three months of confusion and failure convinced Murad that he could not handle the grand vizirate and hold on to his life. He asked to be relieved of his duties, and allowed to make a pilgrimage to Mecca. The grand vizirate was then conferred upon the aging Suleiman Pasha, who now became married to the Sultana Aïsche. This was in mid-August of 1655,[5] however, and we must go back two months, and return to the Dardanelles.

When Francesco Morosini had sailed into the Cyclades in mid-June, he had taken with him 18 Venetian galleys, two galleasses, two sailing ships, and the half-dozen Maltese galleys, leaving Lazzaro Mocenigo with four galleasses, six galleys, and some 26 heavy sailing ships to block the Turks' exit from the Dardanelles. A week after Morosini's departure from the straits the new kapudan pasha Mustafa began to move south into the Dardanelles (on 19 June). His armada was a formidable array of eight galleasses (*maone*), 60 light galleys, 30 large sailing ships (*navi grosse da guerra*), and 45 galliots. Some of his vessels were presumably in poor condition, to judge from the consequences of the second battle of the Dardanelles.

Also, on this occasion, the kapudan pasha was to receive no assistance from the Barbary corsairs, for the attacks of the English admiral Robert Blake upon the Tunisian coast and his threat to Algiers earlier in the year had kept the so-called corsairs at home. And now, deploying his forces in the same order as the kapudan pasha Murad had done the year before, Mustafa began his descent toward the exit from the straits on 21 June (1655) with the sailing ships in his first line, the galleasses following them, and the light galleys in the third line, each division stretching almost from shore to shore as it reached the narrows.

Lazzaro Mocenigo awaited the Turkish armada, planning to employ the same stratagem that his predecessor Dolfin had failed to put into effect the year before. The Venetian forces were to cut their cables only after the Turks had got deep into the straits, and had begun their attack. Now it was Mustafa Pasha's intention to launch his galleasses and light galleys against the Venetian right wing, which consisted of the galleasses under the command of Alvise Foscari. He had been misled into believing that this was the weaker part of the Venetian fleet. As the Turkish galleasses and light galleys, now moving to the forefront of the armada, encountered the heavier Venetian galleasses, they were thrown into a confusion which they transmitted to the galleys and heavy ships behind

---

[5] Von Hammer-Purgstall, *Gesch. d. osman. Reiches*, V, 610–33, trans. Hellert, X, 350–75. Murad, the former kapudan pasha, died on his journey to Mecca.

them. Heeding instructions despite the disarray of the Turkish armada, the Venetian commanders held their lines. As the Turkish vessels veered to the starboard, trying to get past them, the Venetians cut the hawsers securing their vessels, and launched their own attacks.

The outcome of the six-hour battle was a near disaster for the Turks, nine of whose ships were burned, three captured, and two driven ashore and sunk. A Turkish galleass was also sunk, and a galley burned. A large number of Turks were taken captive as well as two captains of flagships (*sultane*) and a Neapolitan renegade named Carlino, who had also commanded a flagship. A contemporary reporter assures us that no one could deny the Venetians had had the blessings of the Almighty in this famous encounter which had instilled terror in the minds of the Turks.[6]

Withdrawing as best he could from the area of the Dardanelles, Mustafa Pasha made his way with his battered vessels to Phocaea, where he set about overhauling the armada. Meanwhile Morosini met the papal commander Stefano Lomellino at Cerigo on 22 June (1655); Lomellino had brought five galleys to add to the Christian armament against the Turks. Having been informed of Mustafa's entry into the Dardanelles, Morosini set sail for the straits, but got no farther than Delos in the midst of the Cyclades when on 24 June Mocenigo arrived to recount his defeat of the Turks. Seeking to profit from the plight of Mustafa's armada, on 3 July Morosini began an ill-advised siege of the fortress town of Monemvasia (Malvasia) on the southeast coast of the Morea. The garrison of Monemvasia was said to be weak, and to lack supplies and munitions, although it could obviously be reinforced by troops from other Turkish strongholds at Corinth, Nauplia, Tripolis (Tripolitza), and Kalamata.

Although Mustafa Pasha was active in the Aegean before the end of July (1655), he put a higher premium on wisdom than valor, and avoided any attempt to relieve the Venetian investment of Monemvasia by sea. Owing to an alleged explosion aboard the Maltese *capitana*, however, the Hospitallers had withdrawn from Monemvasiote waters (on 9 July), and when Morosini had to give up the futile five weeks' siege on 18 August, the papal galleys under Lomellino embarked upon their return

---

[6] *Raguaglio del combattimento seguito ai Dardanelli tra l'armata veneta et l'ottomana a 21 Zugno 1655 sotto la direttione de Lazaro Mocenigo, capitan delle navi venete,* in the *Raccolta diplomatica della guerra di Candia,* MS. Marc. It. VII, 211 (7468), fols. 190ᵛ–194ʳ, a dispatch dated "from the galleass on 26 June 1655:" The writer observes in closing that "non si può negare che questo combattimento non habbia havute tutte le beneditioni del Signor Dio, perchè nove sono stati vascelli abbruggiati, tre presi, et due investiti in terra oltre la maona somersa et la galera incendiata. Gli schiavi sono stati in molto numero oltre due capitani di sultane Turche et un rinegato Napolitano nominato il capitan Carlino. . . . In somma la vittoria è riuscita considerabile mentre i danni inferiti, le navi prese ed incendiate, l'inimico spaventato, non v'è cosa che non renda gloriosa l'impresa et memorabile e grande la direttione dell'armi venete . . ." (*ibid.,* fols. 193ᵛ–194ʳ, at which point the text is disintegrating).

to the papal naval station at Civitavecchia on the Tyrrhenian coast. Finally, about the end of September, Morosini left to take command at Candia, leaving Barbaro Badoer, who was replacing him as provveditore, in command of the Republic's ships and galleys until the advent of Lorenzo Marcello, the late Girolamo Foscarini's successor as captain-general of the sea.[7] The Turks as well as the Venetians began to retire their galleys for the coming winter but, despite the Venetians' constant vigilance, the Turks managed to transport foodstuffs and munitions to their forces at Canea, from which the siege of Candia was being maintained.

With the advent of spring in 1656 the captain-general Lorenzo Marcello sailed from Candia with a fleet of six galleasses, 24 galleys, and 13 ships. His purpose was to resume the blockade of the Dardanelles. If the Turkish armada could not get through the straits, obviously there would be no significant reinforcement of the sultan's army at Canea. Pausing for a while at Andros in the northern Cyclades, Marcello received further men and munitions from Venice on 6 May, and thereafter sailed north to Skyros, east to Mytilene, and thence to the little island of Imbros (Imroz) hard by the mouth of the Dardanelles, where he dropped anchor on 23 May. About three weeks later he was joined by seven Maltese galleys under Gregorio Carafa, who in later years (in 1680) would become grand master of the Hospitallers.[8]

Lorenzo Marcello had been hovering over the exit to the Dardanelles for a full month when on 22 or 23 June (1656) the Turkish armada under the kapudan pasha Chinam, a Russian renegade, began to approach the Venetian fleet with nine galleasses, 60 galleys, and 28 or 29 heavy sailing ships (*poderose navi*). Marcello's fleet was smaller—seven galleasses, 31 galleys, and 29 ships—but, as usual, the Venetian vessels were of heavier, more solid construction. The Turks came down the straits under cover of gunfire from cannoneers on the shores. Undeterred by the Turkish cannon, Marcello's forces advanced to meet them in the area of Çanakkale.

It was Monday, 26 June, at the fourteenth hour, i.e., it was about 11:00 A.M. As the wind shifted from north to the west (*maestrale*), the Turkish vessels became crowded against the Anatolian shore. They suffered severely from the clash of arms and the bursts of Venetian gunfire. Chinam Pasha, aided by the westerly wind, got back up stream with 12 or 14 light

---

[7] Cf. Graziani, *Francisci Mauroceni . . . gesta* (1698), pp. 45ff., who refers to Monemvasia as Epidaurus [Limera], as does Arrighi, *De vita et rebus gestis Francisci Mauroceni* (1749), lib. I, p. 36, whose brief account exaggerates the effects of Morosini's efforts at Monemvasia. See Alberto Guglielmotti, *Storia della marina pontificia*, VIII (1893), 136–41; Anderson, *Naval Wars in the Levant* (1952), pp. 153–56.

[8] On Gregorio Carafa's career, note L. Bertoni in the *Dizionario biografico degli Italiani*, XIX (1976), 576–78, with refs.

galleys to the safety of the Turkish forts on either side of the Dardanelles. It was the worst naval defeat the Turks could remember since Lepanto.[9]

There were minor encounters on the following day, but the Turks lost heart. Indeed, they had lost a good deal more, for the Venetians had captured five galleasses, 13 galleys, two small *pinchi*, and four large sailing ships. They had also sunk or set fire to four galleasses, 34 galleys, and 22 ships. As was to be expected, however, the Venetians did not emerge from the contest unscathed, for they counted several hundred dead and wounded as well as a number of oarsmen missing. Lorenzo Marcello, the captain-general, was killed by a "colpo di cannone." Lazzaro Mocenigo, the victor of 1655, lost an eye as a result of a musket shot, and the Signoria lost three sailing ships, which the Turks had set afire. Carafa's Maltese forces had also suffered some casualties in dead and wounded. In comparison with the Turkish casualties, the Venetian losses could be regarded as small, while a large number of Christian slaves, allegedly 5,000, were freed from the Moslem galleys: "Così s'è ultimata la più bella vittoria che habbia già mai havuta la nostra patria. . . ."[10]

Marcello's death left Barbaro Badoer, the provveditore, in command of the Venetian fleet, but Gregorio Carafa, pleased with the Christian success, now decided to return the Hospitallers' galleys to Malta. He could not accept orders from one of lesser rank than a captain-general. Also he regarded the campaign as over and done with for the year; Chinam Pasha could neither attack the Venetians in Candia nor reinforce the Turks at Canea. Carafa had distinguished himself in the battle, having been largely responsible for Chinam's withdrawal beyond the Turkish fortress of Anatolia. He had also apparently captured eleven of the Turkish galleys which the allies had taken, and now he claimed them as the possessions of his Order. Some of the Venetians, especially Antonio Barbaro, the captain of the Gulf, objected to Carafa's carrying off most of the galleys seized from the Turks as well as the rich booty that had fallen into Maltese hands. The bulk of the Christian force was Venetian. The Signoria should get a corresponding share of the captured galleys.

Carafa had been a Hospitaller all his life; a Neapolitan noble, his family

---

[9] Cf. Graziani, *Francisci Mauroceni . . . gesta* (1698), pp. 51–52.

[10] *Lettera del Signor Marcello su la vittoria ottenuta de Turchi ai Dardanelli a 26 Zugno 1656*, in the *Raccolta diplomatica della guerra di Candia*, MS. Marc. It. VII, 211 (7468), fols. 194–197ʳ, a dispatch "from on board ship at Tenedos on 27 June 1656," and see also, *ibid.*, fols. 210–215: *Relatione della vittoria navale conseguita dell'armi Venete a 26 Zugno 1656 sotto la direttione del già capitan generale Lorenzo Marcello*, according to which the Venetian fleet consisted of seven galleasses, 24 light galleys, and 28 sailing ships. Both sources give the same figures for Chinam Pasha's armada, and their accounts of the battle are similar if not the same. Cf. Anderson, *Naval Wars in the Levant*, pp. 158ff.

was notoriously pro-Spanish. The Venetians had never entertained any affection for either the Hospitallers or the Spanish, but they needed all the help the Order could give them against the Turks. Antonio Barbaro's quarrel with the Hospitallers might have proved damaging. The provveditore Badoer, therefore, yielded to their demands, and on 29 June Carafa sailed off with his Turkish galleys and loot to Malta, where he received a grand reception. Meanwhile Antonio Barbaro had been so obstreperous in his objections that Badoer sent him back to Venice under arrest, although he was soon released for further service against the Turks in 1657 and for more trouble (this time with the captain-general Francesco Morosini) in 1660.

Meanwhile the Venetians were rejoicing in their overwhelming defeat of Chinam Pasha in the narrows of the Dardanelles (on 26 June 1656), and the provveditore Barbaro Badoer had not failed to take full advantage of the success they had enjoyed with the help of the Hospitallers. Posting two galleasses, four galleys, and five ships at the straits to keep an eye on the Turks (on 4 July), Badoer sailed for Tenedos, seizing the island from the Turks (on 8 July). Six weeks later he also ousted the Turks from Lemnos (on 20 August). The latter island was generally known as Stalimene, and was famous for its reddish earth (Lemnian bole), "terra sigillata," which was used as an astringent to treat snake bites and numerous other afflictions. It was pressed into small cakes, stamped with the seal of the Gran Signore, and widely used in the Ottoman empire. Little of it, however, was allowed to go westward into Europe. To the Venetians, therefore, Lemnos would seem to have been a boon to physicians as well as a base for subsequent operations against the Turks.[11]

---

[11] In antiquity the collection of Lemnian earth was accompanied by a religious ceremony, "e [si] la formava in girelle picciole e l'improntava col sigillo di Diana, e questa era detta terra sigillata, terra Lennia e sacra. Questa è quella terra sigillata che tanto è stata celebrata dagli antichi medici e specialmente da Galeno nel libro nono delle facoltà de 'semplici' come quella che sia ottimo rimedio a salvar ferite, a flussi del sangue, a mali pestilentiali, a morsi d'animali velenosi, a far vomitar i veleni già presi, et ad altra infirmità. Questa terra hoggi vien tenuta sotto grande custodia, et è suggellata col suggello del Gran Signore de Turchi, e poca ne viene portata in Christianità" (*Presa di Stalimene . . .* , in *Raccolta diplomatica della guerra di Candia,* MS. Marc. It. VII, 211 [7468], fol. 216). On the magic qualities of Lemnian earth, note Brusoni, *Historia* (1673), I, bk. XIII, p. 306.

My colleague Professor Christian Habicht has called my attention to the large importance of Lemnian earth as illustrated by the following texts: Vitruvius, *De architectura,* VII, 2, ed. F. Krohn, Leipzig: Teubner, 1912, p. 163; Dioscorides, *De materia medica,* ed. Max Wellmann, 5 bks. in 3 vols., Berlin, 1907–14, III, 97, pp. 67–68; English version in Robert T. Gunther, *The Greek Herbal of Dioscorides,* Oxford, 1934, pp. 638–39; Galen, in K.G. Kühn, ed., *Medicorum graecorum opera quae extant,* 26 vols. in 28, Leipzig, 1821–33, XII (1826), 169–78, and cf., *ibid.,* XIV (1827), 8; note also Carl Fredrich, "Lemnos," *Mitteilungen des Kaiserlich Deutschen Archäologischen Instituts, Athenische Abteilung,* XXXI (1906), 72ff., 254–55, and F.W. Hasluck, "Terra Lemnia," *Annual of the British School at Athens,* XVI (1909–1910), 220–31,

The campaign of 1656 had indeed been remarkable, for the two islands, at the very mouth of the Dardanelles, were the *antemurale* of
Istanbul. Providing a foothold in the midst of Turkish waters, they were a
further step toward maintaining the blockade and preventing the shipment of men and munitions from the Turkish capital to Canea and to the
sultan's forces encamped around Candia. Furthermore, with such a
stronghold off the coast of the Dardanelles an attack upon Istanbul itself
was not inconceivable. It is no wonder, therefore, that at this critical
juncture the Porte turned to the redoubtable Mehmed Köprülü, who now
accepted the grand vizirate on his own terms. In fact from mid-September 1656 Mehmed Köprülü was the virtual ruler of the Ottoman
empire.[12]

Leaving sailing ships to block the exit from the Dardanelles, and garrisons to hold his island conquests, Barbaro Badoer sailed to Delos and
thence to Paros, where in February 1657 he yielded command of the
fleet to the one-eyed hero Lazzaro Mocenigo, the newly-appointed captain-general. In March a Turkish armada of some 32 galleys and some
smaller vessels emerged from the Dardanelles, where the Venetian
blockade was inadequate. Their objective was to retake the island of
Tenedos, but they made no attempt to do so, for the Venetians seemed
well prepared to deal with them. In April and May Mocenigo enjoyed
some success in the waters and among the islands off the coast of Chios,
including the occupation of Suazich (on 18 May).[13] He thought of attempting the conquest of Chios, but gave up the idea in view of the
danger which loomed over Tenedos, for (says one of our informants) the
island was threatened by the Turks "con poderosissimo esercito da terra

---

Sultan Mehmed IV now sequestered the English ships in Turkish waters to force them to
serve with his own armada against the Venetians, as we learn from a plea which reached
the English government on 8 January 1657 (Public Record Office, State Papers 97, XVII,
fols. 135–36): "The Ottoman being exasperated and inraged at the advantages gained this
yeare upon his states by the armes of the most serene Republic of Venice, who besides the
totall destruction of a most powerfull fleet have had the favour of God to free from the
Turkish yoke Tenedos and Stalimene, otherwise called Lemnos, principall islands and of
great consequence, making themselves masters of them with small resistance and in a
short space of time, [the Ottoman] doth now practise all diligence to render his forces for
the next service vigorous, formidable, and capable to recover what he hath lost and to
conquer the kingdom of Candia, for which he hath laboured in vaine and troubled himselfe
soe many yeares.

"Besides the orders imposed upon all his Arsenalls for the rigging up of a quantitie of
vessells, he hath begun to offer violence to the English that are in his Porte, pretending to
draw them by force to his owne service, and for that purpose doth deny them that at
present are in his harbours leave to depart," to which (the writer declared) Oliver Crom-
well should make a vigorous objection rather than "to see his ships subjected to soe great a
violence as to be constrained contrarie to their own will to joyne with the Turke against a
Christian prince [the doge of Venice], an awncient and affectionate friend. . . ."

[12] H. Kretschmayr, *Gesch. von Venedig*, III (1934, repr. 1964), 330.

[13] Cf. Brusoni, *Historia* (1673), II, bk. xiv, pp. 7–8.

e con una fortissima armata di mare." In mid-June Mocenigo was joined
by the papal squadron under Giovanni Bichi, a nephew of Pope Alexander VII, and by that of Malta under Gregorio Carafa, the prior of Roc-
cella. Bichi and Carafa had met at Messina (on 18 May), and sailed east
together. Since they could not agree on which held the superior rank—
protocol was always important—they were finding it difficult to confer
or to cooperate with each other.

Giovanni Bichi was lieutenant-general of the pope's brother Mario
Chigi, who was the nominal captain-general of the papal forces on land
and at sea. Mario, however, had no intention of going into the Levant.
Bichi's rank was thus presumably inferior to that of Carafa, but he refused to acknowledge the fact, and he did have Chigi's papal banner on
board. Who would take precedence, Bichi or Carafa? The crisis came in
early July (1657) when the Turkish armada came down into the Dardanelles with ten galleasses, 30 galleys, and 18 sailing ships "plus any number of saïques and caïques." Although Mehmed Köprülü was wrestling
with grave problems on the Bosporus, he was determined to break the
Venetian blockade and recover the islands of Tenedos and Lemnos.

Lazzaro Mocenigo as Venetian captain-general of the sea had planned
to meet the sultan's armada in the straits with Carafa on his right and
Bichi on his left, but the latter found the proposed deployment of the
squadrons unacceptable. He could not yield the right wing to Carafa. He
also claimed that Alexander VII had ordered him to take command in
any direct encounter with the Turks. Truly the hour of decision had
come; Mocenigo and Carafa acted promptly. They yielded the *battaglia,*
the central position of command, to Bichi. Mocenigo took the right wing,
Carafa accepted the left. Delayed by the necessity to get water enough
for those aboard their ships and galleasses, and held up by heavy winds,
first from the north and then from the east, the Christians were not well
prepared to meet the sultan's armada as it approached the mouth of the
Dardanelles on the morning of 17 July (1657). The east winds were tying
most of the Christian galleys to the European shore at the exit from the
Dardanelles. As the Turks moved south and west, aided by the winds,
they were confronted by no more than seven Christian galleasses, four
galleys, and twenty sailing ships. The winds and Turkish gunners had
almost cleared the Anatolian shoreline.

The fourth battle of the Dardanelles (17–19 July 1657) was a series of
hard-fought encounters, costly to both sides. The *cannone turchesco*
took a heavy toll of Christian life, as the winds and the current drove
most of the Turks and their opponents into the northern Aegean. The
Christians took refuge at Tenedos. The Turks went further south, to
Mytilene, having lost several ships and six galleasses. The Turkish losses
exceeded those of the Christians, but the agha of the janissaries was said
to be on hand with 80,000 "combattenti" who were to be employed for

the recovery of Tenedos. When the weather improved, the combat was resumed.

During the evening of 19 July, as Lazzaro Mocenigo went into action with his usual "intrepidity," a cannon ball struck his flagship, igniting the gunpowder, bombs, and grenades which he had aboard. Most of the deck was blown off the ship. Mocenigo was killed. His death led the Venetian crews to believe that fate had snatched a likely victory from them. They recovered his body, the standard of the Republic, the lantern of the flagship, and the banner of the winged lion of S. Mark, but they could only grieve over the loss of so great a commander thus cut off in the "flower of his years." His head had been crushed, apparently by a falling yardarm. Among those whose lives were saved was Mocenigo's brother Francesco, who had served him as a lieutenant, and who (we are told) now desired nothing more than to give his own life for the fatherland "a similitudine del fratello."[14]

---

[14] *Lettera de Barbaro Badoer, proveditore dell'armata, con laquale dà parte del seguito dei Dardanelli con la morte del capitan general Mocenigo* [almost illegible], dated "from the galley at Tenedos on 24 July 1657," in the *Raccolta diplomatica della guerra di Candia*, MS. Marc. It. VII, 211 (7468), fols. 203^r–204^r, and *Relatione del combattimento seguito tra l'armata Veneta et la Turca li 17, 18, e 19 Luglio 1657 sotto la direttione del già illustrissimo et eccellentissimo Signore Lazaro Mocenigo, cavalier, procurator, capitan general da mar*, dated "from the galley at Tenedos on 21 July 1657," *ibid.*, fols. 204^v–210^r. According to the latter text, "Consisteva l'armata nemica in XVIII navi, XXX galere, X galeazze, e numero infinito di saiche e caichi" (fol. 205^v). The writer of this account saves himself and the reader a certain amount of extraneous detail by noting that "basta il dire che emulando nel valore le galeazze le navi e le navi le galeazze, i Turchi [si sono] avviliti dal coraggio de nostri" (fol. 206^v).

We also learn from this *Relatione* the details of Lazzaro Mocenigo's death: "Non per questo [i.e., because of certain losses in the combat at sea] il capitan general rallentò punto quell'ardore che lo renderà glorioso tra tutte le memorie immortali della posterità. Continuava egli il viaggio con tutta intrepidezza quando un colpo fatale di canone portò una palla nella munitione della generalitia [Mocenigo's flagship] dove oltre la polvere v'erano bombe e granate, onde acceso il fuoco la galera si divise per mezo, volando tutta la coperta, non rimanendo che dalla parte del fogone indietro con morte dello stesso generale. . . . Accidente così lacrimabile ha fatto creder perduta la vittoria, e sebene si sono ricuperati il cadavere del capitan generale, lo stendardo, il faro, et la bandiera publica, non per questo si sono punto rallentate le lacrime per la caduta d'un comandante che nel fiore degli anni pareva che havesse rese tributarie la virtù et la fortuna. Fu ritrovato il cadavere con la testa tutta fracassata da qualche gran colpo che si suppone dell'antenna. Tra quelli che si sono salvati nella galera generalitia è stato Signor Francesco Mocenigo, luogotenente e fratello del medesimo capitan generale, che miracolosamente s'è preservato in vita col solo desiderio di sacrificarla alla patria a similitudine del fratello" (*ibid.*, fols. 207^v–208^r). Note also in this connection the *Lettera di raggualio del combattimento tra l'armata veneta e la turca a' Dardanelli sotto il comando del già illustriss. et eccel. Sig. Lazaro Mocenigo, K[avalier], Procurator, Capitan general da mar seguito il 17, 18 e 19 luglio 1657*, Venice, appresso Gio. Pietro Pinelli, *stampator ducale, 1657*. The fourth battle of the Dardanelles and Mocenigo's death aroused much excitement in Venice and elsewhere. Cf. Brusoni, *Historia* (1673), II, bk. XIV, pp. 11ff.

On the Turco-Venetian naval encounters at the Dardanelles, see also E. Ferrari, "Le Battaglie dei Dardanelli nel 1656–57," in the *Memorie storiche militari*, IX (1913), fasc. 3, pp. 1–243, with an appendix of fifty-seven archival and other texts.

Once more Barbaro Badoer, provveditore of the Venetian fleet, had to assume the high command, "procurando almeno di portar il fuoco nelle galere Turchesche,"[15] but the allied campaign of 1657 had ended, and the Venetians soon found themselves on the defensive. Late in the day on 23 July both Giovanni Bichi and Gregorio Carafa began their homeward voyages. On the way back Bichi ran into a Turkish squadron between the mainland town of Parga and the island of Paxos (just south of Corfu), driving them from access to the Adriatic. The Venetians would blame Bichi's early departure for the loss which, as we shall note in a moment, was soon to follow of Tenedos and Lemnos. Upon his return to Rome, however, Bichi was able to convince Alexander VII that the Venetian charges were unfounded, and on 13 March (1658) the pope appointed him prefect and captain-general of the pontifical galleys. The forces of the Republic had not fared so well in 1657: "Basta il dire esser stato ferocissimo e sanguinoso il combattimento," but the author of the *Relatione* of this year still believed "che la vittoria è stata grandissima in faccia si può dire del Primo Visir et dell'Agà gianizzero."[16]

The most dramatic events in the "war of Candia" were the four battles of the Dardanelles. The struggle of the Venetian Signoria to hold on to Candia had become largely a matter of maintaining the reputation of the Republic. The Cretans had never been easy to deal with; the island had been more of an expense than a source of income. While the Venetian forces were hard put to retain possession of Candia, what could they do with Tenedos and Lemnos, which were so far from their chief sources of supply? Strong garrisons would have to be established on the two islands, and large detachments of the fleet would have to be maintained in the northern Aegean. There were those who thought it might be better simply to let Tenedos and Lemnos fall back into the hands of the Turks and to concentrate the maritime resources of the Republic upon holding Candia until a suitable peace could be made with the Turks.

It would certainly be desirable to keep two or three footholds on the island of Crete for naval purposes, but the costs of war were exceeding the capacity of the Republic to meet them. Let the Porte assume the unprofitable responsibility for the island, and restore to the Venetian merchants access to the Turkish markets. Such at least was the view of

---

[15] *Relatione del combattimento*, fol. 208.

[16] *Ibid.*, fol. 209ʳ, and note Anderson, *Naval Wars in the Levant*, pp. 164–67. On Bichi's role in the events of 1657, see the *Relazione del viaggio delle galere pontificie in Levante l'anno 1657 sotto il comando del loro generale balì Giovanni Bichi, priore di Capua* [written by the Hospitaller Marc'Antonio Miniconi of Perugia], edited with a brief introduction by G. Cugnoni, in the *Bulletino senese di storia patria*, IV (Siena, 1897), 345–89. Cugnoni, pp. 381ff., also gives us a poor text of the *Lettera di raggualio del combattimento tra l'armata veneta e la turca a' Dardanelli* mentioned in note 14 above. Note also G. De Caro, on Giovanni Bichi, in the *Dizionario biografico degli Italiani*, X (1968), 349–51, with various references.

the peace party in the Senate, a view apparently shared by the doge Bertucci Valier (1656–1658), but the war party prevailed. When the Turks became involved in a renewal of warfare in Transylvania, they were prepared to make peace with Venice, but their demand for surrender of the entire island of Crete was more than the war party could tolerate.

The problem presented to the Signoria by the north-Aegean islands was, however, solved shortly after the fourth battle of the Dardanelles for, now under the aggressive leadership of Mehmed Köprülü, the Turks recovered Tenedos on 31 August (1657) and Lemnos on 12 November. After the death of Lazzaro Mocenigo, Francesco Morosini was appointed captain-general of the sea. The years 1658 and 1659 were eventful but futile, for the Venetian fleet, despite the usual Maltese and papal reinforcements (especially in 1658), accomplished little or nothing. Although on the whole they tried to maintain the blockade of the Dardanelles, Turkish vessels managed to move in and out of the historic channel to make periodic landings at Canea, Chios, and the Aegean islands. In late August (1658) the Christian forces failed in an endeavor to take the important fortress island of S. Maura. In mid-March 1659, however, Morosini's naval militia occupied Kalamata on the southern coast of the Morea, and thereafter seized Torone on the Chalcidic peninsula as well as Çeşme on the Anatolian coast opposite the island of Chios. On 22 September (1659) the Venetian (and French) forces also took Castel Rosso (Carystus) at the southern end of the island of Negroponte (Euboea), where they destroyed most of the fortifications. The Venetians had no way of holding on to any one of these places, and Morosini's sailing back and forth in the Archipelago accomplished nothing of abiding importance.[17]

Francesco Morosini began the naval campaign of 1660 with failure to take the island fortress of Negroponte (Chalcis), but he did enjoy a small success with the occupation of the island of Skiathos, the westernmost of the Northern Sporades, *Sciathus insula XX m. passus ab Euboeae ora boreali distans*. Graziani makes much of the Venetian seizure of Skiathos, which was hardly an important conquest. At length, however, the Venetian appeals to France bore fruit. After the second treaty of the Pyrenees (1659), when the Franco–Spanish war had ceased, Louis XIV's government decided to assist the Signoria in the defense of Candia by

---

[17] Graziani, *Francisci Mauroceni . . . gesta* (1698), pp. 56–83, in somewhat confusing detail; Arrighi, *De vita et rebus gestis Francisci Mauroceni* (1749), lib. I, pp. 43–58; Kretschmayr, *Gesch. von Venedig*, III (1934, repr. 1964), 330–33; Anderson, *Naval Wars in the Levant* (1952), pp. 167–70; *Relatione del successo de Calamata sotto la condota del generale [Jacques de] Grémonville, sergente generale, del 1659*, in the *Raccolta diplomatica della guerra di Candia*, MS. Marc. It. VII, 211 (7468), fols. 240ᵛ–246ʳ.

sending a fleet with 4,000 foot and 200 horse under the command of Prince Almerigo d'Este. German mercenaries were hired. At the urgent behest of France the duke of Savoy promised to provide another thousand foot, but it was not to be a good year for Morosini. Despite the appearance of Maltese, papal, Tuscan, and French galleys in eastern waters to help the Venetians, almost nothing was to go well. There was dissension within the Christian forces, especially between the papal and Maltese commanders. Within the Ottoman empire, however, order was being restored to no small extent.

In fact during the years 1659–1661 the Turks under the vigorous administration of the grand vizir Mehmed Köprülü were carrying on war against Francis I Rákóczy in Transylvania, against the Venetians in Crete, Dalmatia, and the Archipelago, and against the Cossacks in the area of the Black Sea. The Turks were also continuing their tiresome aggressions in Wallachia and Moldavia. Moreover, they were now at serious odds with the French, arresting Louis XIV's ambassador and confining him in the fortified enclosure of the Seven Towers (Yedikule), "che generalmente si dice essere ciò seguito per causa del soccorso dato dal Re Christianissimo alli signori Venetiani."[18]

Although the French joined Morosini's fleet in April (1660), they were hardly ready for action before August, when Morosini was finally able to set sail from Cerigo to Suda Bay. Entering the bay under the heavy fire of Turkish cannon, the troops disembarked and sought to scale the walls of Fort S. Veneranda, emboldened by the presence of both Morosini and d'Este. The admiral Francesco Grassi and several officers were killed in the attack. The French then moved on to the walls of Canea while the Venetians assailed the forts of Calogero and Calami as well as the Castello dell'Apricorno. Although these lesser forts were taken, the Christian forces were in no position to break the Turkish hold upon Canea.[19]

Moving on to Candia in mid-September, Morosini and Almerigo attacked the Turks at Candia, forcing their way into the Turkish military settlement known as "New Candia," but again little came of it. When the French troops withdrew to Naxos, Almerigo died,[20] and Jacques de Grémonville took over the command of his troops, finally getting them

---

[18] Ivan Dujčev, *Avvisi di Ragusa* (Orientalia Christiana analecta, 101), Rome, 1935, nos. CLXXXVIII–CXCIII, CXCV, CXCVII, pp. 242–55, with the quotation from doc. no. CXCIII, p. 251, dated 21 December 1661.

[19] Cf. *Raguaglio del successo alla Suda sotto 24 Agosto 1660 sotto la diretione del signor capitan general Francesco Morosini e del signor principe Almerigo di Parma*, in the *Raccolta diplomatica della guerra di Candia*, MS. Marc. It. VII, 211 (7468), fols. 257ʳ–267.

[20] There is an impressive monument to Almerigo d'Este, in commemoration of his services to the Republic, in the church of S. Maria Gloriosa dei Frari in Venice, the fourth monument on the right (next to the altar of the Zane family), as one enters the church by the main portal.

back to France. The frustrating events of 1660 soon led to Morosini's being replaced by his relative Giorgio Morosini, of the S. Maria Formosa branch of the family. Francesco belonged to the S. Stefano branch of the Morosini. He had served in the *capitaneria generale* for three years, the usual term that one held the difficult office, and the Signoria now granted his request to return home.[21]

As the allied forces had moved back and forth from Cerigo to Crete and elsewhere, they had tried, as we have noted, unsuccessfully to break up the Turkish encampments at Canea and Candia. Francesco Morosini blamed their costly failure largely upon the alleged incompetence of the provveditore Antonio Barbaro who, while the Franco-Venetian troops were engaged with the enemy at Candia, had disembarked in disorderly fashion the company under his command. Francesco declared Barbaro condemned to death, but the latter escaped from his clutches, returning to Venice, where the Quarantia Criminale absolved him of the charges made against him. When Francesco came back to the lagoon toward the end of the year 1661, he was assailed by members of the peace party as well as by Barbaro's supporters.

Francesco Morosini was denounced for exaggerating his exploits in order to embellish his reputation, which was misleading (his enemies claimed) to both the government and the populace, for they were encouraged to believe that armed opposition to the Turks could lead to victory and the retention of the island of Crete. Morosini was in fact subjected to prolonged vilification, being accused of seeking to profit personally from pillage, piracy, and extortion—the sources, his detractors asserted, of the Morosini wealth. Doubtless depressed, Morosini was still being kept in quarantine at the island lazzaretto (now the isle of S. Lazzaro degli Armeni), along with the officers and crew of his galley, when the charges being made against him were placed before the Senate, the Council of Ten, and the Quarantia Criminale. According to one citation, eighty informants had attested to Morosini's wrongdoing. There was as large a percentage of backbiters among the Venetian nobles in the Grand Council as there is in modern Academe.

Since the proposed indictment had been lodged anonymously, the Senate should not have taken cognizance of it. Nameless would-be informants submitted three documents listing a hundred or so trumped-up charges against Morosini. Many a distracting inquest and trial had been set in motion by detractors against their enemies only to result in defeat for the accusers, not to speak of distress for the accused. Despite the doge Domenico Contarini's cool reception of Morosini and the prosecu-

---

[21] Cf. Graziani, *Francisci Mauroceni . . . gesta* (1698), pp. 85–105; Damerini, *Morosini* (1929), pp. 89–95.

tor's decision to try the flimsy case against him, on 30 June 1663 Morosini was duly acquitted of the charges filed against him.[22]

Giorgio Morosini, who had been recently appointed captain-general of the Venetian fleet, reached the island stronghold of Cerigo on 7 June (1661) to relieve his relative Francesco of the burden he had been bearing with frustration. Little was accomplished this year except that in late August Giorgio broke up the investment of the island of Tenos (between Andros and Mykonos) by a Turkish armada of some 36 galleys. Pursuing the Turks as they fled from the scene, Giorgio seized four of their galleys and sank another five offshore from Melos, the southwesternmost island in the Cyclades. He had had the assistance of the Maltese commander Fabrizio Ruffo who now, like Gregorio Carafa five years before, laid claim to all four Turkish galleys. When Giorgio Morosini would give him only two, Ruffo withdrew in a huff, going back to Malta to a less spectacular reception than Carafa had enjoyed. The year 1662 was frustrating for Morosini, because nothing was accomplished despite his having been joined by papal and Maltese galleys. In late September the Venetians did, nevertheless, disrupt and partially destroy the Alexandria convoy for this year. The convoy regularly carried supplies to Istanbul or Crete.

The Turks showed no aggression at sea throughout 1663–1664, for during these two years there was a serious renewal of warfare between Austria and the Porte, which led to Raimondo Montecuccoli's defeat of the Ottoman forces on 1 August 1664 in the famous battle of S. Gotthard (Szentgotthárd) on the river Raab in western Hungary. The Turkish commander was the astute grand vizir Ahmed Köprülü Pasha, the son and successor of hardy, old Mehmed Köprülü (d. 1661). Although Ahmed lost the battle, he won the peace, which was established by the treaty of Vasvár ten days later. The Turks retained Grosswardein (Oradea, Nagyvárad), which they had taken in 1660 (and were to hold until 1692), as well as Neuhäusel (Nové Zámky) in southern Slovakia, which they had occupied in late September 1663.[23]

While the Turks were thus engaged, one would think the Venetians

---

[22] Graziani, *Francisci Mauroceni . . . gesta*, p. 107; Arrighi, *De vita et rebus gestis Francisci Mauroceni*, lib. I, pp. 82–84; Damerini, *Morosini*, pp. 93–100.

[23] Szentgotthárd is of course in Hungary, now on the Austrian border, about thirty miles west of Vasvár. There is a little museum in Szentgotthárd, where I found on a printed notice a single reference to Montecuccoli and the events of 1664. On going to Vasvár, one drives on the whole through flat lands. The town is set on a slight height amid green trees and well cultivated fields. A house at Vasvár is allegedly being prepared as a museum. My informant stated that the house in question was the site of the treaty of 10 August 1664, which I was inclined to doubt. As for Nové Zámky—a dull, dowdy town—the tourist will find there almost no memorial of the Turkish past. There is a brief summary of the treaty of Vasvár (in French) in Dumont, *Corps universel diplomatique*, VI-2 (1728), no. XI, p. 23, and a Latin version, *ibid.*, no. XII, pp. 23–25, "actum in Castris Turcicis apud Vasvarum, decima mensis Augusti, anno MDCLXIV."

might have accomplished something worthwhile, even though no papal galleys entered the Sea of Crete or the Aegean to assist them. Once more, however, strife between the Venetian and Maltese commanders impeded any decisive action against the enemy. In 1664 neither Maltese nor papal galleys came into the eastern waters to help either Giorgio Morosini or his successor Andrea Corner. The French were active on the northern coast of Africa and even in the area of Samos and Chios in 1665, but without results of any consequence. Yes, it was as Kretschmayr has put it. As far as Turco-Venetian warfare was concerned, the years from 1661 to 1666 were almost a blank: "So sind die Jahre von 1661 bis 1666 kaum wirkliche Kriegsjahre für Venedig gewesen."[24]

Venetian efforts in 1666 were also marked with failure and disappointment, caused in part by very bad weather during the early months of the year. Although the Hospitallers' galleys came east for a while, they soon returned to Malta without taking any effective action against the Turks. As winter came on, the Venetian fleet withdrew to the islands of Andros and Paros. Now that Austria and the Porte were at peace again, the grand vizir Ahmed Köprülü turned his full attention to the siege of Crete, on which the Turks had been engaged for some twenty years. Köprülü apparently dispatched some nine thousand troops to the island to press the siege of Candia. Both Graziani and Arrighi give highly exaggerated figures for the strength of the Turkish soldiery. The Venetians began the year 1667 by blocking the efforts of a Turkish relief force from Alexandria to land men and munitions at Canea, although some months later the Turkish commanders succeeded in landing extensive reinforcements at Canea.

In 1667, however, the Venetians received much more help than usual from their western allies. The French had been contributing considerable sums to the Christian cause. On 26 February 16 western galleys and five galleasses dropped anchor in Suda Bay as well as numerous other vessels with some six thousand soldiers, among them two fine regiments which had arrived on the scene under the command of Giron François, marquis de Ville, who was accompanied by the Swiss master of artillery Johann Werdmüller. De Ville and Werdmüller were officers and employees of the duke of Savoy who, like various other Christian princes, was trying to do his part against the Turks. The troops, having attempted a landing at Canea, were withdrawn to the trenches of the Christian encampment at Candia (on 6 March), and were soon taken into the fortress

---

[24] Kretschmayr, *Gesch. von Venedig*, III (1934, repr. 1964), 332–35; Anderson, *Naval Wars in the Levant* (1952), pp. 172–77; and cf. Graziani, *Francisci Mauroceni. . .gesta* (1698), pp. 108–11, who notes the Venetians' refusal during the Turco-Austrian war to accept peace on the basis of their receiving one half the island of Crete and the Turks (*Thraces*) the other half. Arrighi, who is, to be sure, only writing a biography of Francesco Morosini, has little to say of the period from 1662 to 1666 (*op. cit.*, lib. I, pp. 83–85).

(in June). Both the Christians and the Turks had to maintain their ready access to the sea.

Despite the ever-welcome reinforcements, the Venetian hold upon Candia seemed as threatened as ever. On 16 March 1667 the provveditore generale Antonio Barbaro wrote the doge and Senate that they must increase the corps of bombardiers, "now reduced to only 163," which fell far short of the number needed to handle the five hundred cannon within the fortifications of Candia. After all, as Barbaro stated in another dispatch, heavy artillery was the "istromento principale della difesa." In the same file as that containing Barbaro's dispatches to the Senate one observer begins a letter of 4 April (1667) with reference to Ahmed Köprülü's strange "vagaries" (*li capricii di questo primo visir*). A talented commander, Köprülü doubtless had his oddities. At any rate there were a number of desertions from the Turkish camp at Candia in 1666–1667. The file in question (like others of this period) contains much information about the Turks, from Köprülü to the disaffected soldiery under his command.[25] In any event the year 1667 must have made a deep impress upon the memory of both the Turkish and Christian forces at Candia.[26]

The usual dissension and hostilities manifested themselves among the allied commanders, especially between François de Ville, who finally left Candia in April 1668, and the Venetian Antonio Barbaro, who was replaced in January (1668) by Bernardo Nano. The papal general Giovanni Bichi was supposedly in command of both the pope's galleys and those of the Hospitallers, whose general was Gilberto del Bene. There were four Neapolitan galleys under Giannetto Doria and another four from Sicily under their own commander. The Christian fleet soon consisted of 35 "ships of the line" (*legni di fila*) recruited from five different sources, four of the commanders being concerned with the important fact of precedence in the naval protocol of the time. The fifth commander was

---

[25] ASV, Senato, Provv. da terra e da mar, Filza 815, pages and entries unnumbered. As Antonio Barbaro had written the doge and Senate from Candia on 8 February 1667, "Dipende il mantenimento di questa piazza dalla vigilante providenza dell'Eccellenze vostre, quali se opportuni faranno seguire i ricapiti delle provigioni già ricercate con agiustate espeditioni di denaro per poter animar queste genti, voglio sperare coll'aiuto del Signor Iddio di veder vani tutti li tentatrici ch' è per pratticare la potenza nemica, per il che io non mancarò certamente d'impiegare continuate et indefesse tutte le più possibili diligenze" (*ibid.*, Filza 815, *Candia li 8 Febraro 1666 S[til] N[ovo]*, *more veneto*).

[26] On the violent encounters of the Christians with the Turks at Candia from 28 May to 9 June 1667, see MS. Marc. It. VII, 657 (7481), fols. 23–27; from 23 June to 15 July, *ibid.*, fols. 33ʳ–44ʳ; and through the first half of October, fols. 47ʳ–49ʳ. During the night of 2 July (1667) the papal and Maltese galleys reached Standia, and the following day "comparvero in fossa della città [Candia]: riceverono triplicato il saluto del cannone e moscheto," fols. 36ᵛ–37ʳ.

Francesco Morosini, who had been reappointed captain-general of the Venetian fleet.

The English and the Dutch profited from the struggle, selling the Turks gunpowder and various war materials. The merchants, including the French, often sided with the Moslems; the aristocracy, especially the French, remembered the Crusades, and happily joined the fray against the Turks. The years 1667–1668 were a period of bloodshed. They are well documented.[27] Toward the end of July (1667) the allied fleet saved the island of Cerigo from an attack by the Turks, but managed to achieve nothing else despite Bichi's wandering here and there in Cretan waters and in the southern Aegean. On 20 September the papal and Maltese as well as the Neapolitan and Sicilian (i.e., the "Spanish") galleys left for home. The Turks had proved to be elusive, adding to their strength on the island of Crete and avoiding anything like a decisive battle with the Christian forces.

Every year had brought hardships to both the Venetians and the Turks. Such were the resources of the Porte, with fortresses and ports everywhere in the eastern Mediterranean, that it was impossible for the Venetians to score a "decisive" victory. Francesco Morosini, again in command, was striving to maintain the Republic's hold upon Candia and, always hoping against hope, to recover Canea (the ancient Cydonia) which, after Candia, was the largest city in Crete. The remains of Venetian fortifications are still conspicuous in both places.

---

[27] Cf. *La Guerra di Candia, 1667–1668,* in MS. Marc. It. VII, 2182 (8779), which is almost entirely given over to a day-to-day account—or diary—of the fighting at Candia from 27 May 1667 to the end of April 1668. The volume contains 197 fols., and is very clearly written. One may find here, fols. 183^r to 190^r, a copy of the marquis de Ville's report to the Senate on the condition of the fortress (*piazza*) of Candia, the Venetian *armata da mare,* and the Turkish encampment as of Saturday night, 21 April, when he left Candia. This MS. also provides us with the texts of a brief (in Latin) of Pope Clement IX to Francesco Morosini dated 18 May 1669 and of Morosini's answer (in Italian) dated 19 July 1669. Cf. in general Alberto Guglielmotti, *Storia della marina pontificia,* VIII (Rome, 1893), 277ff.

De Ville's service to Venice can be studied in four texts given in MS. Marc. It. VII, 657 (7481), fols. 2^r–3, 7^r–8, 11^r–12^r, 13^r–20^v. The first three of these texts, all very brief, are concerned with formal, ceremonial gestures; the fourth is a precise, detailed, descriptive account of the fortifications of Candia as of 20 April 1668 (dated 21 April in the copy cited above), with assessments of the condition of the bastions, ravelins, and *mezza luna,* the counterscarp, etc. In general the prospects seemed hopeful to de Ville. Candia was well supplied with artillery, but munitions were in short supply, especially powder, although 2,000 *barili* had arrived from Venice, despite Köprülü's tightening of the Turkish lines. Other military supplies were by and large exhausted. Food was scarce and expensive; a single chicken cost one and a quarter *reali.* The sick and wounded were hard put to find the means of subsistence. The Venetian fleet seemed of adequate strength to de Ville, with enough galleys, galleasses, and other vessels. The Turks were having their troubles, however, with unrest in Istanbul. Apparently only time could clarify the situation for the Turks as well as for the Venetians.

At the beginning of 1668 the grand vizir Ahmed Köprülü took the offensive. Acting apparently upon information which he had acquired from scouts or spies (*con occulte trame*),[28] he decided to launch a surprise attack upon Lorenzo Corner, the Venetian *proveditor dell'armata*, whose seven galleys then in the area of S. Pelagia (an islet northwest of Candia) were an impediment to the Turks' intention to reinforce their troops under the walls of Candia. Selecting two thousand of his "most warlike soldiers," he placed them under the command of a pasha from Anatolia, who was highly regarded by the Turkish troops. Köprülü sent the pasha off toward Retimo (Réthymnon), on the northern shore of Crete midway between Canea and Candia, under cover of night "so that he would not be seen." Planning to seize the seven galleys under the Venetian *provveditore*, Köprülü had assigned the pasha a dozen galleys.

Somehow Morosini had learned of the grand vizir's plans, and despite the shortness of time he was ready to meet the Turks upon their arrival during the evening of 8 March (1668), apparently adding thirteen galleys to the seven under Corner's command. The contest lasted five continuous hours (*cinque continue hore*), a chaos of fire and sword in the darkness of night. Morosini had taken command of the Venetian naval armament. His galley was quickly surrounded by three enemy vessels, two of which soon had to withdraw from the encounter "much damaged." The third was held under attack by another Venetian galley. A contemporary Venetian newsletter identifies the various Venetian officers involved in the battle—Lorenzo Corner, Alvise Contarini, Niccolò Polani, Daniele Zustignan, Alvise Priuli, Girolamo Priuli, Alvise Calbo, Alvise Minio, Piero Querini, Lorenzo Donà, Giacomo Celsi, Nadal Duodo, and a number of others. Having been freed from the enemy assault, Morosini moved off to attack another Turkish galley (he went "where the need was the greatest") which put up a "validissima ressistenza." The Turkish galley "was captured, however, and left in the charge of an official and some soldiers who were the first to board it."

The Turkish pasha and the beys under his command were highly experienced. Their soldiery fought bravely. The battle was perilous; the outcome remained uncertain for some time. In the darkness it was hard to tell who was winning: *Pendeva incerto l'esito, e fra le tenebre non si dicerneva dove piegasse il vantaggio.* The outcome became clear, however, with the death of the chief bey, apparently the pasha's second in command. His galley was taken, "and this was also added to the triumphs of the Republic's arms:" "It was a bloody acquisition, and particularly so because of the death of the noble Daniele Zustignan, the paymaster, who

---

[28] Espionage (and sabotage) were prominent features of the Turco-Venetian wars (and the Venetians plotted many an assassination), on which cf. *Venezia e la difesa del Levante da Lepanto a Candia, 1570–1670*, Venice, 1986, pp. 79–85, with extensive notes.

in the search for glory had embarked upon the galley *Polani,* and was struck by a musket shot among the first volleys. . . ."

As we have noted, the author of the newsletter apparently named all the Venetian officers who distinguished themselves in this battle: *Tutti li capi da mar, governatori, e nobili han dimostrata singolar prontezza nell'azzardarsi nè vi è alcuno che non habbi date chiare prove di devotione verso la patria et di corraggio et intrepideza.* The newsletter had a wide circulation. The writer could not know what would indeed have saddened him. It was to be the last Venetian victory of the Cretan war.

Morosini and his officers captured five Turkish galleys, and sank another. The rest of the Turkish galleys suffered "considerable damage." Many of the Turks were killed. The grand vizir Ahmed Köprülü lost several beys, an abundance of troops, and no end of slaves, "for there were three hundred persons aboard every galley." Among the 410 captives taken by the Venetians, the greater part were wounded, including some of the beys. Others found safety in flight. Eleven hundred Christian slaves were freed, released from the oars. They would be kept with the fleet, "being accustomed to hardships, with some knowledge of navigation, and experienced in the business of the sea." This gain in manpower was offset by five hundred wounded and two hundred killed. There was rejoicing on the island of Standia (Dia) and doubtless at nearby Candia,[29] but the Venetian forces would have no further occasion to celebrate a victory with salvos of cannon fire and musketry, at least not in the Cretan war.

Although the eyes of Europe were constantly cast in the direction of the Turco–Venetian war for possession of Crete, the Franco-Spanish war of 1667–1668 was a serious distraction. It was Louis XIV's first war, the "War of Devolution," by which he laid claim to his Spanish wife Maria Theresa's alleged inheritance of the Belgian provinces. Maria Theresa was the daughter of Philip IV, and Louis declared that the southern Netherlands had devolved upon her. He was obliged to moderate his ambition, however, when Holland, England, and Sweden formed a triple alliance (on 23 January 1668), and by the treaty of Aix–la–Chapelle (on 2 May) Louis returned Franche-Comté to Spain, which recognized his continued possession of a dozen fortified towns on the Franco-Belgian

---

[29] *Relatione del combattimento glorioso seguito tra galere della Serenissima Republica di Venetia et le galere de' Bei, sotto il commando dell'illustriss. et eccellentiss. Signor Francesco Moresini, Cavalier, Capitan generale da Mar, la notte delli 8. Marzo 1668 nelle acque di Fraschia,* Venice, appresso Camillo Bortoli, 1668. The same text was also published in 1668 by Giovanni Pietro Pinelli, *stampator ducale,* and of course both texts were brought out "con licenza de' Superiori."

border. With France at peace, the Venetian Signoria sought and prayed for renewed assistance from France.[30]

The French did send assistance to try to save Crete from the Turks, but Morosini had to wait another year for it. In the meantime, some seven weeks after the Venetian victory offshore from Candia, Morosini moved with most of the Venetian fleet into the Archipelago; the provveditore Lorenzo Celsi remained in the area of Candia with about a third of the Republic's naval strength. In early May (1668) the Turkish kapudan pasha was reported off the western shores of Crete with (it was said) some fifty galleys which he had brought from Chios. Morosini hurried back to Crete, where he anchored the fleet in Canea Bay near the islet of S. Todero, awaiting the expected papal and Maltese galleys.

During the dozen years of his reign Pope Alexander VII Chigi (1655–1667) had rendered Venice such assistance as he could by the sale of ecclesiastical properties, the allowance of tithes, and the dispatch of papal galleys to the east—all this and more despite his financial problems and his prolonged difficulties with both Cardinal Mazarin (d. 1661) and the young King Louis XIV.

On the evening of 20 June (1667), however, when Giulio Rospigliosi was elected Clement IX,[31] Venetian hopes rose, because not only was the new pontiff determined to resist the Turks, but since he was on friendly terms with France, perhaps Louis XIV would add something of French manpower and resources to the unending contest with the Porte. When Clement IX's five galleys set out in May (1668) to join the Venetian fleet in the Cretan waters, they were under the command of his nephew Vincenzo Rospigliosi, whose dispatches or letters form a diary of his experiences during the expeditions of 1668 and 1669, the last expeditions of the Cretan war.

---

[30] On the peace of 1668, note Louis XIV's letter to Pope Clement IX, dated at S. Germain on 16 April (1668), in Bibl. Nazionale Marciana, MS. It. VII, 675 (8209), fols. 5ᵛ–6ʳ. But peace in Europe was not peace in the eastern Mediterranean, for the Cretan war went on, as the Venetian Signoria lamented in a letter congratulating Louis on the peace between France and Spain and appealing for French help against the Turks: "Mentre però li motivi della pietà medesima [di Maestà vostra] ha persuaso l'animo suo nel mezzo delle vittorie alla pace, le presenti afflitioni della Cristianità oppressa dall'armi potenti de Barbari, confidiamo siam per disponer il Christianissimo suo zelo a voglier l'armi contro di essi per assister ad una causa della nostra santa fede. E mentre la piaza di Candia, valido antemurale all'innondationi de Turchi, resiste, benchè fieramente oppugnata con potentissimo essercito dal Primo Visir, è la bontà della Maestà vostra chiamata a sostener con i vigorosi soccorsi delle sue forze la costanza del Senato et animar quella così importante diffesa con i sovegni delle sue armi sempre vittoriose: La congiontura è importante, l'assedio è pertinacce, e le forze estenuate da così lunga guerra van cedendo, onde il solo calore degl'agiuti della sua corona può invigorire la diffesa della religione e della fede, et il Senato stesso dalla di lei bontà hora li confida pronti e copiosi in corrispondenza dell'urgenze, e dispone di più nell'anima l'augumento di quelle obligationi che grate e perpetue si conserverano alla Maestà vostra, alla quale di tutto cuore augura lunghi e felici gl'anni" (*ibid.,* fol. 8).

[31] Arch. Segr. Vaticano, Acta Consistorialia, Acta Miscellanea, tom. 42, fols. 50ʳ–51ʳ.

The Hospitallers also sent seven galleys eastward, this time under Clemente Accarigi, of whom there is frequent mention in Rospigliosi's volume of letters. Upon his arrival at the islet of S. Todero in Canea Bay (on 7 July 1668), Rospigliosi wrote "that the Venetian fleet, here in these waters of S. Todero, consists of five galleasses, 15 light galleys, and ten vessels of different sorts as well as other small boats." Although Rospigliosi had had to spend some days at the various ports he entered on the way to Crete, taking on water and supplies, he had made fairly good time on his voyage to Crete.[32] The so-called Spanish galleys (from Naples and Sicily) were to put in an appearance too late to render any service against the Turks.

When Rospigliosi had become settled offshore from S. Todero, Morosini left him in charge of the fleet, and went off to attend to the troops and fortifications at Candia, which was under constant pressure from the Turks. Rospigliosi wrote letter after letter dated at S. Todero throughout the month of July (1668). To keep up the blockade of Canea it was necessary to provide the crews and troops with water. Since the Turks were everywhere on the land around Canea, it was difficult to get water, for Rospigliosi was unwilling to venture too far afield for it.[33] While he worried about water, the encouraging news of the Franco-Spanish treaty of Aix-la-Chapelle (of 2 May 1668) reached him at S. Todero in late July.[34] He was also pleased with Morosini's apparent attitude toward

---

[32] Arch. Segr. Vaticano, Miscellanea, Arm. XV, tom. 138, *Registro di lettere del Cavaliere F. Vincenzo Rospigliosi, comandante delle galere pontificie spedite in Levante scritte da 24 Maggio 1668 fino adì 30 Luglio 1669:* "Domenica 20 del corrente [Sunday, 20 May 1668] verso le 22 hore [about 7:00 P.M.] giunsi a Nisita [the Isola di Nisida], et hoggi farò la mia entrata in Napoli, restando sopite tutte le difficoltà per mezzo di monsignor nunzio Gallio [Marco Gallio, bishop of Rimini, and apostolic nuncio to Naples from 19 February 1668] . . ." (fol. 9ᵛ, dispatch written over a period of three days, and dated 23 May, 1668, at fol. 13ᵛ). The preceding dispatch is dated at Gaeta on 20 May, the following at Naples on 24 May (fol. 14ᵛ). Rospigliosi was at Messina by 4 June (fol. 27ᵛ), Faro di Messina on the 12th (fol. 39ᵛ), Corfu on the 16th (fol. 41ᵛ), Zante on the 27th (fol. 46ʳ), Cape Matapan on 2 July (fol. 48ʳ), Braccio (Brazzo) di Maina on the third (fol. 49ᵛ), Cerigo on the sixth (fol. 51ʳ), and had reached the island of San Todero on 7–9 July (fol. 53ᵛ), where he noted "che l'armata Veneta esistente in quest'acque di S. Todero consiste in 5 galeazze, 15 galee sottili, e 10 vascelli diversi oltre a brigantini et altri legni piccoli" (fol. 52ᵛ). On the extensive help which Clement IX gave Venice against the Turks during his brief reign (1667–1669), see Pastor, *Gesch. d. Päpste,* XIV-1 (1929), 602–9.

[33] Cf. *Registro di lettere del Cav. F. Vincenzo Rospigliosi* (ref. given above), fol. 63ʳ: "Il tempo fresco di questi giorni passati, che continua tuttavia con notabile accrescimento, ha impedito a queste squadre di poter far'acqua in vicinanza di S. Todero, nè io ho voluto che si vadarà pigliarne alla Calabuse [Grabusa, a Venetian fortress, but west of Cape Spada] o in altrove per non abbandonar questo posto," which letter is dated at S. Todero on 14 July 1668. Rospigliosi also needed ship's biscuit (fol. 64ʳ).

F. Ballerini, "Lettere di Vincenzo Rospiglioso, cavaliere gerosolimitano e capitano generale dell'armata [pontificia] nella guerra di Candia," *Il Muratori,* I (Rome, 1892), 123–26, has published a letter of Rospigliosi dated 9 July 1668 and, *ibid.,* pp. 181–84, three letters dated 25 July, as well as another two letters dated 21 and 25 July (*ibid.,* II [1893], 167–70).

[34] *Registro di lettere del Cav. F. Vincenzo Rospigliosi,* fol. 66ʳ, letter dated 25 July 1668.

him,[35] but made uneasy by the persistent attacks of the Turks upon Candia.[36] Rospigliosi's letters are full of endless, fascinating detail with which we cannot deal here.

Rospigliosi informs us of the allies' numerous difficulties, their large frustrations and small successes, their reaction to reports and rumors, the movements of Christian and Turkish vessels between Otranto and Rhodes, and (among various other data) the minutes of the war council (*consulta*) held aboard the papal flagship at S. Todero on 30 July (1668). The deliberations took place "in presenza degli eccellentissimi signori generali radunati . . . con i signori luogotenenti loro sopra la reale di sua Santità," i.e., Francesco Morosini was present and, of course, so were Rospigliosi and Accarigi.[37] The decision was made for various reasons—especially the fleet's need of water—to take over the little fort of S. Marina on the eastern point of the island near the harbor of S. Todero (*disposizione per l'attacco del forte S. Marina situato nel regno di Candia 4 miglia distante dalla Canea incontro l'isolotto di S. Todero*).

The Turks on S. Todero obviously depended for their defense upon Fort S. Marina for, as we have seen, the other small fortress on S. Todero had been blown to pieces by the stalwart Istrian officer Blasio Zulian in June 1645, although it is clear that the fortress was at least partially restored by the Turks some years later.[38] However that might be, the attack upon Fort S. Marina was scheduled for 3 August; every minute detail had been considered and provision made for it. The time was opportune, for "the Turkish armada is still at Rhodes" (*l'armata Turchesca maritima si trova tuttavia a Rodi*).[39] On the morning of 3 August, in accord with the resolution of the war council, Rospigliosi and others proceeded against Fort S. Marina, occupying the fort and the adjacent harbor with no resistance at all from the Turks, who took flight as the allied forces were disembarking.[40]

---

[35] *Ibid.*, fol. 67^r, letter dated at S. Todero on 25 July 1668.

[36] *Ibid.*, fol. 67^v, 25 July, 1668.

[37] *Ibid.*, fols. 77^v–80^r.

[38] Cf. *Nova e vera Relatione del combattimento novamente seguito in Candia*, publ. in Venice, Bologna, and Ferrara by Giulio Bulzoni Giglio, 1669: "In tanto fabricando li Turchi un Forte à S. Todoro, e postovi sopra il cannone per tener lontana l'armata veneta et assicurare lo sbarco alla turchescha. . . ."

[39] *Registro di lettere del Cav. F. Vincenzo Rospigliosi*, fols. 80^r–83^v.

[40] *Ibid.*, fol. 84^r, *dal Forte S. Marina 3 Agosto 1668:* "Doppo d'haver serrato il mio piego in data delli 2 del presente devo soggiungere . . . che in adempimento della resoluzione di già presa, ci siamo portati stamane al forte di S. Marina senza havervi incontrato alcuna resistenza per parte de' Turchi, quali nel punto stesso dello sbarco da' nostri se ne son tutti fuggiti . . . ," and cf. fol. 85^r: "L'armata veneta nel solito posto a S. Todero per impedire l'introduzione de' soccorsi per la parte di Canea, questa mattina ci siamo impadroniti, senza contrasto, del forte di S. Marina, havendolo vilmente abbandonato i nemici. . . ."

There is an old but well-informed account of the Candian war during the years 1668–

After the capture of Fort S. Marina, the major success of the expedition of 1668, Morosini urged Rospigliosi and Accarigi to move eastward to Candia to assist in the defense of the capital city of the "kingdom." The "deputies of all the squadrons" did leave Canea for Candia, where they made a survey of the Turkish batteries along the shore in the area of the bastion of S. Andrea. They decided that they could do little or nothing "without manifest risk to the galleys and with very little damage to the Turks."[41] It was almost always the same. Naval commanders would not allow their crews and soldiers to become bogged down in the Turks' everlasting siege of Candia. On the other hand, if the Turkish armada avoided any serious encounter with the allied squadrons, what could the Christian forces do? Year after year papal and Maltese galleys would come east to do the Turks some harm (and often did so), but the naval officers insisted upon confining their actions to the sea.

The presence of Rospigliosi and Accarigi on the northwestern coast of Crete apparently made it inadvisable for the Turks to try to land men and munitions at either Canea or Candia, which was not much of a problem, since the Turks could easily land their reinforcements on the eastern end of the island. Nevertheless, in mid–August Rospigliosi feared that the kapudan pasha might well try to land men and munitions "in the waters of Canea," as he warned the Christian corsairs in the area of Suda Bay, the best harbor of Crete, and so every precaution must be taken.[42]

After having spent some days "in the waters of Candia," Rospigliosi was back in the area of Canea by 20 August (1668). Despite his caution and courtesy, as revealed in his correspondence, everything had not been going smoothly. Disagreement and discord between the Venetians and Maltese was almost to be expected. On 22 August Rospigliosi wrote from the waters of Canea that Morosini was sending a felucca to Otranto in order to have a detailed report "on the state of Candia" transmitted from there to Venice, "e per domandar soccorsi massimamente di gente, la penuria di che crescendo ogni giorno colla morte de' defensori vien però ad indebolire non meno le forze che la speranza di quei comandanti."[43] Morosini desperately needed soldiers to combat the Turks laying siege to Candia, and he was "disarming" his galleys to try to get some of the manpower he required.[44]

1669 by Wilhelm Bigge, *Der Kampf um Candia in den Jahre 1667–1669*, Berlin, 1899, pp. 113–227, esp. pp. 136ff., in the Kriegsgeschichtliche Einzelschriften, vol. V, Heft 26. There is also an Italian translation of Bigge's monograph (Turin, 1901).

[41] *Registro di lettere del Cav. Rospigliosi*, fols. 87ʳ, 88ᵛ, 89ʳ, *et alibi*.

[42] *Ibid.*, fol. 92ʳ: "Vien confermato da più parti l'avviso che l'armata nemica possa portarsi in queste acque di Canea per effettuarsi lo sbarco de' soccorsi destinati dal capitan bassà in aiuto del campo del visir . . . ," from a *lettera circolare* of Rospigliosi dated 16 August 1668.

[43] *Ibid.*, fol. 96ʳ, *dall'acque di Canea 22 Agosto 1668*.

[44] *Ibid.*, fol. 96ᵛ.

There would seem to be cause for alarm. At Standia, the Venetian island north of Candia, Morosini had received news of the kapudan pasha's plans to leave Chios for Monemvasia "and Romania," where 8,000 Turks were stationed, most of them sappers (*guastatori*), waiting to be embarked for Candia. The pasha's armada with more than 50 sail was allegedly between Cerigotto and Grabusa which, if true, was indeed a menace to the Venetians. Rospigliosi was glad that he had returned from Candia in time to meet the Turks if they attacked.[45] On 22 August (1668) Rospigliosi noted that three months had passed since his departure from Rome.[46] He was beginning to plan his return home. Morosini had assured him that he would encounter no obstacles at the Venetian-held islands of Zante and Corfu, and he expected to receive the same consideration at Neapolitan-held Otranto. In any event "the Turkish armada has so distanced itself from here" that Rospigliosi was being led to the reluctant conclusion that it might not be necessary "to prolong our stay in these waters."[47]

Naval protocol was again a problem, for the Venetian galleass *Navagero* had failed to salute the flagship of Malta by firing a *salvo*, and so the latter did not respond (*non è seguito tra loro alcun salvo*). The Maltese commander Accarigi was surprised, even scandalized (*formalizzato*), by this failure to show respect to the Maltese cross. Accarigi was deeply offended. After all, it was his flagship, not an ordinary galley, to which the Venetian vessel had failed to give what he regarded as proper ceremonial recognition. He complained to Rospigliosi, who reported the incident to the Venetian *capitan estraordinario,* who explained that Venice required precedence "per conservar il decoro dello stendardo della Serenissima Republica." If Accarigi's flagship had fired first, presumably the Venetian galleass would have replied. That was not good enough for Accarigi. No, the Maltese were leaving immediately, preparing to go aboard their galleys for the voyage westward, and Rospigliosi could not prevail upon Accarigi and his fellow Hospitallers to remain any longer "in the waters of Canea."[48]

Rospigliosi was not able to persuade the Maltese to delay their departure beyond 28 August (1668), i.e., a mere four or five days, despite the fact it was known that every effort was now being made to see that the Neapolitan and Sicilian squadrons should come east "with all possible speed." Their galleys would be loaded with soldiery to aid in the defense of Candia.[49] The papal commander could only acknowledge and lament

---

[45] *Ibid.*, fol. 97ʳ, and cf. fol. 101ᵛ.

[46] *Ibid.*, fol. 102ᵛ, *dall'acque di Canea 22 Agosto 1668.*

[47] *Ibid.*, fol. 104ʳ, also dated 22 August.

[48] *Ibid.*, fol. 105ʳ, *dall'acque di Canea 23 Agosto 1668.*

[49] *Ibid.*, fols. 105ᵛ–106ʳ, *all'eccellentissimo Capitan generale Morosino in Candia . . . dall'acque di Canea 26 Agosto 1668,* and cf. fols. 112ᵛ–113, *et alibi.* The *Navagero* affair is recounted in several of Rospigliosi's letters.

"that my remaining for two months in the fleet has been almost entirely useless as far as service to the most Serene Republic goes," but he was glad of the opportunity to make clear his zeal and dedication to the Christian cause.[50] In any event Rospigliosi left with the Maltese, and reached the island of Zante before 6 September.[51]

About the time of Rospigliosi's arrival at Zante a small boat pulled into the harbor with news that nine Spanish galleys (from Naples and Sicily) had reached Corfu on their way to the Levant. On 7 September Rospigliosi wrote his brother Cardinal Jacopo that when the Christian galleys had got together, he was prepared to return to Candia and go anywhere that the allied forces could do something worthwhile for the public good.[52] In fact Rospigliosi now left Zante with Accarigi for Corfu, only to find that the commander of the Neapolitan and Sicilian galleys, Don Pedro de Toledo, the duke of Ferrandina, had already departed, having inquired about the papal and Maltese galleys. On 9 September Rospigliosi wrote Don Pedro that he had consulted with Accarigi, *generale de' Maltesi,* and that they had agreed to wait at Corfu for word from him as to what the Spaniards' plans might be.[53] Although basic decisions were made at Madrid (or Naples), the crews and soldiery aboard the Neapolitan and Sicilian galleys were in fact almost entirely Italian.

On the evening of 19 September (1668) the duke of Ferrandina returned to Corfu with the four Sicilian and five Neapolitan galleys. As he entered the harbor, his gunners saluted the papal banner with a volley of all his cannon. Rospigliosi sent him some refreshments and a little slave clad in gold brocade. Thereafter he tried to persuade Ferrandina to embark upon some enterprise against the Turks so that, as the season for naval warfare was passing, his mission would not prove wholly useless. He suggested that Ferrandina send the Venetians at Candia 150 or 200 footsoldiers from aboard his galleys. Morosini's situation was perilous. Even a small body of soldiery would be more useful under the circumstances than anything else that Ferrandina could do. The latter claimed, however, that he lacked authority to take such action, while Rospigliosi asserted that he was ready, even eager, to enroll 200 men for assignment to Candia. The pope was prepared to give his benign approval thereto,

---

[50] *Ibid.,* fol. 107^v, *dall'acque di Canea 28 Agosto 1668.*

[51] *Ibid.,* fols. 108^{v}ff. There is a brief summary of events, as seen by Rospigliosi, in this MS. at fols. 108^v–111^v. He left the waters of Canea, heading for Zante, on 28 August (fol. 116^r).

[52] *Ibid.,* fol. 118^r, *Zante, 7 Settembre 1668:* "Giunge una barca da Corfu con avviso che le galere di Napoli e di Sicilia in numero di 9 [i.e., five Neapolitan and four Sicilian galleys] comandate dal Signor Duca di Ferrandina, marchese di Villafranca, si ritrovano in quel porto, onde quanto prima ci saremo insieme, et io per la mia parte m'esibirò prontissimo di tornar' in Candia ed andar per tutto dove le squadre possino operar qualche cosa in servizio della causa pubblica. . . ."

[53] *Ibid.,* fol. 118^v, *al Signor Duca di Ferrandina, marchese di Villafranca . . . Corfu, 9 Settembre 1668,* and cf. fols. 119ff.

given the current crisis and the advantages that could accrue from the proposed move.[54]

To simplify a somewhat complicated situation let us merely say that Ferrandina remained loath to remove any troops from the five hundred that had been recruited in the kingdom of Naples, especially for incorporation into a pontifical regiment.[55] Of course, problems of protocol would arise. On 22 September Rospigliosi wrote at length to Morosini, informing him of everything that had happened since the withdrawal of the papal and Maltese galleys from the waters of Canea, including his willingness to return to Candia and Ferrandina's refusal to cooperate (owing, he said, to the lateness of the season). In any event Rospigliosi made it clear that insofar as he had failed in his obligation to Venice and to the Holy See, he shared the embarrassment with Ferrandina.[56]

Although the commanders of the allied squadrons had fastened upon 21 September (1668) as the date of their departure from Corfu, they were held up by contrary winds, and could not set sail until Monday, 24 September. The following day they passed by the entrance to the Strait of Otranto (*la Bocca dell'Adriatico*) in a thick fog on a calm sea. From the area of Otranto the squadrons went their several ways, the "Spaniards" heading for Gallipoli and Taranto, Accarigi's seven galleys for Malta.[57]

Thereafter we have a flood of Rospigliosi's letters dated 28 September from Reggio di Calabria.[58] On 1 October he wrote Nicolás Cotoner, the Aragonese grand master of the Hospitallers (1665–1680), in commendation of his colleague Clemente Accarigi. The letter was sent from Mes-

---

[54] *Ibid.*, fols. 123ᵛ–124ʳ, *Corfu, 20 Settembre 1668:* "Giunse finalmente iersera in queste acque il Signor Duca di Ferrandina con 9 galere, 4 di Sicilia e 5 di Napoli. . . . Nell'ingresso salutò lo stendardo di Nostro Signore con salva generale di tutti li suoi cannoni. . . . L'ho . . . regalato d'alcuni rinfreschi e d'un schiavetto vestito di broccato d'oro et in tutto procuro di guadagnarmi l'animo suo affine di persuaderlo ad operar qualche cosa in servizio della causa pubblica acciochè non riesca del tutto inutile la di sua missione. . . .

"Per tal riguardo gl'ho proposto di concedere alla Republica 150 o 200 fanti delle sue galere da inviarsi prontamente in Candia, dove quello soccorso nelle presenti strettezze riuscirebbe più considerabile di qualsivogl'altro. . . . Essendosi egli scusato con allegare la sua impotenza per difetto d'autorità, gli ho risposto ch'io m'ero preso ardire di arrolarne 200, e che sua Santità si era degnata di approvar benignamente tal risoluzione, attese le predette angustie et il gran benefizio che si poteva cavare da così picciol rimedio. . . ."

[55] *Ibid.*, fol. 124ᵛ.

[56] *Ibid.*, fols. 125ᵛ–126ʳ, *al signor capitan generale Morosino, Candia . . . Corfu, 22 Settembre 1668:* ". . . Speravo che il signor Duca mi permetterebbe d'arrolare in aumento di cotesto reggimento pontificio un buon numero di fanteria spagnola [who would have been largely Italian], ma essendosi egli scusato d'aderire alle mie istanze, resto con mortificazione di non haver potuto complire all'obbligo mio in ossequio della Serenissima Republica . . . ," and cf. fol. 129ᵛ *et alibi.*

[57] *Ibid.*, fol 120, *Reggio, 28 Settembre 1668*, and cf. fols. 132ᵛ–133ʳ.

[58] *Ibid.*, fols. 127ff. In writing to his brother Cardinal Jacopo on 28 September, Rospigliosi expressed gratitude to Aloysius Pappacorda (d. 1670), the bishop of Lecce, for his helpfulness (fol. 131ʳ).

sina.[59] By 9 October Rospigliosi was on the Isola di Nisida, just outside the port of Naples, at Gaeta by the 13th,[60] and shortly thereafter he was back in Rome, where he gave his mother Lucrezia[61] as well as his uncle Pope Clement IX a detailed account of the expedition of 1668, which he frankly acknowledged had not been a success.

When Vincenzo Rospigliosi and Clemente Accarigi left the Gulf of Canea for the island of Zante (on 29 August 1668), the task force which Morosini had added to the allied fleet was not strong enough to bar the Turks from entering the large harbor of Canea. Also Morosini needed the manpower at Candia, where he now assembled the crews and soldiery aboard the Venetian galleasses, galleys, and ships to help ward off the Turkish assaults. During the fall of '68 Christian shipping suffered some losses owing to attacks by the Barbary pirates as well as by the fleet of the kapudan pasha. If Candia was going to hold out, it would certainly need increased assistance from the western powers. Candia had been under intermittent attack for some twenty-three years, and of late the Turks had been reinforcing the armament of their siege.

---

[59] *Ibid.*, fol. 134.
[60] *Ibid.*, fols. 136ᵛ–144: ". . . Gaeta, dove giunsi ieri . . . ," letter dated 14 October.
[61] Cf., *ibid.*, fol. 144ᵛ.

VII

Alvise da Molin's Embassy to the Porte, Failure of the French to Relieve Candia, Francesco Morosini's Surrender of the City to the Turks

～

he long war had nearly exhausted the naval and military resources of the Venetian Republic. There had been an almost
disastrous erosion of the Levantine trade. On 3 March 1668 the
doge Domenico Contarini wrote Andrea Valier that the Senate had chosen him to seek peace with the Porte as a "gentleman envoy." Valier was
the Signoria's guardian of the Ionian Sea, patrolling the waters of Corfu,
Cephalonia, and Zante. He had had no little experience of the "customs
and manners of the Turks."[1] Thus while Venice sought armed assistance
from the West, she was turning eastward to seek peace. The Senate had
voted by a large majority to send Valier to the Porte or to the grand vizir
Ahmed Köprülü, wherever he might be, but the members now had no
little difficulty agreeing on the procedures to be followed.

On 6 April (1668) the Senate rejected the text of a proposed letter to
Köprülü to the effect that Valier was being sent "per applicare alle occorrenze publiche e per li maneggi della pace." According to the dis-
carded text, the Senate was confident that the grand vizir was "inclined

---

[1] ASV, Senato, Deliberazioni Costantinopoli (Secreta), Reg. 32 (1668–1672), fol. 2ʳ
[93ʳ].

206

to peace" and wanted, like the Signoria, "to put an end to the shedding of so much blood." On the same day the text of another letter to Köprülü as well as that of a letter to Francesco Morosini, *capitan general da mar*, was also voted down in the Senate, where there was clearly a high measure of contention, as a secretary noted several times (*vedi scontro preso*).[2]

The doge wrote Andrea Valier on 22 June (1668), in accord with the Senate's wishes, that he was to go directly to the sultan Mehmed IV, "wherever he was to be found," as soon as the secretary Giovanni Capello, the dragoman Ambrosio Grillo, and a Turkish chavush arrived to join his suite. The necessary passports and other credentials were already in hand. Valier could choose his own road eastward, going either by land or by sea. If he chose the sea route, he could ask the captain-general Morosini for whatever vessels or galleys were necessary. Provision had been made for the purchase of garments (*panni*), satins (*rasi*), and cloths of gold to the extent of 6,000 ducats. Another thousand ducats were being spent on clocks, silverware, and other such gestures of Venetian good will. The Turk had long enjoyed such gifts.

Valier was now to take the considerable sum of 10,000 ducats from funds already available to him; another ten thousand would be sent with the secretary and the dragoman. The *magistrato alla sanità* had been instructed to furnish him with a physician and surgeon (or barber), as was usually done for envoys on the way to the Bosporus. On the same day (22 June) the Senate or rather the doge wrote the captain-general Morosini of the arrival in Venice of "li passaporti per la sicurezza del passaggio del dilettissimo nostro Andrea Valier."[3] The physician chosen to accompany the Venetian embassy to the Porte was to be one Bartolommeo Dandolo, *medico fisico*, who would look after the envoy and the latter's family.[4]

On 14 July (1668) the Senate approved a letter to go in the doge's name to the sultan Mehmed, lamenting the military mishaps of the past, which were not at all consistent with the Signoria's affection and respect for his Majesty and for the Sublime Porte. Now, with the security provided by the sultan's passports, the noble Andrea Valier would soon be on his way to the Turkish court to negotiate with honor and justice a treaty of peace.[5] On the same day the Senate accepted the text of a similar but rather more precise letter to be sent to the grand vizir Köprülü.[6] War had long held the rapt attention of northern Europe as well as of the Mediterranean world.

---

[2] *Ibid.*, fols. 3r–6v [94r–97v].

[3] *Ibid.*, fols. 10v–11 [101v–102].

[4] *Ibid.*, fol. 25r [116r].

[5] *Ibid.*, fol. 14 [105].

[6] ASV, Senato, Delib. Costantinopoli, Reg. 32, fol. 14v [105v]: "L'affettuosa osservanza della Republica verso l'Eccelsa Porta non ha mai havuta alteratione ne gl'animi nostri,

In the summer of 1668 Paul Rycaut's work on *The Present State of the Ottoman Empire* was being published in London. He had been appointed consul of the Levant Company in Smyrna (in 1667), where he was to remain for the next decade or so. Smyrna, the modern Izmir, is at the head of the Gulf of Smyrna on the eastern coast of the Aegean. On 18 July (1668) Rycaut wrote Charles II's secretary of state that he assumed the latter was receiving weekly dispatches from Italy concerning the Turkish siege of Candia, "the most famous and renowned of any of our moderne times." Nevertheless, Rycaut proposed to keep sending his lordship information from Smyrna,

> though for the present I shall only advise your Lordship that the Turkes seeme to be wholy in despaire of effecting the worke this summer which hath caused diverse mutinies and seditions in the camp and part of the Spahees and Janizaries to withdraw from the trenches, to appease whom, it is said that the Vizier hath appointed and determined 40 dayes' time for taking the city, in which terme, if their worke doth not succeed, then wholy to raise the siege. . . .
>
> The force of the Turkes for this campagna hath not beene contemptible. I have made a list of what they have sent from all parts, which by a moderate calculate arrives to seventy thousand effective men, besides those that remained in the camp of the last yeare, but the sword and the pestilence this yeare hath allready devoured a considerable number.
>
> There are great confusions in their councells at the Grand Signor's Court. Some advise that the Grand Signor should goe to the Morea, there to hasten provisions and succours of men for Candia. Others persuade his passage to that island, as once Sultan Solyman did to Rhodes; others would have the Grand Signor to return to Constantinople, there to apply his mind to strengthen and increase his navall forces so as to become master of the seas, as being the only expedient to subdue Candia.

It is hard to say how well informed Rycaut was, but at any rate he did know that "the Venetians are sending out Signor Andrea Vallier for Bailo to the Port, who is Generall of the 3 islands."[7]

---

come pure la stima verso la persona dignissima dell'Eccellenza vostra è in quel posto che la dichiara per prudentissimo ministro con suo merito singolare. Dovemo però prender confidenza che sia per inclinare alla quiete de'sudditi et al risparmio del sangue. Le nostre intentioni sincere di buona, giusta, e sicura pace saranno sempre le stesse, et essendole queste presentate dal dilettissimo nostro Andrea Valier, che con reggie sicurezze se ne passa alla Porta per questo affare, si assicuriamo sarà udito volontieri e prestatole ogni miglior trattamento, come la preghiamo con li augurii alla sua persona delle prosperità desiderate. [de parte] +141, [de non]—3, [non sinceri]—2." The Senate also approved similar letters to the mufti and "the other pashas of the Porte" (*ibid.*, fols. 14ᵛ–15ʳ [105ᵛ–106ʳ]).

[7] PRO, SP 97, XIX, fols. 20ᵛ–21ᵛ. It is a small matter perhaps, but Valier was being sent to the Porte as a "gentleman envoy," not as a new bailie. Rycaut had been elected a fellow of the Royal Society on 12 December 1666. He was to be knighted on 8 October 1685. On the Turkish siege of Candia in the summer of 1668, note *Cal. State Papers . . . , Venice,*

There was a strong sense of urgency in the Senate, which led to the doge's writing Andrea Valier on 28 July (1668) not to leave his post at Cephalonia to come to Venice, but to go directly to Spalato (Split) on the Dalmatian coast. The Senate assumed that Spalato would be a good *point de départ* for Valier, the secretary Capello, the dragoman Grillo, and the Turkish chavush, who should then proceed to the Porte with the various "robbe decretate," the presents for the sultan and the pashas.[8]

By 4 August, however, plans had changed. Capello had gone to Spalato,[9] but owing to the fact a serious illness had come upon Valier, he had had to be replaced as gentleman envoy to the Porte. On 4 August Alvise Molin (or da Molin) was elected "gentilhuomo inviato." At sixty-three years of age Molin, putting aside all his personal interests, accepted the difficult assignment, which was eventually to prove the most trying and arduous task of his life. His embassy was to become famous, but has not been adequately studied.[10]

At length on 8 August (1668), as the secretary Giovanni Capello waited in Spalato for Andrea Valier's arrival, the doge and Senate sent Capello an explanation of the unseemly delay. While the Senate was awaiting word of Valier's departure for the Porte, "we have learned with extreme vexation that having reached the waters of Istria, [Valier] was unexpectedly seized with a most perilous illness, which has rendered impossible his continuing the journey [to the Porte]." (One may ask, What was he doing in Istria, which is far north of Spalato?) Since, however, the Senate was "most anxious to achieve peace with the Sublime Porte," it was obviously necessary quickly to elect another gentleman envoy. The choice had fallen upon the distinguished noble Alvise da Molin, *cavalier, senator di prestanti qualificatissime conditioni,* who had immediately accepted the charge, and was preparing for his departure eastward.

XXXV (1935, repr. 1970), esp. nos. 324ff., pp. 241ff., and on Rycaut, see Sonia P. Anderson, *An English Consul in Turkey: Paul Rycaut at Smyrna, 1667–1678,* Oxford, 1989, readable and reliable.

[8] ASV, Senato, Delib. Costantinopoli, Reg. 32, fol. 18 [109].

[9] *Ibid.,* Reg. 32, fol. 19 [110], doc. dated 8 August 1668.

[10] *Diario della Speditione dell' illustrissimo et eccellentissimo signor Alvise da Molin, Cavagliere, alla Porta del Gran Signore:* "Eletto l'illustrissimo et eccellentissimo signor cavaglier Alvise da Molin gli 4 Agosto 1668, giorno di Sabato, in Pregadi alla Porta con titolo gentilhuomo inviato, generosamente accetò carica tant'ardua, posposto ogni privato interesse tanto di sua persona giunta all'età d'anni 63, come della sua casa più che mai bisognosa in quel tempo della di lui assistenza . . ." (MS. Marc. It. VII, 1608 [7514], p. 1). This MS., written in a fine, clear hand, contains 150 pages.

The *Diario* also appears in MS. Marc. It. VII, 651 (8580), fols. 101–138^r, where on the last folio we are given the name of the author: "Scritto dal Padre Carlo Paganino della Compagnia di Gesù, confessore di sua Eccellenza nella sopradetta ambasciata e spedizione." There is another copy in the Marciana in MS. It. VII, 365 (7935), pp. 1–354: the number of pages is explained by the copyist's larger lettering.

Obviously the sultan and the pashas must be informed, as soon as possible, of this stumbling block which had fallen in the Venetians' path. Also it was necessary to secure another passport for the *gentilhuomo inviato,* replacing Valier's name by that of Molin. Therefore, the Senate now instructed the secretary Capello to have the dragoman Grillo and the chavush go quickly to wherever the sultan and the pashas might be, explain the reasons for the delay in the Venetian envoy's appearance and, of course, obtain a passport for Molin. Capello was to assure Grillo and the chavush that the Republic would reward their diligence.

Having obtained Molin's passport (and any necessary alteration in the others), Grillo was "with the same diligence to go to Zante, just opposite Castel Tornese, where he will find the cavalier Molin, who will leave this city in a few days in order to await him there," after which they were all to proceed forthwith to the Porte. As for the chavush, who would thus be traveling back and forth with Grillo, Capello must show him some especial gesture of courtesy and appreciation, i.e., he was to give him some appropriate gift in the name of the Republic, "as you will also furnish the dragoman with money for the needs of the journey."

Capello would understand the great importance of all this. When he had sent off the dragoman to the Ottoman court, he was to give up to the local provveditore the galley which had brought him to Spalato, take up residence on land, and bide his time until Molin arrived, taking good care of the rich gifts (intended for the sultan and the pashas) which had been entrusted to him. A copy of this letter to Capello was now made available to the heads of the Council of Ten.[11]

On 10 August (1668) a motion was passed in the Senate requiring Alvise da Molin's immediate departure on the galley of the Three Islands, which had just arrived in Venice. The Senate also wanted his assurance that he would reach the island of Zante before Grillo could get to Castel Tornese, after which they would hasten to "dove si ritrova il Gran Signore." Molin was to be given all the official documents which had been prepared for and sent to Valier, and to reach his own judgment as to the best way to proceed with the Turks. He was of course also to receive letters of credence addressed to the Gran Signore, the grand vizir Ahmed Köprülü, the muftis (interpreters of the sacred law of Islam), and the pashas. On his way "to wherever the Gran Signore might be," Molin must stop at Spalato to take on board the secretary Capello, who would turn over to him the gifts for the Turks as well as the money necessary to carry out his embassy.[12]

---

[11] ASV, Senato, Delib. Costantinopoli, Reg. 32, fols. 19ᵛ–20 [110ᵛ–111], doc. dated 8 August 1668, and cf., *ibid.,* fols. 20ᵛ–21ʳ [111ᵛ–112ʳ]. Capello also appears in the texts, as one might assume, as Cappello.

[12] Delib. Costantinopoli, Reg. 32, fol. 21 [112], doc. dated 10 August 1668.

Although the Senate seemed satisfied with the progress being made, it had apparently not been practicable to carry out their directions precisely as Capello had been instructed to do in the doge's letter of 8 August. On the 25th of the month the doge and Senate wrote Capello, who was still at Spalato, that his two letters of the 18th and 19th had come with the arrival of the dragoman Grillo in Venice. Yes, Molin had embarked to begin his mission, and Grillo was coming with him. Capello was to oblige and please the chavush to the fullest extent he could.[13] On the same day the doge and Senate wrote Molin that "we are sure you will use the gentlest manner in dealing with the chavush to make him courteous to you, and you will provide him with some gift to keep him contented and relaxed."[14]

The attitude of the chavush was obviously important for the success of Molin's embassy, and apparently Capello had managed very well with the diplomatic agent from the Ottoman court.[15] Three weeks later (on 15 September) the doge and Senate wrote Molin of their satisfaction in learning that the favor of the Almighty was made clear by the propitious wind which had carried Molin to Spalato in four days, "especially since we understand how much the chavush's disposition has been made more cheerful by your appearance."[16]

We can follow Molin's journey to the Ottoman court in the ducal dispatches sent to him as well as in his own letters and reports to the Signoria. Much more detail may be found in the *Diario* of Molin's eastward passage written by his chaplain, the Jesuit Padre Carlo Paganino, who has left us a fascinating account of every aspect of the well-known embassy and a meticulous description of everything he saw around him. In fact Paganino's record of the last days of the siege of Candia, his survey of the ruined fortifications, his notes on the city and the inhabitants of Istanbul, and his reflections on the past history of the area in which he found himself on a given day are all interesting.

On 31 October (1668) the doge and Senate wrote Andrea Valier, who had apparently recovered from his "most perilous illness," of the progress Molin had been making in his eastward passage. He had curried favor with the Turkish consuls along the way, thus facilitating communication with the Signoria, for his letters of 27 September and 1 October had come directly from Ianina (Ioánnina) and Trikkala (Tríkala) by way of the provveditore at Corfu. He had had, however, a good deal of trouble with one consul, a Greek, who refused to receive or transmit Venetian dispatches. The doge, therefore, requested Valier to see to it that trust-

---

[13] *Ibid.,* fol. 23 [114], dated 25 August 1668.
[14] *Ibid.,* fol. 24ʳ [115ʳ].
[15] *Ibid.,* fol. 27ʳ [118ʳ].
[16] *Ibid.,* fol. 26ʳ [117ʳ].

worthy persons delivered such dispatches by way of Castel Tornese or some other such place. By this time the Signoria had also learned that the sultan and the pashas might be at Larissa (Lárisa) in eastern Thessaly,[17] and so they were.

On 4 November (1668) Alvise da Molin wrote the Signoria from Larissa that Grillo (and apparently certain other dragomans) had been given living quarters apart from, but not far from, those which he was occupying. The Turks found it easier to come and go when Molin was housed separately. He invited them to come and see him, serving them "wines, coffee, and other refreshments." He learned a good deal from these meetings. Even if he had not found this housing arrangement profitable from the standpoint of dealing with the Turks, he would have been forced into it by the skimpiness of the two houses assigned to him. Actually, however, the sultan's first ministers were not much better housed. Although apparently good hunting grounds, which Mehmed "the Hunter" was bound to enjoy, Larissa was hardly a metropolis.

All the houses were made of mud overlaid with straw. Molin's house, which was largely new, was so damp that he suffered continuously from some sort of catarrh or pleurisy, "now in one part of my person, now in another." He prayed that the Dio Signore might preserve him at least to the extent of his mission's being of some value to the fatherland, for he now found himself longing in this world for the everlasting quiet of the other. The dragoman Grillo was working assiduously while Molin furnished him with facts and ideas, inspiring him to ever more intense effort with the assurance that great recognition of his service would surely come.[18]

While Molin was suffering the discomforts of Larissa (and getting nowhere in the negotiations with the pashas), a letter from Heneage Finch, second earl of Winchilsea and Charles II's ambassador to the Porte, finally went off to England after some delay, depicting conditions in Istanbul. Nothing much was stirring at the moment. The Grand Signor remained at Larissa. There had been some talk of his going to Candia, but now the chief topic of interest was the Venetian ambassador's arrival at Larissa, "but how he is received wee know not yet." If there proved to be some news, Winchilsea would be sure to send it. Trade was languishing in Istanbul. Bad money was increasing. The Turks "are making great provisions of men and ammunition against next spring." They were recruiting janissaries by force, "which," according to Winchilsea, "was never done before in Turkey." Whatever was being planned in Larissa, in

---

[17] Delib. Costantinopoli, Reg. 32, fol. 27 [118], doc. dated 31 October 1668.

[18] ASV, Senato (Secreta), Dispacci Costantinopoli (1668–1669), no. 14, fols. 90–91ʳ, dated at Larissa on 4 November 1668. On this "file" (*filza*) or register, see below, note 22.

Istanbul "these here thinke of doing great matters against the Venetians," possibly attacking their strongholds in Dalmatia.[19]

Molin's embassy gave rise to widespread rumors. From Smyrna on 21 November 1668 Sir Daniel Harvey wrote Joseph Williamson, then in Lord Arlington's office at Whitehall:

The Grand Signor is at Larissa, a towne in Achaia between Athens and Thessalonica, where hee has built him a seraglio, and intends to spend this winter. An ambassador from the State of Venice lately went to desire audience, and when he was come within a day's journey of the court, he sent a druggerman to acquaint the Chimacham with his arrivall. Upon the delivery of the message the Chimacham ask'd him if the Doog his master had brought the keys of Candie with him; the fellow answer'd hee was but a poore messenger and knew nothing of his master's business. He bid him bee gone, and told him if his master come neerer the court, or if hee came any more thither from him without the keys, they shoud loose their heads. The ambassador lyes at the same distance from the court, expecting another answer from the Grand Signor, who has sent to advise about this business with the Vizier. Wee heare here that the Venetians in Candy are in a very good condition, that there has lately arriv'd there a thousand Frenchmen, and that there were some more recruits from that nation neere Zante, who are dayly expected there. There is a report that the Grand Signor intends next spring to goe over thither in person. I cannot avow the certainty of it. . . .[20]

On 22 November (1668) the doge and Senate wrote Molin that his diligence and prudence were fulfilling their every expectation. They were glad that when he had reached Corfu, the generals of the "auxiliary" or foreign troops had shown him every sign of honor. They were also pleased that he had maintained in proper fashion the interests of the Republic in his conferences with the generals. The Senate approved of all the expenses he had thus far incurred and all the gifts he had made, both of money and of garments. The Signoria would continue to provide Molin with the necessary funds and other things (as gifts to the Turks), for it was clear that he had not been unduly lavish in disbursing the straitened assets of the state. Molin need not be concerned. His accounts had been settled with no more difficulty than those of other "ambassa-

---

[19] PRO, SP 97, XIX, fol. 49, doc. dated 28 October/7 November 1668. In the same letter, reopened and dated 22 November/2 December (fol. 50^v), "The Grand Signor continues at Larissa, and the Venetian ambassador advanceth not his affayres." Before going to Smyrna, Paul Rycaut, whose works were often reprinted and became well known, was Winchilsea's secretary. On Rycaut, see Sonia P. Anderson, *An English Consul in Turkey: Paul Rycaut at Smyrna, 1667–1678* (1989), referred to in note 7 above.

[20] PRO, SP 97, XIX, fol. 53^r. Henry Bennet, Lord Arlington, was secretary of state from October 1662 to September 1674, when Joseph Williamson succeeded him. Harvey followed Lord Winchilsea as Charles II's ambassador to the Porte.

dors extraordinary and bailies," for he had received the same authority as they, "and with this assurance you must rest assured."

The doge and Senate had learned with satisfaction of Molin's courteous and honorable reception in Turkish territory, especially at Larissa, "chè ivi sia il Gran Signore." The long letter of 22 November to Molin is full of repeated assertions of the Signoria's faith in his ability to manage the arduous (and intricate) negotiations with the Turks. For example, the Senate agreed with Molin that he must insist upon the complete demolition of the fortress of S. Pelagia, on the islet northwest of Candia, but it would certainly be hard to make the Turks accept that. Molin was to take stock of the fact that the Serenissima would be receiving aid from the Christian princes. When the Turks learned of it, they would obviously be impressed.

By this time the forces of the duke of Lorraine should have arrived in the waters of Candia. The emperor was going to send three thousand infantry, as Molin was informed, and presumably seven hundred French volunteers had already reached Candia "con vascelli e bandiere di Malta." The duke of Brunswick was supposed to provide Venice with 2,400 infantry; the bishop of Strasbourg, another three hundred; and, indeed, a further three hundred were said to be on their way from Brunswick. Sixty knightly volunteers and three hundred infantry, with a good deal of munitions, were coming from Malta. The supreme pontiff (Clement IX) had promised assistance, and was appealing to the Christian princes "con religioso fervore." He hoped that when they understood the desperate need, they would quickly send help to Candia, *ch'è antemurale della Chrestianità*.[21]

Indeed, the Signoria hoped that the campaign of 1668 had already drawn to a successful close. The fleet and the armed forces would be added to, not only to make them capable of resisting the Turks, but to be able to take advantage of any favorable opportunity that arose. Surely Molin could thus make clear to the Turks the desirability of peace to put an end to the shedding of blood. Molin was to look into the extent of the Turks' preparations and to get the information into the hands of the

---

[21] When the consistory met in the papal palace on the Quirinal on Monday, 9 July (1668), ". . . dominus noster [Clemens IX] verba fecit de suppetiis, quas principes Christiani offerunt pro Crete defensione hoc ipso tempore quo allatum fuit ingentem Turcarum numerum in eam insulam descendisse, quo Cretam urbem ad deditionem compellerent, quae res Sanctitatis suae animum ingenti sollicitudine onerasset, non minori Sanctitati suae solatio varia in principibus Christianis auxilia oferri, quibus propugnatores adiuti barbarorum impetum solita animi fortitudine et constantia retundant . . ." (Arch. Segr. Vaticano, Acta Consistorialia, Acta Miscellanea, tom. 42, fols. 73ᵛ–74ʳ), and cf. fol. 76ᵛ, where the troops which the Christian princes had promised to send to Crete to help relieve the siege of Candia are listed in rather different numbers. Cf. in general Pastor, *Gesch d. Päpste*, XIV-1 (1929), 603–4.

Carlo Paganino has a good deal to say about Clement IX's nephew Vincenzo Rospigliosi and the papal auxiliaries in the early pages of his *Diario* of Molin's mission to the Turks.

captain–general Morosini, trying also to find out to what extent the travail of warfare could be diverted to Dalmatia.

The Turks might be made a bit less irritated by the knowledge that the Padre Ottomano had been removed from Suda and sent into Italy. Allegedly the son of a sultan, captured as a child, converted to Christianity, and given a clerical role, the Ottoman Father attracted some attention in his time. Further emphasis was given to keeping the Turkish chavush contented as well as to affording the dragoman Ambrosio Grillo adequate appreciation for his services. The dragomans were indispensable. Molin must also take heed of the secretary Giovanni Pietro Cavalli. The news had come that Louis XIV had sent some ships to take the French ambassador from Istanbul. The new English ambassador to the Porte, who had left Livorno, headed for the Bosporus, apparently had instructions favorable to Venice. Molin must cultivate his friendship. The letter ends with commendation of Molin's son Alessandro.[22]

Competitors for the Turkish trade, the English kept a close watch (or as close as they could) upon the course of Alvise da Molin's negotiations with the pashas at Larissa. On 24 December 1668 Sir Daniel Harvey wrote his esteemed friend Joseph Williamson in Lord Arlington's office at Whitehall that

about three days agoe the sultana began her journey hence towards Larissa, from whence there is news come that the Venetian ambassador was in the night time hurried out of his lodging by two chouses [chavushes] and embarqu'd for Candia without any attendance, but his retinue are since sent after him. Whether hee bee sent as a prisoner, or for the sudaine dispatch of some great affaire with the vizier, is not certainly known. 'Tis conjectur'd by some that since the vizier finds hee cannot take the towne, to appease the people a little (whom this siege has exasperated against him), hee will have the advantage of concluding the peace himself upon the place.[23]

Writing to Molin on 9 March 1669, the doge and Senate stated that his last ten dispatches ("nos. 13 to 22") had in every way confirmed their

---

[22] Delib. Costantinopoli, Reg. 32, fols. 27^v–30^r [118^v–121^r], doc. dated 22 November 1668, [*de parte*] +13, [*de non*]—1, [*non sinceri*],—8, but despite the small vote, the cross before the majority vote 13 would seem to indicate the Senate's passage of the motion.

One may find in the ASV, Senato (Secreta), Dispacci Costantinopoli (1668–1669, a "filza" or file once numbered 153) sixty-eight numbered dispatches (one missing and another added here and there) of Alvise da Molin to the doge and Senate, together with letters from the secretaries Giovanni Capello and Giovanni Pietro Cavalli, whose names appear frequently in the diplomatic correspondence of this period, as well as letters to, from, and concerning the Venetian dragoman Grillo and the Turkish dragoman Panagioti. Actually the letters in this file cover the period from July 1668 to February 1670 (*more veneto* 1669). On the Padre Ottomano, see above, Chapter IV, note 16.

[23] PRO, SP 97, XIX, fol. 62^r. On Molin's journey from Larissa and the voyage to Candia, note Paganino's detailed account in the *Diario della Speditione dell'illustr. et eccell. signor Alvise da Molin*, MS. Marc. It. VII, 1608 [7514], pp. 52ff.

high opinion of the courage and prudence with which he was conducting the fateful affairs of the Republic. The way he was facing peril on behalf of the fatherland would live long in the Venetian memory with full praise for "such an outstanding citizen." The Signoria was indeed distressed by "the barbarous manner in which you have been sent to Negroponte and from there to Canea, and as we wish you the best of health, so we also assure ourselves of your indomitable steadfastness." When Molin's letters were not coming to Venice, the Signoria assumed the Turks were preventing him from writing to inform them of certain critical issues. Now, however, they were hearing from Molin, and the Signoria was responding (after a long interval) to give him further instructions as to how the Senate wanted him to deal with the Turks.

By a gift of the Almighty there was now peace in Christendom. Clement IX had been employing his exalted position in most effective fashion. The Signoria had also been laboring to impress upon the princes the dire jeopardy in which Candia found itself and the damage which its loss would cause to all Europe, "which loss may God fend off!" Already they had succeeded in gaining large bodies of troops as well as ammunition, especially from France, where the king had generously resolved "to sustain our interests." Indeed, Louis XIV had pledged his word to the pope "not to molest Spain during the current year." He had in fact assigned to service in the Levant not only a strong force under the duke of Navailles with two lieutenants or marshals, but also a large, fast fleet under the duke of Beaufort, *armiraglio del mare*, which this time would fly the royal, not the Hospitallers', banners. So, at least, the Signoria informed Molin. (Beaufort, as we shall see later on, would be killed soon after his arrival at Candia.) Soldiery had been chosen from the royal guards for conveyance to Candia. Spain, now assured of peace, had promised galleys as well as a certain number of vessels, troops, and cargo ships (*bastimenti*).

The Signoria entertained the hope of receiving further help from other states, "and the Supreme Pontiff will send his own galleys along with those of Malta, while he continues his appeal to all the princes to support our cause, which one must acknowledge to be that of all Christendom." In the meantime Molin was to be consoled by the thought of the Signoria's compassion for his troubles and by the satisfaction they had taken in the information they had obtained from his dispatches. Despite the dangers involved in written communications, they were making their intentions known to him. And they were directing the captain–general to keep him abreast of changes "by means of confidants," but we have no word of who these confidants might be.

Until the doge and Senate sent Molin further instructions, he was to go on observing everything he could among the Turks. He was, however, to make no commitment before he could inform the Signoria of what was afoot (and receive directions), nor was he to send any order to the cap-tain–general Morosini to suspend hostilities since he now lacked the authority to do so. The captain–general had received orders to meet Molin's every request for money. The Signoria would postpone to an-other time the reply to various details in Molin's numerous dispatches, but they did send him approval of all the expenses he had incurred in giving the Turks "gifts and garments" as well as donations to the drago-mans, support for certain Christian slaves in Turkish hands, and his and his family's personal expenses.[24]

On 2 May (1669) Molin wrote the doge from Turkish-held Canea on the island of Crete that "after eight months without letters from your Serenity that of 9 March now comes to me." He felt that his status as the Republic's "gentleman envoy" to the Porte had been abridged by the commanding position of the captain–general Morosini. He was living in misery and "in the abyss of obscurity." The Senate seemed resolved "to cut the thread of the peace" that he had woven with such difficulty, as their Excellencies could understand from his previous dispatches. Act-ing in accord with the terms of his commission, Molin declared that he had been on the point of establishing a secure and enduring peace. Current circumstances had been favorable to his negotiations.

The Republic would have been assured one half the island "kingdom" of Candia, surpassing any concession that the Signoria had ever wrested from the Casa Ottomana throughout the long centuries of the past. The Turks had never before restored territory they had conquered. Molin now had of course, as he lamented, no alternative but to bow to the unwise decision of the Senate, "fatto vitima inocente de' voti di cotesto eccellentissimo Senato, e reso inutile il sacrificio volontario fatto da me con tanta costanza alla Patria." The Senate's change of attitude as to the desirability of peace with the Porte would be ruinous to his family.

Nevertheless, he would continue to sacrifice himself to the dictates of the state. He would strive to protect the Republic's "confidants" and those who risked their lives conveying the secret dispatches back and forth. Molin said he was ready to have the Signoria's dispatches deliv-ered to him through the pasha, which would of course restrict the Si-gnoria's communications to him, and give assurance to the Turks. In any event the dispatch of letters to Venice and the delivery to Molin of those from the Signoria had become a perilous and baffling business. On one occasion a letter had allegedly been thrown upon the balcony of his house during the night. It was found the next morning by his servitors. It contained instructions from Venice.

Molin was facing many difficulties at Canea, among them being the

---

[24] Delib. Costantinopoli, Reg. 32, fols. 32ʳ–33ʳ [123ʳ–124ʳ], *adì IX Marzo MDCLXIX, al dilettissimo nobil nostro Alvise Molin.*

terrible shortage of food. A goose in Canea cost almost ten times what it would cost in Istanbul in times of extreme scarcity. Since Molin had to provide for forty-seven persons, in addition to the secretary Cavalli's people, he could not only anticipate illness, of which he saw signs already, but even death from starvation. The captain–general Morosini could not solve Molin's problems with money, as might have been possible in the past, "because now the times and circumstances are different." Some days ago a Jewish moneylender had offered to loan him 2,000 *reali* "at 95 percent." He had declined the offer. The passage from Larissa to Canea had cost 709 sequins (*cechini*), and so it went. But "the Lord God, who will perhaps have mercy on me, will also instill in the hearts of your Excellencies compassion for my poor underlings to help cure the ills, which will always haunt me [*che anco nelle mie ceneri saranno*], of these sad, unhappy creatures."

Molin was saying prayers that the divine bounty should be such as to fulfill the hopes being raised by the promises of the Christian princes, and not follow in the sad tradition of earlier times,

and this not only in cases of auxiliary troops, but of the most famous leagues, among others that of Paul III and Charles V in 1540, of Pius V and Spain in 1570, which served no other purpose than to make our experience of the first year such as to plunge us into the second and lead us on to unfavorable and woeful peace treaties which cost us states and kingdoms. I hope that in the goodness of the Almighty the Christian princes have changed their ways, and left [the old ways] behind in the annals and histories of the dead.

Well, there was perhaps cause for hope. Old Sultan Suleiman had been one thing. The incompetent Mehmed IV "the Hunter" was another. A warrior sultan would not have tolerated the commotion then going on in Istanbul, nor would his ministers have been ready to sign a treaty of peace unless the Ottoman forces were too weak to carry on.[25]

According to a long letter dated 14 April 1669 which William Winchilsea sent Lord Arlington from Malta, the Ottoman empire did seem to be falling into chaos. Apparently disturbed by the grave unease spreading throughout Turkish Europe and Asia, Mehmed IV had sent a "hatisheriffe" (*hatti sharif*) or imperial command to his mother to the effect that his three brothers should be put to death, which had caused a sudden insurrection of the janissaries. All the shops in Istanbul and Galata were shut. The city gates were closed. However, "the Queene Mother hath refused to deliver up the Grand Signor's brothers to those who were appoynted to receive them, and is backed by the militia."

---

[25] ASV, Senato (Secreta), Dispacci Costantinopoli (1668–1669), no. 37, fols. 254^r–257^r, *Canea 2 Maggio 1669 S[til] N[ovo]*.

There had been a violent encounter "between the French and some Bostangees of one of Grand Signor's seraglios on the Asia side." The *Bostanjis* were gardeners of the palace. "But in the midst of this heat came in the Bostangee Pasha [*Bostanji-Bashi*] himselfe and parted them, or else the French would have been all killed. . . ." There were many reasons for discontent in the empire, and indeed there was discontent everywhere, as Winchilsea makes clear:

All sorts of people lament and cry out for their great oppressions, for the badnesse of mony and decay of trade, encrease of taxes, and new impositions as for powder and other amunition for Candia. Some whole villages are fled both in Europe and Asia, some to the mountaines, others to Arabia, Tartary, and some for Persia. When I was a yeare since at Ponte Picciolo but 20 miles from the great city of Constantinople, I saw bordering upon that lake whole villages destroyed, and I was told by him who gathers the Harrach [*haraç*] that within that jurisdiction or cadee-lick [*kadilik*] there were 1,700 persons that pay'd Harrach before the Venetian war, and that now there were but 700 left, all the rest having abandoned their houses and vinyards, and that those which remaine fly daily because they must pay not only for themselves but for the whole 1,700.

. . . The people of Smyrna openely in the streetes rayled highly against the Grand Signor minding his hunting more then his subjects, and sayed openly that their Emperour was mad, a foole, and that speedily his brother [Suleiman II], who hath more braines and will take more paynes in the management of publike affayres, will be set up in the throne. That Empire is at a very low ebbe, and must have strange changes in a little time; their weakenesse is apparent; they want not only mony, and men too, but braines to governe what they have.[26]

Sometimes letters prepared for dispatch in the doge's name failed to pass the Senate. It is often not clear to the historian why this should have been the case. Thus on 11 May (1669) a letter addressed "to our beloved noble Alvise Molin" was submitted to the Senate, which rejected it, but why? It is, to be sure, highly repetitive of their letter of 9 March, "which by this time will have reached you." Had Molin received the letter of 11 May, he might have taken some slight comfort from the Senate's abiding sympathy for the suffering and hardships he had endured, the strain and exertion the Turks had inflicted on him in requiring him suddenly to leave Larissa at night and take the road to Negroponte in order to board a ship for Canea. But the Senate had already given full expression to their alleged compassion in the letter of 9 March. They prayed for his continued good health so that the fatherland might continue to enjoy the fruits of his abundant talents. The Senate was highly appreciative of Molin's

---

[26] PRO, SP 97, XIX, fols. 75–76, from aboard the *Jerusalem* in the port of Malta the 4/14 of April 1669. Suleiman II eventually did succeed his elder brother Mehmed IV in 1687.

care in dealing with the Turks to avoid any commitment in writing (*et aggiustatissimo sarà sempre il schivar di metter alcuna cosa in scritto*), a practice to which they were certain he would adhere.

For the most part the text of 11 May follows the line of that of 9 March. Louis XIV's troops and naval armament were ready to depart for the Levant. And, in fact, they were. A good many horses had been sent eastward "per montar molti cavalieri." The papal and Maltese galleys were ready to set sail. The emperor "and many other princes" were contributing strong relief forces, munitions, and money to the Christian cause. All the gifts and expenditures, which Molin had made, had received full approval. By this time of course, the Senate assumed, Molin and the secretary Cavalli had got together to distribute the various gifts intended for the Turks. The Senate had learned of the French ambassador's going to Larissa. They would like to assume, they told Molin, that everything was proceeding satisfactorily for him. They could inform Molin, however, that Louis XIV had sent orders to the ambassador that if the Turks obstructed his departure in any way, "immediately to declare himself deprived of the role of ambassador." And finally the Senate approved of Molin's having sent the young Giacomo Tarsia, *giovene di lingua*, back to Istanbul, where he had been studying Turkish. Tarsia had come to Larissa in 1668 to serve Molin, who obviously had in the dragomans all the linguistic assistance he required.[27]

Although by and large news traveled slowly in the seventeenth century, the Signoria knew by mid-August 1669 that, despite the French and other assistance, Morosini was in serious trouble at Candia. They could not know that by mid-August (as we shall see) the French high command had decided to abandon the defense of Candia, and if so informed, they would certainly have been surprised. Except for the safe arrival of the French and other auxiliaries, however, no good news had come from the Levant. On 16 August (1669) the texts of two letters, one to Molin and the other to Morosini, were put before the Senate, which gave a prompt approval to them both. The letter to Molin acknowledged receipt of some thirty dispatches he had sent the Signoria, "molti vostri dispacci numero 13 fin 43," all giving evidence of his indefatigable competence "in the management of the most important affairs of state." The Senate again noted the patriotic manner in which Molin put the interests of the Republic before his own concern and those of his family.

---

[27] Delib. Costantinopoli, Reg. 32, fols. 33ᵛ–34ᵛ [124ᵛ–125ᵛ], doc. dated 11 May 1669, the senatorial vote being—84 [without the cross + signifying passage of the motion to send the letter]—22,—60: *Non publicata presa per esser superior di due soli voti giusta le leggi et mandata ad altro Conseglio*. On Giacomo Tarsia in this context, see *Diario della Speditione dell'illustr. et eccell. signor Alvise da Molin*, MS. Marc. It. VII, 1608 [7514], p. 47.

Reversing the stand taken in their letter to Molin of 9 March, the Senate had again become interested in peace with the Turks. Reducing the contested territorial issues to four or five, the Senate saw the Porte prepared to cede Cattaro (Kotor) on the Dalmatian coast to Venice and, they hoped, the island of Tenos as well. As for the other places in question, Suda and Grabusa, the Turks would certainly give up Grabusa, the small port on the far west of Crete, as well as Spinalonga on the far east. The fortifications at Suda, in the Senate's view, should be demolished, and not rebuilt at any time. These matters had been considered at length in April 1666. There had been some misunderstanding concerning Suda, which the Turks claimed had been formally given up to them. This was not true, however, as Molin could see from certain letters of 22 November 1668, copies of which had just been sent to him.

Molin was informed that after the arrival of the auxiliary forces of France, the Holy See, and Malta in the "kingdom" of Candia, the Christians had inflicted considerable losses on the enemy. The French were anxious to avenge the death of François de Beaufort. More French vessels were expected from Provence. As for the Venetian effort, Bernardo, the *proveditor general da mar,* would soon reach Candia "with good reinforcements of money, munitions, and troops." As Molin knew well, it was important that the French naval armament should not leave the island of Crete before an "honorable peace" (*decorosa pace*) had been negotiated with the Turks, so as to avoid the troubles which would otherwise follow the departure of the French. In fact such was Louis XIV's intention, and such his instructions to his generals, of which the Signoria sent Molin a copy with its statement "di non partire senza vantaggi o proffittevole pace." And, to be sure, the purpose of Molin's embassy was peace with the Porte, "il conseguimento di una buona, honorevole, e sicura pace. . . ."

If the Turks insisted, Molin was to yield to the demolition of the fortress at Grabusa and the withdrawal therefrom of the munitions and cannon. If the Turks demanded Suda, "as it is at present," Molin was authorized to give way on that also, but of course the Turks should remove their munitions and cannon. Molin was to seek "the greatest possible advantages and benefits." The long letter ends with the expectation of seeing Molin eventually "honored once more for outstanding merit and with applause."[28]

The letter of the doge and Senate to Francesco Morosini (of 16 August 1669) was, *mutatis mutandis,* much the same as the letter of that date to Molin. The Senate had chosen with the most Christian king to work for

---

[28] Delib. Costantinopoli, Reg. 32, fols. 35ʳ–37ʳ [126ʳ–128ʳ], *adì XVI Agosto* [*MDCLXIX*], *al dilettissimo nobil nostro Alvise Molin, cavaliere, alla Canea:* +147,—10,—67.

peace with the Turks; the negotiations were being carried on by Molin. The Senate had decided to rescind their militant decision of 9 March, and they were forwarding to Morosini a copy of the letter to that effect which was being sent to Molin. The strictest secrecy must be preserved "sotto il più religioso silentio" to avoid the trouble which would ensue if the facts became known. Morosini was to continue close cooperation with Molin, for after the establishment of peace a suspension of arms must follow.

Louis XIV had declared that the pressure of French arms was intended to force peace upon the Turks. He had ordered his generals not to leave Candia until everything had been "settled favorably" (*prosperamente deffinito*). Copies of the letters making this clear had been made available to the Senate, i.e., letters to the French generals Beaufort and Navailles, together with the texts of their commissions. And now Morosini was sent copies of these texts to assist him in dealing with the French high command at Candia. The king wanted his generals to be included in the prospective peace.

Morosini was to make clear to Beaufort and Navailles, however, the "plans and discussions which we have already had concerning the division of the kingdom" (*li proietti e discorsi già fatti circa la division del Regno*), a reference, it would seem, to Suda, Grabusa, and Spinalonga. The Senate's idea of peace at this time obviously involved the Serenissima's retention of Candia. The Senate hoped that the papal general Vincenzo Rospigliosi would follow the example of the French captains in remaining at Candia. In deference to his Holiness, Morosini must inform Rospigliosi of the negotiations for peace.[29]

It was more than clear that western Europe had not abandoned the Christian cause sending, as Kretschmayr reminds us, "helpers and help" into the Levant—French, Italian, and German money, papal and Maltese galleys, groups of nobles with a crusading spirit, Swedish volunteers, and German mercenaries. As we have just seen, however, the most notable case of this medley of help was French. In July 1668 Louis XIV had empowered François d'Aubusson, duke de la Feuillade, to lead some five hundred knightly volunteers into the Levant to relieve the Turkish pressure upon Candia. La Feuillade had served with distinction in the French forces at S. Gotthard (Szentgotthárd) on the river Raab at the beginning of August 1664, when Montecuccoli had defeated the Turks. As a gesture of appreciation Clement IX gave Louis XIV the right of appointment to the bishopric of Tournai in Hainaut (on 27 August 1668). Tournai had

---

[29] Delib. Costantinopoli, Reg. 32, fols. 37ʳ–38ʳ [128ʳ–129ʳ], *adì XVI Agosto* [*MDCLXIX*], *al capitan general da mar.*

been taken by the French in 1667, and the papal grant was an official recognition of the king's possession of the city.

La Feuillade paid for most of the expenses for his expedition. Three ships and the soldiery assembled in the harbor at Toulon on 25 September (1668), and reached the island of Crete at the beginning of November. The Venetians were encouraged by the French generosity, but five hundred men could accomplish nothing at Candia. In early March (1669) La Feuillade's troops were back at Toulon, having suffered heavy casualties.[30] La Feuillade had sailed under the banner of the Knights Hospitaller, for Louis XIV did not want unduly to ruffle his relations with the Porte. Despite occasional fairly brief lapses the French had maintained a sort of friendship with the Turks for 132 years (since 1536), finding them a useful counterweight against the Hapsburgs.[31]

Worried by the failures of the papal-Maltese and French expeditions of 1668, Clement IX again addressed a general plea to Christendom to help save Candia from the infidel. The government of Charles II of Spain, which had problems enough of its own, promised but failed to provide some twenty ships. Once more, however, the French answered the call to arms. Since Louis XIV was unwilling to risk losing the privileges which the French embassy in Istanbul enjoyed, the French forces were to sail and fight under the papal banner. It was not that the Turks did not easily learn of French participation in the defense of Candia; it was merely that they would almost certainly want to preserve their long-standing accord with France, which had sometimes been useful to the Porte.

Louis XIV moved quickly. As La Feuillade returned from Crete to Toulon, on 15 March (1669) Louis appointed Philippe de Montault de Bénac, duke de Navailles, as general of the land forces and François de Bourbon, duke de Beaufort, as commander of the *armée navale*. Beaufort was a relative of the king; his father, César de Vendôme, was the son of Henry IV and Gabrielle d'Estrées. Beaufort's checkered career would come to an end in the siege of Candia. Navailles' land forces were said to consist of 57 companies of 12 regiments, which apparently meant about 6,000 men, along with three companies of cavalry, 1,400 tents, three months' provisions, and a huge supply of munitions.

The naval armament was supposed to include 15 ships, 13 galleys, and

---

[30] Cf. Kretschmayr, *Gesch. v. Venedig*, III (1934, repr. 1964), 337–38; Pastor, *Gesch. d. Päpste*, XIV-1 (Freiburg im Breisgau, 1929), 604. Surprisingly enough Graziani, *Francisci Mauroceni . . . gesta* (1698), pp. 142–68, makes no mention of Rospigliosi in his account of events of the year 1668. Arrighi, *De vita et rebus gestis Francisci Mauroceni* (1749), lib. II, pp. 115–53, gives much attention to La Feuillade and very little to Rospigliosi.

[31] During the 1660's French relations with the Ottoman Empire were rather ruffled, however, for Louis XIV had trouble deciding upon a consistent policy for dealing with the Turks (cf. W.H. Lewis, *Levantine Adventurer: The Travels and Missions of the Chevalier d'Arvieux*, New York and Amsterdam, 1963, pp. 133ff.).

three galliots under Beaufort, with the galleys and galliots, however, under the direct command of Louis Victor de Rochechouart, count de Vivonne. The ships were equipped with broadside cannon. Thanks to the diary of J.-B. Duché de Vancy, Vivonne's secretary, we have an abundance of detail relating to the galleys. The extent and obvious cost of the undertaking attest to the importance the king attached to preventing the Turkish capture of Candia.

After two months of exacting preparation the French fleet was ready to leave Marseille by 15 May (1669). Almost immediately thereafter the galleys began their eastern voyage, reaching Monaco on 1 June, Savona on the 2nd, La Spezia on the 5th, and Civitavecchia on the 11th. At Civitavecchia the pope saw to it that M. le général Vivonne was given a feast, with wine and fish for the crews. Every time M. le général came ashore, he was honored with a salvo of "twenty and thirty pieces of cannon."

After three or four days of festivity at Civitavecchia the galleys resumed their course, reaching the Isole Lipari on 18 June, Messina on the 22nd, Corfu on the 23rd, and the island of Zante on the 25th. At Zante, Vivonne was joined by Vincenzo Rospigliosi with seven papal galleys and Clemente Accarigi with seven Maltese galleys. The Christian force was further strengthened by four galleys from Venice. The usual problems of protocol arose, but did not unduly delay the eastern progress of the Christian galleys which reached Cerigo on 1 July, and hove into sight of Crete on the 2nd, when the allies encountered sixteen Turkish galleys from Canea. The Turks withdrew quickly, however, and on the following day (3 July) the Christian galleys arrived at Candia.

François de Bourbon, duke de Beaufort, left Toulon with the transports on 5 June (1669). Well provisioned, he apparently had to make few stops. His *armée navale* now consisted of 15 ships of the line along with ten freighters, fire ships, and other boats. There was also a hospital ship with a goodly supply of linens and medicines. All told, the French crews are said to have amounted to 4,670 men, the land forces to 5,198 soldiers with 629 officers. After leaving Toulon and rounding Sardinia and Sicily by the southwest route, the *armée navale* went on to Zante and Cerigo, arriving offshore from Candia on 19 June. They must have had strong winds to make so long a voyage in so short a time.

Conditions in Candia had reached a point of absolute desperation. The siege had grown in intensity month after month, ever since Ahmed Köprülü had taken over direct command of the Ottoman troops, and launched a memorable attack on 24–25 May 1667. By the time the French expeditionary force had reached Candia, the Turks had largely demolished the important bastion of S. Andrea at the northwest corner of the fortifications. Upon his arrival Navailles reported that one saw only dead, wounded, and crippled soldiers; there was neither a church nor a battlement without broken walls. Candia had been torn apart by cannon, bombs, and stones. It no longer had the shape of a city. Although Beaufort and Navailles should probably have taken the time to familiar- ize themselves and their troops with both the terrain and Turkish tactics, they decided immediately to make an attack upon the enemy en- trenched on the east side of the walls, where the Turks had reduced the bastion of Il Sabbionera to a heap of ruins.

The French made their first attack during the early morning hours of 25 June. Taken completely by surprise, the Turks were swept from their trenches, and took to flight, abandoning their batteries. Carried away by success, the French seemed to be getting lost in the outworks and the trenches when suddenly one of the batteries they had taken exploded. Mines had also been laid in the area. Now they were ignited. Turkish reserves from around southern Candia (*Nova Candia*) and the north- west bastion of S. Andrea suddenly appeared on the scene. Forty French soldiers were killed. As panic ensued, the Turks made a counterattack. Beaufort, in the front line of the French assault, was struck with a musket shot, fell from his horse, and was never seen again. The ill-advised attack cost the French 245 officers and 560 soldiers and sailors. The Turks were said to have lost some 1,200 men. Beaufort's death was a severe blow to the expedition. He had been the commander-in-chief. It was a poor beginning.[32]

The Venetians had played no part in the ill-starred venture, but they were of course severely shaken by the catastrophe. Maybe the French *armée navale* with its 840 guns would do no better than the tired Vene- tian forces, which now numbered no more than 6,000 men. On 6 July Rospigliosi disembarked three regiments, after which he and Vivonne decided it would be unwise to leave the ships and galleys huddled to- gether in the harbor of Candia. A Turkish attack with fireships could bring another disaster. Therefore they moved the bulk of the allied fleet ten miles to the north, to the island of Standia, where by digging wells they hoped to find water. Decisive action of some sort would soon be necessary, for the food supplies in Candia were getting low. The Vene- tians and the French were not in accord, having apparently disagreed as to the advisability of the French attack upon the Turks on 25 June, and as the days passed, relations between them were not improving. At a meeting of the war council on Friday, 12 July (1669), it was agreed that on the first fair day after the following Monday a well-planned attack by the combined land and naval forces would be launched against the masses of Turkish troops laying siege to Candia.

When the wind had finally slackened, the order was given on 23 July

---

[32] On the events of 25 June 1669, see esp. Bigge, *Der Kampf um Candia* (1899), pp. 171–77; note also the account of Carlo Paganino, in his *Diario* of Alvise da Molin's em- bassy to the Turks, in MS. Marc. It. VII, 1608 (7514), pp. 80ff., and on the fortifications of Candia, *ibid.*, pp. 107–111.

(1669) to put the galleys and galleasses close to the ships they were soon to tow within firing range of Candia. By sunrise on the following morning the galleys and ships were mostly in place. The ships were towed into positions from which they could bombard the Turkish units that were operating the batteries close enough to be accessible to the Christian cannon. Thus on the morning of 25 July the allied warships began the heavy bombardment of the Turkish encampments, forts, batteries, and trenches to the extent their broadside cannon could reach them. From twelve to fifteen thousand cannon shots were allegedly fired at the Turks. Although the Venetian, papal, and Maltese galleys and ships had participated in the onslaught to the extent they could, eleven thousand shots were said to have been fired from the French vessels. Certainly the cannonading did the Turks some damage, but deep trenches and dugouts had long been part and parcel of Turkish siegecraft.

Offshore bombardment would not bring the siege of Candia to a halt. By some mishap, moreover, the French ship *Thérèse* exploded with 58 guns and 293 men aboard, causing a terrible disruption in the French lineup. Vivonne's flagship, alongside the *Thérèse*, was so shaken by the explosion that one caught a view of the keel. A number of officers, soldiers, mariners, and galley slaves were killed or wounded. The ship *Provençal* also nearby suffered twenty dead and wounded. All told, there appear to have been 28 dead and 56 wounded aboard the six Venetian galleys which had participated in the attack upon the Turks, while the French were said to have suffered 421 dead and 219 wounded. Turkish deserters set the grand vizir's losses at more than 1,200 men although, as Bigge says, this figure is obviously much too high, "doch ist diese Zahl augenscheinlich viel zu hoch gegriffen."[33] It may be, but the bombardment would seem to have cost the French as much as it did the Turks.

Obviously the French offensive had not gone well. The tired Venetians had contributed only six galleys to the French operations. Vivonne complained in his report of 28 July (1669) to Louis XIV that the Venetians failed to keep their word, and that they frustrated the efforts of others to assist them. In any event Vivonne believed that twelve to fifteen thousand cannon shots must have killed two to three thousand Turks, which seems unlikely considering the Turkish trenches and bunkers. The complete failure of the French to weaken the Turkish position at Candia led Navailles and Vivonne to give serious thought to how much longer they

---

[33] Bigge, *Der Kampf um Candia* (1899), pp. 181–84; *Registro di lettere del Cav. F. Vincenzo Rospigliosi*, Arch. Segr. Vaticano, Miscell., Arm. XVI, tom. 138, fols. 184ᵛ–188ʳ, docs. dated 25 July 1669. Having been able almost always to read the manuscript sources in the archives and libraries where they are kept, I have mostly been spared the use of microfilm. Not so, however, in the case of Rospigliosi's letters, for which I have had to depend upon a microfilm I acquired many years ago, and unfortunately the last third or so of this MS. (fols. 147ᵛff.) has apparently been damaged by moisture, making much of the microfilm impossible to read.

could afford to remain there. As Vivonne wrote the French minister Colbert on 25 July, the enemy and illness were causing too many casualties. Sixty to ninety men were being disabled every day in one way or another. The food supplies were becoming a worry. They might last until September, but the high command would have to provide for the return of the surviving manpower to France. One could hardly expect help from the Venetians, for at Candia they were always on the horns of a dilemma.

Gloomy as the outlook was, the French continued their efforts, making an attack on 30 July (1669) upon the Turks ensconced in the ruins of Il Sabbionera, the bastion on the east wall of Candia (more or less corresponding to S. Andrea on the west).[34] It was a bold venture, but nothing came of it. Morosini was said to have promised five hundred men. He provided only fifty. On 1 August Morosini asked the French again to cannonade the Turks from the sea, but Vivonne declined to do so, and Navailles thought it might be a risk to the French fleet. On the other hand, when on 11 August Vivonne was informed that a reinforcement of three thousand Turks was soon to join their fellows in the siege of Candia, he suggested that a flotilla of French and Venetian galleys go out to meet them. Morosini replied that he wished first to consult Rospigliosi (perhaps to enlist papal galleys in the venture); also he must assemble and consult the war council, but he would inform Vivonne that night. He was apparently unable to do so.

Although Morosini beseeched Navailles and Vivonne to postpone their departure from Crete, it was clear before mid-August that the Veneto-French coalition could not last much longer. Morosini held on to the French a few more days by making a considerable quantity of wheat available to them. By 20 August, however, Vivonne was taking the first steps for the embarkation of the French forces, which had accomplished nothing, and suffered a good deal. Of some 5,200 soldiers, only about 3,500 were being put aboard the ships, and of these 1,500 were ill. Sickness among the galley crews and the mariners was keeping pace with that aboard the ships.[35] On 25 August two Turkish attacks were driven

---

[34] On the Turks' battering of the bastions of S. Andrea and Il Sabbionera, cf. *Nova e vera Relatione del combattimento novamente seguito in Candia*, publ. in Venice, Bologna, and Ferrara by Giulio Bulzoni Giglio, 1669. Plans of the bastions of Il Sabbionera and S. Andrea are given in Bigge, *Der Kampf um Candia* (1899), between pp. 154–55, and in *Venezia e la difesa del Levante* (1986), pp. 136–37, 165ff. A Venetian named Barozzi, who deserted as a renegade to the Turks, had helped Ahmed Köprülü in the final period of the siege by making clear the extent of the weakness of the fortifications of both Il Sabbionera and S. Andrea (ASV, Inquisitori di Stato, Lettere da Costantinopoli, Busta 419, *passim*, cited by Dores Levi-Weiss, "Le Relazioni fra Venezia e la Turchia dal 1670 al 1684 . . . ," *Veneto-Tridentino*, VII [1925], 32, note 5).

[35] Cf. *Registro di lettere del Cav. F. Vincenzo Rospigliosi*, fol. 206ᵛ: "Le malattie che regnano generalmente in quest'armata si fanno specialmente sentire sopra la squadra pontificia, dove hoggi si contano 167 infermi oltre a 38 che già son morti . . . ," doc. dated at Zante on 6 September 1668 (*sic*).

back; on the 31st, 1,500 Italians arrived on the scene. When the French left, Morosini had no alternative to surrender. And this he did under appropriate terms on 5 September (1669). Every Venetian citizen could leave the island within fifteen days, taking off with him all his movable possessions. It was the end of four and a half centuries of Venetian rule on the island of Crete.[36]

In a letter to Molin dated at Candia on 8 September (1669) Morosini informed him of the surrender of Candia, but "the fortresses of Suda, Grabusa, and Spinalonga remain [within the domain] of his Serenity,

---

[36] On the French expedition and the fall of Candia to the Turks, see *Stato dell' armata e soccorso reale mandato dalla Maestà Christianissima in Candia contro il Turco l'anno corrente 1669, mosso dal santo e pio zelo della Santità di N. S. Clemente Nono, per diminuire et abbattere le forze ottomane*, Venice, appresso Camillo Bortoli, 1669; Giov. Graziani, *Francisci Mauroceni . . . gesta*, Padua, 1698, pp. 171–96; Antonio Arrighi, *De vita et rebus gestis Francisci Mauroceni*, Padua, 1749, lib. II–III, pp. 153–218, a good account; and see esp. Bigge, *Der Kampf um Candia in den Jahren 1667–1669* (1899) pp. 158ff., 164–201; after reading Bigge, one should take a look at Camillo Manfroni, "I Francesi a Candia," *Nuovo Archivio Veneto* (1902), 385–93. Note also Gino Damerini, *Morosini* (1929), pp. 119–44; Kretschmayr, *Gesch. von Venedig*, III (1934, repr. 1964), 336–41, which does not get us very far; Anderson, *Naval Wars in the Levant* (1952), pp. 181–84; and (among numerous other works) there is a readable narrative of events by H. de Nanteuil, "Le Duc de Vivonne et ses galères à l'expédition de Candie (1669)," *Revue historique des armées*, no. IV (Paris, 1974), 7–31, which I have found useful.

When the sad news of the surrender of Candia reached Venice, the doge Domenico Contarini wrote the captain–general Morosini that he was only too well aware of the bitterness that Morosini had experienced in having to give up the fortress to the Turks, "ma unitamente commediamo l'espediente d'unire ad essa [la necessità di render la piazza] li negotiati della pace e far che Candia rieschi il prezzo della medesima. A questo fine proprie sono riuscite le forme prudenti praticate nella negotiatione medesima, i vantaggi in essa ottenuti con l'inbarco delle militie, munitioni, e cannoni. Questa gloria però che vi adorna nel concetto universale del mondo per haver potuto per il lungo corso di tre anni sostenere la diffesa di Candia a fronte dell'Ottomana potenza, ben anche deve continuarvi ad illustrar l'animo, mentre con la cessione della piazza, ch'era cadente, havete donato alla Patria nello stato dell'emergenti una decorosa et avantaggiosa pace e prestato alle forze languide di essa un commodo respiro, onde per tutti li capi concorre il Senato con applausi di gloria e con singolari commendationi al vostro valore e prudenza che nella diretione dell'armi e del negotiato vi havete così frutuosamente impiegato. . . . Data in nostro ducali palatio anno 1669 [sic]. Agostin Bianchi segretario" (MS. Marc. It. VII, 657 [7481], fol. 151).

For what it is worth, according to the *Trattato politico sopra la pace fatta tra la Republica di Venetia et il Gran Turco l'anno 1669* (MS. Marc. It. VII, 656 [7791], fol. 9ᵛ), "Se la Republica ha perduto molti de suoi nobili, cittadini, e sudditi che gloriosamente hanno consecrato la vita nella diffesa di Candia e della fede, non è stato ch'una picola stilla in paragone del vasto mare del sangue infedele che si è versato da un millione e ducento mille Turchi, che usciti (a conto fatto d'altri) da Constantinopoli su l'armate Ottomane sono periti nel corso di questa guerra, et il solo ultimo attacco di Candia per loro propria confessione è costato alla Turchia le vite di cento e ottanta mille Musulmani, e quanti ne haverà consumati il ferro et il foco nella Dalmatia e nell'Albania e negl'inutili attacci di Cattaro, Sebenico, e di Spalato, e nelle sconfitte datte loro dall'armi Venete e da Morlacci. . . ." In any event the long war of Candia had certainly taken a heavy toll of the lives and resources of both the Turks and the Venetians. On the financial costs of the war to Venice, cf. R.T. Rapp, *Industry and Economic Decline in Seventeenth-Century Venice*, Cambridge, Mass., and London, England, 1976, pp. 149–54.

together with the adjacent reefs, which is a fact of considerable importance."[37] As soon as he had received Morosini's dispatch, Molin informed the doge Domenico Contarini, "Today finally, on 22 September,
the letters, dated the 8th, of his Excellency, the captain–general, have
reached me by land." It had taken two weeks for the couriers to get from
Candia to Canea. Severe storms had caused the delay. A dispatch of the
grand vizir had apparently come more rapidly by sea, however, to the
pasha at Canea. Molin had thus learned of the reasons which had forced
Morosini to surrender the fortress of Candia to the Turks. Peace had
been made "with the concession of the three fortresses in the kingdom
[of Candia] as well as Clissa and the occupied territory in Dalmatia to
your Serenity, along with the other conditions of which his Excellency
will have apprised your Serenity." Although Molin and Morosini had
been in communication with each other concerning the possibility of
Molin's negotiating peace with the Turks, obviously the French and the
auxiliary troops had withdrawn from Candia too quickly for him to retrieve any advantage for the Republic. Believing that Morosini had probably acted too quickly, Molin was clearly distressed, having been out-
done by time and circumstance.[38]

When the Signoria had been informed of the details involved in the
"peace established between our Republic and the Sublime Porte by the
captain–general of the sea with the subscription of the first vizir," senatorial action was required. In similar cases the Senate had always elected
an "ambassador extraordinary," who would betake himself to the court
and to the very presence of the Gran Signore to see to the reciprocal
ratification of the treaty of peace, "la corrispondenza della pace medesima con le consulte forme." The person to be elected could, as usual, be

---

[37] ASV, Senato (Secreta), Dispacci Costantinopoli (1670), fol. 113ʳ. According to articles II–IV of the treaty of 5 September (1669) between Mehmed IV and the Republic of
Venice, negotiated by the grand vizir Ahmed Köprülü and the captain–general Francesco
Morosini (J. Dumont, *Corps universel diplomatique*, VII-1 [Amsterdam and The Hague,
1731], no. L, p. 119): ". . . Omnia munimenta, portus, insulae adjacentes, et alia loca quae
sub ditione Reipublicae in Regno Candiae sunt, eodem modo quo ante bellum sub domina-
tione eiusdem fuerunt, porro manebunt. In quorum numero sunt Suda, Spinalonga, Cara-
buse, et Tini [the island of Tenos] omnesque dependentiae Spinalongae a Regno Candiae
separentur.

"Omnis res tormentaria, et instructus qui in loco erit, sub hac conditione illic in totum
relinquetur, ut tamen supremus vezirius capitaneo generali XL tormenta majora dono det.

"Omnes insulae in Archipelago et aliae, quae ad ipsam Rempublicam pertinebunt, sub
potestate eiusdem maneant eodem modo quo ipsi ante bellum subjectae fuerunt, fortali-
tiumque Clissa et omnia quae Veneti eripuerunt Turcis in Dalmatia et in Albania absolutae
summaeque potestati Serenissimae Reipublicae subdita relinquentur."

The Turks must have been in serious trouble to make the concessions stated in the
above text. The Italian version of articles I, II, III, XII–XIII is given in Dores Levi-Weiss, "Le
Relazioni fra Venezia e la Turchia dal 1670 al 1684 . . . ," *Veneto-Tridentino*, IX–X
(1926), 117–18, and note Paganino's *Diario* of Molin's embassy to the Turks, MS. Marc. It.
VII, 1608 (7514), pp. 84ff.

[38] Senato (Secreta), Dispacci Costantinopoli (1668–1669), no. 49, fol. 399ʳ, dispatch of
Molin to the doge and Senate, dated 22 September 1669.

taken from any governmental office. He could not refuse the charge, being subject to all the penalties involved in the declination of an ambassadorship to any one of the crowned heads of Europe and the Levant.

The Senate took action on 18 October (1669), making provision for this important, at least symbolically important, embassy to the Porte. The ambassador in question would receive for his expenses 400 ducats a month, to be paid in gold, "with no obligation to render account thereof." Another 1,500 ducats would be given to him "as a gift" to help meet the unforeseen expenses he would inevitably encounter. He must take no fewer than fifteen horses with him, including those of his secretary, a servant, and four grooms. He was also to have a physician, to whom a hundred sequins would be given as a gift, and a barber (surgeon), who would receive fifty. The ambassador's chaplain would have "the usual gift and a salary." The "coadjutor" would get a gift of a hundred ducats, and thereafter fifteen ducats a month.

The Signoria would meet the overall costs of the journey to the Porte and back, *le spese di bocca e di viaggio.* Other salaries and expenses were anticipated, for which the Signoria would make adequate provision. Once chosen, the ambassador must leave within fifteen days, go first to Corfu, and thence to the Porte, where he would follow the instructions which would be given him. If he failed to depart within the fifteen days, he would face a heavy fine. As was to be expected, the motion was passed in the Senate with almost no opposition.[39] Such was in fact the usual formula, with the usual emoluments, for the election of an ambassador extraordinary.

Despite the legal rigmarole on 18 October (1669) the members of the Senate doubtless knew who would be elected ambassador extraordinary to the sultan Mehmed IV. It was of course to be Alvise da Molin, now no longer merely a "gentleman envoy" (*gentilhuomo inviato*) to the Porte. As the doge wrote Molin the following day (19 October), the Senate had added to his dignity "il titolo di ambasciatore estraordinario al Gran Signore." The peace with the Turks must receive prompt ratification. Since Molin was on hand at Canea, with the grand vizir Ahmed Köprülü nearby, he was the one to act for the Signoria in his new ambassadorial capacity. The Senate sent Molin a letter for formal presentation to the grand vizir. He was to assure Köprülü of the Signoria's admiration for him, and to praise him for the part he had played in making peace, saving

---

[39] Senato, Delib. Costantinopoli, Reg. 32, fols. 39^r–40^r [130^r–131^r], *adì XVIII Ottobre* [*MDCLXIX*], +89,—1,—3. As for payments to secretaries and coadjutors, some twenty years before (in 1650) Alvise Contarini had referred to "secretarii e coadiutori, questi con sette e quelli con quindeci ducati al mese salarii, che oggidì non bastano a servitori privati degli ambasciatori" (*Relatione . . . per la pace universale al Convento di Münster* [1650], in MS. Marc. It. VII, 1107 [9016], fol. 12^r).

"so many treasures," putting a stop to the bloodshed, and giving thought to the needs of commerce.

Molin was to assure Ahmed Köprülü that "all the conditions of the capitulation will be inviolably adhered to by the Republic." Strict orders had been sent to Dalmatia to put a stop to all hostilities and to reestablish friendly relations with the Turks. Such orders had also been sent to the borders of Albania and to the Three Islands of the Ionian Sea. Possession of the fortresses of the erstwhile "kingdom" of Candia had already been agreed upon, with the reefs or rocky approaches to the fortresses (of Suda, Grabusa, and Spinalonga) belonging to Venice, but such matters should be thoroughly understood and confirmed before Köprülü left the island of Crete.

Molin was to seek the liberation of "our nobles and other slaves," who had been captured by the Turks, fix the precise time of their release, and try to take proper care of them. He was to seek every commercial advantage possible at the Porte. Also he must try to get Venetian vessels renewed access to the wharf at Spalato (Split). The Senate was anxious to have "l'antica corrispondenza" restored, being quite ready to proceed to the election of a bailie to reside in Istanbul. The required letters of credence were being prepared for the Gran Signore and his ministers. When the grand vizir left Crete for the Porte, i.e., Istanbul, Molin must try to go with him, informing the Signoria that he had done so. He would then be sent "those other orders which we shall think necessary." The ducal letter of 19 October, like so many others of the past weeks and months, was full of praise for Molin, with the usual expressions of concern for the hardships he had suffered.

Associating with the grand vizir, as he was now able to do, Molin must try to learn the vizir's "most secret intentions" and the plans and thoughts of the Turks, which would help to guide the captain–general Morosini as well as the Signoria in their next moves. Molin was to use his own judgment (as he had been doing) in distributing *bakhshīsh*, "il far quei donativi e regalli che stimarete proprii," to the Turkish dragoman Panagioti and other helpful persons at the Porte. The doge and Senate were ordering the captain–general to send 3,000 sequins to Molin immediately to help him meet various and sundry expenses. Other funds had and would come from Venice. Along with this dispatch of 19 October the Senate was sending another passport, which would add to Molin's dignity and the security of the voyage to Istanbul.[40]

---

[40] Delib. Costantinopoli, Reg. 32, fols. 40ʳ–42ʳ [131ʳ–133ʳ], *adì XIX Ottobre* [*MDCLXIX*], *all'ambasciator Molin destinato alla Porta*. The harbor of Spalato (Split) was reopened to Venetian vessels, on which cf. Dores Levi-Weiss, "Le Relazioni fra Venezia e la Turchia dal 1670 al 1684 e la formazione della Sacra Lega," *Veneto-Tridentino*, VII (1925), 5, who gives no little attention to Molin. In fact Levi-Weiss has painted a fairly full

On the same day (19 October 1669) the doge and Senate also wrote Ahmed Köprülü of the "affectionate fealty which our Republic has always maintained toward the Sublime Porte" and of "la stima che si porta verso la dignissima sua persona." They confirmed and ratified all the conditions and articles of the said "capitulation of peace," notifying Köprülü that they were now appointing Alvise da Molin as ambassador extraordinary to the Gran Signore to give the Sublime Porte assurance of the Republic's desire always to preserve that peace.[41] On the 23rd similar letters were to go out to the mufti, the kaïmakam, the kapudan pasha, the *capigilar agasi,* "and other pashas of the Porte."

Meanwhile Molin was rusticating in Canea. On 22 October he wrote the doge that no ship was entering the port, and no one was coming from the encampment at Candia. He had not spent his time entirely in vain, however, for at this early stage of the cessation of hostilities more than one unfortunate event might have occurred, given the extent to which fear and jealousy were rife among the commanders. But he had had more than one opportunity to make clear the absolute sincerity of the Republic in wanting to maintain and cherish the peace that had just been made, which had apparently disarmed at least some of the Turks.

The pasha of Canea was a man of integrity and wisdom. He was trying to assure the Turkish adherence to the peace, and was showing Molin every possible courtesy with frequent gifts of fruit, to which Molin responded "with sweetmeats and other things," which he believed appropriate to the occasion. The pasha had gone off to the Turkish encampment at Candia, where he had planned to spend some time, but after a few days he was back in Canea, having been ordered to return by the grand vizir Ahmed Köprülü. The vizir had done so at Molin's request and in accord with the wishes of the captain–general Morosini. Molin had then had the opportunity to discuss with the pasha the expected arrival of Morosini at Suda.

The Turks now made every effort to do honor to the Venetians. Pavilions—large tents—were set up in the field. Molin was provided with a retinue "and with other manifestations of their customs." He was waiting for Morosini with keen anticipation in order to make clear the high esteem in which he held the captain–general as well as to learn *dalla viva voce* details of his negotiations with the Turks "in the important matter of the peace." Molin was anxious to attend to certain diplomatic functions which still had to be observed to meet the protocol of the times, but with these we shall not detain ourselves.

---

picture of Turco-Venetian relations from 1670 to 1684, *ibid.,* VII (1925), 1–46; VIII (also 1925), 40–100; and IX–X (1926), 97–116, with an appendix of unpublished documents, *ibid.,* pp. 117–54. I have tried, on the whole, not to repeat the material in Levi-Weiss's monograph.

[41] Delib. Costantinopoli, Reg. 32, fol. 42 [133].

Molin was very much concerned with the fact that Venetian merchants, especially those who were shipping merchandise under contracts with owners of foreign vessels, were not flying the flag of S. Mark,
la bandiera di S. Marco. He was anxious to preserve or rather to restore
"the important profit that your Serenity used to derive from the 'cassa
del cottimo,' from which were paid all those on salaries in the household
of the bailie [in Istanbul], and from which monies were also sought for
other expenses." At this point, however, a word of explanation will withdraw us from the text of Molin's letter to the doge and Senate of 22
October (1669). He was trying to resurrect a defunct financial practice.

The *cottimo* was a tax of one percent which the Republic's consuls in
certain Levantine ports had levied upon Venetian merchant ships. In
fact, in the good old days of the Republic, the Venetians had maintained
in certain Levantine ports a mercantile superintendency consisting of a
consul and two assessors recruited from the patriciate. Their purpose
was to oversee and protect the ships and merchants. As the institution
dwindled, the last of these consuls were to be found in Damascus, in
Alexandria, and indeed in London. After the war of Candia, with which
Molin had been so much involved of late, the superintendencies imposing the commercial tax were abandoned. Since their personnel had been
drawn from the more or less impoverished patricians, and one wished to
furnish the latter with some means of livelihood, three "superintendencies" had been established (the *provveditori al cottimo di Londra, di
Damasco, e di Alessandria*), which provided pensions to the appoint-
ees, paying thirty ducats a month in silver. These so-called *provveditori*
had no authority, and bore little or no responsibility.

In his letter of 22 October (1669) Molin was insistent that henceforth
Venetian merchants should not ship their goods to Istanbul under any
flag but that of the Serenissima, even though the vessels under contract
were Flemish, English, "or of another nation." Their merchandise should
go to the Bosporus only under the flag of the Republic "in order to
restore the aforesaid 'cassa del cottimo.' " Merchants had been flying
other flags than that of S. Mark to reduce the Turkish customs duty
(*datio*) from five to three percent, which was the toll paid by the Flemings, the English, and the Genoese, as the French were also doing now,
having recently got the Turkish toll reduced on their exports and imports. The Venetians were still paying five percent. Molin grieved that,
alas, Venetian merchants and those subject to Venice had not been flying the lion banner of S. Mark on their vessels, "to the notable loss of
your Serenity."[42] Since the *cottimo* had only been imposed upon vessels

---

[42] Senato (Secreta), Dispacci Costantinopoli (1668–1669), no. 51, fols. 422^r–423^v,
Canea li 22 Ottobre 1669 S[til] N[ovo]. On the financial importance of the *bandiera di S.
Marco* and the *cassa di cottimo,* cf. the Dispacci Costantinopoli (1670), fols. 82, 87.
Money was always a problem to the Signoria throughout the War of Candia, as we have

acknowledging their Venetian identity by flying the lion banner, obviously the merchants were not only avoiding forty percent of the Turkish toll but also the Venetian impost. The times were changing, and however unwillingly, the Signoria would soon have to give up the "cottimo" except as a device for sponsoring certain pensions.

A few hours after Molin had sent off this last dispatch (of 22 October), the news reached him of the captain–general Francesco Morosini's arrival in the Gulf of Suda. Morosini had written him a courteous letter to inform him of the fact. Plans were promptly made for their meeting "yesterday morning," when Molin left Canea

attended by a noble and numerous retinue of janissaries and sipahis, and also honored by the presence of the pasha's "chiaia," who is the first person here after the pasha himself, sent by the latter with others of his court and with many horses for me and for these gentlemen who are with me, all sumptuously outfitted to accompany me on the journey. Mounted on horseback we rode out from the city [of Canea] toward Suda with all the aforementioned retinue and arrived at the place called the "Lontana di Cassain Pasha." There I found some pavilions all ready, but one especially rich, stately, and majestic, furnished with carpets, cushions, and chairs. Having dismounted and entered this pavilion I found therein many servitors of the pasha himself, ready for whatever I might possibly need.

When I had become seated with the said chiaia, the lord lieutenant general Riva came in a moment to find me with many gentlemen, sent by the most excellent captain–general to receive me with many small boats, including feluccas, from the broadside of his ship, which had been put just opposite the aforesaid pavilion for my greater ease and convenience in making my way to express my great esteem [for the captain–general].

Molin then made up to the officers and gentlemen, who had thus come together, and ordered coffee, sherbert, orangeade (*acqua nanfa*), and perfume for them all, after the fashion of the Turks when they wished to honor someone. Having got through these "ceremonies" and his formal meeting with the pasha's chiaia, Molin went aboard a felucca, and was conveyed to the "ship," presumably Morosini's flagship, where the captain–general gave him a most honorable reception to show the Turks the high regard in which one held a minister of the Signoria. When the august conference of the ambassador with the captain–general ended after some hours, Molin returned to land, and going back into the pavilion, he fulfilled his social obligations to the officers, nobles, and other gentle-

---

often stated, and the major part of that problem was in the recruitment and payment of oarsmen and mercenaries. On the importance of the Venetian guilds in recruiting oarsmen (*galeotti*) and the costs involved at the time of the War of Candia, see Richard T. Rapp, *Industry and Economic Decline in Seventeenth-Century Venice*, Cambridge, Mass., and London, 1976, pp. 52ff., 84, 86.

men who had accompanied him. Shortly thereafter Molin mounted his horse along with the retinue with which the pasha had furnished him, and returned to his house in Canea, where the chiaia and the rest of the Turks bade him farewell, "terminata con decorosa et honorevolissima forma la funtione."[43]

On 23 October the doge and Senate wrote Morosini that they were sending back to him the sergeant major Betti, who had just arrived in Venice with letters of Morosini on the *Salvator del Mondo*. The doge was turning over to Betti this brief note to Morosini as well as some dispatches "for the ambassador extraordinary, the cavalier Molin," together with various things, including garments, which Molin would find essential to give as gifts to the Turks to help him achieve success at the Porte. Morosini must see to it that the whole shipment was conveyed safely and quickly to Molin as soon as Morosini could determine precisely where the ambassador was then staying. When he had sent the *robbe* off to Molin, he was to inform the Signoria that he had done so.[44]

On the same day (and by the same vote) the Senate approved a letter to the sultan Mehmed IV, expressing great satisfaction in the peace which the captain–general had negotiated with the grand vizir. The Venetian government would observe every article and detail of the peace, and would rely upon the ministers and representatives of the Porte in the borderlands (of Dalmatia and Albania) to do the same. Every effort was going to be made "per conservare l'antica amicitia che habbiamo havuto con li serenissimi suoi precessori," as would be made clear "with the living voice by our beloved noble Alvise Molin, whom we have elected ambassador extraordinary to your imperial Majesty, and may your years be many and most fortunate."[45]

The Senate approved still another dispatch on 23 October, this time to Molin, who must try to see that in his first audience at Istanbul he was received with the honor and attention accorded to "ambassadors of crowned heads." The Senate was in fact sending to Molin word of how earlier Venetian ambassadors—Badoer, Soranzo, and Foscarini—had been received at the Porte. Molin would present his letters of credence (one hoped to the sultan himself), along with certain gifts, which were

---

[43] Senato (Secreta), Dispacci Costantinopoli (1668–1669), no. 52, fols. 427ʳff. (most of this dispatch being in cipher). It was written shortly after 22 October 1669. On the coffee, sherbert, and perfume of the time, note Carlo Paganino's *Diario della Speditione dell'illustr. et eccell. signor Alvise da Molin*, MS. Marc. It. VII, 1608 (7514), pp. 29, 41, 46, 58, 88, 90, 99, 102, 136, *et alibi*, and on Francesco Morosini's arrival in Suda and his formal meeting with Molin, *ibid.*, pp. 87ff.

[44] Delib. Costantinopoli, Reg. 32, fol. 44ᵛ [135ᵛ], *adì XXIII Ottobre [MDCLXIX], al capitan generale da mar*, the letter being approved by the Senate +81,—1,—4.

[45] Delib. Costantinopoli, Reg. 32, fol. 46 [137], *adì XXIII Ottobre [MDCLXIX], al Serenissimo Sultan Mehemet*, text approved +81,—1,—4.

being packed, and would be accompanied by another 3,000 ducats in silver. Copies of the Veneto-Turkish peace treaties of 1540, 1573, and 1638 were being sent to Molin, and so were the executive orders relating to the corsairs and their places of refuge in Turkish ports. The imposition of restraint upon and punishment of corsairs was a common factor in the Republic's treaties with the Porte. Molin was to see to it that all the ports of the Gran Signore were open to Venetian vessels and merchants, another conspicuous factor in these treaties.

Also Molin must try to lighten the heavy burden of the five percent customs duty which had been levied on Venetian goods. It should be reduced to three percent, which was the payment made (as we have noted) by the Genoese and now by the French. The Turkish government should send "resolute commands" to Dalmatia and Albania, as was done in 1638, to quell disturbances and to suppress piracy. The port of Spalato (Split) should be opened to Venetian traffic, as it was to that of the Ragusei, who thus had a considerable advantage over the Republic's merchants in the Adriatic trade. The Senate was interested, as was Molin, in reestablishing the *cottimo* on a sound basis in certain Levantine ports, since it was a source of some income to the Serenissima and a protective convenience to the merchants.

Among other tasks, Molin was to look into the question of the many documents (*scritture publiche*) which had been left in Istanbul, presumably before the beginning of the war of Candia; some of them were obviously of importance, and Molin must try to retrieve them. He had money enough to fulfill his ambassadorial responsibilities at the Porte, i.e., 20,000 *reali* in cash and another 10,000 in letters of credit. The road from Cattaro (Kotor) should be reopened to couriers. And passing over a few more details as to gifts and money, such were the requests and the instructions which the Senate sent to Molin.[46]

From Canea on 2 November (1669) Alvise da Molin wrote the doge (and Senate) that the grand vizir Ahmed Köprülü had sent the local pasha back to his post, "as I informed your Serenity in an earlier dispatch." After the Turkish occupation of the fortress of Candia and the assurance of peace, the sultan's master of horse had arrived (in Candia) with gifts for Köprülü, the *primo visir*, who had received the sultan's permission to remain in the Cretan "kingdom" for the winter of 1669–1670. As soon as spring came, however, he must come back toward Istanbul with the army. In the meantime twelve of the best Turkish

---

[46] Delib. Costantinopoli, Reg. 32, fols. 42ᵛ–44ᵛ [133ᵛ–135ᵛ], *adì XXIII Ottobre* [*MDCLXIX*], *all'ambasciator estraordinario Molin destinato alla Porta*, +81, —1, —4, and cf., *ibid.*, fols. 48ʳ–50ᵛ [139ʳ–141ᵛ], a longer letter of similar content from the doge and Senate to Molin, dated 20 November (1669), and approved by the Senate +152,—4,—0.

galleys were to be sent on to Negroponte, where the sultan wished to embark for Thessaloniki (Salonika) to avoid the discomfort of a long journey by land.

The sultan intended to spend the winter in Thessaloniki. Some of the remaining galleys would have to go on to Istanbul under the command of one Terzena Chiaiassi, the overseer (*proveditor*), of the Turkish armada. Ten galleys would be retained at Istanbul. The others would stay at Candia. There was no longer any doubt but that Köprülü would remain on the island of Crete, where the kapudan pasha would join him. This information should assist the Signoria, Molin believed, in making plans to send to the Porte the ambassador, "who would be elected for ratification of the peace." Molin may have suspected, but did not yet know, that he was to be that ambassador.

Molin stated that the captain–general Morosini had sent him a copy of all the minutes of meetings of the war council during the final trials of the siege of Candia. Hitherto Molin had seen only the minutes of 4 August. Now he had read with no small emotion the statement of the reasons which had led Morosini to surrender Candia as being in the best interests of the Serenissima, "nell'abbandono massime delle più valide assistenze ausiliarie, compatendo infinitamente la necessità in cui s'è ritrovato constituito."

Far from satisfied with the way things had gone, Molin confined his observation to the fact that at the meeting of the war council on 25 August it was apparently agreed that one should write to him

to take in hand the matter of a peace treaty before the embarkation of the French troops, who were slipping away from evening to evening. As for this last point, namely that the French should be embarking from one evening to the next, if your Serenity will consult the minutes of the war council for 4 August, he will see a formal statement to the effect that the French were furtively embarking thirty or forty soldiers at a time in order to say that they did not have troops enough to stand by, which makes clear their small inclination for military action, but not their actual departure, of which I was never precisely informed, nor had I ever understood it until after the fact and after the surrender of the fortress.[47]

On 31 December (1669) the doge Alvise Contarini, writing to Molin on the Senate's behalf, noted that

in these last days your dispatches from number 50 to 55 have arrived, from which we learn with great comfort the freedom of movement being allowed you

---

[47] Senato (Secreta), Dispacci Costantinopoli (1668–1669), no. 54, fols. 447ʳ–448ʳ, *Canea li 2 Novembre 1669 S[til] N[ovo]*.

and your household as well as the gestures of courtesy and friendship which the pasha has shown as a consequence of the orders of the grand vizir.

The Senate was pleased and gratified to learn of the Turks' "honorific demonstrations" on the occasion of Molin's formal meeting with Morosini. Now one could apparently hope for that "good and lasting peace." The Gran Signore's joy in the Turkish success at Candia, which had brought some measure of tranquillity to his subjects and to those of Venice, did indeed make one believe in his sincere desire to maintain the peace. Molin's task would be to keep not only his Majesty in a peaceful mood but also the important grand vizir and the chief ministers of the Porte.

The Senate set much store by the restoration of trade in the "kingdom" of Candia, in the Morea, and in parts of Dalmatia, all of which were apparently showing some signs of commercial renewal. It was assumed in Venice that the doge's dispatches of 19 October, along with Molin's letters of credence for the grand vizir, had arrived safely, and that "by this time you will also have obtained the royal charter for confirmation of the peace." The doge called Molin's attention to the laments of the prisoners in the Seven Towers at Istanbul. They had been, it was said, "abandoned and left without any help," although the Signoria had tried to assist them by the dispatch of funds to the Bosporus. The Senate advised Molin of an unfortunate incident in which Turkish cannoneers had recently fired at some Venetian vessels as they sailed past Modon. Moreover, since the conclusion of peace, two corsairs' vessels had been allowed entry into the Turkish harbor of Navarino (Pylos) in the southwest of the Morea. Since there was now peace between the Republic and the Porte, obviously such events created an unease in the Senate.

Molin was to try to find out what he could about the results of an audience which the Turkish envoy in Paris had managed to obtain with Louis XIV. At Vienna one continued to hear complaints from the sultan's ministers about the raids of the Hungarians into Turkish territory and about their (or the Austrians') employment of the fortifications in the borderlands. Molin must have received attached to this dispatch (of 31 December) the copy of a letter from Charles II of England to the Signoria with an order to his ambassador at the Porte to cooperate with the Venetian ambassador. When, therefore, Molin arrived in Istanbul, he must establish the appropriate friendly relationship with the representative of the English crown.

The doge informed Molin that the captain–general Morosini had landed on the island of Zante on 9 December, where he was trying to divest himself of many of the important responsibilities that had been weighing him down for so long a time in order to seek some rest and relief in the fatherland. "In the meantime we must let you know in the present letter of the death of the supreme pontiff, Clement IX, on the 9th of the present month, which is lamented everywhere, and which we have felt most keenly. . . ."[48]

The surrender of Candia was to bring almost no end of vexation to the captain–general Francesco Morosini. While contemporary historians and journalists acclaimed his dauntless spirit and the prolonged resistance to the Turks, a gloomy depression gradually pervaded Venice. Morosini's enemies were filled with envy, resentment, and bitterness; they wanted to destroy his reputation, and inflict such other injury upon him as they could. Before the news of the surrender of Candia had reached the Senate, Morosini had been made a Procuratore di S. Marco which, after the Dogado, was the highest office of the state. It had added fuel to the flame of malignity with which Morosini was now beset. He made his formal entrance into Venice on 21 April 1670. His palace, the façade of which gives upon the Rio di S. Maurizio, was richly decorated; the residents of his parish of S. Stefano joined the procession along the Merceria to the Doges' Palace. While Morosini, his relatives, friends, and supporters were basking in the sunshine of his renown, his enemies were spending their time in quiet conspiracy.

Five months after his return to Venice, suddenly and unexpectedly he was denounced on 19 September (1670) by one Antonio Correr at a meeting of the Maggior Consiglio, the Grand Council. Correr seems to have been moved by ambition, perhaps seeking the important office of public prosecutor or advocate of the state (*avogador del Comun, triumvir Reipublicae advocatus*). It has also been suggested that his virulent attack upon Morosini was one more manifestation of the persistent hostility between the old and the new nobilities, which had been much reinforced (as we have seen) by the sale of the patriciate during the Cretan war, the "aggregazioni di famiglie alla nobiltà veneta." Morosini belonged to the old, Correr to the new, nobility. Correr was now assisted by Antonio Barbaro, formerly provveditore of the fleet, whom Morosini had placed under the naval ban. Barbaro had escaped (as we have already noted) from the captain–general's control by flight to Venice, and had managed to get himself pardoned by the Senate.

If Antonio Correr had aspired to the dignity of public prosecutor, as he doubtless had, his desire was soon fulfilled, for on 5 October (1670), he was indeed elected *avogador di Comun* by the Maggior Consiglio. Cor-

---

[48] Senato, Delib. Costantinopoli, Reg. 32, fols. 54ᵛ–57ᵛ [145ᵛ–148ᵛ], *adì XXXI Decembre [MDCLXIX], all'ambasciator Molin destinato alla Porta*, +133, —3, —5.

rer had begun to enjoy a certain measure of popularity as public sentiment appeared to be turning against Morosini. While the young radicals in the Maggior Consiglio, who had had little or no naval or military experience, tended to respond to Correr's unproven charges, the older nobility in the Senate, many of whom knew something of warfare with the Turks and the dire condition of Crete, were inclined to stand up for Morosini.

One of Morosini's more vigorous defenders blamed the French for the loss of Candia. Never having possessed the island, he asserted, they had no intention of saving it from the Turks. Furthermore, let the captain–general's detractors consider the extraordinary fact that he had recovered from the grand vizir Ahmed Köprülü some 350 pieces of heavy artillery, all the ship's biscuit, arms, munitions, sacred vessels and other such things. Also he had preserved the troops, rescuing all persons who wished to leave the island with their movable property. And, of course, he had saved the Venetian fleet, the chief responsibility of a captain–general, "che nei casi estremi l'abbia la mira principal alla preservazione dell'armata, nella quale consiste l'imperio e la libertà."[49]

Under the dark shadow of defeat Venice was becoming filled with charges and countercharges, rumors and accusations of corruption, personal rancors and jealousies. Morosini's supporters levied, in their turn, attacks upon Correr and Antonio Barbaro. In this atmosphere of contention Correr now requested a meeting of the Maggior Consiglio for the morning of 13 November (1670), although the Consiglio usually met in the afternoon. Correr's initial purpose was to divest Francesco Morosini of his recently acquired dignity of procurator of S. Mark on the grounds that his appointment had been contrary to law and tradition, for he had been appointed *supra numerum.* This was not only an attack upon Morosini but also an affront to the Senate, where the captain–general was held in high esteem.

The Senate had ratified the terms of the surrender of Candia which, Morosini's enemies insisted, he had signed illegally. But Correr had gone too far, and although the Maggior Consiglio had seemed to applaud his efforts two months before, this time Morosini's partisans and even his enemies hooted and howled at Correr. Nevertheless, Correr went on doggedly, assailing the impropriety of Morosini's elevation to the procuratorship of S. Mark and the duplicity whereby he had attained it.

Correr claimed that on 11 August (1669) Morosini had written the Signoria to the effect he would die rather than witness the surrender of Candia. On 27 August, however, according to Correr, Morosini began

---

[49] Gino Damerini, *Morosini,* Milan, 1929, pp. 145–55.

negotiations with the grand vizir Ahmed Köprülü. His good intentions had lasted sixteen days, long enough for the Maggior Consiglio to reward his courage and constancy by making him *procuratore soprannumera-rio,* an exceptional honor. Correr also asserted that letters of Morosini had arrived in Venice with a forewarning of the impending surrender on the very day before the meeting of the Maggior Consiglio, but that Moro-sini's family had concealed the letters in order not to impede the Consi-glio's granting him the signal distinction of the procuratorship. Correr insisted that there was no proper, no legal, alternative to the removal of Morosini from the procuratorship. In any event Morosini and his family might well account themselves fortunate, according to Correr, if his only punishment was to be the loss of the procuratorship, for he had already received knighthood (*cavalierato*), and two of his brothers had been brought into the Senate. No commanders in the past had ever received such rewards for victory as Morosini had received for the loss of Candia.

Correr had overplayed his hand. His long discourse was greeted with silence and repugnance. When he had finished, the eloquent Giovanni Sagredo, the Republic's onetime ambassador to France and England, rose to defend his friend Morosini. Sagredo reviewed Morosini's com-mand at Candia where over the years, he said, 130,000 Turks and 100,000 soldiers from various parts of Christendom had perished, to-gether with 280 Venetian nobles. If Candia had been lost, everlasting glory had been won. Sagredo blamed the Venetian surrender of Candia upon the French general Philippe de Montault de Bénac, the duke of Navailles, who withdrew his forces from Candia, abandoning Morosini and the latter's seamen and soldiery in the very hour of need. While the Turks mounted the breaches in the walls, the French gave them up, repairing to their ships. The pros and cons of the surrender of Candia would long be debated.[50]

The proposal to deprive the captain–general Morosini of the procura-torship of S. Mark would merely restore honor to the French, for it would be tantamount to saying they had not failed the Christian cause against the Turks, but that Morosini had fallen short, thus betraying the father-land. Sagredo went on to rebut as outright falsehoods and gross exaggera-tions all the assertions made by Correr. Despite the applause which

---

[50] Cf. the exchange of letters between Bernardin Gigault, marquis de Bellefonds, marshal of France, and the Sieur de Grémonville, commander of the Order of Malta, in the Bibl. Nazionale Marciana, MS. It. VII, 2389 (11721), fols. 176–87. On the twists and turns of justice and politics in mid-seventeenth-century Venice see Gaetano Cozzi, *Repubblica di Venezia e Stati italiani: Politica e giustizia dal secolo XVI al secolo XVIII,* Turin, 1982, pp. 174–216, esp. pp. 205–6 (in the present context), whose general account is interesting and instructive.

Sagredo's speech now won, the case against Morosini was not closed.[51] The vote taken in the Maggior Consiglio was indecisive.

The Consiglio was, therefore, reconvened on 25 November (1670), but as the wind was blowing more favorably for the captain–general Morosini, some of his enemies left Venice for the countryside, some made friendly overtures to him. Others decided to let the issue of the procuratorship drop, relying upon the trial (*processo*) which lay ahead. A verdict would be reached at the trial, based upon the coming inquest into the surrender of Candia and the management of the war chest. When at the assembly of 25 November Correr embarked upon an effort to refute Sagredo's arguments, he was interrupted by catcalls and the stamping of feet, but he was allowed to continue when he asked for pardon if he had gone beyond the bounds of propriety. He was not moved, he said, by personal considerations. He was merely seeking justice for the Republic.

At this point the well-known patrician Michele Foscarini, who had held several important offices of state, rose to refute Correr and to defend Morosini. In later years Foscarini was to produce the important *Istoria della Republica Veneta*.[52] He reminded the members of the Maggior Consiglio that the eyes of Europe were upon them. The reputation of the Serenissima was at stake. The effort to remove Morosini from the procuratorship of S. Mark before a judicial investigation was disgraceful. He was one of the most eminent figures in the Republic. Foscarini also took issue with Correr that there was anything illegal about Morosini's promotion to the procuratorship. He cited certain similar cases—indeed some unusual, even extraordinary cases—from the past which had been accepted as legal and proper. Yes, Morosini had declared his resolve to withstand the Turks at any cost while some thousands of French were helping him to hold on to Candia. When the French departed, what hope was there of warding off surrender? The standards of the Porte were planted on three continents, Italy was a weak, little place, and who could find the meager territory of S. Mark on the map?

Foscarini denied that letters of the captain–general Morosini had been concealed from the Maggior Consiglio. He accused Correr of trickery, maintaining that he had taken out of context snatches from this dispatch or that in order to concoct fallacious evidence. It was the way an anonymous poet, selecting verses here and there from Vergil, had been able to

---

[51] For Correr's attack upon Morosini, note among other sources MS. Marc. It. VII, 656 (7791), esp. fols. 132ᵛ, 133ᵛ, 134ʳ, and for Sagredo's defense of Morosini, *ibid.*, esp. fols. 146ʳ, 148ᵛ–149ʳ, 150.

[52] Foscarini's work comprises the tenth (and last) volume of the series *Degl'Istorici delle cose veneziane*, Venice, 1722.

make the latter sing the praises of the Virgin. If Morosini had held out in Candia to the point of death, he would indeed have let Venice down, for if the Turks had breached the walls and taken the fortress town of Candia, they would have destroyed the armed forces of the Republic, seized the munitions belonging to the state, and captured the fleet, endangering the Venetians' holdings in Dalmatia. The proposed trial should not be restricted to Morosini, but should include all those who were present at the surrender of Candia. Foscarini's proposal met with applause not only from Morosini's supporters, who expected him to be exonerated, but also from Correr's adherents, who wanted to appear impartial and dedicated to the best interests of the state.

The investigation dragged on for eight months, during which period Francesco Morosini and his brothers Michele, Marc'Antonio, and Lorenzo, who apparently all had apartments in the Palazzo Morosini, hard by the spacious Campo S. Stefano, entertained their friends and partisans in lavish fashion. And finally in the summer of 1671, after a prolonged inquest, the Senate made an official declaration of the innocence of Morosini and his codefendants of all the charges of naval and financial mismanagement which had been levied against them.[53]

---

[53] Cf. Damerini, *Morosini* (1929), pp. 155–71, 180–84. On Correr's attack upon Morosini and the defense of the captain–general by Sagredo and Foscarini, see Giovanni Graziani, *Francisci Mauroceni . . . gesta*, Padua, 1698, pp. 180–81, 201–12, and (at long length) Antonio Arrighi, *De vita et rebus gestis Francisci Mauroceni . . .* , Padua, 1749, lib. III, pp. 225–71, with some fictitious oratory.

VIII

Turco-Venetian Relations (1670–1683) and the Turkish Siege of Vienna

༄

fter Francesco Morosini's surrender of Candia to the Turks, there was an uneasy peace between Venice and the Porte. It lasted for some fifteen years. The doge and Senate continued to send dispatches with the current news and with instructions to Alvise da Molin as *ambasciator estraordinario a Costantinopoli* throughout the year 1670 and a large part of 1671. On 22 August (1671) the draft of a letter of the doge to Molin acknowledged the receipt in Venice of the 153rd dispatch which he had sent the Signoria since his appointment as ambassador extraordinary to the Porte.[1] Early in 1671, however, Giacomo Querini, a distinguished noble, was elected to, and accepted, the formidable post of bailie on the Bosporus,[2] but it always took ambassadors and bailies a long time to take their leave of Venice and go off to distant assignments.

Inevitably the ambassadorial dispatches contain both important and trivial data, but both the one and the other help to illustrate the problems and the life of a seventeenth-century ambassador. In a letter to

---

[1] ASV, Senato, Delib. Costantinopoli, Reg. 32, fol. 178^r [269^r], doc. dated 22 August 1671.

[2] On Querini's appointment as bailie, note Delib. Costantinopoli, Reg. 32, fols. 118 [209], 120^r [211^r], docs. dated 5 and 18 March 1671. A year before (in March 1670) Molin had been appointed "bailo ordinario," *che intraprenderà la carica dopo supplite le funtioni dell'estraordinaria ambasciata* (*ibid.*, fols. 67^v–70^r).

Molin of 15 February 1670, for example, the doge and Senate lamented a shipwreck with extensive loss of life and the "perdita di danaro et molte robbe già allestite per il regallo [alla Porta]," which would cause some delay in the delivery of gifts to the pashas, dragomans, and others in Istanbul, but "we are proceeding with all diligence again to supply everything needed, and in a few days all will be ready to put on board a ship."[3] Not very significant information for a modern historian perhaps; shipwrecks and loss of life were occurring everywhere in the Mediterranean. This shipwreck, however, was obviously important to the Signoria and to the worried Molin.

Of obvious importance, however, was the situation of the Christians in Canea after the Turkish occupation of the port. Molin has briefly described their plight for us in a dispatch dated 3 May 1670, which he sent to the Venetian Signoria: "In Canea the vizir has imposed great hardships upon those few Christians who have remained there, for he has confiscated all their houses and properties . . . , allowing them to build themselves habitations only in the villages that existed on the fringes of the city before the war."[4]

Dated documents show that Molin was still in Candia on 25 May (1670), in Chios on 4 June, in Pera (Istanbul) on 24 June, and on the way to Adrianople (Edirne) on 29 July. A few days later, on 3 August 1670, he wrote a dispatch from Adrianopole. As Molin went to Pera in the spring, he was worried about "the perils of the plague."[5] He had found, and was finding, his role as ambassador to the Turks a difficult one, and was never to see his beloved Venice again, for he died in Istanbul in August 1671.

Serious illness was bearing down on Molin. On 30 August (1670) he wrote the Signoria from Adrianopole of "my unfortunate state of health." He could not, he said, digest the lightest meal. He could not sleep. He had lost his appetite completely, he was tired and weak, re-

---

[3] Delib. Costantinopoli, Reg. 32, fol. 58ᵛ [149ᵛ], doc. dated 15 February 1670 (*more veneto* 1669).

[4] Senato (Secreta), Dispacci Costantinopoli (1670), no. 82, fol. 125ʳ, doc. dated at Candia on 3 May 1670.

[5] Dispacci Costantinopoli (1670), fol. 173ʳ. The final "capitulation" of Candia, as accepted by Sultan Mehmed IV in May 1670, is given, *ibid.*, fols. 176ʳ–185ʳ, 191ʳ. On Molin's approach to the Dardanelles and entry into Istanbul, see Paganino's *Diario*, MS. Marc. It. VII, 1608 (7514), pp. 122ff.

The continuation of Molin's dispatches to the Signoria is to be found in the Senato (Secreta, III, formerly Filza 154), Dispacci Costantinopoli (1670), where they range from no. 69, dated at Candia on 2 March 1670, to no. 132, where this last numbered dispatch is dated at Pera, Istanbul, on 13 February 1671 (m.v. 1670). (Molin's dispatches are in the old Filze 150, 152, and 154). Molin had arrived in Istanbul on 18 June 1670. He found the compound of the Venetian consulate general, the *casa bailaggia*, in dreadful condition as a result of the long years of neglect during the Cretan war. On his residence in Istanbul, cf. the ever-useful book of Tommaso Bertelè, *Il Palazzo degli ambasciatori di Venezia a Costantinopoli e le sue antiche memorie*, Bologna, 1932, pp. 208ff., 242–43.

duced to skin and bones. During the last few days he had suffered from an intolerable pain in his arm and right hand, "che per tre giorni e tre noti mi ha portato insofferibili dolori." He had hoped that at long length a "venting of nature" might bring him some relief, but everything had got worse. He had pinned his hopes upon going back to Istanbul "for a month in some little house on the Black Sea, where the air is just right for the diligent purge [of ailments] and to release myself of all responsibility, leaving the stalwart character of the secretary Capello to take care of the burdens of the bailaggio for that period." He hoped for some respite from his maladies, but the restoration of his health would be impossible, "as the physicians have emphasized to me."

Molin needed a rest; his constitution was wholly undone. Having lost his vigor, he collapsed under every weight laid upon him. The bailaggio, the duties of which he was performing, required a strength of body and mind. Seeing death (*eccidio*) inevitable in the continuation of his manifold duties, he had agreed to submit to those extreme remedies which alone could provide medication for his extreme ills. As he wrote the doge, he had to decline the office of bailie at the Porte, "which the benign public has conferred upon me beyond my every merit." Molin's lament was not that he had lost the vigor of life in the service of the Signoria in the land of the Turk, but that he was either destined to die there or to be no longer able to serve the state in some worthy context.[6]

Nevertheless, Molin went on faithfully with his duties as ambassador despite his ill health and general dissatisfaction. On 1 September (1670) he acknowledged receipt of the doge's dispatches of the preceding 21 June and 11 July. He wrote in reply that he had presented to the grand vizir Köprülü the Republic's request to lighten the burdensome tolls being imposed upon merchandise sent from Venice, seeking especially the reduction of the import duty from five to three percent, bringing it into conformity with what certain other nations were paying. He had, however, dealt with the subject gingerly without trying to exert the slightest pressure upon the grand vizir and without committing himself in any way. Molin had also approached the defterdar, the sultan's minister of finance, explaining that reducing the excessive cost of Venetian trade with the Porte would increase the volume of business and thus add much to the sultan's mercantile revenues. The defterdar promised to take the matter up with the grand vizir, "as I believe he has done."

In any event Molin saw little likelihood as yet of Venice's receiving the concession he had requested, for one must wait and see the outcome of the Turks' forthcoming negotiations with the French. The doge had informed Molin that the Marquis Charles de Nointel had left Paris with a

---

[6] Senato (Secreta), Dispacci Costantinopoli, no. 102, fol. 344, doc. dated 30 August 1670.

Turkish envoy to come to Istanbul "a rissiedere in qualità di residente a questa Porta." Nointel would seek confirmation of the French merchants' paying the three rather than the five percent customs duty, but as far as Louis XIV was concerned, this was a minor matter.

The chief reason for Nointel's coming to Istanbul, although Molin does not say so, was to restore the old Franco-Turkish friendship which had suffered a good deal as a consequence of the French support of Venice in the recent war of Candia. Molin assured the doge that he would remain alert to find out not only what the essential purpose of Nointel's commission and instructions might be, but also to learn in detail what requests he was going to make of the Porte. Molin had been reassured by the doge's informing him of Nointel's good intentions toward Venice, and the Signoria could be certain of Molin's full cooperation with the new French ambassador as far as current circumstances allowed.[7]

Three days later, on 4 September (1670), Molin wrote the doge and Senate from Adrianople that the chief ministers of the Porte were still holding "banquets in the field" in honor of Sultan Mehmed IV. Only such leading figures as the grand vizir, the kaïmakam, the defterdar, the mufti, and a few others of the small inner circle (*li soli della stretta Consulta*) attended these feasts. They were the ruling élite which made the decisions as to peace or war. The kaïmakam was Kara Mustafa Pasha; he was to become a famous (or infamous) figure in Ottoman history. "Black" Mustafa was a favorite of the sultan and, incidentally, a brother-in-law of Ahmed Köprülu. Molin entertained some doubt about the overall prospects for peace, inasmuch as the most pressing orders had gone out from Istanbul for the casting of cannon at Cairo, for the production of gunpowder at Belgrade, for bombs and grenades at Bagnaluca, "as well as for every other item necessary for warfare on land." It was difficult to acquire knowledge of the deliberations and decisions of this small group.

Molin had learned, however, that the sultan was allegedly determined to go to war, "and this will have to be in Europe," but what part of Europe? In any case the vizir, the defterdar, and the kaïmakam were doing their best to persuade the sultan not to take the field himself with the army. When the sultan accompanied the troops, financial problems arose. A huge sum of money would be needed in gold for the "extraordinary gifts" which had to be given to the "militias," when the sultan went with them. It was also very expensive to maintain the dignity of the imperial presence in the encampment.

Furthermore, the personal interests of the grand vizir and the defter-

---

[7] Senato (Secreta), Dispacci Costantinopoli (1670), no. 103, fols. 350–351^r, *Andrinopoli, primo Settembre 1670.* Charles Marie François Ollier, marquis d'Angervilliers et de Nointel, was French ambassador to the Porte from 1670 to 1679. He eventually had much trouble with Kara Mustafa Pasha, Ahmed Köprülü's successor as grand vizir.

dar were such as to make them want to keep a safe distance from the sultan to avoid the perils of poor judgment. The kaïmakam Kara Mustafa Pasha and the others would want to stay with the sultan inasmuch as the grand vizir would have to stay with him. Since, however, they too wanted to keep the sultan off the battlefield, "they all joined hands, these ministers who depended upon operating all the machinery of this great empire to their own satisfaction."

The important fact was that the sultan, "enamored of the beautiful hunting in these environs" (of Adrianople), would doubtless settle down comfortably, provided he were not forced to go to Istanbul, as could have been the case, had war been decided upon. If peace remained the order of the day, the grand vizir, who was anxious to rid himself of the yoke of the court and of the sultan, would almost certainly betake himself to Belgrade in the spring. He did not propose to go to war with some prince, when the season came for a campaign, "not while the forces are not strong enough to embark upon a great undertaking."

According to Molin, representatives of the "empire of Poland" were spreading the boastful word in Adrianople that their princes were powerfully armed on the frontiers, "standing with sword in hand," waiting for an opportunity to extend the glory of Polish arms. At this time there was fear of a Turkish invasion of Poland, and the Poles obviously hoped that such propaganda might dissuade the Turks from such a venture. The snatches of news which Molin passed on to the Venetian Signoria are not only interesting when one knows something of the historical background, but sometimes fascinating and valuable, as when he comes to the plight of the "prince" Francis I Rákóczy in 1670. Rákóczy, who was adrift in Hungary, had been putting pressure on Michael I Abafi, the prince of Transylvania (1661–1690), to afford him a safe refuge, but Abafi, a tool of the Turks, denied him access to Transylvania in order not to become embroiled with the Hapsburgs.

Rákóczy had been involved in the conspiracy against the Emperor Leopold I, which the Hungarian palatine Ferenc Wesselényi (d. 1667) had instigated a few years earlier. The conspiracy had undoubtedly been evoked partly by the Turco-Austrian treaty of Vasvár (of 10 August 1664), which the Hungarians rightly regarded as the betrayal of their country.

Francis Rákóczy was desperate. He had recently sent an offer to the Turks to try to turn over to them the fortresses occupied by the imperialists on condition that the Porte should make him prince of Transylvania. Giving heed to Rákóczy's offer, the Turks were inclined for a while to depose Abafi, but they did not do so. Rákóczy would be the only prominent conspirator whose life was spared, owing to the payment of a large ransom and the intervention of his influential mother Sophia Báthory. In the meantime speculation was rife, "but there is certainly no firm decision up to now, and one can well believe that at present Rákóczy himself may be in the hands of the imperialists."

The Turks were negotiating in friendly fashion with the Swedes, which might turn out well for Poland and Germany. The Bosnians were resentful of the Venetian holdings in Dalmatia; a number of them were serving in the seraglio and at the court. They had some influence on Turkish policy. They did not want to see the Veneto-Turkish treaty last a long time, nor see the sultan suffer the fact "that many places which had mosques should have to remain in the hands of your Serenity." Such were the snippets of news that the doge and Senate could glean from Molin's dispatch of 4 September (1670).

Upon his return to Istanbul, if the Almighty spared him long enough to get there, Molin assured the doge and Senate that he would take care to look into the arsenals and to enquire whether the Turks were busy building galleys, for unless they restored their armada, there could be no persuasive evidence that they planned to break the peace. Within a few weeks the sultan would go out on the hunt, and stay away all winter. The kaïmakam would go with him. The grand vizir would remain in Adrianople with the court, attending to the needs of the government.[8]

Four months before Molin's long dispatch of 4 September (1670), George Etherege, secretary of the English ambassador Sir Daniel Harvey (and incidentally a notable dramatist), sent Joseph Williamson at Whitehall a detailed account of conditions at the Porte. In later years Sir George was to serve the English monarchy at Regensburg. Now he wrote Williamson that the sultan Mehmed IV was about thirty years of age. (He had ascended the Ottoman throne as a child in 1648.) Mehmed was of medium stature, according to Etherege, "leane and long visag'd." Of late he had been letting "haire grow on his chin: his complexion is a darke browne." Whereas Etherege found his appearance not disagreeable, Mehmed was generally regarded as ugly. A religious bigot, he was a passionate lover of the hunt: "The fatigue hee undergoes in it is almost incredible; great numbers of poore people are summon'd in to attend him, and many of them perish in the ffeild through hunger and cold—this has cheifly got him the hatred of his subjects."

Etherege declared, however, that Mehmed was moderate in all other

---

[8] Senato (Secreta), Dispacci Costantinopoli (1670), no. 104, fols. 374^r–377^r, *Andrinopoli, 4 Settembre 1670*. Francis I Rákóczy was the father of Francis (Ferenc) II (d. 1735), one of the great figures in modern Hungarian history, who remains to this day a hero among his people, with streets named after him in Veszprém and elsewhere.

As for the fortresses occupied by the imperialists, which Rákóczy proposed to turn over to the Turks, we are informed by a document dated 11 July 1670, "Le cose pure d'Ungheria passavano con quiete. Andava l'Imperator impossessando delle piazze, et il Ragotzi mostrava prontezza nel farne seguir la consegna" (Delib. Costantinopoli, Reg. 32, fols. 82^v–83^r [173^v–174^r]).

recreations and devoted to his "hasachi" (*hāseki*), his mistress so to speak, "and not given to that unnaturall vice with which he has been slander'd." The sultana came from Candia. Although Etherege looked upon the women of the harem as lacking in refinement, the sultana could practice "her little arts to secure her sultan's affection." Indeed, she could "swoone at pleasure." The sultana had given his imperial highness a son and a daughter. . . . The Grand Signor's privy council consisted of only five persons,

the favorite [Culogli], the Chimacam of the Port, the mufti Vani Effendi, a famous Arab preacher, and one of the pashas of the Bench [and counting the grand vizir, there would be five], most of the great men being with the Vizier, who is imploy'd in Candia. . . . This Chimacam's name is Mustapha Pasha; hee was formerly captaine pasha or admirall of the gallies, and has married the Vizier's sister. Yet this allyance keeps them not from secret emulations and hatreds, and it is thought the Chimacam will dispute the Grand Signor's favour with him at his returne. The Vizier, they say, exceeds not the age of two and thirty yeares; hee is of middle stature and has a good mind; hee is prudent and just not to bee corrupted by money, the generall vice of this country, nor inclin'd to cruelty as his father was. The Chimacam is about the age of forty-five, well spoken, subtill, corrupt, and a great dissembler. Hee flatters the Grand Signor in his inclinations, and ever accompanies him in his hunting, a toyle which nothing but excessive ambition and interest could make him undergoe. . . .[9]

Vani Effendi, the "famous Arab preacher," was apparently the friend and confidant of the kaïmakam Kara Mustafa Pasha, and was to go with him in 1683, on the campaign that would lay unsuccessful siege to Vienna.

Joseph Williamson was kept well informed of the antics of Mehmed IV and the affairs of the Porte. On 5 September (1670) milord ambassador Sir Daniel Harvey wrote Williamson from "Belgrade," a village near the Black Sea, in which the English and other westerners used to seek a change from the sometimes unpleasant atmosphere of Istanbul:

I have little more to adde than what I wrote you last, only that the Grand Signor, being desirous to see in what manner the operation of the mines was effected, hath lately caus'd a mine to be made neere Adrianople, and did order thirty guilty and condemmd persons to be blowne up thereby into the aire. Which diversion pleased him so well that he is resolv'd to second it with a greater mine and a greater number of the like persons.

Upon a sermon preach'd not long since by Vani Effendi, that famous Arab preacher, the taverns here are all pull'd downe, the butts broken in pieces, the

---

[9] Public Record Office (PRO) in London, State Papers (SP), 97, XIX, fol. 150, letter dated May 1670.

wine spilt, and the making and selling of it prohibited for the future upon no less penalty than hanging or being putt into the gallies, which hath wrought a great distraction here amongst many thousands of poore people and others who had their dependance thereon.

Here are still consultations held concerning warr, though the result of them bee incertaine. Yet I heare the Grand Vizir in his treaty with the Venetian Bailo hath demanded Clissa and another towne in Dalmatia, pretending they were not included in the capitulations and unless they render them, he says, he will renew the warr this next spring. . . .[10]

The Turkish invasion of Poland, which Molin had hinted at in his dispatch of 4 September 1670, came to pass less than two years later. Harvey described the huge Turkish preparations in a dispatch of 1 July 1672.[11] The war would last until the treaty of Zhuravno, signed on 16 October 1676, by which the Turks took possession of most of long-disputed Podolia and the Polish Ukraine.[12] Suffering reverses against the Poles, as he had against the Austrians and the Venetians, once more the grand vizir Ahmed Köprülü came out on top, but his success brought the Turks into too close contact with the Russians, who would soon take over most of the Ukraine.

In the meantime England and France had joined hands by the treaty of Dover (in May 1670), but the commercial rivalry between the French merchants and the English Levant Company continued unabated. Sir Daniel Harvey, although a good friend of the erratic Marquis de Nointel, maintained his vigorous opposition to Nointel's attempts to improve the French position at the Porte. Trouble was brewing in Europe. It would have its effect upon the Porte, but Harvey was not to see it. On 27 August 1672 his secretary John Newman wrote the Earl of Arlington from the village of "Belgrade:"

Having remained secretarie to his Excellencie, the lord ambassadour Harvey, during his Embassie, I held it espetially of my dutie to acquaint your Lordshipp that last night (so it pleas'd God) hee dyed of a feaver, the sixt day of his sickness, here at his countrie house ten miles from Constantinople. . . .[13]

Thus it was that in November (1672) Charles II notified the grand vizir Ahmed Köprülü that

having received advice of the death of Sir Daniel Harvey, our ambassador . . . , we have made choice of this bearer, our trusty and well beloved servant Sir John

---

[10] PRO, SP 97, XIX, fol. 156, dispatch dated at Belgrade on 5 September 1670.

[11] PRO, SP 97, XIX, fol. 187.

[12] Dumont, *Corps universel diplomatique*, VII-1 (1731), no. CLVI, p. 325, *tractatus pacis* between John III Sobieski and Mehmed IV.

[13] PRO, SP 97, XIX, fol. 189.

Finch K^t, a principal gentleman of our Court and one of our Councell for matters relating to our forreigne colonies and plantations, as one who by the employments he hath held on our part for many years in Courts of severall foreigne Princes, we have judged more particularly qualified to succeed the said Sir Daniel Harvey. . . .[14]

In 1672 Louis XIV went to war for the second time, his purpose being to reduce the States General of Holland to wrack and ruin, but his generals soon had to face not only the Dutch, but also the Brandenburgers, the Austrians, and the Spanish. The war ended in the various treaties of Nijmegen (Nimwegen) and in that of S. Germain-en-Laye in 1678–1679. During this period the young grand vizir Ahmed Köprülü died (early in November 1676); he was succeeded by his brother-in-law, the arrogant and incompetent kaïmakam Kara Mustafa Pasha. Meanwhile, *come al solito,* the Venetians had had trouble with the Turks, especially in Bosnia (with the new pasha in 1670) and, above all, in the village of Risan in southwest Montenegro (in 1671), which Ahmed Köprülü asserted the Venetians had fortified in violation of the treaty of peace.

For a while it was feared that the obstreperousness of the Bosnians and the Turks' annoyance with the Risan affair might actually lead to a renewal of the war. That did not happen, for whatever the threats of the sultan, Köprülü was painfully aware of the extent to which the long war of Candia had undermined the armed forces and depleted the treasury of the Porte. The Turks' armada was in a sad state. The Arsenal at Istanbul was hardly operating. No, the Turks needed peace more than did the Venetians, especially since Köprülü was contemplating the invasion of Poland. As Levi-Weiss has said, "During the five years from 1671 to '76 Venice seemed free of the burden of the Turkish peril."[15]

General histories have often recounted the large events of these years. One can glean from the archival sources minor episodes which illustrate the weekly and monthly state of affairs. Thus when the Venetian captain-general turned over to the vizir Ahmed Köprülü some slaves (*schiavi*), Köprülü replied with a courteous note of thanks dated at Canea on 10 June 1674. He also promised to inform the Porte that *fuste* from S. Maura and Dulcigno were infesting the "Gulf," i.e., the Adriatic, and that action must be taken to make sure neither these pirates nor any others, *ch' infestano cotesto Golfo,* could continue to damage Venetian shipping. The vizir did state, however, that from the (Turkish) slaves turned over to him he had learned another seventeen, *loro compagni,* still remained by some odd chance in Venetian hands. He would await their

---

[14] PRO, SP 97, XIX, fol. 195. On Sir John Finch, see G.F. Abbott, *Under the Turk in Constantinople*, London, 1920.

[15] Cf. Levi-Weiss, "Le Relazioni fra Venezia e la Turchia . . . ," *Veneto-Tridentino*, VII (1925), 11–21.

coming to Canea "con l'altro viaggio de' vascelli." In closing he acknowledged with thanks the receipt of a "little box" (*cassetta*) which the captain-general had sent him, "e per fine le auguro ogni felicità!"[16]

Friendly as relations seemed to be between Venice and the Turks, and trustworthy as everyone knew Ahmed Köprülü to be, one had to remain on guard. Thus the important stronghold of Corfu was protected (according to a dispatch of Antonio Priuli, *proveditor generale da mar*, dated on the island on 6 May 1675) by twenty companies of mariners who served as reinforcements on the galleys, the galleass, the brigantines, and the feluccas. When counted with the officials and soldiers involved, they formed "a corps of 895. . . ." The garrison of Corfu consisted of twelve companies, involving Italians, Greeks, and others, "amounting to 679." In addition to the 1574 men thus listed, there were "le militie ch'armano le publiche navi," consisting of ten companies of 625 infantry with their officers.

Other Corfiote forces amounted to 819 men, *tra ufficiali e soldati,* not counting the nearby garrisons on the islands of Cephalonia and Zante. The sums given for the maintenance of these forces alone make clear the fact that they were a strain on the resources of the Republic, considering the costs of protecting them from the Turks in the Morea, but in the long run the island fortresses were of larger importance to Venice than the Morea would prove to be, for they were bulwarks against the Turks' intrusion into the Adriatic.[17]

Corfu was apparently more of a naval than a commercial center. At the beginning of August (1675) Antonio Priuli wrote the doge Niccolò Sagredo from his island roost that French ships were not putting in an appearance at Corfu, but they certainly were at Zante and Cephalonia as well as at certain ports in the Morea. The French took on foodstuffs, especially wines and wheat, and the way their vessels were making for Cephalonia, Zante, and the Morea was "beginning to cause no small change in the costs of wheat."

A few months before this (on 23 May) Louis-Victor de Rochechouart, the duke de Vivonne (and brother of the Marquise de Montespan), writing from Messina, had requested the right to load "at Zante, Cephalonia, and Corfu wine, vegetables [*legumi*], ship's biscuit, and other kinds of provisions, and in the event that we send ships and merchantmen of his Majesty [we ask] that one should not make them pay any imposts by way of customs' duties."[18] Vivonne had been a major figure in the French expedition to relieve Candia in 1669.

---

[16] ASV, Senato, Provv. da terra e da mar, Filza 941, doc. dated 10 June 1674.

[17] Provv. da terra e da mar, Filza 943, pages unnumbered, doc. dated 6 May 1675. On 9 July (1675) Antonio Priuli wrote the Signoria of the care he was exercising in the expenditure of public funds on the fleet and the "militias" (*ibid.*).

[18] Provv. da terra e da mar, Filza 943, docs. dated 1 and 3 August and 23 May 1675.

Nevertheless, Antonio Priuli issued a public notice at Zante on 7 October (1675) that an impost must be levied on the export of wine in accord with the senatorial decree of 26 January 1580 until, that is, the Senate should choose to alter in some way the practice and legislation of the past.[19] And such from month to month is the sort of material we can gather from the Venetian Archives, nothing exciting to be sure but, for this very reason, so much the better for the seamen and soldiers who were leading their lives on the Mediterranean during the year 1675. Priuli faced recurrent problems, of course, as when on 8 June of this year he wrote the doge of his concern for the lack of wine for galley slaves (*condennati*). Maybe the French were drinking too much Greek wine. But throughout this period the relations of Venice with the Porte were peaceful, as shown by the copy of an undated letter (but certainly of the year 1675), from Ahmed Köprülü, *gran visir,* "all'eccellentissimo Ser Antonio Priuli general. . . ."[20]

The world began to change, however, when the grand vizir Ahmed Köprülü died the following year (in 1676, as we have noted). He was the second of five members of the Köprülü family who virtually ruled and were to rule the Ottoman state in the years between 1656 and 1710. After the war of Candia, as throughout the seventeenth century, the Venetians were harassed by the corsairs who issued from the Barbary coast, from Castelnuovo (Hercegnovi) and Dulcigno (Ulcinj) on the Montenegrin coast, from S. Maura, Lepanto, Scutari, and elsewhere, all places supposed to be under Ottoman rule. Actually Ahmed Köprülü made prolonged and serious efforts to suppress piracy in the eastern Mediterranean, but such was the everlasting corruption of Turkish provincial officialdom that his efforts were largely in vain. In the suppression of piracy and the general maintenance of law and order the Venetians like the Turks were impeded by a constant lack of adequate funds, as Andrea Valier complained to the Signoria in a dispatch dated at Cephalonia on 10 July 1673.[21] Piracy, however, was not the only affliction from which one suffered during these years.

The plague (*il mal contaggioso*) reached alarming heights at Corfu in the summer of 1673, some persons being kept in quarantine, *altri sequestrati nelle case loro, e morsero così ne' lazaretti.*[22] Andrea Valier,

---

[19] Provv. da terra e da mar, Filza 943, doc. dated 7 October 1675.

[20] Provv. da terra e da mar, Filza 943.

[21] ASV, Senato, Provv. da terra e da mar, Filza 941, *di galera, Cefalonia, li 10 Luglio 1673 S[til] N[ovo].*

[22] Provv. da terra e da mar, Filza 941, doc. dated at Corfu, *dal magistrato della Sanità li 29 Agosto 1673,* and cf., *ibid.,* docs. dated 22 September 1673 and 25 April 1674, signed by Andrea Valier, *proveditor general da mar.* According to Valier, the keeper of the lazzaretto at Corfu had died within a period of two days, "ma senz' alcun sospetto di peste, anzi

proveditor general da mar, seemed to have two major concerns, the plague and the Turks.

In a long dispatch to the doge (and Senate) dated at Corfu on 16 March 1674 Valier closed with reflections on the desirability of another union of the Christian princes against "the common enemy," always the Turk. The princes could assemble their forces at Brindisi or Otranto, and then disembark them at various places on the island of Corfu which, Valier said, was a stretch of land only twelve miles "from one sea to the other," from the Adriatic to the Ionian Sea.[23] In looking toward the resumption of warfare with the Turks, Valier was putting it only ten years ahead of its time. If disgruntled Turks at the Porte were dissatisfied with the peace, obviously they were not alone.

The Signoria and the Porte had been getting along well, however, and from April 1672 Venetian merchants had enjoyed easy access to the ports on the Black Sea, especially Caffa (Feodosiya), paying toll on the goods they imported only in the port where they were to be unloaded, not also in Istanbul or Smyrna, the chief points of entry into the commercial zones of the Porte. Despite persistent efforts, the Venetians could not get the Turkish toll reduced but in 1675 owing to the new bailie Giacomo Querini's skillful negotiations, various minor assessments, allegedly amounting to six percent of the total value of the merchandise imported, were disallowed, presumably to the disappointment of the Turkish customs officials to whom these "minuti balzelli" may have been a considerable source of income.[24]

The accession of Kara Mustafa Pasha, the kaïmakam, to the grand vizirate initiated an especially troublesome period for Europeans at the Porte, in Smyrna, and elsewhere in Turkish territory. Molin's diarist Paganino refers to *il caimacan, primo comandante di questa città,*[25] i.e., Istanbul, but now, as grand vizir, "Black" Mustafa was first commander of the entire Ottoman empire. He made life on the Bosporus difficult for the French ambassador Charles de Nointel, the English am-

---

con fede assoluta del medico che era stata appoplesia." Thereafter his father died, and so did a woman of another family which lived in the same house. Thereupon Valier confined all the other householders to the lazzaretto, required all their clothes, etc., to be burned, and also gave orders "purgar con diligenza la casa, mandarvi anco il medico et il barbiere che li havevano tocchi insieme con tutte le familie e robbe, sbarrare affatto quella contrada e sospendere tutte le raduttioni così di chiesa come forensi . . ." (Provv. da terra e da mar, Filza 941, dispatch of Valier to the Signoria, dated at Corfu on 14 April 1674).

[23] In emphasizing the strategic importance of the island of Corfu, Valier wrote, "Per questo io replicherò, serenissimo Prencipe, che la muraglia di legno, così bene interpretata da Temistocle per la salvezza d'Athene, deve esser quella che più che le muraglie de sassi difenda l'isola di Corfu che deve dirsi l'antemurale d'Italia!" (Provv. da terra e da mar, Filza 941, dispatch dated at Corfu on 16 March 1674, and signed by Valier).

[24] D. Levi-Weiss, "Le Relazioni fra Venezia e la Turchia . . . ," *Veneto-Tridentino,* VII (1925), 24.

[25] *Diario,* MS. Marc. It. VII, 1608 (7514), p. 135.

bassador Sir John Finch, and other European envoys. The Venetians also suffered his hatred of Christians and his avarice. So did the Ragusei.

When the bailie Giacomo Querini returned home (in 1676) and gave the Signoria his report on the affairs of Istanbul (the usual *relazione di Costantinopoli*), he described Kara Mustafa as "bold, violent, haughty, and fierce." Time was fully to justify his description.[26] Querini's successor in the bailaggio, Giovanni Morosini (1675–1680), in his report to the Signoria contrasted the two grand vizirs whom he had known. Ahmed Köprülü he had found "veramente benefico e reale," but as for Kara Mustafa "si riconosce tutto venale, crudele e ingiusto."[27] Within a few years of Morosini's report Kara Mustafa was to destroy himself, cripple the Ottoman empire, and help bring about the downfall of the sultan Mehmed IV.

Giovanni Morosini had had a hard time in Istanbul. His successor and co-bailie Pietro Civran had an even harder time, for Kara Mustafa imposed further fines and affronts (*avanie*) upon the Venetians—and others—as he went on with his "grave e continuata oppressione dei Cristiani."[28] The Barbary corsairs became more active under Kara Mustafa;[29] commerce suffered, and the Venetians could obtain no redress of grievances from the Porte. Giovanbattista Donà (Donado) was the last bailie of the seventeenth century to hold the difficult charge, and on 20 August 1684 he gave the Senate the last report of the century on the Porte and conditions in the Ottoman empire.[30] Donà's original text is still preserved in the Archivio Donà dalle Rose, long kept in the Palazzo Donà on the Fondamenta Nuove in Venice. After the recall of Giovanbattista Donà in 1684 the Republic was not again represented in Istanbul until the year 1700 when the treaty of Karlowitz (of 26 January 1699) was finally ratified.

---

[26] Nicolò Barozzi and Guglielmo Berchet, eds., *Le Relazioni degli stati europei lette al Senato dagli ambasciatori veneziani nel secolo decimosettimo*, ser. V, *Turchia*, I-2 (Venice, 1872), 147: ". . . Vi è Carà Mustafà, detto Caimecan, fu bassà in Silistria, general in Valacchia, e parente del Visir [Ahmed Köprülü], nella di cui assenza e lontananza in Candia poteva in sua vece subentrare, ma potè resistere alle tentazioni della vanità. . . . È però genero e favorito del Re [Mehmed IV], ed uomo ardito, violento, orgoglioso e feroce, ma altrettanto in ogni negozio facile e intraprendente, e chi s'appoggia a lui si sostiene e s'innalza, essendo avido oltre misura d'argento e di danaro."

[27] *Ibid.*, I-2, 206–7.

[28] N. Barozzi and G. Berchet, eds., *Le Relazioni degli stati europei lette al Senato dagli ambasciatori veneziani . . .* , ser. V, *Turchia*, I-2 (1872), 251ff. Civran presented his report (*relazione*) to the Senate in 1682.

[29] The Christian corsairs were also active in the eastern waters (Senato, Delib. Costantinopoli [Secreta], Reg. 35 [1682–1700], fols. 18ᵛ–19ᵛ [116ᵛ–117ᵛ], doc. dated 10 December 1682, *al proveditor general da mar*). The Venetians, however, were trying to cultivate the friendship of the Turkish naval command, and on 10 December (1682) the Senate instructed the Raggion Vecchie in Venice to send two telescopes "of the highest quality" to Giovanbattista Donà, the bailie in Istanbul, "per dare in dono al capitan bassà" (*ibid.*, fol. 19ᵛ [117ᵛ]).

[30] Barozzi and Berchet, I-2, 293ff.

Donà's relations with Kara Mustafa Pasha seemed to take a turn for the better after he had spent an awkward first year in Istanbul, for in August 1682 Kara Mustafa asked him for the service of a good physician. The Venetian University of Padua was famous for its medical school; in fact the English ambassador to the Porte, Sir John Finch, had taken a doctorate in medicine at Padua. Kara Mustafa seemed to have become very friendly, bestowing gifts upon Donà. The high officials at the Porte treated him with respect. The rampant hatred of Christendom, however, which was part of the Islamic fanaticism of the later seventeenth century, was persistently fanned by Kara Mustafa, who wanted to enhance his reputation by some great conquest.

Since the Turks were already dominant in the eastern Mediterranean, having occupied the chief islands of the Aegean as well as the coasts of the Balkan peninsula (except for Venetian Dalmatia), Kara Mustafa looked to warfare with the Austrians, the traditional enemy of the Porte. He was encouraged by the anti-Hapsburg stance of the Hungarians, whose leaders had been incensed for almost twenty years by the treaty of Vasvár (of 1664), which was due to expire in 1684. Kara Mustafa had rivals and enemies at the Porte. In the recent war with the Muscovites in the Ukraine, he had not distinguished himself as a commander in the field. The Turkish army had been defeated three times during the dismal years 1677–1678. After another two desultory and uneventful years Kara Mustafa was obliged to accept the unfavorable treaty of Radzin (in 1681), giving up most of Turkish Ukraine to the Russians. Although the sultan Mehmed IV was much in favor of renewal of the treaty of Vasvár, which Ahmed Köprülü had negotiated to the marked advantage of the Porte, Kara Mustafa was opposed to it, alleging that the Austrians had done the Turks no end of damage by their incursions into (eastern) Hungary.[31]

Kara Mustafa's friendly stance toward the Venetian bailie Donà was undoubtedly the consequence of his intention to proceed against the Hapsburgs, who had almost never been allies of the Venetians. The Turks had been at peace with the Republic for more than a decade and, if there was to be war with Austria, it was well that they should remain so. During the year 1682, however, serious strife arose in Dalmatia between certain Turks and the Morlacchi, the latter being to some extent subjects of the Republic. There was hardly ever continued peace in Dalmatia; land tenure and rents of one sort or another were among the various causes of dissension. The Turks had burned some of the Morlacchi's dwellings; the Morlacchi had thereafter killed some of the Turks in the

---

[31] Dumont, *Corps universel diplomatique*, VII-2 (Amsterdam and The Hague, 1731), no. VII, pp. 12–13, gives the text of an "instrument" of peace dated at Istanbul in 1681, which would have extended the peace of Vasvár for another twenty years, but Kara Mustafa Pasha obviously found it unacceptable.

region of Zemonico. Contemporary accounts, the Morlacchi versus the Turks, were at variance one with the other. At any rate this time the contention and the bloodshed produced an uproar in Istanbul in 1683. The divan or Ottoman privy council, over which Kara Mustafa presided as grand vizir, apparently considered war against Venice.

The kaïmakam summoned the bailie Donà, however, to inform him that the Turks would not have recourse to war if 220 or 224 Venetian subjects (that many Turks were said to have been slain) were turned over to the Porte for execution at Istanbul or in Dalmatia in the presence of the armed forces that Kara Mustafa had sent to the disputed border. The bailie was also summoned to appear before the Turkish authorities to learn the divan's judgment as to the required reparation for the damage done. Donà refused to do so, for such procedure was contrary to the capitulations which the Porte had granted Venice.

Thereafter, to be sure, Donà was informed that the problem might be solved by the Republic's payment of 1,500 "purses" (*borse*) or 750,000 *reali* to the Porte. A "purse" was reckoned at 500 *reali*. As Donà declined any such huge payment, the sum demanded was gradually lowered until, without authority, Donà agreed to pay the Porte 175,000 *reali*. He would also give the grand vizir 25,000 *reali* and a like sum to the other ministers of state, making a total of 450 "purses" or 225,000 *reali*, a considerable sum but, in Donà's opinion, much less expensive than warfare.

The Turks had been mustering their naval as well as their land forces. Since there were rumors of an Austro-Turkish accord, they would be prepared for action at sea as well as in Dalmatia and elsewhere. The Venetians must take heed. But Donà's solution was costly economically as well as humiliating morally to the Signoria, and obviously the peace of 1669 would seem to be in jeopardy.[32] The English ambassador Sir John Finch had explained the situation in Istanbul in a letter of 8/18 October 1680 to Robert Spencer, the second earl of Sunderland, who had been made Charles II's secretary of state the preceding year:

> My Lord, affayrs in this country are incredible, indicible [unspeakable], nay rially inconceivable. What is true today, is not so tomorrow. No promise is strong enough to bind, no reasons, be they never so cogent, powerfull enough to persuade. Impetuous passion accompany'd with avarice over'rules all laws and capitulations.[33]

---

[32] Levi-Weiss, "Le Relazioni fra Venezia e la Turchia . . . ," *Veneto-Tridentino,* VII (1925), 35–41. An unsigned and undated letter in the Public Record Office in London, SP [State Papers] 97, XIX, fol. 310, gives a brief account of the "unhappy (as it is like to prove in the end) rancounter which lat'ly happened in Dalamatia between the subjects of Venice and some of the [Ottoman] Empire. . . ."

[33] PRO, SP 97, XIX, fol. 262, letter dated at Pera of Constantinople on 8/18 October 1680.

The affair of Zemonico was a sad illustration of Finch's view of the Porte under Kara Mustafa Pasha. The bailie Giovanbattista Donà's acceptance of the (even reduced) financial dictates of the Turks did not, as far as the Senate was concerned, effect a reconciliation with the Porte. In the Senate Pietro Valier proposed a return to warfare with the Turks. Why keep feeding their avarice with Venetian gold? On 2 July 1683 letters of the doge and Senate, dated the preceding 15 May, reached Istanbul, recalling Donà from the bailaggio. He replied in a letter to the doge on 10 July, dignified but almost desperate.[34] The Senate had removed him from the bailaggio, because in yielding to the Turkish demands, he had exceeded his authority as bailie. He was not replaced, for the Senate now had no intention in sending another bailie to the Bosporus as a hostage on whom the grand vizir and the divan might lay their hands to wring more money from the Venetian treasury. The secretary Giovanni Capello, friend and associate of the dragoman Ambrosio Grillo, would represent the Signoria in Istanbul.[35]

The grand vizir and the divan could easily take offense at the Senate's failure to send another bailie (a consul general in effect) to answer for the Republic. On the other hand the Venetians had never been enamored of the Hapsburgs, and had as yet no interest in joining them in any sort of entente against the Turks. The Venetians had, however, suffered more than enough from the Turks who, for example, in January 1683 had suddenly requisitioned three Venetian ships which were loading merchandise at the docks in Istanbul. Despite the protests of the bailie Donà, the Turks had used the three vessels for the transport of troops from Cairo to Europe. The Venetians did get their vessels back some nine months later, but October was not a good month to load merchandise for shipment to Venice in view of the late-autumn storms in the eastern Mediterranean.

The grand dragoman Tommaso Tarsia had considerable difficulty in securing a passport for Donà's departure after the Senate had recalled him. One sensed a coming storm; rumor had it that Kara Mustafa Pasha was more than hostile to Venice. If the projected campaign against

---

[34] Barozzi and Berchet, *Le Relazioni degli stati europei* . . . , ser. V, *Turchia*, I-2 (1872), 289–91. On Donà's career see the brief but interesting account in Paolo Preto, *Venezia e i Turchi*, Florence, 1975, pp. 340–51.

[35] Giovanni Capello was a secretary of the Council of Ten. He had been assigned to the Porte until the arrival in Istanbul of a new bailie to replace Donà, whose repatriation had been voted by the Senate (Delib. Costantinopoli, Reg. 35, fols. 32ᵛ–39ᵛ). As stated above, however, the Signoria decided not to send a new bailie to the Bosporus. Capello's safe-conduct, dated 19 June 1683, reads, "Universis et singulis, etc.: Partendo da questa città il circospetto, fidelissimo segretario del Consiglio di Dieci Gio. Capello per condursi alla Porta, ricerchiamo gl'amici, e commettemo alli rappresentanti e ministri nostri, di prestargli ogni assistenza e favore, lasciandolo passar liberamente con sue robbe, armi, e bagaglio e facilitandogli il viaggio, pronti a corrisponder a gl'amici, e certi dell'obedienza de rappresentanti e ministri nostri. +103, —3, —41" (*ibid.*, fol. 39ᵛ).

Vienna should fail, would Kara Mustafa be able to employ the forces he had amassed against the Venetians? The Arsenal in Istanbul had come to life in almost furious fashion. While the Turks said they intended to clear the Archipelago of corsairs, the secretary Capello was wondering why so many ships and galleys were required for that purpose.[36]

Of course the future would depend upon the grand vizir Kara Mustafa's success or failure in the siege of Vienna. With the advent of September 1683, however, and Kara Mustafa's catastrophic defeat on the shores of the Danube below the towering height of the Kahlenberg, the history of Venice as well as that of Austria would indeed change and (from the western point of view) very much for the better.

No episode in the history of Europe in the seventeenth century has attracted more attention than the second Turkish siege of Vienna. The centenary "remembrance of things past" in 1983 as well as in 1883 has produced an abundance of literature on the subject. Even a very brief summary of well-known events should help put in perspective both the Austrians' and the Venetians' drive after 1683 to continued warfare with the Turks. It all began with Kara Mustafa Pasha's elevation to the grand vizirate. Seeking glory for himself and wealth for the sultanate, Kara Mustafa appears to have considered an attack upon Vienna at least as early as August 1682.

Although the ulema and Sultan Mehmed IV were opposed to the resumption of armed conflict with Austria, Kara Mustafa Pasha was persistent, and at length won over the sultan to the belief that the Ottoman occupation of the fortress towns of Györ (Raab) and Komárno would help maintain peace between the Porte and the Hapsburgs. The Turks had held Györ in 1594–1598; their occupation is still remembered and resented. Györ is a thriving city today, with massive public housing, located at the confluence of the Raba, the Repce, and an arm of the Danube. Slovak Komárno is on the left bank of the Danube at the mouth of the Váh; Hungarian Komárom, the other half of the old fortress town, is just across the Danube. Komárno-Komárom was taken and pillaged by the Turks in 1543, 1594, and 1669. Kara Mustafa wanted to take it again, and this time to hold it. In Slovak Komárno one finds today an interesting small museum with recollections of the past, especially of Gabriel Bethlen and Francis (Ferenc) Rákóczy, as well as of the Roman past in a notable collection of ceramics.

The Turks' rearmament on a grand scale and the renewal of activity in

---

[36] Levi-Weiss, in *Veneto-Tridentino,* VII, 42–44. The Venetian Senate had been painfully aware of Kara Mustafa's "vast ideas" and his hostility toward Christendom (Delib. Costantinopoli, Reg. 35, fols. 20–21ᵛ [118–119ᵛ], doc. dated 26 December 1682, *al bailo in Costantinopoli*), "i vasti pensieri del primo visir a danni della Christianità."

the Arsenal had caused suspicion and alarm in Vienna and in Venice. By December 1682 the imperialists were quite alive to the possibility of attack by the Turks.[37] In the early spring of 1683 the Ottoman army moved northwestward in an almost straight line from Edirne (Adrianople), reaching Plovdiv (ancient Philippopolis) in Bulgaria on 8 April, Sofia on 17 April, and Niš on 24 April. At the beginning of May, despite heavy rains, the army got to Belgrade, where on the 13th Mehmed IV, who had led the march thus far, gave Kara Mustafa Pasha the sacred insignia of the Prophet. Mehmed remained in Belgrade.

The Army moved on, arriving at Mitrovica on 27 May and at Osijek (Esseg) on 2 June. Then it pushed on directly north, reaching Székesfehérvár (Stuhlweissenburg) in the center of northwestern Hungary on 25 June, where the khan of the Tatars met with the now commander-in-chief (*serasker*) Kara Mustafa. The Turkish army left Székesfehérvár on 28 June, appearing before the Austrian fortress town of Györ (Raab) in the far northwest of Hungary on 1 July.

The scene is, to the modern historian, a bit confusing. Not far northwest of Hungarian Györ was—and is—Slovak Bratislava (Pressburg), then in Austrian hands. The Austrians also held Komárno-Komárom, an important place, as we have noted, on the Danube. Nearby Nové Zámky (Neuhäusel) on the Nitra river, just north of Komárno, was an Ottoman fortress, and so was old Esztergom (Gran). Eger (Erlau) was also Turkish. Although it is a little hard today to understand how Nové Zámky could have been such a strong fortress town, it is easy to see the one-time strength of Esztergom with its Castle Hill (Várhegy), where one always visits the huge (modern) cathedral.

The disagreements in the imperial high command, with the usual differences of opinion between Hermann von Baden of the war council in Vienna (the *Hofkriegsrat*) and the imperialist general Charles V of Lorraine, then in the field of Györ, presented the court with a perilous and perplexing problem. Fearing that Hermann was then as much concerned with Louis XIV's plans for territorial expansion in the West as he was with the impending Turkish danger in the East, Charles felt that he should return to Vienna. He would be needed for the defense of the city. He therefore withdrew from well-fortified Györ. Indeed, the Turks might have laid siege to Györ, as the sultan and the divan had assumed would be the case. Kara Mustafa Pasha, however, decided that it would require too much time and manpower to take Györ, while in the meantime the imperialists would be strengthening the old-fashioned fortifications of

---

[37] Cf. *Récit du secours de Vienne en l'année 1683 . . .* , ed. Ferdinand Stöller, *Neue Quellen zur Geschichte des Türkenjahres 1683 aus dem Lothringischen Hausarchiv* [in the Haus-, Hof- und Staatsarchiv, Vienna], *Mitteilungen des Österreichischen Instituts zur Geschichtsforschung,* suppl. vol. XIII-1 (Innsbruck, 1933), 10.

Vienna, which city, it was now clear, had been Kara Mustafa's objective all along.

Charles of Lorraine made his way northwestward to Vienna, where he knew his presence was needed, for Kara Mustafa Pasha had now come close to the Hapsburg capital. The Turks quickly overran northwestern Hungary, as the Turkish grand dragoman Alessandro Mavrocordato informs us, moving into Pápa, Veszprém, and Tata in early July. Kara Mustafa, however, lessened the driving force of his army by leaving ten to twelve thousand troops in the area of Győr to protect his rear and the Turkish convoys which would bring him supplies.[38] They could also try to cut off the Christian return to Győr and, possibly, take Bratislava. Any large detachment of troops may well have diminished Kara Mustafa's chances of seizing Vienna although his forces, if properly deployed (and employed), would presumably have sufficed to give him the city. In any event the Turkish host pushed on, reaching the town of Schwechat on 13 July, some seven miles southeast of Vienna, and today the site of the city's airport.[39]

---

[38] Such at any rate is the number of troops which the *Récit du secours de Vienne en l'année 1683*, p. 20, says were left at Győr (Raab).

[39] *Das Tagebuch des Pfortendolmetschers Aléxandros Mavrokordátos*, in Richard F. Kreutel and Karl Teply, eds., *Kara Mustafa vor Wien (1683) aus der Sicht türkischer Quellen*, Graz, Vienna, Cologne, 1982, pp. 64–82, in which we may follow Kara Mustafa Pasha's march to Vienna from the beginning of April to his arrival at Schwechat on 13 July. Mavrokordátos (Mavrocordato) was a Greek, educated in Italy, and the grand dragoman of the Turkish expedition. Note also *Das türkische Tagebuch der Belagerung Wiens (1683), verfasst vom Zeremonienmeister der Hohen Pforte, ibid.*, pp. 109–14. Among the numerous contemporary sources the reader may find especially interesting two letters written by an officer (in the service of the duke of Savoy), who was a participant in the siege from beginning to end. The letters have been published with a brief introduction by Henri Marczali, "Relation du siège de Vienne et de la campagne en Hongrie 1683," *Revue de Hongrie*, III (1909), 34–66, 169–98, 276–92. These letters were apparently written by one Count Francesco di Frosasco (d. 1710); the first should be dated immediately after 15 September (1683), the second probably at the beginning of the year 1684.

There is a large literature relating to the siege of Vienna in 1683, inspired to some extent by the centennials of 1883 and 1983, in which context note Onno Klopp, *Das Jahr 1683 und der folgende grosse Türkenkrieg bis zum Frieden von Carlowitz 1699*, Graz, 1882; the valuable, anonymously published little volume on *Der Entsatz von Wien am 12. September 1683, aus einer kriegshistorischen Studie*, Berlin, 1883, 120 pp., with a useful plan of the "order of battle" (*Schlachtordnung*) of the Christian forces on the last day of the siege, together with a detailed outline of the various units of Kara Mustafa Pasha's army; Augustin Sauer, *Rom und Wien im Jahre 1683: Ausgewählte Actenstücke aus römischen Archiven zur II. Säcularfeier der Befreiung Wiens . . .*, Vienna, 1883, a collection of documents almost entirely from the year 1683; and see Johann Newald, *Beiträge zur Geschichte der Belagerung von Wien durch die Türken im Jahre 1683*, 2 pts., Vienna, 1883–84, as well as John Stoye, *The Siege of Vienna*, London, 1964; Thomas M. Barker, *Double Eagle and Crescent: Vienna's Second Turkish Siege and its Historical Setting*, Albany, N.Y., 1967; Ekkehard Eickhoff and Rudolf Eickhoff, *Venedig, Wien, und die Osmanen: Umbruch in Südosteuropa 1645–1700*, Munich, 1970; and Günter Düriegl, *Wien 1683: Die zweite Türkenbelagerung*, Vienna, Cologne, Graz, 1981.

The Emperor Leopold I and the court had begun their retreat from Vienna on 7 July, headed for Krems, Melk, Linz, and Passau, which they reached on the seventeenth,[40] leaving Charles of Lorraine in command of the troops. Meanwhile the Hungarian leader Imre Thököly, after running with the hare and hunting with the hounds month after month, finally sided with the Turks, who seem to have promised him the kingdom of Hungary. Far worse than Thököly, however, was the problem which Louis XIV presented both to the empire and to Europe.

At Louis's behest the high courts of Metz (acting also for Toul and Verdun), Breisach (for Alsace), and Besançon (for Franche Comté) had set about securing for France all the towns and territories that earlier peace treaties had accorded the Crown. The so-called "chambers of reunion" were thus created to look into the historical past and assert the French claims, which brought about the eventual annexation of Saarbrücken, Luxembourg, Zweibrücken, and (above all) Strasbourg (in 1681). Other towns were also added to the French realm. Europe was almost thrown into turmoil. The projected union of Holland and Sweden, Spain and Austria led Louis to moderate his ambition for a while, and the Turks' investment of Vienna led him to postpone military action, but only for a while. Nevertheless, the imperial court obviously had serious cause for concern in the West as well as in the East.

When Leopold I and the court retreated from Vienna on 7 July (1683), with dire misgivings, Count Ernst Rüdiger von Starhemberg was left in defense of the city. His heroic command during the Turks' two months' siege of Vienna was to make him a legendary figure. He was later to be the patron of Eugene of Savoy and to advance the latter's career. Civilian as well as military matters in the city were entrusted to the aging Count Kaspar Zdenko Kaplirs, who faithfully discharged the two commissions which he had done his best to decline. Kaplirs' decisions, however, were subject to Starhemberg's approval. The Capuchin preacher Marco d'Aviano, the spiritual mentor of both Leopold I and Charles of Lorraine,

---

Walter Sturminger, *Bibliographie und Ikonographie der Türkenbelagerungen Wiens 1529 und 1683*, Graz and Cologne, 1955, lists some 650 titles relating to the siege of Vienna in 1529 (nos. 1–534, 3301–3416) and more than 3,300 to the siege of 1683 (nos. 601–3148, 3501–4270), many of the works listed being contemporary with the events they describe or the scenes they depict. Max Vancsa, "Quellen und Geschichtschreibung," *Geschichte der Stadt Wien*, ed. Anton Mayer, IV-1 (Vienna, 1911), pp. 1–108, describes in detail the published sources relating to the first siege of Vienna in 1529 (pp. 23–36) and those relating to the second siege in 1683 (pp. 40–77), with some illustrations in color.

[40] *Ein Tagebuch während der Belagerung von Wien im Jahr 1683* [the diary of Count Ferdinand Bonaventura Harrach, written in 1698 during his fourth sojourn in Spain as the Austrian ambassador], ed. Ferd. Menčík, in the *Archiv für österreichische Geschichte*, LXXXVI (Vienna, 1899), 211–19.

was prominent throughout the siege. Today there is a monument to the revered Marco, hailing him as "die Seele der Befreiung Wiens XII September MDCLXXXIII," beside the Kapuziner Kirche, at the point where the Tegetthoffstrasse runs into the Neuer Markt. The mayor of Vienna, Johann Andreas von Liebenberg, was another stalwart and ever-useful figure; a monument to von Liebenberg, "Bürgermeister von Wien im Jahre MDCLXXXIII," may be seen today on the Ringstrasse across the street from the University. There were in fact many other heroes working in the city, but we shall limit ourselves to these four.

Although it is impossible to determine the size of the Turkish host which laid siege to the Austrian capital (and undoubtedly Kara Mustafa Pasha himself could not have supplied us with an even nearly precise figure), a maximum of almost 90,000 has been thought the likely size of Kara Mustafa's army when the siege began. It is hard to believe it was so large unless we include in the figure such Tatar and Hungarian, Moldavian and Wallachian units as were actually present at the siege.

The Turks had been addicted to the employment of heavy artillery, often cast for them by Hungarian or Rumelian founders, since the earlier fifteenth century, but they lacked heavy artillery at the siege of Vienna. The transport of large cannon from Adrianople to Vienna would have been too difficult. It would also have delayed Kara Mustafa Pasha's westward march too long. All along the way the Turks had had to build or rebuild roads and bridges. Perhaps huge siege cannon (of the sort the Turks had used at Constantinople in 1453) were not thought necessary to take Györ and Komárno, which had been the agreed-upon objectives when the Turkish host went out from Adrianople to Belgrade. It would soon become clear, however, that Kara Mustafa lacked sufficient cannon power to demolish the obsolescent and indeed inadequate fortifications of Vienna. And while the Turks were effective in their mining operations, the besieged Christians showed themselves to be quite competent in the fine art of countermining.

The siege began on 14 July 1683. The Turkish encampment hemmed in the southern, eastern, and western ranges of the Viennese walls, embattlements, and moats, which to no small extent followed the lines of the modern Ringstrasse. The major Turkish pavilions and tents stretched along the area of the southeast and east, from the Mölk and Löbel Bastions (*Basteien*) to the Palace Bastion (the *Burgbastei*) and the Carinthian Bastion (the *Kärntnerbastei*), which are shown on all maps of the siege. The Hofburg or Imperial Palace, one of the major tourist attractions of present-day Vienna, was behind the Palace Bastion. The modern Opera House (the *Staatsoper*) at the southern end of the popular and fashionable Kärntnerstrasse lies of course just north of where the Kärntner Bastion once stood. Despite attacks upon the area of the Scottish Gate (the *Schottentor*) on the west, and various strikes made elsewhere, the Turks concentrated their heaviest assaults, bombardments, and mining operations upon the Löbel and the Palace Bastions.[41]

The Turks had very quickly set about the digging of trenches in the wide expanse of the glacis and directing their light artillery at the defenders whenever the latter emerged to impede them. The siege soon reached the stage of hand-to-hand combat as well as mining and countermining, as the Turks sought to take possession of the counterscarp to bring their artillery and mining operations up to the southern ravelins, the bastions, and the curtain wall. Life in Vienna had not been without difficulties before the advent of the Turks, as we shall note presently, but the crowded conditions of the city became a horror, replete with dysentery and other maladies, during the two months of the siege.

As the Turks prepared their dugouts, trenches, and underground galleries with protective traverses at given intervals, Charles of Lorraine clung with his cavalry forces to the northern shore of the Danube. From the area of Krems and Hollabrunn southeastward to Marchegg (on the Morava), Bratislava, Györ, and Komárno, Charles tried to keep the long stretch of territory clear of the Turks, Tatars, and Thököly's Hungarians. His Christian allies, especially the Poles with the assistance of the Austrian cavalry, frustrated a Turkish-Hungarian attempt to take Bratislava (on 29 July).[42] Thereafter Charles defeated the Turks at the northern end of his military spectrum (on 24 August). The encounter took place at the foot of the Bisamberg,[43] across the Danube from Klosterneuburg. Charles had to keep the area open, because he was waiting, and waiting, for the arrival of the German and Polish troops which, it was hoped, would break the Turkish siege of Vienna.

---

[41] A brief chronology of the siege (from 14 July to 12 September) is given in Mavrocordato's diary in Kreutel and Teply, eds., *Kara Mustafa vor Wien* (1982), pp. 82–89, and in considerable detail in the diary of the master of ceremonies of the Porte, *ibid.*, pp. 115–92. The English reader has easy access to a good account of the siege in Barker, *Double Eagle and Crescent* (1967), pp. 241–334, esp. pp. 254ff., and note Eickhoff and Eickhoff, *Venedig, Wien und die Osmanen* (1970), esp. pp. 359–407. The siege, as viewed by the Christian officers in Vienna, is described day by day in the *Récit du secours de Vienne en l'année 1683*, to which reference has been made above.

During the summer of 1683, while Kara Mustafa Pasha was at Vienna, the Venetians were having financial and other difficulties in Istanbul (Delib. Costantinopoli, Reg. 35, fols. 41–42 [139–140], doc. dated 21 August 1683, *al segretario Capello in Costantinopoli*).

[42] On the Turkish-Hungarian venture against Bratislava (Pressburg), cf. the diary of the Turkish master of ceremonies in Kreutel and Teply, *Kara Mustafa vor Wien* (1982), p. 141; Klopp, *Das Jahr 1683* (1882), pp. 285–87; Barker, *Double Eagle and Crescent* (1967), pp. 287–88; Eickhoff and Eickhoff, *Venedig, Wien und die Osmanen* (1970), p. 391.

[43] *Kara Mustafa vor Wien* (1982), pp. 170–71, 207–8 (note 53), 223–34; Barker, *Double Eagle and Crescent*, pp. 293–94.

The Germans and Poles did respond, even generously, to the appeals of the Emperor Leopold and Charles of Lorraine, despite the financial questions that arose and the diplomatic maneuvering that was inevitable. A large body of troops, with the support of the Catholic court at Munich, moved eastward into Lower Austria under the young Maximilian Emmanuel von Wittelsbach, the elector and duke of Bavaria. Another large contingent (of musketeers and horse), with the approval of the Protestant court at Dresden, made their way south into Lower Austria under Johann Georg III von Wettin, the elector and duke of Saxony. Prince Georg Friedrich von Waldeck commanded detachments of Franconian and Swabian forces which came to the aid of the Austrians, as did a small body of German troops under two sons of Ernst August of Braunschweig [Brunswick]-Lüneburg, to whose willingness to assist Christendom against the Turks we shall come shortly. Friedrich Wilhelm von Hohenzollern, the so-called Great Elector (of Brandenburg), provided no assistance at all. The French influence was strong in Brandenburg, and Friedrich Wilhelm's demands for payment of military service were beyond Leopold's capacity to meet them.

The Polish response under the flamboyant King John III Sobieski was extraordinary. On 31 March (1683) representatives of Leopold I, Holy Roman emperor, king of Hungary and Bohemia, and archduke of Austria, and John III, king of Poland and grand duke of Lithuania, had reached an "everlasting offensive and defensive alliance" (*foedus perpetuum offensivum et defensivum*), for the "daily experience" of their subjects had made manifest the danger which the power of the Ottoman empire posed for Christendom.[44] The Sejm or parliament of the monarchical republic of Poland quickly ratified the alliance, which was almost unusual, for any member of the unruly Sejm could dissolve the parliament and even annul its previous resolutions by his single vote (the *liberum veto*). The Sejm also voted a large increase in the size of the armed forces.

John III Sobieski left Warsaw on 18 July (1683), and went south to Częstochowa to get the blessing of the Black Virgin, the "queen of Poland" on the height of Jasna Góra. He reached Cracow (Kraków) on 29 July, expecting to effect a union with Charles of Lorraine by the first week of September. He left Cracow in mid-August, proceeding westward to Gliwice (Gleiwitz), where he arrived on 22 August, then to Racibórz

---

[44] Dumont, *Corps universel diplomatique*, VII-2 (Amsterdam and The Hague, 1731), no. xxxiv, pp. 62–64. The alliance was ratified by Leopold at Laxenburg on 2 May. About the same time a treaty was made between Sultan Mehmed IV and Count Imre Thököly, promising the latter the kingdom of Hungary (*ibid.*, no. xxv, p. 40). Leopold also made separate treaties with Ernst August of Brunswick-Lüneburg and Max Emmanuel of Bavaria (*ibid.*, nos. xxviii-xxix, pp. 51–55).

(Ratibor) on the Oder on 24 August, and thence to Opava (Troppau) at the Slovak border. He got to Olomouc (Olmütz) in Moravia on 26 August, Brno (Brünn) on the 29th, and Mikulov (Nikolsburg) on the following day. By 30–31 August Sobieski had made it to the area around Hollabrunn,[45] where Charles of Lorraine came to meet him to discuss the Turkish peril and the great military venture which lay ahead. The Poles' arrival in each city had been made a festive occasion with banquets and drinking bouts, which doubtless delayed their progress by more than a day or two, but on the whole Sobieski had in fact moved rapidly.

The imperialists and the Poles, assembling north of the Danube in the region of Hollabrunn, came southward across the river at Tulln. The Bavarians crossed the Danube near the point at which the river Traisen flows into the great waterway, while the Saxons made their crossing at the fortress town of Krems. Moving from Tulln in central Lower Austria eastward to Weidling and Klosterneuburg on the northern slope of the Wienerwald, the allied Christian forces gradually and with much difficulty ascended the Leopoldsberg and the higher Kahlenberg. The "Vienna Woods" was, and is, a mountainous part of the countryside with heavy vines, wild hedges, trees, and thickets, forming in various areas an impenetrable undergrowth, through which in one way or another the Austrians, Germans, and Poles had had to make their way up the slopes of the Leopoldsberg and the Kahlenberg. Klosterneuburg, with its famous Augustinian monastery, is a tourist site today, and so is the top of the Kahlenberg, site of the old Camaldulensian monastery, with its sometimes hazy view of Vienna. The Emperor Leopold, who had come down the Danube with the apparent intention of joining the allied armies, was strongly advised not to do so, for his superior presence (and the picayune protocol of the day) would be distressing to Sobieski, who would have to take a subordinate position. Also Leopold was hardly a soldier, and the Viennese needed the Polish army.

After untold hardships of mountain-climbing up the Leopoldsberg and the Kahlenberg, the allied forces were finally ready to descend upon the enemy by 12 September. Kara Mustafa Pasha had made almost no effort to occupy the heights and thus prevent the Christians' ascent to their strategic vantage point. Early in the morning of the 12th the Austrian, Saxon, and Bavarian troops, forming a straggly left wing under Charles of Lorraine (in so far as a wing could be maintained on the rough terrain), came down slowly from the wooded heights to meet the Turks. Later on, Sobieski and the Poles made their difficult descent, forming the honor-

---

[45] Cf. Ferd. Bonaventura Harrach's *Tagebuch während der Belagerung von Wien im Jahre 1683*, ed. Ferd. Menčík, in the *Arch. f. österreichische Geschichte*, LXXXVI (Vienna, 1899), 244.

ific right wing. Much of the planning and reconnoitering had been done by Charles of Lorraine, who kept the testy Sobieski in good humor by endless tact and acquiescence.[46]

Every schoolboy used to know—or ought to have known—that the allied Christian forces won the "battle of the Kahlenberg." All day on the historic 12th of September in 1683 men were on the move, the Christians coming down the rough and brambly hills and mountainsides, and the Turks feverishly active in the areas to the south of their encampments. Kara Mustafa Pasha withdrew some troops from the trenches, but the siege of Vienna had to be continued. If most of the Turkish men-at-arms had been removed from the dugouts and bunkers, the defenders of the city, however tired by now, might well have emerged to launch an attack here or there upon the rear of the diverse Turkish units then facing the Christians descending from the Kahlenberg and the Leopoldsberg.

The air was rent with musket fire and cannon shots, with rallying cries and exhortations, kettledrums and trumpets. To both the Turks and the Christians war cries and the sound of "ogni sorte d'istrumenti" were an important part of combat. The battle of the Kahlenberg lasted until evening, until the Turkish lines broke, and the enemy began to flee. In their more than hasty retreat eastward in the direction of the fortress town of Györ, Kara Mustafa and most of his various forces got beyond the Rába river well before the Austrian, Bavarian, and Polish armies began their own eastward march. The booty which fell into Christian hands was enormous, the Poles getting much of the treasures which Kara Mustafa and the major Turkish officers had had to leave behind. In fact among the most interesting memorials of Sobieski's role in raising the siege of Vienna are the large, beautifully embroidered Turkish tents which are still to be seen in the castle museum on Wawel Hill in Cracow.

Soon after the flight of the Turks the Elector Johann Georg of Saxony returned to Dresden, the capital of his electorate, which was becoming a beautiful city (and which suffered severely in the Second World War). A strong Protestant, he had helped stop the Turks' westward advance at Vienna, but he resented heartily the Hapsburgs' almost fiercely pro-

---

[46] On the importance of Charles of Lorraine's activities before, during, and after the siege of Vienna, see Paul Wentzcke's biography of Charles, *Feldherr des Kaisers: Leben und Taten Herzog Karls V. von Lothringen*, Leipzig, 1943, esp. pp. 198ff., 221ff. Wentzcke is very well informed, but gives no references in his book to the sources. On 15 September 1683 Charles of Lorraine wrote Francesco Barberini, the cardinal protector of Poland, "Le Roy de Pologne s'est acquis dans ce rancontre une gloire immortelle d'estre venu de son royaume pour une si grande entreprise, e[t] d'y avoir agit en grand roy et en gran capitaine" (Augustin Sauer, *Rom und Wien im Jahre 1683*, Vienna, 1883, doc. no. 64, pp. 62–63).

Catholic policy in the regions of Hungary and Transylvania where they had been able to exercise their will. At least for the time being, he had done with the Hapsburgs. On 13 September John III Sobieski made a triumphal entry into Vienna. He was acclaimed by the populace, but his preceding the emperor into the latter's own capital was a serious breach of dynastic protocol.

Leopold was received into Vienna, however, with all due reverence on 14 September. He met Sobieski in dignified fashion on the following day in a field at Schwechat. The meeting was not a diplomatic success, for Leopold slighted Sobieski's son Jakob when the latter was presented to him. Sobieski and especially his wife Maria Casimira had hoped that Jakob might marry Leopold's daughter, the Archduchess Maria Antonia, which might help secure his election as his father's successor. But now the Hapsburgs were less interested in the Polish alliance, and after no end of marital, diplomatic maneuvering (Maria Antonia was no beauty), she married Max Emmanuel von Wittelsbach, the elector and duke of Bavaria, who had helped a good deal in relieving the siege of Vienna.[47]

Despite the multiple sources we now have at hand, it is difficult to get a clear picture of the extent to which the Turks had done damage to Vienna during the course of the siege. Their lack of heavy cannon seems to have removed much of the interior of the city from the range of their fire. Also Kara Mustafa Pasha had wanted to take the city and revel in its wealth, not necessarily to destroy it, for in the latter case he would only have acquired ruins. Whatever the ruination, restoration was clearly (and remarkably) rapid, for just thirty-three years after the siege Lady Mary Wortley Montagu found Vienna (in September 1716) a "populous city adorn'd with magnificent palaces," with apparently no evidence of Turkish destruction. Lady Mary enjoyed herself in Vienna, almost overwhelmed by "the first people of Quality," the magnificence of the opera, and "the fashions here, which are . . . monstrous and contrary to all common sense." As for the city itself, however, she described it thus on 8/18 September in a letter to her sister Frances Erskine, countess of Mar:

This town, which has the honnour of being the emperor's residence, did not at all answer my ideas of it, being much lesse than I expected to find it. The streets are very close and so narrow one cannot observe the fine fronts of the palaces, tho many of them very well deserve observation, being truly magnificent, all built of fine white stone and excessive high. The town being so much too little for

---

[47] Cf. Ludwig von Pastor (and Rob. Leiber), *Geschichte der Päpste*, XIV-2 (Freiburg im Breisgau, 1930), 770–71, 825–26, 1006–7: "Bei den Heiraten der Fürsten spiele das schöne Gesicht der Braut eine untergeordnete Rolle!" (*ibid.*, p. 771, note 2).

the number of the people that desire to live in it, the builders seem to have projected to repair that misfortune by claping one town on the top of another, most of the houses being of 5 and some of them of 6 storys. You may easily imagine that the streets being so narrow, the upper rooms are extream dark, and what is an inconveniency much more intolerable in my opinion, there is no house that has so few as 5 or 6 familys in it. The apartments of the greatest ladys and even of the ministers of state are divided but by a partition from that of a tailor or a shoe-maker, and I know no body that has above 2 floors in any house, one for their own use, and one higher for their servants. Those that have houses of their own, let out the rest of them to whoever will take 'em; thus the great stairs (which are all of stone) are as common and as dirty as the street. 'Tis true when you have once travell'd through them, nothing can be more surprizingly magnificent than the apartments. They are commonly a suitte of 8 or 10 large rooms, all inlaid, the doors and windows richly carv'd and gilt, and the furniture such as is seldom seen in the palaces of sovereign princes in other countrys: the hangings the finest tapestry of Brussells, prodigious large looking glasses in silver frames, fine Japan tables, the beds, chairs, canopys and window curtains of the richest Genoa damask or velvet, allmost cover'd with gold lace or embrodiery—the whole made gay by pictures and vast jars of Japan china, and almost in every room large lustres of rock chrystal.[48]

---

[48] Robert Halsband, ed., *The Complete Letters of Lady Mary Wortley Montagu*, 3 vols., Oxford, 1965–67, I, 259–60, and cf., *ibid.*, pp. 291ff.

IX

The Conquests of the Austrians in Hungary, the Revolt of the Turkish Army, and the Venetians in the Morea (1684–1687)

❧

he Turkish grand vizir Kara Mustafa Pasha had failed in dismal fashion in the unforgettable siege of Vienna (from 14 July to 12 September 1683), the Ottoman disaster of the century. In their retreat the Turks were badly defeated on 9 October at Parkány (Štúrovo), and after a brief siege they had to give up the city of Esztergom (Gran), the old primatial see of Hungary on the right bank of the Danube opposite Parkány. Several thousand Turks had perished at Parkány, a second great setback for Kara Mustafa, but the Turks surrendered Esztergom (on 26 October) with hardly any loss of life which was, nevertheless, another serious setback for Kara Mustafa, whose future now looked dim. And indeed it was. He was strangled at Belgrade on 25 December by order of Sultan Mehmed IV. On 5 March 1684 the Holy League was ratified at Linz, binding the Emperor Leopold I, King John III Sobieski of Poland, and the newly-elected Doge Marc'Antonio Giustinian to a war against the Turks under the aegis of Pope Innocent XI.[1] The

---

[1] Jean Dumont, *Corps universel diplomatique*, VII-2 (Amsterdam and The Hague, 1731), no. xxxix, pp. 71–72. Leopold and John Sobieski had already been bound together by a *foedus perpetuum offensivum et defensivum*, which was agreed to at Warsaw on 31 March 1683, and ratified by Leopold *in Arce nostra Laxiburgi* (Laxenburg) on the following 2 May (*ibid.*, no. xxxiv, pp. 62–64). On the execution of Kara Mustafa Pasha and the

anti-Turkish activity of the Venetians in the Mediterranean would impede the concentration of the sultan's forces in central Europe. Also, of course, the Venetian fleet in the south would be an important adjunct to the Austrian and Polish armies in the north, and the success of the Austrians now gave the Venetians the opportunity for which they had long been waiting.

As von Hammer-Purgstall has put it, this was to be the fourteenth crusade preached by the popes against the Ottoman Turks. Francesco Morosini had been named captain-general of the Venetian fleet. Having emerged from the cloud cast upon him by the surrender of Candia some fifteen years before (in 1669), Morosini had been considered a likely prospect for the dogate when Alvise Contarini died (on 15 January 1684). But he would serve the Republic best as its commander-in-chief at sea, and Marc'Antonio Giustinian had been elected doge (on 26 January).[2] On Tuesday, 25 April, the feast of S. Mark, when Giustinian was attending mass with the imperial ambassador Francesco della Torre in the basilica a messenger arrived from Vienna with word of the signing of the anti-Turkish treaty. The new allies would render one another all possible aid against the infidel; reconquered territories would revert to their former Christian owners. As always, the other Christian princes would be urged to join the anti-Turkish league.[3]

Christians' acquisition of his skull (allegedly that now in the Historisches Museum der Stadt Wien), see J.W. Zinkeisen, *Gesch. d. osman. Reiches in Europa*, V (Gotha, 1857), 112; note also Thos. M. Barker, *Double Eagle and Crescent*, Albany, N.Y., 1967, pp. 348–60, on the seizure of Parkány and the occupation of Esztergom, and, *ibid.*, pp. 69, 363–64, on the execution of Kara Mustafa Pasha.

On the Turkish peril, the complications of French and Polish diplomacy, the formation of the Holy League, and Innocent XI's persistent efforts against the Turks, note Ludwig von Pastor (and Rob. Leiber), *Geschichte der Päpste*, XIV-2 (1930), 694ff., 725ff., 787–840, and *Hist. Popes*, XXXII, 38ff., 83ff., 168–245.

[2] As noted above, Dores Levi-Weiss, "Le Relazioni fra Venezia e la Turchia dal 1670 al 1684 e la formazione della Sacra Lega," *Veneto-Tridentino*, VII (1925), 1–46; VIII (also 1925), 40–100; IX–X (1926), 97–116, with an appendix of unpublished documents, *ibid.*, pp. 117–54, has described in detail Venetian relations with the Porte from the end of the war of Candia (1645–1669) to the creation of the Holy League in 1684, at which time Francesco Morosini, who had surrendered Candia to the Turks on 5–6 September 1669, was reappointed captain-general of the sea to take command of Venice's reentry into war with the Turks.

Some four years after Morosini's death Giovanni Graziani (*Joannes Gratianus Bergomensis*) published a detailed biography entitled *Francisci Mauroceni Peloponnesiaci, Venetiarum principis, gesta*, Padua, 1698. Antonio Arrighi has also written a biography of Morosini (in Latin), which was brought out at Padua in 1749. We have already made several references to both Graziani and Arrighi. There is a modern biography by Gino Damerini, *Morosini*, Milan, 1929, which we have also cited. Although Damerini provides no footnotes, his work seems to be based on the old Venetian historians listed in his bibliography (Alessandro Locatelli, Pierantonio Pacifici, Pio Tebaldi, Michele Foscarini, *et al.*).

[3] The facts are well known, and have been frequently recounted (cf. von Hammer-Purgstall, *Gesch. d. osman. Reiches*, VI [Pest, 1830, repr. Graz, 1963], 443, trans. Hellert, XII [1838], 160; Romanin, *Storia documentata di Venezia*, 3rd ed., VII [1974], 339; Zinkei-

The Russians might have been effective helpmates, but Moscow was in near chaos during the minority of Peter I and the regency of his half-sister Sophia. Also the Porte was making every effort to pacify and reassure the Russians. The German princes, however, as well as Cosimo III de' Medici, the Hospitallers, and others soon showed their willingness to support the Christian cause against the Turks by contributing (or leasing) the services of their soldiers and seamen to the multiple forces of the Holy League. Bavarian and Hanoverian troops were to be found in the Christian ranks in both Hungary and the Morea. The Turks thus had to face the Poles in Podolia, the Austrians and their allies in Hungary and Transylvania, and the Venetians in Dalmatia, continental Greece, and the Morea.

Although John III Sobieski, along with Charles V of Lorraine and their German allies, had broken the Turkish siege of Vienna, Sobieski did not succeed in rewinning Podolia. After his death, however, it was reassigned to the Poles in the peace of Karlowitz (in 1699), and remained a part of Poland until the second partition (in 1793). Sobieski had had too many problems in Poland to campaign successfully against the Turks, who always found strong support in the Crimean Tatars. The imperialists, on the other hand, seemed to be marching from victory to victory, taking Visegrád on the Danube after a five days' siege (on 18 June 1684) and defeating the Turks near Waitzen (Vác) on 27 June. The imperialists soon occupied Waitzen, some miles east of Visegrád. Upper Hungary was falling into Christian hands.

On 23 July (1684) Charles V of Lorraine wrote the Emperor Leopold of a "gloriosissima vittoria" which the Christian forces had achieved over the Turks "yesterday on the feast of S. Maria Maddalena." Having got word of the whereabouts of the Ottoman army under the command of one Suleiman Pasha, Charles left behind all his infantry and part of the cavalry to the extent they were required to continue the siege of Buda. With the rest of the cavalry, a thousand infantry under the command of Count Franz Karl von Auersperg, and some fifteen hundred Hungarians, Charles went off to meet Suleiman's army, which was then encamped on the height of Ercsi, a small market town on the Danube nineteen miles south of Buda. All night they marched. At the break of day they were within half an hour of the enemy's camp. The Turks emerged from the camp, drawing up for their defense. For four hours they tried to outflank Charles's squadrons, but in vain.

---

sen, *Gesch. d. osman. Reiches*, V, 113–14; Heinrich Kretschmayr, *Gesch. von Venedig*, III [Stuttgart, 1934, repr. Aalen, 1964], 342–43). On the entry of Venice into the Holy League, see also the work of the Venetian noble Nicola Beregani, *Historia delle guerre d'Europa dalla comparsa dell'armi Ottomane nell'Hungheria l'anno 1683*, 2 vols., Venice, 1698, I, bk. III, pp. 88–89, and esp. bk. IV, pp. 110–11, 125–36. Beregani also provides us with a well-informed account of Kara Mustafa Pasha's siege and the failure at Vienna (*ibid.*, I, bks. I–III, pp. 14–82, 91–92).

Finally, thanks to heaven, we threw the Turkish army into the greatest confusion, pursuing them, and this can be compared to the liberation of Vienna, since
all the enemy's camp has been left in our possession, all the tents, barracks,
baggage, cannon, foodstuffs, and munitions. More than four thousand Turks
have been done away with, a large number wounded, and two thousand janissaries all killed. Besides, we have the great standard [*bandiera*], which the Gran
Sultano confers upon the grand viziers to denote their command as general, as
well as the pavilion of the serasker [Suleiman Pasha], who was commanding their
army. Prince Ludwig von Baden has pursued the enemy with two regiments of
cavalry for the space of two hours, and acquired some cannon. Also the Hungarians and Prince [Jerome] Lubomirski's Poles pursued the Turks even farther. I
cannot praise enough to your imperial Majesty the great perseverance of all your
cavalry as well as that of all your officers who took part in this engagement, for
which credit must be attributed to His Divine Majesty. . . .[4]

At Regensburg on 15 August (1684) a treaty or rather an armistice was
finally agreed to by emissaries of the Emperor Leopold I and Louis XIV,
confirmed by the latter at Versailles two weeks later and on the same day
(28 August) by Leopold at Vienna.[5] Whatever a treaty with Louis XIV
might be worth in the long run, it was reassuring at least for the time
being, and Charles V of Lorraine continued the imperialist campaign
against the Turks. Despite his recent victories, however, he was unable
to take Buda (Ofen) in the late summer and early autumn of 1684. Nevertheless, another year lay ahead.

After the doge and Senate recalled Giovanbattista Donà from the bailaggio in Istanbul (in 1683), there was to be no Venetian bailie on the
Bosporus for the next seventeen years. We depend largely upon the
dispatches sent by the bailies to the Signoria for our knowledge of what
was going on in the streets and behind the scenes at the so-called Sublime Porte. No bailies, however, did not mean no news. Other envoys,
rarely so well informed as the Venetian bailies and dragomans, sent reports home to their governments with information often as valuable as it
was interesting. Thus a year after the failure of the Turkish siege of
Vienna, Lord James Chandos, the English ambassador to the Porte, sent
the English secretary of state a long account (dated at Pera on 3 September 1684) of conditions in Istanbul and elsewhere in the Ottoman
Empire.

---

[4] An Italian translation of Charles of Lorraine's letter to the Emperor Leopold appears as
the *Relatione del signor duca di Lorena a sua Maestà Cesarea della vittoria ultima
contro Turchi sotto li 23 Luglio 1684*, in MS. Marc. It. VII, 656 (7791), fols. 54–55, dated
"dal campo vicino a Buda. . . ." On the Turkish defeat, cf. von Hammer-Purgstall, *Gesch.
d. osman. Reiches*, VI, 438, trans. Hellert, XII, 152.
[5] Dumont, *Corps universel diplomatique*, VII-2 (1731), no. XLVII, pp. 81–83. The armistice was supposed to last for twenty years.

Chandos makes much the same observations concerning Sultan Mehmed IV as other governmental agents and travelers to Istanbul:

This Gran Signore by the violent death of his father [Ibrahim] coming to his Empire almost in his infancy hath ere since bin nursed and cajoled in all sorts of effeminacy in so much that he delights in nothing more than his Harem or Women's Company and hunting as they call it, and it hath bin the subtilty of all his cheife visirs (mayor[s] of the Pallace-like) to keep him in the greatest ignorance of all his important affairs. . . . His new visir Azem hath bin for neare forty dayes (or rather hath counterfeited himself so to be) in a sick and dying condition, but now his maske being off, he appeares out of all danger; that which put him in a panic feare was 4,000 mutinous sefferlees who, wanting their pay, demanded no lesse than the visir's head for satisfaction, but were appeas'd againe with 25 dollars a man. . . .

The Turks had heard so much bad news

that [the sultan] is now groane allmost out of patience with it, for indeed ere since their great overthrow before Vienna their hearts have bin more than halfe conquer'd and broke, their fortune and conduct growing every day weaker and weaker insomuch that this Empire is for certaine at this day in as tottering and ruinous a condition as can possibly be imagined.

Chandos found it too much to provide the English secretary of state with a detailed record of

the many great and small victory's the Germans have had over the Turks, and the Poles against both Turkes and Tartars, and the many places th'one and th'other have taken from them, and the great ravage and spoile the Venetians have made in the Morea and on severall considerable Islands. . . . In generall I doe assure you I have not heard that the Christians have missed being victorious in all their attempts on and rancounters with the Turks. . . .

The Turks were indeed in a bad way, for

at present [in early September 1684] the Germans are besieging Buda with a powerful army, the Poles Caminietz [Kamenets-Podolski, onetime capital of Podolia], both masters of the feild, and so like to continue . . . , for the Turks have no where a body of men capable to looke either of them in the face, nor is it possible for the Turks to remedy it, for before they shall be able to raise men and bring them together the summer will be over so that in all probability Buda and Caminietz must fall into the Christians' hands, the consequence whereof is no lesse than all the Kingdome of Hungary to his Caesarean Majesty and the recovery of the better part of the Kingdome of Poland to that king with an addition of Moldavia and Valachia, etc., and yet the Turkes struggle all they can to prevent these misfortunes, the Gran Signore now doing that which never [a] Gran Signore did before him, which is to presse men with a halter, hanging those immediately up that refuse to serve him in his warres, and on the other hand he hath doubled the pay of his Janizary's and Spahis, and yet all in vaine, for his men are so terrify'd and dismay'd that they runne as fast from the warres as they are hauled to it, tho' death is in the case if they are taken flying from their colors.

Chandos was well aware of the fact, however, that the war of the Holy League was not confined to land, for

the Venetians gaule the Turks most sorely by sea, exposing their weake and blind side to all the world, with their powerful armada, for the truth is the Turks are so contemptibly weake at sea that they have not so many as ten men of warre in all the world ready to put to sea to help themselfes, nor seamen to man two of their men of warre, so that the Venetians are patrones of the sea and at liberty to attempt what islands they please. All the Turks aime at in this case is to have fifty or sixty light, nimble galleys that shall outsaile and row the Venetians' galleys with which they fly and steale provisions into what places they think fitt.

In concluding his dispatch, Chandos tried to look into the future and to assess the Ottoman lot, "kismet," in Europe:

My opinion is that the Gran Signore will endeavor his uttmost for a peace with the Christians, nay rather than faile he will buy it with great concessions and money to boot, but if he cannot prevaile, he will bring all the force and power he is able into the feild next summer and have a faire pull for all. If he succeeds, all he lost the two years before will be recover'd. If he miscarry's, all he hath in Europe will be for certaine lost, how ere he faires for the rest.[6]

The war had its ups and downs. For the Turks there were mostly downs. They did recover Waitzen (Vác), but the imperialists under Lorraine with Polish, Bavarian, Hanoverian, Franconian, and other German troops raised the Turkish siege of Esztergom (Gran) on 16 August 1685. Three days later the Christians stormed the fortress town of Nové Zámky (Neuhäusel), where they slaughtered the Turkish garrison.[7] The Christian success at Nové Zámky was celebrated throughout Europe. The imperialist forces also did irreparable damage to the Turks on the

---

[6] Public Record Office (PRO), State Papers (SP) 97, XX, fol. 5, dispatch dated 3 September 1684.

[7] See especially the *Relazione sincera e reale di quanto è occorso nelli regni di Ungheria, Croazia, Schiavonia, ed altri confini de' Turchi, etc., durante la campagna dell'anno 1685, compresavi non solo la battaglia di Strigonia* [i.e., Gran, Esztergom] *e la presa di Neuheusel* [Nové Zámky], *ma anco quella di Coron in Morea . . .* , Vienna, Austria, 1685, published by Gio. Van Ghelen, *stampatore academico,* who wrote a preface to this work, which covers in minute detail the battle at Esztergom, the seizure of Nové Zámky, and Francesco Morosini's occupation of Coron (*ibid.,* pp. 41ff.), to which we shall come later. There is a good map of the siege of Esztergom (*Strigonie*) in Henri Marczali, "Relation du siège de Vienne et de la campagne en Hongrie, 1683," *Revue de Hongrie,* III (1909), pp. 288–89.

Croatian borders. Their success in Upper Hungary was such that the Turks abandoned several strategic sites, including Waitzen, to which they now set fire. While seeking to disarm the Russians in every way, the Turks turned for support to their old friends, the French.

Louis XIV's ambassador at the Porte, M. de Guilleragues,[8] had finally been accorded the "honor of the sofa," which meant that, when received by the grand vizir, he would sit with the latter on the raised floor or divan (leewan), and not be placed at a lower level than the vizir's sofa, to which indignity Kara Mustafa Pasha had reduced Guilleragues's predecessor, M. de Nointel.[9] Shortly before his death Guilleragues also secured an ambassadorial exemption from customs duties. The French were afforded some measure of defense against the Barbary corsairs as well as assistance in the recovery of goods seized by the latter. Among other concessions granted by the Porte, Louis XIV was recognized as protector of the sacred sites in Palestine.

The Turks were dealing gently with the Russians. They wanted peace, and they needed it. When, however, after the fall of Nové Zámky the serasker Ibrahim Pasha sent his emissary Ahmed Chelebi to the imperial commander Charles V of Lorraine with overtures for peace, to which Charles did not reply, Ibrahim was executed at Belgrade for treason. Kara Mustafa's successor as grand vizir, Kara Ibrahim, who had been as ineffective as he was "black," lost the sofa in his turn, and had been exiled to the island of Rhodes, where he was put to death in December 1685. The next grand vizir and serasker Suleiman Pasha, a Bosnian, who was hardly abler than his immediate predecessors, now set about in devious ways to try to repair the military, financial, diplomatic, and political errors of the two Karas.

In May 1686 Suleiman Pasha set out again for Hungary to take command of the frightened Ottoman forces. He sent urgent messages to the khan of the Tatars, who had not yet appeared for the current campaign, as well as to the pashas of Temesvár (Timişoara), Székesfehérvár (Stuhlweissenburg), and Osijek (Eszék, Esseg). Despite his alleged efforts to reorganize the various divisions of the Turkish troops in Hungary, his attempts to break the imperialists' eleven-week siege of Buda (from 18 June to 2 September 1686) were utterly futile. Charles of Lorraine, the young elector Max Emmanuel of Bavaria, and other Christian notables present at the siege were determined to take Buda, the "key to the Ottoman empire," and so they did, with a long night of pillage and

---

[8] Gabriel Joseph de Lavergne, viscount of Guilleragues, died at Istanbul on 5 March 1685.

[9] As stated above, Charles Marie François Ollier, marquis d'Angervilliers et de Nointel, was the French ambassador to the Porte from 1671 to 1679.

slaughter. The Turks had held Buda for almost a century and a half. Certainly a new era seemed to have begun in east, central Europe.[10]

Despite the Turks' long occupation of Buda, one finds today almost no evidence in the streets and squares of the city to attest to their presence. There is one notable exception, however, i.e., the little tomb (*türbe*) of Gül Baba, a famous member of the mendicant Bektashi Order, who is said to have died in Buda on 2 September 1541, the very day that Sultan Suleiman made his triumphal entry into the city.[11] Gül Baba's tomb now stands in a small garden on the southeastern slope of Rose Hill. It was built between 1543 and 1548, and entirely restored in 1962. Apparently every Turk who comes to Budapest today pays a visit to the tomb of Gül Baba, whom Suleiman is alleged to have called "the guardian of Buda."

Székesfehérvár (Stuhlweissenburg) was also taken from the Turks. This came about in mid-May 1688, as recorded by an inscription (*Alba Regalis recuperata 9/19 Mai 1688*) in the center of the city at an entrance to what was the old wall—on Népköztársaság Útja—behind which lie the extensive remains of ancient Roman Alba Regia. A fountain with the dates 1001, 1688, and 1938 in Szabadság Tér stands in commemoration of S. Stephen and the renewals of the city's liberty. Another large plaque on a wall bears the dates 1543–1688, the years of Turkish domination in Széskesfehérvár.[12] One of the oldest and most important cities in Hungary, it stood at the crossroads of the western part of the kingdom, as shown today in striking fashion by the large topographical layout in the Military Museum on Castle Hill in Budapest. Yes, there are reminders of the Turks in present-day Hungary.

---

[10] On the Christian offensive against the Turks from October 1683 until September 1686 (after Kara Mustafa Pasha's defeat by John Sobieski and Charles of Lorraine under the walls of Vienna on 12 September 1683), see (among various other works) von Hammer-Purgstall, *Gesch. d. osman. Reiches*, VI (1830, repr. 1963), 420–76, trans. Hellert, XII (1838), 126–207; Zinkeisen, *Gesch. d. osman. Reiches*, V, 110–24; Onno Klopp, *Das Jahr 1683 und der folgende grosse Türkenkrieg bis zum Frieden von Carlowitz 1699*, Graz, 1882, pp. 338–406; E. Eickhoff and R. Eickhoff, *Venedig, Wien und die Osmanen*, Munich, 1970, pp. 408ff.

The siege of Buda (Ofen) had been hard and costly, but the determined efforts of Charles of Lorraine and his German allies were crowned with startling success on 2 September (1686), as described by Nicola Beregani, *Historia delle guerre d'Europa*, 2 vols., Venice, 1698, II, bk. III, pp. 107–29, 146–47; cf. Paul Wentzcke, *Feldherr d. Kaisers: Leben und Taten Herzog Karls V. von Lothringen*, Leipzig, 1943, pp. 251–78, and note von Hammer-Purgstall, VI, 474–76, 736–38, trans. Hellert, XII, 205–7, 511–14.

Needless to say, the loss of Buda dismayed the Ottoman court, as shown by the *Lamento di Mehemet IV., regnante imperatore de' Turchi, per la perdita fatta della Real Città di Buda nell'Ongaria e della maggior parte del fertilissimo Regno di Morea, occupato dalle forze della Serenissima Republica Veneta* . . . , printed in Venice by Giuseppe Tramontin in October(?) 1686. As seen in Venice, the Christian success at Buda was a victory of the "Lega contro gli Ottomani," which indeed it was.

[11] Cf. Setton, *Papacy and the Levant*, III (1984), 459.

[12] *Ibid.*, III (1984), 472, 479, and IV, 697, 1102.

The Venetians were kept well informed by frequent reports from Ragusa (Dubrovnik). Odd and fragmentary as some of these *avvisi* are, they reflect the current news upon which both the imperial government and the Venetian Signoria sometimes had to base their decisions. Also these *avvisi* have never been published, and (as far as I know) they seem never to have been used; in any event the Venetian Senate regarded them as important enough to be entered into their official records. Thus letters from Ragusa dated 26 October 1686, which apparently reached Venice on or just before 13 November, brought the news that entire families of Turks were fleeing from Belgrade, taking with them in boats going down the Danube their most valuable possessions. Terror reigned among the Turks in Bosnia and the Herzegovina. The messenger whom the grand vizir Suleiman Pasha had sent to Sultan Mehmed IV "con la nuova della caduta di Buda" had returned with a "catiscerif," ordering Suleiman to "hold on to what remains." According to the letters from Ragusa, the sultan had removed from office the grand mufti who had given Kara Mustafa Pasha the fetva or authorization to attack the Christian emperor "contrary to the disposition of their laws, inasmuch as he [had] asked for peace."[13]

The Ragusei lived on a precipice. The Turks might easily have pushed them over the edge, but they never did. The Porte preferred the annual tribute and the various imposts which they levied upon the Ragusei (at not infrequent intervals) to the possession of another half-dead city, of which they had too many. Although rivals in the trading depots of the Levant, the Venetians and the Ragusei had generally maintained friendly relations. Fear of the Turks had helped to keep them at peace with each other. The Ragusei were thrilled by the imperialists' victories in Hungary and by those of the Venetians in the Morea. If, conceivably, the Venetians could clear the Turks and the Barbary corsairs out of the Adriatic, Ragusan life and commerce might begin anew. In letters of July 1686 the rector and councilors of Ragusa gave eloquent expression to their devotion to Venice and to their high hopes for the continued success of the Holy League "con gloriose imprese contro il commune nemico."[14]

---

[13] ASV, Senato, Deliberationi Costantinopoli (Secreta), Reg. 35, fol. 67ᵛ [165ᵛ], *avvisi* reported in Venice on 13 November 1686, based upon letters from Ragusa of 26 October, and cf., *ibid.,* Reg. 42, *portano le lettere da Ragusa delli 26 Ottobre 1686,* a defective copy confusing the *Re* (the sultan) with a *Bè* (a bey).

[14] Senato, Delib. Costantinopoli (Secreta), Reg. 35, fols. 63ᵛff. [161ᵛff.], docs. dated July 1686, in which the Ragusei protested their friendship and loyalty to Venice—"quell'inalterabile et humilissima divotione, che dal corso di tanti secoli sempre li eccellentissimi Rettore e Consigliari dell'eccellentissima Republica di Ragusa . . . hanno proffessato alla Maestà di questa Serenissima Republica, anima il loro proffondissimo ossequio a sperare dalla regia mano della Serenità vostra [the doge Marc'Antonio Giustinian] la continuatione di quelle gratie che al mantenimento della loro libertà hanno sempre conosciute dirette.

Facing setbacks everywhere in Hungary and in the Morea, the Turks had already had recourse to various subterranean ways of seeking peace. If they could stop Morosini from going too far in the Morea and in continental Greece—for in the past the Venetians had usually been anxious for peace and trade with the Porte—they could concentrate on the recovery of their losses in Hungary. This seems to lie behind a letter sent to the Venetian noble (and erstwhile bailie) Giovanbattista Donà by a confidant in the Turkish subcapital of Adrianople (Edirne). The letter is dated as early as 3 March 1685. Its contents were serious enough to be brought to the attention of the Senate, which directed Donà to say no more in reply than "I have received your letter of the 3rd of last March, and having studied the contents thereof, I must tell you that, because of the laws of this government, it is forbidden to private citizens to meddle in these affairs and to continue with such communications. I shall therefore make no reply to other such letters as may come to me. I must make this known to you, and I wish you well."[15]

On 18 July (1686) the Venetian Senate passed a motion, prepared as usual in the Collegio, to request the Capi of the Council of Ten to make proper provision in Venice for the young Antonio Olivieri "because of the long service rendered by his father as dragoman of the Turkish language in Constantinople." Antonio, who was himself proficient in Turkish (a *giovine di lingua*), had also been a faithful servitor of the state, and he was now in Venice "per li successi della guerra presente." In due time, however, he would presumably return to the Bosporus to serve Venice at the Porte.[16]

Not yet, however, for the war went on, to the continued joy and astonishment of Christendom. After the imperialists' acquisition of Buda, they advanced to take Simontornya in west-central Hungary and, of more importance, Siklós and Fünfkirchen (Pécs) in the south. Szeged, also in southern Hungary at the juncture of the Theiss (Tisza) and Maros (Mureş) rivers, yielded to the force of Christian arms after a siege of some three weeks. The grand vizir Suleiman Pasha took up his winter quarters in Belgrade, and the commander of the Tatars did so at Temesvár, about seventy-five miles northeast of Suleiman's encampment. Since the Christians showed no interest in the peace feelers which Suleiman extended to Hermann, the margrave of Baden, president of the

---

. . . : S'assicuri vostra Serenità che non può esser maggiore nè l'infinita nostra devotione nè più intento il desiderio che habbiamo di vedere colmate le glorie della Serenissima Republica con tutte le maggiori felicità, e che la Sacrosanta Lega sempre più s'avvanzi con gloriose imprese contro il commune nemico . . ." (*ibid.*, fol. 64ᵛ).

[15] Senato, Deliberationi Costantinopoli (Secreta), Reg. 35, fol. 63 [161], doc. dated 8 June, 1686.

[16] Senato, Delib. Costantinopoli (Secreta), Reg. 35, fol. 63 [161], doc. dated "1686, a 18 Luglio in Pregadi."

imperial war council (*Hofkriegsrat*), the Turks began preparations on a grand scale for continuance of the war in 1687.[17]

On or just before 1 March (1687) a Ragusan vessel, a *marciliana,* brought to Venice letters from Istanbul dated the preceding 8 January. As soon as the letters arrived, the secretary of the Ragusan envoy to the Signoria brought them to the door of the Sala del Collegio in the Doges' Palace. These letters confirmed the reports which had already reached Venice of a revolt in Istanbul against Sultan Mehmed IV and the kislar- agà or chief of the black eunuchs. The rebels were bent upon taking the lives of both of them as a consequence of the fetva of the grand mufti, reproving the sultan for having lost the most important fortresses in the Ottoman empire. The grand mufti had also chided Mehmed for having given himself over entirely to the pleasures of the chase. The kislaragà was upbraided for having spent his time accumulating treasures while letting the interests of the Ottoman monarchy lapse into disaster. It is not, however, clear what the kislaragà could do in a society dominated at this time by grand vizirs, pashas, aghas of the janissaries, and other military figures at the Porte.

It was being said that the Gran Signore, to try to avoid the impending danger, had taken a solemn oath to abandon the futile sport of hunting. In order to assure the people of his good intentions Mehmed had had all his dogs killed, and had given the necessary orders for the massing of troops throughout all Turkish territory in Europe, *in tutta Rumelia.* To save his hide the kislaragà made a show of contributing all his available funds to help meet the costs of the war, "and has sent into Anatolia to raise troops."

The people in Istanbul had written Mustafa Köprülü Pasha, son of the rugged old grand vizir Mehmed (1656–1661) and brother of the latter's adept successor Ahmed. Mustafa was then serving as serasker at the Dardanelles. The populace wanted him to come to Istanbul to take over the reins of government, but since their letter did not bear the sultan's seal (*reggio sigillo*), he replied with exhortations for them to calm down. In due time he would assuredly come, he said, but they must keep within the limits of allegiance to the state and the confines of the law.

It was also reported that the messenger sent by the Gran Signore to Sulaimān I, the shah of Persia, brought back word that "when Babylon had been restored to him, he might be induced to assist him, but that otherwise, when the war with the Christians was over, his objective would be to get back that fortress which belonged to his domain of old." The Turks were sinking into a sea of troubles. Although they appeared to be preparing "militie grandi" for the coming campaign, "non si vede-

---

[17] Von Hammer-Purgstall, *Gesch. d. osman. Reiches,* VI, 476, trans. Hellert, XII, 207–8, and cf. Zinkeisen, *Gesch. d. osman. Reiches,* V, 124–25.

vano provisione di vettovaglia." There were no provisions in sight. The grand vizir Suleiman Pasha was basing his hopes largely on the help of the Tatars. He had sent one of his dervishes to the great khan to get him to make every possible effort to amass troops and push forward with them quickly.[18]

The Ragusan envoy in Venice was keeping the Signoria abreast of what was happening among the Turks. Although the Ragusei prided themselves upon their independence, which they skillfully maintained for centuries, they were almost subjects of the Porte, and were always knowledgeable when it came to Turkish affairs. They knew what was going on in Belgrade as well as in Istanbul. On or just before 29 March (1687) the Ragusan envoy turned over to the Venetian Collegio letters sent from the grand vizir Suleiman Pasha's headquarters at Belgrade. The letters were dated 23 February, and brought the news that two weeks before (on 10 February) a certain Mehmed Agha, whom Suleiman had tried to send to the Hapsburg court with proposals for peace, had just returned to Belgrade.

Suleiman had addressed his letters to the Emperor Leopold I, and although Mehmed Agha was courteously received by the imperialist general Donat Johann Heissler at Dobrodzień (Guttentag) in Upper Silesia and by his colleague Antonio Carafa at Eperjes (Prešov) in eastern Slovakia, he was not allowed to go on to Vienna. Since the letters Mehmed carried were not written by the Gran Signore, Carafa informed him, he could not carry them to the imperial court. Inasmuch as it was the grand vizir who had sent Mehmed, however, the latter could discuss his mission with Carafa "as if with the vizir of his imperial Majesty."

Having turned over the grand vizir's letters to Carafa, Mehmed Agha had been obliged to wait for a reply. In the meantime the grand vizir had sent other letters from somewhere below "Varadino" (Grosswardein, Nagyvárad, now Oradea). In response to the Turkish overtures Carafa informed Mehmed that if the Turks were longing for peace, the Gran Signore must himself write the Emperor Leopold, and have a pasha convey his letters directly from the Porte to Vienna. These letters must be subscribed by the grand vizir, the agha of the janissaries, the spahilar agasi, and the other military commanders, and then it might be possible to negotiate treaties of peace.

The imperialist letters which Mehmed Agha took back to the grand vizir Suleiman Pasha seemed unlikely to lead to a cessation of hostilities.

---

[18] Senato, Delib. Costantinopoli (Secreta), Reg. 35, fols. 68–69ʳ [166–167ʳ], doc. dated 1 March 1687, which text may also be found *ibid.*, Reg. 42. The *marciliana*, i.e., *marcigliana*, referred to in the text, was a vessel common in the later sixteenth and seventeenth centuries. Equipped with both square and lateen (triangular) sails, it was still seen in the Adriatic in the later nineteenth century (cf. the *Dizionario di marina medievale e moderno*, Rome: Reale Accademia d'Italia, 1937, p. 435).

They required "that if the Turks desired peace, they must surrender to the emperor all the fortresses in the kingdom of Hungary, the fortress of Kamenets-Podolski to King John Sobieski along with the entire province of Podolia, and the kingdom of Candia to the most serene Republic of Venice."

The grand vizir was alleged to have summoned the agha of the janissaries, the spahilar agasi, and other commanders to a meeting of the war council. They apparently all agreed (*con voti universali*) that peace was essential, and affixed their signatures and seals to a statement which they intended to send to Carafa. Some of those present, however, advised that they await the sultan's decision (*un reggio catiscerif*). Thereupon they designated a pasha with the dignity of two horsetails (*di due tuii*) to take such an answer to the Christian encampment at Eperjes (Prešov). Considering the later attitude of the war council, this report seems more than doubtful.

A monk who had arrived in Belgrade from Moscow reported that the "grand duke"—Sophia Aleksyeevna, the half-sister of Peter I, was then ruling Russia—was gathering a large army to move against the Turks, "and that the khan of the Tatars was excusing himself for not being able to serve the vizir in the next campaign, being compelled to guard his own frontiers." At Belgrade the word now was that general Heissler had put to flight a troop of Tatars and Turks. The troop had been serving with Imre Thököly, the pro-Turkish aspirant to the throne of Hungary, to guard a baggage train of provisions and munitions intended for Erlau (Eger, Agria).

The grand vizir was reported to be putting in order the mint at Belgrade, which had not yet begun to produce coinage. He was causing trouble for himself as well as for merchants and artisans, for he had already corrupted coinage at the Porte (as we are told) by adding forty ounces of copper to every hundred ounces of silver.[19]

The Ragusei kept feeding the Venetian Signoria reports and rumors. Details might be wrong, as we have noted, but the general tenor of the news bulletins (*avvisi*) that they passed on usually proved to be accurate. There is often some truth in the talk of the town. Letters from Belgrade dated 10 April (1687) brought word that the grand vizir Suleiman Pasha had sent the aforesaid Mehmed Agha, now called Mehmed

---

[19] Senato, Delib. Costantinopoli (Secreta), Reg. 35, fol. 69 [167], doc. dated 29 March 1687, which text may also be found, *ibid.*, Reg. 42. On the career of Donat Johann Heissler, note the *Allgemeine Deutsche Biographie,* XI (1880, repr. Berlin, 1969), 671–72, and on Antonio Carafa, see the account of G. Benzoni, in the *Dizionario biografico degli Italiani,* XIX (1976), 485–94, with a full bibliography relating to Carafa's career. On Suleiman Pasha's corruption of the Ottoman coinage, cf. von Hammer-Purgstall, *Gesch. d. osman. Reiches,* VI, 467, trans. Hellert, XII, 194.

Pasha, to the general Carafa for the second time in an effort to make peace,

but the [Turkish] ministers clearly placed slight hope in such negotiations, and the vizir himself was making quite a show of the diligence he was exercising to amass troops for the battlefield. Sermons were being preached every day in the encampments of the ablest troops, encouraging them all to fight courageously for Mohammed and to free themselves once for all from the Christians' oppression or to give their lives in the effort to do so.

It was being bruited about in Belgrade that within six days Suleiman Pasha would have

to exhibit the *tuì,* that is the horsetail, the signal for his departure, and after another fifteen days, as soon as the troops arrive, which they say are expected to be numerous, [he would have] to get the tents and pavilions ready for the march. Letters from Constantinople dated 14 March bring the news that the kaïmakam [Redjeb Pasha] was preparing troops and munitions to help the grand vizir.

In fact the kaïmakam Redjeb Pasha had issued such rigorous orders for the recruitment of troops in Anatolia that if and when they were fully carried out, "those realms would remain deserted." Word was spreading abroad in the Turkish capital that the next campaign was going to end the war either to the advantage of the Turks or to the total destruction of the Ottoman empire. Officials at the Porte were saying that the ten galleys and thirty ships which had been armed in the Arsenal at Istanbul were to be united with the thirty ships from the Barbary coast "in order to meet the fleet of the most serene Republic of Venice."

The Venetian captain-general Francesco Morosini, to whom we shall come presently, had been doing almost unbelievably well both on land and at sea. At any rate word had come to the Bosporus that the Turks had managed to get aid in the form of money and provisions into Kamenets, which should help protect the stronghold against the rising aspirations of the Poles.[20] As usual in the *avvisi,* the news came piece by piece. Although the surviving archival texts, dispatches and *avvisi,* do not provide us with the smooth, literary continuity of the contemporary and later chroniclers, they usually furnish us with firsthand, reliable data, uncolored by the chroniclers' brushes. To be sure, they are not always wholly reliable (what sources are?), but they tend to be more factual and objective in content than the work of the chroniclers who have had time to mull over the consequences of this event or that.

---

[20] Senato, Delib. Costantinopoli (Secreta), Reg. 35, fols. 70^v–71^r [168^v–169^r], doc. dated 7 and 9 May, 1687, according to an *avviso* transmitted to the Venetian Signoria by the Ragusei in "le lettere di Belgradi delli 10 Aprile." On the kaïmakam Redjeb Pasha (*Redscheb*), note von Hammer-Purgstall, *Gesch. d. osman. Reiches,* VI, 477–78, 493–95, trans. Hellert, XII, 208–10, 233–37.

About mid-June (1687) one Zuanne Vincenzi delivered to the Venetian Collegio in the name of the Ragusei further letters, one in Turkish
accompanied by a translation. The grand vizir Suleiman Pasha was still
at Belgrade. According to reports of 27 May he then had at his command
60,000 troops, although the Turks were contending that his army far
exceeded that figure. They claimed that he had 30,000 troops with him,
and that there were 15,000 Tatars in the "fields of Sriem" (Srem) commanded by the son of the Great Khan. Furthermore, they maintained
15,000 Turks were quartered in the villages of "Samun" beyond the
Sava, while troops were continually coming in from Istanbul. It was
alleged that the kulkiaya or lieutenant-general of the janissaries was
expected with 25,000 foot, which suggested an addendum of some thousands of soldiers to the grand vizir's forces. Foodstuffs, however, were in
short supply in the area between Belgrade and Esseg, and so the vizir
would have to bring them from Belgrade.

At the grand vizir's court it was said that, first of all, the Turks would
try to help Eger (Erlau), which was entirely without supplies of any kind.
The vizir had apparently decided upon two avenues of approach to Erlau
without identifying either one of them. It was also being said that when
the vizir had got the Ottoman army into the fields of Srem, he planned to
cut the bridges to force the soldiery into combat.

Upon the return of Mehmed Agha to Belgrade five days before (on 22
May) with letters from Hermann von Baden and the general Antonio
Carafa, word soon got abroad that the Emperor Leopold's demands entailed, as we know, the return of the so-called kingdom of Candia to
Venice, Podolia to the Polish king, and all the fortresses in Hungary to
the Hapsburgs. If the Porte wished to continue to hold Belgrade, it must
pay tribute. The grand vizir had the imperialist letters read to the council
of his *capi di guerra* who, angered by the pretensions of von Baden and
Carafa, were now reported to have sworn with tears in their eyes to rid
themselves of these Christian vexations with scimitar in hand and no
sparing of bloodshed.

The grand vizir declared that during the first days of the new moon,
which would be about 9 June, he ought to have the army move into the
fields of Esseg (Osijek). He had gone there on 24 May with the agha of
the janissaries [Mustafa Pasha of Rodosto] and the defterdar [Esseïd
Mustafa Pasha] to pick out the best places for his encampment. Although
the vizir was putting on a good front, and appeared to be full of courageous resolutions, it was clear that he was suffering an inner consternation, "which one also observes in all his other leaders."[21]

The grand vizir Suleiman Pasha now wrote the Ragusei, from whom he

---

[21] Senato, Delib. Costantinopoli (Secreta), Reg. 35, fol. 72 [170], doc. dated 19 and 21
June 1687.

had just received a dispatch which the Ragusan envoy Marino Caboga had delivered to him. In his reply Suleiman stated that he had had the Venetian dragoman write a letter for him to the *signori di Venetia*, obviously with suggestions of peace. Having received no reply to the letter, he blamed the Ragusei for failing to see to its delivery. He was well aware, he said, that this was not the consequence of the Ragusei's negligence, reminding them that the Turks' loss of a few fortresses did not in any way indicate the diminution of the Ottoman empire. It was merely taking a few drops of water from the sea. Obviously he wanted the Ragusei to bear in mind the power and extent of the Ottoman empire. The Venetians, deceived by the governmental instability of a year or two, had embarked upon their enterprise of conquest with "untimely indecision" (*irressolutione immatura*), contrary to their usual practice. He seemed to have no doubt that the Venetians would pay the price of their rashness.

If after the death of the late grand vizir Mustafa Pasha, the Venetians had come forward with the claim "our money has been taken from us," and their request for its return had been rejected by the Porte, Suleiman could have understood their failure to abide by their promise of peace. Then they would not have been so severely censured but, no, they had made their hostility manifest with such arrogance that it might appear they had never enjoyed the friendship of the Sublime Porte and the advantages it had brought them. Their brazen insolence was bringing the wrath of the Almighty down upon them. If in the future the Venetians intended to continue with such ambition and hostility, one might hope that affairs would take a different course, and that the Venetians would be doubly defeated.

If the unruly Venetians gave sincere thought to renewing their friendship with the Porte, however, the most serene, invincible, and powerful sultan would certainly exercise toward those people, who were the servants of God, his clemency and grace. As for the Ragusei, they must not delay for another hour the payment of the tribute which they owed the Porte "in conformità dell'antico costume consignato al publico errario." Suleiman, therefore, instructed the Ragusan government to send another ambassador to Belgrade with the tribute so that the latter might join Marino Caboga in making the customary payment.[22] The letter seems a little confused. Did it reflect Suleiman's state of mind?

As Suleiman Pasha gave the Ragusei to understand that hard times lay

---

[22] Senato, Delib. Costantinopoli (Secreta), Reg. 35, fols. 72ᵛ–73ᵛ [170ᵛ–171ᵛ], entry made on 21 June 1687, "data nellà custodita città di Belgrado, tradotta da Giacomo Fortis, traduttione consegnata dal Vincenti." Two other versions of this letter are given, *ibid.*, fols. 73ᵛ–75ᵛ [171ᵛ–173ᵛ], in one of which "Marino" is identified as Marino Caboga. For other (Italian) translations of this text, see, *ibid.*, Reg. 42.

ahead for the imprudent Venetians, he had of course no inkling of the disaster which would soon overtake him and the Ottoman army under his command. On 12 August 1687, however, the Turks suffered a crushing defeat near the village of Darda, about five miles north of Esseg (Osijek) and directly south of Mohács, where the Turks had overwhelmed the forces of Louis II of Hungary one hundred and sixty-one years before (on 29 August 1526).[23] It was the Turks who were facing hard times, for a seven months' drought had produced famine. A small measure of grain cost two ducats. On 25 August a fire swept through Istanbul, destroying a thousand houses and three hundred and twenty-five shops. A week later (on 1 September) the fire burned down part of the Seraglio.[24]

It was not long before the imperialists took Esseg (Osijek) and Valpovo some fourteen miles to the northwest, near the Drava, terrifying the Turks in Croatia, Slavonia, and southern Hungary—not to speak (as we shall do shortly) of the Venetians' success in the Morea and in Attica. As the imperialists advanced, the Ottoman troops became rebellious, demanding the removal of the grand vizir or the deposition of the sultan. Whether Mehmed IV could survive these setbacks was a question, but very shortly it became clear that Suleiman Pasha could not.

As the imperialists approached the Turkish encampment near Peterwardein (Petrovaradin), Suleiman Pasha convened his war council, which decided to send a company of sipahis and silihdars across the Danube as a first line of defense. For two days a relentless rain poured down upon the troops, soaking them to the bone, for they had been sent out without tents or a baggage train. Lacking food and forced to bivouac in the mud, as von Hammer-Purgstall says, they gave vent to their bitter resentment of the supreme command. Upon retracing their steps to come back over the river, the sipahis and silihdars discovered that the bridge had been barricaded by order of the grand vizir who, at ease in his encampment, was leaving them stranded.

When their commander, the vizir Jafer Pasha, also returned to the

---

[23] On the Christian defeat at Mohács in 1526, cf. Setton, *The Papacy and the Levant*, III (1984), 248–50, with notes on the sources, and on the dramatic victory of the Christians near Mohács in 1687, see the contemporary newsletter *Distinta e verissima Relatione della segnalata vittoria ottenuta dalle armi cesaree sotto la condotta del serenissimo duca Carlo di Lorena contro l'esercito del gran visir, combattuto e disfatto nelle vicinanze di Darda colla morte di otto mila Turchi, quantità di Schiavi, presa di tutto il bagaglio ed acquisto di cento pezzi di cannone, con altre distinte parlicolarità, seguita li 12 Agosto 1687, giorno della festività di S. Chiara*, Venice, [1687], printed by Gio. Francesco Valvasense. The battle of 12 August, in which the Turks were crushed, is sometimes called the battle of Harkány (some miles northeast of Darda). It broke the Turkish ascendancy in Hungary.

[24] Von Hammer-Purgstall, *Gesch. d. osman. Reiches,* VI, 480–81, trans. Hellert, XII, 213–14.

encampment, the troops tore down the barricades, recrossed the river, and came on toward the ornate pavilions of the high command. The grand vizir tried to appease their fury with provisions or gold. The rebels would allegedly have neither, but demanded that Suleiman Pasha surrender to them the seal and sacred standard of the grand vizirate. Dismayed by the obstreperousness of the troops, Suleiman fled to nearby Peterwardein and was soon followed, in early September (1687), by some of his chief officers, including the vizir Jafer Pasha, the defter-dar Esseïd Mustafa Pasha, and the agha of the janissaries Mustafa of Rodosto.[25]

An *avviso* from Istanbul, dated in the suburb of Pera on 17 September (1687), provides the immediate sequel to Suleiman Pasha's flight. Advised that the troops were not only on the point of revolt but had resolved to strangle him, Suleiman abandoned the army at Peterwardein, and having embarked on the Danube with a small following, he sailed down to Belgrade. From there in four or five days he reached the frontier of Wallachia where, taking post-horses, he hurried on to Adrianople (Edirne) "to await the orders of the Gran Signore." Suleiman's courier arrived in Istanbul the evening of 16 September, and departed the following morning. Some were saying that Mehmed IV had ordered Suleiman to come to Istanbul, others that an executioner had just left (on the night of 17 September) "to take his head."

Siavush Pasha had been chosen as Suleiman's successor "per capo della militia," and Mehmed had ordered the kaftan and sword to be sent to Siavush "per la sua confirmatione." In the meantime the report was circulating "that the rest of the troops are disbanding, and that the new serasker [Siavush] is in no position to offer any resistance: the mutiny, once begun, could have grave consequences!"

Furthermore, "the vessels of the Gran Signore are at Tenedos, where they claim that the aberrant recruits have mutinied; they have killed their commander, who is named Mehmed Pasha, and have wounded Marra Bey, the captain of their squadron. The kapudan pasha is at Samos with a part of the galleys."[26] The spirit of revolt was spreading. It would soon reach the capital.

The rebellious troops in the encampment near Peterwardein prepared an indictment to be sent to Sultan Mehmed, to which all the major officers subscribed. Suleiman Pasha was accused of having promised the

---

[25] Von Hammer-Purgstall, *Gesch. d. osman. Reiches*, VI, 490–91, trans. Hellert, XII, 228–30, and cf. Zinkeisen, *Gesch. d. osman. Reiches*, V, 126–28.

[26] Senato, Delib. Costantinopoli (Secreta), Reg. 35, fols. 75^v–76^r [173^v–174^r], entry in the register dated 23 October 1687: "Pera di Costantinopoli 17 Settembre 1687," which text may also be found, *ibid.*, Reg. 42.

troops three aspers at Esseg and five at Székesfehérvár (Stuhlweissenburg) to make up for their lack of victuals. He had assured the volunteers
enrolled to help relieve the siege of Buda a full twenty aspers. In each
case he had broken his word, and had then struck from the roles a large
number of soldiers on the flimsiest excuses. Various other charges were
lodged against him, notably that he had abandoned the army.

As indicated in the *avviso* of 17 September (1687), even before receiving the emissaries of the mutinous soldiery, Mehmed had confirmed
their election of Siavush Pasha as serasker, the first news of the revolt
having frightened him into submission. As usual in a political or military
turmoil among the Turks, heads began to fall. Death was meted out in the
main encampment, now under the walls of Belgrade, and on the shores of
the Bosporus. The army was moving eastward, making for Istanbul. Suleiman Pasha's head was sent to the rebels along with a letter from the
sultan, urging them not to continue on to Istanbul but to take up their
winter quarters at Sofia and at Philippopolis (Filibe, Plovdiv), for the
advance of the Christian enemy was a serious menace to the Porte. As for
the new serasker Siavush Pasha, he was soon to die at the hands of
rebellious troops in Istanbul, as he tried to defend the harem which, alas,
fell into the hands of the military mob.

Once more Mehmed IV turned to the family of the Köprülüs to help
him resolve the crisis, summoning Mustafa Pasha, the son of Mehmed
and the brother of Ahmed, from his command over the castles on the
Dardanelles. Mustafa Köprülü was named the kaïmakam, and as the in-
surgent army moved eastward from Adrianople, he summoned the
ulema, scholars of Moslem law and religion, to a meeting in the mosque
of Hagia Sophia (on 8 November 1687). There he told the silent audience that, as they all knew and as the rebels had insisted, Mehmed the
Hunter had no thought of anything but the chase. For some years he had
avoided the appointment of men capable of rectifying the defeats of the
Ottoman army and the frustrations of government.

Why, then, did the mullahs have no word to say? The Padishah must be
removed from the throne. The ulema gave its consent by continued silence, well aware that the decision had already been made. Leaving
Hagia Sophia, the assembly went to the iron-barred apartment in the
Seraglio, where princes of the house of Osman were confined. Mehmed's
elder brother Suleiman was released from his long imprisonment, and
placed upon the throne.

Suleiman II spared his worthless brother's life. Mehmed had come to
the throne as a child in 1648, as von Hammer-Purgstall says, "the play-
thing of the opposing parties of the harem and the aghas, until [Mehmed]
Köprülü's iron hand broke the back of revolt [in 1656], and for five years
paved with heads the groundwork, upon which the dominance of his

great son [Ahmed] was based for fifteen years."[27] That was a bygone era. The Ottoman empire would have to stumble along into the next century, suffering severe blows during the military hegemony of the Austrians.

The news on the Rialto was of Austrian success and Turkish dismay. Venetian participation in the anti-Turkish drive began in the summer of 1684 when (on 18 July) the fleet under the captain-general Francesco Morosini left the island of Corfu, heading for the Turkish-held island of S. Maura (Leucadia, Levkas). The Venetian forces arrived off shore on the evening of the twentieth, and on the following morning the galleys and galleasses entered the harbor on the northern end of the island under Fort S. Maura. The Turks had taken the island in 1479.[28] While the mercenaries under the command of Carlo di Strassoldo were being disembarked, the Turks made no effort to prevent or even hinder their landing. On Sunday morning, 23 July, the captain-general Morosini attacked Fort S. Maura from the sea. He had sent the Turkish garrison a letter the previous evening, threatening them with "absolute slaughter" (*l'estremo eccidio*) if in the course of that day they did not surrender the fortress.

The Turks replied that they intended to maintain the fortress for the sultan, its lawful owner, and so Morosini and Strassoldo had to go on with the operations they had just begun. On Monday, 24 July, Morosini resumed his attempt to batter the walls from the sea. He did better this time, *essendo buona calma*, "but the effect was not such as one hoped for, since there was little damage done." In fact the Turks in Fort S. Maura were encouraged, believing that the Venetian forces could cause them no more damage than the fleet had already managed to do.

Morosini now ordered a dozen pieces of heavy artillery to be put ashore, "and so our men kept at it with trenches, batteries, and mortars to shoot bombs and cannon balls, continually harassing the fortress with

---

[27] Von Hammer-Purgstall, *Gesch. d. osman. Reiches*, VI, 491–98, trans. Hellert, XII, 231–41, and cf. Zinkeisen, *Gesch. d. osman. Reiches*, V, 143–44. On the coronation of Mehmed IV's brother, Suleiman II [III], on 27 November 1687, note Nicola Beregani, *Historia delle guerre d'Europa*, II (1698), bk. VII, pp. 372–74.

[28] On the Turkish seizure of S. Maura (Leucadia) from Leonardo III Tocco, the last Christian ruler, in 1479, see K.M. Setton, *The Papacy and the Levant (1204–1571)*, 4 vols., Philadelphia: American Philosophical Society, 1976–84, II, 514–15. After elaborate ceremonies Morosini, accompanied by a large suite, had sailed with the fleet from the Lido on 10 June 1684, his first stop (on the twelfth) being the port of Rovigno (Rovinj) in Istria (Alessandro Locatelli, *Racconto historico della veneta guerra in Levante diretta dal valore del Serenissimo Principe Francesco Morosini . . . dall'anno 1684 sino all'anno 1690*, 2 vols. in one, Colonia, 1691, I, 9–12). Thereafter the fleet (or parts thereof) stopped at Lesina (Hvar), Cattaro (Kotor), Curzola (Korčula), and Corfu. On the fleet, the commanders, and the volunteers, cf. Beregani, I, bk. V, pp. 137–40. Carlo di Strassoldo was attended by his brother Niccolò, who is sometimes improperly described as "the General."

every sort of attack." Though it proved to be short-lived, the siege of S. Maura was a fatiguing venture, as the soldiers dug trenches and raised bunkers. Not the least of their difficulties was that they did not even have enough water to drink. Some days later, however, a large breach was opened in the landward wall of the fortress. Again Morosini sent the Turkish garrison a demand to give the fortress up to him. This time the Turks responded with the white flag of surrender, and one evening between 7:00 and 8:00 P.M. (*verso le 23 e mezza della sera*) their emissaries emerged to arrange the terms of the capitulation. It was agreed that they might leave the island with their wives and children, their arms, and as much baggage (but only as much) as each one could carry.

On the morning of 7 August (1684) the Turkish-held slaves came out of Fort S. Maura first, and were given their freedom. Toward midday the Turks made their exit, some of whom were embarked that same evening, while others stayed up all night waiting for their embarkation. They were gathered in the lee of Morosini's flagship to protect them from injury. On the morning of 8 August they were sent the dozen or so miles north to Prevesa (Preveza), where they did not wish to go, for the Prevesani had given them no assistance during the siege. Furthermore, as they had issued from Fort S. Maura, the Turks had received little protection from the rapacious Christian soldiers, who seized some of their black slaves, and robbed them of arms and other things. Within the fortress there was hardly a house that had escaped untouched by the showers of bombs and cannon balls that were rained upon them. Nevertheless, an eyewitness to the siege and seizure of Fort S. Maura has left us his assurance that, "fortificato in buona forma," the fortress would prove impregnable.[29] Well aware that the Venetian hold upon S. Maura would not be secure as

---

[29] *Relatione dell'acquisto di S. Maura*, in MS. Marc. It. VII, 656 (7791), fols. 31–32, which text informs us that Morosini's forces included Dalmatian *oltramarini*, Greeks, papal troops (*papalini*), Florentines, and other Italians. Girolamo Corner, Morosini's chief military and political rival (each entertaining hope of ultimate elevation to the dogate), had sailed from Corfu in early July (1684) in a vain attempt to take S. Maura before Morosini could reach the island (Francesco Muazzo, *Storia della guerra tra li Veneti e Turchi dal 1684 al 1696*, Bibl. Nazionale Marciana, MS. Ital. VII, 172 [8187], bk. I, fol. 4ᵛ). Corner's ill-advised venture was apparently costly to his reputation (cf. James M. Paton, *The Venetians in Athens [1687–1688], from the "Istoria" of Cristoforo Ivanovich*, Cambridge, Mass., 1940, pp. 48–49, with notes on pp. 93–94).

On Morosini's occupation of S. Maura, see also Locatelli, I, 53–64, and on Carlo di Strassoldo and his brother Niccolò (a volunteer), *ibid.*, I, 23, 46, 51, 58, 63–64, 75, 84, 93, *et alibi*. As for S. Maura, Beregani, I, bk. VI, pp. 188–97, gives a full and accurate account of Morosini's capture of the island fortress, as does Graziani, *Francisci Mauroceni . . . gesta*, lib. III, pp. 225–33, who gives S. Maura the earlier name Leucadia (Levkas). There is also, among other sources, a day-to-day account of the siege with a description of the island in Gio. Battista Moro, *Prime Mosse dell'armi venete contro l'impero Ottomano nella campagna, MDCLXXXIV* (MS. Marc. It. VII, 171 [8308], fols. 10ʳ–19ʳ), which work is also given in MS. Marc. It. VII, 400 (8310).

long as the Turks held the nearby mainland port of Prevesa, Morosini moved toward the port during the night of 20 September (1684), and forced the Turks into surrender nine days later on Michaelmas.[30]

As the Venetians now looked toward renewed warfare with the Turks on land as well as at sea, they turned to a large extent to the Germans to supply them with a field army. They were soon negotiating with the dukes of Brunswick-Lüneburg and Württemberg, the elector of Saxony, and other princes in the northland. The rulers of Brandenburg and Bavaria were not interested in employing their troops in Greece, but several princes were. The Venetians would provide an occupation for the German forces at loose ends, pay their wages, and remove them from the streets and taverns of the principalities. The military contracts tended to follow much the same lines, and so let us look at the contract dated 13 December 1684, which the Venetians negotiated with Ernst August, duke of Brunswick-Lüneburg, prince of Osnabrück, and (from December 1692) the first elector of Hanover. Of Ernst August's half-dozen sons the eldest, Georg Ludwig (born in 1660), would become George I of England in 1714.

Ernst August agreed to send to the Serene Republic for service against the Turk three regiments of infantry, each consisting of 800 combatants in eight companies, "veteran soldiers, well-clad, and armed with muskets and swords." With these troops must come, as nominal commander, one of the duke's sons, and so one did. Ernst August's third son, Maximilian Wilhelm, was appointed general of the Brunswick-Lüneburg troops who, at least at first, would be under the actual command of an experienced officer. The latter would receive his orders from the captain-general Morosini. As the campaign advanced, Maximilian Wilhelm was to play a prominent role in the conduct of military affairs. The Venetians' contract with his father was signed on his eighteenth birthday. His mother, of course, was Sophia, daughter of Friedrich V of the Palatinate and Elizabeth, the daughter of James I of England. There are frequent references to Maximilian Wilhelm, the "prince of Brunswick," in Morosini's dispatches to the Venetian Signoria. Brunswick became a Catholic in 1692, entered the service of the Empire in warfare on the Rhine, in Hungary, and elsewhere, and died in Vienna at the age of sixty in 1726.

To revert to the contract, the troops of Brunswick-Lüneburg were to

---

[30] *Vera e distinta Relatione dell'acquisto della fortezza di Prevesa fatto dall'armi della Serenissima Republica di Venetia nel giorno di S. Michel' Arcangelo sotto la prudente valorosa condotta dell'illustriss. . . . Francesco Morosini . . .* , Venice, 1684, newsletter printed by Gio. Francesco Valvasense in the Frezzeria at S. Marco. Note also Locatelli, I, 65–66, 73–79; Beregani, I, bk. vi, pp. 198–200, 227–29; and Gio. Battista Moro, *Prime Mosse dell'armi venete*, MS. cit., fols. 23ʳ–24ᵛ, 29ᵛ–30ʳ. R.C. Anderson, *Naval Wars in the Levant, 1559–1853*, Liverpool, 1952, pp. 194–236, has followed the Venetians' naval activity from 1684 to 1698.

serve on land, on *terra ferma,* wherever required, and were to be put aboard ships only for the necessary transport to the scenes of action. They were to be kept together under their own banners, in their own units, and not dispersed. If any of these German soldiers deserted to the Venetian forces, they were to be returned to Brunswick's command, "e così reciprocamente." They were to be allowed full freedom of religion, and if they died, they were to receive an honorable burial "no less than for those of the Roman Catholic religion." The German commander was to have military jurisdiction over his troops in both civil and criminal cases. He was supposed to notify the Venetian captain-general of the deaths of any and all Brunswick-Lüneburg officers, and present their successors to the captain-general. The Venetians had had a long experience of paying the wages of dead officers and non-existent troops.

The Republic was to provide the necessary artillery and munitions, and must also make payment for arms broken or lost in hostile engagements with the Turks. The sick and wounded were to be put without delay into military hospitals or other proper places to receive the necessary care "at a reasonable price." Once the campaign had started, the Venetians must make available food for the troops and fodder for the horses. In the meantime the foodstuffs and the cloth necessary for clothing which the Brunswick-Lüneburg troops would bring with them into Venetian territory were to be free of import duties. Also the prices of all items necessary for the campaign, especially the costs of food, were to be set at appropriate levels, so that the Brunswick-Lüneburg troops "might enjoy without discrimination the same advantages and conveniences as those of the Republic."

When the Brunswick-Lüneburg troops joined with the Venetian forces in an engagement against the Turks, they would divide the booty "according to the usual practice." When they fought the Turks by themselves, without the Venetians, they would get all the profits of plunder, "intendendosi pratticar con loro il medesimo vicendevolmente." All the captured cannon and munitions, as well as all the Turkish captives, were to be given up to the Venetians. The latter agreed to a monthly stipend of 233¾ "Hungarian ducats" (*ongari*) for each German company of one hundred combatants which, when the wages for the colonel and his staff were added, would amount to 2,010 Hungarian ducats a month for a given regiment of eight companies. The so-called Hungarian ducats were widely coined in various north-Italian mints.

The Venetians promised to make payments three months in advance, together with a "gift" of another month's wages to help the troops meet the "extraordinary expenses" of their journey to the Venetian Lido. Further financial concessions would be made to help the troops get started on the expeditions to the Morea. The Signoria regularly made large advances in the wages of soldiers and seamen, for expeditions almost always got under way much later than expected, and the mercenaries had usually spent in Venice (and at the Lido) a large part of their wages before their departure from the city.

The first review of the Brunswick-Lüneburg troops would be held at the Lido, and deductions would be made in payments to the extent that the soldiers in each company fell short of the required one hundred. Thereafter reviews would be held every month throughout the duration of the coming campaign to adjust payments to the numbers of surviving combatants. Besides the wages to be paid, the Venetians were to provide the troops with ship's biscuit (*biscotto*), "for every head a monthly portion of forty pounds," and to furnish them with satisfactory lodgings, baggage trains, and boats to take them to the Lido for some days of rest and restoration from the hardships of the long journey to Venice.

The Signoria's treaty of December 1684 was to last for one year, beginning with the day the Brunswick-Lüneburg troops arrived at the Lido, for which an allowance of at least two and one-half months had to be made "for the journey of the troops from Hanover to the Lido." The treaty might remain in effect for a longer period than a year, depending upon the wishes of the high contracting parties. Upon the termination of their service the troops were to be supplied first with naval transport and then with baggage trains to take them to the northern borders of the Veneto "verso il Tyrol." If peace should be made between the Republic and the Porte before the expiration of the treaty, the Signoria must adhere to all the terms of the contract. Upon reaching Venice, the Brunswick-Lüneburg troops were to "promise fealty" to the Republic for the period of their service.[31]

---

[31] Léon de Laborde, *Athènes aux XVᵉ, XVIᵉ et XVIIᵉ siècles*, 2 vols., Paris, 1854, II, 74–78, and *Documents inédits ou peu connus sur l'histoire et les antiquités d'Athènes*, Paris, 1854, pp. 128–32, doc. dated "in Venezia li 3/13 Dec. 1684." For almost 140 years these two works have remained indispensable for the period they cover. Selections from Francesco Morosini's dispatches and the minutes of his war council are given in the second volume of Laborde's *Athènes* and republished, together with other material, in the companion volume of *Documents*. Although, unfortunately, Laborde claims that he himself transcribed Morosini's dispatches from the signed originals, the facts are demonstrably otherwise.

In *Athènes*, II, 219, and *Documents*, p. 192, Laborde reproduces Morosini's signature from a formal document, which had nothing to do with any dispatch sent from the Morea or Athens. The signature appears thus:

Francesco Morosini had made a good start in the Venetians' war with the Turks by the capture of the fortress and island of S. Maura on 7–8 August 1684 and by that of the mainland port of Prevesa some seven weeks later (29 September). He resumed his offensive in the early summer of the following year with an army (as usually stated) of some 8,200 combatants, consisting of 3,100 Venetian mercenaries, 2,400 soldiers from Brunswick-Lüneburg, 1,000 Maltese under the banner of the Hospi-

---

Laborde transcribes the above as *Francesco Morosini Capitan generale*, reproducing the original (he says) for two reasons—first, to share with his readers that sense of "intimate communication which autographs establish between the one who reads and the one who has written, whatever the distances of time or place, an intimacy which I have enjoyed in holding in my hands all the correspondence of the great captain; the other reason being, in my own interest, to excuse the errors that I may have made in deciphering and copying this wretched handwriting."

First of all, Laborde's transcription of Morosini's signature is incorrect. It should read *Francesco Morosini, Cavalier, Procurator, Capitan generale*. Secondly, Morosini did not himself write the dispatches in question; they are all in the hand of a secretary. Although Morosini signed the dispatches (not the minutes of the war council), it was never in the formal fashion given above. Obviously Laborde employed a copyist (sometime after 1845) to whom, for whatever reason, the Venetian archivists did not make the original texts available. They gave the copyist an inferior text.

A note dated 1829 and inscribed at the end of the volume or "file" (*filza*) of the original dispatches and minutes of the war council makes it clear, however, that the archivists were well aware they possessed the originals of Morosini's dispatches. Perhaps the fact that Laborde had received access to the Archives by order of Prince Metternich, who had been a friend of his father, was the reason for the originals' being withheld from his copyist. The Austrian domination of Venice was not popular on the lagoon. For the archival reference to the originals of Morosini's dispatches and the minutes of the war council, see below, Chapter X, notes 3–4, and cf. Setton, IV, 1101–2, note 211.

I have based this account largely upon the signed originals of Morosini's dispatches, which (as far as I know) have never been used before, and also upon the contemporary "newspapers," which usually carried accurate reports of current events.

As for military "treaties" or contracts, it is of course well known that warfare was a business in which the services of professional mercenaries and other hirelings had been bought and sold in the military market from the time of the Italian condottieri in the fourteenth century. Eventually the Swiss, Germans, Bohemians, Swedes, Scots, and others also made the practice of arms their major occupation, and by the middle of the seventeenth century the German princes (and others) were leasing regiments of their native veterans and recruits in "commercial enterprises" (*Soldatenhandel*), a source of profit as well as a solution to certain social problems. See in general Fritz Redlich, *The German Military Enterpriser and His Work Force: A Study in European Economic and Social History*, 2 vols., Wiesbaden, 1964–65 (*Vierteljahrschrift für Sozial-und Wirtschaftsgeschichte*, Beihefte 47–48).

Warfare was also a grim, demoralizing business. On the dismal character of some of the dominant figures in the Thirty Years' War, see Redlich, I, 200–205. As the "standing army" gradually came into existence, it led to the standardization and increased production of arms, gunpowder, clothing (including uniforms in due time), artillery, transport, and other necessities brought about by military operations. On the furnishing of supplies by contract to the armies of the later seventeenth century, note Redlich, II, 21–24; on the salaries and various other sources of income gleaned by generals, colonels, captains, and lieutenants, *ibid.*, II, 27–66. On the reigning princes of the later seventeenth and eighteenth centuries as military entrepreneurs, see Redlich, II, 88–111. Incidentally, Duke Johann Friedrich of Brunswick-Lüneburg (d. 1679) was one of the first German princes to lease his regiments to a foreign power, which power in fact happened to be Venice (*ibid.*, II, 95–96).

tallers, 1,000 Slavs, 400 papal troops and 300 recruits from the grand duchy of Tuscany. Coron (Koróni) fell to the Venetians on 11–12 August 1685 after a siege of forty-nine days,[32] and thereafter they occupied Vitylo (under the fortress of Kialepha) and Passavá on the west and east coasts of the central prong of the southern Morea. The Venetians also took the town of Kalamata at the northern end of the Gulf of Messenia. The old castles erected on the hills at Passavá and Kalamata—castles whose beginnings went back to the early thirteenth century—were demolished by Morosini's orders, but the ruins are still there to remind the traveler of a turbulent past.

In the following year (1686), after the death of Carlo di Strassoldo, Morosini was joined by a distinguished Swedish soldier, Count Otto Wilhelm von Königsmarck, the third son of Johann Christoph von Königs-marck (1600–1663), who had been a prominent figure in the Thirty Years' War, one of Gustavus Adolphus's commanders. Otto Wilhelm accepted an annual stipend of 18,000 ducats to take command as general of the land forces of the Republic, made up largely of Italians, Hanoverians, and Saxons, with some Swedes, French, and others. He was accompanied by his wife Catharina Charlotta, countess von Königsmarck, and a large household, which included Catharina's lady-in-waiting Anna Akerhjelm, whose letters and journal are an important source for the Moreote and Athenian campaigns.[33]

Von Königsmarck took ship at Venice on 13 April (1686), and landed

---

[32] *Relazione del glorioso acquisto della fortezza di Coron, capitale del regno della Morea, fatto sotto il prudente valoroso commando dell'eccellentissimo Signor Cavalier e Procurator Francesco Morosini, capitan general da mar, il giorno di 11 Agosto 1685,* Venice, 1685, printed by Gio. Francesco Valvasense: ". . . doppo 49 giorni di duro ostinatissimo assedio. . . ." Cf. the detailed account in Locatelli, I, 124–52, and on the Venetian occupation of Vitylo (Kialepha), Passavá, and Kalamata, as noted below in the text, see, *ibid.,* I, 172–77. Beregani, I, bk. VIII, pp. 293–99, and bk. IX, pp. 315–30, has also described at length the siege and seizure of Coron as well as the near destruction of Kalamata by Morosini's forces (*ibid.,* I, bk. XI, pp. 362–63, 370–72), on which note Graziani, *Francisci Mauroceni . . . gesta* (1698), lib. III, pp. 249–70, 276–77.

[33] Laborde, *Athènes,* II, 256–349, and *Documents,* pp. 214–307, has republished Anna Akerhjelm's letters and journal (with a French translation) from Giörvell's *Svenska Bibliotheket,* III (Stockholm, 1759). Redlich's two volumes on *The German Military Enterpriser* (1964–65) contain ten references to Otto Wilhelm's father, the well-known Swedish general Johann (or Hans) Christoph von Königsmarck; on Otto Wilhelm, see Locatelli, I, 201ff., and Beregani, I, bk. XIII, pp. 413, 424–25, and II, bk. I, pp. 2, 10ff., *et alibi.*

Although Francesco Morosini's experience of warfare had been largely confined to the sea, he was well aware of the basic technical, social, and economic changes which had transformed the military in Europe in the later sixteenth and seventeenth centuries. If as a seaman Morosini was not entirely at home in the world of Dutch-Swedish-German warfare, his field commander Otto Wilhelm von Königsmarck was, having learned a good deal from his father and the Swedish military tradition.

Turkish tactics on the battlefield changed very little from the mid-sixteenth to the mid-eighteenth century, whereas "in Europe technological advance led to tactical revolution," on which note V.J. Parry, "La Manière de combattre," in Parry and M.E. Yapp, eds., *War, Technology and Society in the Middle East,* London, 1975, esp. pp. 227–28, 247–56, with a rich bibliography of contemporary sources.

with German reinforcements at S. Maura on 5 May in good time to begin
the Venetians' third campaign against the Turks, again in the Morea.
When further units arrived from Italy on 23 May, an army of some 10,800
men went into action, taking Navarino Vecchio (Zonkhio, ancient Pylos)
on 2 June with almost no resistance on the part of the Turkish garrison.
Two weeks later, on the fifteenth, the Venetian forces obtained Navarino
Nuovo despite a valiant defense of the port by its commanders Jafer
Pasha and Mustafa Pasha. The Turkish serasker or commander-in-chief
in the Morea, Ismaïl Pasha, had made an ineffective effort to relieve
Navarino Nuovo (to the south of il Vecchio), and when he failed, Jafer
and Mustafa surrendered. Moving a little to the south, von Königsmarck's troops invested the fortress of Modon (Methóni) on 22 June,
while Morosini hovered offshore around the island of Sapienza.[34] Modon
succumbed to the force of Christian arms on 10 July and now, possessing
both Coron and Modon, Venice had recovered the "chief eyes of the
Republic" (*oculi capitales Comunis*).[35]

Having won the southwest of the Morea, Morosini and von Königsmarck turned their attention to the northeast. On 29 June (1686) the
latter took possession of Argos while the serasker retreated to Corinth.
The Venetian commanders' objective was to take Napoli di Romania

---

[34] Morosini has given us a rough sketch of the Moreote campaign of 1686 in a letter
which he addressed from on board his galley on 26 June 1686 to the Turkish commander
Ahmed Agha "Desdar" and the other Turks in Modon, rejoicing in the Venetians' conquest
of "Vecchio e Novo Navarino, che fanno a pieno comprendere non potersi più Monsulmani
contrastare l'invito valore di queste poderose forze, che dal potente braccio del
Grand'Iddio sono guidate. Voi pure sapete a qual fine sia qua comparsa questa formidabil
armata ch'in terra et in mare v'ha immediate ristretto tra l'angustie d'un miserabile assedio. . . ."

The failure of Ahmed Agha and his fellow Turks to surrender promptly the fortress of
Modon would have no other effect "che a rinovare l'horida memoria delle straggi e scem-
pio attroce di Coron—e siamo certi che havete veduto le sette navi partire con li Turchi
medesimi dell'una e dell'altra fortezza di Navarino per dove meglio è a loro piacciuto." The
Turkish serasker or commander in the Morea, Ismaïl, was a frightened failure, "tante volte
batuto, rotto, e disperso da nostri valorosi soldati, e che sempre più s'allontana da cimenti.
. . . Lo dicano quelli spetialmente di Navarin Novo, ch'hanno veduto presto disperato il
caso d'haver dalle sue mani alcun soccorso, et imparino li commandanti da Seffer Bassà
[the commander at Navarino Nuovo] a non resistere con imprudente ostinatione alla volontà e salvezza de gl'altri habitanti di queste fortezze, che non devono esser più del Gran
Signore, ma dell'eccelsa nostra Republica. . . ." Morosini was prepared to mount a bat-
tery of twenty mortars to fire bombs at Modon as well as another of twenty cannon, and
"tutta la città dovrà in breve esser arsa e destrutta e col sagrifitio di voi tutti incenerita.
. . . Di galera, aque di Modon, li 26 Zugno 1686" (Bibl. Nazionale Marciana, MS. It. VII,
675 [8209], fols. 13ᵛ–14ʳ, and note MS. Marc. It. VII, 657 [7481], fols. 66–67ʳ).

Ahmed Agha, *castelano di Modon,* returned a brief reply to Morosini. The Turks also
depended upon the Almighty, and they would fight to the last man, "e quando non potremo
più, poneremo focco, e si abbrucciaremo, e così la fortezza non sarà nè vostra nè nostra!"
(*ibid.,* fol. 14ᵛ), which did not happen.

[35] Cf. Setton, I, 178, and on the Venetian seizure of Navarino Vecchio (on 2 June, 1686),
Navarino Nuovo (on 15 June), and Modon (on 10 July), see Locatelli, I, 210–37; Beregani,
II, bk. I, pp. 4–19, 22–23, 26–34; and Graziani, lib. III, pp. 283–98.

(Nauplia), an important and well-fortified port. They encountered no little difficulty in their quest for Nauplia, but while the serasker was said to be awaiting their advance at Lepanto and Patras, von Königsmarck seized the height of Palamidi, which looms over Nauplia. Never one to lose time, the Swedish field marshal kept the city under a heavy bombardment, according to Anna Akerhjelm, so that a fire raged within its walls for fourteen days. Von Königsmarck repelled several attacks by the serasker's forces as well as sorties from Nauplia.

The Venetians' success was assured, however, when on 6 August (1686) von Königsmarck defeated the serasker Ismaïl near Argos. It was the last encounter in which the Turk had assembled all his available forces to stop the Christian advance in the Morea. Von Königsmarck had had his horse shot out from under him in the engagement, but he immediately mounted another, and continued in the fray. If it was a glad day for von Königsmarck, it was also a sad one, for his nephew Karl Johann had just died of the pestilence which was ravaging the Venetian army. Many others also succumbed to the several illnesses afflicting the host, as Anna Akerhjelm wrote her brother Samuel Månsson from the island of Zante on 18 December (1686).[36] The campaign was much harder going for the Christian soldiery than it has sometimes been depicted. Nevertheless, by the end of the season the Venetian forces, having occupied several strategic ports and islands, had gained control of most of the Morea.

The campaign of 1687 fulfilled the highest hopes of the Venetian Signoria, for Morosini, von Königsmarck, and Max Wilhelm of Brunswick now took possession of all the strongholds in the Morea but one. Venice and the German princes, however, had been paying a high price for this success. The polyglot army was still rent with various maladies, including the bubonic plague,[37] to such an extent that the Elector Johann

---

[36] Letter of Anna Akerhjelm to her brother Samuel Månsson Akerhjelm, dated at Zante on 18 December 1686, in Laborde, *Athènes*, II, 264–69, and *Documents*, pp. 222–27; in general note von Hammer-Purgstall, *Gesch. d. osman. Reiches*, VI, 484–88, trans. Hellert, XII, 219–25; Laborde, II, 85–95; Kretschmayr, *Gesch. von Venedig*, III, 344–46. See also Locatelli, I, esp. pp. 243–69, and Beregani, II, bk. II, pp. 75–84, who dates the battle of Argos on 6 August 1686 (*ibid.*, pp. 80, 82). The Turks surrendered Nauplia (Napoli di Romania) on 29 August (*ibid.*, pp. 98–101): "La conquista di questa importante quanto famosa piazza, metropoli di vasta e seconda provincia, che portò seco il dominio di più di trecento villaggi, abbattè del tutto nella Peloponneso le speranze de' Turchi." Cf. Graziani, *Francisci Mauroceni . . . gesta*, lib. IV, pp. 303–11.

[37] On the existence of the bubonic plague in the Venetian forces, note Morosini's dispatch of 17 December 1687, as cited by Laborde, *Athènes*, II, 208–9, *una specie d'epidemia accompagnata da bugnoni* [Venetian for *bubboni*] *e da flussi di sangue*, and note below, pp. 314–15, 333–34, 342–43, 347, 352–53. Beregani, II, bk. II, p. 89, says that in the late summer of 1686 the Venetian forces were being assailed by "una mortale disenteria, accompagnata d'acute febbri, che molto più delle scimittarre de' Turchi mietevano le vite de' più riguardevoli comandanti," and on the *mal contaggioso* in the summer of 1687, see, *ibid.*, bk. VI, pp. 285–86. Graziani, *Francisci Mauroceni . . . gesta*, lib. III, pp. 240–41, 244, and lib. IV, pp. 315–16, 339, also emphasizes the peril of the pestilence from 1684 to 1687.

Georg III of Saxony finally cancelled his military contract with Venice. Apparently 3,350 Saxons had been recruited for service in the Morea in 1685; by the time the contract was cancelled in 1687 there were 800 left, of whom many had become crippled. Every year more military hirelings were needed, and every year they came. The months of June and early July of 1687 were spent in the basic training of an army of 7,000 men and in planning for the coming campaign.[38]

On 23 July the bulk of the Venetian army was landed near Patras, defeated the main Turkish force remaining in the Morea, and promptly occupied the city of Patras, an important acquisition.[39] Thereafter the Christian troops seized the twin forts of "Rumelia" and "Morea" on the north and south shores of the entrance into the Gulf of Corinth. Next they took the castle at Lepanto, the ancient (and modern) Naupactus. The Turks set fire to the lower town of Corinth before abandoning the seemingly impregnable fortress of Acrocorinth. They also withdrew from the historic ramparts of Castel Tornese on the northwest coast of the Morea opposite the island of Zante. Their resistance to the Venetians had crumbled everywhere in the peninsula,[40] and they had to pull out of Mistra, capital of the old Byzantine despotate of Mistra.

In Christendom it was a time for celebration, and festivities were held

---

[38] On the preparation of troops and ships for their departure eastward, the expected arrival at the Lido of "another regiment of Brunswick," and the imminent embarkation of Antonio Mutoni, count of S. Felice, and his bombardiers for the voyage to Greece, see Archivio di Stato di Venezia, Senato Mar, Reg. 153, fols. 129 [167], 131^v–132^r [169^v–170^r], docs. dated 28 and 31 May, 1687. Mutoni sailed from Venice on 28 June, headed for S. Maura, to join the Venetian fleet under Morosini, as the campaign of 1687 was getting under way.

A survey of Morosini's activities and the Venetian campaigns from the occupation of S. Maura (1684) to that of Athens (1687) is given in Antonio Arrighi, *De vita et rebus gestis Francisci Mauroceni Peloponnesiaci, principis Venetorum* . . . , Padua, 1749, lib. IV, pp. 292–344. Arrighi, however, adds little to our knowledge of these campaigns. On the events of June and early July 1687, see Locatelli, I, 321ff.

[39] The battle of Patras was fought on 24 July (1687), the day after the Venetian forces were landed (cf. James M. Paton, *Mediaeval and Renaissance Visitors to Greek Lands* [1951], pp. 124–25, 128; see also Locatelli, I, 330–36, and Beregani, II, bk. VI, pp. 289–96).

[40] These events were well reported by the journalists of the time: *Verissima e distinta Relatione della vittoria ottenuta dalle armi della Serenissima Republica di Venetia dell'acquisto fatto delle quattro piazze Patrasso e Lepanto con li due Dardanelli et altri acquisti sotto il prudente valoroso comando dell'illustrissimo et eccellentissimo Signor Cav. e Proc. Francesco Moroseni, capitan general da mar*, Venice, 1687, which tract was reprinted and the type reset at least once. Another *relatione* on the same subject was printed by Leonardo Pittoni at Venice in 1687.

The occupation of Acrocorinth was a great event for, with the exception of Monemvasia, it had cleared the Turks out of every fortress in the Morea by 21 August 1687, as described in the *Nova e distinta Relatione della conquista della famosa città di Coryntho in Morea e d'altri diversi luochi fatta dall'armi della Serenissima Republica . . . sotto il comando dell'illustriss. . . . Francesco Morosini . . . , con la total espulsione del Seraschier da quel Regno, comandante de' Turchi, li 21. Agosto 1687*, Venice, 1687, published by Antonio Pinelli, *stampator ducal*, and cf. Locatelli, I, 346ff.; Beregani, II, bk. VI, pp. 300–303; and Graziani, lib. IV, pp. 317–32.

in various Italian cities, glorying in the victories of Charles of Lorraine over the Turks as well as in those of Francesco Morosini. On 12 August (1687), as we have noted, Lorraine had inflicted an overwhelming defeat upon the main Turkish army under the grand vizir Suleiman Pasha near the village of Darda, just south of historic Mohács. By 21 August Morosini and von Königsmarck had crushed the Turks in the Morea. Celebrations were held in Rome, Ferrara, Padua, and elsewhere.[41] There can be no question, however, but that Lorraine's success made that of Morosini possible.

The Venetians now possessed all the Morea except for Monemvasia, the rugged, island fortress on the southeast coast of the peninsula. Monemvasia remained in Turkish hands until 1690. It was known as Malvasia in Venice, where the name is still attached to several *rii* and *calli* on the lagoon. The Morea was an impoverished land, but the inhabitants realized some return on the export of currants, almonds, fruit, olive oil, and tobacco. The wine of "Malvasia" was, however, probably the chief Moreote product in which the outer world was interested. Monemvasia and the wine were known as "Malmsey" in England, where the wine had been popular for centuries, long before the year 1478 when Duke George of Clarence, the brother of Edward IV, was allegedly drowned in the Tower in a "barell of Malmsey wine."[42]

---

[41] *Verissima e distinta Relatione delle solenissime feste e fuochi fatti nell'Alma Città di Roma in occasion delle presenti vittorie nell'Ungaria* [especially at Darda on 12 August] *sotto il comando del serenissimo duca Carlo di Lorena e in Levante sotto il comando dell'illustriss. . . . Gio. Francesco Morosini . . . per la Serenissima Republica di Venetia,* Venice, 1687, and cf. the *Distinta e verissima Relatione della segnalata vittoria ottenuta dalle armi cesaree sotto la condotta del serenissimo duca Carlo di Lorena contro l'esercito del gran visir, combattuto e disfatto nelle vicinanze di Darda, . . . seguita li 12. Agosto 1687 . . . ,* Venice [1687]; *Descritione delle feste fatte in Ferrara dalla pietà e generosità de suoi concitadini per le gloriose vittorie ottenute dall'armi imperiali e Venete contro il Turco . . . ,* printed by Bernardino Pomatelli in Ferrara [1687]; and (among other such newsletters) *Vera e distinta Relatione delle solenni allegrezze e fuochi fatti dalla magnifica città di Padova per le gloriosissime vittorie ed acquisti fatti dall'armi invitissime della Serenissima Republica di Venetia* [which celebration took place at Padua on the night of 26 November 1687], Padua, 1687.

[42] E. F. Jacob, *The Oxford History of England: The Fifteenth Century, 1399–1485,* Oxford, 1961, p. 581.

X

Francesco Morosini, the Invasion of Attica, and the Destruction of the Parthenon

A fter encircling the Morea in triumph, following the victory at
Patras, the Venetian fleet under the captain-general Morosini
reached the area of Corinth on 13 September 1687. In the
meantime the troops had gone by land from the Gulf of Corinth to the
Saronic Gulf to wait for him. Two days after his arrival Anna Akerhjelm
noted in her diary that the captain-general had proceeded on horseback
to Corinth "to see the place," being well received by von Königsmarck.
"I obtained permission on this occasion to go to Corinth," Anna now
wrote. "I should have been most distressed not to have been able to say
that I have been there." Von Königsmarck was then entertaining certain
officers as his guests. They were all in a merry mood, according to Anna,
and "his Excellency spoke to them of Aristotle in Latin and in Greek.
They have all agreed that they will send for the captain-general at Athens
in order to teach him to speak Latin!"[1] Doubtless the wine was flowing
freely.

Morosini's prime consideration was now the protection of the Isthmus
of Corinth, as he emphasized at a meeting of the war council (*consulta di
guerra*) held at the isthmus on 17 September. One must prevent the
entry of Turkish troops into the Morea. The Venetian forces had also to

---

[1] Anna Akerhjelm, *Journal [Dagbok]*, in Laborde, *Athènes*, II, 314–15, and *Documents*,
pp. 272–73, entry dated 15 September, 1687, and cf. Beregani, II, bk. VI, pp. 305ff.

301

provide security for the peasantry in the fields, for their labors would redound to the "public good." Having taken all the Morea except for Monemvasia, the question before the war council was how best to employ the remaining weeks of September and October. There were those who advocated an attempt to take Athens, and others who thought that their next objective should be the island of Negroponte (Euboea), which Venice had lost to the Turks in 1470.[2]

Having approved of the idea of trying to seize Athens when meetings of the war council were held on 12 August and on 14 September, Morosini had now changed his mind. At the war council on 17 September he declared that if Athens were in fact taken, and the troops lodged in the city for the coming winter, it would be difficult to supply them with provisions, for the Turks lorded it over the surrounding countryside. Indeed, the serasker, the Turkish commander-in-chief, had his station in Thebes, a little more than a day away from Athens. One would have to face the wear and tear of defending the three miles of roadway from Athens to Porto Lion, as Morosini always called Piraeus, in order to convey provisions and munitions from the fleet to the city. Contemporary sources estimate the distance from Piraeus to Athens at from three to six miles. Forage would be so scarce, Morosini said, that the mounted men would lose their horses. Furthermore, he did not see how the occupation of Athens could prevent the Turks from moving back into the Morea, for they still held Megara, which gave them control over the road from Athens to Corinth.

The captain-general Morosini thus regarded "the enterprise of Athens" (*l'impresa d'Atene*) as likely to be unprofitable, since the Venetian forces might be obliged very quickly to abandon the city and destroy it, which would mean the uprooting and ruination of the poor Greeks as well as the loss of an annual subvention of 9,000 *reali* which the latter had promised to pay the Venetians if Athens were spared. Morosini was convinced it would be better for the Republic's forces to remain in Corinth, where they would have easy access to food and forage. The cavalry and horses could be lodged safely at Tripolitza (Tripolis), "which is a wide area in the middle of the kingdom [of the Morea] possessed of handsome and commodious dwellings, with very fertile fields producing

---

[2] On the Turkish seizure of Negroponte, cf. Setton, II, 300–3. In an entry in her diary dated 19 August 1687 Anna Akerhjelm informs us that the field marshal Otto Wilhelm von Königsmarck had considered cutting a canal through the Isthmus of Corinth to divide the Morea from continental Greece and to move the troops by water from one gulf to another, "but his Excellency, becoming convinced that this was not as easy as one had imagined, it was decided that the troops would be sent by land to the other gulf" (*Journal*, in Laborde, *Athènes*, II, 306–9, and *Documents*, pp. 264–67). Massimiliano Pavan, *L'Avventura del Partenone*, Florence, 1983, p. 185, mistakenly puts the Turkish conquest of Negroponte in 1540.

a quantity of hay, of which there is a goodly harvest already reaped [for us] by the Turks." Unless the cavalry wintered at Tripolis, it would not be possible to supply every horse with four pounds of fodder (*biada*) every day.

Morosini believed that his views rested on firm foundations for, as he emphasized, it was of vital importance to have and to hold the "kingdom." The letters he had just received from the Senate in August, sent (as always) in the name of the doge, had made that fact more than clear. The war council finally agreed, therefore, that the troops should remain in winter quarters at Corinth to the extent that the fortress of Acrocorinth could hold them (*che dentro la fortezza capir vi potesse*). The cavalry and the remainder of the German troops, in accord with Morosini's wishes, would make Tripolis their haven for the winter, whereas the Venetian fleet with the seamen and certain mercenaries (*oltramarini*) would take cover in the harbor of Napoli di Romania (Nauplia) where it was alleged that, thanks to the Almighty, all signs of the pestilence had been "totally extinct" for the past fifty days.

Although acceding to Morosini's desire for the soldiers and seamen to spend the coming winter at Corinth, Tripolis, and Nauplia, the war council decided that before going into the aforesaid quarters they should try to take Athens. However hesitant, Morosini went along with the idea. The conquest of the important island of Negroponte (Euboea) would have to be postponed until the spring of 1688. As a prelude to the Athenian venture, however, it was now proposed that the Venetian ships (*navi*) should first sail toward Negroponte to arouse the fears of the Turks and draw them to the island. Thereafter the galleasses and galleys should carry all the soldiery in good health to the "shores of Athens," i.e., to Piraeus, to see whether, before taking action, it might be possible to extract from the Greeks "a contribution of 50,000 to 60,000 *reali* as a subsidy for the state coffers."

If nothing came of this endeavor, then the Venetian forces ought to launch an attack upon "that walled enclosure" (*quel recinto*), i.e., the Acropolis, and to employ all possible force to take the place by storm in order to wrest from the Turks such a convenient shelter. It would in fact be highly worthwhile also to destroy all the nearby Turkish villages in Rumelia, i.e., on the mainland, and drive the Turks from the area of the Isthmus of Corinth, for this would lead to peace and quiet in the Morea.[3]

---

[3] The minutes of the meeting of the war council on 17 September 1687 are to be found in the Archivio di Stato di Venezia (ASV), Senato, Provveditori da terra e da mar, Filza 1120: *Armata, Capitan general, da 20 Settembre* [actually from the 17th] *1687 sin 19 Maggio 1688: Francesco Morosini, Cavalier, Procurator*, without pagination, and cf. Laborde, *Athènes*, II, 122–26, and *Documents*, pp. 155–59.

The Turks had added to "that walled enclosure" (in 1686?) by demolishing the little temple of Athena Niké on the southwest corner of the Acropolis and incorporating the

More than once, moreover, in the next six months, Morosini and the Venetian high command would also consider the complete destruction of Athens.

As Morosini reported to the Venetian Signoria from the "gulf of Aegina, at the strait of Corinth," in a dispatch of 20 September (1687), he had explored with Otto Wilhelm von Königsmarck and the war council the problem they faced in determining their next move. There was general agreement that the season was too far advanced for an attempt upon Negroponte. Cold and rainy weather lay ahead. The soldiers, especially those who had been recruited some time before, were clad only in the usual garb and lacked warm cloaks. The fortress of Negroponte was defended by a garrison of some 5,000 combatants; it was well supplied with no end of military equipment, foodstuffs, and everything else necessary. The Turks had built a new fort [Kara Babà] near the bridge connecting Euboea with the mainland, putting about forty pieces of artillery into the fort to cover the area of the bridge and the nearby shoreline. Obviously Negroponte was too much for the Signoria's weary troops.

Athens, however, was another matter. A feigned approach toward Negroponte, as was suggested, might lead to the serasker's withdrawing troops from Attica, Boeotia, and the Megarid. Nevertheless, after these meetings of the war council Morosini continued to mull in worrisome fashion over the decision to try to take the Acropolis, as he informed the doge and Senate in his dispatch dated 20 September, for what purpose would the possession of Athens serve? The surrounding region was inhabited by Turks, who would allow neither food nor fodder to come from the countryside.

In Morosini's opinion it was a mistake to believe that Athens could serve as an outpost for the protection of the Morea, for the city was two days' march from the Strait of Corinth and more than thirty miles from Megara, "which is the direct route by which one goes from Rumelia to Corinth." To Morosini's satisfaction, however, as we have just seen, the council had agreed with his proposal that the major portion of the soldiers and seamen should be lodged in the strongholds of Acrocorinth, Tripolis, and Nauplia. This would, he thought, assure the peasants of the safety of their own homes and make it possible for them to return to the land, "which has remained in large part uncultivated for so long a time."

As for Athens, if the Greek inhabitants, most or all of whom dwelt in

---

stones into the western bastion covering the approach to the fortress. When the bastion was removed by Ludwig Ross and the architect Eduard Schaubert in 1835–1836, as every student of Greek history knows, the stones were found, and the temple was reerected on its old foundation. Owing to the faulty reconstruction, however, the Athena Niké had to be rebuilt in 1935–1940 (Adolf Michaelis, *Der Parthenon*, Leipzig, 1871, p. 88; Martin L. D'Ooge, *The Acropolis of Athens*, New York, 1908, pp. 192–95; Ida Thallon Hill, *The Ancient City of Athens: Its Topography and Monuments*, London, 1953, pp. 164–65).

the lower city, did not produce the 50,000 to 60,000 *reali* which Morosini was going to demand, the Venetian forces would (despite his doubts) try to seize the Athenian fortress, the Acropolis, from the enemy. Morosini was always beset, he says in this dispatch (of 20 September), by two problems, *danaro e biscotto,* money and ship's biscuit. Without money there was no way to feed the soldiers and seamen, no way to support the Republic's military operations in continental Greece and the Morea. The glorious triumph thus far achieved could turn to ashes. Long-winded as usual, Morosini was also (as frequently) in deep despondency. Complaining of his "depressed and battered health," he feared the charge of captain-general was becoming too much for him. Perhaps, *force majeure,* he would have to withdraw from the scene, recommending that Girolamo Garzoni, *proveditor dell'armata,* should take over the responsibility of the war with the Turks. In the meantime he was sending the present dispatch by a fast felucca to Venice, and he appealed to heaven to cure the ills that assailed him.[4]

In another dispatch dated 20 September (1687), Morosini wrote the doge Marc'Antonio Giustinian that immediately upon his arrival in the Gulf of Aegina, in accord with his instructions from the Signoria, he had bestowed gifts and expressions of gratitude upon the Count von Königsmarck, the prince of Brunswick, and Louis de la Tour d'Auvergne, lord of Turenne, as well as the other officers in conformity with their rank, in thankful recognition of their outstanding service "nell'insigne vittoria di Patrasso." Von Königsmarck's stipend was increased from 18,000 to 24,000 ducats; Max Wilhelm of Brunswick was given a jewel worth 4,000 ducats; and Louis de Turenne a sword of honor valued at 2,400 ducats. The officers received promotions and various other appropriate considerations, including jewelry and gold chains, while the troops were given their reward in an extra month's salary.[5]

Everyone assumed there was small likelihood of the Athenians' finding so large a sum as 50,000 to 60,000 *reali.* In any event Morosini, von Königsmarck, and their officers emerged from the Gulf of Aegina during the evening of 20 September (1687), sailed quietly through the night with a fair wind, landed in Porto Lion the following morning, and disembarked some 8,000 infantry and 600 horse with no interference from the Turks. At the risk of repetition—and Morosini's dispatches are very

---

[4] ASV, Senato, Provv. da terra e da mar, Filza 1120, dispatch dated "di galera, golfo d'Egena, stretto di Corinto, 20 Settembre 1687 s[til] n[ovo]," and signed by Morosini, and cf. Laborde, *Athènes,* II, 126–31, and *Documents,* pp. 159–63.

[5] Senato, Provv. da terra e da mar, Filza 1120, dispatch also dated "di galera, golfo d'Egena, stretto di Corinto, 20 Settembre 1687 s[til] n[ovo]," and signed by Morosini; as to the rewards in question, see Laborde, *Athènes,* II, 97, 119, 275, and *Documents,* p. 232, on which note also Locatelli, I, 354; Beregani, II, bk. VI, p. 300; and Arrighi (1749), pp. 343–44.

repetitious—we shall return shortly to their historic entry into Porto Lion. Piraeus was called Porto Lion, as everyone was aware at the time, because of the great marble lion which then stood on the inner shore of Piraeus, not at the entrance to the port. Morosini, as is well known, sent the lion to Venice, where it now stands before the Arsenal.[6]

At the appearance of the Venetian fleet in the enclosure of Piraeus, the leading Greeks of Athens came down to make obeisance to Morosini in the harbor. They offered their property and their lives, says Cristoforo Ivanović, "per le maggiori glorie della Republica." They were benignly received, and assured of defense against the Turks. They told Morosini and von Königsmarck that there were six hundred Turks capable of bearing arms in the fortress, determined to hold out against the Venetian forces, because they believed the serasker in Thebes would come to their assistance. Morosini promptly ordered that the army march upon Athens, which Ivanović puts at a distance of five miles from the harbor.[7] The Turkish residents of the city had taken refuge in the fortress, which henceforth we shall call the Acropolis.

Having thus landed at Piraeus on Sunday morning, 21 September, the Venetian land forces under von Königsmarck's command were put on the road to Athens that very afternoon. Morosini has given us a detailed account of what followed in his long, important dispatch to the doge and Senate on 10 October (1687), to which we shall come in a moment, for it was not until then that Morosini sent a full report to Venice. We shall deal with the facts in the chronological order in which they are given in the texts.

The earliest statement we have of the Turkish surrender of Athens to the Venetian forces appears in the minutes of a meeting of the war council aboard the captain-general Morosini's flagship in Porto Lion on 29 September (1687). It was in this context we first hear from Morosini that

---

[6] On the size of the Venetian forces, note James M. Paton, ed., *The Venetians in Athens (1687–1688), from the "Istoria" of Cristoforo Ivanovich*, Cambridge, Mass., 1940, pp. 9, 67. Laborde, *Athènes*, II, 133, and William Miller, "The Venetian Revival in Greece," in *Essays on the Latin Orient*, Cambridge, 1921, repr. Amsterdam, 1964, p. 406, both follow Alessandro Locatelli, *Racconto historico della veneta guerra in Levante*, 2 vols. in 1, Colonia, 1691, II, 3, in putting the size of Morosini's army at 9,880 foot and 871 horse. On the bibliography relating to the late medieval and early modern history of Athens, cf. K.M. Setton, *Catalan Domination of Athens*, rev. ed., London, 1975, pp. 261–301 (and in the present context), pp. 297ff., and see esp. Paton's notes to his edition of Cristoforo Ivanović (cited above) and his volume on *Mediaeval and Renaissance Visitors to Greek Lands*, Princeton, 1951. Paton's two slender volumes are very valuable. Note also the attractive book by Massimiliano Pavan, *L'Avventura del Partenone: Un Monumento nella storia*, Florence, 1983, and the brief survey by Peter Topping, "Venice's Last Imperial Venture," *Proceedings of the American Philosophical Society*, CXX-3 (1976), 159–65.

[7] Paton, *The Venetians in Athens*, p. 10.

in the brief span of the eight days employed in the conquest of Athens we have effected, thanks to the Divine Providence, the surrender of the fortress itself with ever greater glory attending our arms. It seems that the calmness of this clear weather, in contrast to the other miserable and rainy periods of these past weeks, offers us the incentive to consider whether we ought to pursue some other important and profitable enterprise. In the present period of success perhaps we should not entirely lose sight of a possible attempt upon Negroponte, especially in view of the present consternation of the serasker, who has allowed this already sadly battered fortification miserably to perish without having the heart to try to relieve it.

In summoning the present meeting, however, my sole motive has been zeal for the public good, as I have not made any judgment in advance as to what specific enterprise I should propose to you. Thus I have desired that the most useful and expedient decision should be pondered and assessed with sage and thorough debates as to what the season might allow us to do [as winter lay ahead] in order to put an end to this so fortunate and renowned campaign with the addition of new and happy events.

After a good deal of reflection and argumentation, as we are informed, "ben essaminato ogni punto sopra la materia importante," although there were those who did not wish to abandon the idea of an attack on Negroponte since things were going so well "nella presente favorevol congiontura," others were strongly opposed to the venture. The taking of Negroponte would be an arduous and difficult affair. The winter was on its way; the weather would be unreliable. Negroponte was defended (as we know) by a garrison of 5,000 combatants, not to speak of the assistance which the serasker might well render Negroponte, even if he had not helped the Turks in Athens. The Venetian forces numbered at least 9,000 men, including the soldiery aboard the ships. It was, therefore, finally agreed that before trying to reach a decision in the council the captain-general Morosini should discuss the problem in private with the lord general von Königsmarck to sound out his views for while, conceivably, the latter might not disagree with the proposed assault upon Negroponte, the war council could only reach a "mature and stable" decision after learning at the next meeting how von Königsmarck and the other generals assessed the situation. Von Königsmarck was not present at the session of the council on 29 September.

Among those present at this meeting were of course Morosini who, as we have noted, had begun the debate over the critical question of Negroponte, as well as his friend Girolamo Garzoni, the *proveditor d'armata,* who was to lose his life the following year when the Christian forces did seek to take Negroponte. Garzoni's sepulchral monument may still be seen at Venice in the church of the Frari, over the main entrance. Also on hand at the meeting were Pietro Querini, *capitan estraordinario* of the galeasses; Agostino Sagredo, captain of the galeasses; Benetto Sanudo, captain of the Gulf, i.e., the Adriatic; Carlo Pisani, *governator de' condannati*, i.e., commander of the vessels rowed by galley slaves; and Zorzi Emo, commissioner of the fleet.[8] There is no evidence that any one of them brought up the sad fact of the explosion in the Parthenon, the temple of Minerva, which had occurred three days before this meeting of the council.

From 2 October, taking the important texts in chronological order, we have the minutes of another meeting of the war council, at which Morosini stated that he had gone to Athens the day before to confer with von

---

[8] Senato, Provv. da terra e da mar, Filza 1120, minutes of the war council dated "1687, 29 Settembre stil novo, Porto Lion:" "Ridotti d'ordine, etc., in questa galera capitana generalitia gl'infrascritti illustrissimi signori che col voto deliberativo e consultivo al presente formano la consulta di guerra, l'illustrissimo et eccellentissimo signor Francesco Morosini, cavalier, procurator, capitan general, così disse:

"Nel breve giro d'otto giorni impiegati all'espugnatione d'Atene conseguitasi, mercè alla Divina Providenza, la resa della fortezza medesima con gloria sempre maggiore di quest'armi, pare che la tranquillità de' tempi sereni a differenza degl'altri sinistri e piovosi corsi nelle settimane passate porga eccitamento di pensare se si debba prosseguir ad alcun'altra operatione di proficuo rimarco, e forse anco nella presente prosperità a non perder totalmente di vista qualche attentato sopra Negroponte, attesa massime l'attual costernatione del seraschier, che lasciò miseramente perire questo già debellato recinto senza haver cuore di soccorrerlo.

"Io però nel convocar di presente questo congresso col solo motivo zelante del publico bene, come non mi son preffisso di proporle qual si sia positiva intrapresa, così ho desiderato che sia con savii e maturi dibattimenti ponderata e discussa la più utile e conferente risolutione, a cui permettesse il tempo di potersi ancora dar di mano per chiuder con nuovi aggregati di felicissimi eventi il fine di sì fortunata e celebre campagna.

"Con sodezza de pesati rifflessi e di vive ragioni, ben essaminato ogni punto sopra la materia importante, di che si tratta, fu considerato che quanto veramente militan per un capo degl'essentiali vantaggi nella presente favorevol congiontura per non abbandonar l'impresa di Negroponte, che si farà sempre più ardua e difficile, così dall'altro canto s'apprese per gagliardo l'ostacolo della staggione, che non promette stabilità de tempi propitii, e l'oppositione insieme vigorosa d'haver a contender con un pressidio di 5 m. combattenti senza il soccorso, che fosse per introdurvi il seraschier, quando il nostro accampamento non sarebbe maggiore di otto in nove mille huomini, compresa la militia delle navi, e senza il dibattimento di quei che d'ordinario mancano dalle fattioni, s'è perciò d'unanime sentimento rissolto prima di devenire a qual si sia deliberatione che dall'eccellentissimo signor capitan general sia tenuto nel proprio stesso particolar discorso coll'eccellentissimo signor general Konismarch a fine di scandagliar il preciso delle sue intentioni per doversi poi doppo, mentre non dissentisse egli dall'attentato predetto, maturare e stabilire in nuova sessione col suo intervento e degl'altri generali il decisivo di questo gravissimo punto, che merita d'esser con tutta la pesatezza equilibrato e concluso.

"Francesco Morosini, cavalier, procurator, capitan general.
Gierolamo Garzoni, proveditor d'armata.
Pietro Querini, capitan estraordinario delle galeazze.
Agostin Sagredo, capitan delle galeazze.
Benetto Sanudo, capitan di Golfo.
Carlo Pisani, governator de' condannati.
Zorzi Emo, commissario d'armata."

This document is misdated 27 September (1687) in Laborde, *Athènes*, II, 163–65, who gives a rather defective text, which is repeated and also misdated in his *Documents*, pp. 164–66.

Königsmarck. They had discussed at length a number of problems, especially the army's next move. The Turks had been thrown into such fear and trembling by the fall of Athens that Morosini was, to be sure, wondering whether it might not be well to attempt "la bella impresa di Negroponte." He told von Königsmarck that in Venice the government and the populace were said to be living in anxious expectation of news of some truly great conquest. Von Königsmarck, however, as we shall be told again in Morosini's dispatch of 10 October, objected to the very thought of directing the campaign toward so hard and hazardous an enterprise as an attack upon Negroponte at so late a date. But he did suggest, since Athens had been taken, perhaps they should remain where they were, taking up winter quarters in the city. Then they could try to drive the serasker from Thebes, and destroy that Turkish outpost so close to the Morea. The fleet might well pass the winter in Piraeus.

Although Morosini had reminded von Königsmarck that the war council had already fixed upon Corinth, Tripolis, and Nauplia for the winter quarters, he added that the most discouraging news had come of late that the pestilence was rampant in more than a dozen places in the Morea. It was therefore agreed that Athens was probably the best place for the troops to remain in during the winter. Also they would not attempt to take Negroponte. Not only was the season late, but they lacked adequate manpower, and they could not risk a failure. They must wait for reinforcements. Yes, now one could clearly see that the attack upon the Acropolis, *la fortezza d'Atene*, was truly the work of divine inspiration. The taking of the city was a glorious achievement. The troops would be safe in Athens, and the fleet secure in Piraeus.

The shattered Turkish garrison, having unfurled the white flag of surrender, was to come down from the Acropolis "the day after tomorrow" (*posdomani*), 4 October, and then the Christian garrison would take over immediately. As for von Königsmarck's proposal to attack and drive the serasker from Thebes, the war council would have to settle that question at a later session.[9] As in the minutes of the war council held on 29 September, so in those of the session of 2 October, also held in Piraeus, there is no mention of the destruction of the Parthenon.

In the long and important dispatch of 10 October (1687) Morosini finally informed the doge and Senate of how the Venetian fleet emerged from the Gulf of Aegina during the evening of 20 September, landed in Porto Lion the following morning, and disembarked the infantry and cavalry with no interference from the Turks. It was all done "nel breve

---

[9] Minutes of the meeting of the war council on 2 October 1687, in Senato, Provv. da terra e da mar, Filza 1120, without (as always in this "file") pagination, and cf. Laborde, *Athènes*, II, 167–71, and *Documents*, pp. 166–70.

giro d'una notte." Upon the appearance of the fleet in Porto Lion the Turks had shut themselves up "nella fortezza," i.e., they had taken refuge on the Acropolis, resolved to defend themselves, declaring that they would not and could not surrender the Ottoman fortress.

The Venetian high command decided, therefore, immediately to launch an attack "with the fury of arms," and the general von Königsmarck went quickly to work. By the morning of 23 September two batteries had been set up to fire at the upper reaches of the Acropolis, one of six cannon and the other of four mortars (*mortari da bombe*), as Morosini says, "to harass the besieged." In the meantime an inspection of the fortress had made clear that it was unassailable on three sides. An assault was possible only on the western slope of the Acropolis "against the entrance at the fortified gateway." The Venetian cannoneers directed a continuous barrage of artillery at the western approach to the fortress to reduce the damage which the Turks' artillery was beginning to do their Christian assailants, and which made impossible any likelihood of erecting earthworks to approach the gateway and upper walls of the fortress.

The ceaseless bombardment of what Morosini calls that "barbarous site" (*barbaro luogo*) continued for four days, from 23 to 26 September (1687), under the direction of Antonio Mutoni, the count of S. Felice, and finally "one had the satisfaction of seeing one bomb fall, amid the others, with a lucky strike [*con fortunato colpo*] on the evening of the twenty-sixth."[10] Morosini does not mention the fact in this context, but

---

[10] In this dispatch of 10 October Morosini clearly gives Mutoni credit for firing the "lucky strike" which destroyed the Parthenon: "Col getto poi delle bombe continuatosi a flagellar dal sopraintendente Conte di S. Felice l'interno del barbaro luogo, s'hebbe il contento di vederne fra le altre a cader una la sera di 26 con fortunato colpo. . . ." A certain Major Sobiewolsky in his account of the Hessian regiment at Athens says that the fatal shot was fired by a lieutenant from Lüneburg in one of Max Wilhelm's three regiments (cf. Adolf Michaelis, *Der Parthenon*, Leipzig, 1871, p. 346, no. 18). The Florentine agent in Venice, Matteo del Teglia, seems to attribute the shot to his friend Rinaldo de la Rue, who was later killed at Negroponte in mid-September 1688 (Paton, *Mediaeval and Renaissance Visitors to Greek Lands* [1951], pp. 125–26, 128). Still others have been given credit for the shot that was soon to be heard round the world, on which see T.E. Mommsen, "The Venetians in Athens and the Destruction of the Parthenon in 1687," *American Journal of Archaeology*, XLV (1941), 544–56, esp. pp. 549ff. As Mommsen notes, however, the account given by Sobiewolsky seems convincing, although Mutoni was in general charge of the heavy artillery.

Mutoni's cannonading of the Acropolis was subjected to a good deal of harsh criticism as being wasteful and incompetent (*il conceto della sua pocca habilità e la credenza ch'habbia più parole che fatti*). Morosini constantly defended Mutoni, with whom von Königsmarck had become dissatisfied and angry. In fact, according to a (somewhat inaccurate) contemporary account, von Königsmarck was removing Mutoni from command over the artillery in order to replace him by another *bombista* (Sobiewolsky's Lüneburger?) at the very moment when the "lucky strike" ignited the day's supply of gunpowder which the Turks were storing in the Parthenon:

"Il Chinismarch gli levò la sopraintendenza ai mortari con sostituirli un altro bombista, ma nel punto ch'era per farne la consegna una bomba getata a capricio e senza regola andò

the bomb had fallen on the Parthenon, igniting what he describes as a goodly quantity of gunpowder which the Turks had stored therein, *un deposito di buona quantità di polvere.* The fire spread quickly, burning for two entire days, as Morosini wrote the doge and Senate, and destroyed the Turkish dwellings on the Acropolis, causing great loss and untold misery. Still the Turks would not surrender, displaying a fearless courage that won the Christians' admiration.

The forlorn folk now stranded in the hot ruins of their houses placed all their hopes in their local commander-in-chief, the serasker of Thebes, and in fact after the siege of the Acropolis had lasted eight days, a large body of Turkish horse appeared in the vicinity of Athens.[11] Von Königsmarck soon put them to flight, however, and within the hour the besieged lost all their spirit. From the height of the Acropolis they had watched the wretched failure of the serasker. Hoisting the white flag of surrender (on the Frankish Tower), they sent down the west slope of the Acropolis five of the chief figures among them as hostages. Now there was a suspension of arms.

Von Königsmarck referred the five Turks to Morosini "for the conclusion of terms." The Venetian captain-general had decided to accept no terms (*patti*). It was to be an unconditional surrender. The Swedish general von Königsmarck remonstrated, however; in one way or another they had to take the fortress. Its rock-bound height would make its assailment the most difficult he had ever encountered in any campaign. Reluctantly Morosini gave way, agreeing to sign the terms of capitulation in accord with von Königsmarck's wishes. It was 29 September.

The Turks must give up the Acropolis within five days, which meant 4 October. Morosini granted them a "gracious indult," an amnesty. They were required to leave the Acropolis unarmed, each one carrying off a single bundle of his possessions on his back. In order to prevent their

---

a cadere sul tempio di Palade dentro alla Fortezza, e diede il fuocco a molta polvere che per giornaliero deposito tenevano in quel locco [if true]. Il danno fu molto, e fu grande anco il pericolo che prendesse fuocco anche il gran deposito ch'era pocco distante [if true, but the fire was to last for two full days], e grandissimo fu il timore degl'habitanti, che restarono con molta confusione, come può figurarsi . . ." (*Relatione dell'operato dall'armi Venete doppo la sua partenza da Corinto e della presa d'Atene*, ed. Spyridon P. Lampros, "Two Accounts of Athens toward the End of the Seventeenth Century" [In Greek], *Deltíon tēs Historikēs kaì Ethnologikēs Hetairías tēs Helládos*, V [Athens, 1897], 223, and cf. Laborde, II, 145–46, note, who gives selections from a modernized text of the MS. in the Bibl. Nazionale Marciana, It. VII, 656 [7791], fols. 102–4).

On the problems presented by this *Relatione*, see T.E. Mommsen, "The Venetians in Athens and the Destruction of the Parthenon in 1687," pp. 549ff., who seems not to have had access to Lampros's transcription of the original. The second "account of Athens," which Lampros, *Deltíon*, V, 225–27, has published (from the same MS. Marc. It. VII, 656 [7791], fols. 104ᵛ–106), is a historico-archaeological survey of the late seventeenth-century city. It is of some interest but of slight value.

[11] Cristoforo Ivanovich, *Istoria della Lega Ortodossa contra il Turco*, ed. J. M. Paton (1940), p. 11, places the Turkish incursion at daybreak on 28 September, and says that the enemy relief force consisted of 2000 horse and one thousand foot.

joining their fellow Turks at Negroponte (Euboea), as they would certainly have done in the event of their being given the opportunity to leave Athens by land, Morosini obliged them to take passage from Piraeus in certain foreign vessels which they had to charter at their own expense. They were in fact to be conveyed to Smyrna aboard an English *pinco,* three Ragusan *pettachi,* and two French *tartane,* all of which happened to be immediately available. By the evening of 5 October about 3,000 Turks, of whom five to six hundred were capable of bearing arms, were embarked on these vessels headed for the Anatolian coast. More than 300 Turks, male and female both, chose to remain in Athens "to cleanse their impure souls with the waters of the sacred baptism."[12]

When the Turks came down from the Acropolis, as Morosini informed the doge and Senate, they were subjected to insults and injuries inflicted on them by the "insolent rapacity of the officers and soldiers of the nations" which made up the Venetian army. He was in no position to control the soldiers, he said, to see that justice was done. The Turks' wives and children as well as their belongings were taken from them by force despite the fact that von Königsmarck had ordered an escort for them, as Morosini had recommended, suspecting some mishap on the long road to Piraeus. All the Christians' evil doing and foul play took place before the Turks could reach the port, where Morosini tried to make some amends for the injuries they had suffered and to make them understand his resolve to see that no further wrong was done them.

---

[12] The quotation comes from Morosini's dispatch of 10 October (see the following note), which seems to have been made available to the author of the *Vera e distinta Relatione dell'acquisto della città e fortezza d'Athene fatto dall'armi della Serenissima Republica di Venetia sotto la valorosa diretione dell'illustrissimo et eccellentissimo Signor Francesco Morosini . . .,* Venice, 1687, which was published by Antonio Pinelli, *stampator ducale:*

". . . Per il corso di otto giorni si continuò con il cannone e con il fulmine delle bombe a daneggiar l'interno [of the Acropolis] et accender il fuoco, et una di esse caduta in un deposito di polvere uccise molto numero di nemici con universale confusione. . . . Si effettuò doppo cinque giorni l'uscita delle genti in numero di circa tre mille, e tra questi cinque in sei cento huomini d'armi, e sopra cinque bastimenti furono fatti trasportar a Smirne. Oltre di essi però altri trecento del corpo dello stesso pressidio inspirati dal vero lume del Cielo volsero trattenersi per mondare l'impurità dell'anime con l'acque del santo battesimo!"

On the movement of the Venetian forces into Athens, the destruction of the Parthenon, and the surrender of the Turks, note Locatelli, II, 2–9, who says that Morosini and von Königsmarck landed 9,880 foot and 871 horse at Piraeus in order to take the city (cf. above, note 6). On the Venetian occupation of Athens, cf. also Beregani, II, bk. VII, pp. 335–39; Graziani, *Francisci Mauroceni . . . gesta* (1698), pp. 334–39; and Arrighi, *De vita et rebus gestis Francisci Mauroceni* (1749), lib. IV, pp. 345–49.

Toward the end of 1687 one could also buy on the Rialto Bridge in Venice a copy of the *Relatione delle cose più curiose ed antiche che si ritrovano in vicinanza di Atene,* which Antonio Bosio had produced at S. Maria Formosa. This latter tract was apparently written by Rinaldo de la Rue, on which see Paton, *Mediaeval and Renaissance Visitors to Greek Lands* (1951), pp. 84, note 1; 126; and 150–54, where the tract has been reprinted. Paton used the copy in Florence; I first met this text in the Marciana in Venice.

"Thus there has also fallen into the power of the august domain of your Serenity," Morosini wrote the doge,

the illustrious and renowned fortress of Athens [the Acropolis] along with its famous city of wide extent which, adorned with eminent buildings and antiquities, evoking famous and learned memories, has boundaries exceeding three miles in circumference.

Here the Greeks are blessing with voices of exultant joy the hand which has freed them from the enfeebling harshness they have suffered for so long a time, all the more so as they see themselves rescued from the pillage and the vindictiveness [the Turks] brought to bear upon their persons, dwellings, and possessions. They have not failed up to now to give sturdy proof of their contentment and their faithful devotion [to us] in view of the fact that if we face some other Turkish raid upon our camp, they have bestirred themselves to the extent of five hundred men and more to enter the conflict with arms, adding themselves to the soldiers under the command of the lord general [von Königsmarck], which has rendered futile the enemy's every attempt at ambush.

Morosini had words of high praise for the two *provveditori di campo* Zorzi Benzon and Daniele Dolfin, who had acted throughout the siege "with their accustomed, indefatigable ardor," rendering every possible assistance to the cavalry, attending to the needs of the gun emplacements (*batterie*), and fulfilling all other requirements for the attack upon the Turks. He also spoke with the highest approval of the nobles Niccolò Capello, Andrea Pisani, Alessandro Valier, Ferigo Marcello, and Pietro Emo, "who have all shown themselves desirous of rendering the most helpful service to the fatherland with an enhancement of their extraordinary and distinguished merit."

As for Morosini himself, he acknowledged in his long letter of 10 October to the doge and Senate that now he longed for a still greater advance in the triumph of Venetian arms. He could not refrain from asking the war council whether, after the fortunate surrender of Athens, they should not "take heart and take counsel to launch some other invasion elsewhere." The weather remained propitious, and therefore he thought of "how glorious it might be to close the current campaign with some marvelous and great exploit at Negroponte." But consultation with the general staff concerning such a weighty decision led Morosini to leave his flagship at Piraeus, where he had stayed through most of the siege, and under the pretext of a review of the troops he went to von Königsmarck's headquarters amid the tents at Athens.

As soon as Morosini broached the subject of Negroponte, von Königsmarck replied with strong objections to any attempt to take the stronghold on the well-fortified island, "not so much because the season was far advanced, but chiefly because of an inadequate number of troops." He had no way of knowing, he said, that the Turkish garrison at Negroponte, when combined with the serasker's troops from Thebes, would be inferior in numbers to the mercenary forces of Venice. By sorties alone the Turks could prolong any attempt to put their stronghold under siege, reducing still further the declining strength of the Serenissima's army. Keeping the troops thus on call at all hours (*a tutte l'hore sotto l'armi*), amid hostile encounters and harsh living conditions, would cause further deaths and increase the persistent pestilence that had beset the army. Their plight would lead to their withdrawal from Negroponte with further losses of manpower, damage to their reputation, and a lessening of the "public glory" they had thus far achieved.

From these prudent and well-based reflections, says Morosini, von Königsmarck went on to observe that by establishing their winter quarters here in Athens they could provide the troops with much-needed "quiet and repose," to which Morosini says he now gave his full agreement. Without von Königsmarck's presence, however, and his command of the army, Morosini declared that one could not agree to leave the Venetian forces in an exposed position on *terra ferma*, six miles from the sea. Von Königsmarck responded favorably to the captain-general's statement. Yes, he would remain at Athens, and watch over all the troops to try to avoid the "pernicious disorder" which threatened the army if the foreign mercenaries should leave to take up winter quarters in the islands, as their officers had already decided to do.

Having settled the important question of winter quarters, which Morosini had found a constant worry, he reported to the members of his staff the discussion with von Königsmarck, to whose views they quickly acceded. There seemed to be no alternative to abandoning an attempt to take Negroponte. Thus a conceivably successful trial of arms with the Turks for the greatest prize in Greece was not going to take place, for the Venetian forces were believed to be not strong enough to oust the Turks from the important stronghold of Negroponte. It was withal a bitter disappointment to Morosini, "because considering the present consternation of the enemy, a more favorable opportunity could never be hoped for again."

In any event the decision had been made. The army would spend the winter of 1687–1688 in Athens. The Venetian fleet would remain in Piraeus, "Porto Lion," where the seamen could easily tar the keels, repair their vessels, and have an immediate access to the sea.

This decision as to the plans for winter quarters was quite different from that taken by the war council a month before (on 11 September), but it had been necessary to yield not only to von Königsmarck but also to the wishes of the other field commanders and their troops. One great worry remained, however, for the plague had broken out again in several parts of the Morea. The quarantine at Modon had not yet been cleaned up; according to dispatches of the provveditori of Corinth and Patras the plague had spread to Trikkala (northwest of Argos) and to Tripolitza (Tripolis) as well as to ten villages in the region of Kalavryta. The provveditore of Maina had also reported that the dread disease had become much worse in Mistra, causing discord and misery in a poverty-stricken area with a population of more than ten thousand.

Morosini was gravely worried by the extent of the plague in Mistra, *dal che facendosi più sempre fastidioso l'inviluppo di quel molestissimo imbarazzo.* He was as embarrassed as he was distressed by the plight of the Mistriotes, for he had already ordered that the available supply of millet should be parcelled out on a basis of cash payments. The poor should be assisted by those who were well off, and in this connection he declared he would not go along with the impost being paid by the Jewish community of a hundred households. It amounted to no more than the "feeble sum" of 2,000 *reali,* paid with the annual tribute of 100 sequins (*cechini*) to the provveditore of Maina.

Leaving Morosini to worry about the millet and the money, we may note that in the history of early modern warfare the various types of pestilence—especially the bubonic plague, typhus fever, cholera, malaria, and dysentery—were usually as important as cannon and musketry. The plague or pestilence did not assist Morosini's troops, recruited from various nations, to get along with one another. Insubordinate officers were always a troublesome problem. As the plague spread, Morosini ordered contaminated houses and goods to be burned. The elders, *vecchiardi,* of infected villages were warned not to allow their people to carry the plague elsewhere through trade or travel. Morosini had forbidden the peasants to move in or out of the Strait of Corinth. He was leaving no stone unturned, as he assured the Venetian government, to uproot the dreadful malady, but only the hand of God could slay the "perfidious monster with which I have had to struggle for so long a time."

Despite the peril and hindrance of the plague, Morosini made it clear that the important fortress at Corinth was not being neglected, for the Venetian government was apparently following his advice to send a strong force to the shores of "the other Gulf," that is, of Corinth. If the need arose, they could take the passes and close the entranceway to such incursions as the Turks might attempt. Since it had been possible to burn in their entirety the outskirts and the town of Megara, which the Turks had abandoned in the area of the Strait of Corinth, von Königsmarck seemed to be thinking also of an attack upon Thebes to destroy the serasker's stronghold, from which with irritating madness the Turks would send out troops of cavalry to ravage the countryside. Von Königsmarck's idea was of course well worth considering, but such action had to be postponed, as the minutes of the meetings of the war council would make clear to the Venetian government.

The doge and Senate would understand from Morosini's report that Athens must be made into an armed fortress with sufficient provisions. Without a strong military force one could never undertake the conquest of Negroponte, "upon which the possession of Achaea depends entirely as well as the peace and security of the kingdom of the Morea." The taking of Negroponte, therefore, should be the prime concern of the Venetian government. Although Morosini does not mention the fact in the present context, the Maltese, papal, and Florentine troops had not (as expected) joined his forces, owing to the plague in the Morea. Furthermore, the regiments recently enrolled by the Signoria had been diverted to Dalmatia for the same reason. His failure to receive the needed reinforcements was a stroke of ill fortune for, as he declared, a splendid opportunity had been lost which might have brought undying fame to the triumphant glory of Venetian arms, *certo pur essendo che per colpa d'un tal e tanto diffetto hora si prova la disgratia d'essersi perduta sì bella occasione che immortalato havrebbe la gloria trionfante di quest'armi.*

Morosini regarded certain foreign recruits (*oltramarini*) as the best and most profitable of the military investments that Venice was making. He thought that the more such recruits the Signoria could enlist "at any price," the better, for the experienced soldiery of "the bellicose nation bore fruit both on land and at sea" (. . . *per il buon frutto che da sì bellicosa natione in terra e sul mare se ne ricava*). It is clear that the *oltramarini* referred to were the Dalmatians. Certainly the Germans were also a bellicose nation, well trained since the Thirty Years' War, but Morosini had constant difficulty with them, as we shall observe again, and of course they did not come from "beyond the sea." Young recruits were a problem; they became ill and fell by the wayside. The plague had wreaked havoc in the Venetian forces, but a company of Neapolitans had just arrived to fill up the depleted ranks of a regiment. The Venetians, however, must keep their promise to the Holy See to send back to Rome two companies of infantry provided by Pope Innocent XI, now that the campaign of 1687 was drawing to a close.

The perennial problem remained, however, of the Signoria's paying the wages of dead soldiers whose names were retained on the enrollment lists as a means of enriching their officers. Morosini's worries were manifold, and he closed his letter to the doge and Senate with facts and figures to illustrate the difficulties he faced.[13]

---

[13] Senato, Provv. da terra e da mar, Filza 1120, dispatch dated "di galera, Porto Lion, 10 Ottobre 1687, s[til] n[ovo]," and signed by Morosini; and cf. Laborde, *Athènes*, II, 157–61, misdated 4 or 5 October, and *Documents*, pp. 170–73, also misdated, transcribed from a poor copy and incomplete in both of Laborde's works. This dispatch was published with the correct date by Nicolò Varola and Francesco Volpato, *Dispaccio di Francesco Morosini, capitano generale da mar, intorno al bombardamento ed alla presa di Atene,*

In a dispatch of the following day (11 October) Morosini wrote the doge and Senate from Piraeus that, inasmuch as Venice had now acquired Athens, he believed the Greeks should continue to make their annual "contributione" of 9,000 *reali* to the Signoria, especially if in the pact they had made with the Venetian government they had agreed to assist in the taking of Athens from the Turks. They had every reason to rejoice in the expulsion of the Turks, "et han ben motivo di riconoscere la somma loro felicità in sì dolce cambiamento di vassalleggio." Certainly little or no harm, he said, had been done them in the assault upon the fortress. Also he had raised their spirits by naming Daniele Dolfin, the *proveditor in campo,* as governor of the city. The admirable Dolfin had not hesitated to add the weight of governance to his other responsibilities.

To the fortress on the Acropolis, Morosini intended to appoint a Venetian noble "che sostenga la reggenza del recinto." As soon as the Turks had come down from the fortress, he had sent Count Tomeo Pompei up with a garrison to clear away the ruins and to cleanse the place of the putrifying corpses, "of which there were more than three hundred, of both sexes, killed by that one prodigious bomb that caused the desolation of the majestic temple dedicated to Minerva, which had been converted into a heathen mosque." At last we have a reference to the Parthenon, two weeks after its destruction.

Morosini noted that he had chosen a chaplain, presumably for the garrison, as well as a Capuchin father of the province of France, apparently for Catholics in the encampment. The Capuchin was a missionary who had resided in Athens ever since his arrival there fifteen years be-

---

l'anno 1687, Venice, 1862 (per le nozze Morosini-Costantini), from the copy of the *Dispacci del Capitan Generale Francesco Morosini, 31 Maggio 1686–19 Maggio 1688* in the Biblioteca Correr (Venice), MS. Correr, I, 299 (Colloc. 772), on which cf. Adolf Michaelis, *Der Parthenon,* Leipzig, 1871, pp. 345–46, and Paton, *The Venetians in Athens,* p. xii, with the refs., *ibid.,* pp. 71, 76, 82, 89, 99, and on the destruction of the Parthenon, note Michaelis, *op. cit.,* pp. 345–47, and Paton, pp. 69–71. Having missed the work of Varola and Volpato as well as the notices in Michaelis and Paton, Pavan still dates the dispatch in question on 4–5 October in *L'Avventura del Partenone* (1983), pp. 171, 174. Since Mommsen, in the *Am. Journ. Arch.,* XLV (1941), 548, puts Morosini's second dispatch (of 11 October) "about a week after this first account [of 29 September] of the conquest of Athens," he also misdates the latter text on 4-5 October. Damerini, *Morosini* (1929), pp. 259–60, has the correct date (10 October, 1687).

On the siege and taking of Athens note, among the various contemporary literary sources, Francesco Muazzo, *Storia della guerra tra li Veneti e Turchi,* Bibl. Nazionale Marciana, MS. Ital. VII, 172 (8187), bk. III, fols. 54ᵛ–56ᵛ, who puts the destruction of the Parthenon on 27 September; Michele Foscarini, *L'Istoria della Repubblica veneta,* in *Degl'Istorici delle cose veneziane,* X (Venice, 1722), 250–51. On 18 October Anna Akerhjelm wrote her brother Samuel Månsson of "how repugnant it was to his Excellency [von Königsmarck] to destroy the beautiful temple which has existed for three thousand years [!], and which is called the temple of Minerva, but in vain. The bombs had their effect, and so never in this world can the temple ever be replaced" (Laborde, *Athènes,* II, 276–77, and *Documents,* pp. 234–35).

fore. These were not, strictly speaking, appointments, for Morosini could not make abiding ecclesiastical decisions without the authorization of the Venetian government. As an aside we may note that the Capuchin hospice in Athens included the choregic monument of Lysicrates, known for centuries as the "lantern of Demosthenes" (at the foot of the east slope of the Acropolis), which Fr. Simon de Compiègne had acquired for the Order in 1669.

But to return to October 1687, von Königsmarck had just sent the captain-general twenty-two male "blackamoors" (*Mori*) and forty-one negresses (*nere*).[14] The blackamoors Morosini had divided between the naval commanders and certain superior officers (*capi da mare e sopraintendenti*), "according to the usual custom." To please von Königsmarck he had returned the female slaves in order that they might be of some use to the soldiers, even though the latter had already carried off diverse slaves of every sort. As for other matters, Morosini wrote that the Venetians had acquired from the fortress eighteen cannon, among them twelve of bronze, with two mortars, *un petrier . . . et una gran bombarda*, the latter of huge caliber designed to shoot stone cannon balls.

As we have had several occasions to note, Morosini was continually beset by a shortage of funds. Like an accountant, he had to weigh the cost of each next move. Now that the campaigning season of 1687 was drawing to a close, he sought to relieve his coffer (*cassa*) of the heavy costs of chartering vessels. As he reported to the doge and Senate in his long dispatch of 11 October, he had terminated the leasing of fifty-three ships (*bastimenti*) of various kinds, especially *pettachi* and *marciliane*, and had confined himself to the retention of five *pinchi*, six *navi*, nine *pettachi*, two *brulotti*, and fourteen *marciliane*.[15] He was keeping vessels of larger tonnage since they would be able to hold the munitions and matériel (even if "with great difficulty") which were being unloaded from the other vessels. It would certainly be more of a chore thus to distribute the needed materials among the squadrons, but anyhow Morosini was saving 200 ducats a month, reducing the costs of convey-

---

[14] As one example of the many minor but (I think) misleading flaws in the text of Morosini's dispatches used by Laborde's copyist, we find that "ventidue furono li schiavi e quaranta una le schiave prese dal signor Konismarch" (*Athènes*, II, 162, and *Documents*, p. 174). Actually, however, the passage in question appears in the original signed dispatch as "venti due furno li Mori e quaranta una le nere inviatemi dal signor Konismarch . . ." (ref. in note 16). While certain modernizations of spelling are obvious in the texts published in Laborde's two works, I have no inkling as to why such changes as we find in the present instance should ever have been made.

[15] On the various vessels mentioned, see the *Dizionario di marina medievale e moderno*, Rome: Reale Accademia d'Italia, 1937.

ance from 1,500 to 1,300 ducats a month, and all without altering any of the Signoria's contractual obligations.

In the meantime it was apparently unclear whether the regiments of Brunswick veterans would remain with Morosini's forces or leave at the close of the campaigning season. The overbearing Morosini had had trouble with the various branches of his German troops, over whom discipline could be exercised only by their own officers, who were not always cooperative. In some ways he would have been as glad to see them go as to remain with him in Greece, but in either event, when the spring came, he would need reinforcements. Most of all he needed money, and at times he thought a convoy might appear bringing the needed financial subventions. He expressed bitterness that the amount he had expected had been reduced to 200,000 ducats, although a like amount was supposed to be sent "on a new voyage." Winter was coming, however, and Athens was far from Venice; "di sì lungo tratto di camino sa il Cielo quando potran capitare."

The doge and Senate would understand from Morosini's account the dire needs of their forces at Athens. In order to help maintain the fortresses of Maina, Coron, Modon, Navarino, Castel Tornese, Patras, and "Lepanto and its Dardanelles," he was allocating to them the taxes collected (*le scossioni*) on the islands of Zante and Cephalonia. This would provide the said fortresses with their monthly allotment of funds as well as of bread; for the required transport he was going to assign two of the fourteen *marciliane* he had retained in his service. The fortresses of S. Maura, Prevesa, Corinth, and one or two other places seemed to be provided for adequately. As galleys were being outfitted in the Arsenal at Istanbul, so also did Morosini and von Königsmarck require skilled carpenters to set in order the Venetian fleet.

Morosini had acquired an intercepted letter which the Monemvasiotes had sent to the Turkish commandants at Canea on the island of Crete. He was pleased to learn how badly off the Monemvasiotes were as they implored the commandants to send them some relief. In the meantime the Venetian siege of the towering, rock-bound fortress continued, with the local peasants apparently assisting the besiegers to add to the Turks' "tormento della disperatione."

Toward the close of "this most reverent dispatch" (of 11 October) to the doge and Senate Morosini expressed in his usual baroque style his gratitude for the honors done him and for the appointment of a second nephew to a post of dignity. With an equal fervor, however, he went on to lament the fact that he was being harassed by a "monstrous fatality," which was not at all allayed by the recognition being accorded to him and his family. Indeed, he was beset by a "pitiless destiny which is always seeking to pull me down with insidious affronts!" He had reason to grieve, he said, when at the very apogee of success he saw no escape from disparagement.

One source of Morosini's discontent lay in the fact that the first of his nephews [Piero Morosini]

who, while he remains here with me exposed to ceaseless toil, suffering, and peril, was almost degraded from the position of captain of the Gulf. Well do I understand that my long tenure of this exalted, important post with the obligation of exercising that justice which does not please everyone is a veritable bellows emitting noxious fumes for one's descendants. . . . In the end I shall trust that the pious humanity of your Excellencies may be moved to deliver me from this deplorable state which, without provident and solicitous aid, can only lead me to ultimate destruction. . . .

This was not the first time Morosini had asked in one way or another to be relieved of his charge as captain-general of the fleet of the Republic. In Venice his opponents, adherents of the ambitious Girolamo Corner, then commander of the Signoria's forces in Dalmatia, had doubtless sought to disparage Morosini by the flippant treatment of his nephew. Corner was generally believed to be Morosini's chief rival for the dogate if the ailing Giustinian should die. He was doing well in Dalmatia, having just taken Castel Nuovo from the Turks (on 30 September 1687). Another source of Morosini's exasperation was the fact that Corner had received contingents of troops diverted from Morosini's command for fear of the plague in the Morea, with which troops Morosini felt he might well have taken Negroponte.

Misfortune always resulted from the troublesome political commotions of the sort that had involved his nephew, as Morosini noted at the conclusion of his dispatch of 11 October. The law was disregarded to the prejudice of the naval captains (*capi da mare*) who might seek advancement in rank and the procurement of reserves they richly deserved. Certainly everyone of them was risking his life and crew to the hazards of warfare to help increase the glory of the Venetian state. They should be encouraged with gestures of privilege and distinction which under the current circumstances would enliven their spirits so much the more to sacrifice their all "to the adored service of the fatherland."[16]

---

[16] Senato, Provv. da terra e da mar, Filza 1120, dispatch dated "di galera, Porto Lion, 11 Ottobre 1687 s[til] n[ovo]," and signed by Morosini; and cf. Paton, *The Venetians in Athens* (1940), pp. 48–55, 98–99. An addendum to the dispatch of 11 October, dated "1687 a dì 6 Ottobre s[til] n[ovo], Porto Lion," provides a "Nota degl'arteglieria rittrovata nella fortezza d'Attene acquistata dall'armi gloriose della Serenissima Republica di Venezia." The list includes bombs, cannon, columbines, and falconets.

Francesco Muazzo, *Storia della guerra tra li Veneti e Turchi*, in the Bibl. Nazionale Marciana, MS. It. VII, 172 (8187), bks. I–III, fols. 1–43ᵛ, has covered the war in Dalmatia up to "l'acquisto di Castel Nuovo." On the career of Girolamo Corner, note the account

While Morosini worried and fretted over his problems, glorying in the victories thus far achieved and complaining about the lack of money and supplies, the rest of the world was almost as impressed with the Venetians' advance in the Morea as with the Austrians' triumphs in east-central Europe. On 25 October (1687), for example, the doge Marc'Antonio Giustinian returned a brief but courteous reply to the Ragusei in acknowledgment of their letter of 10 September (even before Morosini's penetration into Attica), congratulating the Signoria "upon the successes granted by the Lord God to our arms in the Levant." Giustinian assured the Ragusei that the Venetian Signoria entertained the same "kindly disposition" toward them as they had expressed toward Venice.[17]

In another long dispatch prepared at the end of the month (30 October 1687) Morosini wrote the doge and Senate that the troops had been quartered "nella città d'Atene" in apparently seemly fashion with the assistance of the lord general, the Count von Königsmarck. Their housing was a problem, however, and Morosini had taken up with the lord general the question whether it might be possible to make the inhabitants of the city provide maintenance for the troops so that the Venetian government would carry little or no further burden during the coming winter than the funds which must be given to the officers, who paid their troops. As always, the captain-general was seeking to reduce expenses; they preyed upon his mind with ever-lasting intensity. The few houses of the well-to-do had already been taken from them, however, and "all the rest are living by their own sweat." Von Königsmarck also found "other insuperable difficulties in allowing the dispersal [of the troops] in such close proximity to the enemy, with the disruption of military discipline which would result from our few units' being in so many habitations, mixed up among the families of the Greeks. . . ."

It might have been a good way, if practicable, of saving money, but von Königsmarck's objection had rendered Morosini's idea futile. Also one wonders to what extent the poor Athenians could have supported the troops bivouacked upon them. "But just as I have had with inexpressible sorrow to put up with planning so different from my strongest desires, which I had set about putting into effect," as Morosini informed the Signoria, "just so with equal distress do I already have to witness the considerable flights from the encampment, even though the cost of

---

given by R. Derosas, in the *Dizionario biografico degli Italiani,* XXIX (1983), 243–47, with a good bibliography, and on Corner's success at Castel Nuovo, see Beregani, II, bk. VII, pp. 325–33.

[17] Senato, Delib. Costantinopoli (Secreta), Reg. 35, fol. 76, doc. dated 25 October, 1687, the text of which was approved by the Senate +73, 1, 2. After this letter no further entries were made in this register for more than two years, until 15 December, 1689.

arresting deserters has risen from the four sequins current in the kingdom of the Morea to ten sequins here in the more open country."

In these past days Morosini had had two men hanged on a yardarm,
and had arrested three others on orders of the lord general. In fact the
latter three culprits, guilty of the heinous crime of desertion, were still
hanging from trees in the countryside as an example of the punishment
that awaited other such treasonous wretches. The evil was mostly to be
found "among the soldiers of the new levies, and especially of the French
nation, unstable of themselves and given by nature to always wandering
off " (*nei soldati di nuove leve e massime di natione francese istabile
per se stessa et avezza al genio di sempre vagare*). To help improve the
situation Morosini suggested that all or most of "the soldiery should be
incorporated in the large corps of the old regiments."

As the doge and Senate were well aware, however, such was the nature
of the military contracts that discord was inevitable, inasmuch as justice
was administered to all the mercenaries by the various officers commanding their units. If it were possible to modify the "despotic authority" of the officers, Morosini believed it would also be possible to hold
down the desertions and to establish a proper discipline among the
troops. He had already apprised the Signoria of the fact that three redoubts, now manned with task forces, had been built along the road from
Athens to Piraeus to assure access to the sea.

Meanwhile to keep the cavalry supplied with fodder it was necessary
for von Königsmarck to combine horse and foot in frequent excursions to
provide for such needs from the countryside, where one always had to be
on the alert against an enemy attack. There was a report that the serasker was now more quickly gaining strength as a result of reinforcements. To keep him from the environs of Athens, Morosini had proposed
to von Königsmarck "the idea of invading and sacking the villages of
Livadia, which are furnishing him with provisions, and thus also to put in
some want the large garrison of Negroponte, which has probably been
obtaining therefrom the abundance of its foodstuffs."

Since von Königsmarck had approved of the idea of striking at Livadia
—and it would presumably be necessary first to attack Thebes—Morosini believed it essential to issue orders to the Venetian authorities everywhere in the Morea to put their forces in readiness for the coming
venture. They were to gather at the Strait of Corinth by 7 November,
having collected as many Greek auxiliaries as they could to increase the
force of the projected onslaught upon Livadia which, if successfully
carried out, would certainly be an immense blow to the Turks. Morosini
proposed Zorzi Benzon, who had recently been appointed one of the two
proveditori estraordinarii of the Morea, as commander of the Moreote
forces to sally forth against Livadia.

Morosini was also still worrying about "that most troublesome embarrassment," the plague, as well as the penury, of the inhabitants of Mistra. The provveditore of Maina, however, had succeeded by a new accord with the Jews in extracting from them immediately some 5,000 *reali* [instead of 2,000] and the assurance of an annual "contribution" of 50,000 aspers. Morosini had directed the provveditore of Maina (also named Morosini) to see to the collection of every possible source of revenue. For the rest, thanks to the Almighty, the fortress of Modon was now said to be free of the plague, although one still looked forward to seeing the neighboring villages rid of the dread affliction.

It was still a question whether the old regiments of Brunswick-Lüneburg under Prince Maximilian Wilhelm would remain with the Venetian forces or not. In any event Morosini was reserving the vessels necessary to transport them to Venice if in fact they were leaving. Assailed meanwhile by repeated requests made in the names of the lord princes of Brunswick and Württemberg no less than by those made in the name of Louis de Turenne, Morosini was trying to find the ways and means of pleasing them. To overcome every difficulty he had decided to set aside the ships *S. Giovanni di Villafranca* and *Madonna di Belveder* to make easier the passage of their subjects. But it was not easy to please everyone or, for that matter, anyone; life was a laborious business for Morosini during these months.

Besides the problems of desertion and discipline the captain-general's dispatch of 30 October (1687) deals with the abuse of the soldiery by certain commanders, financial difficulties relating to payments to the mercenaries, the rank to be given to certain officers, and the accounts to be paid under the various contracts that he was trying to manage. The sergeant-general Corbon was ill, and preparing to depart for Curzola (Korčula); the lieutenant-general Davila had simply bowed out; others had been lost since the beginning of this year's campaign. A replacement of senior officers was needed. The mere thought of being supplied with ship's biscuit only until December horrified Morosini, and yet he waited and waited for the convoy that did not come.

Morosini thought that provisions could be obtained for the coming winter by impinging upon the Levantine trade, but in the meantime everything that could be procured in the surrounding countryside must be sent directly to Porto Lion (Piraeus), for he could not divert ships from the fleet to pick up foodstuffs. He had already notified the doge of the munitions he needed, but now he sent a more precise list, specifying the amount of gunpowder required as well as the number of bombs, fuses (*michia,* presumably for matchlocks), and cannon balls "so that the most essential implements for warfare will not be lacking in time of need."

In one of his recurrent dilations upon the obvious, Morosini explained to the doge and Senate that without large and strong reinforcements the Venetian mercenaries could never keep pace with the "grandi operationi" which lay ahead, for illness and desertion had depleted their ranks. The army must be rebuilt for action before the first week of May (1688). As he had already notified the doge, the kapudan pasha had been summoned to Istanbul, but now reports came from Smyrna that having gone beyond the "Castelli" into the Dardanelles (of Istanbul) with the galleys and ships, the Ottoman grand admiral had apparently soon departed. He had refitted his armada with all the ships at Fochies (Foça, Phocaea) along with nine vessels of the sultan and three of the Barbary corsairs. It was hard to know what the Turks intended to do next. Morosini assumed that they would remain at Fochies to keep an eye on the Venetians if they should venture out of Piraeus. As winter approached, the Turkish armada would doubtless withdraw into the Dardanelles. There was, however, a rumor, which Morosini doubted, that the armada might stay through the winter at Fochies.

As for the campaign of 1688, the Venetian fleet must make as good a showing in the Archipelago as it had the year before. Anti-Turkish corsairs should be encouraged. The Venetians would have less trouble with, and the Turks less assistance from, the Barbary corsairs, because the Algerians would now "have to defend themselves from the indignation of France."

Morosini closed the dispatch of 30 October with the note that he was entrusting its delivery to the captain of the *Belvedere*

together with a drawing of the fortress and city of Athens prepared with great care by milord superintendent [of artillery, Antonio Mutoni], count of S. Felice, who must take much credit for their conquest. He has added diverse annotations concerning the celebrated monuments which are still resplendent in their ancient remains, and which seem to me worthy of the careful consideration of your Excellencies.[18]

Morosini's life seemed, at least to him, a compound of double toil and trouble, as he explained in his dispatch of 14 November (1687). After a long and worried wait for the convoy he needed so badly, he finally

---

[18] Senato, Provv. da terra e da mar, Filza 1120, dispatch dated (by Morosini) "di galera, Porto Lion, li 30 Ottobre 1687, s[til] n[ovo]," and signed by Morosini. As is well known, soldiers in the seventeenth century—often recruited, sometimes forcibly, from the poor peasantry and the riffraff of society—led miserable lives, as emphasized by Redlich, *The German Military Enterpriser*, II (1965), 191–230, and so desertions were widespread and expected (*ibid.*, II, 213–19, 228–30). In October (1687) the foreign princes and some of the chief officers apparently did return to Venice or to other places in the West for the coming winter (Locatelli, II, 10–11).

received a report that the convoy, consisting of only two English ships, had landed on 29 October (1687) at the island of Zante. Despite the diligence of the Venetian commander involved, thirty-two days had been wasted, and then it was necessary to disembark at Zante, setting ashore two companies of mercenaries as well as the money scheduled for delivery to Morosini. With the assistance of the English consul every effort had been made—but all in vain—to induce the captains of the two vessels to continue the voyage to Athens. Even the ship's biscuit had had to be unloaded from the vessel carrying it.

Morosini was "agitato et afflitto;" his problems had mounted into "ineffable torments." Failure to feed the soldiers and seamen would lead to disaster, threatening the apparent good fortune of Venice. Having no alternative, Morosini had decided to ration the available ship's biscuit, doling out smaller quantities to the land forces and to the oarsmen and gunners of the fleet. He was, however, giving them all a lira a day at the rate of five soldi per lira in cash in addition to their regular wages. The other seamen were to receive three soldi. The officers of the Brunswick regiments, however, refused to go along with any such arrangement, and to avoid the risk of an "insufferable scandal," Morosini had to yield to the Germans' "having insisted upon the exchange of enough rice to make up for the shortage of bread, [and lacking rice?] I have had to give them wheat, measure for measure, to effect this compensation."

To lessen the task of distributing the ship's biscuit and to lessen also the consumption of his limited stores, Morosini had decided to send the four galleys of Corfu, Zante, and Cephalonia back home with orders to the officials on the islands to discharge the seamen immediately, but with the understanding that they should be rehired and rearmed before the coming March (of 1688). Morosini had hoped that he might first employ their labor at Coron and Modon, but now it was not to be so. These penurious procedures were detrimental to the best interests of the state, and made a poor showing, especially with the troops in winter quarters so close to the enemy and with so many desertions taking place among the Venetian forces. The sad fact was that every day the deserters kept the Turks aware of what was going on in Athens and at Piraeus.

Morosini lacked ship's carpenters, tanners, and other workmen; the constant postponement of maintenance was proving harmful to the fleet. On "the day before yesterday" (12 November 1687) only two small vessels—the pettachio *Madonna del Rosario* and the saïque *Madonna di Loreto*—had arrived in Piraeus with tents for the winter and some other equipment, but with less than a week's supply of bread.

The weather had been stormy. It would get worse. Morosini was preparing a squadron of seven of the more worn and shoddy ships to send to the island of Curzola (Korčula), whither he had already sent the *S. Giovanni Battista* with Max Wilhelm, the prince of Brunswick, aboard. Nu-

merous other vessels had also to be sent westward for repair and recon-
ditioning so that when the spring came for the next campaign, they might
be ready for "un vigoroso et utile servitio." Morosini had already dispatched two other ships, the *S. Iseppo* and the *Pace Abbondanza,* to the
remaining Venetian fortresses on Crete—those at Suda, Spinalonga, and
Grabusa—as well as to the stronghold at Cerigo. He was supplying Grabusa and Cerigo at least with money enough to last through March
(1688) and ship's biscuit enough to see the garrisons into April. In this
connection Morosini was relying upon the able Alessandro Valier, "who
through the entire course of the present war has always labored as a
volunteer both in these well-known hazards and in the perils of
Dalmatia."

Morosini then discharged from service another half-dozen or more
ships "for some respite to the public coffers," but he was still keeping in
reserve the five *pettachi,* one *nave,* and one *pinco* "for the voyage of the
three veteran regiments of Brunswick if they should have to leave here in
accord with the contract." In some doubt as to public policy, now that
mid-November had come, Morosini was trying to prolong the stay of
various mercenary troops and officers, although the sergeant-general
Hermann Philipp von Ohr was always pressing him for the means of
departure. Indeed, trying to keep him satisfied with plans and preparations for embarkation

has been the best way to keep him in suspension, and although it may be said
truly that I do not know how I can get him removed from the fixed notion he has
had up to the past week that vessels should be got ready and the troops put
aboard them, for he has been terribly frightened by a false rumor spread abroad
with mischievous skill by the Turks that one suspects the infectious disease to be
at Thebes.

Ohr remained, however, until the end, and would participate in the siege
of Negroponte the following year, as would Max Wilhelm, the prince of
Brunswick.

Rumor was a weapon which the Turks were now using to their advantage, having seen how great a distraction it had proved to the Venetian
forces during the campaign of 1687. They were likely to continue trying
to reap some benefit in the coming campaign from their false and venomous reports. Apparently the Curia Romana especially needed reassur-
ance. A recent Venetian venture into the "canal" or channel of Negroponte, however, had excited the anti-Turkish feelings of certain local
leaders in the area of Thessaloniki, along the Bulgarian border. They
were much moved by the success of Christian arms against the common
enemy. Actually two of the principal leaders involved had come to Athens, and had shown themselves ready to join in the next campaign when-

ever the Venetian fleet should move into the vicinity of Thessaloniki. They would come out to join the Venetian forces with three hundred or more horsemen, and serve like an enrolled militia with no more drain on the public treasury than the daily biscuits and the required arms and munitions. Upon the departure of the two leaders Morosini presented each of them with some sort of medal, "che riceverono con indicibil contento," and gave them assurance of rewards to come in keeping with the value of their service.

As autumn was approaching winter, the new serasker Mehmed Pasha settled his troops into winter quarters. He had gone to Talanda, "a city in the vicinity of Negroponte toward the Gulf of Volo." To keep the Venetian Signoria informed, Morosini identified the Turkish commanders in Greece—Emir Pasha was at Livadia (just west of Lake Copais), Saïm Pasha at Zeitounion (Lamia, inland from the Gulf of Malis), Jusulderem Ahmed Pasha at Trikkala in western Thessaly, and Ismaïl Pasha, Mehmed's predecessor as serasker, at Thessaloniki. All told, the Turkish forces would now amount to about 5,000 foot and 3,000 horse besides the large garrison of 4,000 to 5,000 at Negroponte, while Mustafa Pasha at Thebes had 800 foot and 500 horse at his immediate command. Mustafa was making frequent and furtive raids from Thebes, trying "to infest the countryside" and sometimes falling into conflict with the Venetian troops, who were setting traps for his cavalry. The agility of the Turkish horse, however, was such as to carry them off into instant flight and safety.

As a consequence of the serasker's great increase of Turkish soldiery in the province of Livadia, Morosini judged it wise to give up the "meditata invasione" of the region. It was not practicable to send a corps of peasants into so dangerous an enterprise with the evident risk of serious defeat, considering the ease with which the enemy had added to his strength and reorganized his troops so that within a few short hours he could bring them together for action.

For the rest much might depend upon the results of the clamorous excitement then raging in Istanbul, where the populace was becoming ever more incensed at the abhorrent figure of Sultan Mehmed IV so that conspiracies were being hatched against his life. Mehmed's supporters were being eliminated. His opponents were divided into two factions, one seeking to elevate his young son [Mustafa] and the other, his elder brother [Suleiman II or III] so that some change of fortune for the better might accompany the new occupant of the throne. Morosini had not yet learned the fact, but on 8 November (1687), six days before the date of this dispatch to the doge and Senate, Mehmed had indeed been deposed, and his brother Suleiman was reigning as sultan.

Other news from the Porte was to the effect that the kapudan pasha had lost his head by order of the sultan (*d'ordine reggio*) for his failure to meet the Venetian captain Lorenzo Venier at the harbor of Rhodes. For the same reason, but there was some uncertainty about the report, the Turkish commander of the ships that had been restored at Fochies had also been decapitated. Morosini was disposed to urge Venier on to "fruitful attacks" upon the Turks every time they ventured out to sea although, in view of the number of vessels he had had to discharge, Morosini was not sure he could provide Venier with sufficient reinforcements to meet every Turkish attack. Nevertheless, it was important that the Venetians should maintain an adequate armament in the northwestern Cyclades, "in the waters of Zia [Kea]," to interrupt the access of Turkish galleys to the island of Negroponte. It was important to prevent the Turks from adding to the fortifications on the island. In any event the Turks would avoid the approach to Negroponte by way of the channel (off the shore of Marathon), for they would be in peril of having the Christians cut off their exit.

Morosini would have wished to support with money, as justice demanded, the squadron then at sea, but considering his impoverished state, he was powerless. From time to time he had struggled to assist the ships in question in every way he could, but he seems to have had only 80,000 ducats left which, considering the obligations he faced, was an almost negligible sum. The captains were consoling themselves by the trust they placed in the provident hand of the doge. When in times of crisis money was needed, the Signoria often sold titles of nobility, and despite the poverty of the state one could always find at least some citizens rich enough to buy the coveted titles at high prices. When it had become clear that the Holy League, binding the Austrians, Poles, and Venetians against the Turks, was going to be formed, the Signoria knew that money would be needed, and titles of nobility were put up for sale.[19] One's candidacy for the *nobiltà*, however, was dependent upon certain requirements which not every rich citizen could meet, and so there were limits to the amounts of money that could thus be raised.

To go on with Morosini, however, he could not refrain from stating that all the galleasses and galleys, to the infinite regret of the gunners, were behind in four wage payments, which would be met in five days,

---

[19] There are more than forty *Suppliche per aggregazioni alla nobiltà veneta* in MS. Marc. It. VII, 682 (7891), beginning in the Collegio on 10 February 1684 and ending on 17 September 1704 with the votes taken in the Senate (*in Pregadi*) and the Grand Council (*in Maggior Consiglio*), with a careful record of each case. The first applicants for the costly distinction of nobility (to have their names inscribed in the Golden Book) were the Bettoni family, the last (as listed in this MS.) the Fracasetti, with such notable families as the Benzon, Rezzonico, Martinengo, Trevisan, Ottobon, and Pignatelli listed among them.

this being a passionate resolution to which I must adhere so that if it is at all possible, payment must be made to the military, and now especially, since they are on land, and in an exposed area, which compels us so much the more to keep them satisfied. I confess the truth of not knowing how to understand what mischance [*fatalità*] has produced this miserable distress with regard to both money and bread. . . .

And again Morosini closed a long dispatch on a doleful note with facts, figures, and financial lamentations, leaving to the mature and sublime understanding of the doge the needs of the Serenissima's threatened forces overseas.[20]

Besides the sad recollections of the destruction of the Parthenon, the Venetians have left us the priceless drawings which Giacomo Verneda did of "the fortress and city of Athens." Morosini sent at least one of these drawings to the doge and Senate along with his dispatch of 15 November (1687). He also enclosed a petition from Verneda addressed to the Signoria for an increase in his stipend,

which it seems to me we owe him for his laborious and valuable service. Likewise in order to be able some time to send [you] a plan of [Napoli di] Romania also, I have ordered the engineer [Giovanni] Bassignani who, besides his commission to sketch the plan of the fortress with all its works and the fortifications which have been added to them, has the further assignment of applying himself to their restoration.

Morosini feared that certain aspects of the fortifications might have suffered some impairment from the excessive heat of summer so that when the imminent rains came more serious damage might follow.[21]

On Christmas day (1687) Morosini wrote from Piraeus to the doge and Senate that, two days before, the "ducal letters" of 22 November had arrived by way of Otranto, enjoining him to let go the three veteran

---

[20] Senato, Provv. da terra e da mar, Filza 1120, dispatch dated "di galera, Porto Lion, 14 Novembre 1687, s[til] n[ovo]," and signed by Morosini. On the unrest in Istanbul, cf. Locatelli, II, 16–21.

[21] Senato, Provv. da terra e da mar, Filza 1120, dispatch dated "di galera, Porto Lion, 15 Novembre 1687, s[til] n[ovo]," and signed by Morosini: ". . . Perfettionato dall'ingegner capitan Verneda il dissegno della fortezza e città d'Atene, lo accompagno unito alla supplicatione che porge alla publica munificenza per impetrare quell'aumento di stipendio che al suo faticoso e proffittevole servitio parmi dovuto. Così parimente per poter una volta anco trasmetter quello di Romania ho spedito colà nella settimana passata l'ingegner [Giovanni] Bassignani, che oltre la commissione di rillevar la pianta della piazza con tutte l'opere e fortificationi che se le son aggionte, tiene l'incarico d'applicarsi al ristauro delle stesse in caso rissentito havessero dagl'ardori della staggione spirata qualche detrimento, onde poi dall'imminenti pioggie non le succedessero più dannose rovine, tutto contribuir dovendosi, per mantenere quella fortissima piazza nell'ottima struttura, in che fu nel passato verno costituita" [which passage comes at the end of the dispatch].

regiments of Duke Ernst August of Brunswick. He had not lost a moment in putting the orders into effect. Everything that had to be done, had been done in two days, "but with that grave discontent entailed in the loss of such a seasoned body of troops." The new levy would not compensate for the loss of the hardened veterans. The three regiments comprised 24 companies with 1,373 soldiers. Their wages had been taken care of for the current month of December. They had all been provided with a twenty days' supply of ship's biscuit. Also the Venetian provveditore of the island of Zante would help look after them. Morosini was attending to the problem of arranging for the transportation of the Brunswick regiments back to Venice. It is not clear, however, how many of these troops departed, if any, for we shall note the return homeward of the "three old regiments" of Brunswick-Lüneburg in early November 1688 after the failure of the Venetian siege of Negroponte.

In the meantime, in accord with the directions Morosini had received in a ducal order of 15 October, he had sent Captain Giacomo Verneda, the engineer, to Corinth with instructions to draw a topographical plan of the Isthmus of Corinth for its entire length of ten or twelve miles. His plan or plans must include the fortress enclosure of Acrocorinth as well as the villages which lay below it, everything to be done with that exactitude of measurement and with such detailed descriptions as Verneda thought necessary. The latter had gone off to Corinth to set about his task, although Antonio Mutoni, count of S. Felice, claimed that the plan he had made (which had already been sent to Venice) contained all the details and data which Verneda was seeking, "and now he has given me another copy of it with the addition of various annotations." This was also being submitted to the Signoria.[22]

Such plans and drawings as those of Verneda and S. Felice were useful for the maintenance as well as for the improvement of the fortifications. They helped architects and engineers to understand their problems and to provide the Signoria with estimates of projected costs. They also satisfied the curiosity of those back home, for many of these plans and drawings were soon published. The sixteenth and seventeenth centuries were an age of journalism, and just as the *giornalisti* of earlier generations had covered the battle of Lepanto and the war of Candia, so now the journalists covered the Austrian successes against the Turks and the Venetian occupation of Athens.

---

[22] Senato, Provv. da terra e da mar, Filza 1120, dispatch dated "di galera, Porto Lion, 25 Decembre 1687, s[til] n[ovo]," and signed by Morosini.

XI

The Venetians' Withdrawal from Athens, the Removal of Antiquities, and Morosini's Failure to Take Negroponte

Despite the publications of the contemporary literati, the history of the Venetian occupation of Athens in 1687–1688 is best gleaned from the dispatches of Morosini and the minutes of the war council over which he presided. At a meeting of the council held on 31 December (1687) Morosini reviewed the major decisions and events of the preceding three and one half months. He began with the resolution agreed to by the council (on 14 September) to demand a large sum from the Athenians and (in the event of their failure to pay) to make an attack upon their city. The primary purpose of the attack would be to remove the Turks from proximity to the Strait of Corinth and thus protect the "war-torn kingdom of Morea." Morosini emphasized the fact that, when Athens had been taken, the council decided on 2 October to establish winter quarters in the city and the harbor of Piraeus, giving up the idea of wintering in the Morea because of the outbreak of the plague. Dwelling on the advantages of Athens and Piraeus, he mentioned the appointments of Tomeo Pompei to the garrison in the fortress and of Daniele Dolfin to governance in the city, while of course von Königsmarck remained in command of the army. Redoubts had been built along the road from the city to Piraeus to assure the army of access to the sea.

The question would soon arise, however, what to do with Athens, for when the Venetian high command had occupied the city, it was not their intention to hold it indefinitely (*cosí non vi era allora intentione di sostenerlo*). If they gave up the city, what would happen to the Athenians? Debating the pros and cons of their problems, Morosini stated that the heads (*li primati*) of the Greek community both by personal visits and by letters had implored the high command to have pity on them and help them to maintain permanent residence in their city. The Greeks offered to give their property and their lives, to the fullest extent they could, to help the Venetians hold Athens. There were about 3,000 men capable of bearing arms, including the Albanians who had sought refuge in the city, but for the most part they were unarmed, and could not hope to hold out against the Turks without the aid of a military force capable of offering a "valid resistance" to the enemy after the departure of the Venetian forces.

As he contemplated the possibility of trying to hold on to Athens, Morosini had had S. Felice and the Venetian engineer Giacomo Verneda draw plans of the city and the fortress, which he had been studying along with their notes. The fortification of Athens was impracticable. The inhabited area was too extensive; the work would cost too much, and there was too little time to do it. Indeed, time was getting them into trouble. Whether the Venetians chose to maintain their forces in Athens or to abandon the city, either alternative would involve them in several months' effort. If they gave up the city, they would have to settle the Greeks elsewhere to protect them from the vindictive Turks. If the Venetian forces remained in Athens, they ran the serious risk of the Turks' receiving large reinforcements which, considering the toll the plague had taken of his troops, Morosini was most reluctant to have to meet in any sort of battle. He was unwilling "to retreat in hasty disorder and then leave this poor people miserably to perish in a slaughter of barbarian cruelty."

If the Venetian high command tried to move the populace from Athens by water, it would be a question of providing transport for more than 6,000 Greeks, not to speak of the Albanians. The people might, of course, be taken from Piraeus to some safe landing, and thereafter make their own way by the mountain roads into the Morea. If the Greeks remained in the city, and one tried to make a stronghold of it, how would they ever get food, especially in view of the widespread poverty under which they were laboring? The Greeks had informed Morosini that they could find the means of maintaining themselves for some time, if the Turks withdrew to try to meet the Venetians' further invasions.

Morosini told the war council that a decision must be reached on three points: Were they to maintain the fortress (the Acropolis) or simply to demolish every structure on it? As for the lower city, were they to try to keep it or just abandon it? And, finally, if they were going to hold on to the city, to what extent must they limit the area to be fortified? Athens as such was far too large for enclosure within battlements of any kind. If the high command proposed to leave Athens, would they destroy the city or merely pull out their forces? In either case they would have to provide some form of conveyance for a large number of people, and make up their minds where they were going to settle them.

Yes, Morosini was long-winded, but he was thorough. Having discussed these matters in full detail, the war council came to the unanimous conclusion that it was utterly impracticable to set to work fortifying Athens. A makeshift defense would serve no purpose. It would require more than 3,000 workers, and "entire years" of the crews' traveling the six miles back and forth from Piraeus. Troops could not be left behind to defend the peasants when the spring came, for the fleet and the soldiery would have to move on to their next objective (which would be Negroponte).

The Swedish general von Königsmarck also believed it best to give up all thought of trying to retain Athens, which would prove a useless expenditure of labor and money. Von Königsmarck advised the war council to give up the idea of laying waste to the city and its houses in order not to push the poor Greeks into desperation, for some day they might try to return to the homes they could not dwell in safely after the Venetian departure. Nevertheless, that the Greeks might know of the great sympathy and affection which Venice felt for them, the war council recognized that they must be given safe passage to a refuge in the Morea or in other places which the Venetians might take, where they could be given houses and provisions according to their need "so that they may be consoled in every respect in the gentle care of this august, most kindly Signoria."[1]

At the next meeting of the war council (held on 2 January 1688) Morosini lamented the terrible spread of the plague in the Morea. At first it seemed as though, with the aid of heaven and the advent of winter, the *mal contagioso* would "mitigate its ardor," and one would see the flame of pestilence extinguished. But, no, it was burning more fiercely than ever, and reaching such lengths that Morosini feared for the good health and safe survival of the army. From Napoli di Romania (Nauplia) and Modon the dread disease had made its insidious way into the villages "because of the free commerce of the peasants" who without the slightest regard for the danger had gone everywhere despite Morosini's incessant restrictions and prohibitions. Conditions had become especially

---

[1] ASV, Senato, Provv. da terra e da mar, Filza 1120, minutes of the war council dated "1687, 31 Decembre s[til] n[ovo]," and cf. Laborde, *Athènes*, II, 191–98, and *Documents*, pp. 174–80.

bad at Mistra with the dispersal of various goods and spoils acquired from the Turks.

The plague had thereafter spread to Patras, Castel Tornese, and the fortresses of Lepanto and Rumelia, and now once more it had been discovered in a house in the city of Napoli di Romania. It had also been found in a Venetian vessel on the shore at Corinth. The fearful malady had spread to Thebes, Talanda, all through the channel of Negroponte, and into the island of Skopelos in the Sporades. It had spread "in such fashion that on all sides these naval and military forces are surrounded by the imminence of disaster, which has become so much closer, as in these past days the suspicion of contagion has appeared in Athens, which has forced me to have three houses burned down immediately!"

Now two persons had died on the island of Aegina with every indication of the contagion. In view of the encroaching peril it was the unanimous decision of the war council that "one ought in the first place to urge and hasten the departure of the Greeks from Athens and provide for their transportation elsewhere." Above all, of course, the army needed protection, so the war council decided to establish a "magistracy for health" (*magistrato alla sanità*) composed of three "patrician subjects," who should have full and absolute jurisdiction in matters relating to the general health of the Venetian forces.[2]

In a dispatch of 2 February (1688) Morosini reminded the doge and Senate, who hardly needed reminding, that their army had taken Athens to remove the Turks from easy access to the Isthmus of Corinth "for the greater security and tranquillity of the conquered realm of the Morea." The dispatch is a lengthy rehearsal of facts and fears with which we are well acquainted. But the plague had indeed entered Athens, and the exposed populace must be kept apart from the troops. Furthermore, Morosini needed mariners and soldiers, gunpowder, bombs, and a large quantity of fuses (*michia*) to ignite firearms. He denounced the trickery of officers in charge of the mercenaries for retaining on their enrollment lists the names of deceased soldiers, whose wages they put in their own pockets, but he was encouraged by the five companies of Albanians whom he had enlisted in the service of the Republic.[3] The Venetians had had a long experience of the military prowess of the Albanians, who tended to be anti-Turkish although they had provided the Porte with many a grand vizir.

The Athenian problem was disconcerting. The Venetian forces had wrested the Acropolis from the Turks. It seemed, to some at least, almost

---

[2] ASV, Senato, Provv. da terra e da mar, Filza 1120, minutes of the war council dated 1688 [1687 *more veneto*], 2 January, at Porto Lion; Laborde, *Athènes*, II, 198–201, and *Documents*, pp. 180–82.

[3] Senato, Provv. da terra e da mar, Filza 1120, dispatch dated 2 February, 1688 (1687 *more veneto*); Laborde, *Athènes*, II, 202–4, and *Documents*, pp. 182–85.

dishonorable to pull out and leave the great fortress to the enemy. The subject came up again at an interesting meeting of the war council on 12 February (1688), when Morosini presented to the council the general von Königsmarck's views as set forth in letters of 30 January. These letters had, of course, been written at the Venetian encampment in Athens.

Von Königsmarck pointed out that an effective garrison on the Acropolis would require 300 soldiers. Since so many Greeks had been loath to leave Athens, von Königsmarck suggested that some "families of peasants" might be admitted into the demolished houses on the Acropolis (and possibly in the higher areas of the Plaka) if they were willing to take refuge therein, and able to pay for the rebuilding of the houses at their own expense. They would also have to guarantee their own food supply for sixteen months despite the fact that would be a difficult and almost futile obligation if the surrounding countryside were to be "always infested by the Turks."

The Acropolis itself would need military equipment and foodstuffs for at least one year if the fortress were to be held against the Turks. Besides the 300 infantrymen one would have to take account of another one hundred persons—officers, bombardiers, secretaries (*ministri*), hired help, and gunners. In a recent letter of 8 February von Königsmarck had noted that the 400 persons involved would need 200,000 ship's biscuits, which would be hard to furnish, considering the limited supplies and slow service that Venice had hitherto provided.

Morosini then presented the requirements of wine, which for the period specified would amount to 1,440 casks, and if the Greek peasants remained with the garrison, the need would rise to 2,160 casks. The occupants of the fortress would consume some 36,000 measures of rice and 20,000 casks of oil. The officers and other folk of their ilk would need meat and salt fish, cheeses, and other such items. As often noted in Morosini's dispatches, foodstuffs could only come by sea, and Athens was quite a distance from Piraeus.

On the Acropolis water was a problem. There were sixteen cisterns, and when they were all full and functioning, they did not yield more than 12,200 *mezzarole*.[4] Such a water supply, divided among a thousand persons (counting the Greeks), would only last for about three months. The largest cistern, however, was that in the "theater of Bacchus" (i.e., the theater of Dionysus), which was outside the walled enclosure of the fortress. The Turks might easily take it or render it useless, which would

---

[4] The *mezzarola* (*mezzaruola, mezarola,* etc.) was a measure to indicate the quantity of water, wine, and oil in Italy, Sicily, and Sardinia, usually denoting about 100 pints or two casks (*barili*), on which see Ronald Edw. Zupko, *Italian Weights and Measures from the Middle Ages to the Nineteenth Century,* Philadelphia: American Philosophical Society, 1981, pp. 146–47.

mean a loss of 5,800 *mezzarole*. When one added the aquatic needs of the animals and the kitchens, the water supply would not last more than fifty days. These were matters, said Morosini, "carefully to be pondered."

It was possible that the great cistern under the Parthenon, "il tempio famoso della moschea," had not suffered serious damage when the roof was blown off by the incendiary bomb. But how potable would the water be, and what its effect upon the health of the "poor soldiers" dependent upon it? The limited supply of water on the Acropolis makes clear the reason why the fire which followed the explosion in the Parthenon had burned for two entire days. The Turks had hardly had water enough to drink, let alone put out the fire.

An effective garrison would have to be made up of the best officers and the most stalwart veterans. When the spring came, such soldiery would be needed for the siege of Negroponte. The reason for employing the Venetian forces against Athens, as was well known, was to remove the Turks from a stronghold so near the entrance into the Morea. When that purpose had been achieved, they would have abandoned the city, had not the widespread plague in the Morea required them to winter in Attica. And so after another thorough (and repetitious) weighing of the pros and cons the war council voted unanimously "that for now we ought to leave the fortress of Athens just as it is at present." They would remove all the cannon, munitions, and other military accoutrements, but they would not dismantle the walls for, with the aid of the Almighty, they might reoccupy Athens at some time in the future if it were to serve the interests of the Republic.[5]

---

[5] Senato, Provv. da terra e da mar, Filza 1120, minutes of the war council dated 1688 [1687 *more veneto*], 12 February at Porto Lion; Laborde, *Athènes*, II, 210–16, and *Documents*, pp. 185–90.

As Morosini noted in his dispatch of 18 March (1688) to the doge and Senate (referred to in the next note): "Si meditorno poi con seria pesatezza le altre essenziali circostanze d'esser la fortezza predetta [the Acropolis] sei e più miglia dal Porto [Lion] discosta, che portava l'obligo di provederla per un anno almeno de munitione da viver e da guerra con 300 scielti fanti italiani oltre gl'offitiali et altri stipendiati e serventi, così che nel corpo tanto debole delle militie e nel scarso requisito del biscoto si sarian multiplicate maggiormente le angustie all'armata.

"Anco la mancanza dell'acqua fu riputata a rilevantissimo diffetto e di grande rimarco l'urgenza che poteva nascere [nascere] di doverla soccorer ad onta d'ogni premunimento con sbarchi vigorosi e col più precipitoso sconcerto nel bollore dei nuovi conflitti e quando tutte le forze ad ardue imprese stessero intente. . . ."

Some eighteen or nineteen months after the Venetian withdrawal from Athens, Morosini's rival Girolamo Corner, then *proveditor general da mar con autorità di capitan general in terra*, presided over a meeting of the war council at the Strait of Corinth (on 26 or 28 October 1689), in which the condition of Athens was discussed. The walls of the fortress (the Acropolis) were intact with but little damage, which could easily be repaired. There were four gates with iron gratings, one of wood; they lacked bolts, and some of them lacked hinges. Of three cisterns, two were full of ruins; the third had some water, which

As Morosini remained through the winter at Piraeus, sending detailed reports to the doge and Senate, he could not be entirely certain that his every communication would reach its destination. His dispatches were considered in the Collegio before their submission to the Senate. The membership in both bodies, especially the Collegio, would change from one month to another, which may help to explain the constant repetition in his dispatches, for he wished to keep the government fully informed. Thus once more on 18 March (1688) he wrote that the most stringent reasoning had persuaded the war council to vote for "l'abbandono della città d'Atene." Also it had been determined once for all that the fortress could not be held when the troops were withdrawn to embark on the next campaign, which would be against Negroponte.

Most of the Greeks would have to be removed from Athens, and shipped to Napoli di Romania (Nauplia) and to other fortress towns in the Morea. The Albanians and some of the poorest Greeks were expecting to seek refuge in certain grottoes in the mountains near the Strait of Corinth, and to raid Turkish territory as a means of livelihood. All these people were, however, gravely disturbed by the doleful fate which was forcing them to flee from their homes and their fatherland. The dislodged Greeks could hardly pay the agreed-on tribute [of 9,000 *reali*]. Morosini might well be obliged to assist them with some measure of charity.

Patras and Castel Tornese were ports of abundant trade. Venice could not afford to let them go "and much less the 'Dardanelles' of Lepanto," which stood at the entrance to and kept watch over "that famous Gulf" [of Corinth], sharing in its way with Acrocorinth the defense and custody of the kingdom of the Morea. Morosini sent the Signoria the plan of the Isthmus of Corinth, with all its miles and measurements plus a detailed description prepared by the lieutenant-general Giacomo Verneda, which were proofs of the latter's experience and skill. They also pro-

---

had been put into it. There were some wellsprings in the city. A recent exploratory survey of the city had, however, revealed "l'habitato quasi tutto demolito, solo sussistervi in una parte da cinquanta case capaci d'alloggiarvi circa 500 huomini: Che nella città vi esistono qualche numero d'Atheniesi condotivi dall'Ivadia [i.e., from Livadia] per procacciarsi il sostentamento pronti però di sempre ritirarsi."

While the reoccupation of Athens was considered, it involved too many problems, and the reduction of Monemvasia would be of greater service to the Republic. The inhabitants of Aegina wanted a garrison of some 25 to 30 soldiers for their protection and to help maintain possession of the island. While Corner's war council did not want the Turks to take over Athens again, it was adjudged necessary to seek some expedient other than that of the Venetians' doing so themselves (ASV, Senato, Provv. da terra e da mar, Filza 948, doc. dated 26/28 October 1689).

Athens allegedly remained almost uninhabited for some three years after the Venetian withdrawal from the city (on 8 April 1688), on which cf. Paton, *Mediaeval and Renaissance Visitors to Greek Lands* (1951), p. 157, note 6, and this despite the fact that Sultan Suleiman II had apparently pardoned the Athenians for "whatever they had done" (Locatelli, II, 152–53).

vided striking evidence that no time should be lost, and every effort made, to guarantee the security of the isthmus, upon which the peaceful possession of the great kingdom of the Morea depended.[6]

One can picture the captain-general Morosini pacing back and forth in the little cabin of his flagship, dictating a dispatch to the doge and Senate, pausing frequently, rewording this and that, and leaving a verbal tangle for his secretary to unravel. Often one wishes that the secretary had been more adept at unraveling the skein, as in Morosini's long dispatch dated at Piraeus on 19 March (1688). Here the captain-general expressed concern for the Cerigotti, whose island was ever exposed to the "infestationi" of the Turkish galliots, as well as for the inhabitants of Vatika on the southeastern prong of the Morea, not far from the Turks of Monemvasia. The plague was a greater problem in the Morea, however, than the attacks of Turkish galliots.

The Jews in Mistra had agreed to increase their annual contribution to the Venetian coffers to a thousand *reali*—they had no alternative—in addition to the payment of 5,000 *reali* which they had already made to the "publica cassa." Upon his departure from Argos after a recent trip to the area of the picturesque fortress of the Burdzi, Morosini had ordered Zorzi Benzon to return to Mistra to see to the transport to Kialepha (on the eastern shore of the Gulf of Coron) of a number of weapons stored at Mistra—falconets, springals, and mortars "of various kinds"—as well as some 28,000 measures of gunpowder, which the Turkish kapudan pasha had left behind at the time of his "defeat and shameful flight." Morosini sent the Signoria a design and plan of the lofty old Byzantine castle of Mistra, which was being garrisoned by local peasants until other arrangements could be made.

Aside from the transport of arms and gunpowder Morosini was directing his attention to the production and available supplies of olive oil at the three neighboring fortresses of Coron, Modon, and Navarino, and especially at Coron, where large shipments were commonly loaded aboard vessels. Benzon would hasten to Nauplia and to Corinth to confer with Morosini. The Isthmus of Corinth was to be made the "piazza d'armi" where, in conformity with the views of the lord general von Königsmarck, all the apparatus of warfare was to be assembled for the coming campaign. The assemblage of men and munitions must be effected before the Turks could employ their large increase in manpower in an attack upon the isthmus.

The Morea would thus be covered before the Venetian forces began another invasion of Turkish territory. Provisions must be amassed on the

---

[6] Provv. da terra e da mar, Filza 1120, dispatch dated "di galera, Porto Lion, 18 Marzo 1688, s[til] n[ovo]," and signed by Morosini, with a poor text in Laborde, *Athènes*, II, 217–19, and *Documents*, pp. 190–92.

Isthmus of Corinth, and horses collected from the whole of the Morea. The pastures were good around the plains of Nauplia. Shipments of bread must be made in *marciliane* from the island of Zante into the Gulf of Lepanto, i.e., of Corinth. Morosini prayed that the Almighty would prevent recurrence of the terrible shortages from which the seamen and soldiery had been suffering for some time. Also, alas, the pestilence had reappeared in Athens. It had become necessary to bring the troops to Piraeus to shield them from the spreading infections.

In retrospect Morosini felt no small distress at not having shared sufficiently his limited supplies of bread with the Greeks. He had had to provide for the fleet first of all. The burden had been weighing on his mind for the forty-five months since he had assumed the supreme naval command in Greek waters. He deplored the fact that he had been unable to help the Greeks in the barren area of Vatika. They had been forced to live on a mixture of olive pits, grape seeds, and the grass of the fields "di modo che disperrati per vivere è mancato il principal vigore d'angustiar Malvasia." The poor folk of Vatika had been too hungry to give the Venetians much assistance in the prolonged beleaguerment of Monemvasia. Except for the damage caused by the lack of food (*la penuria del biscotto*) in the Vatikan peninsula the Turks probably could not have endured the siege.

During his trip to Argos, Morosini had taken the opportunity to visit Nauplia, where he was pleased to see in good condition "all those great works [of fortification] which I had had erected there last winter." The small items that he found awry could quickly be corrected. He was also pleased with the triple fortress which had been constructed on the great height of Palamidi, which towers over Nauplia and the little island fort of the Burdzi. Two centuries after Morosini's historic visit brass guns with the Venetian lion of S. Mark and the date 1687 were still to be seen amid the crumbling ruins of the fortifications.[7] The engineer, Captain Giovanni Bassignani, had given the final touch of perfection to the design and plans of the walled enclosure of Palamidi—and presumably also of Acronauplia below it—which was a "glorioso preciosissimo acquisto." Enclosed with a copy of Bassignani's plans Morosini sent the Signoria the engineer's petition for some financial recognition of his exemplary service to the state.

Finally, at the conclusion of this dispatch of 19 March, Morosini noted as an afterthought that since the abandonment of Athens lay just ahead, he had wanted to carry off some of the city's most noble ornaments. He had ordered the detachment (from the west pediment of the Parthenon) of "the figure of a Jove" (*la figura d'un Giove*) with which one might

---

[7] Cf. the *Handbook for Travellers in Greece*, London: John Murray, 1854, p. 258.

have enhanced the lustrous beauty of Venice. Actually it was not a Jupiter (or Zeus), but rather a Neptune (or Poseidon) of which Morosini had ordered the removal from the west pediment, where for more than two millennia Athenians and visitors to their city had admired the portrayal in marble of Poseidon's unsuccessful contest with Athena "for the land," i.e., for the possession of Attica. Pausanias identified the scene for us about the year 174, and an artist in the suite of the Marquis Charles de Nointel, Louis XIV's ambassador to the Porte, sketched it for us in 1674—just in time.

Morosini also wanted to remove from the west pediment, as he tells us, "the reliefs of two most beautiful horses from the frontispiece of the Temple of Minerva, on which one sees the most remarkable sculptures." But he then goes on to say that

hardly had one put his hand to the surface of the great entablature to remove [the sculptures] than everything came crashing down from that extraordinary height. It was a miracle that no one of the workers was injured. One attributes the reason [for the downfall] to the structure's being without mortar, the stones having been joined together one to the other by an ingenious artifice but, then, they all came apart as a result of the blast of the airborne bomb.

The impossibility of setting up a scaffold there and of carrying up to the Castello the masts of galleys and other implements to construct a windlass does away with any idea of moving on to other perilous endeavors, to which I am putting a stop, the more so because all the rest is inferior, with nothing of particular interest and [some figures] lacking limbs which have been eaten away by time. In any event I have decided to take a lioness, done in beautiful fashion, although damaged in the head which, however, can be perfectly repaired with a piece of similar marble that I intend to send off with it.[8]

---

[8] Provv. da terra e da mar, Filza 1120, dispatch dated "di galera, Porto Lion, 19 Marzo 1688, s[til] n[ovo]," and signed by Morosini: ". . . Nell'abandono che seguir deve al presente di Atene studiai levarvi alcuno de' suoi più nobili ornamenti, con cui s'havesse potuto accrescere il cospicuo lustro alla Dominante, e fattasi anco l'esperienza di staccar la figura d'un Giove [actually Poseidon] e li rissalti di due bellissimi cavalli dal frontispitio del Tempio di Minerva, in cui le sculture più riguardevoli s'osservano, apena si pose la mano a levar la superfitie del gran cornisone che tutto da quell'estraordinaria altezza precipitato a basso, fu miracolo non sia negl'operarii accaduto del male. Si ascrive la causa dall'esser la fabrica senza calcina e di pietre l'una all'altra con industrioso artifitio assieme connesse, ma poi dal conquasso della volata munitione tutte scatennate.

"L'impossibilità di piantarvi armatura e di trasportare sopra il Castello arbori di galere ed altri istrumenti per far cavrie toglie l'addito ad altri perigliosi tentativi che io sospendo, tanto più che mancando ciò v'era di più singolare, tutto il resto è inferiore e mancante di qualche membro dal tempo corroso.

"Ho destinato prender in ogni modo una leonessa di belissima struttura, benchè diffettosa della testa, quale però si potrà perfettamente accomodare col pezzo di marmo simile che seco sarò per trasmettere. . . ," and cf. Laborde, *Athènes*, II, 225–26, and *Documents*, p. 193. For a late seventeenth-century survey of the antiquities of Athens, see Locatelli, II, 24–34.

According to a letter of 8 June (1688), written by a Venetian officer from the island of Poros, just south of Aegina, Morosini had pulled the army out of Athens, *la fortezza e città,* on the preceding 4 April. The soldiers had gone en masse (*in isquadrone*) to Piraeus, and embarked three days later for "Porto Porro" on the southern tip of Poros. Something of a classical scholar, the officer had not reached Athens until 18 December (1687). He made an enthusiastic tour of the city which he said, with no little exaggeration, contained some six thousand houses. He was quite enthralled (*estatico*) by the Parthenon enshrined in its ruins.[9] A week after the withdrawal from Piraeus, Morosini sent the doge and Senate two dispatches, in the first of which he states, as we shall note shortly, that the embarkation of all the Venetian forces took place on the morning of 8 April (1688).

Distressed by the continuance and apparent increase of the plague in Athens, and intent upon preserving "il capitale precioso di tutte queste forze di mar e di terra," as Morosini wrote in his first dispatch of 15 April 1688, he had at last moved the fleet and the army to Porto Poro. The war council had been discussing the action for weeks. Now they had done it. Morosini wrote the doge and Senate that Porto Poro was an appropriate site in which the fleet could take cover because of the many inlets on the island, the abundance of fresh water, the easy availability of food from the Argolid, and the proximity of the port to Corinth. The move had been a difficult and fatiguing operation for, first of all, they had had to see to the evacuation of the Athenians "in order not to leave them in the rabid clutches of the Turks after the departure of our militias."

It had indeed been a laborious task, requiring the conveyance of the families and their possessions the "five or six miles" to the shores of Piraeus, from which they were moved in barks towed by galleys to the islands of Aegina and Koluri. Others had been sent to Zante on the pinco *S. Zorzi,* and still others to Nauplia aboard various vessels, some of which were *tartane.* All went under the strictest quarantine (*sotto le risserve di rigorosa contumacia*), but assisted in every way by the paternal charity which the glorious Signoria of Venice never failed to display. And now the Athenians would be free from the barbarous servitude to which they had been reduced under the Turks. They would also be impoverished and homeless.

Morosini had warned von Königsmarck they would have to take care that their own soldiers did not move into the abandoned houses of the Greeks to avoid further misfortune. The capital punishment meted out

---

[9] Laborde, *Athènes,* II, 187–90, and *Documents,* pp. 194–96.

to the first delinquents had served as a restraint on the others. In this connection the fear was not of deserters concealing themselves in the houses, which would have been well nigh impossible, but of the spreading peril of the plague. The provveditore Dolfin had been vigilantly burning the most contaminated habitations together with their contents. Considering the wide expanse of the city, however, it was impossible to put guards everywhere. When one added the soldiery to the local population, some 20,000 persons were said to be caught in the confusion. The burning of the infected dwellings was apparently not proceeding fast enough, and soldiers were being struck every day by the plague.

The most serious problem had been discovered among the foreign troops who, being under their own commanders, had concealed for some time the appearance of the disease among them. It was especially widespread in the regiment of Hessians, for they had deceived themselves as to the malign nature of the affliction, and had neglected to take such precautions as segregating infected persons and burning contaminated objects. The pestilence thus became more virulent among them, and more Hessians died of the disease than any of the other troops.

Morosini included with his dispatch a copy of the physicians' report as to the nature of the pestilence which was pursuing them. The besetting evil was a kind of epidemic contagion produced by the perverse influx which had afflicted those regions for so long a time, striking all the more severely those with weakened or badly formed bodies nourished with poor food, the only remedy being that of expelling its venomous malignancy with cordials and sweat inducements.[10] Despite this learned appraisal of the malady and the way to treat it, the trouble continued without abatement, and quarantine seemed the only effective way to deal with it.

Morosini and von Königsmarck got all the "militias," regiment by regiment, along with the Acropolis garrison, aboard the galleasses, galleys, and ships. The horses and mules went aboard too, well washed with salt water. Morosini encountered more than a little hardship in finding places for the rest of the troops, having set aside the flagship *S. Zuanne* for von Königsmarck and the *Scala di Giacob* for the sergeant-general Ohr to protect them from the perils of contagion. During the conveyance of the soldiers and seamen to the island of Poros, however, it was impossible to set those who were well apart from those suspected of illness, for the latter formed the majority.

The wounded were put together in barks to be towed to their destination,

---

[10] The attending physicians' report may be found in the Provv. da terra e da mar, Filza 1120, *copia di consulta de medici,* doc. undated, with the subscription of a half-dozen medicoes, confirmed by Lorenzo Braga and Emmanuele Sepilli, chief physicians of the Venetian fleet.

and truly it was a gift of the Divine Providence that the embarkation was carried out on the morning of the eighth of the current month [8 April], and that we have landed here [at Porto Poro] safely on the same evening so that the troops were kept aboard the fleet for no more than two days and one night. Thus further losses did not occur among them except in the ships *Pace, Abbondanza, S. Domenico, Postiglione,* and the pinco *S. Nicolò,* where some sailors were found to be infected. The others remained in their previous state of good health.

Morosini had got the soldiers and seamen safely to Porto Poro, but the pestilence had become a roaring flame which he found no means of putting out: *s'è di presente sparsa l'infettione a termine tale che non so qual regola potrà valere all'estintione di tanto incendio.* Sixty to seventy men were becoming ill every day, and more than thirty of these were dying. The only relief from the pestilence seemed to lie in the exercise of divine mercy when the Almighty should decide to intervene. The distribution of bread was another problem, for the foreign troops were being defrauded by their own officers. At least the pinco *Maria Inglese* had brought rice; and money, "the soul of warfare," had come from Venice. Six vessels had arrived with ship's biscuit. Morosini had also received gunpowder, bombs, anchors and other moorings, and skilled workers as well as medicines, physicians, and surgeons along with a reinforcement of eighty-six galley slaves (*condannati*) who would serve as rowers aboard the galleys, which were already well supplied with enslaved Turks from Mistra. Morosini could in fact increase his armament by one more galley if another hull should become available.

Morosini had found the Mistriotes a "most troublesome embarrassment." He had offered them their freedom for 200,000 *reali* (in late August 1687), which Francesco Muazzo thought they might have managed (*summa considerabile non impossibile alle facoltà Mistriotte*), but they had said they could not pay such a sum. Although other terms of surrender were soon arranged, the plague remained a severe problem in Mistra, and the town was put in quarantine. In February (1688) the *provveditore* Zorzi Benzon forced the Mistriotes to surrender the town when it seemed that the pestilence had abated. The Turks were discovered, however, to have violated the terms of the capitulation, withholding arms they were supposed to have given up, stealing millet from the Venetian supplies, and (among other charges) escaping to Monemvasia in disregard of the quarantine. The result was that in March the able-bodied males were consigned to the galleys, 312 children (*putti*) were divided as slaves between the fleet and the army, and women and elderly males were dumped on the shores of Porto Lion, leaving them there "for the greater confusion of the enemy" (shortly before the departure of the Venetian forces on 8 April). The survival of the women and the elderly males would depend upon their receiving aid from Thebes or Negroponte, but Morosini was rid of his "embarrassment."

Morosini closed this first dispatch of 15 April with a fierce attack upon the "sinister procedures" of the French, who never ceased to assist the Turks. The sad fact was, according to Morosini, that the French had carried to Monemvasia munitions as well as food to the Turkish garrison on the rocky height despite the Venetian effort to keep the town under siege. Morosini found the pro-Ottoman sympathies of the French very strange, for recently a French *tartana* in Porto Gaurio (Gavríon), on the northern end of the island of Andros, had been attacked by a Turkish galliot "under the mantle of friendship" with no regard for the king's flag. The entire French crew was cut to pieces by the barbarians. The cargo was removed and sent to the Turks at Negroponte, and the French vessel was sunk outside the breakwater at Porto Gaurio.[11] Such was the Turks' friendship for the most Christian king.

Morosini began his second dispatch of 15 April (1688) to the doge and Senate with renewed reference to Giacomo Verneda's plans for the fortification of Corinth. These plans, which contained precise measurements and detailed notes, Morosini assumed must by mid-April have reached Venice aboard the pettachio *Redentor*. He stated that he now agreed with von Königsmarck and Verneda that it would be best to increase the defenses of Acrocorinth by extending the fortifications on either side of the huge stronghold. This would provide a more effective barrier against the Turks' reentering the Morea than trying "to set up fortifications on the strait."

Morosini was contemplating excavations at the east end of the Gulf of Lepanto (Corinth), if the Venetian Signoria would provide the essential tools and engineers, in order to prepare a necessary shelter for the coming winter for at least a whole squadron of galleys. It was a less ambitious project than he and von Königsmarck had once considered (in mid-August 1687) of constructing a canal from the Gulf of Corinth to the Saronic Gulf.[12] Mariners would have to wait another two hundred years for the Corinth Canal (until 1881–1893).

In submitting to the Signoria the account which the doge Giustinian had requested of the expenses incurred during the year in the maintenance of all the Venetian garrisons in the Morea and of the revenues collected in the so-called Regno during the same period, Morosini wrote that he could only refer to the records received from the Venetian offi-

---

[11] Provv. da terra e da mar, Filza 1120, dispatch dated "di galera, Porto Poro, 15 Aprile 1688, s[til] n[ovo]," and signed by Morosini. On Morosini's difficulties with the Mistriotes, note Muazzo, *Storia della guerra tra li Veneti e Turchi dal 1684 al 1696*, in the Bibl. Nazionale Marciana, MS. It. VII, 172 (8187), fols. 51ᵛ, 59ᵛ–62ʳ, and cf. J.M. Paton, *The Venetians in Athens* (1940), pp. 32–36. On Morosini's abandonment of Athens, cf. Locatelli, II, 48–53.

[12] Cf. Laborde, *Athènes*, II, 119, 306–9, and *Documents*, pp. 264–67, an entry in Anna Akerhjelm's *Journal* (*Dagbok*), dated 19 August, 1687, and see, above, Chapter X, note 2.

cials. Whatever figures he supplied the doge are not given in his dispatch. The garrisons, however, stood in dire need of reinforcements of soldiers, bombardiers, and every sort of gunners. The voluminous registers of reports written from every place in the Morea could be sent for inspection. They would seem excessively detailed, for Morosini had always imposed the strictest financial vigilance upon everyone. Benzon, who was then trying to control the pestilence in the fortress town of Coron and the adjacent area, had always been on the alert. But the pestilence, also to be found in the region of Patras and at Lepanto, was of course the major reason for the sparse revenues which had been collected in the Moreote kingdom.

In the long run, however, the revenues from the Regno would far outweigh the then current burden of expenditure. From olive oil alone considerable sums were bound to accrue, for in every nook and cranny in the Morea there was a copious supply of oil, especially in the area of Coron, where in the local levies and appropriations from the Turks Benzon had obtained 960 barrels of oil. Salt could also become a good source of income.

In the meantime Morosini urged the doge and Senate not to delay the projected expedition of the *proveditor general dell'armi* and the other officials who had been "appointed for the good government of that upset kingdom [of the Morea]," into which all the Athenians would be going to seek refuge. Unarmed they needed protection, and the longer the delay in giving it to them, the greater would be their distress and resentment. Morosini could not provide for all contingencies, and "therefore I protest to your Serenity that, groaning under this grievous burden, my battered spirit will be a miracle of heaven if I have the stamina still to hold out in this fifth campaign, which I look upon with anguish and the woeful afflictions I have already described to you."

Morosini closed this second dispatch of 15 April (1688) in a tone of grievous self-pity. As we have seen, he frequently felt sorry for himself. Invoking the assistance of the Almighty at every turn, however, he wrote the doge and Senate he would keep his steadfastness of heart, bear the yoke of fatigue, and meet emergencies of any sort that might arise in his "adored service to the fatherland." But he had had enough, more than enough,

and at this point with profound respect, renewing my humble appeals to the royal throne of public Majesty, I beg for a ray of that charitable benevolence which I see granted to so many citizens with generous concessions, and meanwhile I ask as an act of charity for the election of the successor which the most excellent Senate has benignly promised me several times. Therefore at the end of the campaign I shall be forced, if the Almighty [*il Supremo Motore*] allows me to live, to relieve myself of the burden as a consequence of being weak and weary-laden. I need feel no regret at the denial of due regard, nor [regret] after five years of arduous toil and honest sweat poured out for the public glory at appearing in the sublime presence of your Serenity in the guise of presumed unworthiness. . . .

While his conscience and the Signoria's view of justice might be at variance, Morosini now signed the dispatch to the doge,[13] obviously with a sigh.

This dispatch reached Venice on 7 May. As we have stated more than once, it was dated 15 April. The doge Marc'Antonio Giustinian had died on 23 March (1688).[14] Morosini had been chosen his successor on 3 April. Morosini might thus almost seem to be writing, complaining, to himself. The Signoria made haste to inform Morosini of his accession to the dogate. If his dispatch reached Venice in twenty-two days, one could be sure that he would receive the good news of his election and the ducal *berretta* before the end of April, and in fact the news reached Morosini and the Venetian fleet on 28 April.[15] Long an object of veneration in

---

[13] Provv. da terra e da mar, Filza 1120, dated "di galera, Porto Poro, 15 Aprile 1688, s[til] n[ovo]," and signed by Morosini.

[14] Giustinian's eventful dogate is commemorated by a plaque in the chapel to the left of the high altar in the church of S. Francesco della Vigna in Venice. He is said to have taken over responsibility for the state in a difficult period, "Rempublicam difficili tempore acceptam, Castro Novo, Leucade, Nicopoli, Naupacto, Athenis totaque Peloponeso auctam reliquit." His funereal monument is very modest, reflecting perhaps the financial stringency of the Republic during Morosini's expensive campaign. On Morosini's election as doge, cf. Locatelli, II, 57, 61–65; Graziani, lib. IV, pp. 342–44; and Arrighi (1749), lib. IV, pp. 350–52.

[15] The letter of the Signoria notifying Morosini of his election as doge may be found in the Bibl. Nazionale Marciana, MS. It. VII, 588 (9513), fol. 35, *Al serenissimo Signore Francesco Morosini, elletto doge di Venezia, capitan generale da mar*, dated 3 April 1688: "Chiamato dalla supremma dispositione agli eterni riposi il serenissimo Marc'Antonio Giustiniano, prencipe di sempre degna ricordanza, si sono da noi convocati li soliti consigli, perchè in conformità del prescritto dalle leggi li fosse destinato il sucessore, radunati però li 41 ellettori et invocato il nome dello Spirito Santo, riflettendo essi nel singolar merito ch'adorna la Serenità vostra dal valor insigne, della quale ha ritratto la patria moltissimi essentialissimi vantaggi in tante cariche, e particolarmente nella supremma di capitan generale da mare, che hora ella per la terza volta con vera laude sostiene, sono questo giorno d'unanimo consenso e con universale consolatione et applauso concorsi ad ellegerla in principe e capo della Republica nostra.

"Noi che sperimentiamo vivo contento di vederla collocata nel posto e nella dignità ch'era ben dovuta alle sue eminenti virtù, se ne rallegriamo con noi medesimi, come lo facciamo grandemente con la Serenità vostra, sotto li di cui felici auspicii confidiamo di vedere sempre più prosperato le cose publiche. Siamo certi ch'ella si compiacerà di continuare alla diretione di coteste gravissime occorrenze, come lo troviamo necessario fin che venga da noi diversamente disposto . . . , mentre noi insisteremo nelle applicationi e nelli studii più attenti per assisterlo con li possibili rinforzi, onde ella habbia li mezi più aggiustati all'importanti militari intraprese e corrispondenti alla dignità del capo della Republica, che deve dirigerle. Il di più che ci occorre d'aggiungere a questo caso, si contenterà d'intenderlo dal segretario nostro Giuseppe Zuccato, che lo spediamo con le presenti e con la baretta ducalle, a cui presterà fede, come farebbe a noi medesimi. Fra tanto preghiamo Sua Divina Maestà che doni alla Serenità vostra lunga e felice vita. Data nel Palazzo Ducale li 3 April 1688." A somewhat different text of this appears in MS. Marc. It. VII, 657 (7481), fols. 152–153[r], where eight other documents relating to Morosini from 1669 to his death in 1694 may also be found (fols. 148ff.).

Venice where his triumphal arch still stands at the far end of the Hall of the Scrutinio in the Doges' Palace, Morosini bequeathed a grim legacy to history. In the two hundred days of Venetian dominance in Athens and on the Acropolis, more serious damage was done than in the preceding two thousand years.

The dogate was the supreme dignity in the Venetian Republic but the doge, although he might be personally influential, was a ceremonial figurehead, long since stripped of the authority to make important decisions. In addressing his dispatches month after month to the "serenissimo principe," Morosini was actually writing to the Collegio, which would submit his messages to the Senate. Even after his election as doge, therefore, Morosini continued to direct his dispatches to the "most serene prince." But, then, he had to write to someone, and officers rarely if ever wrote directly to the Signoria or Senate. Morosini's next long dispatch, dated 6 May (1688), began with the usual expression of obeisance to the "most serene prince," and keeping his two offices quite apart from each other, he made no reference to the letter he had just received informing him of his election. Francesco Muazzo, among others, notes that shortly after Morosini's withdrawal from Athens he received the news of his elevation to the dogate (*li giunge la nuova d'esser fatto doge*).[16]

Morosini followed a more cheerful line in his dispatch of 6 May. The Signor Dio had opened up the treasures of his merciful benevolence to the harassed soldiers and seamen. The death rate of those struck by the plague had now fallen from sixty or seventy a day to a more compassionate twenty. Conditions had been slowly improving for a month, ever since Easter (18 April), and the peril of contamination was now disappearing from the vessels in the fleet but, alas, there was still the sad fact "that in each of the two galleys *Bembo* and *Corner* an oarsman has been discovered with the bubonic infection" (*che nelle due galere* Bembo e Corner *in caduna de quali s'è un remigante col bubone scoperto.*).

The plague had been at its worst when the Venetian forces withdrew from Athens, and therein one could clearly see a sign that the decision to leave the infested city and its citadel had come from the Almighty, *il Supremo Motore*. According to the records compiled after the abandonment of Athens, 574 persons had died in the encampment and 52 in the fleet at Piraeus. Morosini mentioned the names of a dozen outstanding soldiers who had lost their lives to the plague, a more formidable opponent than the Turk. Despite all the hardships, at a meeting of the war

---

[16] *Storia della guerra tra li Veneti e Turchi*, MS. Marc. It. VII, 172 (8187), fol. 62ᵛ. On the many political institutions in the Republic of Venice from the dogate (697–1797) to the lesser magistracies, note the helpful survey in Jean Georgelin, *Venise au siècle des lumières*, Paris and The Hague, 1978, pp. 571–618.

council (on 18 April) it had been decided to strike at Negroponte as soon as it might seem practicable, with a preliminary feint toward Thessaloniki to distress the Turks. At the same time a squadron of Venetian light galleys in the Archipelago was to make a quick attack upon certain Moslem galleys to create as much confusion and fear as possible. As soon as the order was signed, Lorenzo Venier, *capitan estraordinario delle navi*, set out with eight of the best warships and an armed, two-masted merchant ship (*palandra*). The palandra was often used to carry cannon, which were of course mounted broadside. It was left to Venier's judgment, as he sailed for Thessaloniki, to make a trial of bombing the port city in order to extort whatever he could from the inhabitants "to aid the public coffer."

Ever vigilant, Morosini was keeping in mind the possible peril in being unprepared to meet, if necessary, the Turkish vessels which in mid-May were likely to go from Istanbul through the Aegean to Alexandria, where workmen could tar their keels and arm them. He hoped that the Christian corsairs would become properly united at Chios in order to pursue the noble objective of harassing the Turks. Leaving Querini, captain of the galliots, to look after the fleet and von Königsmarck and Daniele Dolfin to attend to military affairs, Morosini set out from Porto Poro on the morning of 26 April with nineteen galleys, heading for the island of Andros and then for Capo Doro, just north of Mt. S. Elias on the southeastern tip of the island of Negroponte (Euboea). Thereafter he moved westward to the southern entrance to the "canal" of Negroponte, stopping for a while off the shores of Castel Rosso (Carystus) and the Petalies or Spili Islands, where under the very eyes of the barbarians and to their distress Morosini's galleys took on water.

For four full days Morosini hovered in the region, sailing through the neighboring areas. Finally he withdrew from the scene, but in such fashion (he said) that the Turks could not be very quickly assured of his departure. Also he left them (he said) with the lingering fear that the Venetian forces might reappear at any moment to embark upon the invasion of the "realm" of Negroponte. Actually, however, there was little Morosini could do at the time, for his forces were still in weakened condition (*in debole costitutione*).

There was little doubt in Morosini's mind that this unexpected display of naval prowess had caused confusion among the Turks, who would be less likely for a while to try to attack the Isthmus of Corinth. But the Signoria must send him all the necessary apparatus of warfare or no worthwhile operation against the Turks would be practicable. The first serious encounter with them was likely to lead to a battle, which one could hardly risk at the beginning of the campaigning season. When the decision was made to invade the island of Negroponte, one could be sure of a harsh conflict and an arduous siege of the fortress town of Negroponte, i.e., Chalcis. The Turks had fortified the stronghold with exterior works and trenches lined with stockades. They had erected an outpost upon the rocky mound of Kara Babà ("Black Father") on the mainland at the entrance to the bridge leading to the town of Negroponte.[17]

According to Morosini (and to other sources), all the works on the mainland outpost of Kara Babà were proposed and directed by a certain Girolamo Galoppi of Guastalla, who had been a dragoon in Corbon's regiment. At the time of the attack upon Napoli di Romania (Nauplia), "mosso da diabolico istinto," Galoppi had fled in outrageous fashion to the Turks [at Negroponte], and abjured the Catholic faith, for which treachery Morosini was sure that heaven would bring down upon him the avenging sword of Venetian justice. Although on 6 May, as he wrote this dispatch, Morosini could not know what was to come, Galoppi's fortification of Kara Babà would lead to the failure of the Venetian forces to take Negroponte in the late summer and fall of 1688.

Upon Morosini's return to Porto Poro with the nineteen galleys he had taken to the shores of Castel Rosso and the Petalies (Spili Islands), he immediately had the keels tarred, the work being done in various well-chosen places. He had been pleased to find that the admiral Pietro Zaguri had returned from Zante with the ships *Venere Armata, Guglielmo, David,* and *Costà* as well as two other vessels commanded by Filippo Petrina and Simon Benedetti, the *Genova* and the *Duca di Lorena,* which had been repaired at Corfu after suffering damage from a storm. They came with five hundred infantry taken from the fortresses of S. Maura and Prevesa besides the five companies which had been aboard the other ships mentioned by Morosini, along with military equipment and a huge store of bread. And with a few other details relating to ships and bread Morosini brought another long, informative dispatch to an end.[18]

The last text signed by Morosini in the register of his original dispatches in the Venetian Archives is dated 19 May (1688). As he now wrote the Signoria, the season was advancing at a rapid pace, making it all the more urgent to hasten the delivery of the troops and provisions which would be indispensable for the campaign in the offing. Despite the shortage of funds which was upsetting him, Morosini had gone ahead and chartered a merchant vessel of sizable tonnage (of the Smyrna trade) as well as the Dutch pinco *S. Anna.* He had recently decided to remove from

---

[17] On the Turks' mainland outpost of Kara Babà, note Anna Akerhjelm's letter to her brother Samuel Månsson, dated aboard the ship *S. Johannes* (in the channel at Negroponte) on 7 August, 1688 (Laborde, *Athènes,* II, 286–87, and *Documents,* pp. 244–45).

[18] Provv. da terra e da mar, Filza 1120, dispatch dated "di galera, Porto Poro, 6 Maggio 1688, s[til] n[ovo]," and signed by Morosini, who says he had tried to effect Galoppi's repentance with "rich allurements," *per quanto s'habbi da me contribuito per farlo coll'altrui essortatione ravvedere dall'essecrando errore e con vivi allettamenti rimoverlo dal malvaggio passo, tutto è riuscito vano.* . . . On Galoppi and the fortifications at Kara Babà, cf. J.M. Paton, *The Venetians in Athens* (1940), pp. 84–85.

the fleet the two state-owned ships *S. Nicolò* and *Venere* along with the pinchi *S. Nicolò* and *S. Iseppo*. He was sending the squadron off to the island of Zante under the command of the admiral Zaguri, which could now be done without much risk. The pinco *S. Zorzi* was being held up at Zante for lack of a cargo.

All together, however, these vessels might bring to Greece as much as the ships hired for the Venice-to-Zante run would carry to the latter island. The thought encouraged Morosini to believe that presently the great convoy would arrive under Corner, the *proveditor general dell'armi;* Morosini awaited Corner and the convoy with great anxiety in view of the current circumstances, expressing a high regard for Corner's "elevantissimi talenti." Morosini also looked forward to the arrival of other officials whom Corner was bringing with him, for they were to assume the heavy responsibility of "the economic and political governance of the conquered kingdom of Morea so that those grave impairments may cease which without the proper authorities have been productive of disorder and confusion."

Morosini had often written the doge and Senate that he had certainly not failed in vigilant attention to Moreote affairs to the fullest extent that distance had allowed him while in Athens. The disturbed state of the Morea filled his soul with grief. He had commissioned Zorzi Benzon, *proveditor estraordinario* in the Morea, to turn the ardor of his spirit to the problem of the coming harvest. The wheat crops, to which the state had ultimate title (*di publica ragione*), should not be scattered, but kept under the control of the government so that wheat (and other grains) should not be taken from the Morea "in the mercantile traffic."

The primary objective should be the distribution of a proper ration of bread, at least to maintain the garrisons and to prevent the lavish consumption of ship's biscuit. Morosini wanted "the third and the tithe" of crops which were to be taken from the Turkish stores as well as the "universal tithe" of all the other crops exacted from the peasant holdings. An abundant harvest was in prospect everywhere in the Morea as a result of the willing efforts and suffering this past winter of the country folk (*villici*), "who have buried in the ground that which should at this very time provide them with enough to eat." Underground storage was a common practice.

A stockpile of wheat in reserve would be very valuable for sales (*per le comprede*) when it was decided to put up buildings in the Morea intended for the production of ship's biscuit. In Morosini's humble opinion the fortress town of Napoli di Romania (Nauplia) would be the best place to establish such bakeries. Nauplia was also the place where Morosini believed it best to build powder magazines, deposits for every sort of munitions, and warehouses for food as well as the equipment of warfare. All would be of easy access for the fleet, and the concentration of such resources at Nauplia would bring relief from the heavy expense which one was now forced to undergo in the chartering of so many vessels.

In the actual production of ship's biscuit, however, Morosini feared no drawback other than how much the prevailing shortage of labor would allow to be made. In every district there were of course some mills lacking the advantage of real rivers which in other places provided power for the grinding process, and which at times could scarcely meet the needs of the state. Yes, one could easily see that this would be one of the chief obstacles to the realization of so useful a plan as he had in mind. Morosini always had his eye on the almighty ducat, and was also concerned about the collection of tolls on the sale and shipment of olive oil.

As more important for the moment, however, Morosini was pressing Benzon to waste no more time in repressing the audacity of the Turks in Monemvasia who, instead of meeting in combat the irregular troops laying siege to the fortress town, would make unseemly raids on the countryside. Morosini was relieved, however, that the discord among the inhabitants of Vatika was caused not by disaffection but by hunger, as a result of which they had been constrained to withdraw from their position in the siege before the arrival of the commander Lascari with the troops of Maina and Laconia. The Vatikani should have joined or followed him. Morosini decided that the most needy among the Vatikani should receive some measure of assistance in the form of ship's biscuit until the next harvest or be aided with a moderate allotment of money instead of bread if the fleet required the latter.

Morosini was trying to push Lascari into tightening the siege of Monemvasia to drive the Turks into desperation by deploying at the entrance to the causeway (*al ponte*) some strong combatants to contest the exit of the Turks from the towering fortress town. When the besieged did get out onto the mainland, Lascari was to see that they were cut to pieces. For the rest, Morosini had received from Basadonna, the *proveditor estraordinario* of Navarino, the plan of the castle of Arcadia (Kyparissia) together with a report relating to it by the governor Napoleon. He was sending both the plan and the report to Venice, where the Signoria would have to make the next move.

Morosini regarded the construction of proper fortifications at Arcadia as important, "especially since the inhabitants of the place have restored at their own expense the devastation caused by the explosion which the Turks set off when they abandoned [the town]." The castle of Arcadia, on the west coast of the Morea, was a notable site and of high strategic value. Captain Bartolommeo Salamón was stationed there with a dozen soldiers. His purpose was above all to guard the five large bronze cannon, the fifty-nine bronze gunbarrels, and nine iron cannon as well as some "male mortars" (*petriere mascoli*) and other things listed in a note which Morosini was sending with his dispatch. At any rate the data pertaining to Arcadia indicated the importance of the place, and so the need of its being defended at least by one of the "ordinary companies."

As Morosini was preparing this dispatch (of 19 May 1688) Lorenzo Venier, the *capitan estraordinario delle navi,* had just returned from his voyage to Skiathos and Thessaloniki to try to extort money from the Turks. Morosini gathered from Venier's report that the latter had managed well, but he had got no money from the inhabitants of the city owing to the presence of Ismaïl Pasha, the former serasker of the Morea, who was then resident at Thessaloniki as the first commander. Ismaïl would not consent to the Venetian demand for a "contribution." Venier had sought to exact the funds by every possible means, including a heavy bombardment of the port to harass the people, but all to no avail. In any event the "few bombs" that Venier could fire into the "vast enclosure" of the well-walled city had had the "good effect" of setting a number of houses on fire which burned for half a day and a night, and "non può che riputarsi considerabile il danno e l'afflittioni che havran gl'animi loro concepito."

Venier had shown good judgment in knowing when to stop the bombardment of Thessaloniki, for an officer and four mariners aboard the two-masted gunboat (*palandra*) had fled from his squadron in a caïque before he had got out of the harbor. They were well aware of the poor armament of Venier's ships, and would inform the Turks. Nevertheless, his mission had been accomplished to the full credit of Venetian arms and the disturbance of the city and its surrounding area. Morosini's views are not always consistent. While Venier's venture had certainly upset the neighborhood of Thessaloniki, he had acquired no money for Morosini's *erario,* and the five deserters had revealed the vulnerability of a part of the Venetian fleet.

Morosini rejoiced, nonetheless, in the seamen's widespread recovery from the plague, although it was a fact that after some four to six days of reassuring freedom from infection, some cases had turned up in the army. It was clear, to Morosini at least, that the "Dio delle misericordie" did not intend to allow the resurgence of the grievous malady. The small residue of pestilence had appeared in a regiment of the prince of Brunswick, who was confident that he would soon be entirely rid of the affliction. Morosini feared most of all "the late arrival here [at Porto Poro] of the armament of all the forces which is delaying the start of the campaign [against Negroponte]." Be that as it might, he was rejoicing in the restoration of the health of the seamen and soldiers, which he obviously thought boded well for their next undertaking.[19]

---

[19] Provv. da terra e da mar, Filza 1120, dispatch dated "di galera, Porto Poro, 19 Maggio 1688," and signed by Morosini.

A month later, on 20 June (1688), Anna Akerhjelm, lady-in-waiting to the Countess von Königsmarck, wrote her brother Samuel Månsson that "we have been frightened by the plague," but it had slackened. The quarantine had been almost entirely lifted, although some people were still in confined isolation. The Venetian armed forces, which numbered 16,000 men,[20] were kept busy in constant military exercises, awaiting orders to learn where they were to go next. Anna had already written her brother that the captain-general Francesco Morosini had been elected doge of Venice, but he would remain in eastern waters until the end of the campaign. When Morosini had received the news of his election, he had remained aboard his galley. The field marshal Otto Wilhelm von Königsmarck and two or three of the other most important personages in the armed forces went aboard to pay him their compliments.

When von Königsmarck expressed pleasure in Morosini's elevation to the dogate, the doge replied, "If you rejoice in my honor, I have reason to thank you, for it is the consequence of your own valor." While we cannot linger over the interesting details in Anna Akerhjelm's letter, we must note that as part of the fireworks and other displays attending the celebration of Morosini's election, the model of a fortress with a mosque in the center was set adrift on the water. "I am not sure that they have wanted to represent Negroponte by this tableau, and since this is not yet decided, I refrain from conjecture." The doge had left Porto Poro for Candia, where there was said to be an insurrection. As Anna added in a postscript to her letter, however, Morosini returned to Porto Poro on the evening of 19 June, but one still awaited the arrival of the Maltese.[21]

On 7 August (1688) Anna Akerhjelm wrote her brother from on board the *S. Johannes* offshore at Negroponte, informing him that

we embarked at Porto Poro on 6 July, according to the new calendar, with a splendid armed force. The Maltese were with us, but they started to fall ill in large numbers. . . . We left the port on 7 July. Most of the soldiers, officers, and

---

[20] Francesco Muazzo, *Storia della guerra tra li Veneti e Turchi*, MS. Marc. It. VII, 172 (8187), fol. 67ʳ, puts the total at 16,600, *esercito il maggiore avuto dalla Republica nella guerra presente*, with 8,000 Germans, 4,000 Italians, 1,500 Slavs, 800 dragoons, 300 Milanesi, and 2,000 Swiss. He does not include, however, either the Florentines or the Maltese, and one always hesitates to accept the numbers of troops as given by the historians and war correspondents of the seventeenth century. However, according to Locatelli, II, 102, ". . . finalmente fattosi interamente lo sbarco [on 23 July 1688], era il nostro campo composto di tredici mila settanta combattenti (oltre il battaglione de' Maltesi), cavalli 892, e sopra le navi del Venier [the Venetian naval commander] per guarnigione soldati 1605, e si rendeva più poderoso per li venturieri, e molti isolani concorsivi." Cf. Arrighi (1749), lib. ɪv, p. 353.

[21] Letter of Anna Akerhjelm to her brother Samuel Månsson, dated at Porto Poro on 20 June 1688 in Laborde, *Athènes*, II, 280–85, and *Documents*, pp. 238–43, and see Damerini, *Morosini* (1929), pp. 271–73, 275.

volunteers had to be reembarked on galleys and galliots in order that the contrary wind, which had started and lasted for some days, should not impede their arrival. One knows that this wind, at this time of year, can last a month and even longer. . . . We reached Cape Colonna with the ships on 9 July.

The unfavorable winds continued. The various vessels in the fleet had to seek refuge in one port or another; some even returned to Porto Poro to take on fresh water. Presently the *S. Johannes* made Porto Raphti on the east coast of Attica. Galleys were sent here and there along this shore and that to locate ships which had gone astray. The Count and Countess von Königsmarck disembarked on the island of Negroponte on 13 July; there were the usual complaints (for whatever reasons) among the members of their suite. The Turks did not try to prevent their landing. Von Königsmarck became entrenched near the fortress town of Negroponte (Chalcis) on two hills, upon which he erected fortifications buttressed with cannon of large caliber. It would be hard to dislodge him. Across the "canal" or channel of Negroponte was the Turkish citadel of Kara Babà (Black Father); Anna Akerhjelm wrote her brother that "it is the father of the two daughters Morea and Negroponte."

The question would be asked, when the siege of Negroponte had been abandoned, why had not the Venetian high command reduced Kara Babà, which was at the northern end of the road from Thebes to Negroponte, before bearing down upon the latter town? If a mistake was made in this context, it was certainly Morosini who made it.

The ships, apparently following the galleys and galliots, arrived on 23 July, with Anna aboard. "The batteries have been ready since the 30th, and we are continually discharging twenty-eight pieces of artillery of large caliber as well as eight mortars which hurl bombs. God, who bestows victory, will also deign to bless the arms of Christendom for the love of Jesus Christ." Although the admiral Venier had cast anchor with a large number of ships in the channel of Negroponte, the Turks in the island fortress were getting all the assistance they wanted from the mainland citadel of Kara Babà. Von Königsmarck was not at all reassured with the manner in which Negroponte was being assailed, and

the worst of it is that the army is suffering more and more from illnesses. Among the Knights of Malta there are sixty who are ill in addition to their general. The other generals are also all struck with violent fevers so that the situation takes on an evil aspect in our eyes.

Worst of all, as Anna Akerhjelm saw it, von Königsmarck himself had now come down with a violent, intermittent fever.

Morosini tried to persuade the field marshal to go back aboard his ship so that he would be less upset and more removed from anxiety, thus making more effective the medicines he was taking. Von Königsmarck was loath to do so, but finally yielded to his wife's entreaties. On the day that Anna Akerhjelm was writing—7 August—von Königsmarck's fever had abated somewhat. He bore a heavy responsibility. The army was striving constantly to push closer to the town of Negroponte. The Turks were making nighttime sorties which did no harm. Some Turks had deserted their fellows, and come to the Christian encampment. They had not been paid for months. Reinforcements had arrived at Kara Babà, "which our men had seen," but they had gone off again. The Christians' cannonading was doing the enemy much damage. The Turkish deserters assured "our men" that there were no mines planted in the walls and earthworks of Negroponte. One need not believe it.[22]

As the days dragged on, Morosini became increasingly troubled and, as one Alessandro S. Angeli wrote the provveditore Zorzi Benzon from Negroponte on 23 August (1688),

Last Friday, which was the 20th of the current month, his Serenity decided to launch a general assault upon the Turkish trenches contrary to the advice of all the commanders. But fortune, which has always been favorable to his Serenity, did not desert him any less on this occasion so that, having overcome with vigor the difficulties which have greatly hindered our advance, and having overwhelmed the Turks with a mass of gunfire and the force of courage, he compelled the enemy to give way. They lost everything. Many Turks were cut down by our cavalry, which met theirs in a frightful clash. Some were left on the field dead, their casualties being reckoned at about two thousand, counting those we took as slaves. We'll add to their aches and pains by bombardment and cannonades. . . . We have acquired twenty-six bronze cannon and four mortars of 500 caliber as well as some other muskets [*spingarde*]. Believe me, your Excellency, neither in past nor present warfare has a more difficult, and one can say more impracticable, enterprise ever been undertaken. There are about eight thousand stalwart defenders [in Negroponte], and anyone who has not seen their defense works can hardly understand [our problem].

According to Alessandro S. Angeli, the Christian losses in dead and wounded amounted to some one hundred and fifty. Girolamo Garzoni,

---

[22] Letter of Anna Akerhjelm, who had also been ill since leaving Porto Poro, to her brother Samuel, dated on board the *S. Johannes* on 7 August 1688, in Laborde, *Athènes*, II, 284–91, and *Documents*, pp. 242–49; cf. the *avvisi* in the Bibl. Nazionale Marciana, MS. It. VII, 588 (9513), fols. 13–15, 25–26^r, docs. dated at Negroponte on 7 and 10 August, and note, *ibid.*, fols. 29 and 11^v–12, *avvisi* of 19 September and 8 October 1688, which do not appear in chronological order in the MS. Locatelli, II, 93, 96, informs us that there were 6,000 Turkish soldiers in the fortress town of Negroponte and some 6,600 in the mainland fort of Kara Babà.

the *proveditor d'armata,* was killed; his impressive funeral monument, as we have noted, may still be seen in the church of the Frari at Venice. The prince d'Harcourt was wounded, and so were the princes of Turenne and Brunswick. The serasker Mustafa Pasha and his son were apparently both killed. Corbon emerged as hero of the engagement which, if far from decisive, seemed to the Christian reporters quite promising,[23] but the promise was not to be kept.

Anna Akerhjelm wrote her brother again, presumably on 13 September (1688), noting that von Königsmarck had been beset by the current fever eleven times, although now it seemed to have left him. She also describes the great attack of 20 August upon the Turks, informing us that the Venetian forces had succeeded in taking the borgo or faubourg of the town, "where our men made a great slaughter of the enemy," whose losses she puts at more than a thousand. Alessandro S. Angeli also mentioned the encroachment upon the borgo in his letter to Benzon.[24]

---

[23] Bibl. Nazionale Marciana, MS. It. VII, 656 (7791), fol. 117, *copia di lettera scritta dall'illustrissimo signor Allessandro Santi Angelli da Negroponte sotto li 23 Agosto 1688,* which is the basis of an *avviso* also dated 23 August, which may be found in MS. Marc. It. VII, 588 (9513), fol. 27: "Arriva lettera dell'armata scritta da un corrispondente al nobile huomo Benzon per via di Zante, spedita per Ancona a Venezia all'illustrissimo Signor Morelli, quale porta che li 23 sudetto li nostri s'abbino impadronito di tutti li colli e forti esteriori d'intorno la città di Negroponte, e che il saraschiero con 23 pezzi di cannone e 4 mortari avesse fatto trinciera con le sue truppe ben fortificato, ma che il generale di battaglia Corbon e Chinismargh con la loro cavallaria e fantaria l'abbino attaccato et fatta giornata, quali venuti a fiera battaglia tra loro doppo molto contrasto di diverse ore li nostri generali e soldati s'abbino portati valorosamente, massime il Corbon, quale ha fatto segnalatissimi fatti da vero soldato, havendosi cimentato col saraschiere, et alla fine rottolo con la morte del medesimo suo figlio, et obligati gl'altri alla fuga con aver tralasciato nelle nostre mani tutti li cannoni e mortari che si ritrovavano nel trincieramento, onde veduto il conflitto e la perduta de Turchi, il bassà e commandante della città sortito fuori nel medesimo tempo, s'attaccò fierissima la battaglia, quale per diverse ore non sapendosi da che parte piegarsi alla fine dal coraggio dei nostri e de' principali, cioè Prencipe Turrena, Bransvigh, e generali di battaglia Corbon e Chinismargh, a quali molte volte gli sono restati morti sotto li cavalli fecero conoscere con le loro armi il suo gran coraggio, massime il Corbon, quale azuffattosi col sudetto bassà doppo molti colpi tra loro restò il bassà colpito et atterrito da sì valoroso soldato, parimente il nobile huomo Gierolimo Garzoni, seguendo li fuggitivi sino fuori delli aprocci fu assalito da numero da quei barbari, e preso fu trucidato, lasciando per la fede l'alma al Signore . . . ," and cf., *ibid.,* fol. 29ʳ, where Garzoni's death is also mentioned.

Locatelli, II, 80–120, has described the siege of Negroponte during the months of July and August (1688) in much detail, dwelling (as might be expected) on the Christians' attack of 20 August, which Locatelli places on the nineteenth, and giving much attention to the death of Garzoni (*ibid.,* pp. 112–17). Owing to the printer's error, the pagination in Locatelli's second volume goes from 80 to 91, but there is no break in the text. And of course Morosini's biographer Graziani deals with the Venetian failure at Negroponte (Chalcis) in *Francisci Mauroceni . . . gesta,* lib. IV, pp. 348–63.

[24] There is another account of the Christian attack upon the Turks' palisaded trenches in the borgo of Negroponte on 20 August in MS. Marc. It. VII, 656 (7791), fols. 118–119ᵛ, *Copia di lettera venuta dall'armata veneta sotto Negroponte in data di 13 Settembre*

Anna says, however, that three hundred Christians were killed, and many wounded. On 22 August the Turks made a strong sortie from the walls of Negroponte; they struck at the Florentine contingent which, lacking adequate strength, had to fall back. The Turks almost recovered one of the fortified heights of the borgo, but aid arrived in time to force their retreat into the town. One night, a week or so earlier, the Turks had made a sortie which forced the Florentines to abandon their entrenchment, with many killed and wounded, although the major general Hermann Philipp von Ohr and the brigadier Charles Sparre arrived in time to force the enemy back behind the walls.

Fearful for the well-being of the troops, the ailing von Königsmarck left his ship, apparently on 23 August (1688), bringing joy and some measure of confidence to the hard-pressed troops. The following day, being told that the Turks were preparing one of their frequent sorties, he actually mounted a horse to set himself at the head of the troops. It was a false alarm, which was just as well, for the fever returned, lasted for several days, and forced von Königsmarck into bed in his tent. Again the doge Morosini urged him to go back aboard his ship, as he was constrained to do on 28 August. From time to time von Königsmarck was so weak that he could neither speak nor understand what anyone said. His illness was serious, divided the command of the troops ashore, and obviously did not bode well for the Venetian effort to wrest Negroponte from the Turks.

Anna Akerhjelm's important letter to her brother (of 13 September) is inconsistent within itself. The letter was probably written over a period of several days, and doubtless under great strain. She begins by saying that von Königsmarck's fever had abated, then informs us that "today is the twenty-first day of his last fever," and immediately thereafter states that "the fever, which has held him without cease from 30 August to 13 September, comes back again every day at different hours," all in a letter

---

1688 all'illustrissimo signor Antonio Soderini: "Si portassimo però con tanta velocità a petto scoperto alle dette palizate che strapati li palli a forza con le mani, spaleggiati da un continuo fuocco di moschetaria, granate, bombe, e canone che mediante l'agiuto divino superassimo e s'introducessimo nelle loro trincere, e doppo due hore di sanguinoso combatimento piegò l'inimico che fu seguitato sino alle porte della città, e dal spavento che hebbero ch'ancor noi trasmischiati con loro non s'introducessimo nella piazza, serorono le porte, lasciando fuori circa 400 Turchi che vedendosi in quel stato getorono nell'agua, ove restarono da nostri tagliati.

"Questo fatto costò molto sangue dell'inimico e la perdita de loro canoni e mortari, e di noi la morte dell'eccellentissimo Gerolamo Garzoni da moschetata nel petto. . . ." Of the Christian soldiers 130 were killed in the encounter, and more than 300 wounded. . . . "Il general Conismarch è gravemente amalato, e li giorni passati fu al punto di morte, il sargente general amalato. Al presente commanda il principe di Bransvich, li migliori officiali sono stati amazati, onde quando Dio non ci agiuta, le cose vano male. Mentre la stagione si avanza, la pertinnaccia de' nemici è grande. . . ."

misdated 3 September in both Laborde's editions.[25] In any event despite the care that the Countess Catharina Charlotta von Königsmarck lavished upon her husband day and night, neither eating nor sleeping, as Anna had reason to know, the field marshal died on 15 September (1688).[26]

The Venetian galleys in the channel of Negroponte and the troops ashore kept watch over all the assistance which the Turks in the beleaguered town received through their mainland outpost of Kara Babà. The Christians were doubtless disheartened when on 27 August (1688), as Anna Akerhjelm states in her *Journal (Dagbok)*, a Turkish reinforcement of 1,500 men arrived on the scene. There was little or no good news. The valiant Marquis de Corbon was killed by a musket shot fired from Kara Babà on 8 October. Although the doge Morosini wanted the troops to fortify their encampment at Negroponte, and remain in the field all winter, the princes refused to do so, especially milord of Darmstadt, who had four or five regiments under his command. It was clear that the siege of Negroponte had failed.

The embarkation of the sick and wounded began on 18 October, at which time the soldiers started also to load the artillery aboard the ships. The troops in good health maintained their order of battle before the borgo until the night of 20–21 October, but during the very early morning of the twenty-first they were all put aboard the galliots and galleys. They pulled out as the sun rose. The weather was calm. The doge Morosini appeared with his galley to tow the *S. Johannes* out of the channel of Negroponte, for the now widowed Countess von Königsmarck and Anna Akerhjelm were on board the ship. Most of the Greeks remained on the shore, contemplating their ominous future. Those who had boats or could find transport accompanied the Christian forces. Held up for a day and two nights by bad weather, the countess and Anna Akerhjelm reached Castel Rosso (Carystus) at midday on 24 October. There they found the galleys and galliots with the Christian forces on board.

The next day, 25 October, the countess, Anna Akerhjelm, and their suite reached

a port located between Hydra and the Morea, near the citadel of Kastri, about forty miles from Napoli di Romania. We landed on the coast of the Morea, where

---

[25] Letter of Anna Akerhjelm to her brother Samuel, written in the harbor of Negroponte and misdated 3 September, 1688, in Laborde, *Athènes*, II, 290–97, and *Documents*, pp. 248–55. Anna has dealt with the great engagement of 20 August and the Turkish sortie also in her *Journal*, II, 318–21, and *Docs.*, pp. 276–79.

[26] Anna gives the date in her *Journal*, in Laborde, *Athènes*, II, 324–27, and *Documents*, pp. 282–85, as does Locatelli, II, 126–27.

we spent three or four hours, waiting for the orders to depart. The Florentines had already left us during the night. It was believed that, had it been possible, the doge would have wanted to attack Castel Rosso in order to have a foothold on the island, and since there were those who understood that negotiations had been started for peace, the Venetians would thus have had stronger claims on Negroponte. . . .

The troops were divided on board ships which were to go, some to Napoli [di Romania], the rest to Modon and to Navarino. The time was spent in waiting, and we reached 4 November. We went ashore twice. There was an abundance of edible mushrooms. The prince of Turenne sent to inform the countess that he intended to leave that night, not wanting to wait any longer for the convoy. He inquired whether she wished to leave with him. The countess could not make this decision without receiving orders from the doge, who wished to entrust letters to her. On 5 November, early in the morning, the galleys made their exit from the port, the "captain of the ships" [Lorenzo Venier] having given signals with which they complied. At the tenth hour of the morning the anchors were raised. The weather was calm. We were obliged to tack between the islands of Hydra and Deserta for an entire day and an entire night.

In the forenoon on 6 November we finally caught sight of [the island of] Spezzia, where we had to await orders again. The galleys were then hard by this island. The doge's secretary [Felice] Gallo came in the afternoon, bearing a large dispatch addressed by the doge to the Republic. He wished the countess, on behalf of the doge, a safe and pleasing voyage.[27] Then we continued our voyage with a favorable wind, with three ships before us and another three after us. Sailing with the first [three ships], aboard the *S. Anna*, was the prince of Turenne. The other three were carrying the three old regiments of Lüneburg, which were returning to Venice after having served their time. The princes of Darmstadt with their troops were on board some other ships, headed for winter quarters at Modon and Navarino.

Thereafter the Countess von Königsmarck and Anna Akerhjelm sailed past Turkish-held Monemvasia "with the best wind one could hope for," into the waters of Cerigo, on to Coron, Modon, and Navarino, the island of Prodano, and that of Zante, "and there we caught up with the ship of the prince of Turenne, which had cast anchor before us." The ladies of Zante came to pay a visit to the countess, who spent two nights on their island. And so the voyage went on, and so does Anna Akerhjelm's *Journal*, a diary of great value, covering the Venetian venture into the Morea, Attica, and Negroponte from September 1686 until the failure of the

---

[27] Morosini's secretary Felice Gallo, in whose hand I suspect most of the captain-general's dispatches were penned, was among those who lamented the destruction of "il Tempio dedicato a Minerva, qual'era prima dell'espugnatione intatto, ma hora dalle bombe distrutto" (Paton, *Mediaeval and Renaissance Visitors to Greek Lands* [1951], p. 70). On Gallo, cf. Locatelli, I, 16, 96, 112, 321–22, and II, 80, 126, 216, and for the months of October and November 1688, *ibid.*, II, 134–56.

long, hard siege in the fall of 1688. Toward the end of November '88 the countess and Anna reached Malamocco, and were confined to the quarantine on the island of S. Lazzaro for almost seven weeks. "We remained there until the evening of 14 January, and then we entered Venice." On 22 February ('89) Anna recorded in her diary, "The carnival is ending today with great gaiety. I have gone out twice to see the masks, and sometimes I have gone to the Opera. I have also been to the church of the Salute, a temple of great beauty."[28]

The siege of Negroponte had been a costly failure. Morosini and the princes had hardly withdrawn the troops when speculation began on the causes of the lamentable outcome. The brilliance of the Moreote campaigns of Morosini and von Königsmarck had been tarnished and, when something over a year later (on 10 January 1690) the ailing Morosini returned to Venice (amid celebrations), he still had reason to resent the harsh criticism of the leadership of the Negropontine expedition.[29] Such criticism begins with a letter dated 4 November (1688), written by a participant (or one who claimed to be a participant) in the expedition. The writer of the letter was certainly well informed, providing us with details not to be found elsewhere. Aside from his disparagement of the leadership of the expedition (and he is especially hard on the young Maximilian Wilhelm of Brunswick-Lüneburg), the writer reproached the high command for not having first dealt with the Turkish garrison on the hill of Kara Babà to halt the flow of men, munitions, and provisions to Negroponte.[30]

---

[28] Anna Akerhjelm, *Journal,* in Laborde, *Athènes,* II, 322–41, and *Documents,* pp. 280–99. On the carnival in Venice, note Beregani, II, bk. v, pp. 188–89.

[29] On the elaborate ceremonies attending Morosini's return to Venice (on 10–11 January 1690, *more veneto* 1689), see Locatelli, *Racconto historico della veneta guerra in Levante,* II (1691), 267–79; Graziani (1698), lib. IV, pp. 370–71; and Arrighi (1749), lib. IV, pp. 379–80.

[30] On the failure of the Venetian forces to take Negroponte, see the long, anonymous letter dated 4 November (1688) in the Bibl. Nazionale Marciana, MS. It. VII, 588 (9513), fols. 3–9: "Qui siamo al termine della campagna non coronata dalle solite glorie, anzi resa funesta nella vanità dell'impresa, in cui si sono inutilmente logorate forze poderose e consumate senza frutto sino le monizioni e l'artigliarie delle galere e delle navi medesime con publico infinito dispendio. . . ." The writer of this letter could only wonder "se fosse più facile il tentativo o nella terra ferma, in cui s'opponeva un solo forte di poco rilievo [i.e., Kara Babà] che domina Negroponte, o nell'isola, in cui v'erano trincierati e muniti 9,000 soldati per difender la piazza . . ." (*ibid.,* fol. 3ʳ).

Whatever the reasons for this sad discomfiture, one fact was obvious. There was a deficiency of leadership in the land forces from the beginning. Many experienced officers had been rendered hors de combat by wounds or maladies, but princely rank had given the young and (allegedly) incompetent Maximilian Wilhelm of Brunswick-Lüneburg a command he could not manage: "La mancanza de' generali primarii facendo cader il commando nel Prencipe di Branswich ha rese languide sin da principio l'operazioni perchè, inesperto e privo di stima, o non ha saputo dirigere o ha mancato di far fedelmente ese-

Why, then, did Morosini and von Königsmarck not take action against the hilltop fort of Kara Babà before proceeding against Negroponte? The answer to be given to the critic would seem obvious: they would have exposed their forces to attack from the Turkish strongholds at Thebes and Livadia as well as to sorties from Negroponte, where there was a large garrison. One judges military ventures by the results, and from a military standpoint the campaigns in the Morea and against Athens had gone remarkably well. Considering the wear and tear on the Christian forces caused by the plague, perhaps Morosini should not have undertaken the siege of Negroponte. But nothing ventured, nothing gained,

---

guire ciò che li suggeriva il buon zelo e li dettava l'ottima sua volontà . . ." (fol. 4ʳ).

"Rimasero feriti il Prencipe d'Hermstat, il Baron Spar [Chas. Sparre], et altri di minor conto. . . . Qualch'altro officiale restò nella baruffa, dalla quale si ritirassimo doppo un'ora e mezza d'ostinato contrasto con perdita di 1,200 in circa tra morti e feriti [presumably on 20 August 1688]? Tal fu l'esito di quest'importantissimo tentativo reso vano più dall'inesperienza di chi lo commandò che dalla costanza di chi vi s'oppose . . ." (fol. 6ʳ).

"Sparsasi fra tanto nell'isola [di Negroponte] la voce che si sciogliesse l'attacco, corsero molti vescovi e vecchiardi a piedi di sua Serenità, offerendo 7,000 Greci per quest'inverno armati et alimentati averebbero a costo delle lor vite diffese le trinciere e mantenuta la bloccazion della piazza. Ma gl'aiuti prima incerti sull'infedeltà, poi inutili nella viltà de' Greci discorragiti anno avuto un'intiera ripulsa fra tanto la milizia, li commandanti, e le monizioni fu necessità il decampare. I più vicini alla marina prevedendo nella vittoriosa crudeltà de gl'infedeli la loro morte presero a gara l'imbarco sopra l'armata per passare in Morea, abbandonando le sostanze e la patria per non perder la vita.

"Fuggirono due schiavi di fortezza che usciti doppo l'assalto riferirono il pocco numero de' difensori [but the writer has just said the Turks had '9,000 soldati per difender la piazza'!], la rovina della distrutta piazza, e la necessità che averebbero avuto d'arrendersi se non fossero stati in particolare di polvere puntualmente soccorsi, e così rendesi sempre più chiara la cagione e più manifesto il disordine che ha fatto perder inutilmente la campagna col non aver applicato a Cara Babà e vietati a difensori i soccorsi . . ." (fol. 7ᵛ).

Thereafter the author of this letter, who had apparently witnessed the abandonment of Negroponte, describes the embarkation of the troops, the difficulty of one hundred ships tacking their way out of the channel, and Morosini's ordering the fleet to start for the Spalmadori "20 miglia distanti dalla bocca del canale et 80 dalla fortezza per far colà la rassegna delle milizie, il riparto de' quartieri, e l'espedizione di bastimenti bisognosi di concia a Venezia." At the Spalmadori the fleet picked up some Greeks in the area of Castel Rosso, and continued the voyage with those who were to be assigned to winter quarters in the Morea and those who, "terminato il tempo dell'impiego," were returning to their own countries.

The tragedy of warfare and the pestilence was only too apparent in the number of survivors, ". . . computando il numero delle forze che restano in universale ascende fra sani et ammalati ad 8,000. I Suizzeri fra tutti non son più che cinque in seicento, et i Vittemberg sono ridotti a 2,200 di 3,700 che sono venuti. Le malatie n'han'esterminato la maggior parte, come succede annualmente alle truppe di nuova leva, che poi partono con scapito esenzialissimo dell'armata quando sono assuefatti al fuoco et al clima," a fact of which Morosini often complained in his dispatches to the Signoria.

Other pertinent dispatches may also be found in this MS. in the Marciana (It. VII, 588 [9513]), docs. dated 7 August 1688 (fols. 13–14), 2 September (fols. 19–20), 19 September (fol. 29), and 8 October (fols. 11–12). There is no dearth of material on the Negropontine expedition.

and in those days soldiers and seamen, like gamblers, were well aware of the fact.

The historian is aware of another fact. Venice could not afford the vast expenses of Morosini's campaigns from 1684 to 1688, and not without reason was he always concerned about his empty coffers (*cassa, erario*). The Venetian success in the conquest of the Morea, confirmed by the treaty of Karlowitz in 1699, was due very largely to the Austrians' even more startling success against the Turks, who were obliged to send their best troops into Hungary and Transylvania to meet the Hapsburg offensive which Charles V of Lorraine (and thereafter Eugene of Savoy) was leading against the tottering Ottoman empire. In the meantime Morosini's onetime rival Girolamo Corner had done very well in Dalmatia and, as we shall see presently, would soon capture Monemvasia, the last fortress still in Turkish hands in "the kingdom of the Morea."

XII

Girolamo Corner's Success at Monemvasia, Domenico Mocenigo's Failure in the Aegean, and the Death of Francesco Morosini

❧

he war of Candia had been destructive of Venetian commerce in the Levant. The patriciate had to no small extent withdrawn from trade, the *nobiltà* assuming the social stance of the aristocracies in other parts, indeed in all parts, of Europe. The Venetian patriciate tried to maintain its social status, and on the whole did so, by acquiring large tracts of land by marriage and by purchase. Northern Italy and the Veneto suffered from wars and epidemics. The Venetian plague of 1630 is too well known for comment. As the plague declined and ceased, the grateful Republic saw to the construction of the majestic church of S. Maria della Salute.

Piracy was a constant impediment to the continuance of prosperous trade. Convoys became larger and more expensive. Marin Gritti, *direttore di convoglio*, in a dispatch to the doge and Senate dated 3 November 1684 pays tribute to the "zelante pontualità di questi nobili huomini Ser Zorzi Benzon et Ser Andrea Navagier." Benzon, as we have seen, was conspicuous in Morosini's Greek campaigns. Morosini was often distressed by the failure of a convoy to arrive when he expected it and needed it. The large convoy was difficult to maintain and to keep on any sort of schedule.

363

On 20 December (1684) Gritti's convoy was delayed, arriving at Corfu only *doppo quaranta giorni di molesto viaggio contrasto sempre da venti contrarii.* There were everlasting complaints about *la contrarietà de' tempi nella intemperie della stagione, il vento furioso di sirocco,* etc. Contemporary documents inform us of convoys under Marin Gritti, Iseppo Moresini, Pietro Bembo, Alvise Priuli, Daniele Dolfin, Giacomo da Mosto, Niccolò Vendramin, Angelo Bembo, Zorzi Querini, Alvise Mocenigo III, Antonio Canal, Girolamo Priuli, Antonio Bollani, Marco Calbo, Bartolo Moro, Giacomo Contarini, and Girolamo Marcello. These convoys carried supplies and funds as well as German and other troops to Morosini, "et altri publici apprestamenti per l'occorrenze dell'armata."[1] The Venetians' two wars with the Turks (1645–1669, 1684–1699) were costly, and reduced the Republic's commercial revenues to disastrously low levels. And of course during this period the English, Dutch, and French came into possession of a large part of the Levantine trade.

The Austrians had fared well, very well, in the Holy League and, as we have seen in some detail, between 1685 and 1689 they had wrested Esztergom (Gran), Nové Zámky (Neuhäusel), Buda[pest], Simontornya, Siklós, Fünfkirchen (Pécs), Szeged, Osijek (Esseg), Eger (Erlau), Petrovaradin (Peterwardein), Belgrade, Székesfehervár (Stuhlweissenburg), Nish (Niš), Vidin, and a score of other fortified towns from the Turks.[2] These years also marked the beginning of one of the most daring, brilliant, and successful military careers in the long history of Europe—that of Eugene of Savoy—but it was some time before he could make his enduring impress upon the generations yet to come.

After Francesco Morosini's election as doge (on 3 April 1688) and his return to Venice (on 10–11 January 1690), Girolamo Corner, *proveditor general da mar,* was the Republic's chief commander in Greek waters. Corner had been maintaining a tight siege of Monemvasia (Malvasia), and on 25 September 1689 Antonio Molin, *proveditor estraordinario in Regno* [*di Morea*], wrote Corner that he had received valuable information "from a Greek Christian who fled this morning from Malvasia."[3] However valuable Molin's information may have been, it was apparently not very useful to Corner, who did not succeed in taking the great fortress of Monemvasia for another year.

While the siege of Monemvasia went on, Corner became interested in

---

[1] The dispatches of the *Nobili direttori di convogli da 29 Ottobre 1684 sin 8 Maggio* [actually *3 Maggio*] *1694* are preserved in the ASV, Senato, Provv. da terra e da mar, Filza 880, interesting, on the whole clearly written, and valuable for the detail they contain.

[2] See above, pp. 273–80; note also pp. 366–69; and cf. von Hammer-Purgstall, *Gesch. d. osman. Reiches,* VI, 507ff., 515ff., 543ff., trans. Hellert, XII, 252ff., 264ff., 296ff.; Max Braubach, *Prinz Eugen von Savoyen,* 5 vols., Munich, 1963–65, I, 115ff., 122–23, 129–30, 135–37, 143–44.

[3] Senato, Provv. da terra e da mar, Filza 1123.

Athens, which had suffered severely from the Venetian occupation. Corner sent a "persona confidente . . . in Athene per esplorar gl'andamenti de' Turchi." Apparently the result was a report dated 6 October 1689 to the effect that some three thousand Christian peasants and foreigners were taking up residence in the city. They were keeping up good relations with the Turks,

considering the necessity they felt of having a garrison in the fortress [the Acropolis] to protect them from being molested by Christians and galley-slaves on the loose. They are thinking of putting eight cannon into the fortress, and the galleys must go to Porto Raphti, from which place Ibrahim Pasha is coming by land to the fortress, but the Athenians say it is not well advised to go as long as [Corner's?] fleet does not withdraw. The serasker [the Ottoman commander-in-chief] is of the opinion that he might spend the winter in Athens when the fortress has a garrison. He has with him 800 horse and about 1,400 foot. A pasha had arrived in Athens with another 500 troops. I do not know where he is . . . , but one believes that only the vizir can settle the inhabitants into that place. This is as much information as I have been able to get about the area [of Athens].[4]

These were the years during which Sir William Trumbull, the friend of Dryden and Pope, was the English ambassador to the Porte. A cautious and rather crusty character, Trumbull was a classicist, and had been well trained as a lawyer. His appointment to the embassy had been made in November 1686; he had set out for Istanbul on 16 April 1687; and going, as one usually did, by way of Smyrna, he had arrived at the Turkish capital on 17 August 1687. He pleased the English merchants on the Bosporus and at Smyrna to such an extent that he was nominated again as ambassador to the Porte in November 1689, and continued in the post until the end of July 1691. Some four years later he was to be appointed secretary of state (on 3 May 1695). Trumbull had thus been in Istanbul for a full two years when on 31 October 1689 he sent to Whitehall the following report on Austrian successes and Turkish problems:

. . . Since the last rout att Nissa [Niš] and the taking the place by the Germans, Arab Regeb Bacha, the serasquier, was strangled, and Ibrahim Bacha, who was formerly Jannissar-Aga, afterwards Bacha of Bagdat [Baghdad], and who the last yeare defended Negropont, was put into his place. The Vizir allso, fearing the Imperialists might advance to Sophia, sent orders to Osman Bacha, serdar att Viddin [Vidin in Bulgaria], and to Teckely [Imre Thököly] to come with their forces to him.

On the 9th instant Teckely arrived with about 80 horse, and was met with the same ceremony as ambassadors usually are, vizt by the chiaus-pachi and several chiauses; onely he alighted att the tent of the Vizir's kiah, and was thence conducted on foot to the Vizir who (after usuall complements) ask'd what newes he had of the imperiall armie. He said, They were neer Viddin when he came away.

---

[4] Provv. da terra e da mar, Filza 1123, doc. dated 6 October 1689.

And while they were speaking a courier arrived from the Tartar Han (who, with his son, was come to Nicopolis from Walachia), bringing newes that Viddin was taken, upon which the Vizir ordered Teckely and Osman to returne with all speed to Nicopolis (whether he would follow them), and consult with the Tartar Han about the best means to repulse the Germans from Viddin and for securing those parts.

He [the Vizir] gave Teckely very faire words, assuring him of the Grand Sei-gneur's particular favor, and that he should not faile of being rewarded for his faithful services to the Port. He presented him allso with a sable vest, a topas ring, a horse well furnished, and 2,000 dollars. He asked leave of the Vizir to speak with the French ambassador, but the Vizir told him it was not now conve-nient to loose time in talke, but to follow his journey with all expedition. How-ever, about 4 houres in the night (after he had suppt and dranke plentifully at the Vizir's kiah's tent) he went privately to the French ambassador's lodging at So-phia, where he stay'd till towards morning and so departed. . . .[5]

The end of Sultan Mehmed IV's long and costly reign was filled with a turmoil which continued into the short period of his brother Suleiman II's succession (1687–1691). In mid-December 1687 the imperialists took Eger (Erlau) in northern Hungary. The Turks had held the city for almost a century (from 1596). The main mosque became the church of S. Leopold and, as von Hammer-Purgstall noted a century and a half ago, a lonely minaret still stands (as it does), a reminder of the Turkish past.[6] The Ottoman government was almost hopelessly unstable. After sixty-nine days of authority as grand vizir Ismaïl Pasha was replaced on 2 May 1688 by the former agha of the janissaries, Mustafa Pasha of Rodosto (Tekirdag on the Sea of Marmara), who had been the executioner of Kara Mustafa Pasha at Belgrade after "Black" Mustafa's failure before Vienna. There was a further corruption of coinage. Tobacco was taxed. In fact imposts and taxes of one sort or another were levied almost everywhere in the Ottoman domains. Such measures added to the widespread unrest.

The most stunning blow the Turks received at this time, however, was the imperialists' occupation of Belgrade, their chief fortress in Europe. The city was taken on 6 September 1688, as we have noted. It was the Turks' most important loss, but the imperialists now acquired a number of other Turkish cities and towns. Sultan Suleiman I had taken Belgrade in August 1521.[7] The Turks had thus held the city for more than a cen-tury and a half. The Austrians soon lost it, but got it back in 1717,

---

[5] Public Record Office (PRO), London, State Papers (SP), XX, fols. 150, 153ᵛ–154ʳ. There is an informative sketch of Trumbull's career by Wm. P. Courtney in the *Dictionary of National Biography*, XIX (repr. 1937–38), 1192–94.

[6] Von Hammer-Purgstall, *Gesch. d. osman. Reiches*, VI (1830, repr. 1963), 507, trans. Hellert, XII, 252.

[7] Setton, *Papacy and the Levant*, III (1984), 199, and on the imperialists' occupation of Belgrade, note Max Braubach, *Prinz Eugen von Savoyen*, I, 143–44.

holding it from the peace of Passarowitz (in 1718) to the peace of Belgrade (in 1739). Again the Turks recovered the beleaguered city, and again the Austrians seized it (in 1789). The checkered history of Belgrade was symptomatic of the history of the Balkans over a period of some centuries. In fact during the First World War the Austrians moved into the city again (in 1914, 1915–1918). Now the capital of Yugoslavia and Serbia, Belgrade seems more secure than hitherto.

In the last two decades of the seventeenth century nothing in the Ottoman empire seemed secure. After six years of warfare (1683–1688), almost constant setbacks (and seditions) had exhausted the Turkish treasury, and neither the army nor the administration had a single outstanding person in their ranks. An Ottoman embassy, headed by Sulfikar Effendi and the influential grand dragoman Alessandro Mavrocordato, had waited upon Max Emmanuel, the elector of Bavaria, who was in command of the imperialist forces at Belgrade in September 1688, when the city fell to the Christians. The Porte wanted peace under honorable terms.

Months of protocol, however, held up the Ottoman embassy's access to Vienna and the imperial presence, the ambassadors being detained at Pottendorf, to the south of Vienna. After having agreed to follow certain ceremonial requirements, Sulfikar Effendi and Mavrocordato were allowed to enter Vienna (on 8 February 1689), and were thereafter admitted into the imperial presence. Sulfikar was accompanied by five Turks,[8] Mavrocordato by four Greeks, including the Venetian dragoman Tommaso Tarsia. The Tarsia family had long served the Signoria as dragomans.

Leaving aside details of protocol and ceremonial, important in those days and under such circumstances, there was the question, to start with, whether the two Turkish envoys were truly ambassadors or merely internuncios, for in their letters of credence Sulfikar and Mavrocordato were designated negotiators, with no indication of the extent of their responsibility. As for Mavrocordato, he was well known to westerners, one of the chief statesman in Istanbul. Years later (in 1709–1710) Mavrocordato's son Niccolò was to become the first Phanariote hospodar of Moldavia.

The ministers plenipotentiary of the Christian alliance, who had gathered in Vienna to represent Austria, Poland, and Venice, agreed to regard Sulfikar and Mavrocordato as ambassadors. The two ambassadors had a letter from Sultan Suleiman II and another from the grand vizir, which letters gave them instructions, but no authority to commit the Porte. At a meeting on 12 February (1689) the Turkish envoys began by

---

[8] The Turkish envoy appears as Sulfikar in von Hammer-Purgstall (ref. below), but as "Suflicar Efendi" in a Ragusan *avviso* later given or sent to the Venetian Signoria (Senato, Delib. Costantinopoli [Secreta], Reg. 35, fol. 85ʳ).

demanding the return to the Porte of various fortified towns as the first step toward a treaty of peace, which of course the imperialists refused, demanding instead the payment of indemnities. Sulfikar declared that the Emperor Leopold could keep his conquests provided he gave up Transylvania, which the imperialists had no intention of doing.

Conferences went on each week, all to no avail, but finally on 12 March the Austrians presented their requirements to the Turkish delegates: the imperialists must receive possession of Hungary with its dependencies, the right to fortify their frontier towns, freedom of trade, an exchange of prisoners, custody of the Holy Sepulcher in Jerusalem, an indemnity for Venice, and the restitution of all territory the Tatars had taken in Moldavia. These conditions had to be accepted within thirty days, and put into effect within six months. The imperialists also expected to see the Turks depart from Transylvania. Even if Sulfikar and Mavrocordato had possessed full authority, which they did not, obviously they could not have yielded to the imperialist demands.

Toward the end of March (1689) the Turkish delegates received the Venetian prerequisites for peace: the Signoria demanded, besides full recognition of the Republic's conquests, the Turkish withdrawal from the fortress town and island of Negroponte as well as from Athens and other places. The Signoria must also have all the territory between Obrovac and the river Bojana up to the mountains of Bosnia and the Hercegovina, along with Antivari (Bar) and Dulcigno (Ulcinj). The tribute which the Signoria had previously agreed to pay for possession of the island of Zante must be abolished, and the Porte must return the money —225,000 *reali*—which the grand vizir Kara Mustafa Pasha had wrung from the bailie Giovanbattista Donà in 1683. Venice would have the right to fortify her frontiers and later on, to negotiate with the Turks concerning commerce, the bane of piracy, and other matters of importance to the Signoria and the Porte.

At long length, upon instructions from John III Sobieski and the Sejm, the Polish delegates presented the Turkish envoys with their requirements for peace: the Poles must receive an indemnity for the damage done them by the Cossacks and the Tatars, the latter of whom must withdraw immediately from the Crimea and from certain other areas of importance to Poland. The Poles also wanted the restitution of the holy places (including apparently the return of the Holy Sepulcher to the Franciscans), as guaranteed by the treaty of Zuravna.[9]

The Polish demands included the freedom to build new churches and repair old ones, the right to ring church bells (to which the Turks always objected), and permission to go to Jerusalem without the payment of any

---

[9] For the treaty of Zuravna of 16 October 1676, between John III Sobieski and Mehmed IV, see Dumont, *Corps universel diplomatique*, VII-1 (1731), no. CLVI, p. 325.

tax or toll. Finally, the Poles insisted upon the Turks' freeing Polish prisoners and, above all, upon the return to the Polish crown of Kamenets, the capital of Podolia. They also insisted upon the Turks' evacuating wide areas of the Ukraine. Upon hearing a renewal of certain demands of the imperialists, the Turkish envoys were said to have asked, "Why do you not also demand Constantinople?" Even if Sulfikar and Mavrocordato had been authorized to make large concessions, peace would have been extremely difficult, for the Empire, Venice, and Poland had all committed themselves to making no separate treaty with the Turks, and the Porte could never accede to the sweeping demands of all three allies.[10]

Since there was no prospect of making peace with the Christian allies, Sultan Suleiman II (or III) had his pavilion set up before the seraglio at Adrianople (Edirne). He was going to participate in the coming campaign. The command of the army on the Danube had been given to Arab Redjeb Pasha, the governor of Sofia, but he did badly and was soon beheaded. Turmoil was rife in the Ottoman government; heads fell, and commanders were replaced. The sultan encountered discouraging events in the warfare of 1689. As we have already noted, the important town of Niš in southeastern Serbia fell to the Austrians. While the Turks held their own against Russia, Poland, and Venice, the Austrians inflicted heavy losses upon them. The Poles were forced to give up the

---

[10] Note, however, the letter of the doge Morosini and the Senate addressed to Sultan Suleiman on 23 December 1689 concerning the failure of these negotiations for peace, which is rather at variance with the above account (from von Hammer-Purgstall). The letter is given in Senato, Delib Costantinopoli (Secreta), Reg. 35, fols. 77ᵛ–78ʳ [175ᵛ–176ʳ], "Al Sultan Soliman, Gran Signore: Con la lettera cortesissima di vostra Maestà, che da gl'inviati suoi alla corte cesarea è stata consignata all'ambasciatore nostro, che ivi rissiede, e da noi ricevuta con la dovuta estimatione, habbiamo inteso assontione sua al sublime soglio Otthomano con sentimento ne' nostri animi di una somma essultanza. Se ne rallegriamo però con la Maestà vostra con tutta la sviseceratezza de nostri cuori, e porgemo voti che a così felice successo siano accompagnate anco quelle gratie che alla rettitudine de suoi sentimenti et alle giuste brame possino esser più confacenti e più convenevoli.

"Non minore anco è stato il contento nostro nel rimarcare nella Maestà vostra una vera dispositione di ridonare con una sincera pace la quiete ne' sudditi del suo felicissimo Imperio e di quelli della Republica nostra, ma perchè gl'ablegati suoi hanno chiaramente fatta conoscere irragionevole la qualità delle loro propositioni, e che non ostante che il ministro nostro e quelli de collegati siano concorsi a dare le possibili facilità per avvanzamento de trattati, hanno insistito gl'inviati nelle prime inadmissibili propositioni siamo stati per necessità costretti a concorrere nel loro licentiamento, restando essi colpevoli del discioglimento d'un negotiato che poteva ristabilire l'antica corrispondenza da noi sempre coltivata con l'Eccelsa Porta e con li gloriosi progenitori della Maestà vostra, verso la di cui dignissima imperial persona nodrimo una particolar' osservanza con desiderio di terminare, con una sincera e sicura pace, ogni differenza con l'Eccelsa Porta. Nel resto brameremo sempre le occasioni di dar prove del nostro rispetto verso l'insigne merito di vostra Maestà, alla quale auguriamo in tanto molti anni di salute e di vita. +87, —2, —12," and cf. the letter of the same date addressed "a Mustafà Bassà, primo visir," *ibid.,* fols. 76ᵛ–77ʳ [174ᵛ–175ʳ]. The next entry in this register is dated 3 June 1692, leaving a gap of almost thirty months (1689–1692).

siege of Kamenets-Podolski, however, and Francesco Morosini failed to take Monemvasia, leaving the siege to his onetime rival Girolamo Corner. The grand vizir Mustafa Pasha of Rodosto was removed from office, and replaced by Mustafa Köprülü, who had been largely responsible for the dethronement of Mehmed IV.

Then about fifty-two years of age, Mustafa Köprülü was admired as a staunch defender of the laws of Islam; he was, as we have had occasion to note, son of the doughty old Mehmed and brother of the astute Ahmed, the conqueror of Candia. An enemy of the Christians, *abstemio nemico del vino,* Mustafa Köprülü had had a good deal of political but little military experience (*politico ma non ha nissuna prattica di guerra*). When he had done homage to the sultan, Mustafa Köprülü summoned the leading figures of the court and the empire to a meeting of the divan, the state council, reminding them of their duty as Moslems and of the perils which endangered the Ottoman empire. The next campaign, he said, might see the enemy under the walls of Istanbul. He annulled various taxes, but confiscated the properties of various rich malfeasants, executing them as a reward for their misdeeds. The central and provincial administrations of the Ottoman empire were almost entirely reorganized.[11] But the Turks were at war with Christendom, and how would they fare, for the new grand vizir was not a warrior?

It was at this time (on 6 November 1689) that Sir William Trumbull, the English ambassador to the Porte, wrote Charles Talbot, the earl (and later duke) of Shrewsbury, about Mustafa Köprülü's elevation to the grand vizirate and about some of the governmental changes which it entailed. The letter was addressed to Shrewsbury during the latter's first and rather brief period as secretary of state under William and Mary. Trumbull had just been "informed of the change of Vizir, which oblig'd us to stop this ship (bound for Venice) for transmitting this short account:"

After the late defeats the Vizir [Mustafa Pasha of Rodosto] had dismiss'd all most all the souldiers, both spahees and Janisaries, that were left in the army near Sophia, fearing a mutinie might begin among them, as he had great reason to apprehend from their extravagant talke, most of them publickly railing att the Grand Seigneur and him (the Vizir) and cursing their owne Law and Prophet. But he was wanting to secure the cheif point, which was to keep the person of the Grand Seigneur neer him, who being seiz'd with a panick feare (upon the taking of Nissa) was easily persuaded by the Kislar-Aga (his cheif eunuch) and such other favourites of the Seraglio to run away to Adrianople and to leave the Vizir behind to give necessarie orders and to consult with the Tartar Han and Teckely [Imre Thököly] of what was to be don against the Germans. As soon as the Grand

---

[11] The foregoing has been taken from von Hammer-Purgstall, *Gesch. d. osman. Reiches,* VI, 528–48, trans. Hellert, XII, 279–301.

Seigneur had left him and was gott to Adrianople, the Turkish principle of judging according to successe was presently sett on foot, it being hardly ever known that a Vizir has not been turn'd out after their armie has been beaten.

I cannot yet learne the particular intrigues or who have been the authors of this change (some thinking the Tartar Han was the cheif contriver, who put the caddees [*kadis*, judges] and lawyers upon it, and may have some further designs upon this Empire) or how farr it may be carried on. But I am certainly informed that the Grand Seigneur ordered a galley to go for Kuperli [Köprülü], who was Bacha of Scio, to bring him thence to Gallipoli, and so to go post[haste] to Adrianople, that the Bostangi-Bachi was allso dispatch't away for Mustapha, the late Vizir, to Sophia to take the seales from him and bring him as a prisoner to Adrianople. Kuperli was alreadie arriv'd there, and is declar'd Vizir. Whether the late Vizir will be strangled or banish't is not yet known, but they will call him and his officers (some whereof are putt in prison) to a severe account for all the treasure pass'd through their hands and of the late extraordinary taxes rais'd for the payment of the souldiers.

This Kuperli Ogle is younger brother to the famous Ahmet Bacha (better knowne by the name of Kuperli Vizir) and now (beyond all example in the Turkish histories) succeeds in the place of supreme minister, as his said brother had don to his father. He is esteemed a verie strict and just person, greatly skill'd in their Law and a rigid observer of it, free from covetousnesse and extortion, and it is thought was advanc'd to the vizirat rather from a popular opinion of his integritie than any inclination of the Seraglio. The former Vizir is allready as much spoke against as a man given to sodomie and wine with great excesse and of much negligence in the publick affaires, suffring himself to be wholly govern'd by his officers about him, who tooke great summes of mony from all pretenders. In short, that he was unfitt and uncapable of that trust. . . .

The new Vizir has alreadie declar'd his intention to settle this government according to their antient methods by having all wayes 7 Vizirs of the Bench with him and consulting with them and holding publick divans in all matters of importance, a thing left off many yeares since, the successive Vizirs having assum'd to themselves an arbitrarie power and acted absolutely as their humour, passion, or interest led them.

Last weeke the Grand Seigneur's fleet came into this port [Istanbul], consisting in all but of 9 men of warre (such as they are) and 15 galleys, together with the prize of Capt. Paolos, a Leghornese (taken by the Algerines, but by them deliver'd to the Capt. Bacha as a present to the Grand Seigneur) with a Venetian galley and 2 brigantines, which has been all the effect of this campagne att sea. . . .[12]

In a long dispatch dated at Monemvasia on 23 May 1690 Girolamo Corner sent the doge Francesco Morosini and the Senate a detailed account of his disagreements with an allied commander "per l'intrapresa dell'attacco del borgo di Malvasia." He also described the state of his finances, supplies, artillery, and munitions, as well as his military and

---

[12] PRO, SP 97, XX, fols. 151–52, 154.

naval problems, including a somewhat costly encounter with the enemy at Monemvasia. He gave notice also of the arrival of an important convoy, the movements of the Turkish commanders and their troops at Tenedos, Negroponte, Larissa, Thebes, and elsewhere. On the whole, despite the length and cost of the siege, Monemvasia still remained in the hands of the Turks,[13] and their holding on to the fortress in this obstinate fashion was one of their few successes.[14]

Month after month Girolamo Corner, the Venetian *proveditor general da mar*, continued the siege. It was, as he reminded the doge Francesco Morosini, a tiring business, but he never relaxed his efforts to take the stronghold from the Turks. Monemvasia had been provided with more foodstuffs (and with a larger armament) than the Venetians had realized, which was obviously the reason for the long duration of the siege or rather the blockade.[15]

---

[13] ASV, Senato, Provv. da terra e da mar, Filza 1123, dispatch no. 37. On 30 April 1690 the Venetian forces had defeated and captured Zin [*che in lingua Albanese significa Diavolo*] Ali Pasha of Hercegovina, killing 700 Turks—300 sipahis and 400 infantry—in his militia which then consisted of 3,000 men, plus 500 sipahis which the pasha of Bosnia had sent to assist him. The engagement took place in Dalmatia, not far from Cattaro (Kotor), and is described in the newsletter *Verissima e distinta Relazione del combattimento et vittoria ottenuta dall'armi della Serenissima Republica di Venetia . . . li 30 Aprile 1690 in Dalmatia ne' confini di Cattaro con la priggionia dello stesso bassa*, Venice, 1690.

[14] There are a number of letters and other texts from the year 1689 in a fragmentary "file" in the Provv. da terra e da mar, Filza 948 (docs. unnumbered), which relate to the siege of Monemvasia (Malvasia), the problems which the commander Girolamo Corner was facing, financial reports, and especially conditions in Nauplia, Naxos, Chios, and elsewhere, one of the more interesting being a report dated 24 November (1689) concerning the chaos in Negroponte (Euboea) when Ibrahim Pasha left the island, having been summoned by the sultan to Istanbul.

This same report (by one Grani da Idra) speaks of the unrest in Istanbul which was being increased by the discovery of an inscription written in Bulgarian letters on a slab of marble to the effect "che nell'anno 1691 doverà Costantinopoli cader in mano de' Christiani, e del 1693 sarà tenuto un concilio per l'union delle chiese, e che ciò havesse aumentato fra Turchi la confusione!"

[15] From a galley "nell'acque di Malvasia, 2 Luglio 1690," Girolamo Corner wrote the doge Morosini and the Senate, "Assunto dalle mie debolezze questo gravissimo peso, non ho mancato di prestar tutta la mia più fissa attentione al proseguimento del blocco di questa piazza in conformità dei decreti della Consulta [the war council] . . ." (Provv. da terra e da mar, Filza 1123, dispatch no. 39).

On 25 July 1690 Girolamo Corner reported to the doge Morosini and the Senate (*ibid.*, disp. no. 41): "Capitato con celere viaggio il convoglio condotto dalla diligenza e zelo del nobil' huomo Ser Giacomo Contarini, governatore estraordinario di nave, ricevo l'honore di varie riverite ducali di vostra Serenità, et capitate pur col medesimo le reclute dei regimenti Spar e Stiron [the commanders, Sparre's regiment consisting of 333 men, Stiron's of 113, but Sparre's men were something of a problem:] tutta buona e brava gente, ma desertori, et al solito insolenti, per il che mi convien tenerli sopra le navi, sino che dal signor general Spar, che con tutto fervore adempisce le sue parti, siano posti in qualche regola. . . . S'è ricevuto col detto convoglio buona quantità di polvere e qualche portion di biscoto per quest'occorentie, alle quali la publica generosità si compiace contribuirvi un'attentione tanto propensa, scorgendo con contento quanto m'accennano per l'espeditione copiosa de' biscotti, che sarà praticata con ogni convoglio a provedimento d'un sì importante requisito per il sopraveniente verno in particolare. . . ."

At long last on 12 August 1690 Girolamo Corner could write the doge Francesco Morosini and the Senate that Monemvasia, *piazza dell'importanza ben nota,* had been taken with the help and favor of the Almighty. Now the entire "kingdom" of the Morea was subject to his ducal Serenity and the Signoria. The long contest for the fortress had made it famous, "e tanto più hora per la lunga sua ressistenza." The blockade had lasted a full seventeen months. Monemvasia had been a nest of evil outlaws, a shelter for the Barbary corsairs who infested the eastern waters, and disrupted Venetian commerce with Romania.

Upon the surrender of the fortress 1,200 Turks had emerged, of whom 300 were capable of bearing arms. Corner had taken seventy-eight cannon, some of bronze, others of iron, as well as two mortars, ship's biscuit enough for some months, gunpowder, and various other pieces of military equipment. No more than about four hundred "of these brave Venetian forces" could be counted among the dead and wounded, "and the wounded will all recover with the good-will of the Lord God." As soon as the Venetians had entered Monemvasia, Corner had converted the larger mosque in the upper enclosure of the fortress into a church dedicated to the Blessed Virgin, which had been Morosini's intention when he first began the blockade, and Corner was pleased that he had been able thus to fulfill Morosini's intention.[16]

Girolamo Corner waited, however, for another thousand men and 200,000 ducats, all badly needed. In the meantime, "fatto seguir il scarico di tutte le munitioni da vivere e da guerra et altri effetti di ragion de' Turchi, ch' esistevano sul vassello [di] Capitan Rebuti, ho anche subito rilasciato gl'ordini neccessarii all'eccellentissimo ser proveditor general Corner acciò facci consegnar il medesimo con tutti li suoi armizzi e attreci al capitano o a chi capitasse per suo nome a riceverlo giusto le publiche prescritioni. Ho pur subito dato gl'ordini proprii perchè sia rilevata nel meglior modo fosse permesso la qualità e quantità delle genti che si ritrovavano sopra le due navi perite nel combattimento con le sultane, come di quelli si sono sottratti con la fuga e degli altri caduti in schiavitù per tutto rassegnar poscia a riflessi di vostre Eccellenze . . . , Di galera nell'acque di Malvasia 25 Luglio 1690." There was clearly increased action amid the Venetian forces at Monemvasia.

[16] Provv. da terra e da mar, Filza 1123, disp. no. 42, "di galera a Malvasia, 12 Agosto 1690 S[til] N[ovo]." Monemvasia had apparently been taken at considerable cost, as described in the newsletter *Distinta Relatione dell'acquisto di Napoli di Malvasia fatto dall'armi della Serenissima Republica di Venetia sotto il prudente, valoroso commando dell'illustriss. et eccellentiss. Signor Cav. e Proc. Girolamo Cornaro, capitan general da mar, li 12 Agosto 1690,* published by Antonio Pinelli in Venice in 1690.

With the fall of Monemvasia Corner had captured "quel capo Francesco fugito dall' armata," a renegade cannoneer, who had shot to death the important Lorenzo Venier in 1689, and had aided and encouraged the Turks to hold out. Corner had had the said Francesco drawn and quartered "tra quattro galere," as a lesson to other renegades and traitors.

The Turks were allegedly content with the good treatment which Corner had accorded them. They had in fact been escorted to the islet of S. Todero in Canea Bay (at Crete) by Captain Dolfin. The Venetian fleet had been reconstituted, Monemvasia well fortified, and supplied with enough munitions, ship's biscuit, and other foodstuffs to last until March 1691. Other armaments had been found among the ruins in Monemvasia (Prov. da terra e da mar, Filza 1123, disp. no. 43, written from Coron on 20 August, 1690, as indicated in the following note).

The season was getting on (now we have reached 20 August 1690), and although the Venetians always dreamed of recovering long-lost Negroponte (Euboea), the fortress was too well defended for Corner to try to take it, "piazza da Turchi ben premunita, risarcite le fortificationi, e guardata da numeroso pressidio." On the other hand, as Corner assured the Signoria, the Isthmus of Corinth was being well protected against any possible Turkish intrusion. Unfortunately, however, there were not funds enough available to pay the troops for the month of September, despite which fact Corner was contemplating an attack upon Valona, which the Turks had taken from Venice in 1464, "if it is decided in the name of the Lord God to proceed with the fleet to Albania to undertake an attack upon Valona or some other of those [Turkish] fortresses." So he informed the doge and Senate, and this despite the lateness of the season, the strong north winds, and other obstacles and uncertainties. And despite other important facts given in this long dispatch, we must pass on.[17]

In a dispatch of 9 September (1690) Girolamo Corner informed the doge Morosini and the Senate that he had left the waters of Monemvasia the previous evening, reaching Cape Matapan "con prospero vento." He was seriously short of money, but had managed along the way to pick up what (considering his needs) could only be regarded as small sums. In passing by Venetian-held Coron and Modon, Corner had learned that both fortress towns were sadly lacking in supplies. The walls and fortifications were "in a bad state and in need of further restoration." Taking note of every chink in the Venetian naval armament and in the fortress towns,[18] Corner was headed for Canina (Knin) and Valona, although the month of September had now come upon him. His almost rash decision to continue his aggressive policy was fully justified, for on 19 September he could write the doge and Senate that (two days before) he had taken both Valona and Canina.[19]

---

[17] Provv. da terra e da mar, Filza 1123, disp. no. 43, "di galera nell'acque di Coron, 20 Agosto 1690, S[til] N[ovo]."

[18] Provv. da terra e da mar, Filza 1123, disp. no. 44, "di galera nell'acque del Saseno, 9 Settembre 1690 S[til] N[ovo]."

[19] Provv. da terra e da mar, Filza 1123, disp. no. 45, "di galera a Valona, 19 Settembre 1690 S[til] N[ovo]." It was a remarkable achievement: "L'acquisto importantissimo della piazza di Valona e fortezza di Canina in Albania superiore, hora in potere di vostre Eccellenze, fa ben spiccare quanto sia grande la confluentia delle celesti beneditioni alle glorie della Patria, distinta la protetione che il Signor Dio si compiace donar alle medesime. Voluto con nuovi miracoli insignirle di vittorie e trionfi, ove che la consistenza d'un paese vivo d'huomini bellicosi e di tanta conseguenza rendea al maggior segno ardua e difficile ogn'intrapresa unico effetto di sua omnipotenza, dalla quale tutto deve riconoscersi et dovuti anche al medesimo altretanto maggiori i rendimenti di gratie.

"Tenuto coll'armata per due giorni sequestrato al Saseno da impetuosa fortuna di vento e mare, che non m'ha permesso poter avanzare in quest'acque che solo il giorno di ii corrente [2 September]. Vista nel mentre da Turchi la medesima et valso loro il beneficio del sforzoso ritardo per ricever i soccorsi circonvicini, aumentate le forze in un valido

Now the lateness of the season did discourage Corner from attempting to lay siege to Durazzo and, apparently succumbing to the "malignant fevers" widespread at the time, he died on 1 October 1690. Domenico Mocenigo was then given command at sea as the captain-general. He was not made of the same stuff as a Morosini or a Corner, and the period of his captaincy became a misfortune for Venice.[20] Corner had apparently intended to hold on to his conquests by adding to their fortifications. The engineer Giovanni Bassignani was active in the region of Canina and Valona at the beginning of January 1691 when Mocenigo was embarking upon his captaincy-general.[21] Bassignani was examining the fortifications of both towns in an effort to assess the practicability of holding them against the Turks.

The archival sources allow us to enter the war councils of the Venetian captains-general as well as the halls of the Senate and the Grand Council. As for the captains-general, only the archival detail will reveal the extent of their indecision while in the throes of a campaign, as we have already observed in Francesco Morosini's case during the years 1684–1688. Uncertainty as to the route to take, concern for the next attack, the enemy's plans, his strength, and so on were all as characteristic of a naval expedition as of a campaign on land. The complications were increased when one decided to disembark the naval forces to meet the enemy on land. Like Morosini before him, Mocenigo had his problems.

Mocenigo presided over a meeting of the war council at Corfu on 20

---

corpo di circa sette mila huomini, et sopra 2,500 cavalli, et preoccupate coll'infanteria tutte l'eminenze che sovrastano al lithorale intorno Valona e tutti i posti più avantaggiosi alle rive tenute dalla cavalleria con vigilanza battute fu trovato tutto disposto per impedirci e contrastare vigorosamente il sbarco. . . ."

Nevertheless, after Corner's extensive preparations on 13 September the Venetian forces (much assisted by Maltese and papal troops) forced the surrender of the Turks in Valona on the seventeenth, and thereafter those in Canina also hoisted the white flag: "Sortirono da questa [fortezza] sopra tre mila anime, oltre 546 huomini d'armi, et furono sino al loro campo pontualmente scortati senza che gli sii stata inferita molestia alcuna [which, if true, was unusual]. Il campo de' Turchi si fece novamente vedere in quel giorno, e s'avicinò di maniera che l'uno e l'altro degl'eserciti stettero in battaglia fin tanto che evacuata la piazza si retirorono con gl'usciti dalla medesima."

Tucked into this "file" is a finely drawn map (in color) of Canina, "conquistata dall'armi della Serenissima Republica di Venezia nel mese di Settembre 1690 sotto il prudentissimo comando dell'illustrissimo e eccellentissimo Signor Cavaliere, Procurator Girolamo Cornaro, Capitan General." Cf. the newsletter *Distinta Relatione dell'acquisto delle celebri fortezze di Cannina e piazza della Vallona fatto dall'armi della Sereniss. Republica di Venetia sotto il prudente e valoroso commando dell'illustriss. . . . Girolamo Cornaro, capitan general da mar, li 17 Settembre 1690,* also published by Pinelli in 1690.

[20] Unfortunately many of the dispatches in the ASV (Archivio di Stato di Venezia), Senato, Provv. da terra e da mar, Filza 1125, sent by Domenico Mocenigo as captain-general of the sea to the Signoria from the end of 1690 throughout the year 1691 are withering into fragments, owing to the disintegration of the paper caused by dampness.

[21] Provv. da terra e da mar, Filza 1125, letter dated at Corfu on 1 January 1691 (m.v. 1690).

January 1691 (m.v. 1690). Fearful of the enemy, he had ordered the demolition of Canina on 26 December (1690). The fortress town was thus partially in ruins by the time he met with the council. Reports from Valona and from the Morea concerning "the resolute intentions of the enemy and their preparations" worried him, as did the elevation of Khalil Pasha "to the superior command in Albania." Khalil had already arrived at "Beratti" (Berat), a day's journey from Valona, with 6,000 janissaries, plus a "great multitude of Albanians," cannon, and other accoutrements of warfare, which had been brought from Negroponte for an attack upon Valona. Berat is only thirty miles northeast of Valona; Mocenigo had reason for concern, but not perhaps dismay. Carlo Pisani, commander of the convicts' galleys (who could not attend the meeting of the war council, owing to his absence), had written Mocenigo that Kaplan Pasha had appeared in the area of Canina "to interrupt the work of demolition at Canina and impede the transport of materials." Kaplan had with him a force of some two thousand men, "which, even if driven back by the courage of our men, serves to make clear the increasing numbers of the enemy and their plans for even greater ventures."

In Mocenigo's opinion the continued defense of Valona imperilled the Venetians' hold upon the Morea. The engineers had allegedly found the fortifications inadequate. The Turks were gathering strength. Conditions had been much different four months before, according to Mocenigo,

when the prudence and zeal of the war council, the valor and courage of the most illustrious lord captain-general Girolamo Corner settled the question of the venture into Albania. At that time the Turks were to be found in a state of consternation. The imperialists were in possession of Belgrade, victorious in the field, having reached these very borders [they had taken Niš]. His Excellency was also very sure that the people would declare themselves on his side, and he believed that he could easily advance into the interior of the province [of Albania],

but Corner's death had brought that dream to an end.

The times had changed, and the Venetians must adjust their employment of resources to that change: "Tutte queste ragioni mi danno motivo di proponere alla maturità del congresso," Mocenigo finally concluded, "che anche la Vallona si demolisca . . . ," and his decision was accepted by Agostino Sagredo, *proveditor dell'armata;* Alvise Foscari III, *capitanio estraordinario delle galleazze;* Benetto Sanudo, *capitanio delle galleazze;* Alessandro Bon, *capitan del Golfo* [the Adriatic]; and Filippo Donà, *commissario pagador.*

A letter of Carlo Pisani, *governatore de' condannati,* dated at Valona on 17 January 1691 (m.v. 1690), informed Mocenigo in some detail of Turkish movements in the Canina-Berat-Valona area, as does an anonymous letter of 15 January. In fact the various letters and dispatches in the Mocenigo file are loaded with information concerning the Turks, with in fact more than a little attention given to the Greeks and the Albanians.[22]

Mocenigo informed a meeting of the war council (*la consulta di guerra*) on 23 January 1691 that word had come from Pisani at Valona "that the serasker [the Turkish commander-in-chief], having departed from Berat, was already on the march with all his forces and with six cannon, headed for Valona." Mocenigo was confident, however, that Pisani had already begun "la demolitione di Vallona." The Venetian high command was soon of two minds about Valona, for owing to the current "state of things" it might prove impossible to demolish the fortress town. It would thus be better to defend it, as Mocenigo wrote the doge on 30 January. No, Valona was not yet reduced to ruins, and Pisani along with the general Charles Sparre was obliged to defend the town with a garrison of 1,200 veterans against a Turkish force of some 16,000 men, of whom 8,000 were "huomini scielti, parte cavalleria, parte infanteria," as Mocenigo now informed the doge in a dispatch of 7 February.

The Turkish siege of Valona was a fearful trial to the Venetians. Sparre was killed, Pisani held out "con intrepido fervore." So Mocenigo wrote on 1 March (1691).[23] In mid-March the Venetians finally withdrew from Valona, in fact demolishing it, and thereafter the Turks moved in, "havendo demolita totalmente quella piazza [i.e., finishing the destruction of the fortress town], e fortificata Canina con pallificate in quella parte, dove erano fatte le brecchie."[24] Although, as we have noted, the demolition of Canina had been ordered "by the decree of 26 December [1690]," obviously the town had not been entirely destroyed, and the Turks now gave it temporary fortifications by means of palisades. Girolamo Corner's Dalmatian-Albanian venture had come to nothing. On 22 April (1691) Mocenigo described a reunion of Charles Sparre's relatives and fellow officers, held at Corfu on 7 April, in which they paid homage to the deceased warrior.[25]

A month or so later (on 16 May) Mocenigo prepared an interesting report to the doge and Senate on the condition of the Venetian fortress towns in the Morea and elsewhere. He had recently made a tour of inspection:

Having left Corfu the night of the 7th [of May], I have been able in these few days to make hasty visits to Prevesa, S. Maura, and Lepanto, and to catch a

---

[22] Provv. da terra e da mar, Filza 1125, without pagination, but the docs. are easily located by their dates.

[23] Provv. da terra e da mar, Filza 1125, disp. no. 16, and of course all the material concerning Mocenigo comes from this file.

[24] Provv. da terra e da mar, Filza 1125, doc. dated 29 March 1691.

[25] *Ibid.*, disp. no. 23.

glimpse of the Two Castles [of "Rumelia" and the "Morea," the ruins of which still guard the Strait of Lepanto], and continuing the voyage toward Navarino, I have been able to see also the fortress of Patras. Prevesa in the opinion of the engineers whom I brought with me is not a fortress able to put up any great resistance, the exterior fortifications, which were added after we acquired the place, being narrow and weak.

The houses within Prevesa are largely in ruins and falling down, so that I should think it better to do away with them entirely and to use the material to build others much lower to serve as barracks [*quartieri*] around the walls as lodgings for the garrison. There are four towers outside, within a musket shot of the walled enclosure, where a few soldiers stand on guard, not without the danger of their being surprised and made slaves [by the Turks], especially at nighttime. I believe that when the towers were built, they were of some use, but now they serve no purpose, and in the judgment of the engineers it would be better to dismantle them.

Lepanto is laden with defects, battered on all sides, and quite beyond refortification, nor could one maintain it [under siege] except with an army in the field either superior or at least equal to that of the enemy. Thus the Two Castles and that of Patras can put up but a slight defense. All the fortifications are in poor condition; it would be difficult to make good their shortcomings. Only at S. Maura can one establish a firm base, so long as one attends to the outer fortifications, for there is but little land on both sides, [either] toward the island or the mainland, all the rest being closed off by marshes and swampy areas. Access will be most difficult for the enemy, and improved in proper fashion, S. Maura could be considered an enduring acquisition for the Republic.

In all the aforesaid fortresses I have observed many shortcomings, especially in S. Maura, Prevesa, and Lepanto, which I have found to have only fourteen barrels of good gunpowder. Therefore I have written to the most excellent lord provveditore generale Navagero that he provide 200 barrels of powder from that which exists in the supply depots of Corfu, and likewise with lead and fuses, of which there was a lack. The artillery in these strongholds has almost all been taken apart. Therefore I am urging his Excellency to see to its restoration, and to remove and send to Venice at the first opportunity many pieces of Turkish cannon, muskets, and other useless arms, and also to have transported to Corfu the spoilt Turkish gunpowder which one finds in the strongholds, to look to its improvement, putting it in a state of usefulness in case of need.

Mocenigo had found the *proveditor straordinario* at S. Maura, Bartolo Gradenigo, and his predecessor Girolamo Priuli both active in their devotion to the public service. All the villages in the jurisdictions of both Lepanto and S. Maura, however, had sent their elders (*vecchiardi*) to Mocenigo to complain of the fact that neither their lives nor their properties were being protected from the incursions of the Mainote leader Liberio Gerachari, known as Liberacchi, and the raids of one Captain Elia, who in most oppressive fashion were wringing from the veins of these poor folk a tribute of more than 50,000 *reali* every year.

A Mainote Greek, Liberacchi had joined the Turks, who made him the "bey of Maina." He figures prominently in Locatelli's history of the "Venetian war in the Levant."[26] Later on, Liberacchi abandoned the Turks, and threw in his lot with the Venetians who, having ample reason to distrust him, put him into prison at Brescia, where he died.

Mocenigo had promised to help the distressed Greeks of Lepanto and S. Maura, and now recommended sending to the threatened areas sizable squads of infantry and cavalry. Two of the island galleys and four galliots, he wrote the doge, should be stationed at S. Maura.

Recruiting the manpower of the Morea, the islands, and the region of Lepanto, Mocenigo believed that a corps of from four to five thousand troops could be assembled, which could easily destroy or drive from the countryside "those evil folk who hold it in subjection." After all, there were not many Turks in these areas. Mocenigo proposed that the Signoria should pay every soldier a monthly wage of two sequins (*cecchini*), provide saddles for the cavalry, "and arms to be paid for at a monthly rate of four lire per person." The cavalry must do no violence to the peasantry, which had shown a willingness to provide them with forage and fodder "in order to see themselves once more free of the oppression of criminals, and I shall try to increase the garrison at Lepanto to seven hundred infantry and to send there two hundred cavalry, if not immediately, at least at the end of the campaign."[27]

With no Venetian bailie sending dispatches to the doge and Senate, we rely upon the English ambassador's reports to Whitehall. On 15 June (1691), as Sir William Trumbull was preparing to leave Istanbul (where Sir William Hussey was to succeed him), he sent Daniel Finch, earl of Nottingham and secretary of state for military affairs, an interesting account of the tension which the death of Sultan Suleiman II had caused on the Bosporus.

"I venture these few lines," wrote Trumbull,

att great uncertainties to acquaint your Lordship that the Grand Seigneur, after a lingring distemper of a dropsie and a rupture (whereof I formerly wrott to your lordship), dy'd on the 10th instant at night or the 11th in the morning att Adrianople, and yesterday his body was brought hither and buried in the mosque of Solyman the Magnificent.

The Vizir, being informed of his approching death, departed from Adrianople in great hast with those few souldiers he had (hardly 4,000) to prevent all designs among them of setting up the deposed Sultan Mahomet [Mehmed IV] or one of

---

[26] Alessandro Locatelli, *Racconto historico della veneta guerra in Levante diretta dal valore del Serenissimo Principe Francesco Morosini . . . dall'anno 1684 sino all'anno 1690*, 2 vols. in one, Colonia, 1691, II, 164, 173, 193–201ff., 219–20, 236.

[27] Provv. da terra e da mare, Filza 1125, disp. no. 25, "[di] galera, acque del Zante, 16 Maggio 1691 S[til] N[ovo]."

his sons, for the elder of which (Mustapha) both the army and people were generally dispos'd, and would have obtain'd it in all probability in case his death had happened before they left that town. The Vizir's interest was against any one of this family, and so he obtained of the Muftee and those others of the law, whome he left behind him att Adrianople for that purpose, to declare Achmett, the younger brother of the deceased, to be Grand Seigneur.

Sultan Ibrahim left 5 sons—Mahomet, Solyman, Orcan, Achmet, and Selim. Orcan and Selim dy'd severall yeares ago. Mahomet and his 2 sons are alive and in prison. This Achmet is about 45 yeares old, has been kept under confinement all his life, and said to be an idiott, and to divert himself cheifly by beating of a drum and severall frantick actions, whereas the Grand Seigneur deceased was an idiot of a quieter temper, imploying all his time in reading of the Alcoran.

How the present necessity of their affaires will make the army and the people submitt to this Emperor cannot be foreseen, nor how the Vizir will be able to raise mony to give the souldiers their customary donative, which by a moderate computation will amount to 2,500 purses, though it is affirm'd that the Vizir (foreseeing this) carried a good summe with him in order to buy off the army. However, there is certainly an universall discontent by the choice of such a person so that it cannot possibly submitt long, and if the court of Vienna should have any more dispositions towards a peace than what appeared in their instructions to my successor, I should think the Vizir might incline to it. Sir William Hussey [Trumbull's successor] will be here on Thursday the 18th. I shall not need to trouble your Lordship with his negotiations at Adrianople, he having sent your Lordship an account thereof. . . .[28]

It was Ahmed II, of course, who succeeded Suleiman II. It made little or no difference to the Venetians, who were at war with the Porte. On 16 June (1691) the war council met, as it usually did, aboard Domenico Mocenigo's galley, this time in the harbor at Nauplia. Mocenigo noted that the coming of the Maltese galleys to join the Venetian fleet—plus the expected arrival of four more galleys under the captain of the Gulf— should set the council to thinking what could be done in the current campaign "a beneficio publico, decoro dell'armi, difesa de'stati, et offesa de' nemici." According to the last information which had come to Mocenigo the Turkish armada had recently left the Dardanelles (*i Castelli*). It comprised only twenty-two galleys, ten *sultane,* and three vessels from the Barbary coast. The Turkish land forces then in areas into which the Venetians might venture were not very large; the garrisons in their fortress towns were of only middling strength (*mediocri*). It would

---

[28] PRO, SP 97, XX, fol. 182, letter dated at Constantinople (or Istanbul, as I usually call it after the year 1453) on 15 June 1691. The letter was received at Westminster (London) on 21 September. Trumbull's successor as ambassador to the Porte was Sir William Hussey, whose death was reported by Thomas Coke in a letter dated at Adrianople (Edirne) on 17 September 1691 (*ibid.,* XX, fol. 207ʳ). Daniel Finch, second earl of Nottingham, was a nephew of Sir John Finch, who had been (as we have seen) the English ambassador to the Porte a decade or so before.

seem that an opportunity might be awaiting the Venetian fleet in Moreote waters.

The Turkish serasker in mainland Greece had hardly more than five
hundred men at his disposal. The government in Istanbul was directing
its attention toward Hungary. Although Mocenigo had no way of knowing, the Porte was in something of a quandary, owing to the death of
Suleiman II. One was not likely to see very strong Turkish forces in the
area of the Morea for some time. Nevertheless, Mocenigo thought it
unwise "to distance ourselves too far from the Morea" and launch forth
to bear arms beyond the Archipelago. They could not go too far afield,
for it would not serve the "public good." Also it would be unwise, he
thought, to seek conquests on *terra ferma,* "perchè sono più facil a
perdersi," for they would be more fully exposed to Turkish attack. Any
places acquired on land would require large garrisons to maintain them.
No, the Venetian forces must adhere to the sea, where they could assume
that their conquests would be more lasting. They must look to the islands
being held by the Turks.

"As for the enterprises which can be attempted among the islands,"
Mocenigo told the war council,

I am thinking of the kingdom of Candia, Negroponte, Chios, Mytilene, Tenedos,
Lemnos, and Stanchiò. Our forces consist of about eight thousand infantry, including the auxiliaries, with seven to eight hundred horse. What requires the
most serious consideration, however, is the fact that we are without a military
general to direct operations during a campaign on land, especially when there
may be doubt concerning some engagement with the enemy. I regard it as essential to employ the fleet [and most of its manpower] only at sea.

It will never be sound policy to disembark all the troops and leave the fleet
exposed to the mercy of the enemy which could, *restando padrone del mare,*
either overtake us by surprise or by their mere appearance oblige us precipi-
tously to reembark [our forces] during what seemed like a promising enterprise.
That would mean a loss of reputation and a grave peril which might entail serious
consequences. At least three thousand infantry are needed to guard the fleet, so
there would only be about five thousand men to put ashore.

Such was the war council's problem. The safety of the fleet must be the
primary consideration in any plans they made. From Venice they could
not expect more than another thousand men. In any event the men
would come late or, *com'era solito,* "with many ill and in a state to
render little or no service."

Then one by one Mocenigo dilated on the almost insuperable problems that would be involved in "l'impresa del regno di Candia." As for
Negroponte, the reports which he had received suggested that the island
fortress was being defended by no more than 1,500 men, "and I should
think it not difficult to occupy the heights which dominate the place."

Past experience had shown, however, that it would be necessary to attack two forts, first Kara Babà and then the island stronghold of Negroponte itself. It would be too much to make the two assaults at the same time. Having taken Kara Babà, it would be advisable to leave a detachment of at least two thousand men in the hilltop fortifications, which would mean hardly more than five thousand to take the main stronghold of Negroponte and guard the fleet at the same time. They might also end up in a hostile encounter with the serasker who, although Mocenigo does not mention the fact, could recruit troops from Thebes, Livadia, and elsewhere.

Chios seemed a reasonable objective. It was easy to disembark on the island, and the accustomed place of landing was not far from the fortress. The Turkish garrison was said to number only 1,300 men. The inhabitants of Chios were of course largely Greeks, "ben affetti al dominio turchesco per le grandi esentioni e privilegi che godono." The active Greeks were, to be sure, largely merchants, not accustomed to the use of arms. One need entertain no fear of them. With the Venetian fleet at sea, Mocenigo thought it would be easy to impede the delivery of assistance to the Turkish garrison. Mocenigo had sent a trustworthy person, a good judge of fortifications, to shed "some more light on this place," as also on Mytilene, "which I understand to be even less strong than Chios, and by and large they are both good islands." Neither enterprise—against Chios or Mytilene—would be very costly to the Republic. Success would deprive the Turks of the two ports, which were among their chief shelters in the Archipelago.

Tenedos, "che occupa gran concetto nell'opinione degl' huomini, impressi che per la sua situatione possa causar penuria di viveri alla città di Costantinopoli," was in Mocenigo's view a much over-rated island. It was not a site from which one could impede the delivery of foodstuffs to the Porte: that would require the long maintenance of ships at the mouth of the Dardanelles to prevent the entrance into and the exit from the waters of the Turkish capital. Almost the only inhabitants of Tenedos were those within the fortress, "which being full of defects would be easy to take," but in Mocenigo's opinion it would still be more trouble than it was worth (*ma più d'impegno che d'utile*).

As for Lemnos and Stanchiò, they would almost "fall by themselves, but I do not consider them of such importance that they should be made our objectives in the present campaign." Perhaps the best thing for Venice would be to defeat the Turkish armada at sea but, according to Mocenigo, the Turks were timorous and sought to avoid risks. "Also it appears that the kapudan pasha has orders to avoid combat and to reserve the armada for safe opportunities, and so the doubtful question is whether in seeking out their armada we should not be wasting the best part of the campaigning season." Nevertheless, upon due reflection, the war council decided, each member having stated his opinion, that it would be best, if possible, to meet and attack the Turkish armada at sea (*doversi applicar a combattere l'armata nemica*), for after all they did lack a commander for an engagement of the enemy on land.[29]

On 6 July (1691) Mocenigo wrote the doge Francesco Morosini and the Senate that he was continuing to sail in pursuit of the Turks: "On the assumption of being able to find them at Foça [Phocaea] or at Mytilene [Lesbos] I have put myself within sight of these ports, the usual places of refuge for the Turkish armada."[30] Three days before (on 3 July) Mocenigo had informed the war council that all inquiries had so far led him to believe that there were twenty-two galleys and twelve ships [*navi*] within the Dardanelles. He therefore suspected that, considering the Turks' naval "weakness," they were not likely to venture out into the open, "and consequently our plan of attacking them is unlikely to come about, hence it would seem a more productive use of our time to think of some other more profitable undertaking." They had already discussed the fact and decided that their forces were not sufficient to win back the important island of Negroponte.

Mocenigo still remained, moreover, uncertain of the wisdom of an attempt upon the island of Chios. It was, to be sure, one of the most conspicuous islands in the Archipelago, fertile and rich, and the Gran Signore drew large revenues therefrom. If the Republic could take Chios, even part of those revenues would easily maintain a garrison there. Even so, "what I regard as still more important," Mocenigo told the war council (on 3 July), "is that we should take from the enemy one of the chief ports they have in the Archipelago, where they find shelter for their armadas, and where the 'caravans' sail from Constantinople to Syria and to other places as well. . . ."

Having outlined the "advantages" the Venetian fleet might enjoy in any worthwhile venture, including the desirability of seizing Chios, Mocenigo went on to the "disadvantages," the *svantaggi*, which were much greater than those he had stated to the war council on 16 June:

The fortress [of Chios] is not so badly provided with men-at-arms as appeared from our first reports, and although Chios lacks cavalry and enough Turks to

---

[29] Provv. da terra e da mar, Filza 1125, "adì 16 Giugno 1691 S[til] N[ovo], porto di Napoli di Romania." Presently word came from Istanbul "che i Turchi abbiano spedito per amassar gente nelle parti della Natolia [Anatolia] a difesa de' loro stati d'Arcipelago, dove dubitano di qualche tentativo, e massime Scio, Metelin, e Tenedo, aggiungendo qualche altra particolarità dell'armata nemica, che si vociferava sortita da Castelli . . . ," but uncertainty still attended the movements of the Turkish armada (*ibid.*, disp. no. 29, from Mocenigo to the doge and Senate, dated "in the waters of Mytilene 26 June 1691"). It looked as though the Porte was getting ready to deal with Mocenigo's "campaign."

[30] Provv. da terra e da mar, Filza 1125, dispatch no. 30.

form an army to put up resistance in a campaign, there are so many men there that they could render our attack, if not uncertain, at least difficult and bloody. The island is inhabited by a multitude of Greeks, who are not ill disposed toward the Turkish rule, under which they enjoy very ample privileges, for they are merchants, not soldiers. . . .

The Greeks were quite content to submit to Turkish domination and preserve their lives and their property. They were indeed unlikely to make any move on behalf of the Venetians. In fact the pasha of Chios had shut up a goodly number of Greeks in the fortress to engage them in defense of the place, and he was holding six of the most prominent inhabitants of Chios as hostages. The Venetians' available soldiery was very limited; military service and desertions took their toll. And, perhaps most of all, the lack of an experienced commander of land forces, once the Venetian troops had landed on Chios, caused Mocenigo much concern, as it did the war council, which decided not to go forward with the proposed attack upon Chios.[31]

The war council met again in the waters off Tenedos on 17 July (1691). This time the general of the Maltese galleys was present. Mocenigo again spoke at length on the difficulty of getting to do battle with the Turks, who always took refuge within the "mouths" of the Dardanelles, whenever the Venetian fleet appeared on the scene. Rumor had it that the Turks had disarmed some ships in order to transfer the crews to the garrisons of Mytilene and Chios. Their galleys were seen anchored at the Castello di Rumelia (on the European side of the Dardanelles). Entering the canal to do battle with them required the "most serious reflections" (*gravissimi riflessi*). One would have to await a very strong wind to outdo the current, and then pass between the firepower of batteries on both the European and the Asiatic side of the canal. The risks would be great, and they were not worth it, because the enemy would use the time it took the Venetians to enter the canal to withdraw still further to the east (from Çanakkale into the Sea of Marmara). They would "frustrate our diligence with flight." Penetration into the Dardanelles was "more perilous than prudent." Obviously, however, the Venetian high command must find some other way to strike at the Turks, "so that we do not go through the campaign without having inflicted some loss of consequence upon the enemy."

Since the Venetian fleet was already "nell'acque del Tenedo," seizure of the island fortress would be a "sensible blow" to give the Turks. It would not seriously impede "l'ingresso e l'uscita dai Dardanelli," but it would take from the enemy a convenient haven into which to escape

---

[31] Provv. da terra e da mar, Filza 1125, minutes of the meeting of the war council "adì 3 Luglio 1691 S[til] N[ovo], Scogli de' Spalmadori."

from attacks by the Venetian fleet. Indeed, an assault upon Tenedos might bring the Turkish ships and galleys from behind the protective wall of the Dardanelles. The military captains and engineers had agreed with Mocenigo. Tenedos could easily be taken. The fortress was in miserable condition, and surrounded by hills upon which the Venetian forces might plant their batteries. The garrison at Tenedos was usually no larger than three to four hundred men. They could not long resist an attack.

Tenedos was different from Chios. The village was small, inhabited by but a few *villani,* who would abandon it at the first appearance of the Venetian forces. Tenedos was a famous place; an outcry arose every time it was taken. "I should think it a public service," Mocenigo told the war council, "to demolish it, and be content with having taken from the Turks this place of refuge under the very eyes of their armada, with an advantage to the reputation of our arms." There was no point in holding on to Tenedos, for it was useless to Venice.

The Morea and various other places must be defended first of all. When Mocenigo had finished, every member of the war council had something to say, giving vent to "the most weighty reflections." Even weak fortresses could put up resistance when they were well garrisoned. The war council decided the greatest diligence must be exercised to try to ascertain "the quality and size of the garrison which at present may be in Tenedos," in order to make clear whether the proposed attack was well advised. In the meantime the Venetian fleet must advance to the mouth of the Dardanelles "in order of battle," putting themselves within sight of the Turks, which was necessary in view of the decisions and orders already decided upon and, of course, as a means of maintaining the honor of the Signoria at sea.[32]

At the next meeting of the war council on 23 July (1691) Mocenigo declared that he had indeed exercised diligence in an effort to shed some "new light" upon conditions in Tenedos in accord with the recent decision of the council. He had sent a brigantine the other night to disembark a few men on the island. They had learned from three "slaves," whom they had presumably captured, that in fact the size of the Turkish garrison had risen to more than three thousand. The Turks had also added to the fortifications, dug trenches before the main gateway as well as "at the mills," and were clearly ready to defend the island against an attack.

Mocenigo acknowledged that he and "the military captains and engineers" had been mistaken in their assumption that Tenedos could easily be taken. Now it was clear that the "imperfections" of the garrison and the fortress had been rectified, "but I do not," he said, "regard Tenedos of such importance as to justify the fatigue [of an attack] and the shed-

---

[32] Provv. da terra e da mar, Filza 1125, minutes of the meeting of the war council, "adì 17 Luglio 1691 S[til] N[ovo], aque del Tenedo."

ding of blood." It was better to abstain from any undertaking "dove si possa perdere più di quel che s'acquista." Everything possible had been done up to now so as not to allow the campaigning season to slip by without some worthwhile accomplishment. The Venetian forces, however, were limited; they lacked experienced military captains. It had been the part of wisdom to make no attempts upon either Chios or Mytilene.

Having thus given up all thought and hope of taking Tenedos, Chios, and Mytilene, what if anything lay ahead for the Venetian fleet? At least they had achieved the "riputatione d'essere stati alle Bocche [de' Dardanelli] ed haver provocato a battaglia l'armata Turchescha." They lacked the military leadership (as we have heard several times) as well as the manpower for a large enterprise on land, and so the war council now decided "that for this reason we must not undertake the attack upon Tenedos nor risk troops for a conquest which is considered useless, unsubstantial, and not to be attempted except to destroy [the fortress]."

Since there thus appeared to be no other enterprises which would be easy, *altre imprese facili,* the war council decided that they must save the Signoria's exiguous forces in the hope of a better year in 1692. Nevertheless, to keep the Turkish armada confined within the Dardanelles the Venetian forces would remain in position for some time, "and in the meantime repair to Mykonos and Paros [in the Cyclades] in order to increase the stores of wine and foodstuffs to relieve the hardship in which the fleet now finds itself."[33]

In the fall of 1691 there was a mutiny of French troops aboard the flagship of Bartolo Contarini, the *capitan ordinario* of the sailing ships. Contarini was wounded; the mutiny was suppressed. Disorder among the French troops must have been expected, for Louis XIV was no longer maintaining his neutrality in the Christian war with Islam. He was supporting the Turks in clandestine, and in not so clandestine, fashion. In December (1691) the disaffected garrison at Grabusa on the far west of the island of Crete surrendered the fortress to the Turks. After further meetings of the war council it was decided to make an attempt upon Turkish-held Canea, also in western Crete, and on 17 July 1692 Mocenigo landed his forces at Canea with little interference from the Turks. He had more or less at his command 34 galleys and 27 ships, including four papal and eight Maltese galleys, which fact limited somewhat his overall authority.

The Christian allies frustrated a Turkish attempt to relieve the siege on 8 August. When, however, Turkish prisoners informed Mocenigo that the kapudan pasha was headed for Canea with a large naval force, his

---

[33] Provv. da terra e da mar, Filza 1125, minutes of the meeting of the war council, "adì 23 Luglio 1691 S[til] N[ovo], acque del Tenedo."

usual caution overtook him, and he decided to withdraw the Venetian fleet and the allied squadrons. Although the papal and Maltese generals suggested that all three should employ their maritime strength against the armada of the kapudan pasha when and if it arrived on the scene, he declined their offer as putting the Venetian vessels in undue jeopardy. On 29 August (1692), therefore, the allies gave up the siege of Canea. And so the papal and Maltese commanders sailed westward with their galleys, while the Venetian fleet soon got under way for Nauplia, where it was intended to spend the winter. Mocenigo was recalled to Venice and brought to trial. He was found innocent of betrayal, but timidity and incompetence had ended his naval career.[34]

The significance of Domenico Mocenigo's spiritless abandonment of the siege of Canea was well understood in Istanbul, as Thomas Coke makes clear in a dispatch of 29 October 1692 to the earl of Nottingham at Whitehall:

. . . The Venetians have rais'd their seige at Canea with losse and disreputation, which is imputed to the French, who gave notice of their designe to the Turks, and severall hundreds of them in the Venetian army, as soon as disbarkt in Candia, went over to the Turkes, and helpt to defend the place. This good successe on their side, and the Imperialls' having donne nothing in Hungary, I feare will elevate the Turks. The greatest harme they have rec'd has been from the Haiduds or theives in the mountaines betwixt Sofia and Belgrad, who did great mischeife on that road, taking 100 m. dollars sent from Adrianople to the army, convoy'd by 400 men. . . .[35]

After the sad failure of Domenico Mocenigo, the eyes of Venice became fastened upon the doge Francesco Morosini as the next captain-general of the sea. When the Senators gathered in the Sala dello Scrutinio in the Doges' Palace on Christmas day in 1692 to make their nominations, Morosini received 95 votes, Girolamo Dolfin 27, and 22 others shared the remaining 46 votes. At seventy-four years of age and in poor health, Morosini did not want to accept the onerous charge, but he finally yielded to tears and entreaties. Returning to the Sala del Maggior Consiglio, the Senators did not have to wait for the formal vote to act upon the assumption of his election. When the vote came, moreover, with 847 nobles present, there were 797 votes favorable (*de parte*), 34 opposed (*de non*), and 12 without commitment (*non sinceri*). The next

---

[34] Cf. Anderson, *Naval Wars in the Levant* (1952), pp. 213–14, who as usual tries to follow the Venetian galleys here and there from month to month; note also Romanin, *Storia documentata di Venezia*, VII (3rd ed., Venice, 1974), 354; Kretschmayr, *Geschichte von Venedig*, III (1934, repr. Aalen, 1964), 350; and *Diario dell'assedio della Canea l'anno 1692 sotto il capitan general Domenico Mocenigo*, MS. Marc. It. VII, 656 (7791), fols. 84–100, covering the seven weeks from 12 July to 29 August 1692.

[35] PRO, SP 97, XX, fol. 254^v, dispatch dated 19/29 October 1692.

day in the Senate Morosini rose from his chair, removing the horned hat of the doge (as was done when the newly elected doge gave thanks for his elevation to the dogado), and offered his life to the Republic.

After elaborate processions and ceremonies in the Piazza and the Church of S. Marco on 24–25 May 1693, Morosini went to the Lido in the Bucintoro, the ornate state galley, on the 26th, accompanied by his two councilors Zorzi Benzon and Agostino Sagredo, his lieutenant Francesco Mocenigo, and other officials. He boarded his flagship at the Lido, and then sailed some days later for Monemvasia, where the Venetian fleet had assembled. It was his fourth call to arms as captain-general of the sea.

Morosini reinforced the garrisons of certain fortress towns in the Morea, especially that of Corinth. Thereafter he thought of proceeding to the Dardanelles, but the opposing winds were too strong. He pursued Algerian pirates, and having learned of the approach of the Turkish ser-asker of Livadia, he hastened to the defense of Corinth. He needed more men, money, and ship's biscuit, however, to achieve any appreciable success. He did occupy a few small islands in the Saronic Gulf and in that of Argolis, but he suffered from the afflictions of old age, including kidney stones and a defective bladder (. . . *adeo vehementer sub ipsum saevientis mali exordium, quod a calculi vi asperabatur, vexari incepit*).

Retiring to Nauplia (Napoli di Romania), where he intended to spend the winter, Morosini died on 6 January 1694.[36] Today as the tourist comes into the Sala dello Scrutinio in the Doges' Palace, he sees at the far wall a triumphal arch (built in 1694) enclosing the doorway leading to the great stairway which goes down to the courtyard. The arch bears the memorial inscription *Francisco Mauroceno Peloponnesiaco Senatus MDCVIC*. Morosini was later buried with great ceremony in the church of S. Stefano, where the tourist encounters (as soon as he enters the main portal) a great bronze seal in the pavement, with the inscription *Francisci Mauroceni Peloponnesiaci, Venetiarum principis, ossa 1694*. Francesco Morosini and old Enrico Dandolo are probably the most famous of all the doges of Venice.

---

[36] Giovanni Graziani, *Francisci Mauroceni Peloponnesiaci, Venetiarum principis, gesta*, Padua, 1698, pp. 378–85, who dates the *publicae supplicationes* on 14/24 May 1693, and Morosini's death on 6 (not 9) January 1694; Antonio Arrighi, *De vita et rebus gestis Francisci Mauroceni Peloponnesiaci, principis Venetorum. . .* , Padua, 1749, pp. 386–91, who also puts what Graziani calls the *supplicationes* on 24 May (*IX Kalendas Junias*), and Morosini's death on 6 January (*VIII Idus Januarias*); Romanin, *Storia documentata di Venezia*, VII (3rd ed., 1974), 354–56, who gives 9 January as the date of Morosini's death; Gino Damerini, *Morosini*, Milan, 1929, pp. 306–32, who dates Morosini's death on 6 January; Kretschmayr, *Gesch. v. Venedig*, III (1934, repr. 1964), 350, who puts Morosini's death "in der Nacht auf den siebten Jänner 1694."

XIII

Louis XIV, the Turks, and the War of the League of Augsburg, the Treaties of Ryswick and Karlowitz, and the Uneasy Peace between Venice and the Porte

◦～

When the imperialists finally took Belgrade (on 6 September 1688), Louis XIV put behind him the treaty or "truce" of Regensburg (of 15 August 1684), whereby he had bound himself to an armistice with Leopold I for twenty years (*armistitium viginti annorum*).[1] At the French court it was said that Louis had been too generous. Immediately after the fall of Belgrade, Louis had sent troops into the Rhenish Palatinate, where they embarked upon widespread destruction. Early in the year 1689, as we have seen, the Turkish envoys Sulfikar Effendi and Alessandro Mavrocordato had tried to arrange a truce or peace with the imperialists, the Venetians, and the Poles, but nothing had come of their efforts. With Louis XIV as their near ally the Turks were no longer interested in peace with the Empire unless Leopold I gave up Belgrade and left Transylvania to the Porte.[2]

According to Thomas Coke, the French had helped the Turks defend Canea. By the end of October 1692, as Coke informs us, success ap-

---

[1] Dumont, *Corps universel diplomatique*, VII-2 (1731), no. XLVII, p. 82.
[2] Cf. Pastor, *Gesch. d. Päpste*, XIV-2 (Freiburg im Breisgau, 1930), 837–38.

389

peared to have swung to the side of the Turks, ". . . the Imperialls' having donne nothing in Hungary." As the French gradually diverted the attention of the imperialists from the eastern front, the Turks did become more successful, and indeed they had already done very well during the year 1690, recapturing Niš and Belgrade and driving the Christian enemy for the most part out of Serbia, Bulgaria, and Transylvania.[3] On 19 August 1691, however, Ludwig von Baden defeated the Turks in an almost decisive battle at Slankamen, on the Danube in northern Serbia. The grand vizir Mustafa Köprülü was killed. The battle was disastrous for the Turks and costly for the Austrians,[4] but it secured the Hapsburg possession of Hungary and Transylvania. In another half dozen years Eugene of Savoy would add the decisive mark in his overthrow of the Turks at Zenta.

In the meantime, although the imperialists carried on war with the Turks, Louis XIV was a serious distraction. Actually, however, as we shall see, Austria was not to be the chief opponent of France in the War of the League of Augsburg (1688–1697). Although we may regard Leopold I as the main author of the basic pacts of the League, William III of Great Britain was to be Louis XIV's most conspicuous and determined opponent. Louis was anxious to retain the areas in Alsace and Lorraine that he had gained at Westphalia (in 1648) as well as the "reunions" that he had seized in 1680–1681, none of which Leopold I had recognized as valid in the Truce of Regensburg.

Louis had been much concerned by the formation of the League of Augsburg on 9 July 1686, which was to last for three years and longer if necessary. The league consisted of the emperor, the king of Spain as duke of Burgundy, the crown of Sweden for the provinces which it held in the Empire, the elector of Bavaria, the "circles" of Bavaria, Franconia, and Swabia, the dukes of Saxony, and the other princes of the empire "beyond the Rhine," all pledging themselves to maintain the truce concluded at Regensburg in 1684 between France and the empire for the preservation of peace and tranquillity throughout the empire and for the common defense of the rights and interests of the high contracting parties.[5]

The League of Augsburg was an alliance against France. If the imperialists succeeded in adding Hungary and Transylvania to the Hapsburg domains, and could then make peace with the Porte, obviously Louis

---

[3] Cf. Braubach, *Prinz Eugen von Savoyen*, I, 176–77. For Coke's letter of 29 October 1692, see above, p. 387.

[4] Cf. von Hammer-Purgstall, *Gesch. d. osman. Reiches*, VI (1830, repr. 1963), 561–63, trans. Hellert, XII, 319–21.

[5] As summarized in Dumont, *Corps universel diplomatique*, VII-2, no. LXXII, pp. 131–39, with the German and French texts defining the establishment of the League of Augsburg, "so gegeben und geschehen in Augspurg den 29 Jun. [9 Jul.] 1686."

XIV was in trouble, for Leopold would be in a position to transfer his military resources from the eastern to the western front. Louis knew that he had to strike while the iron was hot, and he did so, with a public declaration that as soon as the emperor had ceased hostilities with the Turks, he would undoubtedly attack France, and that the League of Augsburg was merely a German "association" against the rights and the crown of France.[6]

The Venetians found the years 1692–1693 difficult. The failure to take Canea had been disappointing, and there was constant fear of Turkish attack.[7] The unease in Venice and elsewhere was not unjustified. Every year a new army seemed to emerge from Turkish soil. On 19 February 1692 Thomas Coke described the Ottoman state of mind to the earl of Nottingham in a dispatch from Istanbul:

> . . . Notwithstanding their great losses, they [the Turks] never faile of an army next yeare and their souldiers are constantly pay'd, nor will the Empire ever want men or mony sufficient, tho not in such a degree as when it was in its meridian, and they think the Germans will be tyr'd before them, and should they gett but one victory in the field, they should soon recover their losses. . . .
>
> These people are of a very proud, obstinate humor, zealous, looking on the warre now as more of religion than state, and think as the present state of Christendome is, they can't loose more, and may recover what [is] lost. In discourse with a great minister, judicious, not Frencheify'd, I told him our first alliance with the Port was not, as it now seemes, only for commerce, but the power of the house of Austria being then as formidable as France is now, wee united with [the Port] in opposing it and stoping its encrease, it being their true interest as well as ours, that the power of Christendome should not fall under one monarch, who

---

[6] *Mémoire des Raisons, qui ont obligé le Roy de France Louis XIV à reprendre les Armes et qui doivent persuader toute la Chrétienté des sincères intentions de Sa Majesté pour l'affermissement de la tranquilité publique, [fait] à Versailles le 24. Septembre 1688,* in Dumont, *Corps universel diplomatique,* VII-2, no. XCIV, pp. 170–73, with the assertion "que [Sa Majesté] ayant tousjours esté bien avertie du dessein que l'Empereur a formé depuis long-tems d'attaquer la France, aussitost qu'il aura fait la Paix avec les Turcs. . . . On avoit assez remarqué qu'à peine ce Traitté de Trève [of 1684] fut ratifié de part et d'autre que Sa Majesté voulut bien encore donner de nouvelles marques de sa modération, et quoy qu'elle eut appris que les Ministres Impériaux employoient tous leurs soins et tous leurs efforts dans la pluspart des Cours d'Allemagne pour porter les Princes et Estats de l'Empire à entrer dans de nouvelles Ligues contre la France: Que par le Traitté fait à Ausbourg ils avoient engagé un nombre considérable de Princes et d'Estats a souscrire cette Association. . . ."

[7] Summaries of letters and reports, so-called "rubrics," dated at or issuing from Corinth, Argos, Tripolitza (Tripolis), Karytaina, Kalamata, Navarino Vecchio and Novo, and Arcadia from July 1692 to June 1693 are given in ASV, Senato, Provv. da terra e da mar, Filza 840, pages and entries unnumbered. They range from rumors of a projected Turkish invasion to the distribution of benefits (*l'assignationi de' beni publici*) to some of the inhabitants of Monemvasia in recognition of their loyalty to Venice (*in riconoscimento della loro fede*). During this period one worried about the rumored increases in the size of the Ottoman army, *vedendosi ingrossare sempre più l'esercito nemico,* for the Turks seemed indefatigable.

would envolve them in the common destruction, and (which is the solidest argu-
ment) if they did not make use of this opportunity for peace, the warre in Christendome was too hot to continue long, and if it ware struck up there, then the
whole torrent would bee turned upon them. He answered these are your Frank
braines and speculations. You mistake us. Wee looke on the present circumstances which turns us to account and not on remote consequences which may
bee some yeares hence. If God will have it so, it must bee so, and all our precautions can't prevent it. These are their notions, and I feare wee shall see peace in
Christendome before it's made here. . . .[8]

The international scene was complicated by many factors—the debili-
tation of Charles II of Spain, who was living longer than anyone had
expected; the suspicious death of his French wife Marie Louise
d'Orléans (on 12 February 1689); the Bavarian claim to the Spanish
throne, owing to Max Emmanuel's marriage to Maria Antonia, the daughter of Leopold I; Leopold's own efforts to secure the throne for his
younger son, the Archduke Karl; and Louis XIV's ambition to add the
Spanish kingdoms to the domains of the house of Bourbon. Louis had,
however, embarked upon a rougher sea than he realized, for now the
anti-Catholic, parliamentary forces in England brought about the
Glorious Revolution (1688–1689), the deposition of James II, and the
accession of William III and Mary II.

At last William could give vent to his long-standing hostility to the
French. On 12 May (1689) Leopold I accepted at Vienna a defensive and
offensive alliance with the United Provinces of Belgium. The alliance was
directed against the French, owing to their recent invasion of the imperialist Palatinate and their slippery failure to adhere to treaties they had
signed (*lubrica Gallorum in observandis tractatibus fides*).[9] At Hamp-
ton Court five days later (on 17 May) William and Mary declared war
upon the king of France in response to his invasion of the states of the
emperor and the Empire as well as his outrageous violation of the
treaties confirmed by the English crown.[10]

---

[8] PRO, SP 97, XX, fols. 246ᵛ–247ʳ, dispatch dated 18 February 1691/1692. Francesco
Muazzo, *Storia della guerra tra li Veneti e Turchi dall' 1684 al 1696*, MS. Marc. It. VII,
172 (8187), bks. viii–ix, has much to say about Venetian naval affairs during the years
1692–1693, and for a summary of Ragusan *avvisi* concerning Turkish affairs (in 1691–
1692) vis-à-vis the unrest of the janissaries, the financial difficulties of the Porte, Imre
Thököly and Transylvania, and the Turks' reestablishment in Belgrade, see ASV, Senato,
Delib. Costantinopoli (Secreta), Reg. 35, fols. 83ᵛ–85ᵛ [181ᵛ–183ᵛ].

[9] Dumont, VII-2, no. cxii, pp. 229–30, *actum Viennae 12. Maii 1689.*

[10] Dumont, VII-2, no. cxiii, pp. 230–31, *donné en nôtre Cour à Hampton-Court le 17.
Mai 1689 et de nôtre Regne le premier:* "Lorsque nous considérons le grand nombre
d'injustes moiens dont le Roi des François s'est servi depuis quelques années pour satis-
faire son ambition; qu'il n'a pas seulement envahi les États de l'Empereur et de l'Empire à
présent en amitié avec nous, désolant des provinces entières et ruinant leurs habitans par
ses armées, mais qu'il a déclaré la guerre à nos alliez sans y être provoqué, violant mani-
festement par là les traitez confirmez par la garantie de la Couronne d'Angleterre—nous
ne saurions moins faire que de nous joindre à nos alliez pour nous opposer aux desseins du

Warfare between England and France was not confined to armies and navies, but extended also to merchantmen, dominating international commerce as well as politics. In 1695, for example, the French attacked English merchantmen in Turkish waters at Salines, the important harbor on Larnaca Bay in Cyprus, at Smyrna, and elsewhere, as Sir William Paget, the English ambassador to Istanbul, reported to the duke of Shrewsbury, William III's secretary of state. Neither England nor France was at war with the Turks; the Ottoman domain was neutral, and should not have been the scene of such armed conflict. Paget, who was soon to distinguish himself in the negotiations which led to the peace of Karlowitz, wrote Shrewsbury in September 1695: "While the Grand Signor is abroad [Mustafa II was at Belgrade], I have not the means to repress this insolence, and when he returns, the partiality of the Court for the French makes me apprehend that we shall hardly obtain satisfaction, tho I will try to procure it by all possible means."[11]

Paget was an enterprising ambassador, having established friendly relations with Constantine Brancovan, the prince of Wallachia, so that "my letters pass better and more securily then they could do formerly." He wanted William III to write a formal letter of thanks to Brancovan to "encourage him to continue his offices."[12] With almost everyone at war, Paget doubtless thought of the old adage that a friend in need was a friend indeed.

At Whitehall on 22 August (1689) the deputies of William III of Great Britain and those of the States General of the Protestant Netherlands signed another treaty against France, whereby both England and the Netherlands forbade all sorts of trade and commerce with the French, and undertook to reestablish a just and reasonable peace in Christendom.[13] Four months later (on 20–23 December) William joined the defensive and offensive alliance which the Emperor Leopold had made (on

---

Roi des François, que nous regardons comme le Perturbateur de la Paix et l'enemi commun de la Chrétienté:" The most Christian king of France had become "the common enemy of Christendom."

[11] PRO, SP 97, XX, fol. 15, doc. dated at Adrianople on 2/12 September 1695, with a postscript dated 2 October 1695, and cf. a letter of one James Paul addressed to Whitehall on 23 August 1698, on Venetian involvement in the Anglo-French commercial warfare in Greek waters (SP 97, XXI, fol. 14).

Paget had been received in an audience by the grand vizir on 18 February 1693 and thereafter on 7 March by Sultan Ahmed II (d. 6 February 1695), at which time the English and Dutch were trying to persuade the Turks to make peace with the Hapsburgs and their allies, while the French were doing their best to keep the Turks at war (von Hammer-Purgstall, *Gesch. d. osman. Reiches*, VI [1830, repr. 1963], 587–88).

[12] PRO, SP 97, XX, fol. 347ʳ, letter dated 26 April 1696. On Constantine Brancovan (d. 1714), see B.H. Sumner, *Peter the Great and the Ottoman Empire*, Oxford, 1949, pp. 42–44, and von Hammer-Purgstall, *Gesch. d. osman. Reiches*, VII (1831, repr. 1963), 68–70.

[13] Dumont, VII-2, no. cxviii, p. 238, *fait à Wittehal le 12/22 jour d'Août 1689*, and cf. no. cxl.

12 May) with the Allied (Catholic) Provinces of Belgium.[14] Some six months later Charles II of Spain and Vittorio Amadeo, the duke of Savoy, entered into an alliance (on 3 June 1690), "comme il est venu une Armée Françoise en Italie à dessein d'agir ouvertement contre l'État de Milan, et qu'elle s'est tenue dans les États de son Altesse royale de Savoye."[15] The next day (on 4 June) a treaty of alliance against France bound Vittorio Amadeo to the Emperor Leopold I; two days thereafter Charles II of Spain entered the "federation" of 12 May 1689 in a new accord with Leopold against France.[16]

The Grand Alliance was growing. Friedrich III, the elector of Brandenburg, added his name and the promise of 20,000 troops (with an imperial subvention) to the anti-French coalition (on 6 September 1690),[17] and a month later Vittorio Amadeo entered into the Grand Alliance with William III of Great Britain and the States General of the Netherlands (on 20 October 1690).[18] Imperial, royal, and princely deputies had been conspicuous as they moved from one center of power to another, negotiating and signing pacts against the French. Later on, these pacts were renewed, and a number of others were made against France. Louis XIV had to face an almost united Europe. The war against the Turks continued, with a subsidy here and there from a German prince,[19] as did the war in the West, with the periodic exchange of prisoners. So many states were caught up in the War of the League of Augsburg (1689–1697) that the Venetians had no hope of finding much assistance against the Turks throughout the last decade of the seventeenth century, but when peace was finally made, they were actually to do quite well.

Military historians have taken a large interest in the various battles fought both on land and at sea during the War of the League of Augsburg, especially the French marshal François de Luxembourg's victories at Fleurus on 30 June 1690 (over the Dutch), Steenkerque on 24 July 1692 (over William III), Neerwinden on 29 July 1693 (again over William III), as well as the French admiral Anne-Hilarion de Tourville's defeat by the British and Dutch naval forces offshore from Saint-Vaast-la Hogue in the Cotentin peninsula (in May 1692) and his defeat of the British fleet off Lagos a year later (on 30 June 1693). William III, distracted by the British war in Ireland, did badly in the field, but after a three months' siege he captured Namur, causing delight in London and distress in Paris, "the one great victory of his sixteen campaigns."[20]

---

[14] *Ibid.*, VII-2, no. cxx, pp. 241–42, and note no. cxii, pp. 229–30.

[15] *Ibid.*, VII-2, no. cxxv, pp. 265–66.

[16] *Ibid.*, VII-2, nos. cxxvi–cxxvii, pp. 266–69, docs. dated 4 and 6 June 1690, the latter treaty being ratified by Leopold at Vienna on 17 June.

[17] *Ibid.*, VII-2, no. cxxviii, pp. 269–70, and cf. no. cxxxvii.

[18] *Ibid.*, VII-2, no. cxxx, pp. 272–73, and cf. no. cxxxvi.

[19] Cf. *ibid.*, VII-2, no. cxlv, pp. 306–7, doc. dated at Vienna on 22 March 1692.

[20] Cf. G.N. Clark, *The Later Stuarts, 1660–1714*, Oxford, 1949, pp. 154–68.

Owing to the heavy pressure which the Austrians and their German allies had exerted upon the Turks, Francesco Morosini and Otto Wilhelm von Königsmarck had done singularly well in their campaigns of the 1680's. The Venetians had not fared so well in 1692–1693, as we have noted, but under the unfortunate command of Antonio Zeno they did take the island of Chios from the Turks in 6–18 September 1694, but had to surrender the island on 21 February 1695 after suffering severe losses.[21] As in the abandonment of the siege of Canea, the relinquishment of Chios was detrimental to the reputation of Venice. On 22 March [O.S., i.e., 1 April] 1695 William Raye, the English consul in Smyrna, wrote a friend in England,

"I doubt not you'l have heard of the Venetians' shamefull abandoning Scio with very many particulars which cannot with any certainty come to our knowledge, the cheife informations wee receive being from the Turcks themselves." According to what Raye had learned in Smyrna,

the Grand Signor's fleete of 20 shipps and 23 gallyes, being well reinforced with men and all things necessary, did on the 30th January [O.S., i.e., 9 February] attack the Venetians' fleete, in which through want of good conduct or the misfortune of a calm, few of the Venetian shipps being able to come up, their admirall and vice admirall shipps were burnt and one or two more destroyed.

Not content with this success, as Raye informs us, ten days later [on 19 February] the Turks forced the Venetians into a second engagement,

in which the Venetian fleete was so shattered and disabled that they were glad to retire under the shelter of their Castle, and doubting [not] a third attempt might be made on them, took up hasty resolutiones of abandoning the isleland, which they did on the 11th past [O.S., i.e., 21 February] in the night in so great confusion and consternation that they not only left the Castle entire with those additional fortifications they had made, but allso many horse and men and great quantityes of ammunition, cannon, mortars, bombs, arms, mastick, and what not.

One ship ran aground, and all those aboard were made slaves. Most of the Latins fled with the Venetians—Chios had been a Genoese colony from 1346 until 1566, when the Turks occupied the island. Of the Latins who remained on the island six or seven of the most prominent were "hung up by order of the seraschier." The Greeks were exposed to the insolence and plunder of the Turkish soldiery, but were apparently let

---

[21] Philip P. Argenti, *The Occupation of Chios by the Venetians (1694)*, Oxford, 1935, introd., pp. xxix–xxxv, lviii–lxviii, and see the *Relatione del nobile huomo Signor Bartolo Contarini, capitan estraordinario delle navi Venete, dell'occorso nel combatimento sotto Scio con l'armata maritima Turca l'anno 1694, il mese di febraro* [m.v., i.e., 1695], MS. Marc. It. VII, 656 (7791), fols. 108–114.

alone after a day or two, "but 'tis said the Grand Signor has confiscated the estates of all manner of inhabitants, appropriateing the whole isle-land to the Crown."

Most of the Latin churches were converted into mosques, the people reduced to misery, "and all this occasioned by the discontent or ambition of some few zelotts of the Roman Church, who have thereby enslaved their cuntry which before continued very happy in the enjoyment of many extraordinary priviledges under this government." It was only two weeks before the Venetian loss of Chios "that the Grand Signor [Ahmed II] died at Adrianople of a dropsy [on 6 February 1695], and that his nephew Sultan Mustapha [II] was advanced to the throne, which being immediately attended with such successes mightily raises the Turks' spirits." The new sultan was said to be planning to go in person to the wars, and "their shipps are allso fitting up at Constantinople with all exspedition to proceed for the Morea, so ere long wee shall see whither these late successes will encouradge them againe to encounter the Venetians, who 'tis hoped will not againe committ so great errors. . . ."[22]

As time passed, one wondered at the continuing life span of the ever-ailing Charles II of Spain. By the year 1696 one could only assume that he did not have much longer to live. Even in the Empire attention was turning from the eastern front to Spain. Louis XIV did not want the question of the Spanish succession to arise while he was at war with England and the Netherlands, the Empire, various German principalities, and of course with Spain. First of all Louis removed Vittorio Amadeo from the Grand Alliance by the treaty of Turin (of 29 August 1696), accepting "pour toujours une Paix stable et sincère entre le Roi et son royaume et Son Altesse Royale M. le Duc de Savoye et ses États, comme si elle n'avoit jamais été troublée. . . ."

---

[22] PRO, SP 97, XX, fol. 294, letter dated at Smyrna on 22 March 1694/95 O.S., i.e., 1 April 1695, also to be found in Argenti, *The Occupation of Chios . . . (1694)*, doc. no. 54, pp. 224–25, and cf., *ibid.*, docs. nos. 53, 55–56. Argenti's various works on Chios are detailed and valuable.

The military reputation of the Venetians must have been slightly redeemed when they frustrated the efforts of Ibrahim Pasha, who had defended Negroponte some years before, to establish a foothold in the Morea in June 1695. Ibrahim's forces had apparently exposed Argos and Monemvasia to some danger, but he was defeated with "molta quantità de morti, tra quali due agà de gianizzeri e Bechir Passà, genero del Seraschier [Ibrahim], con poca perdita de Veneti oltre qualche numero de feriti" (*Nova, vera, e distinta Relatione della vittoria ottenuta dall'armi della Serenissima Republica di Venetia contro gl'Ottomani nella campagna d'Argos, il giorno de' 10 Giugno 1695, sotto il prudente e valoroso comando dell'illustriss. et eccellentiss. Signor Alessandro Molin, capitan general da mar*, printed by Girolamo Albrizzi at Venice in 1695). Cf. Anderson, *Naval Wars in the Levant* (1952), pp. 220–22. Also the Venetians were not doing too badly in Dalmatia and Albania (cf. Senato, Delib. Costantinopoli [Secreta], Reg. 35, fol. 95 [193], doc. dated 3 July 1694 and, *ibid.*, fols. 96^v–97^r [194^v–195^r], doc. dated 21 August, 1694).

Vittorio Amadeo gave up all the commitments he had made to the allies at war with France. Louis promised him the restitution of all places the French had occupied in Savoyard territory as well as the fortress town of Pinerolo and the forts dependent on it. Various forts were to be demolished at the expense of France, all the territory in question being restored to Vittorio Amadeo, whose daughter Marie Adelaïde was to marry Louis's grandson, also named Louis, the then duke of Burgundy.[23]

In early October 1696 there was a suspension of arms in Italy. The imperialist, Spanish, and Savoyard troops were to refrain from hostilities with the Crown of France.[24] Vittorio Amadeo had of course already given Louis XIV a pledge of neutrality. At length the long-expected peace treaties, many of the terms having already been agreed upon in secret negotiations, were signed in William III's château at Ryswick (Rijswijk), three miles southeast of The Hague.

On 20 September 1697 a treaty of peace was signed between Louis XIV and the States General of the United Provinces of the Netherlands. It was to be "une Paix bonne, ferme, fidelle et inviolable," along with "un oubli et amnistie générale de tout ce qui a esté commis de part et d'autre à l'occasion de la dernière guerre." Louis would allow the Emperor Leopold I until 1 November to accept such articles as those in the Netherlandish treaty, after which period the articles would be put into effect whether they had the emperor's approval or not. A separate treaty of commerce and navigation was also signed on 20 September by the envoys and plenipotentiaries of Louis XIV and the States General of the United Provinces.

A separate treaty of peace between Louis XIV and William III of Great Britain was also signed at Ryswick on 20 September (1697) "to stop the war by which of late a large part of Christendom was being assailed" (*de sopiendo bello quo magna pars orbis Christani nuper affligebatur*), with the usual waiting period for Leopold I's acceptance. All territories, fortresses, islands, and lands taken during the war were now to be restored to their former owners. On the same day at Ryswick a treaty was duly signed between the envoys of Louis XIV and Charles II of Spain, by which all territories and "reunions" taken by Louis from Charles, in Spain as well as in the (Catholic) Netherlands, since the peace of Nijmegen (Nimwegen, in 1678–1679) were to be restored, except for eighty-two towns, villages, and other places to be identified in a separate list.[25]

---

[23] Dumont, VII-2, no. cxc, pp. 368–71, *fait à Turin le vingt-neuf d'Août, 1696,* treaty ratified by Louis XIV on 7 September 1696, and cf. no. cxci.

[24] *Ibid.,* no. cxcii, pp. 375–76, *donné à Vigevano le septième Octobre 1696,* ratified by Louis XIV at Fontainebleau on 22 October, and by Leopold I at Vienna on 29 October.

[25] *Ibid.,* nos. cxcv–cxcviii, pp. 381–420, docs. dated 20 September 1697 at Ryswick, with later ratifications signed at other places, together with other relevant data.

On 22–23 September (1697) a "cessation of arms" between Leopold I
and Louis XIV was agreed upon, envoys of the latter assuring the imperialists that French troops would not attack the domains of the Empire
until 1 November.[26] At last on 30 October, the day before the cessation
of arms would end, the envoys of Leopold and Louis signed a treaty
which was supposed to establish a lasting peace and a true friendship
between the Empire and France, using the earlier treaties of Westphalia
and Nijmegen as the building blocks of a new tranquillity in
Christendom.

Louis gave up to Leopold and the Empire all the "reunions" except
those in Alsace (*quae extra Alsatiam sita. . .sunt*), which the imperialists never regained; he also gave up to the king of Sweden as count
palatine of the Rhine the duchy of Zweibrücken (*avitus ducatus Bipon-
tinus liber et integer cum appertinentiis et dependentiis*). Leopold was
obliged to cede to Louis the important city of Strasbourg (*urbs Argen-
tinensis*) "and whatever belongs to this city on the left bank of the
Rhine." Louis had taken Strasbourg in 1681.[27] He was happy to retain it,
but he now surrendered Freiburg and Breisach to Leopold (by articles
XIX–XX) as well as Philippsburg to the Empire (art. XXII). He also gave
back the duchy of Lorraine to Duke Leopold I, with various concessions
and restrictions (arts. XXVIIIff.)[28] In this treaty, as in the others signed at
Ryswick, there were of course many other provisions of which we cannot
take account here.

Although the Venetians had not been involved in the War of the
League of Augsburg, they were much relieved by the treaties of Ryswick.
The withering health of Charles II of Spain and the international intrigue
it gave rise to, however, caused a widespread unease in Europe. The
Spanish question remained unsolved, and there was nothing the Venetians could do about it. They could, however, try to do something with
the "kingdom" of the Morea, which Morosini, von Königsmarck, and
Corner had won for them. The Morea was divided into four provinces—
Romania, Laconia, Messenia, and Achaea—with their capitals in Nauplia (Napoli di Romania), Monemvasia (Malvasia), Navarino Nuovo, and
Patras. Each province had a provveditore for military ventures and the
larger problems of administration, a rettore for civil and judicial affairs,
and a camerlengo for financial detail. Another provveditore, governor of

---

[26] *Ibid.*, VII-2, no. CXCIX, p. 421, [*datum*] *in Arce Ryswicensi 22 Septembris 1697.*

[27] Cf., *ibid.*, VII-2, no. x, p. 15, doc. dated 30 September 1681, "pour la reduction de
ladite ville [de Strasbourg] à l'obeïssance du Roi de France, Louis XIV."

[28] *Ibid.*, VII-2, no. CC, pp. 421–39, *acta haec sunt in Palatio Riswicensi in Hollandia
trigesima die mensis Octobris A.D. 1697,* the sixty articles of the treaty, with the usual
detailed addenda: ". . . Pacis hujus basis et fundamentum sit Pax Westphalica et Neoma-
gensis . . ." (art. III).

the "Three Islands" of Corfu, Zante, and Cephalonia, also held the reins of S. Maura and in Lepanto.

During the course of the year 1698 and thereafter Venetian officials in the Morea looked carefully into the current problems relating to agriculture, the fisheries, the mines, the functioning (and non-functioning) of the water mills, the condition of local Greek (and some Turkish) inhabitants, and the attempts here and there at reforestation. The officials compiled cadastral surveys, paid particular attention to the care and restoration of fortifications, reported on the available artillery and munitions in the Moreote strongholds (*piazze*), and sought to ensure the provision of bread for the militias, taking stock of the numbers of soldiers who were well (*sani*) and of those who were ill (*amalati*). Assessing the various expenditures and sources of income, the officials in question considered the costs of physicians and hospitals.[29] And, as might be expected, they recorded all the accounts and concessions which were to be registered in each provincial archive (*nell' archivio della loro provincia*). Inevitably there were of course troubles with the mainland Turks.

According to a statement of 16 April (1698) the Greek clergy in Tripolitza (Tripolis) or at least the Greek bishops seemed to be doing well: "vi soggiornano alcuni vescovi del rito greco, et godono publici assegnamenti." At Corinth, in the light of a report of 18 July, we learn that the first (or lowest) enclosure of the massive town-fortress was inhabited by Greeks, "et hanno alcune habitationi contigue alle mura del secondo contro la buona regola." The habitations in the upper reaches of the rocky height had been "in large part destroyed." Artillery was scarce at Corinth, and despite the height [of Acrocorinth] the walls were ruinous and capable of but slight resistance to attack. Indeed, a widespread inspection had revealed the fact that all the fortesses in the "kingdom" were in sad need of immediate attention. In the garrison at Corinth there were 26 men in apparent good health, while 34 were ill. The hospital was not being well maintained. The security of Corinth was especially important, for it protected the entry from the mainland into the Morea. There were, however, serious problems everywhere in the Venetians' Moreote kingdom, but within the next few years the contemporary texts give little or no evidence of notable improvements.[30]

---

[29] When the doge Silvestro Valier gave Giovanni Grimani his commission as "commissario sopra i confini in Dalmatia et Albania" (on 25 February 1698), the latter was directed to take with him Dr. Pompeo Sacco, professor of medicine in the University of Padua (Senato, Delib. Costantinopoli [Secreta], Reg. 35, fol. 107ᵛ [205ᵛ]). Dr. Sacco was presumably to have much larger responsibilities than the care of Grimani and his staff.

[30] Detailed summaries of the exhaustive investigations of the needs and resources of the Morea from 1698 to 1705 (with very little material after 1700) are to be found in the ASV, Senato, Provv. da terra e da mar, Filza 837, with "rubrics" of some thirty documents, all dated and numbered. The "file," which is coming to pieces, carries the dates "from 16 February 1697 to 28 March 1701." The year 1698 receives the most attention. Chas. [Karl]

The Morea prospered under the Venetians, as time went on, but eventually and inevitably the religious antagonism between Latin Catholics and Greek Orthodox was bound to express itself. At first the Greek clergy did indeed do well, and not only in Tripolitza. The nineteen bishops in the Morea enjoyed the *publici assegnamenti*. Before the Venetian governance of the Morea, the oecumenical patriarch in "Constantinople" had appointed the bishops, but now the local communities chose their own bishops. The patriarch had also appointed the heads of the *stavropegia* (σταυροπήγια, monasteries "fixed with the cross"), monasteries over which he exercised certain proprietary rights. They were an important source of income to the patriarchate, with their landed properties, tenancies, exemptions, market rights, and privileges, but now the patriarch lost much of the revenues he had derived from this source.

Before the period of Venetian rule in the Morea the required gifts made to the Church by the priests and their parishioners had been equally divided between the episcopate and the patriarchate. Morosini had cut these gifts (φιλότιμα) in half, the remaining sums going entirely to the bishops, which was another financial loss to the patriarch who was, like the entire Greek quarter of Istanbul (the Phanar), always under the close surveillance of the Ottoman government. Also the wealthy and well educated Greeks in the Phanar, the Phanariotes, who were often profitably employed by the Porte, preferred the incompetent Moslem rule in the Morea to the more efficient Catholic rule. As the years passed, the Venetian provincial administration did become more efficient, and increased efficiency meant increased taxes. Although the Signoria imposed restrictions on Moreote commerce and industry, lest they become in any way competitive with those of Venice, the governmental revenues and the incomes of Greek traders and agriculturists did increase markedly during the thirty odd years that the Serene Republic was to hold the peninsula.

To the confusion caused in western Europe by the numerous participants in the War of the League of Augsburg must now be added an element of further confusion in the East. On 28 July 1696 Peter the Great of Russia had captured the Turkish stronghold of Azov, at the mouth of the river Don, giving him easy access to the Sea of Azov. He

---

Hopf, *Chroniques gréco-romanes*, Berlin, 1873, pp. 385–90, gives the names of the rettori and provveditori of Achaea, Messenia, Romania, and Laconia, as well as those of local officials from 1692 to 1715. In this context, see also Gaetano Cozzi, "La Repubblica di Venezia in Morea: Un diritto per il nuovo Regno (1687–1715)," in *L'Età dei Lumi: Studi storici sul Settecento europeo in onore di Franco Venturi*, 2 vols., Naples, 1985, II, 739–89, dealing especially with Venetian legislation relating to the Morea.

also established a naval base at Taganrog in the northeast corner of the Sea of Azov. Although the Turkish base at Kerch, the southern outlet from the Sea of Azov, prevented Peter's entry into the Black Sea, it was all too clear that Russia had become a serious threat to the Porte.[31] After all, the Russians had launched attacks upon Constantinople as early as the years 860 and 941, and who could be sure that they might not soon do so again? As we have already observed (in a footnote), the English and Dutch had been trying to persuade the Turks to come to terms with the Hapsburgs and their allies, while Louis XIV's emissaries had urged the Turks to remain at war.

Although the treaties of Ryswick had ended the War of the League of Augsburg, the Spanish question was fast coming to need an answer. It seemed clear that the Bourbons and the Hapsburgs would be the chief contenders for the Spanish crown when Charles II died, despite the Bavarian claim (which eventually disappeared when the elector's little son died in 1699). It would obviously be helpful to the French if the Turks continued their warfare with the Hapsburgs, which they apparently had every intention of doing. The history of eastern Europe and that of Turkey were about to change, however, and one of the truly decisive battles of the seventeenth century was about to take place.

As the sun was beginning to set on 11 September 1697 a large Turkish army under Sultan Mustafa II and the grand vizir Elmas Mehmed Pasha encountered the imperialist forces at Zenta (Senta) on the banks of the river Tisa (Tisza, Theiss) in northern Serbia. The imperialist commander, as every student of history knows, was Prince Eugene of Savoy, then thirty-four years of age, one of the most remarkable military figures of modern times. With his usual boldness of direct attack, Eugene inflicted an overwhelming defeat upon the enemy. The Turks lost 25,000 men, including the grand vizir, the vizirs of Adana (Seyhan), Anatolia, and Bosnia, plus more than thirty aghas of the janissaries, sipahis, and silihdars, as well as seven horsetails (symbols of high authority), 100 pieces of heavy artillery, 423 banners, and the revered seal which the sultan always entrusted to the grand vizir on an important campaign. The grand vizir wore the seal hanging from his neck. There were many who believed that it had never fallen into the hands of an enemy before the

---

[31] Cf. B.H. Sumner, *Peter the Great and the Ottoman Empire*, Oxford, 1949, pp. 17–24. In the late seventeenth and early eighteenth centuries the Russians were at war with the Turks three times (1676–1681, 1687–1699, and 1710–1713). After making peace with the Turks in 1700, Peter soon found himself at war with Charles XII of Sweden, whom he defeated at the battle of Poltava (on 8 July 1709). Thereafter, however, Peter was himself defeated by the Turks on the river Prut, and lost both Azov and Taganrog (in 1711–1712), which he never recovered (*ibid.*, pp. 24–26, 40).

battle of Zenta. The Christians suffered a loss of 28 officers and 401 men killed as well as 133 officers and 1,435 men wounded. To contemporaries it seemed like a small price to pay for such a striking victory. Sultan Mustafa never took the field again.[32]

The Thirty Years' War and the Austro-Turkish strife after 1683 had wrought havoc in eastern Europe. Lady Mary Wortley Montagu had been charmed by the magnificent palaces and the social life of Vienna (in September 1716), as we have noted, but as she continued her travels, she found that "the kingdom of Bohemia is the most desart of any I have seen in Germany, the villages so poor and the post houses so miserable; clean straw and fair water are blessings not allways to be found and better accommodation not to be hop'd [for]." Prague, to be sure, retained some of its royal past, and those who could not afford to live in Vienna "chuse to reside here, where they have assemblys, music, and all other diversions (those of a Court excepted) at very moderate rates, all things being here in great abundance, especially the best wild fowl I ever tasted. . . ."[33]

When Lady Mary went northward into Saxony, she was charmed by Dresden, for "the town is the neatest I have seen in Germany—most of the houses are new built, the Elector's Palace very handsome. . . ."[34] When she finally got into Hungary, she found Raab [Györ] acceptable. The cathedral was large and well built, "which is all that I saw remarkable in the town." As she moved on, however, to the area of Komárno-Komárom, milady's buoyancy was dampened:

Leaving Comora on the other side the river, we went the 18th to Nosmuhl, a small village where, however, we made shift to find tolerable accomodation. We continu'd 2 days travelling between this place and Buda, through the finest plains in the world, as even as if they were pav'd, and extreme fruitfull, but for the most part desert and uncultivated, laid waste by the long war between the Turk and Emperour, and the more cruel civil war occassion'd by the barbarous persecution of the Protestant religion by the Emperour Leopold. That Prince has left behind him the character of an extrodinary piety and was naturally of a mild mercifull temper, but putting his conscience into the hands of a Jesuit, he was more cruel and treacherous to his poor Hungarian subjects than ever the Turk has been to the Christians, breaking without scruple his coronation oath and his faith solemnly given in many public treatys. Indeed, nothing can be more

---

[32] The battle of Zenta, which finally brought to an end the War of the Holy League, has been described in some detail by a number of historians from von Hammer-Purgstall, *Gesch. d. osman. Reiches,* VI (1830, repr. 1963), 634–41, trans Hellert, XII, 416–25, to Max Braubach, *Prinz Eugen von Savoyen,* I (1963), 256–61.

[33] Robert Halsband, ed., *The Complete Letters of Lady Mary Wortley Montagu,* 3 vols., Oxford, 1965–67, I, 280, letter dated at Prague on 17 November O.S. [27 or properly 28 November] 1716.

[34] *Ibid.,* I, 282, letter dated at Leipzig 21 November O.S. [2 December] 1716.

melancholy than travelling through Hungary, refflecting on the former flourish-
ing state of that Kingdom and seeing such a noble spot of earth allmost
uninhabited.

Lady Mary found Buda depressing,

once the royal seat of the Hungarian kings, where their palace was reckon'd one
of the most beautifull buildings of the age, now wholly destroy'd, no part of the
town having been repair'd since the last seige but the fortifications and the
castle, which is the present residence of the governour. . . .

As she proceeded on her journey, going south toward Mohács, she noted
two places,

both considerable towns when in the hands of the Turks, . . . now quite ruin'd;
only the remains of some Turkish towers shew something of what they have
been. This part of the country is very much overgrown with wood, and so little
frequented 'tis incredible what vast numbers of wild fowl we saw, who often live
here to a good old age "and, undisturb'd by guns, in quiet sleep."

When Lady Mary reached the area of the Danube between Karlowitz
(Sremski Karlovci), where the treaties of 1699 were signed (as we shall
see in a moment), and the city of Petrovaradin (Pétervárad), where Eugene of Savoy had defeated the Turks in the battle of "Peterwardein" (on
5 August 1716), and thereafter retook Belgrade, she was stunned by the
sight of the battlefield:

. . . We pass'd over the feilds of Carlowitz where the last great victory was
obtain'd by Prince Eugene over the Turks. The marks of that glorious bloody day
are yet recent, the feild being strew'd with the skulls and carcases of unbury'd
men, horses and camels. I could not look without horror on such numbers of
mangled humane bodys, and refflect on the injustice of war that makes murther
not only necessary but meritorious. Nothing seems to me a plainer proofe of the
irrationality of mankind (whatever fine claims we pretend to reason) than the
rage with which they contest for a small spot of ground, when such vast parts of
fruitfull earth lye quite uninhabited. . . .[35]

From the last decades of the sixteenth century England and Holland
had maintained ambassadors at the Porte. The English embassy in fact
began in the year 1583 with the appointment of William Harborne as
agent of the recently established Levant Company. For almost two and a
half centuries the English ambassador, whether at Istanbul or Adriano-

---

[35] *Ibid.,* I, 298–301, 305, two letters, one dated at Petrovaradin on 30 January O.S. 1717,
and the other at Belgrade on 12 February O.S.

ple, played a dual role as envoy of the Crown and as agent of the merchants who paid his salary. The Venetian bailie and the French ambassador had been resident on the Bosporus for a much longer period, the Venetians largely for commercial reasons (which led the British and Dutch to follow suit) and the French as a pivot in their anti-Hapsburg policies.

The Austrian and Polish envoys came and went, as their governments sent them on one mission or another. Turkish embassies were much less frequent and, as von Hammer-Purgstall reminds us, the envoys of the Porte came back home "without having learned anything." It was only from the beginning of the eighteenth century that Turkish envoys returned to scatter in Ottoman soil some of the seeds of European culture, custom, and convention.[36] In this context the year 1699 becomes especially important.

For some years Lord William Paget had been suggesting the desirability of peace to the Ottoman government. The battle of Zenta had certainly made the Turks more receptive to his oft-repeated advice. After some fourteen months of dickering and deliberation and some three months of arduous negotiation,[37] Paget could finally write the secretary of state at Whitehall from the town of Karlowitz (Sremski Karlovci) on the Danube in northern Serbia (on 26 January 1699):

This Express is dispatched to give His Majesty the news of the conclusion of the treatyes of Peace which have ben debated here above 3 months, with danger of breaking off severall times. The Moscovite seal'd his agreement the 14/24th. The Emperor's ambassadors plenipotentiaries and the ambassador of Poland have subscribed and seal'd their articles this day and, tho the Venetian ambassador [Carlo Ruzzini] has not subscribed and signed his, nor seems to like them, yet they have ben so well and carefully drawn with the intervention, assistance, and industry of the imperial ambassadors that 'tis not doubted but the State of Venise will readily approve them, but because that ambassador has not orders to conclude, time is allowed for his subscription to this treaty. So it is not doubted but the Peace will be generall so soon as that plenipotentiary can hear from Venise. . . .[38]

---

[36] Cf. von Hammer-Purgstall, *Gesch. d. osman. Reiches,* VII, 3–4, with text altered in Hellert, XIII, 5–6, and see A.C. Wood, "The English Embassy at Constantinople, 1660–1762," *English Historical Review,* XL (1925), 533–61, a valuable article.

[37] On the involved negotiations preceding the peace of Karlowitz—36 conferences in 72 days—see von Hammer-Purgstall, *Gesch. d. osman. Reiches,* VI, 648–49, 652–78, trans. Hellert, XII, 435–37, 439–75.

[38] PRO, SP 97, XXI, fol. 37, dispatch from Lord Paget, dated at Karlowitz 16/26 January 1699. In this context note the contemporary MS. Marc. It. VII, 407 (7494), *Scrittura intorno al Congresso di Carlovitz,* 70 fols., which begins with the observation that "seguita la Pace tra la Francia e le potenze collegate l'anno 1697 li 30 Ottobre nel Palazzo di Riswich all'Haiji [The Hague]," and goes on to discuss the background of events leading to the Peace of Karlowitz, the principal negotiators being the Turkish emissaries Mehmed

Paget and the Dutch envoy Jacob Colyer (Coljer) had been largely responsible for the important Peace of Karlowitz, which preserves the formal date 26 January 1699, involving the Emperor Leopold I, Sultan Mustafa II, King William III, the Allied Provinces of Belgium, and the Protestant Netherlands, ending some sixteen years of savage warfare and bloodshed (. . . *per sedecim hucusque annos saevum, exitiale et multa humani sanguinis effusione cruentum adeo bellum* . . .). King

---

Reis Effendi and the chief dragoman Alessandro Mavrocordato, who of course represented the Porte, the imperialists Wolfgang Etting and Leopold Schlich, the Venetian Carlo Ruzzini, together with Polish, Russian, and other plenipotentiaries, with Lord William Paget and the Dutch Count Jacob Colyer as the mediators who finally helped bring about the peace of late January 1699.

As usual coffee, pipes, sherbets, etc., helped to lubricate the meetings and solve various problems. This text was probably written by a secretary of Carlo Ruzzini. It is also to be found (with some variations) in MSS. Marc. It. VII, 902 (8220), fols. 48–77; 1255 (7968), fols. 256–319, to which we shall return in a moment; and 2217 (9202), 67 fols., with a drawing at fol. 13ᵛ of the housing arrangements prepared for the plenipotentiaries and other participants in the congress at Karlowitz (the Turks, imperialists, Venetians, Russians, Poles, and the "mediators").

There is a huge collection of documents and letters (both originals and copies) now available in a large vellum-bound volume in the Marciana, MS. It. VII, 399 (8625), *Congresso di Carlowitz (1699) e Carte relative a missioni di Carlo Ruzzini*, with more than 650 pages of texts. They were apparently all drawn from the collection of Ruzzini, who carefully assembled all the material he had access to before and after Karlowitz. This volume contains letters of Franz Kinsky, Wm. Paget, J. Colyer, Alessandro Mavrocordato, Leopold I, Robt. Sutton, William III of England, the doge Silvestro Valier, Wolfgang von Ettingen (Etting), Leopold Schlich (Schlich), Francesco Loredan, the Venetian ambassador at Vienna, the dragomans Tommaso and Giacomo Tarsia, and numerous others. A summary of the contents of this volume may be found in the *Inventari dei manoscritti delle Biblioteche d'Italia*, vol. LXXXI [Venezia, Marciana], prepared by Pietro and Giulio Zorzanello (Florence, 1956), pp. 143–55.

There is also a *Relatione del Congresso di Carloviz e dell'ambasciata di Vienna di Carlo Ruzini Cavalier (1699)* in MS. Marc. It. VII, 381 (7782), 79 fols., with a detailed map in color put at the end of the volume, locating Karlowitz, Petrowardein, and other important places as well as the quarters occupied by the Turks, the imperialists, the English and Dutch mediators at Karlowitz, together with the *domus conferentiarum* and the seating of the conferees. This work has been published by J. Fiedler, as noted in the *Inventari*, vol. LXXXI, cited above, pp. 126–27. The Peace of Karlowitz was the high spot in the latter-day history of Venice.

Some of the major difficulties encountered at Karlowitz in achieving the short-lived peace are covered from 25 September 1698 to 8 March 1699 in the *Relatione delle cose passate al Congresso di Pace tenuto in Carlovitz* in the volume of *Relazioni di ambasciatori*, MS. Marc. It. VII, 1255 (7968), fols. 256–319, referred to above. This dated diary of negotiations, with the seating arrangements provided for William Paget, Jacob Colyer, Carlo Ruzzini, the Ottoman Mehmed Reis Effendi, Alessandro Mavrocordato, and the secretaries of the English and Dutch mediators as well as those of Venice and the Porte adds no end of interest to a detailed text.

And finally there is a careful summary of contemporary events (beginning with the memorable years 1683–1688), ranging over the whole of Europe but with especial emphasis upon Austria and Venice, in the *Relatione del Congresso di Carlolivitz e dell'ambasciata di Vienna di Carlo Ruzini, Kavalier*, in MS. Marc. It. VII, 892 (7799), 180 fols., which Ruzzini presented to the doge in the year 1700, with an apology at the end (on fol. 179ʳ), "Di me, Serenissimo Principe, non posso scriver che con dolore di non haver posseduto talento eguale al destino di quei grand'affari. . . ."

Augustus II and the Republic of Poland as well as the Serene Republic of Venice also quickly became signatories to the peace.[39] As Russia now became involved in another war with Sweden, Peter the Great also made peace with the Porte when his possession of Azov was accepted.[40] From the time of Karlowitz the spirit of European statecraft fastened itself upon the Turks, and thereafter Ottoman policy and practice entered the byways of western diplomacy.

During the critical period Paget's strength of character, defiant honesty, and diplomatic skill endeared him to the Turks, and in March 1699 the sultan and the grand vizir wrote William III, requesting Paget's continuance at the Porte as the British ambassador. Reluctantly Paget remained at the Ottoman court until May 1702, when he left Adrianople, "laden with presents." In July he reached Vienna, where he had also been ambassador, and where he seems to have settled a dispute between Leopold I and Mustafa II concerning their borderlands in Bosnia. Paget left Vienna with "several rich gifts," going on to the court at Munich to employ his bargaining skill in an effort to remove certain difficulties between Leopold and Maximilian Emmanuel, the elector of Bavaria. Paget finally got back to London in April 1703, bringing Queen Anne twelve Turkish horses which Sultan Mustafa had given him.[41]

Meanwhile from Belgrade, which the Austrians had taken in 1688, and the Turks had soon recovered, Paget sent home a letter briefly describing something of the sequel to the signing of the first Treaties of Karlowitz. The letter is dated 11 February 1699. In a modest way it also depicts the importance the Turks had attached to his mediation in the negotiations for peace.

After the publication of the Peace of Carlowitz [on] January 16/26 the Turkish ambassadors stay'd there 'till Wensday of 25 January/4 February in expectation of the arrival of an expresse from Venice, who should have brought the ambassador's power to subscribe and seal his articles, but nothing appearing in that time, they were obliged to set forward for Adrianople that the Port's ratification might be remitted to me within the time appointed, so that they left Smirna [Sremska Mitrovica? ancient Sirmium] the 25th O.S. [4 February], and made towards Belgrade, where they arrived the 26th at night. We set out with them, but went more leasurely, so that we got not in till Friday morning of 27th O.S., but then I was received with extraordinary ceremonies and unusual circumstances. . . . The Dutch ambassador [Jacob Colyer] came up some hours after me, and was likewise well entertained.

---

[39] Dumont, *Corps universel diplomatique*, VII-2, nos. CCVIII–CCXI, pp. 448–59.

[40] On 25 December 1698 a two years' armistice had been arranged between Mustafa II and Peter I of Russia "by the mediation of his royal Majesty of Great Britain," which means William Paget's involvement (Dumont, VII-2, no. CCVII, pp. 447–48).

[41] These facts have been taken from the brief sketch of William Paget's career by Gordon Goodwin, in *The Dictionary of National Biography*, XV (repr. 1937–38), 64, and see Wood, "The English Embassy at Constantinople," *EHR*, XL (1925), 546–48.

Since my arrivall here, I am induced to think (from certain expressions, which some of [the Venetian ambassador's] retinue who came with the Dutch ambassador to see this place, let fall) that the Venetian ambassador [Carlo Ruzzini] had no mind to expedite his concerns, for they complained of the German and Polish ambassadors for being to easy. They say'd that if those had stood off a while, they might have had much better terms, so that it seems that's his opinion, but mine is that if others had been as full of fancy as he was, we had parted long 'eer this without doing anything. It were to be wished that he might receive expresse orders from his principals to sign his articles either before or at the arrival of the imperial ratification, else that business will remain uncertain, and meet with the same unexpected and perhaps ungratefull accidents, which may make its going on uneasy, and the Emperor may be engaged in unnecessary inconveniences.[42]

In due or perhaps in Paget's opinion undue time, the Venetian Signoria sent the Republic's "ratification of the treaty made by the imperial ambassadors for them at the late Congress." According to Paget, "it was dispatched to mee (signed by the Doge), and came to my hands the 13/23 February." So Paget reported from Belgrade on 20 March (1699), and

the imperial ratifications were exchanged (by us) at Slankamen the 4/14 instant [14 March]: With the ceremonie the difficult business is happily ended, with the satisfaction of all parties, and I am preparing to return to Adrianople and to go from hence to Constantinople, where I expect and hope to find my successor. . . .[43]

When the Venetian Senate had accepted the articles of the proposed peace of Karlowitz, after weighing the pros and cons in numerous dispatches from Carlo Ruzzini, the Republic's *ambasciatore plenipotentiario*, the motion was made and passed (on 12 March 1699) to elect an "honorable noble" as *ambasciatore estraordinario* to the Turks. The person chosen for the post was to leave promptly for the Porte to effect the final, formal ratification of the Turco-Venetian treaty. He would receive 400 ducats a month for his expenses, "with no obligation to render account thereof," as well as a gift of 5,000 scudi at the rate of seven lire to the scudo. He was to take with him fifteen horses, including those of his secretary, a servant, and four grooms. He was also to take with him a physician, to whom a hundred sequins (*zechini*) would be given as a gift,

---

[42] PRO, SP 97, XXI, fol. 43, letter dated at Belgrade on 1/11 February 1699. In England the Gregorian calendar (of 1582) was adopted in 1752, omitting ten days from the Julian calendar up to the year 1700, thereafter eleven days to 1800, twelve days to 1900 (and thirteen days to 2100). References to both the Julian calendar (Old Style) and the Gregorian (New Style), with their ten-day difference, are common in the seventeenth century. On the disputes and complications attending the introduction of the Gregorian calendar, see F.K. Ginzel, *Handbuch der mathematischen und technischen Chronologie*, III (Leipzig, 1914), 266–79.

[43] PRO, SP 97, XXI, fol. 49, letter dated at Belgrade on 10/20 March 1699.

and a barber-surgeon, who would receive fifty sequins. The physician would have a servant. The Signoria assumed the costs of their "traveling expenses," *le spese di bocca e di viaggio.* The provisions made for the coming embassy, which was to include (in addition to the ambassador's secretary) a coadjutor, an accountant, and a chaplain, were almost exactly the same as those accorded Alvise da Molin upon his election as ambassador extraordinary to the Porte thirty years before (on 18 October 1669).[44]

Lorenzo Soranzo was elected ambassador extraordinary to the Porte. After the usual expressions of appreciation for his past services and confidence in his proper fulfillment of the manifold responsibilities of his forthcoming mission, the doge Silvestro Valier and the Senate issued his commission on 27 June 1699. The ships *Croce* and *Iride* were going to convey him to the Dardanelles, where he would find other vessels and other ministers, the Austrians apparently having made most of the necessary arrangements. On 27 June the Senate also approved the dispatch of appropriate letters to the sultan, the mufti, the grand vizir, the kaïmakam, and other vizirs, as well as to the sultan's mother and "alla regina sposa del Gran Signore."[45]

Upon his arrival at the Porte, Soranzo was to present the doge's letter to the grand vizir, making clear to the latter that the purpose of his mission was indeed ratification of the peace negotiated at Karlowitz. He was to express pleasure and satisfaction in the renewal of tranquillity which would save so many treasures and stop the shedding of blood, "considerando il vantaggio del commercio e raffermando che dalla parte della Republica sarano inviolabilmente osservate le conditioni di essa [pace]." The Signoria wished to see the old friendship restored between Venice and the Porte, and to help maintain this it had been decided to appoint a bailie who, as in the past, would be resident on the Bosporus. Soranzo was to assure the grand vizir of the high esteem in which the doge and Senate held him. If the grand vizir was not in Istanbul, Soranzo must go to Adrianople to confer with him, and there must be observed "il più decoroso trattamento solito con ambasciatori di teste coronate," i.e., Soranzo must receive the same honorable reception as had in the past been accorded the ambassadors Badoer, an earlier Soranzo, Foscarini, and Molin.[46]

When Soranzo was received by Sultan Mustafa II (as the Signoria

---

[44] Senato, Delib. Costantinopoli (Secreta), Reg. 35, fols. 108–109^r [206–207^r], doc. dated 12 March 1699, the vote being +187 [*de parte*], —3 [*de non*], —5 [*non sinceri*], and on the remuneration for the ambassador's staff, note also, *ibid.,* fols. 129^v–130^r [227^v–228^r]. On the terms of Alvise da Molin's election as ambassador extraordinary to the Porte, see above, pp. 229–30.

[45] Delib. Costantinopoli, Reg. 35, fols. 126^r, 124, and 125.

[46] Lorenzo Soranzo's commission as ambassador extraordinary to the Porte is given in the Delib. Costantinopoli Reg. 35, fols. 126–130 [224–228], dated 27 June 1699.

hoped he would be), he was to give him the customary greeting "in the name of our Republic," deliver his letters of credence, and present the sultan "with the usual gifts." He was to speak of the solemn confirmation of the peace and the Turco-Venetian friendship of past years "in grave and appropriate words." Before his departure Soranzo would be given a copy of the Republic's treaty with the Porte, "that is, of the sixteen authentic articles in the Turkish language signed at Karlowitz."[47] He was also to receive a copy of the peace which Alvise da Molin had made with Porte in 1670. Soranzo was to seek whatever further advantage he could while he was at the Turkish court, and effect the exchange of prisoners, lists of whose names he was to take with him. He must find out the method, time, and place of the liberation of these prisoners, "especially of the nobleman [Pietro Antonio] Bembo."[48]

Soranzo must look to the commercial advantages he could gain for the Republic, taking care to see that all Turkish ports were opened to Venetian merchants, who should not be required to pay higher tolls than those paid by other nations, i.e., the five percent toll paid by the Venetian merchants should be reduced to the three percent which certain others were paying. Until the new bailie arrived in Istanbul, Soranzo must take care of the "familia ordinaria" of the bailaggio at Pera. Besides certain dragomans Soranzo was to take with him six "giovani di lingua," Venetian students of Turkish who would live at the bailaggio, doing their best to master the language for subsequent employment by the Signoria.

At least one of these students must always accompany whatever dragoman goes to the Porte to assist him in any way possible as well as to acquire some experience and further knowledge of the Ottoman court to make him of greater service to the Signoria. In fact Soranzo must see to the reestablishment of the Turkish school at the bailaggio, and inform the Senate of which sons or nephews of the dragomans might later be employed by the Signoria. Some of them should be enrolled in the school in accord with an enactment of the Senate (of 27 December 1670).[49]

---

[47] The sixteen articles of the Turco-Venetian treaty of Karlowitz are given (in Italian and French) in Dumont, *Corps universel diplomatique*, VII-2 (1731), no. CCX, pp. 453–58.

[48] On Bembo, note the Delib. Costantinopoli, Reg. 35, fol. 180^r, doc. dated 11 March 1700. Bembo had been captured when his galley was sunk on 6 July 1697 (Tommaso Bertelè, *Il Palazzo degli ambasciatori di Venezia a Costantinopoli*, Bologna, 1932, p. 333, note 17).

[49] On the need of providing the manuscripts and instruction necessary for the study of Arabic and Turkish (*per lo stabilimento d'una scuola della lingua Araba e Turca*), one may consult the memorandum addressed to the Venetian Senate by one Salamone Negri sometime early in the year 1706 (ASV, Senato III [Secreta], Dispacci Costantinopoli, Filza 169 [21 March 1706 to 21 May 1710], fols. 39–44, 593, at which time Carlo Ruzzini was ambassador and Ascanio Giustinian bailie to the Porte). On the long history of the Tarsia family as interpreters or dragomans, cf., *ibid.*, fols. 74ff., 360; and on Christoforo Tarsia, of whom mention is made elsewhere, see, *ibid.*, Filza 171, fols. 483ff., and esp. Filza 172, fols. 136–145^r, a dispatch of the bailie Andrea Memo dated 20 December 1714. Also on the ignorance of Turkish at Venice (and the lack of instruction therein), the "school" of

Soranzo must see to the reconstruction of the church of S. Francesco di Pera in Galata, which had always been maintained by Venice despite its destruction by frequent fires in the past. He must also extend the protection of Venice to the Fathers of the Holy Sepulcher of Jerusalem, as had been done in the past. And of course Soranzo was to pay the usual wages, and give the usual provisions and appropriate gifts to the janissaries who made up the guard at the "casa bailaggia" in Pera.[50]

Soranzo did not arrive in Istanbul until 13 November (1699), having sent the Venetian dragoman Giacomo Tarsia ahead when his ship came in sight of the island of Tenedos. He received an almost royal reception with five salvos of Turkish cannon fire "all'arrivo in facia del Tenedo." The Turks had shown great respect for the Venetian ambassador.[51] In fact the pasha of Tenedos paid Soranzo a visit, bringing him refreshments, to which courtesy he responded by giving the Turk confections and candles, of which the Signoria informed Soranzo they would send him a further supply. As Soranzo came to the Dardanelles, he was greeted with another salvo of cannon fire, and the kapudan pasha sent a chavush and his adopted son to bid the ambassador a welcome to Istanbul. Soranzo entered the Turkish capital incognito, whereupon the grand vizir immediately sent his agha to him with further refreshments, and the other pashas made similar gestures.[52]

The Senate was pleased that Soranzo, following the example of the other ministers and the custom of the Turks, had sent the new French ambassador his greetings with a word of welcome to the diplomatic colony on the Bosporus, "not waiting until he should give you notice of his arrival," as his predecessor had done. The courteous response of the

---

Turkish at Istanbul (and its failure on several occasions), the dragomans (and the perils to which they were subjected), the *giovani di lingua* (and their occasional temptation to become Turks because of "la lussuria di quelle donne turche"), etc., see Paolo Preto, *Venezia e i Turchi*, Florence, 1975, pp. 95–115, and cf., above, Chapter I, note 41.

[50] As noted above, Lorenzo Soranzo's commission is to be found in the Delib. Costantinopoli, Reg. 35, fols. 126–130, and cf., *ibid.,* fols. 131ff., 147ff., 149ᵛ–150, *et alibi.* Gifts were always an important part of placating the Turks (fols. 136ʳ, 156ᵛ–157ʳ, 162ʳ, *et alibi*).

The bailie's house in Istanbul had fallen into serious disrepair during the recent war, and required serious attention, on which see the Delib. Costantinopoli, Reg. 35, fol. 166ʳ [264ʳ], *all'ambasciator estraordinario alla Porta:* "Sopra gl'avisi del [Tomaso] Tarsia [the Republic's grand dragoman in Istanbul] che la casa bailaggia si ritrovasse bisognosa di risarcimento, savia rileviamo la speditione ch'havevate fatta per via di terra a Costantinopoli, ordinandoli l'allestimento d'alloggio capace al vostro numeroso seguito" (doc. dated 20 November 1699, and note, *ibid.,* fols. 179ᵛ–180ʳ, on Tarsia and the need to repair the casa bailaggia, doc. dated 11 March 1700). Cf. Bertelè, *Il Palazzo degli ambasciatori di Venezia a Costantinopoli* (1932), pp. 253ff., 332ff., and note pp. 82, 85. "As for the church of S. Francesco in Galata," according to a ducal letter to Soranzo of 8 May 1700 (Delib. Costantinopoli, Reg. 35, fol. 190ᵛ), "it has already been turned into a mosque."

[51] The doge and Senate had learned with pleasure "che ne'discorsi tenuti con voi da Turchi habbiano mostrato la degna impressione ch'ha lasciato nell'animo loro la valorosa condotta de nostri commandanti nella decorosa guerra . . ." (Delib. Costantinopoli, Reg. 35, fol. 179, doc. dated 11 March 1700).

[52] *Ibid.,* fol. 179ᵛ.

French ambassador was important to the Signoria, for tact and courtly gestures were the lubricants of protocol and diplomacy. But of course ambassadors always had problems to deal with and, as the Senate warned Soranzo, "important are the maneuverings of the representatives of Muscovy who, it appears, are awaiting the arrival of the imperial ambassador to make some new proposals, about which you must make every effort to find out whether they are tending toward a truce or the conclusion of a complete peace."[53]

On the whole Lorenzo Soranzo was successful in procuring information for the Signoria. What is more, however, he not only easily effected the ratification of the Turco-Venetian treaty of Karlowitz (signed so reluctantly by the Republic's so-called plenipotentiary Carlo Ruzzini), but succeeded in making a number of addenda thereto which, long kept secret, renewed in large part the more favorable "capitulations" of the earlier Turco-Venetian treaties. But not the least of Soranzo's worries, during his years in Istanbul, was the restoration of the *casa bailaggia*, which had received little attention during the recent fifteen years of warfare.[54]

Venice fared well in the Peace of Karlowitz, retaining the entire "kingdom" of the Morea, the seven Ionian islands, the two Cretan fortress towns of Suda and Spinalonga, Butrinto, Parga, Cattaro (Kotor), Castelnuovo (Herceg Novi), and Risano (Risan) on the Dalmatian coast, plus the islands of Aegina and Tenos in the Aegean. She was to give up all claim to *la fortezza di Lepanto,* and the *castello detto di Rumelia,* near the entrance to the Gulf of Corinth, was to be demolished.[55] As for the Empire, Leopold I held on to the kingdom of Hungary, all Transylvania

---

[53] Delib. Costantinopoli, Reg. 35, fols. 180^v–181^r, doc. dated 11 March 1700.

[54] Bertelè, *Il Palazzo degli ambasciatori di Venezia a Costantinopoli* (1932), pp. 253–58, 332–33. Soranzo's reception at the Porte seems to have surprised the Signoria, on which cf. the Delib. Costantinopoli, Reg. 35, fols. 188^v–191^v [286^v–289^v], doc. dated 8 May 1700: "All'ambasciator estraordinario alla Porta Ottomana, Cavaliere Soranzo: . . . Il vostro solenne ingresso, la visita al primo visire, l'audienza ottenuta dal Sultano, l'altre visite de'principali ministri, e quelle date e ricevute da ministri dell'estere nationi non potevano essere esseguite respettivamente con più proprietà nè con maggior splendore. . . .

"Godiamo intendere che in ognuno dell'accennati incontri oltre li caftani distribuiti in numero maggiore del solito a quelli del vostro seguito, habbiate esato la corrispondenza quale ben si conveniva alla dignità della Republica et al decoro della publica rappresentanza, godendo particolarmente ch'il Gran Signore con la voce propria habbia dato la risposta alla vostra prudente espositione, significandovi le commissioni rilasciate per l'estesa della ratificatione alli capitoli accordati in Carlovitz."

[55] Dumont, VII-2, no. CCX, pp. 254–58, and on the Venetians' continued possession of the island of Aegina, cf. Delib. Costantinopoli, Reg. 35, fol. 160^v [258^v], doc. dated 5 November 1699, a dispatch of the doge and Senate to the ambassador Soranzo. There were always problems in the confirmation of a treaty, and on the difficulties now involved in establishing the Turco-Venetian boundaries in Dalmatia, with the approaches to Castelnuovo, Cattaro, and Ragusa, see the Delib. Costantinopoli, Reg. 35, esp. fols. 161ff. [259ff.], 183ff. [281ff.], 191ff. [289ff.], 196^r [294^r], 204^{v}ff. [302^{v}ff.], *et alibi,* docs. dated 1699–1700.

then in his possession, Croatia, and Slavonia, while Sultan Mustafa II kept the banat of Temesvár (*Arx Temisvariensis*), the city of Belgrade, and certain other territories. The treaty or "armistice" was to last for twenty-five years.[56] And, finally, the Turks recognized Poland's right to Podolia and the western Ukraine.[57]

The question must have arisen in many a mind as to how long these agreements would last, for the projected twenty-five years of peace were emphasized only in the Turkish agreement with the Empire, not in those with Venice and Poland. The Austrians had done well through the years. Since raising the siege of Vienna in 1683 they had won nine notable victories in fourteen campaigns. Also they had either taken or retained their hold upon nine fortress towns of importance, including Györ (Raab), Esztergom (Gran), Buda[pest], Székesfehérvár (Stuhlweissenburg), Osijek (Esseg, Eszék), Petrovaradin (Peterwardein, Pétervárad), and Oradea (Grosswardein, Nagyvárad). It was a goodly haul.

One often pays a price for success, and so did milord Paget for, as we have noted, at the request of Sultan Mustafa II his appointment as ambassador to the Porte was to go on for another three years. In 1701 he was succeeded by Sir Robert Sutton, whose dispatches to Whitehall show that by the spring of 1702 there was a high state of tension between Venice and the Porte as a result of the Venetians' seizure of a Turkish vessel with goods aboard worth 200,000 dollars. The French and Dutch consuls were also incensed at the Venetians, for their principals "had concerns in [the vessel] to the extent of 20,000 dollars each." Furthermore, as Sutton wrote the secretary of state at Whitehall on 4 May (1702), "This accident serves to sour the minds of the Turks against the Republick, whereas it was before observable that they are not able to brook the loss of the Morea to the Venetians."[58] Nevertheless, peace did continue between Venice and the Porte for another dozen years.

The Turks, however, were adding to their armada, as Sutton informed the secretary of state, piling up "peculiarly great magazins of ammunition and provisions near the Morea." They had also sent their best and oldest troops to areas close by the Morea. The Sultana Valide, the mother of Mustafa II, "who has a great ascendant over the Grand Signor, her having lost a great part of her rents which lay in that kingdome," was obviously anxious to see the Turks retake the Morea. Sutton thought it "doubtfull how long the Republick will be able to keep friends with this

---

[56] Dumont, VII-2, no. CCVIII, pp. 448–51.

[57] *Ibid.*, VIII-2, no. CCIX, p. 452.

[58] PRO, SP 97, XXI, fol. 96, letter dated at Adrianople on 23 April 1702, O.S. or, after 1700 adding ten days [it should be eleven] 3 May, but the ten-day difference lingers on for some time into the eighteenth century. Sutton was knighted in 1701, and thereafter sent to Istanbul, where he remained as ambassador for fifteen years (until 1716).

Empire [the Porte], which is not insensible of the fair opportunity they have by all Christendome being embroyled in a war," i.e., the War of the Spanish Succession had just begun. Sutton wished to know, therefore, if the Turks chose to go to war, "whether his Majesty will be pleased to allow that endeavours may be used to shew them that it is more their interest to break with the Muscovites then the Venetians. . . ."[59]

The Venetian ambassador was trying to calm the wrath of the pashas by the payment of money "for reparation of the affront and dammages . . . , but there is a new dispute arisen which will imbroil them further." A sea rover had in fact just seized a Turkish saïque near Negroponte. Some of the men aboard had managed to escape and make their way to Adrianople, "where they have made their complaints," and apparently produced some measure of proof "that the corsair belongs to the Morea and is consequently a subject of Venice."

According to Sutton, the French were stirring the embers, apparently seeking to "ingage the Port[e] in a war against the Republic if not against the Germans, whom they know to be weak in Hungary, having their hands full elsewhere." The Germans, i.e., the Austrians, had sent no envoy or minister to Istanbul, and seemed to have little interest in Turkish affairs. However, as Sutton wrote the secretary of state, "I must not omit to acquaint your Lordship that the Venetians, but more especially the French, give any considerable sums of mony at the Port to obtain their ends, which is an advantage generally denied to us."[60]

Except for the periods during which the Köprülüs were dominant in Istanbul, the grand vizirs, kaïmakams, reis effendis, and other high officials of the Porte put in an appearance and made their departure with disturbing rapidity throughout the seventeenth century.[61] In a dispatch of August 1702 Sir Robert Sutton takes us through some of the rocks and reefs endangering the Turkish government. The mufti or chief jurisconsult of the sacred law in Istanbul [Seïd Feïzullah], "hath found the secret of so managing the Queen Mother [the Sultana Valide] that she is come entirely into his interests, and they two joyning together, which happens as often as the one hath the least need of the other's assistance, carry all

---

[59] Sutton, *ibidem.*

[60] PRO, SP 97, XXI, fol. 100, dispatch dated at Pera of Constantinople on 30 May O.S. [9 June] 1702, and received at Whitehall on 12 August.

[61] Note the turmoil at the Porte and the changes in Turkish officialdom when Mustafa II ascended the Ottoman throne, as described in the Venetian Delib. Costantinopoli, Reg. 35, fols. 101–102ʳ [199–200ʳ], entry under 25 June 1695, relating to events which took place in early May. In fact Sultan Mustafa informed a timorous pasha who was trying to avoid the responsibilities of the grand vizirate, *rappresentando la propria debolezza et inhabilità per la direttione del commando,* "If you do not accept the ministry, you will die now, and if you accept it and govern badly, you will die somewhat later. Therefore accept it to live a while longer. Also Köprülü was much younger than you, but my father, along with Köprülü's prudent governance, quietly enjoyed eighteen years of proper imperial rule!"

things at pleasure." The reis effendi, who served under the grand vizir [Amudshazade Hussein Köprülü] as a sort of chancellor, was very astute, and being only too well aware of the mufti's influence over the court, he tried to win his favor. For some time the reis effendi [Abdul Kerimbeg] had succeeded in keeping the mufti and the grand vizir on good terms, but he knew that, as the two major figures at the court, they would inevitably fall apart. The reis effendi, therefore, soon threw in his lot with the mufti.

At first Abdul Kerimbeg, the reis effendi, dealt cautiously with the grand vizir. When the latter, however, resigned from his exalted post [on 5 September 1702], the reis effendi, "a person like the mufti, alwaies ready to follow interest without any reguard to publick faith or engagements," acquired a large part of the grand vizir's power of governance. The grand vizir, a man of character in Sutton's opinion, had made peace with the enemies of the Porte. He had followed the course of justice. Now he had been set aside, "because there are designs laying which he may be too just to approve." The mufti had taken over.

The Grand Signor's master of the horse, his nephew, had been strangled. His favorite kiaya, "an officer who does almost all the business under him," had been removed; another kiaya, an underling of the mufti, had been put in his place. The Grand Signor [Mustafa II], in Sutton's view, really had no future, considering "his own age and infirmities, he now lying under an obstruction in his liver, all these have brought him down to so low a condition that he probably cannot last long." In this regard Sutton was to be proved quite right.

With the change of vizir, Sutton thought " 'tis much too be feared it will not be long before a war is begun by the Port[e] on one side or another." The war would most likely be directed against the Venetians for, as Sutton had already informed the secretary's office at Whitehall, "the Turks cannot brook the loss of the Morea, and do not scruple to say openly that they cannot leave that Republik time to digest so rich a morsel." It would be easy, Sutton believed, for the Turks to wrest the Morea from the Venetians. The Austrians, Poles, and Muscovites were wrapped up in their own struggles. A large part of the Sultana Valide's income had been derived from the Morea. She was presumably seeking its return. Indeed, that the Morea was the Turks' major objective seemed clear as a consequence of "their having sent their oldest and best troops to the frontiers of the Morea and taken particular care to furnish well their magazins there with ammunition and provisions, great quantities whereof have been transported to Lepanto, Negropon[te], and elsewhere."

The Turks were also increasing their fleet, to which they intended to add 40 ships, while "those they have already amounting to about 30, are almost all very large ships." A new ship in the Arsenal, now ready to be launched, had "holes pierced for 120 guns." There was another on the stocks at Istanbul which would carry between 50 and 60 guns, and five or six more of the same size were abuilding on the coast of the Black Sea. "The disputes witch the ministers of the Port continually raise with the Venetians show the aversion they have to that Republic and their readiness to quarrel with it." The Turks had also become angry with the Emperor Leopold of late, for "the Emperor neglects his concerns with the Port as much as if he were indifferent whether he was to continue in peace with this [Ottoman] empire or not." The French were using "all imaginable artifice as well as mony" to embroil the Turks in renewed warfare with the Austrians or the Venetians,[62] which would be of obvious advantage to the French, as the War of the Spanish Succession gained momentum.

The longer Sutton watched the political drama in Istanbul, the more downhearted he became. On 12 January 1703 he wrote the secretary of state at Whitehall that "there are two or three crafty ministers present in this government who are heaping up immense riches by the most indirect means." He would seem to be referring to the mufti and the reis effendi, whose names he does not give. In any event the unholy two (or three) were selling "their protection to those who commit the greatest injustices towards the Frank nations," i.e., the western Europeans, for the safety of whose properties and persons Sutton now entertained no little doubt. The two or three ministers in question had such a capacity for deception that they "never give any satisfaction but in fair words, contriving to defeat the effect of their own orders and commands for redresse of injuries."

Such violations of justice seemed never to have been done in the past, in times of high prosperity, despite the haughtiness of the vizirs. The ministers in question paid no heed to the letters of ambassadors and made "a sport of the remonstrances of our druggermen." If they continued in this arrogant fashion, Sutton feared they might ultimately be drawn "to invade the countries of their neighbors," which evoked Sutton's concern that the interests of her Majesty's subjects—merchants and ship-owners—might be "in a much worse state then ever they used to be when the Port was engaged most in war."[63]

As Sir Robert Sutton warned the British government that the intrigues and turmoil within the Ottoman government posed a danger to the Levant Company, just so did Antonio Nani, *proveditor general in Morea,* warn the Venetian Signoria (from Argos on 28 May 1703) that one must

---

[62] PRO, SP 97, XXI, fols. 86ᵛ–88, dispatch dated at Pera of Constantinople 7/18 August 1702.

[63] PRO, SP 97, XXI, fol. 118, dispatch dated at "Pera of Constantinople," 12 January 1702/3.

keep a watchful eye upon the Morea, *l'antemurale del publico dominio in Levante.* Their powerful neighbor, the Turk, who was always alert to profit from opportunity, would certainly aspire to seize possession of the so-called kingdom. Therefore the best use of peace was to prepare for war. Nani describes, as others had done before him, the strengths and weaknesses of the chief fortress towns of the Morea—Nauplia-Palamidi, Monemvasia, Modon and Coron, the two Navarinos (*Vecchio e Nuovo*), and the important Castle of the Morea, "situato all'imboccatura del Golfo di Lepanto e in se stesso un posto riguardevole, e la vicinanza in cui è di Patrasso, piazza totalmente mancante, lo rende più accreditato e considerabile."[64]

Nani also called attention to the Mainotes of Brazzo di Maina at the southern end of Mt. Taygetus in the Morea, "people who are restless and fierce [by nature], and have always aroused apprehension in the mind of whoever has had dominion over them."[65] The Mainotes had long been well known for their sustained hostility to the Turks. How would the Venetians make out with them?

In August 1702 Sutton had informed the secretariat of state at Whitehall that the Grand Signor Mustafa II probably could not last much longer. And he was quite right. On 4 September 1703 Antonio Nani wrote the doge and Senate that as the consequence of a "noisy revolt at the court of Constantinople [on 22 August 1703] the rebels have put the scepter in the hand of Mustafa [*sic*], brother of Sultan Mehmed, having cut to pieces the mufti [Feïzullah] and the agha of the janissaries [Tshalik], while the grand vizir [Rami Pasha] fled with the minister [Alessandro] Mavrocordato. . . ." The provveditore of Achaea had confirmed the report which Nani had received, adding that for three days at Lepanto forty shots of cannon had solemnized the "new coronation." Such a crisis in the Ottoman government required serious thought on the part of the Venetian Signoria: *popoli malcontenti, genii desiderosi di novità, monarca d'età giovanile, di spiriti superbi e feroci, piantato sul trono da sudditi ribelli al frattello, armi in moto formano un infelice aspetto. . . .*[66]

---

[64] The dispatches of Antonio Nani from 22 April 1703 to 27 December 1705 may be found in the ASV, Senato, Provv. da terra e da mar, Filza 852. The letter from Argos, dated 28 May 1703, is the third entry in this "file." Despite the peace of Karlowitz piracy remained an unceasing menace (cf. Delib. Costantinopoli, Reg. 35, fol. 187^r [285^r], doc. dated 15 April 1700).

[65] *Ibid.,* Filza 852, entry no. 5, dispatch dated at Kalamata on 4 August 1703.

[66] *Ibid.,* Filza 852, entry no. 6, dispatch of Antonio Nani to the doge and Senate, *Romania li 4 Settembre 1703 S[til] N[ovo]*, which text is followed by an account from Corinth, dated 2 September, of the deposition of Sultan Mustafa II. On the uprising in Istanbul, see also, *ibid.,* entry no. 7, dated 2 October 1703. Obviously either Nani or his secretary was confused as to the name of the sultan deposed and the name of his successor.

The rebellion had arisen on the Bosporus and in Adrianople, extending over some thirty-six days, from 17 July to 22 August 1703, ending on the latter date when Mustafa II, who died the following year, was replaced by his younger brother Ahmed III.[67] As for the latter, Antonio Nani wrote the doge and Senate in mid-May 1704 that according to word which he had recently received from a confidante, who paid constant attention to the goings-on in Istanbul, the new sultan was much concerned with military preparations. The army was already on the way to Adrianople, where an armed fortress had been established. Some thought that the new kapudan pasha [Osman] was to go with the armada to the Black Sea "to give a hand to the construction of the castle" which had been started the year before. The serasker was allegedly instructed to go by land with a body of troops to assist in the building of the castle and to protect the kapudan pasha.

The attention which the sultan was giving to strengthening the Turkish "maritime armament" was certainly worrisome. Despite assurances of the sultan's good intentions, Nani was apprehensive, for there could be no doubt as to his fierce and warlike spirit, and Christians knew that the oath of a barbarian prince was worthless. Also the young Ahmed III was fired with ambition to embark upon some undertaking to make a name for himself and perhaps avail himself of Venetian weakness in the Morea.[68]

Antonio Nani did indeed see weakness in the Venetian forces stationed in the Morea. The old discipline, which had been so well maintained during the late war, had grown "rusty and lax as a result of the idleness of peace." Nani therefore took the officers under him to task. The effectiveness of the soldiery had declined owing to the inattention of their captains; the men had been unnerved by their "listless leisure" (*languido riposo*), and they must learn again to bear the heavy weight of armaments.[69] In the meantime Nani was trying to keep track of the turn of events in Adrianople and Istanbul.

On 22 February 1705 Nani wrote the doge and Senate that the report had been confirmed of the removal from the grand vizirate of Kalaïlikoz Ahmed Pasha, who had been replaced by Baltadji Mehmed Pasha. Kalaïlikoz had fallen from power on 25 December 1704. Nani had learned the news from the Venetian bailie on the Bosporus. Mehmed appeared to be a lover of tranquillity, for he was placid by nature, and was clearly

---

[67] Von Hammer-Purgstall, *Gesch. d. osman. Reiches,* VII (1831, repr. 1963), 73–86, trans. Hellert, XIII (1839), 110–29.

[68] Provv. da terra e da mar, Filza 852, entry no. 14, dispatch dated at Mistra on 17 May 1704.

[69] *Ibid.,* Filza 852, entry no. 15, dispatch dated at Tripolitza on 30 May 1704.

enjoying the peace which then obtained under Sultan Ahmed III, who had been looked upon as a would-be warrior (and indeed he would eventually turn out to be so). In the meantime Nani as *proveditor general in Morea* was trying to maintain the best possible relations (*la migliore corrispondenza*) with his Turkish neighbors so that Venice should not be subjected to any undue hardship.[70]

In the meantime life was peaceful in the Morea. On 1 September 1705 Antonio Nani acknowledged receipt of a "revered ducal letter," dated 10 June, which the Senate had sent him, along with a decree relating to the alms which had been collected in the Veneto "for the maintenance of the Holy Sepulcher of Jerusalem." Nani had distributed a copy of the text of the decree to all the prelates and parish priests in the Moreote provinces, "those of the Latin as well as of the Greek rite," seeking to enlist their support of the Signoria's pious objective of raising money for the upkeep of the church (built on the assumed site of Christ's burial). Nani assured the Signoria he would do his best to see that money was indeed raised and taken care of for the sacred purpose which the Senate was fostering. In this letter, however, he also dilates on the necessity of maintaining "that sound discipline which, acquired at the price of blood in the last war [with the Turks], now requires all our attention. . . ."[71]

Like his predecessors and successors, as *proveditori generali in Morea*, Antonio Nani had had many worries and responsibilities. The dispatches to the Signoria are concerned with problems relating to mariners, galley slaves, and shipwrecks, garrisons, available troops, and shortages of manpower, tolls, taxes, contraband, and the lack of funds needed for various purposes, with particular attention to the correspondence between the local pashas and the Venetian officials. The weakness of the three regiments of dragoons and the other forces in the Morea was worrisome. In fact from 10 January to 26 March 1706 there appear to have been only 2,045 infantry at Corinth to stop the entry of Turks into the Morea. There were hardly a thousand cavalry at Corinth.[72]

The pashas of Negroponte and Lepanto were alleged to be at some odds owing to the "gelosia imaginabile entro il nuovo bassà in Lepanto con sole 40 persone di seguito e non più."[73] Apparently the Turkish

---

[70] *Ibid.*, Filza 852, entry no. 24, dispatch dated at Patras on 22 February 1705 (m.v. 1704), and cf., *ibid.*, no. 28, dated at Romania on 4 July 1705: "S'è verificata la caduta del primo visir Calailico, e dagl'avisi de' quali m'honora il zelo dell'eccellentissimo signor cavalier bailo Giustinian, rilevo che vi si habbia sostituito Mehemet Calfa . . ." (entry no. 24). On Kalaïlikoz Ahmed, see von Hammer-Purgstall, *Gesch. d. osman. Reiches*, VII (1831, repr. 1963), 107–109ff., trans. Hellert, XIII, 159–61ff.

[71] *Ibid.*, Filza 852, entry no. 29, dispatch dated at Romania on 1 September 1705.

[72] ASV, Senato, Provv. da terra e da mar, Filza 838, entry no. 5, pages unnumbered. Filza ("file") 838 covers the period from 1705 to 1708.

[73] *Ibid.*, Filza 838, no. 8, dated March–May 1706.

command on the border of the Morea was now as hard-pressed for man-power as that of the Venetians, who had many other complaints. The tithes were not being properly paid in Arcadia (Kyparissia), Phanari, Androusa, Karytaina, Leondari, and Kalamata.[74] There was always some-thing wrong, but after having spent the usual two years or more as *prove-ditor general* in the Morea, Antonio Nani was happy to contemplate the apparent success of his administration.

As Nani wrote the doge and Senate (on 20 October 1705), he was giving up his post with the good fortune of leaving the Moreote frontiers in complete quiet without any conceivable reason for dissatisfaction as well as with an excellent relationship with the Turks who were in com-mand at the borderlines. The kingdom of the Morea was thus free from all molestation, even that often suffered from criminal raiders (*anche de' malviventi*). Also Nani was leaving the revenues of the "public patri-mony" of the Morea in a better state than he had found them. In fact he said that the revenues had risen to "the sum of four hundred ninety-seven thousand, seven hundred fifteen and a half ducats."[75] When one still has the data upon which budgets of the distant past were allegedly based, the totals are rarely in accord with modern calculations. We do not (as far as I know) possess the facts and figures from which Nani derived his total of the revenues of the kingdom, but that last half-ducat was obviously his way of making clear to the Senate the meticulous attention he had devoted to the provincial budgets of the Morea.

In early May 1706 Sultan Ahmed III managed to curtail the extortion-ate practices of governmental officials and to reduce the unrest in Istan-bul by the appointment of Tchorlulu Ali Pasha as the grand vizir. Bring-ing reason and justice into the administration of Ottoman domestic and foreign policy, Tchorlulu Ali made no attempt to profit from attacks upon either Venice or Austria despite the opportunities which the War of the Spanish Succession and the "Great Northern War" seemed to be offering the Porte. Ahmed III's government remained neutral, adhering to the treaties of Karlowitz (1699) with the states of the Holy League and to the truce of 1698–1700 with Russia. The situation changed, however, when on 8 July 1709 Peter the Great defeated the Swedes under Charles XII and the Cossacks under the hetman Mazeppa in the Ukraine, in a battle some three miles northeast of the city of Poltava on the right bank of the Vorskla river.

Charles XII had established Stanislaus I Leszczynski as king of Poland, but Poland was now full of Russians and being held largely under Peter's

---

[74] *Ibid.,* Filza 838, no. 9, May–July 1706, and the tithes were not being properly paid at Patras (no. 28).

[75] *Ibid.,* Filza 852, entry no. 30.

warlike dominance. In Istanbul Tchorlulu Ali's non-aggressive policy was interpreted as pro-Russian in some quarters, and he soon fell a victim to the intrigues of the Seraglio (on Sunday, 15 June 1710). He was succeeded as grand vizir by Numan Köprülü Pasha, the son of Mustafa Köprülü, whose death we have noted at Slankamen (in 1691). Although honest and just, after the fashion of the Köprülüs, Numan seemed unable to delegate authority. He tried to do everything himself, but there was too much to do. His grand vizirate lasted only two months. His life was spared, however, and he returned to Negroponte as governor, which position he had previously occupied. Numan was the fifth and last member of the Köprülü family to serve as grand vizir of the Porte.[76]

Now, once more, the grand vizir was Baltadji Mehmed Pasha, who yielded to the anti-Russian feeling which had grown up in the Seraglio. The Russians were becoming much feared in Istanbul. The Tatars of the Crimea had also become hostile to the Russians, who were infringing upon their territories. After his defeat near Poltava, Charles XII had sought shelter in the Turkish fortress of Bender on the river Dniester. Friedrich Augustus, elector of Saxony (1670–1733), who had become king of Poland as Augustus II (in 1697), had just driven Charles's ally Stanislaus Leszczynski out of Poland (in 1709). Charles's affairs were not prospering, but he was much encouraged when, quite to the surprise of the British ambassador Sir Robert Sutton, the Porte declared war upon Russia on 20 November 1710.[77] Thereafter, on 17 January and 22 February (1711), Czar Peter I promptly made indignant responses to the Ottoman declaration of war, for Ahmed III and his ministers had violated the recently renewed treaty of peace between Russia and the Porte.[78]

According to a dispatch of 8 December (1710) which Sutton sent Lord Dartmouth, who had recently become the secretary of state at Whitehall, he had had a meeting a day or two before with the grand vizir Baltadji Mehmed Pasha. The latter was quite willing to discuss the Russian problem as seen by the Turks and the Swedes. In fact Baltadji

---

[76] Von Hammer-Purgstall, *Gesch. d. osman. Reiches*, VII, 136–48, trans. Hellert, XIII, 203–23.

[77] Akdes Nimet Kurat, ed., *The Despatches of Sir Robert Sutton, Ambassador in Constantinople (1710–1714)*, Camden Series III, vol. LXXVIII (London, 1953), nos. 8–9, pp. 25–29, dispatches dated 16 and 20 November 1710. Sutton attributes the Turkish declaration of war against Russia entirely to the influence of Devletgerey (Davlat Giray), Tatar khan of the Crimea (1698–1702, 1707–1713), which was undoubtedly the case. Sutton kept himself very well informed; his dispatches are detailed, important sources for the history of the Porte in the early years of the eighteenth century.

[78] Jean Dumont, *Corps universel diplomatique*, VIII-1 (1731), docs. nos. CV, pp. 259–64, dated 17 January, and CVIII, pp. 266–69, dated 22 February 1711. According to Sutton's dispatch to Dartmouth dated 20 November 1710 (Kurat, *Despatches*, no. 9, p. 28), the sultan had "excused himself for having renewed the Truce with the Muscovites, laying the blame of it on [Tchorlulu] Ali Pashaw the late Vizir, who had misrepresented things to him and diverted him from thoughts of war."

enlarged very much upon the motives of their present resolutions and ran into complaint against the Muscovites, blaming the conduct of the late ministers [Tchorlulu Ali Pasha and Numan Köprülü Pasha] for suffering themselves to be amused by them. He shewed great jealousy of the growing power and ambitious designs of the Muscovites, saying that they had already reduced the Suedes to a low condition, and that the Port had certain information that they intended to fall upon them in another year.

Baltadji was indignant

that [the Muscovites] had committed great insolencies on the frontiers, and been guilty of many infractions of the Peace. That they had cut in pieces a great many Tartars, and carried away their horses, cattle and goods. That the Czar had pretended precedence of other Kings and taken upon himself the title of Emperour. That they knew he promised himself to be one day Master of Constantinople, and that he had said he hoped to be buried in the Church of Sancta Sophia, and held other discourses to the same purpose.[79]

Although Sutton believed that the sultan, his ministers, and most of the populace were entering the war with reluctance, "the chief men of the Law [the ulema] and the Soldiery [especially the Janissaries]" refused to consider any alternatives. On 7 January (1711) Sutton wrote Dartmouth that the Turks were anxious to maintain peace with western Christendom, "for which reason they are positively resolved to dispatch envoys to Vienna and Venice with letters from the Sultan and Prime Vizir full of assurances that his Highnesse will religiously observe and maintain the Treaties of Carlovitz."[80] Sutton was certain, however, that if the war should go on "without any notable successe," the Turks would grow weary of it "in a few years" because of the cost of maintaining their fleet, the hardships the army suffered "in a desert country and inclement climate," as well as the poverty of the pashas and timariots "who serve at their own expense." Ahmed III had a good deal of money, but he was loath to part with it, and if he were "forced to bring it out," it would not last long, and there would seem to be no way of replacing it.[81]

The Turkish court was relieved for a while of its uncertainty and confusion when on or just before 25 July (1711) the news reached Istanbul of the defeat of the Russians in a sometimes violent two-day encounter with the Turks on the banks of the river Pruth (on 9–10 July), in the long-disputed province of Moldavia. When the Russians took fright, Czar

---

[79] A.N. Kurat, ed., *The Despatches of Sir Robert Sutton, Ambassador in Constantinople* (1953), no. 10, p. 29.

[80] Kurat, *Despatches*, nos. 10–11, pp. 30, 32, docs. dated 8 December 1710 and 7 January 1711.

[81] Kurat, no. 15, p. 49, dispatch to Dartmouth, dated at Pera of Constantinople 29 May 1711.

Peter sent two "plenipotentiaries . . . with a white flag to the Vizir offering him peace on such terms as he himself could desire for the Port."[82] The grand vizir Baltadji Mehmed Pasha, the commander of the Turkish forces at the Pruth, dealt generously with Czar Peter and the Russians, to the annoyance of King Charles XII and the Tatar Khan Davlat Giray.[83] According to the treaty of Pruth, Peter was to give up the fortress of Azov, destroy that of Taganrog, and henceforth not meddle in Polish affairs.[84]

The treaty of Pruth did put an end to the war between the Turks and Russians, but inasmuch as it did not terminate the disputes and differences between them, "on est convenu de part et d'autre de requérir et prier les nobles seigneurs Mons. Robert Sutton, Chevalier, et Mons. Jacob Colyer, Comte de l'Empire Romain, Ambassadeurs . . . , d'employer leur médiation au nom de leurs Hauts Souverains pour terminer et ajuster les dits différens. . . ." By and large Czar Peter had met the requirements of the treaty of Pruth in which it had been agreed, however, "que le Czar ne se mêlera plus des Polonois ni des Cosaques qui dépendent d'eux. . . ."[85] Since Peter had not relaxed his hold upon Poland, the "said differences" were inevitable, and the result was another treaty of peace and friendship between Russia and the Porte (on 5/15 April 1712).

Peter now agreed once more to withdraw all Russian troops from Poland; if the Swedes entered Poland with the intention of attacking him (or for any reason at all), his reentry was not to be regarded as an infraction of the treaty. But when the Swedes withdrew from Poland, he must do so also. The Porte would see to Charles XII's return to Sweden "without doing any wrong publicly or secretly to the subjects and lands of the Muscovites."[86] Despite this formal agreement there was still unease

---

[82] Kurat, *Despatches*, no. 18, pp. 58–59, doc. dated 25 July 1711, in which Sutton also gives Lord Dartmouth the articles of peace. On Moldavia, see esp. Demetrius Cantemir (Dimitrie Cantemir), *Descriptio Moldaviae*, Bucharest, 1973, Latin text with Rumanian translation, notes added by D.M. Pippidi.

[83] On the background to the battle on the Pruth, the battle itself, and the Turco-Russian peace of 21 July 1711, see Kurat, *Despatches*, nos. 16–21, 23, pp. 53–70, 75–76, docs. dated from 25 June to 1 October 1711.

[84] Cf. Dumont, *Corps universel diplomatique*, VIII-1, no. CXIV, pp. 275–76, *fait au Camp des Turcs près de la rivière de Pruth le 6. de la lune Gemaiel-Achir* [Jumadâ al-äkhirah] *l'an de l'Hégire 1123 et le 10 ou 21 de Juillet 1711*.

[85] *Ibid.*, VIII-1, no. CXIV, p. 275a.

[86] *Ibid.*, no. CXXVIII, pp. 297–98, *signé et scellé par le Grand-Vizir Jusuf Bacha* [who had succeeded Baltadji Mehmed Pasha as grand vizir on 9 December 1711] *à Constantinople le 5. Avril 1712*. Cf. Kurat, *Despatches* (1953), no. 33, p. 113, dispatch of Sir Robert Sutton to the British secretary of state Lord Dartmouth dated 7 April, 1712, "I have now the honour to acquaint your Lordship that on the 5th instant a Truce for the term of 25 years was concluded between the Czar and the Sultan, and the same evening the Treaties were exchanged in the Turkish and Russe languages. . . ."

enough on the eastern fronts to require its full confirmation at Adrianople on 5/16 June 1713 and now, despite the Swedes, the Porte and Russia had finally made peace, which was supposed to last for twenty-five years.[87]

Sir Robert Sutton was well informed throughout his fifteen years as the British ambassador in Istanbul, maintaining close relations with Ottoman officials, members of certain ambassadorial staffs, and various dragomans. His dispatches are often lengthy and detailed. From December 1711 to April 1712 he was engaged with his colleague Jacob Colyer, the Dutch ambassador, in efforts to make secure the peace between Russia and the Porte. In fact both the Russians and the Turks made such demands upon the time of both Sutton and Colyer that they seem to have done little else for the almost four months in question.[88] Sutton appears to have favored the Russians, from whom he received both money and gifts. Indeed it is apparently well known that the Russian P.B. Shafirov gave Sutton 6,000 ducats and a sable coat.[89] The British government did not approve of his meddling in Russo-Turkish affairs, but he found it difficult not to do so. Although Sutton received his salary from the Levant Company, he has little to say about English

---

On the long sojourn of Charles XII in Turkish territory, note the dispatches of Alvise Mocenigo, the Venetian bailie in Istanbul, to the Signoria in ASV, Senato III (Secreta), Dispacci Costantinopoli, Filza 170, fols. 108–10, 136–38, 202ᵛff., 236ff., 510ʳ, docs. dated 1 May, 15 June, 17 August, 6 September 1710, and 15 September 1711, and finally on "il passaggio del Re di Suezia per li stati Cesarei" (*ibid.*, Filza 172, fols. 71ff.). On Charles XII and the Turco-Muscovite peace as well as the Turks' insistence that the Czar Peter withdraw from Poland, see, *ibid.*, Filza 171, fol. 166ʳ, doc. dated 22 July 1712, and note fols. 269ff., doc. dated 6 December 1712; fols. 317ʳ–320, doc. dated 15 February 1713 (m.v. 1712); *et alibi* in this file of the bailie Mocenigo's dispatches and various other documents.

The text of the final, formal treaty of peace between the Porte and Russia, concluded at Adrianople on 5/16 June 1713, is given in an Italian translation in Filza 171, fols. 429–34, but of course the troubles continued (*ibid.*, fols. 463–66, a dispatch of Mocenigo dated at Pera di Costantinopoli on 12 October 1713, and cf. fols. 479–482, dispatch dated at Pera on 25 November 1713). Poland, however, remained a problem (Filza 171, fols. 498–503, dispatch dated at Pera on 20 January 1714 [m.v. 1713], also fols. 526–530, 555–558ʳ, *et alibi*).

[87] Gabriel Noradounghian, *Recueil d'actes internationaux de l'Empire Ottoman*, I (Paris, 1897), no. 18, pp. 203–7, with a summary of the treaties of Ahmed III (1703–1730) on pp. 59–64. On the prolonged negotiations leading to the Turco-Russian treaty of 16 June 1713 as well as the endless difficulties which Charles XII caused Sultan Ahmed III in the latter's efforts to get him safely out of Turkey, see Kurat, *Despatches* (1953), nos. 34–74, pp. 123–204, Sutton's dispatches to Dartmouth from 19 April 1712 to 7 October 1714, with a French text of the treaty, *ibid.*, no. 60, pp. 180–81. On the Polish-Swedish-Russian-Turkish problems and relations, see the report to the Venetian Senate of the Republic's ambassador to Poland, Daniele Dolfin (in 1715–1716), which has been published with an introduction by Marino Zorzi, "Daniel Dolfin 3⁰, ambasciatore in Polonia," *Ateneo Veneto*, vol. 20, nos. 1–2 (1982), pp. 267–302 (Dolfin's *relazione* is dated 10 August 1717).

[88] Cf. Kurat, *Despatches*, nos. 28–33, pp. 85–123, Sutton's dispatches to Dartmouth from 20 December 1711 to 7 April 1712.

[89] *Ibid.*, p. 8.

trade or, for that matter, any trade at all. His reports to Whitehall are concerned with his own diplomatic, political, and military interests, all of which were of large importance while he represented Queen Anne on the Bosporus.

During the years of the War of the Spanish Succession (1701–1714) the English were anxious to see to the preservation of peace in eastern Europe, whereas the French wanted to rekindle the old hostility between Vienna and the Porte to weaken the Grand Alliance against France. The War of the Spanish Succession involved the major states of Christendom. The attention of Europe was fastened upon it to a far greater extent than upon the Turco-Russian-Swedish difficulties. Despite its great importance, however, the War of the Spanish Succession lies outside the sphere of our Venetian-Austrian-Turkish interests.[90] It did make its mark in Istanbul. Sir Robert Sutton was at constant odds with the French ambassadors, the baron Charles de Fériol, and (from 1711) his successor, Pierre Puchot, the count Desalleurs. The Venetian Signoria shared the views of the French government to no small extent. Thus Sutton wrote Lord Dartmouth on 1 October 1711:

> The Venetians here have taken an allarm at the discourses of the people of a war with that Republick. There are hitherto no further grounds to fear it then

---

[90] I have therefore deleted from the text what I had initially written on the War of the Spanish Succession involving, as it did, the notable careers of Prince Eugene of Savoy, Duke John [Churchill] of Marlborough, Nicolas Catinat, François de Villeroi, Louis Joseph de Vendôme, Claude Louis de Villars, and others. Nevertheless, it seems worthwhile to give thought to some of the more important documentation involved, which of course did bear upon eastern Europe and Italy, where in fact the war actually began with Prince Eugene's invasion of the peninsula and his defeat of Catinat at Carpi and of Villeroi at Chiari in 1701.

The British declaration of war against France and Spain was announced at S. James' Palace in Westminster (London) on 4/14 May 1702 (Dumont, VIII-1 [1731], no. xxviii, p. 115); that of the States General of the Netherlands was published at The Hague on 15/25 May (*ibid.*, VIII-1, no. xxvi, pp. 112–14). On 15 May the Emperor Leopold I issued his declaration of war against the king of France and the latter's grandson, the duke of Anjou, now Philip V of Spain; the imperial seal was affixed to Leopold's decree of warfare in the castle at Laxenburg on the Schwechat some ten miles south of Vienna (*ibid.*, VIII-1, no. xxix, pp. 115–16).

Louis XIV responded with his own declaration of war against the emperor, Queen Anne of Great Britain, the States General, and their allies, which he signed on 3 July (1702) in the château at Marly-le-Roi to the west of Paris (*ibid.*, VIII-1, no. xxxi, p. 118). The more important documents relating to the War of the Spanish Succession (1701–1714) are most conveniently found in Dumont, VIII-1, nos. xxxiv–xxxv, xxxix, xlii, xliii, xlv–xlvii, xlix, lxxxv, cxix–cxx, cxxi, cxxxi, cxxxiv, cxxxvi–cxxxviii, cxlii, cxlv, and cxlvii, pp. 120ff.

The War of the Spanish Succession was concluded in the treaties of Utrecht of 31 March/11 April 1713, which are given in Dumont, VIII-1, nos. cli–cliii, clvi–clvii, clxiv, and cf. no. clxix, pp. 339ff., and in the treaties of Rastatt (6 March 1714), *ibid.*, VIII-1, no. clxx, pp. 415–23, and Baden (7 September 1714), no. clxxiv, pp. 436–44, and note nos. clxxx, clxxxvi. Although some of these documents do relate to the main themes of this book, their relevance has not seemed sufficient to deal with them in any detail.

that the Turks bear them a particular ill will accompanied with contempt, and will certainly grow very insolent and haughty after the execution of the peace with Muscovy. The extreme partiality of the Venetian bailo to the French and his intimacy with the Embassadour of that Crown as well as certain practices, whereof I formerly gave your Lordship an account, administer occasion to several to suspect that they will unite their endeavours to imbroil the Port with the court of Vienna, especially if the bailo should flatter himself by those means to divert a war with the Republick.[91]

A month later, on 8 November (1711), Sutton again informed Dartmouth that "the people [in Istanbul] already begin to talk of a war with the Venetians, and there is evidently a great propension to it in the soldiery and the navy, which much allarms the Venetians, tho' there be yet no other grounds of fear." After the conclusion of the treaty with the Russians, however, Sutton believed that "we shall be better able to discover whether the Port inclines to a war with the Republick or not."[92]

---

[91] Kurat, *Despatches*, no. 23, p. 74.
[92] *Ibid.*, no. 26, p. 81.

XIV

*The Turkish Reconquest of the Morea,
the Victories of Eugene of Savoy,
Von Schulenburg's Defense of Corfu,
the Peace of Passarowitz, and Venice
as a Playground of Europe*

❧

hen the Turks had made a final peace with the Russians in June
1713, settling various issues (including certain questions relating to the frontiers), the ministers of the Porte once more turned
their attention to Venice. Turkish and Venetian ships had been as usual
in collision, and the Signoria had allegedly encouraged an insurrection in
Montenegro during the Russo-Turkish war. The last straw had been the
Venetians' seizure of a vessel carrying the treasures of the erstwhile
grand vizir Damad Hasan Pasha (1703–4) to his wife, the sultana Kha-
didje. The Hospitallers' seizure of a Turkish vessel on the way to Egypt in
1644 had led to the Cretan war and the loss of Candia, and now a like
venture on the part of the Venetians brought about another Turco-Venetian war and the eventual loss of the kingdom of the Morea.

The revolt of Montenegro was a serious matter. When the rebels were
defeated, their leader, the vladika Gikan, who had distributed some
35,000 ducats (supplied by the Russians) among his people three years
before, now fled to Venetian-held Cattaro (Kotor). Despite the fact that
the Venetians were said to have promised the Porte not to give refuge to

426

rebels, they received Gikan in Cattaro, and refused to turn him over to the Turks. The result was the Turkish declaration of war on 9 December 1714, with a "manifesto" in fourteen articles, of which the first was concerned with the pillaging of the vessel belonging to the harem of Damad Hasan Pasha, the last with Venetian support of the Montenegrin insurrection, the remaining twelve relating to the Venetians' alleged harassment of Turkish ships at sea.[1]

About five weeks later (on 11 January 1715) the horsetails were put up on display at the imperial Seraglio in Istanbul in the presence of the vizirs and emirs, the sheikhs and the ulema, proclaiming the outbreak of war. Ahmed III left the Seraglio in mid-March to convey the awesome standard of command to the grand vizir Damad Ali Pasha, with whom he began the westward journey to Thessaloniki (Salonika), and went with him into northern Greece. At Thebes the grand vizir, now the serasker, held a council of war to decide upon which Moreote fortress they should first put under siege. No member of the council would venture an opinion, however, and at length the grand vizir directed Kara Mustafa, the beylerbey of Diarbekr (Diyarbakir), to take the Venetian-held castle of the Morea at the southern entrance to the Gulf of Lepanto (Naupactus). To carry out this objective the grand vizir is said to have given the beylerbey command of some forty thousand men, but most such figures are suspect, whether we are dealing with numbers of troops in the East or in the West.

Fate seemed to be working on the Turks' behalf when the news came to their army in Greece that the provveditore Bernardo Balbi had surrendered the Venetian town of Exoburgo (τὸ Ἐξώβουργον) on the fortified height of Tenos. Balbi had given up the island without a struggle in June 1715. It was a small island, but a large blow, for the Venetians

---

[1] By late January 1714 the bailie Alvise Mocenigo had become painfully aware "che s'era sparsa la fama d'essersi deliberato in consulta secreta di farsi in quest'anno un poderoso armamento maritimo," which some people thought might be directed against the Maltesi, others to hold the Tripolini in check, "ma la maggiore parte pretendeva che ciò riguardasse la Morea" (Senato, Dispacci Costantinopoli, Filza 171, fol. 504ʳ, dispatch dated at Pera di Costantinopoli on 23 January 1714 [m. v. 1713]). The Turks had been building up their armed forces at an alarming rate, as Mocenigo's successor Andrea Memo (Memmo) had more than once warned the Signoria (*ibid.*, Filza 172, fols. 102–111, dispatch dated at Pera on 24 October 1714, and cf., *ibid.*, fols. 164–173).

The bailie Andrea Memo and the Venetian dragomans were harshly treated at the Porte after the Turkish movement toward the Morea (Dispacci Costantinopoli, Filza 172, fols. 134–145ʳ, dispatches of the bailie dated 13 and 20 December 1714). In fact on 7 August 1715 Memo informed the doge "from the waters of Zante" of his release "from the terrible prison in which I was shut up for four months" (*ibid.*, fols. 205ff., and cf. fols. 216–218ʳ). The secretary Domenico Franceschi was also confined to prison, in the Seven Towers (Yedikule), *ibid.*, fols. 238–240, 258ᵛ, letters dated 8 December 1714 and 28 March 1715, and note Amy A. Bernardy, *L'Ultima Guerra turco-veneziana (MDCCXIV–MDCCXVIII)*, Florence, 1902, pp. 89–97, letters of Memo dated 28 April and 7 August, 1715.

had held Tenos from the year 1390, and it had become a Latin stronghold. The Turks removed thirty-five cannon from Tenos, which they put aboard fifteen of the vessels in their fleet, and two hundred Catholic families were carried off to North Africa. Many a Turkish kapudan pasha had tried through the years to take Tenos, but now Djanüm Khoja Mehmed Pasha was the first to do so. He had acquired the position of lord high admiral in December 1714, and was to lose it in February 1717, acquire it again for a few days and lose it in 1730, and hold it for the third time from 1732 to 1736. Djanüm Khoja was a Turk, originally from Coron on the southern coast of the Morea. Captured in the last war, which had ended with the peace of Karlowitz (in January 1699), Djanüm had spent seven years as an oarsman slave on the Venetian galleys. Ransomed at the cost of a hundred ducats, he was now serving the Porte with distinction, and enjoying the opportunity to strike back at the Venetians.

Clearing the roads from Thebes to Corinth, the grand vizir-serasker Damad Ali Pasha entered the Isthmus by way of Megara about 10 June, and came down into the Morea some two weeks later. Turkish transports were soon unloading supplies (brought from Negroponte) in the Bay of Cenchreae. The fortress of Acrocorinth was put under siege, but the valiant days of Francesco Morosini and Girolamo Corner were no more, and to the shame and distress of the Signoria, Acrocorinth passed into the hands of the Turks after a mere five days of heavy bombardment. They would hold it for more than a century. The fortress had been surrendered with the understanding that the garrison would withdraw without harassment, but owing to the sudden explosion of a powder magazine, for which the Venetians and Turks blamed each other, the latter tossed the terms of capitulation to the winds, and began slaughtering the local Greeks as well as the Venetian mercenaries. The *provveditore straordinario* Giacomo Minotto, who had been in command at Corinth, was carried off a prisoner to Anatolia, where the efforts of Frau von Hochepied, wife of the Dutch consul in Smyrna, finally secured his release.

On 12 June 1715 Sir Robert Sutton wrote a long letter from Istanbul to be sent to Whitehall, where it arrived on 28 July, informing the secretary of state that he had been in consultation with the Dutch ambassador Colyer concerning the possibility of "an accomodation between the Port and the Republik of Venice." Sutton was acting in accord with instructions from the Crown; George I had become the king of Great Britain the year before. Sutton and Colyer were encountering difficulties, however,

upon consideration that the Vizir [Damad Ali Pasha] is already advanced very near to the Isthmus of the Morea, that he is the principal author and promoter of the war, that he is in greater credit and power then any minister in his post has been known to be, insomuch that no other minister dares to represent a matter of that nature to the Grand Signor without his knowledge and leave, and that we are not empowered to make any overtures for the satisfaction of the Port in the several articles of injuries and dammages, whereon the declaration of war is grounded.

Sutton and Colyer decided to convey their instructions from England and the States General to the kaïmakam, whom they saw separately, offering their "interposition and mediation for accomodating the differences between the Grand Signor and the Republik of Venice." They sought to persuade the kaïmakam that their "overture proceeded from our masters' friendship to the Grand Signor and concern for the preservation of the peace of Carlovitz." The kaïmakam

received our presentations very civilly as a token of our masters' friendship to the Grand Signor, and said it was a pity [that] these offers were not made sooner; that the Grand Signor would have hearken'd to 'em, but that matters were carried too far to give room to any negociations this year. . . .

The kaïmakam was courteous, but evasive. His kiaya, however, "explained himself more clearly by saying that the mediation might take place at another time, when they should be masters of the Morea."

Sutton had also discussed the matter with the "head gardener" (the *bostanji-bashi*), an important official, who had met him secretly:

He stands so much in fear of the Vizir that, tho' he did not know the subject upon which I desired to confer withe him, he came in disguise to the place where I had appointment to meet him, and I was confident he dares not let it be known that he hath had any conversation with me.

Sutton informed the recipients of his letter that the Grand Signor and the vizir were so far committed to the seizure of the Morea "that there is little doubt but they will look upon all overtures of accomodation at this time to be no other then an artificious endeavour to deprive them of the conquest of the kingdome. . . ."

In fact, according to Sutton, the Turks would seek "to recover all that they lost in the late war with the Christian powers." All that could be expected of them "will be to observe the peace with the Emperour 'till they find an opportunity which they shall esteem favorable to break with him." The French had assured the Porte "that the Emperour's affairs are in such a situation that he can not give them any disturbance this year," with the further encouragement that the king of Sweden would not only divert the arms of the czar of Muscovy and the king of Poland from any sort of aggression against the Porte, but also those of his imperial Majesty.

Although Damad Ali Pasha was confident that he could deal with the Austrians' intervention, if indeed they should intervene, Sutton was not so certain of Turkish success. Maybe the emperor could bring the Turks to reason.

If the conjuncture were favorable, I humbly conceive it to be necessary to humble them, which would be no difficult matter for the Emperour. They are arrived at so high a pitch of presumption, insolence, and perfidy that there is no reasonable hope of their remaining quiet 'till they have received a severe mortification, for which they are more than abundantly ripe.

Sutton continued, however, with the news that "there has run a report here that the capitan [pasha] has taken Tino, which is hitherto without foun[dation], but 'tis believed he either has [made] or will make a d[escent] on this island. . . ."[2] Yes, the Turks had taken Tenos, as we have just seen.

The Venetian fortresses were beginning to fall like dominoes, for when news of the surrender of Corinth reached the Greeks on the island of Aegina, they asked the kapudan pasha Djanüm Khoja Mehmed Pasha to deliver them from the heavy hand of Venice, which he did on 7 July 1715. The surrender of Corinth was also followed by that of Argos. Now the grand vizir Damad Ali Pasha divided his Moreote forces into two divisions, one to attack the castle on the height of Palamidi, which looms over Nauplia (Napoli di Romania), and the other to assail the fortress town of Nauplia itself and, of course, the little island fortress of the Burdzi in the harbor of Nauplia. Sari Ahmed, the beylerbey of Rumelia, and the agha of the janissaries were assigned to the considerable task of taking Palamidi, while Turk Ahmed Pasha and the lieutenant-general of the janissaries were to force their way into the lower town and, doubtless, to take the Burdzi.

On the height of Palamidi (τὸ Παλαμήδιον), more than seven hundred feet above sea level, the Venetians had constructed huge fortifications. The Palamidi was inaccessible on all sides except in one area on the east, where a series of hills made an ascent possible. There were actually two forts on the height (Morosini speaks of three), Palamidi and Acronauplia, with huge cisterns which would allegedly keep a garrison supplied with water for three years. The grand vizir Damad Ali Pasha was doubtless well informed. He saw no point in bogging down the troops in trenches, from which artillery fire could do the Venetian garrison little damage. He decided upon attacks rather than a siege, promising rewards to those whose feats of arms might earn them. One soldier, who wrenched a lion

---

[2] PRO, SP 97, XXIII, fols. 173–76, letter of Sir Robert Sutton, dated at Pera of Constantinople on 12 June 1715.

banner of S. Mark from a rampart, was given a purse full of silver, and was authorized to put an emblem on his turban (on 14 July 1715). Another, a sipahi, received a reward of two hundred piasters and an increase of ten aspers in his daily wage for a minor exploit. At length on the eighth day of the siege, if such it was, the Turks stormed the fortifications on the height of Palamidi.

When the Turks had taken the forts on the towering hilltop, they could bombard the lower town of Nauplia with no possible interference from the beleaguered garrison of some seventeen hundred men. The Greeks, most of whom preferred the governance of the Turks to that of the Venetians, gave the invaders such help as they could. During these thirty years of Venetian rule in the Morea it had become painfully apparent that Latin Catholics and Greek Orthodox could not get along together. The Turks moved into Nauplia and, as in their entry into other Moreote towns, they slaughtered the inhabitants, collected booty, and enslaved the commanders. Tradition allotted the grand vizir an army of 120,000 men. The loot they seized in Nauplia was said to be sufficient to satisfy them, some of them even gaining as much as ten to twenty purses of silver from their plunder. The Turkish high command acquired an immense store of munitions as well as 126 cannon and twenty muzzle-loading mortars. As for the Venetian high command, Alessandro Bon, the last provveditore generale of the Morea, was wounded, died in Megara, and was buried in Thebes. Angelo Balbi, Giovanni Badoer, and Niccolò Barbaro were sent to the Bosporus to be imprisoned in the Seven Towers (Yedikule) at the southern end of the walls of Istanbul.

Sultan Ahmed III was so impressed by the news of the Turkish occupation of Nauplia that he came to see the town and the forts of Palamidi. The churches were turned into mosques. Osman, the agha of the sipahis, was assigned to the defense of Nauplia. (Osman was the son of Sulfikar Effendi, who with Alessandro Mavrocordato had tried in vain to make peace with the Holy League at Vienna in 1689.) Toward the end of July (1715) the kapudan pasha Djanüm Khoja Mehmed Pasha was ordered to go with the armada to Coron. The artillery used at Nauplia was embarked for Modon. On 30 July the grand vizir himself arrived in Messenia, the southwestern spur of the Morea between Modon (Methoni) on the west and Coron (Koroni) on the east. The distance from Modon to Coron is about seventeen miles or about a five hours' ride at a leisurely Turkish pace over the hills and the mountainous passes north of Cape Gallo, now Cape Akritas. The bellicose Mainotes put up no resistance, nor did the inhabitants of Kialepha and others in the vicinity.

The Turkish encampment had been located near the mills of Begoghli north of the flat land of Modon (and between Navarino and Coron). The Turks were allegedly informed that the Venetians were not prepared to defend Coron and Navarino, and that they had removed their more valuable possessions to Modon, which seems strange, for unless the Venetian fleet was assembled in great strength off the island of Sapienza, Coron was a far easier place to defend than Modon. In any event the Venetian mercenaries as well as the Greeks were in rebellion. The Turks entered Modon without difficulty.

The grand vizir Damad Ali Pasha had the Venetian captives put in chains. The Venetian commander Vincenzo Pasta was then taken over by the "levends," the brigands in Turkish employ. They hauled him off to the kapudan pasha Djanüm Khoja, who remembered that in the days of his travail as a galley slave Pasta had been kind to him. In fact Djanüm not only pled Pasta's cause before the grand vizir but received with compassion the other Venetian officers who had been brought aboard the Turkish fleet. He gave each one of them clothes and ten imperial dollars, while Pasta received a slave to attend to his needs. The cruelty of the grand vizir stood out in sharp contrast to the kindliness of the kapudan pasha, for in mid-August 1715 Damad Ali was paying thirty imperial dollars for every Christian brought to him in order to enjoy their decapitation one after the other before his tent at Modon.

Kara Mustafa, the beylerbey of Diabekr, now took the Venetian-held castle of the Morea at the beginning of August (1715). Thereafter the fortress town of Suda in western Crete surrendered (on 25 September), and when the garrison at Spinalonga on the eastern end of the island gave up, the Venetian presence on Crete became but a memory. Monemvasia surrendered to the Turks, as did Cerigo and Cerigotto. When news of the fall of the castle of the Morea and the fortress towns of Navarino and Modon reached Sultan Ahmed at Serrai (Turk. Siroz) in Macedonia, northeast of Thessaloniki, three days of celebration began, as envoys of the friendly powers offered the Padishah their congratulations (in late August 1715).

In the meantime the grand vizir Damad Ali had set about the administration of the Morea, where there were said to be some two thousand villages. Eight commissioners were appointed to make a survey of the peninsula, and another two to make an assessment of the sixty-two villages on the island of Tenos. The grand vizir also required an inspection of the muster-rolls of the sipahis and silihdars, and instituted a rigorous, overall discipline. Renegade Turks, who had embraced Christianity under the Venetians, were put to death. Governors were appointed to the Moreote fortresses. And while the grand vizir was at Nauplia, he received the silihdar of Sultan Ahmed, who came with swords of honor and fur cloaks as well as with letters of high praise for the grand vizir and all the officers of higher rank.

The Venetians had, however, been doing well in Albania and on the Dalmatian coast despite the destructive inroads of the Turks. But in the

Morea the overwhelming success of the Turks led the Venetians to fear
that the enemy would extend his aggression to Corfu. This led them to
destroy the fortifications they had built on the island of S. Maura, for
they feared they might not be able to hold the island against the Turks,
who would use it as a point of departure for an assault upon Corfu. With
the fortifications gone, the Venetians had to give up S. Maura. As they
did so, the grand vizir broke camp at Nauplia, leaving the Morea on 3
December 1715, after the hundred and one days which had sufficed for
him to conquer the entire peninsula. Thereafter he hastened back to
Adrianople.[3]

At the beginning of the Moreote war one Ibrahim, a *müteferrika* (a
member of the Ottoman palace elite), had been sent to Vienna with a
letter from the grand vizir Damad Ali Pasha to Prince Eugene of Savoy.
Damad Ali expressed the hope that the imperialists would remain neutral while Venice and the Porte were at war, just as they had during the
recent conflict between the Turks and the Russians. Eugene received the
Turkish envoy on 13 May 1715, presumably in his palace on the Him-
melpfortgasse (which leads off the Kärntner Strasse between the Ste-
phansdom and the Staatsoper). When Ibrahim returned to the Porte four
months later, he brought with him a letter from Eugene, in which the
latter offered for a second time the assistance of Austria to reestablish
peace between Venice and the Porte, but the Turks did not reply.[4]

In Europe the political scene was complicated. The Emperor Charles
VI did not recognize Philip of Anjou as king of Spain, and claimed the
kingdom for himself while Philip refused to accept Charles's possession
of the Spanish Netherlands, Naples, Sardinia, and Milan. The treaties of
Rastatt and Baden (of 1714) had not brought about peace between the
Bourbons of Spain and Austrian Hapsburgs. Pope Clement XI had been
doing his best to enlist the aid of the imperialists on behalf of Venice,[5]
but Charles had feared that if he ventured into war with the Turks (in
Hungary), his Italian states might be exposed to Spanish attack. Louis
XIV's death on 1 September 1715 now added to the difficulties of the

---

[3] Von Hammer-Purgstall, *Gesch. d. osman. Reiches*, VII, 173–84, trans. Hellert, XIII,
262–77; Romanin, *Storia documentata di Venezia*, VIII (3rd. ed., 1975), 28–33; Kretschmayr, *Gesch. von Venedig*, III (1934, repr. 1964), 356–57; and cf. Amy A. Bernardy,
L'Ultima Guerra turco-veneziana (1902), pp. 17–34.

[4] Von Hammer-Purgstall, *Gesch. d. osman. Reiches*, VII (1831, repr. 1963), 193–94,
trans. Hellert, XIII, 291–92.

[5] Giovan Francesco Albani was elected pope on 23 November 1700, and received the
tiara on 18 December. There is a detailed survey of his reign by Francesco Pometti, "Studii
sul pontificato di Clemente XI (1700–1721)," in the *Archivio della R. Società Romana di
Storia Patria*, XXI (1898), 279–457; XXII (1899), 109–79; and XXIII (1900), 239–76,
449–515. Pometti deals with the Turco-Venetian war in the Morea and the Turks' attack
upon Corfu (in 1716) as well as with papal relations with France, Austria, Spain, and
Savoy.

time. He was succeeded by his five-year-old grandson Louis XV under the regency of Duke Philip of Orléans, who declared that Charles had no cause for apprehension as far as France was concerned, but the Hapsburgs feared, not without some reason, that the French might adhere to their friendship of almost two centuries with the Porte.

When Philip V of Spain became reconciled with the Holy See, largely as a result of his marriage to Elisabetta Farnese, he finally gave Pope Clement assurance in a letter of 25 November (1715) that the Spanish would make no move against Charles VI's Italian possessions in the event of the latter's going to war with the Porte. Clement now renewed his appeals to the Christian princes to take up arms against the Turks. He granted Charles VI the sum of 500,000 florins to be collected from church lands in the Hapsburgs' *Erblande,* and another hundred thousand to Venice, but Charles was still hesitant. Clement promised to do everything he could to protect Charles's Italian states. Venice agreed to defend Naples (against the Bourbons), and as a consequence of further financial and other concessions to Charles, on 13 April 1716 the Austrians and Venetians made an offensive and defensive alliance against the Turks, with the pledge that war would be declared forthwith against the Turks. Appeals were made to King Augustus of Poland, Czar Peter of Russia, and to other Christian princes. If the Turks should attack Naples, Venice must help defend the capital of the south-Italian kingdom with 6,000 infantry and eight ships of the line, while Charles VI promised to send an auxiliary force of 12,000 men as soon as any part of Venetian territory was attacked.[6]

At the time of the Austrian decision to join the Venetians in the war against the Porte, Prince Eugene of Savoy had warned the Turks (in a letter of 2 April 1716) that to maintain peace with the Hapsburgs they must abide by the treaties of Karlowitz and restore to the Republic of Venice all the territories they had taken. Despite the constant demands made by Charles VI for guarantees as to the safety of his Italian possessions as well as for ever-increasing financial support, the imperialists had been preparing for war both in Hungary and in Transylvania. Indeed, at the beginning of February 1716 the grand vizir Damad Ali Pasha had reproached Anselm Franz Fleischmann, the imperial envoy at the Porte, with the fact that the imperialists' increasing military readiness was causing unease at the Ottoman court. Prince Eugene had given the Turks until 15 May (1716) to reply to his ultimatum. The imperialists, however, made no declaration of war against the Turks, leaving that formality to the Porte, and in June the grand vizir wrote Eugene with adequate invective that the Sublime Porte would emerge victorious with the help

---

[6] Ludwig von Pastor, *Geschichte d. Päpste,* XV (Freiburg im Breisgau, 1930), 81–90, and *Hist. Popes,* XXXIII, 110–23.

of the Almighty from this war which the Turks had neither wanted nor caused. And Damad Ali and the divan persisted in the assertion that it was the Austrians who were breaking the peace.

The Austrian high command was given, as was to be expected, to Eugene of Savoy, who was also the president of the imperial war council (*Hofkriegsrat*). Eugene left Vienna on 2 June (1716), and reached the village of Futog (Futak), north of the Danube and west of the fortress town of Peterwardein (Petrovaradin), within a surprisingly short time (on 9 June). The imperialists' field army was believed to number from 80,000 to 90,000 men, with some 40,000 men in Transylvania. On 26 and 27 July the Turks crossed the Sava, and advanced on the right bank of the Danube in the direction of Peterwardein, as far as the area of Slankamen (where the Margrave Ludwig von Baden had defeated the Turks in 1691). Eugene now informed Vienna (in a dispatch of 28 July) that according to the last news he had received the enemy forces amounted to 200,000 men or (as some reports had it) even 250,000 men.[7]

The first encounter of the imperialists with the Turks occurred on 2 August (1716), an unfortunate four-hour engagement in the area of Karlowitz, a grievous if minor defeat. It would have been better if it had not happened, "das besser nicht geschehen und unterblieben wäre." The imperialists lost about 700 men, and the Turks went on toward the fortress town of Peterwardein, of which Damad Ali Pasha apparently demanded the surrender, rather an arrogant gesture under the circumstances. In a dispatch of 4 August Prince Eugene informed the emperor that he expected to attack the enemy on the morrow "with a part of the infantry and all the cavalry." Orders were issued on the afternoon of the 4th as to the disposition of the imperialist forces, including those within the fortress of Peterwardein. Eugene had resolved upon offensive action to recover the initiative in maneuverability. He moved swiftly, putting in order as best one could some 70,000 men in 64 battalions and 187 squadrons to face the various military corps of Damad Ali's army of allegedly 200,000 men. The offensive strategies of the western tacticians, as we have had more than one occasion to emphasize, were rarely matched by the Ottoman commanders.

As Braubach has observed, however, one cannot say that in the battle of Peterwardein, which now took place (on 5 August 1716), all went according to plan, and that good fortune attended the Germans through-

---

[7] Max Braubach, *Prinz Eugen von Savoyen*, 5 vols., Munich, 1963–65, III, 308–9, 312, 314–15, and cf. Pastor, *Gesch. d. Päpste*, XV, 91–92, not without error, and on the opinions expressed by the Turkish leadership and on the Porte's preparations for the coming war, cf. von Hammer-Purgstall, *Gesch. d. osman. Reiches*, VII, 194–99, trans. Hellert, XIII, 292–300.

out. Nevertheless, the speed of the Christian operations did take the Turks by surprise in the early hours of the morning. The Christians had their setbacks, but those which the Turks suffered were far worse. In the heat of combat the grand vizir Damad Ali Pasha was laid low by a gunshot; his attendants took him to nearby Karlowitz, where he died. His troops fled south in disorder to Belgrade. Prince Eugene now wrote a dispatch in the tent (or "pavilion") of the grand vizir to the dramatic effect that the enemy had been completely defeated, "totaliter geschlagen," whereupon Count Ludwig Andreas Khevenhüller, the young commander of the cuirassiers, rode off on horseback to bring the news to Vienna, where he was received on 8 August with understandable jubilation.[8]

Spectacular victories frequently inspire awesome but unrealistic accounts of battles. Thus one could hardly believe that the Turks lost 30,000 men at Peterwardein, although their casualties were very likely nearly twice those of the imperialists, who would seem to have suffered the loss of almost 5,000 dead and wounded. The janissaries had fought bravely, but they were poorly led. The sipahis were a flighty horde, and their horses enhanced their capacity for escape. We have already noted Lady Mary Wortley Montagu's visit to "the fields of Carlowitz," very close to Peterwardein (Petrovaradin), where she observed that "the marks of that glorious bloody day are yet recent, the feild being strew'd with the skulls and caracases of unbury'd men, horses and camels."[9] Lady Mary had seen the widespread evidence of carnage some seven months after the battle. Damad Ali Pasha's ornate pavilion was taken (Prince Eugene had penned his dispatch announcing the victory as he sat among the treasures of the grand vizir). The imperialists had captured 156 banners, five horsetails, 172 cannon, and a huge supply of ammunition.[10] When it was all said and done, the extent of Eugene's success at Peterwardein was almost unbelievable. He not only wrote to the Emperor Charles VI from the grand vizir's pavilion, but also to Pope Clement XI, and the Christian triumph was celebrated in Rome with almost the same fervor as in Vienna.[11]

Whatever Eugene of Savoy's failings may have been, procrastination was not among them. He pulled the imperialist army out of the area of Peterwardein during the night of 13–14 August; by the 16th he had reached Zenta (Senta) on the river Theiss (Tisza); and before the end of the month his army was gathered around the fortress town of Temesvár

---

[8] Braubach, *Prinz Eugen von Savoyen*, III (1964), 315–20, with a map of the area of Peterwardein and Karlowitz, the location of the Turkish camp, and the placement of the imperialist forces.

[9] See above, p. 403.

[10] Pastor, *Gesch. d. Päpste*, XV (1930), 91, who gives the likely figures of 6,000 Turkish dead, while the imperialist forces suffered 3,000 dead and 2,000 wounded.

[11] Pastor, XV, 92–93.

(Timișoara), which the Turks had held since the year 1552.[12] The capital of the Banat of Temesvár—an extensive, fertile area between the Transylvanian Alps and the Danube, the Theiss and the Mureș (Maros)—the stronghold was in its day of great importance. As the Austrians stood under its walls, it was being defended by a body of ten to fifteen thousand men, apparently superior troops. On 23 September a large Turkish relief force attacked the camp of the imperialist general Johann von Pálffy, one of the commanders of the Christian troops which had put Temesvár under siege. The Turks were beaten off, and although their return was expected, they did not come back. On 1 October a Christian squadron got across the Turkish trenches and the moat, pushing their way into an important part of the stronghold. On 12–13 October (1716) the large Turkish garrison surrendered, and Charles VI was virtual ruler of the Banat.[13]

Satisfying as his success was, it was not enough for Eugene of Savoy to overwhelm the Turks at Peterwardein and thereafter seize the capital of the Banat of Temesvár. Eugene's desire to continue the offensive against the Turks was, however, hardly the only motivating force in Christendom, for troops and funds were soon forthcoming from Prince Maximilian of Hesse, the Elector Max Emmanuel of Bavaria, Pope Clement XI, and of course the Venetian Signoria. Pope Clement was committing the resources of the Church in liberal fashion to help effect the undoing of the Turks. In 1716 he had granted the Emperor Charles VI a tithe to be collected from the ecclesiastical properties in the hereditary lands of the Hapsburgs, as well as a subsidy of 400,000 florins, and now for the year 1717 he imposed a tax on the clergy in Naples, Milan, and Mantua, which was supposed to produce some 500,000 scudi within a period of five years to support the imperialists against the Turks. Venice received papal permission again to impose a tax of 100,000 gold scudi on the ecclesiastical holdings in the domain of S. Mark, which would amount to 200,000 scudi for the years 1716–1717. Portugal assured the Holy See of assistance against the Turks. Philip V of Spain took it upon himself to provide six ships of the line, four galleys, and 8,000 men to reinforce the Christian naval armament against the Turks, in return for which Clement was to give the king authority to exact an annual subsidy of 150,000 ducats from the Spanish clergy for a term of five years. The Spanish fleet was to go into action, but not against the Turks.[14]

In the meantime (on 5 June 1716) Edward Wortley Montagu, Lady Mary's husband, had been appointed the British ambassador extraordinary to the Grand Signor. His mission, like that of Sutton, was to try to make peace between the Austrians and the Turks. The Montagus had left

---

[12] Setton, *The Papacy and the Levant*, IV, 584.
[13] Braubach, III, 323–28, and cf. Pastor, XV, 95.
[14] Cf. Pastor, XV, 93, 96–97, 100.

London with their little son at the end of July, and had got as far as Vienna by September. On 20 January (1717) Montagu wrote the secretary of state at Whitehall,

Tomorrow I hope I shall receive the orders to the governours of the places thro which I am to pass, and I intend to set out the next day. I hope in a very little time to let this Court know how far the Turks are inclined to a peace, if they desire it before they have made another campagne. This Court is of opinion that whatever they may offer concerning a cessation of arms is absolutely to be rejected, and need not be communicated. . . .[15]

It looked as though Wortley Montagu had embarked on a difficult mission. He reached the Ottoman court at Adrianople on 13 March (1717).[16] The imperialists had been making every effort to help Eugene of Savoy raise the large army which he hoped to put into the field in the spring of 1717. He had been tarrying for a while in Vienna—until the Empress Elisabeth Christine gave birth to a daughter, Maria Theresa, now heiress to the Empire. On the following day, 14 May (1717), Eugene took leave of Charles VI, who gave him a jeweled cross, and admonished him not to take undue risks. The imperialist army was now said to number 100,000 men capable of bearing arms. On 15 May Eugene went aboard a ship which carried him down the Danube past Pressburg (Bratislava)—later a favorite haunt of Maria Theresa—to Ofen (Buda), where on the 16th he was greeted with a salvo of cannon fire, disembarked, heard mass, and inspected the fortifications and a new supply depot. After five hours in Buda he resumed his journey, and on 21 May arrived at Futak (Futog) which, as in 1716, had been fixed upon as the rendezvous for the troops and their point of departure for what lay ahead.

There had been no movement on the part of the Turks by the time Eugene had reached Futak. One knew nothing of the Turks except that they were building up their manpower little by little. What their numbers might prove to be and the quality of their troops remained a question. In the meantime the imperialists were directing their course southeastward toward the village of Páncsova where, veering southwestward, they crossed the Danube in late June, and some days thereafter Eugene's army, now entirely united, settled under the walls of Belgrade at the confluence of the Danube and the Sava. The imperialists had already taken the city (on 6 September 1688), as we have stated more than once, but soon lost it back to the Turks. Now they would get it again—and eventually lose it again.

---

[15] PRO, SP 97, fol. 9 [6], dispatch dated at Vienna on 20 January 1716/17.
[16] *Ibid.*, fol. 11, dispatch dated 10 April 1717.

The garrison in Belgrade, the Turks' major stronghold on the eastern frontier, was very large, 30,000 men under the redoubtable Mustafa Pasha. The Turks made sorties from the fortress town, but by mid-July the imperialists began a heavy bombardment of the walls from the left bank of the Danube and from the left bank of the Sava, i.e., from across the river in both cases. After a few days a large part of Belgrade had apparently been reduced to ashes. The imperialists had brought a good deal of heavy artillery on their numerous transports which had come down the Danube. The grand vizir Damad Ali Pasha who, as we have seen, had been killed at the battle of Peterwardein, was soon succeeded by Khalil Pasha. The latter now had had to assume the formidable task of assembling a large army for the defense of Belgrade.

Khalil Pasha was not much of a soldier, although he now found himself in command of a straggly army of some tens of thousands of janissaries, sipahis, Tatars, and others. The first units, all horsemen, of Khalil Pasha's massive forces came in sight of the Turkish soldiery atop the walls of Belgrade on 28 July. They were greeted with jubilant cries by the besieged. As the days passed, the numbers of Turks arriving on the embattled scene increased enormously. On 1–2 August they began shelling the imperialist forces, having taken their stand on the high ground to the west of Prince Eugene's campsites. While the Turks seemed content with cannonading the various parts of the imperialist army, Eugene saw that his position was becoming perilous. If the Turkish cannon dislodged his troops and caused confusion among them, they could be exposed to attack, for his campsites were between the fortress of Belgrade (on the west) and Khalil Pasha's forces (on the east), between the upper and the nether millstones, as it were. Eugene almost always solved a tactical problem on the battlefield by an immediate, all-out attack, and when early in the morning of 14 August a bomb struck the main munitions depot in Belgrade, bringing down several defense towers and adding no end to the destruction of the fortress town, Eugene knew that the hour had come.[17]

Having alerted the numerous generals in his high command, Prince Eugene began the attack upon Khalil Pasha's vast hordes of soldiery during the night of 16 August (1717):

Alles sass auch gleich zu Pferde,
Jeder griff nach seinem Schwerte,
Ganz still rückt man aus der Schanz';
Musketier wie auch die Reiter
Täten alle tapfer streiten:
'S war fürwahr ein schöner Tanz.

---

[17] Braubach, III, 340–53; Pastor, XV, 102–3; von Hammer-Purgstall, VII, 217–19.

A fog helped conceal the imperialist troops as they withdrew from their encampments, putting the Turks at a marked disadvantage although, it is true, Christians also went astray. They ventured out, however, in as orderly fashion as the hazy night allowed, but the Turks were caught at loose ends. It was a ruthless, bloody battle. As the ghastly hours passed, Khalil Pasha knew that he had been defeated, that Belgrade was lost. He gave the orders for retreat, which became a tumultuous flight. The surrender of the garrison, now twenty thousand strong, was ratified by both sides on 18 August. The Turkish soldiers were free to depart, but must leave all war materials behind. Prince Eugene made his formal entry into Belgrade on the 22nd, and the Turks streamed out in the days that followed with drums beating and flags flying.

It was an extraordinary victory. The imperialist army had seemed imperilled for some time. Even those who had shared the risks and gained the rewards of the battle could hardly believe what had happened. Turkish casualties have been estimated as high as 13,000; it is unlikely that they fell much below some 9,000. Large numbers were wounded or made captive, becoming losses to the Porte in either event, while the imperialists suffered only 2,000 dead and somewhat more than 3,000 wounded. The Christian forces won nine horsetails, insignia of Ottoman rank and authority. They also acquired 131 cannon, 35 mortars, 20,000 cannon-balls, 3,000 bombs, 30,000 grenades, 600 casks of gunpowder, 300 of lead, and various minor trophies and treasures, some of them to be displayed at social gatherings in Vienna, Munich, and elsewhere. Within the walls of Belgrade the victors found another 650 or so cannon and on the banks of the Danube fifteen Turkish galleys and some armed boats. As at Peterwardein, Prince Eugene acquired the ornate pavilion of the grand vizir, this time that of Khalil Pasha, who lost the grand vizirate as a consequence of his defeat. Eugene's victory was celebrated by poets and painters, historians and journalists, who enhanced his reputation and spread his glory.[18]

A full two months before the fall of Belgrade, the Turks had become ready to make peace with the imperialists. In June (1717) Edward Wortley Montagu had written the staff at Whitehall from Istanbul,

The day I left Adrianople I sent a courier by Belgrade to Vienna with a general proposal to enter upon a treaty at such time and place as shall be named by the ambassadors of the mediators. . . . This Court is desirous of a Peace if they can have one without great danger of the Grand Signor's being deposed; leaving Temiswar in the hands of the Enemy without endeavouring to recover it would bring him into much danger. If he cannot defend himself in this campaigne against the Emperour, and the Germans can take Belgrade, it is likely this Court

---

[18] Von Hammer-Purgstall, VII, 219–20; and cf. Braubach, III, 354–61; Pastor, XV, 103.

can agree to a Peace by which Belgrade is to be demolished, but no conjecture about this Court or Government is to be depended on. A new Grand Signor or new Ministers will continue the War. If a correspondence between the Imperial Court and the ambassadors of the mediators be kept open, we shall be able to make use of the first opportunity that offers to hasten a peace, and an opportunity here, where changes are frequent, is not to be neglected. It is thought there is even now some danger of the Grand Signor's being deposed.

Tho the Turks say it is not consistent with their safety to make a peace unless Temiswar be restored, they onely mean as the state of affairs now is, which will probably be alter'd before the return of my courier, and if a Congress is agreed to, the demands on both sides will be according to the state of affairs at the time of the Congress. The French ambassador doth his utmost to engage the Turks to continue the war. The Emperour's ministers were of opinion I should send such proposals as were made, tho never so unreasonable. I have communicated what I have done to the Dutch ambassador, who thinks a very great point is gained, and that there is a greater prospect of peace than cou'd have been imagined there would be so soon. . . .[19]

The attention of Europe had been diverted from the Venetians' struggle with the Porte when the Emperor Charles VI and Prince Eugene of Savoy reentered the war against the Turks. On 8 July 1716, however, the kapudan pasha Djanüm Khoja Mehmed landed a large force on the Venetian island of Corfu, the gateway into the Adriatic, *l'antemurale d'Italia.* The Venetian fleet, hovering in the waters of Zante, off the northwestern shore of the Moreote peninsula, had been waiting more than a month for the appearance of a Christian auxiliary fleet made up of papal, Spanish, Genoese, and Tuscan vessels, which were late in getting themselves together. In fact they did not convene in the papal harbor of Civitavecchia until 16 June (1716), which was late for rendering assistance to the Venetians at Corfu.

Nevertheless, the situation was saved by the Saxon general Count Matthias Johann von Schulenburg, now in the employ of Venice. He had had a long experience of warfare, having begun his military career under

---

[19] PRO, SP 97, XXIV, fols. 37–38ʳ, letter in cipher (certainly by Wortley Montagu), dated at Pera of Constantinople on 8 June O.S. [19 June] 1717. According to a letter of Sir Robert Sutton, dated at Vienna on 5 January 1718 (PRO, SP 97, XXIV, fol. 45), it would appear that, as of that date at least, the Turks were not convinced of the desirability of peace: "The delay of the answer expected from the Port [as to the proposed peace] joined to the advices which the [Emperor's] ministers have lately received from Wallachia of the Turks' having changed their dispositions to peace and making great preparations for carrying on the war gives this Court [at Vienna] some pain, and some of the ministers begin to cast reflections upon Mr. Wortley as if he had marred their businesse. . . ."

On 28 October (1717) Wortley Montagu had received from the secretariat of state at Whitehall letters of recall from the Porte, but he chose to remain at Istanbul until 6 June 1718 (cf. the sketch of Lady Mary Wortley Montagu by Leslie Stephen, in the *Dictionary of National Biography,* XIII [repr. 1937–38], 706ff.). Despite his social and financial advantages Wortley Montagu did not achieve great distinction.

the dukes of Savoy and King Augustus II of Poland. During the Great Northern War von Schulenburg had fought against Charles XII of Sweden, and had shared in the defeats at Punitz (Poniec) in 1704 and at Fraustadt (Wschowa) in 1706. Thereafter von Schulenburg had served under Marlborough and Eugene of Savoy in the battles at Audenarde (Oudenaarde) in 1708 and Malplaquet in 1709. After other commissions he had entered the service of Venice in October 1715 as field marshal of the Republic's land forces for three years, and arrived on the lagoon in December to take the overall command.

The fortress town of Corfu on the eastern shore of the island had been neglected for years. After the war of Candia and Francesco Morosini's Greek campaigns the Venetian treasury was almost empty. When von Schulenburg set to work on Corfu, he girded the town with palisades, trenches, and other outworks. He also appealed for more men and money to the Signoria, which responded with taxes on craftsmen and merchants as well as with the sale of titles of nobility and various offices. The Venetian captain-general Andrea Pisani had adjudged it unwise to attempt to put a halt to Djanüm Khoja Mehmed's disembarking the Turkish troops from some 250 vessels, for when all the troops had gathered, including some from Gomenizza (Igoumenitsa) in southern Epirus, they apparently amounted to almost 30,000 foot and 3,000 horse. The serasker Kara Mustafa and the kapudan pasha had brought with them an armament of allegedly 2,000 cannon. Nevertheless, von Schulenburg was determined to stand fast, and he did so.

Having landed on Corfu, the Turks' first attempts were against the forefront barrier of Monte Abramo, but they were beaten back. Both the besiegers and the besieged spent the month of July (1716) in making preparations. The Turks erected two batteries, bombarding the fortifications with one and the town itself with the other. Andrea Pisani had to keep the Venetian fleet out of their range. The Turks repeated their efforts against Monte Abramo, and finally took the outpost; they also breached a ravelin in the new fortress by the seaside. For the most part the Turkish operations on land were presumably in charge of the serasker Kara Mustafa.[20] It was hard to believe that the Venetian forces could hold out on Corfu, but von Schulenburg believed it.

---

[20] There is a stirring and well written account of the Turkish siege of Corfu in the *Diaria relazione dell'attacco della Piazza di Corfù formato dalle armi Ottomane l'anno 1716*, in MS. Marc. It. VII, 1619 (8412), fols. 1–46ᵛ (unnumbered). Inc. "Monsieur, Già con più precedenti lettere in pontuale adempimento di quanto vi ho promesso, non ho mancato di avanzarvi quelle notizie de' miei viaggi che ho creduto meritevoli della vostra attenzione . . . ," and indeed the author's account merited the attention of every European in 1716. There is a description of the Turks' finally taking Monte Abramo on fols. 26ᵛff.

This MS. also contains a *Copia di lettera scritta da Staggi Meemet Chozà* [the kapudan pasha Djanüm Khoja Mehmed], *gran Bassà, all' eccellentissimo Signor Vettor da Mosto III, proveditor e capitano di Corfù nell'assedio di questa Piazza . . . , 1716 al proveditor della Città 6 Luglio* (fol. 47), with da Mosto's reply dated from the city of Corfu on 8

At last the papal, Spanish, Genoese, and Tuscan vessels did become united with the Venetian and Maltese galleys, in the waters of Corfu. All told, there were a hundred Christian vessels to launch attacks upon the Turks in early August, but this and that prevented their doing so, and on 20 August a severe storm scattered their squadrons. The storm also raised difficulties for the Turks. But sometimes bad news comes quickly. The battle of Peterwardein (on 5 August 1716) was bad news to the Turks, nor were they pleased by the appearance of the Christian auxiliary fleet. During the night of 21–22 August they put all their horse and foot aboard their ships, sailing off to the mainland, leaving cannon and mortars, grenades and bombs in the remains of their encampment. Pisani might have pursued the Turks, and done them some damage between Corfu and the Albanian-Greek coastline, but he did little or nothing.[21] It may have been just as well, for experience had often shown it

---

July (fol. 48). There is also an *Altra lettera scritta da Mustafa Bassà, serraschier, al Comandante della Piazza di Corfu e suoi capi principali. . . , data dalla Campagna di Corfù li 5 Agosto 1716* (fols. 49–50ʳ), together with the Venetian commandant's reply dated "from the city of Corfu the sixth of August 1716" (fols. 50ᵛ–51). The Turkish letters contain the usual threats (cf., above, the exchange of letters between Francesco Morosini and Ahmed Agha "Desdar," p. 297, note 34) and (as the case may be) Christian or Turkish defiance. In the present case the serasker Kara Mustafa declares his intention "liberarla [la Piazza di Corfù] dalle vostre mani per abbattere le chiese e i templi destinati al culto degl'idoli e costruire in loro luogo moschee e templi di vere adorazioni per seguire i precetti della vera fede . . ." (fol. 49ʳ).

There is another copy of the *Diaria relazione dell'attacco della Piazza di Corfù* in MS. Marc. It. VII, 1618 (8267), 126 pp., which also provides us with the Turco-Venetian exchange of letters (*ibid.*, pp. 117–26). There are other MSS. of this text (Marc. It. VII, 584 [8498], 1533 [8826], and 2247 [9629]): it was originally written in French, and translated into Italian by one Lorenzo Molin.

[21] F. Pometti, "Studii sul pontificato di Clemente XI (1700–1721)," *Arch. della R. Società Romana di Storia patria*, XXIII (1900), 269–74; Pastor, *Gesch. d. Päpste*, XV (1930), 93–94; Kretschmayr, *Gesch. von Venedig*, III (1934, repr. 1964), 358; *Vere e distinte notizie dell'assedio e liberazion di Corcira, oggi detta Corfu, . . . dall'armi ottomane, seguita in Agosto del corrente anno 1716, raccolte e date alla luce da Andrea Caputi*, Naples, 1716, and cf. *Al Serenissimo Doge Giovanni Cornaro ed all'illustrissimi ed eccellentissimi Signori Senatori dell'inclita e libera Signoria di Venezia . . .* , with a preface by Andrea Caputi, dated at Partenope [Naples] on 30 November 1716, esp. pp. 11ff., a detailed account.

There is a brief but detailed account of the encounters both on land and at sea in *Veridica Narratione di quanto è successo in Levante tra l'armata della Serenissima Republica di Venezia e quella dell'Ottomano, incominciando dall'anno 1715 sino all'anno 1718 che si fece la Pace*, MS. Marc. It. VII, 563 (7692), 167 pp. of text, with particular attention given to von Schulenburg's defense of Corfu, *ibid.*, pp. 27–49 and ff.

The sources for this period available in the Marciana and the Venetian Archives are too numerous to deal with, but attention should be called to the *Relazione o sia Trattato di quanto è successo trà l'Armi Venete e l'Ottomane, l'anno 1716*, in MS. Marc. It. VII, 385 (7148), fols. 1–14ʳ, which, just before the arrival of the Christian auxiliaries, puts in place 26 Venetian ships (*navi*) "a romper un cordone di 64 Turchesche" (fol. 4ʳ), and describes the heavy losses suffered by the Turks in their naval engagements with the Venetians, the late arrival of the Christian auxiliary forces, the struggle for Monte Abramo, which the Turks at long last managed to take, the parts played by von Schulenburg and his Venetian officers, the Turks' eventual "vergognosa fuga" (fol. 11ᵛ) on 21–22 August, and thereafter the operations of the Venetian fleet in the waters of Zante and S. Maura until mid-October

was difficult to manage the auxiliary Christian squadrons sent against the Turks, with their several commanders, awareness of protocol, and tendency to disagree with one another.

Matthias Johann von Schulenburg had become the hero of the day. The Signoria bestowed on him a lifelong appointment at 5,000 Venetian ducats a year, gave him a costly sword of honor, and ordered the erection of a monument to him as a lasting tribute. The monument was put up in 1718 on the esplanade at Corfu before the gateway to the old fortress. After saving Corfu for Venice, von Schulenburg seized Butrinto on the mainland across the channel from Corfu. He also reoccupied the island of S. Maura, and was embarking upon the invasion of Turkish Albania when the war came to an end, but it was not the end of von Schulenburg's Venetian career, for he remained in the service of the Signoria until his death in 1747.

After his dramatic successes against the Turks (who labored under the colossal strain of Eugene of Savoy's victories), von Schulenburg never ceased to worry about the defense of the fortress towns of Butrinto, Cattaro, Spalato, Zara, Budva, Traù, and others. He feared the possibility of the Turks' using Knin (Canina) as a *point de départ* for an attack upon the coast. He was much concerned about the safety of the island of Cerigo and especially the safety of Cephalonia. Most of all, however, the defense of the island of Corfu remained uppermost in his mind, as he made clear in a long report to the doge, which he prepared at Venice on 1 October, 1718, ten weeks after the Venetians had made peace with the Porte.[22]

1716. This MS. also contains a diary of related events from 8–9 May to 17 August (fols. 18–34^r, fols. unnumbered) as well as three other items of some interest.

A large, slender fol. volume entitled *Motioni marittime della flotta Veneta e squadre ausiliarie per la campagna MDCCXVI e MDCCXVII sotto la direzione delli capitani estraordinarii delle navi N. H. S. Andrea Corner, 1716, N. H. S. Lodovico Flangini, 1717 morì, N. H. S. Marc' Antonio Diedo, 1717* (MS. Marc. It. VII, 384 [10048]), provides us with detailed plans of the siege of Corfu, with the placement of the Venetian and Turkish fleets from 5 July to 26 August 1716, showing the location of Mts. Abramo and S. Salvador, with views of Imbros, Tenedos, and other islands with the positions taken by the Venetian and Turkish fleets in various precisely dated engagements between 1716 and 1718.

[22] MS. Marc. It. VII, 1210 (9026), fols. 73–98, 106^r, *et alibi*. Von Schulenburg also made it clear that he needed men and money (*ibid.*, fol. 86^r): "Per dimostrare quanto è neccessario di fortificare le piazze [strongholds] di frontiera sudette, e perchè non giovi migliorare le altre per la diffesa della provincia, Vostra Serenità mi permetta che supponga 10 mila huomeni, truppe regolate, destinate alla diffesa della provincia in una guerra. . . ." In fact, all told, von Schulenburg stated he had need of more than 30,000 men for the defense of Venetian possessions along the frontiers of possible Turkish attack (*ibid.*, fols. 90^r, 91^r, *et alibi*). And as the years passed, his letters, reports, and memoranda continued always to emphasize the need for more troops here and still more there (cf., *ibid.*, MS. Marc. It. VII, 1211 [9027], fol. 242^r, doc. dated 4 May 1731). The overwhelming importance of defending Corfu against the Turks was forever in his thoughts (cf. his letter to the doge, dated at Venice on 6 June, 1733 [*ibid.*, fols. 363ff.]). Of less importance than the defense of Corfu was that of Cattaro, which also greatly concerned von Schulenburg, however, as did a sustained vigilance along the Albanian frontier (MS. Marc. It. VII, 1210 [9026], fols. 505ff.).

In the meantime, although the captain-general Andrea Pisani had been held up to some opprobrium, he also became active. One can understand his fear of subjecting the Venetian fleet to what he regarded as undue risk. In view of the Republic's straitened finances, galleys and ships with broadside cannon had become almost too expensive to replace. Collaborating with von Schulenburg and with the assistance of his brother Carlo Pisani, the captain-general did move south of Corfu in October 1717, and took possession of the Turkish ports of Prevesa (Préveza) and Vonitza (Vonitsa), the latter place being on the south shore of the Gulf of Arta, about eight miles southeast of Prevesa. Actually the Venetian occupation of Prevesa was largely due to von Schulenburg, and when Prevesa was taken, the Turks had to surrender Vonitza.[23] Although Andrea Pisani did redeem his reputation to a fair extent, von Schulenburg was to receive the lasting acclaim of the Venetians.[24]

---

[23] *Relazione dell'acquisto della fortezza di Prevesa, ottenuta dall'armi della Serenissima Republica, sotto la valorosa condotta del capitan gen. Andrea Pisani,* Venice, 1717, published by Girolamo Albrizzi, in the Campo della Guerra hard by the Church of S. Giuliano, and cf. the *Relazione delli combattimenti seguiti trà l'armata Veneta e l'Ottomana nell'acque d'Imbro ed in quelle di Santo Stratti e Monte Santo nei giorni 12, 13, e 16 di Giugno 1717* for further Venetian naval activities which began when Lodovico Flangini, the *capitan estraordinario delle navi,* set sail from Zante on 26 May (1717). Also published by Albrizzi (and two associates) in 1717, this tract describes events which attracted attention at the time, but are of no historical consequence as we review the year 1717 from a modern standpoint. For details, see von Hammer-Purgstall, VII, 222ff., and on the Venetians' occupation of Prevesa and Vonitza, note the *Veridica Narratione di quanto è successo in Levante tra l'armata della Serenissima Republica di Venezia e quella dell'Ottomano . . . ,* MS. Marc. It. VII, 563 (7692), pp. 128–41. Von Schulenburg has left us a long account of past events in a letter of 15 August 1718 written to the doge Giovanni Corner (MS. Marc. It. VII, 1210 [9026], fols. 46–72). Needless to add, he continued to worry through the years about the safety of Butrinto, Prevesa, and Vonitza (*ibid.,* fols. 279–80, letter to the doge Corner dated at Corfu on 5 September 1721).

[24] On Schulenburg's career, see the article by P. Zimmermann, in the *Allgemeine Deutsche Biographie,* XXXII (1891, repr. Berlin, 1971), 667–74. Schulenburg was born on 8 August 1661 at Emden in the onetime Prussian province of Hanover. He died at Verona in the Veneto on 14 March 1747. As I have already observed in *The Papacy and the Levant,* IV (1984), 1103, note 220, two large volumes of copies of Schulenburg's letters to the doge, relevant decrees of the Senate, plans for the recruitment of troops, data concerning the deployment and organization of the Republic's forces on land and at sea, requirements of artillery and munitions, warehouses for supplies, *biscotto* for the troops and *foraggio* for their horses, *ospedali e quartieri per la conservatione de soldati,* financial facts and figures, the needed fortifications at Corfu, in Dalmatia, and elsewhere—all this and more may be found in the Bibl. Nazionale Marciana, MSS. It. VII, 1210–11 (9026–27), which contain documents dated from 3 December, 1715, to 30 October, 1733, a few of which have been cited above. Incidentally, Schulenburg closes a memorandum to the doge, dated at Venice on 26 November, 1729, "con quello antico ma saggio consiglio: Chi desidera la pace, si prepari alla guerra" (*ibid.,* vol. II, fol. 6ʳ).

Schulenburg, whose name is also given as Johann Matthias, was well known in his own day as an ardent collector of paintings and as a patron of artists in Venice. The records of his career are partially preserved in the Niedersächsisches Staatsarchiv in Hanover. Cf. the survey of Schulenburg's collection by Alice Binion, "From Schulenburg's Gallery and Records," *The Burlington Magazine,* CXII, no. 806 (May 1970), 297–303, and the brief notice of his career by Antonio Morassi, "Un Ritratto del Maresciallo Schulenburg dipinto da Antonio Guardi," *Arte veneta,* VI (Venice, 1952), 88–91. And now see especially A.

The Turks had fared as badly in the war with Austria as they had done well in that with Venice. Now having suffered defeats at Peterwardein, Temesvár, and Belgrade, they had also failed in the effort to take Corfu, and thereafter had lost Prevesa and Vonitza. The Turks were ready to make peace, and so doubtless were the Venetians, for they had become exhausted. But astride the steed of victory, Prince Eugene of Savoy and his friend the Emperor Charles VI had no interest in peace with the Turks. They would go on to further conquests of territory and the further ruination of the Ottoman empire.

Suddenly, however, the winds of warfare changed. The Spanish fleet of six ships of the line, four galleys, and 8,000 men which Philip V had offered to assist Venice against the Turks was still at anchor in the harbor of Barcelona at the beginning of July 1717. There was word afloat, however, that the fleet which had been fitted out largely with papal money was in fact not going to set out against the Turks, but rather against the Hapsburgs' Italian possessions. Ministers of the Spanish Crown denied the rumor. Held up by contrary winds for a brief while at Mallorca, the fleet soon sailed eastward, and on 25 July was moored in the gulf and harbor of Cagliari, the capital of Sardinia. The Spanish landed troops, and soon had taken over the entire island.

Pope Clement XI and the Curia Romana were shocked. The treachery of Philip V was incredible, but there it was. Sardinia was now held by the Spanish. The fleet which had laid siege to Cagliari and occupied the island had been financed by tithes levied upon ecclesiastical lands and revenues with the solemn assurance that its sole use would be against the Turks. The Emperor Charles VI and the Viennese court were furious, accusing Clement of betraying them, for the pope had indeed promised Vienna that the Hapsburg possessions in Italy would be safe. The Venetians had added their own assurances to those of the Holy See that Naples and presumably the islands would be protected.

The ambition of Philip V and the Spanish government had not only aroused the indignation of the Austrians but also the concern of the French and British. The regent of France, Philip of Orléans, and the British statesman Lord James Stanhope now got together to prevent the outbreak of war between the imperialists and the Spanish. They also wanted to clear up some unsatisfactory provisions in the treaties of Utrecht, Rastatt, and Baden.[25] Joining the imperialists, they were soon

---

Binion, *La Galleria scomparsa del maresciallo von der Schulenburg: Un mecenate nella Venezia del Settecento*, Venice, Ateneo Veneto, 1990.

[25] The treaties of Utrecht (in 1713) and Rastatt-Baden (in 1714) had ended the War of the Spanish Succession, but in complicated fashion. In MS. Marc. It. VII, 401 (7424), 400 pp., the doubts, differences and dissatisfactions attending the important congress at Utrecht (in 1712) are made more than clear by the numerous copies of the dispatches which Carlo Ruzzini addressed to the doge of Venice and other officials of state, plus various other relevant documents, including a letter to the pope dated at Utrecht on 8 June

to form the Quadruple Alliance, the *Quadruplex Foedus,* at London on 2 August 1718, whereby Charles VI, Louis XV of France, and George I of Great Britain (who were supposed to be joined by the Dutch as the fourth participant) would lay down the terms by which peace would be established between the imperialists and the Spanish.

The Emperor Charles would at long last recognize Philip V as "the legitimate king of the Spains and the Indies." Philip's ambitious wife Elisabetta Farnese, who would be the heiress to both Parma and Tuscany (upon the coming extinction of the male lines of the Farnesi and the Medici), had put in the claims for her little son Don Carlos. Charles acceded to her request with the overall insistence that Parma and Tuscany were and must remain fiefs of the Empire. Philip V would be required to give up his claims to Sicily and Sardinia. Charles VI would receive Sicily from Vittorio Amadeo II, the duke of Savoy, and the latter would now acquire the so-called kingdom of Sardinia from Charles. Vittorio Amadeo had been assured possession of Sicily in one of the treaties of Utrecht, and Charles VI's rights to Sardinia and the Spanish Hapsburgs' holdings in Italy had been acknowledged in the treaty of Baden.[26] If Philip refused to agree to the terms being thus imposed upon him by the Quadruple Alliance, the signatories to the Alliance would have recourse to arms, and force him into acceptance.[27]

Philip V and his Italian prime minister Cardinal Giulio Alberoni were certain to reject the terms being imposed upon Spain by the Quadruple Alliance. They had added to the size and strength of their fleet with every intention of continuing their aggression in the Mediterranean, their purpose being to complete the conquest of Sicily and to make an attempt upon Naples. By violating the recent treaties of Utrecht and Baden, and bringing Europe to the brink of warfare, the Spanish had done the Turks a great service. Under the circumstances the Austrians now became

---

1712 (*ibid.,* p. 154). Ruzzini's first dispatch was written at Treviso on 11 February 1712 (m.v. 1711); the next to the last at Utrecht on 25 November 1712 (p. 394); the last dispatch (no. 53), which is to the doge, remains undated, for it breaks off in the middle of a sentence. Obviously p. 401 (at least) has been lost from the bound volume. The issues were important to the Venetians although they were not directly involved (cf. Kretschmayr, *Geschichte von Venedig,* III, 307–8).

[26] On 11 April 1713 Louis XIV of France and his grandson Philip V of Spain had accepted art. v of one of the treaties of Utrecht, "reconnoissant dès à présent en vertu de ce Traité son Altesse royale de Savoye pour seul et légitime Roy de Sicile" (Dumont, *Corps universel diplomatique,* VIII-1 [1731], no. CLV, p. 363), and in the treaty of Baden which was ratified on 7 September 1714 Louis XIV had promised and pledged "quod suam Caesaream Majestatem [Charles VI] relinquet in tranquilla et pacifica possessione omnium statuum et locorum quae in Italia modo tenet, et quae antea a regibus Domus Austriacae possessa erant, videlicet [possessio] Regni Neapolitani . . . , ducatus similiter Mediolanensis, regni insuper et insulae Sardiniae, . . . ," etc. (*ibid.,* no. CLXXIV, art. XXX, p. 440). Charles VI and Philip V would have nothing to do with each other.

[27] The terms of the Quadruple Alliance, the imperial, French, and British ratifications thereof, and the various *articuli separati* are given in Dumont, VIII-1, no. CCII, pp. 531–41, *actum Londini die 22 Julii (v. st.), 2 Augusti (n. st.) anno Domini MDCCXVIII.*

willing to consider peace with the Porte in order to look to their interests in Italy.

Toward the end of June 1718, during the period of negotiations which would lead to the Quadruple Alliance, a large Spanish fleet of eighteen warships and some smaller vessels set sail from Barcelona, headed for the island of Sicily. The Spanish moved into Palermo, took Catania, and laid siege to Messina, which according to the Quadruple Alliance was to become the property of the Emperor Charles VI. At this point the interest of the British in the Alliance had become especially important, for Sir George Byng, who had just been raised to the rank of admiral (in March 1718), was sent into the Mediterranean to give effect to the intentions of the Alliance, which meant that he must put a halt to the Spaniards' efforts to take Messina. On 21 July Byng reached Naples, where he conferred with Charles VI's viceroy.

By the end of the month Byng was in communication with the Spanish commander, to whom he proposed a cessation of arms in Sicily for two months, i.e., until the negotiations in progress had determined the steps to be taken to preserve the peace. The Spanish commander apparently had no alternative to declining Byng's offer. His purpose in the Mediterranean was to win the island of Sicily for the king of Spain. The result was the naval battle off Cape Passero at the southeast corner of Sicily (on 31 July 1718). The Spanish fleet was poorly organized and badly led. The English captured or sank every ship. In August 1720 the Spanish had to withdraw from Italy. Byng later helped arrange for the surrender of Sardinia to Vittorio Amadeo. The ambitions of Philip V and his minister Alberoni had come to nothing.[28]

By the time Spain made peace with the Quadruple Alliance, Austria and Venice had already made peace with the Turks, who had gained a good deal from the territorial aspirations of Philip V and his minister Alberoni. The treaties of these years tended to be repetitions and modifi-

---

[28] On the admiral Sir George Byng, who was raised to the peerage as Viscount Torrington (on 9 September 1721), and the naval battle off Cape Passero, see the article by J.K. Laughton, in the *Dictionary of National Biography*, III (repr. 1937–38), 567–70. The major events involving Spain, the Empire, Clement XI's efforts against the Turks, and the Quadruple Alliance between the years 1716 and 1720 (which I have tried to compress as much as possible) are dealt with in some detail by Pastor, *Gesch. d. Päpste*, XV, 93, 99–100, 104–23; Pometti, "Studii sul Pontificato di Clemente XI," *Arch. della R. Società Romana di Storia patria*, XXIII (1900), 483–512; von Hammer-Purgstall, *Gesch. d. osman. Reiches*, VII (1831, repr. 1963), 220–37; Braubach, *Prinz Eugen von Savoyen*, IV (1965), esp. pp. 20–39, 55–64; and cf. Kretschmayr, *Gesch. von Venedig*, III, 426; Romanin, *Storia documentata di Venezia*, VIII (3rd ed., Venice, 1975), 43–44.

Mary Lucille Shay, *The Ottoman Empire from 1720 to 1734, as Revealed in Despatches of the Venetian Baili*, Urbana, 1944, Illinois Studies in the Social Sciences, XXVII-3, repr. Westport, Conn., 1978, has given us a narrative of Turco-Venetian relations as reported by the bailies Giovanni Emo, Francesco Gritti, Daniele Dolfin, and Angelo Emo from 1720 to 1734 with accounts of the uprisings in Istanbul in 1730 and 1731, the succession of grand vizirs, fires and plagues on the Bosporus, the ceaseless giving of gifts to the vizirs, the

cations of those of the recent past. Thus according to the Austro-Turkish treaty of Karlowitz (of 1699), as we have seen, the Emperor Leopold I had retained the kingdom of Hungary and all Transylvania then in his possession as well as Croatia and Slavonia. Now by the terms of the treaty with Sultan Ahmed III, "set forth in the pavilion at Passarowitz on 21 July in the year 1718," Leopold's son Charles VI not only kept all the imperialist gains recognized by the Turks at Karlowitz but added to them. The treaty of Passarowitz (Požarevac) was supposed to last for twenty-four years. The Ottoman government, represented by the plenipotentiaries Ibrahim Effendi and Mehmed Pasha, gave up to the Hapsburgs the Banat of Temesvár (Timişoara) and the western parts of Wallachia and Serbia, the fortress town of Belgrade [which the Turks were to recover in 1739], and most of Bosnia. Again, as at Karlowitz, peace had been made by the intervention of Great Britain and Holland and so, as *legati mediatores,* Sir Robert Sutton and Count Jacob Colyer signed the treaty on behalf of King George I and the States General of the Netherlands. It was the most impressive and profitable treaty that the Hapsburgs had ever concluded with the Porte.[29]

When judged by the Austro-Turkish treaties of the past, the accord of

---

kapudan pashas, reis effendis, etc., the decline of Venetian commerce, and the weakness of the Serenissima in naval matters. Her book ends with a jumbled account of the difficulties which the Turks, Persians, and Russians had with one another.

[29] Dumont, VIII-1 (1731), no. cxcix, pp. 520–24: ". . . Provinciae Moldaviae et Valachiae, partim Poloniae et partim Transylvaniae limitibus conterminae, interjacentibus, ut ab antiquo, montibus distinguantur et separentur, ita ut ab omni parte antiquorum confiniorum termini observentur, nulláque in his nec ultra, nec citra fiat mutatio, et cum partes Valachiae cis Alutam fluvium sitae [i.e., west of the river Olt or Oltul] cum locis et munimento Temeswarini in potestate et possessione Sacrae Romano-Caesareae Regiaeque Majestatis sint, juxta acceptatum fundamentum pacis *Uti Possidetis,* in eiusdem potestate et dominio permaneant ita ut praedicti fluvii ripa occidentalis ad Romanorum, ripa vero orientalis ad Ottomannorum Imperatorem pertineat," i.e., the imperialists owned all the area west of the Oltul, and the Turks the area east of the Oltul (art. i).

"Cum a Drina fluvio [the river Drina in eastern Bosnia] usque ad Unnam [the Unac or Unats in western Bosnia] in utraque ripa fluvii Savi sitae, sive apertae sive occlusae arces et palankae Romanorum Imperatoris milite munitae sint, cum antiquis suis territoriis juxta fundamentum pacis in Ejusdem Sacrae Caesareae Regiaeque Majestatis potestate permanento, quare etiam integer fluvius Savus cum suis ripis ad Eandem pertinet," i.e., Charles VI possessed the entire valley of the Sava (art. iii), plus certain other territories specified in the treaty (arts. iv–vi). The signatures of Sutton and Colyer as representing George I and the Netherlands are given, *ibid.,* p. 524 b. Having been left out of the negotiations which led to the peace of Passarowitz, Abraham Stanyan, Wortley Montagu's successor as the British ambassador to the Porte, was quite disgruntled (cf. his letter to the secretary of state at Whitehall in PRO, SP 97, XXIV, fols. 257–58, "at the Grand Vizir's camp at Sophia, 20th July 1718 O.S." [i.e., 31 July], and note, *ibid.,* fol. 260).

There is a large volume in the Marciana (MS. It. VII, 383 [7733], 154 fols., with 15 blank fols.), containing the dispatches of Carlo Ruzzini to the doge Giovanni Corner, i.e., to the Signoria, from 21 March to 10 November 1718, with other relevant addenda and numerous texts signed at Passarowitz by the mediators Robert Sutton and Jacob Colyer (fols. 1–114), plus letters written by Ruzzini to various princes, diplomats, and others relating to the peace of Passarowitz from 16 April to 15 October 1718 (fols. 127–51, and numbered separately as fols. 1–25) as well as two (original) letters of credence on parchment issued

Passarowitz was indeed extraordinary, a source of pride and satisfaction to the court at Vienna, but one wonders what further gains the imperialists might have made if Philip V and Alberoni had not interrupted Prince Eugene of Savoy's campaigns against the Porte. The intervention of Austria had certainly reduced the losses which Venice would otherwise have suffered. In any event the Serene Republic had to give up the entire Morea and the islands of Tenos and Aegina, but she did retain the seven Ionian islands, including S. Maura as well as the mainland strongholds of Butrinto and Parga, Prevesa and Vonitza.[30]

Austria had done well in the years preceding and including 1718; in a moment we shall look at the subsequent history of Venice. In the meantime, however, we should note that at the assembly of Pressburg (Bratislava) in 1687–1688 the kingdom of Hungary had been recognized as a hereditary possession of the Hapsburgs. Ten years later Transylvania was added to Hungary, and after the War of the Spanish Succession the Austrians had little cause for complaint in the treaties of Utrecht, Rastatt, and Baden (in 1713–1714). The scattered lands with disparate languages over which Charles VI now ruled would involve the Austrians in many difficulties in the years to come, but fortunately they lie beyond the scope of this volume. When Lady Mary Wortley Montagu first arrived in Vienna (on her way to Turkey with her husband), she found that the city "did not at all answer my ideas of it, being much lesse than I expected to find it."[31] As the days passed, however, she became much impressed with the city and the court, and as the years passed, Vienna would become one of the artistic centers of Europe.

---

to Ruzzini in the doge's name on 12 March and 28 April (1718), and signed by the secretary Giovanni Francesco Busenello. On Passarowitz and the results thereof, see Amy A. Bernardy, *L'Ultima Guerra turco-veneziana* (1902), pp. 53–71.

[30] Dumont, VIII-1, no. cc, pp. 524–28, *actum sub tentorio ad Possarovitz XXI. Jul. MDCCXVIII,* esp. arts. I–IV on the Venetians' retention of parts of the Dalmatian coast with Butrinto, Prevesa, and Vonitza on the basis of *uti possidetis,* The *bailaggio* was restored in Istanbul (art. XIV), and various judicial, maritime, and other problems were dealt with at length in the Veneto-Turkish treaty of Passarowitz, which had also been negotiated through the mediation of Sutton and Colyer (*ibid.,* p. 524 b). Cf. Setton, *The Papacy and the Levant,* IV, 1103–4.

Despite the gains which the Ottoman empire had won from Venice in the treaty of Passarowitz, the Turks had embarked upon a period of difficulty and decline, although they made some effort at administrative and military reform, which the Venetians followed with close attention (Paolo Preto, *Venezia e i Turchi* [1975], pp. 357–77). The successes of Austria and the growth of Russian power were, however, too much for the Turks to contend with, especially in view of their failure to make much progress in military technology and the extreme conservatism of Islam. Nevertheless, the advance of Austria and Russia moved Venice to ever closer ties to the Porte (*ibid.,* pp. 380–92).

[31] *The Complete Letters of Lady Mary Wortley Montagu,* ed. Robert Halsband, I (1965), 259, letter dated at Vienna on 8 September 1716, and for Lady Mary's letters from Vienna, see, *ibid.,* I, 259–79, 291–97; for those from Adrianople and Istanbul (Constantinople), I, 308–415.

The Viennese succumbed happily to the grandeur of Baroque palaces and churches with their fresco paintings and fine sculpture. They enjoyed the Italian drama and opera, the French comedy, and even returned to the German theater and German literature. In the later eighteenth century Austria was remade in remarkable fashion by the reform and reconstruction of governmental institutions, by a marked improvement in the lot of the peasantry (owing to the efforts of Maria Theresa and her son Joseph II), and by the well-planned promotion of trade and industry. There was a notable enrichment in the curricula of the primary schools and those of the universities. Ecclesiastical privilege was almost drastically abridged, monasteries were suppressed, and monastic wealth reduced.

Maria Theresa's ministers, Wilhelm von Haugwitz and Wenzel Anton Kaunitz, managed (more or less) to organize an imperial bureaucracy, a standing army of considerable size, a workable treasury, and an almost efficient judiciary. The estates of the Hapsburg realms (those of Bohemia and Moravia, Styria and Carniola, Gorizia and Gradisca) were drawn into a system of general taxation, from which neither the clergy nor the landowning nobility was any longer to be exempt. The reluctant Carinthians were forced to pay taxes, and although the Hungarian estates contributed considerable sums to the military budget, by and large the Magyar nobility escaped general taxation for almost another two centuries. The Hapsburg *Erblande* were on the whole taxed as were the other component parts of the Empire, but in the governmental intricacies of the time it is difficult to make entirely reliable generalizations. Although Maria Theresa (d. 1780) initiated many of the reforms which helped to establish the Hapsburg empire upon a more solid foundation, the more radical and perhaps far-reaching changes for the better were brought about by Joseph II (d. 1790). He was moved by the thought of the time, the period of the so-called Enlightenment. Although mother and son often disagreed, their combined effect, despite subsequent disruptions, was certainly beneficial to Austria and the Empire.

Despite the Crown's adherence to Catholic orthodoxy, non-Catholics and Jews were finally given access to the universities. Torture was abolished in 1776, and so was the death penalty a decade later. Early in the reign of Joseph II the huge general hospital (the Allgemeines Krankenhaus) was built in Vienna, as was the large academy of military surgery (the Josephinum), where the tourist may now visit the Museum für Geschichte der Medizin. These buildings, important in the history of medicine and surgery, are to be found between the Sensengasse and the Van Swieten-Gasse.

A highly cultivated bourgeoisie grew up in Vienna and elsewhere in the Hapsburg domains. Music flourished. Haydn and his friend Mozart were, needless to say, as joyously received in the *salons* and drawing rooms of the well-educated bourgeoisie as in those of the nobles of

Vienna. Their work was also very popular in public performances, especially that of Mozart. Freedom of the press became widespread in Austria until the political pamphleteers aroused Joseph II's not entirely unjustified fears toward the end of his reign. The events in France in 1789 made censorship inevitable in Austria. The Austrian Enlightenment almost came to an end in the reactionary and repressive regime of Francis II [I] (1792–1835), but an intellectual renaissance lay ahead in the Vienna of the later nineteenth century.[32]

As for Venice, she held on to the Ionian islands and the four towns on the mainland until the dissolution of the Republic in 1797 (when Napoleon gave up Venice and part of the Veneto to Austria in the treaty of Campo Formio). For some time after Passarowitz, however, the Venetians feared an attack by the Turks,[33] but the Porte (like Venice) had embarked upon years of decline and, holding on to the Morea, the Turks were more interested in recovering Belgrade from the Austrians than in seeking to regain territory from the Venetians. The Signoria's administration of the islands and the mainland ports was poor. The state was financially exhausted. Venetian officials exploited the islanders to the fullest extent they could. Conditions on the island of Zante were especially oppressive. They were rather better at Corfu, which remained the chief naval station for Venetian vessels plying the Adriatic and Ionian

---

[32] Cf. in general the excellent little book by Ernst Wangermann, *The Austrian Achievement, 1700–1800*, London, 1973, and note the selections from the sources (in English translation) in C.A. Macartney, *The Habsburg and Hohenzollern Dynasties in the Seventeenth and Eighteenth Centuries*, New York, 1970, esp. pp. 94ff. There is a detailed study of the mercantile policies of Maria Theresa and her son Joseph II by Adolf Beer, "Die österreichische Handelspolitik unter Maria Theresia und Josef II.," *Archiv für österreichische Geschichte*, LXXXVI (1899), 1–204, and on Maria Theresa and the early years of Joseph, see Derek Beales, *Joseph II*, I, Cambridge Univ. Press, 1987.

[33] Cf. ASV, Senato III (Secreta), Dispacci Costantinopoli (1719–1720), fols. 18ʳ, 19ʳ, a dispatch of Carlo Ruzzini to the doge dated at Corfu on 25 June 1719: "Apertamente si professa [according to the *ambasciatori mediatori*, the Dutch and British ambassadors Colyer and Stanyan] che l'intentione della Porta sia di ricuperar quelli non solo dell'ultima, ma dell'antecedente guerra di Morea, motivo che potrà servir a quelle ulteriori comissioni che la publica prudenza conoscesse opportune per scansare le dilationi che per altro seguirebbero sopra l'intiera libertà de schiavi nostri . . . ." [Colyer and Stanyan soon secured the release of a number of Venetian "slaves," *ibid.*, fol. 47, and note fols. 626ff.].

"L'occhio unito alla memoria delle passate contingenze è andato osservando il sito delli pericoli e delle gloriose diffese non meno che lo stato, in alcuna parte, migliorato delle fortificationi. A queste però ben molto vi manca, onde si possan creder rimosse le facilità e per conseguenza gl'allettamenti nel cuor de' nemici, ben stabilito e sicuro l'unico antemurale della Patria e dell'Italia, che chiama dalla somma sapienza dell'eccellentissimo Senato un'assidua se ben dispendiosa cura per condur'alla perfettione opera di tanto valore."

There were allegedly various Turkish violations of the treaty of Passarowitz, *ibid.*, fols. 48ff., a dispatch of Ruzzini dated at Pera di Costantinopoli on 5 September 1719, and cf. fols. 97ʳ, 99, 101, 103, *et alibi*, as well as fols. 224, 232–233, etc., with many parts of many dispatches in cipher. Sometimes, however, Ruzzini's meetings with the Turkish leadership were very friendly (*ibid.*, fol. 324ʳ).

Seas. During the Russo-Turkish wars (1768–1774, 1787–1792) the Greek islanders made manifest their hostility to the Turks by assisting the Russians in every way they could despite the sustained efforts of the Venetian Signoria to remain neutral. These two wars made a deep impression upon Europe, and certainly upon Venice; indeed the war of 1768–1774 was the first Greek revolt against the Sublime Porte.[34] In fact, after Passarowitz (1718), Venice tried to detach herself from all the conflicts in Europe for, with so many problems at home, she could not do otherwise.[35]

---

[34] Franco Venturi, *Settecento riformatore*, 4 vols. (so far published in five parts, Turin, 1969–84), III, 22–73, 90–91, 92–96, 100–6, 111ff., trans. R. Burr Litchfield, *The End of the Old Regime in Europe, 1768–1776: The First Crisis*, Princeton Univ. Press, 1989, pp. 23–73, 91, 93–96, 100–6, 111ff.

[35] With a mastery of the sources and the secondary literature Marino Berengo, *La Società veneta alla fine del Settecento*, Florence: Sansoni, 1956, chaps. I–III, has traced in some detail the historical background to the decline of Venice—the economic difficulties, political unease, administrative corruption, and social instability of the Republic—during the course of the later eighteenth century. Various troubles arose in the Signoria's relations with the complicated network of the "states" which made up the Republic (Bergamo, Brescia, Padua, Verona, Udine, Crema, Vicenza, Treviso, Rovigo, Feltre, and others). Berengo has described the social classes (*nobili, cittadini, popolani,* and the *incerta classe borghese*), the divisions and hostilities among them, and the parts they played in government, the professions, agriculture, commerce, various industries (and *artigianati*), fisheries, etc., as well as the helpless, hopeless class of wandering vagabonds: "Il povero doveva restare povero, ed il ricco conservare le sue richezze." The ruling patriciate could not see the problem, and so the Republic of S. Mark started to go down hill.

Berengo has also depicted with painstaking care the miserable foodstuffs available to the masses; rural life in the Veneto; problems of land ownership (by the nobles, the monasteries, and the Church); leases, rents (in kind), and the labor needed for cultivation of the land; the "rustiche insurrezioni" often caused by famine, tolls, and taxes; the governmental monopoly of tobacco (an important source of income for the Republic), the illegal cultivation of the profitable plant, and its clandestine sale in Venetian territory. Violation of the tobacco contraband could bring the offender three years on the galleys.

The smugglers of tobacco often had recourse to brigandage. In the poorer areas of the Republic, where surveillance was less thorough, the brigands moved to and fro not without some support from the local residents. Highway robbery added to the tribulations of merchants, travelers, and the police, especially in the Alpine regions from Friuli and Gorizia to the plains of Bergamo as well as in the hinterland of Istria where the people, always happy to evade the salt and tobacco monopolies, were in constant conflict with the law.

In dealing with the intellectual life of the Venetians in the eighteenth century Berengo, chap. IV, has emphasized the cleavage between the traditionalists, some of whose works were limited by a scholarly attention to detail (*pedantesca minuziosità*), and the small number of *illuministi veneti*, whose activities were limited by the censorship of books, especially when they ventured into religion and politics. Thus the sale of Rousseau's works was officially prohibited in Venice, but Benjamin Franklin's works were quite acceptable. On the whole, however, the discreet Venetian could acquire, read, and keep almost any book he wanted. The influence of the French Enlightenment had pervaded the Veneto, and spread throughout Italy, which became increasingly open to the currents from England, Holland, and Germany. As for the so-called religious "tolerance" of the Venetians, it is perhaps better to think of their "indifference," of which in the latter half of the century Freemasonry (involving nobles and the bourgeoisie) was a rather important part.

The rationalist and revolutionary ideas of the French Jacobins, the deism of the Freemasons (sometimes deviating into atheism), and the heretical determinism of the Jansenists caused no end of political and religious dissension in Venice and the Veneto. In fact, since

To look back for a moment, Venice had managed to sustain some measure of economic prosperity (despite a prolonged period of inflation) after she had lost her dominion over the island of Cyprus to the Porte (in the war of 1570–1573). The island declined rapidly after the Turks had taken it. From the early years of the seventeenth century, however, Venice began to suffer some measure of economic deterioration, owing to the huge increase in English, Dutch, and French commerce in the eastern Mediterranean. Also the circumnavigation of Africa had already ruined the Venetian spice trade, which the Portuguese, English, and Dutch had quickly taken over. Venetian trade with the commercial centers in Germany had been a rich source of revenue, but this was of course vastly reduced by the Thirty Years' War.

The long war with the Porte for possession of the island of Crete (1645–1669) had drained the Venetian treasury. Taxes and tolls of all kinds were increased during the Cretan war; titles of nobility were sold (for 100,000 ducats per family); but these funds were spent on warfare, not invested in commerce. Later on, whatever resources the Signoria could assemble were spent in support of Francesco Morosini's conquest of the Morea which, as we have seen, the grand vizir Damad Ali Pasha had reconquered in one hundred and one days in the latter part of the year 1715.

During the last half century or so a large literature has grown up relating to the decline of the Venetian Republic in the seventeenth century, of which we cannot take any detailed account here.[36] Despite the set-

---

the time of Paolo Sarpi relations between the Signoria and the Curia Romana had been weighed down by disagreement and conflict despite the fact Venetians were all supposed to be good Catholics. There was now a wide gap between the patricians of Venice and the revolutionaries of Paris. Many liberal ecclesiastics had come to believe that the rights of man were embedded in the Gospels. They defended the Jews, on whom the indignity of the ghetto had been imposed. The breach between old Venice and the new France could never be bridged, and even the nobles of the terraferma, cut off from the centralized government of Venice, welcomed the advent of Napoleon, who liberated them from the rule of the Signoria. So much for the effect of the "new ideas" of the Enlightenment and the French Revolution upon Venice, which Berengo, chaps. V–VII, has explored in full, and cf. Bruno Caizzi, *Industria e commercio della Repubblica veneta nel XVIII secolo*, Milan, 1965, pp. 12ff., concerning the restrictions on the trade in tobacco (and woolens, raw silk, foreign cloths of all kinds, coffee, oil, salt fish, indigo for dyeing cotton, wool, and silk, etc.), "il tema del contrabbando domina la tematica dell'economia veneziana del Settecento," with which Berengo has dealt at length. Note also the slender volume of Franco Venturi, *Venezia nel secondo settecento*, Turin, 1980, who gives brief (but instructive) synoptic views of life in Venice and the Veneto in the eighteenth century, concentrating upon prominent persons and the principal problems of the time. On the costumes (and to some extent the social customs) of eighteenth-century Venice, see *La Moda a Venezia nel Secolo XVIII*, with notes by G. Morazzoni, Milan, 1931.

[36] In listing the names of historians who have dealt in recent years with the latter-day history of Venice there come to mind (among others) Daniele Beltrami, Marino Berengo, Wm. J. Bouwsma, Fernand Braudel, Carlo Cipolla, Bruno Caizzi, Gaetano Cozzi, Jas. C. Davis, Jean Georgelin, Felix Gilbert, Frederic C. Lane, Gino Luzzatto, Brian Pullan, Donald E. Queller, Ruggiero Romano, Guido Ruggiero, Domenico Sella, Federico Seneca, Aldo Stella, Alberto Tenenti, Gianfranco Torcellan, Franco Venturi, and Stuart J. Woolf.

backs in warfare, local manufacturers and artisans remained at work in the Veneto as well as in Venice. In fact they sometimes retreated to the Veneto. The silk mills and paper mills prospered. Rice was grown in the Veneto, and exported in fair quantities. Sugar was refined, and soap was made. Maize had become an important product in the later sixteenth century, and still remains so in the Veneto to this day. The woolen industry had grown remarkably in the sixteenth century, and declined in sad fashion in the seventeenth. Labor was a persistent problem in Venice and the Veneto. So were exports and imports.[37] The overall decline of the Ottoman empire had made the Turks less dangerous enemies (they were preoccupied with the Austrians), and had also made them less

---

[37] Bruno Caizzi, *Industria e commercio della Repubblica veneta nel XVIII secolo* (1965), has made a careful study of the various work-forces in Venice and the entire Veneto. Labor was generally held under strict discipline, and a day's work might well amount to fourteen hours. The woolen and silk mills were especially important; so were the glass works on the island of Murano, exporting beads, mirrors, glass plates, and window panes. Cloth was woven for garments and the long hose of the time. Paper was manufactured, and exported in large quantities. A good many men were employed in the lead- and iron-works as well as in the production of soap, wax, ceramics, porcelain, and tobacco. Although the Signoria strove to keep peace with every state in Europe with which she could become involved, arms were manufactured in Venice and the Veneto but, as Caizzi makes clear (p. 192), "foreigners had no access to the forges; every cannon that was produced had to bear the name of the manufacturer and the seal of S. Mark. Customers could not have recourse to individual master craftsmen, but could only make contracts with trade-unionists among the master workers [. . . *coi sindaci delle maestranze*]."

The Venetian customs duties had been generally high and the surveillance of labor almost rigid, but as the eighteenth century and the independence of the Republic were gradually drawing to a close, there was some oscillation between the protectionism of the past and a certain measure of free trade. The distinction was drawn between such goods as were produced within the boundaries of the Venetian Republic, which remained subject to heavy customs duties, and essential imports which remained exempt from high tariffs. It was not always easy, however, to set the one apart from the other, which caused difficulties both within the Venetian state and with those bringing goods into the Veneto.

During the Turco-Venetian war, which ended in 1718, the Republic had been obliged to allow certain foreign traders to do business on more or less equal terms with the local residents. Upon the restoration of peace between the Porte and the Venetian government, it proved to be impracticable to revert to the old restrictions placed by the Signoria upon the foreign traders, who had taken over a large part of Venetian commerce, and now held on to it, "leaving the locals the crumbs of commerce" (Caizzi, pp. 217ff.). After 1758 Ottoman ships appeared in ever larger numbers at the docks in Venice, bringing goods from the Levant. Venetian merchants often chartered ships from Missolonghi (Mesolóngion), as the consul in Thessaloniki reported in September 1790, preferring them to Venetian ships, for they were lighter and less expensive. While Venice lost much of her trade to competitors, she continued to find profit in tobacco, soap, salt, and wax. Although the Levantine trade declined on the whole, Turkish coffee and cotton became of prime importance; wool also came from Turkey and Albania, as did linen (made from the fiber of flax). But generalizations are difficult, for conditions varied markedly (and so did customs' regulations) from one generation to the next. The subject can only be dealt with in some detail, as Caizzi, pp. 219–66, has done. The Venetians remained suspicious of (and hostile to) the Turks until the end of the century, and sometimes they even entertained silly ideas of reconquest, but accommodations were made, and peace obtained between the Signoria and the Porte to the end of the century, on which cf. Paolo Preto, *Venezia e i Turchi*, Florence, 1975, pp. 378ff.

profitable customers. The Russians had become an important force in eastern Europe in the early years of the eighteenth century, as we have seen, and the Venetian Signoria looked happily upon their military ventures, for they were inimical toward both the Turks and the Austrians.

The plagues of 1576–1577, 1630, and 1657 had brought about marked increases in wages, while the Venetian guild system apparently made production too costly for both manufacturers and merchants to compete in Istanbul, Smyrna, or elsewhere with the English, Dutch, and French. Over the years commercial enterprise and arranged marriages had concentrated wealth in the hands of various patrician families, whose sons came to avoid the labors and risks of navigation. As their commercial opportunities declined, these families turned to the countryside, to the reclamation of the marshlands in the Veneto, became agriculturists (not without profit), and built themselves luxurious villas, *facendo la bella figura.* Various aspects of the economic and social consequences of the patriciate's acquisition of large landed estates still remain obscure, however, and until further archival research can furnish us with instructive detail, it seems best to confine ourselves to general statements of apparent accuracy.[38]

After the peace of Passarowitz, despite economic hardship, life went on in Venice with some measure of tranquillity. Possessing a wide range of talents, Venetian craftsmen were highly respected. They maintained the iron foundries which produced (among other things) the bells for the campanili which still sound the hours in Venice. More refined workmen manufactured mechanical clocks which, one generation after another, Venetian ambassadors and bailies took as gifts to the sultans and the pashas. The Turks loved clocks, but they could never repair them when

---

[38] Undoubtedly agriculture, viticulture, and the rents derived from the large landed estates on *terra ferma* helped fill the gap caused by the decline of Venetian industry, although the export of Venetian glass, paper, and silk cloths, especially the *panni d'oro,* for the most part remained strong. The Venetian economy certainly had its ups and downs throughout the eighteenth century, on which cf. in general Jean Georgelin, *Venise au siècle des lumières,* Paris and The Hague, 1978, pp. 86ff., 157ff., 237ff., 303ff., *et alibi,* whose weighty tome contains a vast amount of factual detail sometimes at odds with itself.

Georgelin has dealt with the production of grains (especially maize), the breeding of cattle, pigs, sheep, goats, and horses, as well as with changes in the weather from one period to another and their assumed effect upon the price of grains. He has also dealt with the history of Venetian coinage, the building and rebuilding of palaces, theaters, hospitals, and villas in the eighteenth century. He moves back and forth in time, going from one country to another to make comparisons with the Venetian economy, causing rather a jumble of the abundant statistical data he has collected.

Franco Venturi, *Venezia nel secondo settecento,* Turin, 1980, pp. 6–7, believes that Georgelin has been misdirected by the precepts of the *Annales* school in his analyses of the connections between changing economic conditions and the political difficulties of the Venetian government. In any event Georgelin has the decline of Venice and the Veneto constantly in mind at the same time as he combats the idea of decline. I must, however, add that I have found his book lively, interesting, and instructive.

they went awry. Craftsmen also constructed fine organs for use in churches as well as for secular purposes. Venetian goldsmiths and jewelers were highly esteemed in Europe, and today there are several well-known jewelry shops on the Piazza S. Marco. Venetian craftsmen gave much time to the manufacture of pottery, the blue-and-white majolica, and (from the early eighteenth century) fine porcelain. Examples of their work, collected by the Venetian noble Teodoro Correr (d. 1830), may now be seen in the Museo Civico Correr (in the Procuratie Nuove on the Piazza S. Marco).

The glassworks of the island of Murano are as well known today as they were in the late seventeenth and eighteenth centuries, for there has been a renascence in glass-making at Murano since the 1920's, when Paolo Venini and Giacomo Capellin revived the artistry of the sixteenth century in their production of vases, goblets, and other glassworks. The Aldine press became famous; its works are still treasured. As the years went on, despite some measure of censorship, the Venetian book business prospered. Popular editions were inexpensive. The literate populace followed local events and foreign affairs in the newspapers, the *gazzette* and *gazzetini*, which we have cited from time to time. Today every Venetian reads *Il Gazzettino*, the chief newspaper on the lagoon. Learned academies were established in Venice and the Veneto, and today the Ateneo Veneto remains one of the more highly esteemed and productive learned societies in Europe. From one generation to the next the Venetians have continued to build up the Library of S. Mark, the Biblioteca Nazionale Marciana (now in the old Zecca or Mint), which gradually became a most important library after Cardinal Bessarion gave the Signoria his large and valuable collection of manuscripts (in 1468). The Venetians have always maintained the Marciana with the greatest care (despite some spoliation and disruption by Napoleon after the fall of the Republic in 1797), and today scholars from much of the learned world come together to use the manuscripts, incunabula, and other works assembled in the Marciana, where they are always accorded help and a generous reception.[39]

---

[39] On the French and Austrian plundering of the Venetian libraries, those of the churches, monasteries, and convents, and to some extent that of S. Marco in 1797, 1806–7, 1810–1812, and thereafter, see the important work of Marino Zorzi, *La Libreria di San Marco*, Venice, Ateneo Veneto [Milan, 1987], esp. pp. 319–64, and ff. For a brief survey of the intellectual and social life of Venice in the eighteenth century, see Georgelin, *Venise au siècle des lumières* (1978), pp. 705–81, who puts some emphasis upon the Venetians' interest in mathematics and the sciences, libraries and the public press as well as upon convents and the feminism of the Enlightenment, the popularity of clubs and cafés, fêtes and religious processions, along with the growth of deism, the decline of the priesthood, the widespread political unrest, and the corruption, disarray, and gradual enfeeblement of the Venetian governmental institutions. Cf. also Gianfranco Torcellan, *Settecento veneto e altri scritti storici*, Turin, 1969, esp. pp. 149ff.

Holidays and festivities, enlivened by fireworks, were long popular on the lagoon, and indeed they still are. As the masses turned out to witness the regattas, so did the nobility. The nobles also gave large banquets when they could afford them, and won and lost money at the gaming tables, which often took up the time and attention of the younger patriciate, whose employment abroad had been curtailed after the year 1718.

Learned Venetians, of whom there were many in every generation, occupied themselves with the close study of maps, topography, geography, astronomy, astrology, navigation, anatomy, medicine, and history. The University of Padua, a Venetian institution, was famous. Sir John Finch, the English ambassador at Istanbul from 1674 to 1681, had taken a doctorate in medicine at Padua, and so had his friend and constant companion Sir Thomas Baines. The humanists had long thrived in Venice, where one continued to pursue the study of philosophy and theology, write poetry and compose dramas, ending up with the works of Pietro Chiari, Carlo Goldoni, and Carlo Gozzi. Of these Goldoni is the most famous, especially for his comedies; he wrote in Venetian, and his statue now stands in the busy Campo S. Bartolomeo.

The theater and theatrical companies became especially popular in Venice in the eighteenth century. The Teatro "la Fenice," built in 1790–1792, was largely destroyed by fire in 1836, but having been restored, it is still the revered scene of the opera, always a high spot in the Venetian year. The first public opera house had opened in Venice in 1637. We have already noted Anna Akerhjelm's enjoyment of both the opera and the carnival in February 1689, and they remain much the same three centuries later, the carnival with its masks and masquerades. Hotels and travelers, some of them "tourists," had been common in Venice from the fourteenth century, often complaining about the prices.

Music gradually became an indispensable part of the social as well as of the religious life of the Venetians. Some names stand out in the record of the past. Andrea Gabrieli (d. 1586), Venetian composer and organist, became well known for his choral and instrumental music on ecclesiastical and state occasions as well as for festive gatherings in the palaces of the patriciate. Andrea's nephew Giovanni Gabrieli (d. 1612) also became famous as a composer and an organist. Both Andrea and Giovanni distinguished themselves as organists in St. Mark's, by far the most important church in Venice (although it did not become the cathedral until 1807 when the church of S. Pietro di Castello had to give up its primacy). Claudio Monteverdi (d. 1643), the great avant-garde composer of madrigals and operas, spent the last thirty years of his life in Venice, where he now lies buried in the church of the Frari. Monteverdi furnished composers in Venice with the model to which they would adhere in the years to come. In the more modern era there come to mind Gioacchino Rossini (d. 1868) and, above all, Giuseppe Verdi (d. 1901), the outstanding operatic composer of the nineteenth century.

After the peace of Passarowitz the "grand tour" began slowly to bring tourists to Venice. The city gradually became what has been called a playground for the wealthy. On the whole it would appear that the tourists and the wealthy did not see much of one another. Among the wealthy was Lord Byron (d. 1824), who had an apartment on the Frezzeria (in 1816–1817). After January 1818 he took a three years' lease on one of the Palazzi Mocenigo on the Grand Canal as well as on a villa at La Mira on the river Brenta. Byron's letters depict his views of Venice (and of course give much attention to his personal affairs and literary problems). While living on the Frezzeria he wrote his friend Thomas Moore (on 24 December 1816) that, as for Venice, "the nobility, in particular, are a sad looking race—the gentry rather better."[40]

The tourists enjoyed riding in gondolas up the Grand Canal and under the Rialto bridge; when they went along the entire Canal, they passed a dozen churches and some two hundred palaces. The elegant Ca d'Oro caught their attention, as it had that of all visitors to Venice since the mid-fifteenth century (it is now a museum). Many of these palaces were and are famous. Travelers of the later eighteenth century were bound to be impressed by the huge Palazzi Pesaro, Rezzonico, and Grassi (all museums now). The Palazzo Corner-Loredan (now the Municipio) would interest historians who knew something of the annals of the Corner family, and historians could not fail to seek out the Palazzo Dario, which the Signoria had given to the Venetian secretary Giovanni Dario, who had ended sixteen years of warfare with the Porte in the renowned treaty of January 1479. All these palaces are on the Grand Canal.

The architecture of Venice reflected both eastern and western styles, the major buildings being the Lombardo-Byzantine basilica of S. Mark and the Veneto-Gothic Doges' Palace. Visitors were taken to see the church of S. Maria Gloriosa dei Frari (where the Archives of State were eventually assembled in the Franciscan convent after the fall of the Republic), the Dominican church of SS. Giovanni e Paolo (where a number of doges are entombed), the church of S. Stefano (where Francesco Morosini lies buried), the huge church of the Salute (built to commemorate the Venetians' escape from the plague of 1630), the tiny church of the Miracoli (which the Germans have recently restored), and so on and on. Many visitors ventured to the far north of the city to see Tintoretto's house and the handsome church of the Madonna dell'Orto. There was no end of things to be seen in Venice and, as time went on, no end of visitors came to see them.

---

[40] *The Works of Lord Byron, Letters and Journals,* ed. Rowland E. Prothero, 6 vols., London, 1898–1901, IV, 29, and note Rosella Mamoli Zorzi, "Lord Byron e Venezia," *Ateneo Veneto,* CLXXV, n. s. XXVI (1988), 243–55. And of course the Americans were to join the British in their love of Venice, in which context note Zorzi, *Robert Browning a Venezia,* Venice, 1989, and *Henry James, Lettere da Palazzo Barbaro,* Milan, 1989.

Uppermost in the minds of at least some travelers and tourists were the works of art in Venice. Anticlericalism was part of the eighteenth-century Enlightenment, and when the fall of the Republic came in 1797 thousands of paintings and pieces of sculpture were bought, stolen, and otherwise dispersed from unprotected palaces, closed churches, bygone guilds, and suppressed monasteries. Nevertheless, in the Venice of today the works of more than a thousand painters, sculptors, and architect-builders may be seen in palaces, churches, and museums. Important paintings were collected in large part in the Accademia, built from the old Chiesa della Carità and the Scuola di S. Maria della Carità, one of the six Scuole Grandi or "Great Guilds" in the city.

The Accademia was not established until 1807, after which works were gathered from various churches and elsewhere, gifts were made by Venetian nobles, and through the years the collection grew to include the works of Gentile and Giovanni Bellini, Piero della Francesca, Andrea Mantegna, Cima da Conegliano, Jacopo Palma il Vecchio, Vittore Carpaccio, Giorgione da Castelfranco, Jacopo Bassano, and the *maestri del Rinascimento* Titian, Tintoretto, and Paolo Veronese. To see such works, the legacy of the old Republic, the earlier travelers and tourists had had to go from one church or palace to another, hoping for admission. In the Scuola Grande di San Rocco, despite the spoliation after 1797, the extraordinary series of paintings done by Jacopo Tintoretto in the sixteenth century still remains one of the major attractions of modern Venice.

In a letter to his friend Samuel Rogers, Lord Byron wrote from the Palazzo Mocenigo (on 3 March 1818),

The Carnival was short, but a good one. I don't go out much, except during the time of masques; but there are one or two *conversazioni*, where I go regularly. . . . The city, however, is decaying daily, and does not gain in population. However, I prefer it to any other in Italy; and here have I pitched my staff, and here do I purpose to reside for the remainder of my life [which of course was not to be the case]. . . .[41]

Venice had become a dissolute city, and Byron fitted well into the life of the social élite. As he wrote another friend on 8 September 1818:

Venice is not an expensive residence (unless a man chooses it). It has theatres, society, and profligacy rather more than enough. I keep four horses on one of the islands, where there is a beach of some miles along the Adriatic, so that I have daily exercise. I have my gondola, and about fourteen servants . . . , and I reside in one of the Mocenigo palaces on the Grand Canal; the rent of the whole

---

[41] *Letters and Journals*, ed. Prothero, IV (1900), 208.

house, which is very large and furnished with linen, etc., etc., inclusive, is two hundred a year (and I gave more than I need have done). In the two years I have been at Venice I have spent about *five* thousand pounds, and I need not have spent a *third* of this, had it not been that I have a passion for women which is expensive in its variety every where, but less so in Venice than in other cities. You may suppose that in *two years*, with a large establishment, horses, house, box at the opera, gondola, journeys, women, and Charity (for I have not laid out all upon my pleasures, but have bought occasionally a shilling's worth of salvation), villas in the country, another carriage and horses purchased for the country, books bought, etc., etc.,—in short everything I wanted, and *more* than I ought to have wanted, that the sum of five thousand pounds sterling is no great deal, particularly when I tell you that more than half was laid out in the Sex;—to be sure I have had plenty for the money, that's certain.[42]

As Byron played, he also worked, and as he began the fourth canto of *Childe Harold's Pilgrimage,* his thoughts turned from the profligate present to the historic past:

> I stood in Venice, on the "Bridge of Sighs;"
> A Palace and a prison on each hand:
> I saw from out the wave her structures rise
> As from the stroke of the Enchanter's wand:
> A thousand Years their cloudy wings expand
> Around me, and a dying Glory smiles
> O'er the far times, when many a subject land
> Looked to the wingéd Lion's marble piles,
> Where Venice sate in state, throned on her hundred isles. . . .

> In Venice Tasso's echoes are no more,
> And silent rows the songless Gondolier;
> Her palaces are crumbling to the shore,
> And Music meets not always now the ear:
> Those days are gone—but Beauty still is here.
> States fall—Arts fade—but Nature doth not die,
> Nor yet forget how Venice once was dear,
> The pleasant place of all festivity,
> The Revel of the earth—the Masque of Italy!

---

[42] *Ibid.,* IV, 255–56.

INDEX